ESSENTIAL
Chinese
Grammar

WRITE AND SPEAK CHINESE LIKE A NATIVE!

VIVIAN LING & WANG PENG

TUTTLE Publishing

Tokyo | Rutland, Vermont | Singapore

"Books to Span the East and West"

Tuttle Publishing was founded in 1832 in the small New England town of Rutland, Vermont [USA]. Our core values remain as strong today as they were then—to publish best-in-class books which bring people together one page at a time. In 1948, we established a publishing outpost in Japan—and Tuttle is now a leader in publishing English-language books about the arts, languages and cultures of Asia. The world has become a much smaller place today and Asia's economic and cultural influence has grown. Yet the need for meaningful dialogue and information about this diverse region has never been greater. Over the past seven decades, Tuttle has published thousands of books on subjects ranging from martial arts and paper crafts to language learning and literature—and our talented authors, illustrators, designers and photographers have won many prestigious awards. We welcome you to explore the wealth of information available on Asia at www.tuttlepublishing.com.

Published by Tuttle Publishing, an imprint of Periplus Editions (HK) Ltd.

www.tuttlepublishing.com

Copyright © 2020 by Vivian Ling and Wang Peng

Library of Congress Cataloging-in-Publication Data

ISBN 978-0-8048-5140-4

First edition
27 26 25 24 23   6 5 4 3   2307CM
Printed in China

TUTTLE PUBLISHING® is a registered trademark of Tuttle Publishing, a division of Periplus Editions (HK) Ltd.

Distributed by

North America, Latin America & Europe
Tuttle Publishing
364 Innovation Drive
North Clarendon, VT 05759-9436 U.S.A.
Tel: 1 (802) 773-8930
Fax: 1 (802) 773-6993
info@tuttlepublishing.com
www.tuttlepublishing.com

Japan
Tuttle Publishing
Yaekari Building 3rd Floor
5-4-12 Osaki Shinagawa-ku
Tokyo 141 0032
Tel: (81) 3 5437-0171
Fax: (81) 3 5437-0755
sales@tuttle.co.jp
www.tuttle.co.jp

Asia Pacific
Berkeley Books Pte. Ltd.
3 Kallang Sector #04-01
Singapore 349278
Tel: (65) 6741-2178
Fax: (65) 6741-2179
inquiries@periplus.com.sg
www.tuttlepublishing.com

Contents

PART TWO
254 Chinese Sentence Constructions You Should Know

Why We Wrote This Book

Correct, natural grammar usage is important for communicating beyond an elementary level in any language. Yet the study of grammar tends not to be a very popular aspect of Chinese language learning. However, language learners who wish to progress beyond the "daily survival" level and are not content with their Chinese ability being stuck at a "pidgin" level will find the study of Chinese grammar extremely rewarding and fruitful. This book is designed for learners who are motivated to boost their skills beyond the current level, perhaps even up to a professional or university graduate level. For such motivated learners, this book aims to make the study of Chinese grammar efficient and interesting. It provides a systematic overview of the grammar with a special focus on issues and pitfalls that affect English speakers.

Do not blame yourself if you feel your current grasp of Chinese grammar is weak. The current trend in teaching foreign languages has shifted away from the old-school grammatical orientation to a modern communicative approach. Both methods have their pluses and minuses, and the ideal approach actually combines the two. The advantages of the communicative orientation are clear in the early learning stages; however, its disadvantages begin to emerge at the intermediate level. The opposite is true of the grammatical structure approach.

Students who have learned Chinese mainly by following the communicative approach often find themselves acquiring more sophisticated vocabulary at the intermediate level, while lacking the grammatical frameworks to hang it on. Some may actually be able to use their newly-acquired vocabulary, but lack self-confidence and feel as though they are "winging it." Some may choose to simply to stay within their "safety zone," using only the tried-and-true can't-go-wrong sentence patterns they already know, while avoiding the more complicated patterns that make one's language lively and articulate. This book aims to remove this bottleneck, and to provide you with the grammatical apparatus to continue building your proficiency in Chinese beyond the beginner level.

Learning a foreign language is a two-pronged "fact-act" endeavor. Knowing the "facts" of the language is essential, but putting that knowledge into action is the real key to building communication skills. This book provides both the "facts"—in the form of grammatical explanations—as well as the materials for practicing the "act," in the form of copious usage examples and exercises with answer keys. Explanations of grammar points are unavoidably abstract or technical, but the examples that follow the explanations make them concrete and clear. The answer keys are intentionally located immediately after the exercises to provide quick feedback.

The "act" part of your learning process is implemented by the examples and exercises. To be effective, the sentences must be authentic and interesting, which means their vocabulary will necessarily be above the basic level. While we try to minimize the use of vocabulary beyond the intermediate level in this book, you will inevitably encounter some words that are outside your repertoire. But don't let this unfamiliar vocabulary become a stumbling block. By all means, look up unfamiliar words and turn this inconvenience into an opportunity to grow your vocabulary.

All Chinese expressions in this book are represented in characters and *pinyin*. While this is cumbersome, it is designed to accommodate readers with varying levels of character literacy, including those who have learned only to speak but not read Chinese. To those readers who have no use for *pinyin*, we would like to congratulate you and thank you for putting up with this unnecessary encumbrance.

The parsing of words in *pinyin* deserves a note here. Native speakers of languages with phonetic writing systems—such as the European languages and Vietnamese—have a clear sense of what constitutes a "word" in their language because it is clearly indicated by the writing system. But the Chinese writing system, which uses characters, provides no such intuitive sense of what constitutes a "word." In this book, we have adopted a compromise between the official Chinese system and our own Chinese-English bilingual sense.[1] For the purpose of reinforcing grammatical points in the book, we use hyphens to link elements that form units, such as set phrases (成语 **chéngyǔ**), verb-complement combinations, and structural words. On the other hand, the *aspect marker* 了 **le**, when written in *pinyin*, is attached to its associated verb to indicate a completed action. Similarly, the modifier-particle 的 **de** is attached to its preceding word, even in cases where the modifier is an extended phrase.

This book is designed for use by self-study learners as well as in the classroom. If used in self-study, it would be best if the learning is not solitary. Given that communication normally involves two people, it is very helpful to have a partner or tutor as you practice the speaking "act." This is like learning to play tennis. You can practice against a backboard or practice serving the ball alone, but it is so much more effective and fun to have a player on the other side, at least some of the time. A tutor or language partner not only brings the communication to life, but can also serve the essential function of correcting your faults. Knowing grammar "facts" does not guarantee that you will automatically "act" them out correctly in your day-to-day conversations, because bad habits and your original linguistic mindset die hard. However, once you have learned the "facts" presented in this book, you should be able to self-correct when given a signal from your language partner. In fact, a language partner who is vigilant for errors and willing to prod you to self-correct is more effective than one who hands you all the correct expressions on a platter.

This book may also be used as the grammar component within a formal Chinese language course, in which case the materials provided here will be enhanced by a task-master and coach, which is to say, by a professional language teacher.

—Vivian Ling and Wang Peng

---

[1] China has promulgated a set of official rules: http://pinyin.info/readings/orthography.html. However, TCFL experts are not in agreement as to its efficacy for the purpose of teaching Chinese to foreigners.

Part I Basic Grammatical Features of Chinese

1 Some Fundamental Characteristics of the Chinese Language

The typical first impression that Chinese makes on an English speaker is that it sounds musical, because it has four tones (plus a neutral tone), and a distinctive rhythm. Indeed, these are the two most important elements of the language for a learner to master in order to sound authentic. Correct rhythm comes naturally with vocabulary and sentence structure, which leaves tones as the most challenging aspect, so we will tackle this first in this section.

1.1 What Chinese sounds like

While the tools for continuing self-study of Chinese are now widely available, pronunciation, particularly the tones, requires some hand-holding by a teacher who speaks standard Chinese, and is able and willing to exercise tough love. The teacher's function is not only to model correct pronunciation, but more importantly to give you constructive feedback. You may have noticed that many of your native Chinese friends speak with regional accents, so what's wrong with learning to speak like them, or to speak with a bit of a foreign accent for that matter? The answer is: Learning any version of Chinese requires more or less the same amount of time and effort, and standard Chinese will give you better returns by far. Furthermore, the regional-accented versions of Chinese still carry Chinese tones and rhythm, and the speakers sound like members of the Chinese-speaking community, whereas a Western accent immediately marks the speaker as a foreigner.

On the matter of tones, getting each of the four tones right is only the beginning. Far more important is getting the tones in a sequence of two or more syllables "internalized." Start with 2-syllable tonal pairs, then after you have mastered all 20 of them, progress to phrases with three syllables and four syllables in different tone sequences. Soon these pairs, triplets, and quads will become internalized as short tunes that ring in your ear and you will be able to attach different words (like lyrics) to them.

To get started, the 20 tonal pairs are listed here with example words familiar to you:

	+ first tone	+ second tone	+ third tone	+ fourth tone	+ neutral tone[1]
first tone	yīshēng 医生 *doctor*	jīnnián 今年 *this year*	gōngxǐ 恭喜 *congratulations*	tiānqì 天气 *weather*	dōngxi 东西 *things*

---

[1] The neutral tone occurs in the second syllable of many common words when they are pronounced in the standard way, but most native speakers also use it optionally elsewhere in their speech. Language teachers, when speaking "instructional Chinese," tend to eschew the neutral tone when it is optional. In rapid speech bordering on slurring, the neutral tone is used extensively. The inconsistent tonal markings in textbooks reflect this reality.

	+ first tone	+ second tone	+ third tone	+ fourth tone	+ neutral tone[1]
second tone	zuótiān 昨天 *yesterday*	chúfáng 厨房 *kitchen*	nánnǚ 男女 *men & women*	tóutòng* 头痛 *headache*	xuésheng 学生 *student*
third tone	Běijīng 北京 *Beijing*	Měiguó 美国 *America*	yǒuhǎo** 友好 *friendly*	kǎoshì 考试 *take an exam*	hǎoba 好吧 *okay, fine*
fourth tone	màishū 卖书 *sell books*	liùshí 六十 *sixty*	ài nǐ 爱你 *love you*	tài guì 太贵 *too expensive*	mèimei 妹妹 *younger sister*

* Non-native speakers of Chinese, even some very proficient ones, find the second tone particularly challenging, especially when followed by a 4th tone (´ + `). Check your pronunciation with a teacher to see if the second row in this chart warrants extra focus.

** In the case of the ˇ + ˇ tonal pair, there is a regular "tone change" (called "tone sandhi" by linguists) whereby the first syllable in the pair changes into second tone. Thus, for example **yǒuhǎo** in the above table is actually pronounced as **yóuhǎo**. Most books, including this one, expect the user to know this rule, but some textbooks mark the first syllable in a ˇ + ˇ tone sequence as a second tone. Aside from this regular tone change, in standard Chinese (not including certain regional versions of Chinese), there is one other kind of tone change that involves two specific words, i.e. 不 **bù** and 一 **yī**, which are each pronounced in the 4th tone when followed by a syllable having a 1st, 2nd, or 3rd tone, and in the 2nd tone when followed by a 4th tone syllable.[2] Here are some examples:

yìtiān 一天 *one day*	**yìtiáo** 一条 *one line of*	**yìqǐ** 一起 *together*	**yíbàn** 一半 *half*
bùgāo 不高 *not tall*	**bùlái** 不来 *not coming*	**bùjiǔ** 不久 *not long*	**búzài** 不在 *not at...*

You may find additional tonal pair exercises on the internet, some even with YouTube videos. Resources for practicing 3-syllable tone sequences are more scarce, and here's where a teacher can help. When you progress to 4-syllable phrases, you will have at your disposal a large repertoire of set phrases (成语 **chéngyǔ**), which are a marvelous window into Chinese culture. Mastering these set phrases will not only improve your tonal pronunciation, it will also help you speak like a well-educated Chinese person. Again, guidance from a teacher on identifying the most useful 4-syllable phrases will be very useful.

The other major difference between the sound of Chinese and English is that the rhythm of the two languages is very different. This rhythm is affected by how words are formed. Chinese vocabulary is dominated by two-syllable words, and four-syllable phrases are also prevalent. This characteristic of Chinese, together with its tonal system, creates a "flow" which is very different from English, in which the rhythm of an utterance hinges on its intonation and the accented syllables.

---

[2] Some textbooks mark the tones on 不 **bù** and 一 **yī** as 4th and 1st respectively in all cases, some as they are morphed in actual practice. This book will follow the latter practice to provide a more accurate model for students.

In terms of the vowels and consonants of the languages, which are the elements most commonly associated with pronunciation, Chinese is really not all that different from English, and is actually simpler than English. There are no consonant clusters like *st-/sch-/chr-/pl-/fr-* in Chinese. Of the 21 consonants in Chinese, only five are not found in English: *zh, ch, z, c, x.* As an aside, even though *zh, ch,* and *sh* are represented by two letters of the alphabet in *pinyin* romanization, they are actually single sounds, just like *z, c,* and *x.*[3] Of the vowels in Chinese, only one—*ü* (written as u when preceded by *y, j, q, x*)—is not found in English, but it does exist in many other European languages including German and French. In sum, an English speaker only needs to learn these five new consonants and one vowel to produce the entire range of Chinese sounds.

Chinese pronunciation is best mastered at the early stage of learning the language, but it is never too late to make improvements. Whatever your level of Chinese, if you want to pronounce the tones and rhythm of Chinese more accurately, the "Addendum: Common Measure Words and Their Associated Nouns" will provide some helpful techniques.

1.2 How Chinese words are formed

All Westerners know what a word is. If you ask a random group of native Chinese how to say "word" in Chinese, most of them will give you the knee-jerk answer "字 zì," a few might say "词 cí" after a moment of thought. If you showed them a sentence written in Chinese characters, such as "我希望我的公司明年会派我去中国工作 Wǒ xīwàng wǒde gōngsī míngnián huì pài wǒ qù Zhōngguó gōngzuò. (*I hope my company will send me to China to work next year.*)" and asked them to pick out the words in it, some may just pick out each character as a word, but some may identify certain two-character combinations as words, e.g. 希望 xīwàng, 明年 míngnián, 公司 gōngsī, 中国 Zhōngguó, and 工作 gōngzuò. But if you showed them the sentence in romanized form, e.g. "Wǒ xīwàng wǒde gōngsī míngnián huì pài wǒ qù Zhōngguó gōngzuò," most likely all of them will come up with the words as they are parsed in the romanization. Any Chinese can tell you what a *character* (字 zì) is, but not so with a *word* (词 cí), because this is an acquired concept for native Chinese speakers. With the exception of linguists and language teachers, Chinese speakers in general are not analytical about how words are formed from the sub-units represented in writing by single-syllable characters.

For convenience in the present discussion, we will introduce the linguistic term "morpheme" to refer to the smallest meaningful unit in a language. Each morpheme in Chinese is one syllable and is represented in writing by a single character. The present discussion focuses on the spoken language, so we will use the term "morpheme" rather than the more familiar word "character." Some morphemes are stand-

---

[3] In a Chinese phonetic script system called 注音符号 zhùyīn fúhào, all initial consonants are denoted by single symbols, thus representing these sounds more accurately than all existing romanization systems, including *pinyin*.

alone words in their own right while others are like building blocks that combine with other morphemes to form a countless number of words in the rich Chinese vocabulary, and some are both. In fact, the flexibility and boundless capacity for combining single-syllable morphemes into words is a key aspect of the beauty and genius of the Chinese language. The total number of single-syllable Chinese morphemes—and the characters that represent them—are finite and relatively fixed, while the much larger repertoire of words created by combining the morphemes is enormous and constantly expanding.

The average well-educated native Chinese speaker knows about 3,000 morphemes, although the number used actively in everyday speech is considerably smaller. A non-native learner familiar with the ways in which words are formed from morphemes can function quite well in daily life communication with about 1,000. Moreover, the morphemes learned early in the study of Chinese are the ones occurring most frequently in everyday communication, and are the most prolific in word formation. This is good news for the learner, because it means the language-learning curve starts out very steep and levels off as one becomes more advanced. After the learner becomes familiar with the various patterns of word formation, each new morpheme learned brings into reach many more new words. Compared with learning new words in English one by one, the process by which one's vocabulary grows in Chinese is actually more efficient. While we may lament that knowing English does not help you very much when learning Chinese, we should rejoice that the basic "morphemes" in Chinese are useful building blocks which help you to quickly expand your Chinese vocabulary once you learn them.

Chapter 2 will provide a more detailed discussion of Chinese vocabulary. In this overview, we will provide just two simple pointers.

1. Learn the individual components of words

Whenever you learn a new word in Chinese, learn the meanings of its individual syllables or components (the morphemes) whenever possible, because this will help you remember the word and will help you understand other words using these morphemes later. Most morphemes have one root meaning, but may have additional derived meanings which are logically associated with the root meaning. For example, the root meaning of 进 **jìn** is *to advance*, although the first meaning a student normally learns is *to enter*. The combination 进步 **jìnbù** means *to improve*, but if you think of it as *to advance a step* (the way a native Chinese speaker does), then it becomes very easy to remember and also to learn other words containing the components 进 **jìn** *to advance* and 步 **bù** *step*, for example:

进行 **jìnxíng** *to proceed*	前进 **qiánjìn** *to go forward*	快步 **kuàibù** *quick paced*
进展 **jìnzhǎn** *to develop*	先进 **xiānjìn** *to advance*	初步 **chūbù** *beginning*
进口 **jìnkǒu** *to import*	改进 **gǎijìn** *to improve*	让步 **ràngbù** *to yield*
进军 **jìnjūn** *to advance troops*	推进 **tuījìn** *to promote*	步行 **bùxíng** *to go on foot*
	上进 **shàngjìn** *to advance*	

If you think of morphemes as word components, then learning new vocabulary is largely a matter of learning how new words are generated from the basic components of Chinese—i.e. which is easier than sheer memorization.

2. How bisyllabic words are formed

As mentioned earlier, bisyllabic words consisting of two discrete morphemes joined together dominate the Chinese vocabulary. The vast majority of bisyllabic compounds fall into the following categories:

- **verb + object:** 毕业 **bìyè** *to graduate*; 投票 **tóupiào** *to vote*
- **modifier + noun:** 高校 **gāoxiào** *college/university*; 动物 **dòngwù** *animal*
- **noun + noun:** 父母 **fùmǔ** *parents*; 人口 **rénkǒu** *population*
- **adverb + verb:** 微笑 **wēixiào** *to smile*; 慢跑 **mànpǎo** *to jog (slow run)*
- **verb + verb:** 学问 **xuéwèn** *learning*; 行动 **xíngdòng** *action*
- **verb + complement** (see Chap. 12): 听懂 **tīngdǒng** *to hear & understand*; 打破 **dǎpò** *to break*
- **two synonyms:** 喜欢 **xǐhuan** *to like*; 练习 **liànxí** *to practice*
- **two antonyms:** 长短 **chángduǎn** *length*; 先后 **xiānhòu** *first and later (order)*
- **contractions:** 文革 **Wén-Gé** (文化大革命 **Wénhuà Dàgémìng** *Cultural Revolution*); 高铁 **gāotiě** (高速铁路 **gāosù tiělù** *high-speed rail*)

Knowing the meanings of the individual morphemes and understanding the above patterns of word formation give you a leg up in learning new vocabulary. For example, if you know the meanings of the morphemes 要 **yào** and 就 **jiù**, then it should be relatively easy for you to grasp the meanings of the underlined words in the following sentences, or to guess them correctly.

a. 要 **yào**: *important, essential*

深圳在1980之后成为了中国当代经济发展的要地。

Shēnzhèn zài 1980 zhīhòu chéngwéile Zhōngguó dāngdài jīngjì fāzhǎnde yàodì.

After 1980, Shenzhen became an important site in China's modern economic development.

b. 就 **jiù**: *to undertake*

我相信双语能力会给我带来更多、更好的就业机会。

Wǒ xiāngxìn shuāngyǔ nénglì huì gěi wǒ dàilái gèngduō, gènghǎode jiùyè jīhuì.

I believe bilingual ability will bring me more and better employment opportunities.

Among the various types of bisyllabic compounds listed above, words that are formed by combining *verb + object* and *verb + complement* are more flexible than the others, since the two components can sometimes be separated and other elements inserted in between. Examples:

毕业／毕了业 **bìyè/bì-le-yè** *to graduate/have graduated*;
投票／投过两次票 **tóupiào/tóuguo liǎngcì piào** *to vote/to have voted twice*;
听懂／听得懂 **tīngdǒng/tīng-de-dǒng** *to hear and understand/able to hear and understand*;
打破／打不破 **dǎpò/dǎ-bu-pò** *to break/cannot be broken*.

EXERCISES:

1. What is the meaning of the first morpheme below in the context of the words that follow it?

   a. 本 **běn**: 本地 **běndì**, 本人 **běnrén**, 本性 **běnxìng**

   b. 易 **yì**: 易经 **yìjīng**, 贸易 **màoyì**, 改名易姓 **gǎimíng-yìxìng**

   c. 从 **cóng**: 从事 **cóngshì**, 从商 **cóngshāng**, 从母 **cóngmǔ**

   d. 帮 **bāng**: 黑帮 **hēibāng**, 四人帮 **Sìrén Bāng**

   e. 张 **zhāng**: 张开 **zhāngkāi**, 扩张 **kuòzhāng**

   f. 身 **shēn**: 本身 **běnshēn**, 立身 **lìshēn**

   g. 修 **xiū**: 进修 **jìnxiū**, 修身 **xiūshēn**

   > **ANSWERS:**
   >
   > | | | |
   > |---|---|---|
   > | a. basic, original | c. follow | e. spread, expand | g. cultivate (person) |
   > | b. change, exchange | d. gang | f. self | |

2. Figure out the meanings of the underlined words from their contexts alone. (Look up words that are unfamiliar to you.)

   a. 别管<u>他人</u>之事。(What is meaning of 他 **tā** in 他人 **tārén**?)
   Bié guǎn tārén zhī shì.

   b. 这个童话听起来很简单，但它的思想<u>内容</u>很丰富。
   (What is the meaning of 容 **róng** in 内容 **nèiróng**?)
   Zhège tónghuà tīng-qǐlai hěn jiǎndān, dàn tāde sīxiǎng nèiróng hěn fēngfù.

   c. 越战时期有不少越南政府的<u>政要</u>移民到美国来了。
   Yuèzhàn shíqī yǒu bù shǎo Yuènán zhèngfǔde zhèngyào yímíndào Měiguó láile.

   d. 如果说美国是个先进的国家，那么为什么有那么多的人民得重病时无法<u>就医</u>？ **Rúguǒ shuō Měiguó shì ge xiānjìnde guójiā, nàme wèishénme yǒu nàme duōde rénmín dé zhòngbìng shí wúfǎ jiùyī?**

   e. 丝绸之路是中国古代通往罗马的贸易<u>要道</u>，也是当时东西文化交流的<u>要道</u>。 **Sīchóu-zhī-lù shì Zhōngguó gǔdài tōngwǎng Luómǎde màoyì yàodào, yě shì dāngshí dōng-xī wénhuà jiāoliúde yàodào.**

   > **ANSWERS:**
   >
   > | | | |
   > |---|---|---|
   > | a. other | c. important political figures | e. an important route |
   > | b. to contain | d. to seek medical treatment | |

1.3 Essential features of Chinese sentences

The Chinese linguistic mindset tends to be more "efficient" than English, in the sense that certain elements which are considered absolutely necessary in an English sentence can be dispensed with in Chinese. In this regard, there are two notable sentence-forming tendencies of Chinese speakers that a non-native should adopt in order to sound more like a native.

1. The "topic + comment" structure in Chinese

In English, the **subject + predicate** sentence pattern is the norm. When a speaker wishes to draw attention on an element other than the subject, he may want to mention it first, but then needs to add other words or phrases that are cumbersome or inelegant. Examples:

A. *I finally saved enough money to buy that smartphone that I've been longing for.*
B. *You know that smartphone I've been longing for? Well, I finally saved enough money to buy it.*

A. *I'm really disappointed that the new Chinese restaurant in town doesn't even have a Chinese menu.*
B. *About that new Chinese restaurant in town, I'm really disappointed that it doesn't even have a Chinese menu.*

A. *I haven't had time yet to think about the problems you raised with me yesterday.*
B. *As for the problems that you raised yesterday, I haven't had time to think about them yet.*

The corresponding mechanism in Chinese is much simpler and more direct. Chinese speakers conceptualize the substance of a sentence in two parts: the **topic** and the **comment**. The way to focus on any particular element of a sentence—regardless of whether it is the subject—is simply to state it first as the **topic**, and the rest of the sentence then becomes a **comment** on that topic. This **topic + comment** pattern is used frequently in Chinese colloquial speech, and it appears in formal speech and writing as well. A common sentence topic is actually the object, which can be stated first to either give it greater prominence, or when the object is very complex, to "set it aside" at the outset.

- *Who can remember things that happened so long ago?*
  那么久以前的事情，谁还会记得呢？
  Nàme jiǔ yǐqiánde shìqing, shéi hái huì jìde ne?

- *I've learned all the vocabulary before Lesson 10, but I have no confidence about those that came after Lesson 10.*
  第十课以前的生词，我都学会了。可是第十课以后的，我完全没有把握。 **Dìshíkè yǐqiánde shēngcí, wǒ dōu xuéhuìle. Kěshì dìshíkè yǐhòude, wǒ wánquán méiyǒu bǎwò.**

♦ *We can perhaps tell a little bit about someone's personality from her appearance, but it's from her actions that we can understand more.*
一个人的性格，也许可以从她的长相看出来一点，但是从她的行为能了解得更多。
Yíge rénde xìnggé, yěxǔ kěyǐ cóng tāde zhǎngxiàng kàn-chūlai yìdiǎn, dànshì cóng tāde xíngwéi néng liǎojiěde gèng duō.

♦ *Colleagues in the department all have different views on the character of the department chair.*
对系主任的为人，系里的同事们各有各的看法。
Duì xìzhǔrènde wéirén, xìlǐde tóngshìmen gè yǒu gède kànfǎ.

Translate the following sentences using the **topic + comment** pattern:

1. How can you remember the names of all those 50+ students so quickly?
2. Which of the five Chinese restaurants nearby do you think is the best?

> **ANSWERS:**
>
> 1. 那五十几个学生的名字，你怎么能那么快就记住了呢？
>   **Nà wǔshíjǐge xuéshengde míngzi, nǐ zěnme néng nàme kuài jiù jìzhùle ne?**
> 2. 这附近的五个中国餐馆，你觉得哪个最好呢？
>   **Zhè fùjìnde wǔge Zhōngguó cānguǎn, nǐ juéde něige zuì hǎo ne?**

2. Omissions of nonessential words in Chinese sentences

Nouns and pronouns can often be omitted in Chinese when they are understood from the context. The noun or pronoun that is omitted can be either the subject or the object, or something that is modified.

♦ *It's raining, we can't go now.* 下雨了，去不了了。
Xiàyǔle, qù-bu-liǎole. (subjects of both phrases omitted)

♦ *Throw it out! I don't want it anymore!* 扔了吧！我不要了！
Rēngle ba! Wǒ bú yào le! (objects in both phrases omitted)

In the following sentences, the nouns modified by ...的 **de** are omitted:

♦ *I never buy imported things.* 我从来不买进口的。 **Wǒ cónglái bù mǎi jìnkǒude.**

♦ *What you said is totally correct.* 你说的完全正确。 **Nǐ shuōde wánquán zhèngquè.**

♦ *Those in our line of work must rise early and go to bed late, and that's extremely tough.*
干我们这行的要早起晚睡，辛苦极了。
Gàn wǒmen zhèhángde yào zǎo-qǐ-wǎn-shuì, xīnkǔ-jíle.

♦ *My Chinese is very poor, so if I say anything incorrectly, please point out my errors.*
我的汉语很差，如果我有<u>说错的</u>，请多多指教。
Wǒde Hànyǔ hěn chà, rúguǒ wǒ yǒu shuōcuòde, qǐng duōduō zhǐjiào.

♦ *Those who repair shoes, sell tofu, or sweep the streets, are all odd jobbers.*
<u>修理皮鞋的</u>、<u>卖豆腐的</u>、<u>打扫街道的</u>，这些都算是零工。
Xiūlǐ píxiéde, mài dòufude, dǎsǎo jiēdàode, zhèxiē dōu suànshì línggōng.

In complex sentences containing two or more clauses, stating the subject of each clause is unnecessary in Chinese when it is understood from the context. Similarly, pronouns are typically omitted. Below are just two of the many examples that you will see throughout this book. Note that the underlined pronouns in two English sentences are omitted in the Chinese translation.

♦ *It was ten years ago that my husband passed away, and at the time <u>he</u> was only 58 years old.*
我先生是十年以前去世的，那时才五十八岁。
Wǒ xiānsheng shì shínián yǐqián qùshì de, nà shí cái wǔshíbā-suì.

♦ *Chinese is not my native language. If <u>I</u> don't speak <u>it</u> for a couple of years, <u>I</u> will forget it all!*
中文不是我的母语。如果两年不说，就会完全忘记了！
Zhōngwén bú shì wǒde mǔyǔ. Rúguǒ liǎngnián bù shuō, jiù huì wánquán wàngjìle.

EXERCISES:

Translate the following sentences, omitting nouns or pronouns that are understood from the contexts:

1. Of the five Chinese restaurants here, there is not even a single good one.
2. What you are capable of doing is not difficult; what's difficult is only what you are not capable of doing.
3. He can retire this year, but he wants to work five more years.

ANSWERS:

1. 这里的五个中国餐馆，连一个好的都没有。
   Zhèlǐde wǔge Zhōngguó cānguǎn, lián yíge hǎode dōu méiyǒu.
2. 会的不难，难的不会。**Huìde bùnán, nánde búhuì.**
3. 他今年就可以退休了，可是想再工作五年。
   Tā jīnnián jiù kěyǐ tuìxiū le, kěshì xiǎng zài gōngzuò wǔnián.

1.4 Chinese parts of speech

Parts of speech in Chinese are more flexible than in English. Most words in English are identified as a particular part of speech (e.g. a noun, verb, adjective, etc.), and grammatical inflexions make this clear. For example, nouns must be either singular or plural, verbs have tenses, adverbs often have the suffix *-ly*, etc. While some English words can be used in different ways as more than one part of speech (e.g. *burden* can be either a noun or a verb, as in *a long-term burden* and *to burden someone with something*), this kind of grammatical flexibility is much greater in Chinese, in which grammatical inflexions don't exist. Most basic Chinese textbooks mark parts of speech for Chinese words in vocabulary lists and students learn the vocabulary that way. But in both formal and colloquial speech, familiar Chinese words will often appear in parts of speech different from those the student has learned. Once you come to appreciate the grammatical flexibility of Chinese words, you will be delighted rather than confused when you encounter a familiar word used in a new grammatical function. In the following examples, the original meanings of the underlined words are presented in parentheses. As you read these sentences, figure out how the meanings of these words in their new contexts derive from their original meanings.

◆ *That classroom is very small, it can only seat 30 students.*
那间教室很小，只能坐30个学生。（坐 zuò: *to sit*)
Nèijiān jiàoshì hěn xiǎo, zhǐ néng zuò 30 ge xuésheng.

◆ *Last year's earthquake at that place killed over 300 people.*
去年那个地方的地震，死了三百多人。（死 sǐ: *to die*)
Qùnián nèige dìfangde dìzhèn, sǐle sānbǎiduō rén.

◆ *That problem is hard to fix, we must send several of the most capable people.*
那个问题不好解决，得去几个最能干的人才行。（去 qù: *to go*)
Nèige wèntí bù hǎo jiějué, děi qù jǐge zuì nénggànde rén cái xíng.

◆ *Waiter, bring us two more bottles of beer!*
服务员，再来两瓶啤酒！（来 lái: *to come*)
Fúwùyuán, zài lái liǎngpíng píjiǔ!

◆ *Several drug dealers suddenly came upon this little peaceful community of ours.*
我们这个治安很好的小社区突然来了几个卖毒品的。（来 lái morphed into a transitive verb)
Wǒmen zhèige zhì'ān hěn hǎode xiǎo shèqū tūrán láile jǐge mài dúpǐnde.

◆ *We can't go wrong if we do it like Old Wang says.*
按照老王的说法去做，肯定错不了。（错 cuò: *wrong*)
Ànzhào Lǎo Wángde shuōfǎ qù zuò, kěndìng cuò-bu-liǎo.

◆ *The policeman didn't give him a ticket, only a warning, so he let him off easy.*
警察没给他罚单，只给了个警告，算是便宜了他。（便宜 piányi: *inexpensive*)
Jǐngchá méi gěi tā fádān, zhǐ gěile ge jǐnggào, suànshì piányile tā.

♦ *Cultivate oneself, <u>put the family</u> <u>in order</u>, govern the nation, <u>bring peace to</u> the world.*
修身、<u>齐家</u>、治国、<u>平</u>天下。(齐 **qí**: *orderly*; 平 **píng**: *calm, peaceful*)
Xiúshēn, qíjiā, zhìguó, píng tiānxià.

Although in general, there are more similarities than differences between English and Chinese in terms of the ways that parts of speech operate within sentences there are many critical differences. The following is a brief overview of these differences that can also serve as a roadmap of the pitfalls that native English speakers should avoid when speaking Chinese.

1.5 Common grammatical errors made by English speakers

A. Adjectives

1. In Chinese, an adjective that describes the subject of a sentence follows the subject directly, without the verb "to be". (For this reason, some Chinese textbooks call these adjectives "stative verbs" instead of using the term "adjective.")

- *She is very smart.* 她很<u>聪明</u>。 **Tā hěn cōngming.**
- *Is it easy to learn Chinese?* 学中文<u>容易</u>吗？ **Xué Zhōngwén róngyì ma?** (In this sentence, the subject is a verb phrase: *to learn Chinese.*)
- *Is Chinese easy to learn?* 中文<u>容易学</u>吗？ **Zhōngwén róngyì xué ma?**

2. When an adjective precedes a noun, the particle 的 **de** is added between them to indicate their relationship. This usage of 的 **de** applies to all forms of noun modification, including simple adjectives, possessives and long modifying phrases (refer to "Noun modification" below).

♦ *<u>Expensive</u> things are not necessarily good.*
贵的东西不一定好。 **Guìde dōngxi bù yídìng hǎo.**

♦ *The cellphone <u>I ordered on the web 10 days ago</u> still hasn't arrived.*
我十天前在网上订的那个手机到现在还没到呢！
Wǒ shítiān-qián zài wǎngshàng dìngde nèige shǒujī dào xiànzài hái méi dào ne!

B. Adverbs and adverbial phrases

1. The most common adverbs in Chinese—都 **dōu**, 也 **yě**, 再 **zài**, 又 **yòu**, 就 **jiù**, 才 **cái**—often have no direct English translations and can be surprisingly confusing. Mastering the use of 就 **jiù** and 才 **cái** requires adopting a certain mindset; but once that is done, they are simple (see Chapter 5).

2. English adverbs formed by adding the suffix -*ly* have no Chinese equivalents. This type of adverb is expressed through word order in Chinese.

3. Adverbial phrases serve two special functions in Chinese: to describe how an action is done, and to request that an action be done in a particular way (e.g.

Grandma speaks slowly and *Please speak slowly*). These two different functions are expressed by different word orders in Chinese (see Chapter 6).

C. Auxiliary verbs

Auxiliary verbs in English are used generally to convey some aspect of the verb (primarily tense) rather than to express meaning. These aspects are expressed differently in Chinese than in English.

◆ *He <u>has</u> already exerted his best effort.* 他已经尽<u>了</u>最大的努力。
  Tā yǐjīng jìnle zuì dàde nǔlì.

◆ <u>*Would*</u> *you like some milk in your tea?* 你的茶要加点牛奶吗？
  Nǐde chá yào jiā diǎn niúnǎi ma?

There are a few exceptions where the English auxiliary verbs carry meaning (e.g. *may* and *can*), and these do have Chinese equivalents.

◆ *You all <u>may</u> sit down now.* 你们<u>可以</u>坐下了。 **Nǐmen kěyǐ zuòxiàle.**

D. The use of measure words (M)

In Chinese, a "measure word" is a grammatical requirement before a noun whenever it is preceded by a specifier or by a number. Sometimes the measure word indicates quantity (e.g. a <u>bag</u> of…, two <u>stacks</u> of…) and sometimes it is simply a "dummy" that fills in the grammatical slot, in which case it does not convey additional meaning. Because measure words are often associated with the shape of an object, they are also called "classifiers." Similar words are also used in English, for example: *a sheet of paper*; *a school of fish*. For example: 一块蛋糕 **yíkuài dàngāo** *a piece of cake.*

Measure words exist in English as well, but they generally do measure something, e.g. *a <u>bushel</u> of corn, a <u>roomful</u> of people, a <u>ton</u> of homework.* But in some cases they do not really carry any meaning, e.g. *a <u>head</u> of cabbage, two <u>loaves</u> of bread.* This kind of usage in English is the norm in Chinese; that is, whenever a noun is stated with a specifier or number, a measure word tags along too (see Chapter 4).

E. Differing uses of the negative with cognitive verbs

English speakers often mistakenly express the negative in connection with "cognitive verbs" (*to think* 想 **xiǎng**; *to feel* 觉得 **juéde**; *to consider* 认为 **rènwéi**; *to believe* 相信 **xiāngxìn**) by negating the verb rather than what will or will not happen. This problem lies on the English side of the linguistic divide. Consider the following pairs of sentences. Which one is more correct and more logical?

  I don't think it will rain today.   vs   *I think it will not rain today.*

The Chinese mindset aligns with the latter, because logically the negation does not apply to what you are thinking about but to what will or will not happen. Therefore, the correct way of stating this in Chinese is:

✓ 我想今天不会下雨。   ✗ 我不想今天会下雨。[4]
Wǒ xiǎng jīntiān búhuì xiàyǔ. and not **Wǒ bùxiǎng jīntiān huì xiàyǔ.**

In Chapter 2, we will discuss the differences in nuance between 不觉得… **bù juéde…** and 觉得…不 **juéde…bù….**

F. Noun modification in Chinese

Noun modification takes on many different grammatical forms in English. In the following phrases, the noun "watermelon" is modified in a wide variety of ways:

- a *big beautiful ripe* watermelon
- *Farmer John's* watermelons
- *that* watermelon *on top* of *the heap*
- the watermelon *you bought from the Farmer's Market the other day*
- the watermelons *available in the winter*
- the watermelon *that your aunt brought to the picnic*

In Chinese, noun modification adheres to a very simple "one size fits all," formula and all the above English examples are translated into Chinese using the form **modifier + 的 de + 西瓜 xīguā.** The only exceptions to this pattern are where specifiers and numbers are added, in which case they can appear as part of a modified noun phrase in two ways:

- *Those three watermelons you bought from the farmers' market yesterday*
  A 你昨天在农贸市场买的那三个西瓜 (preferred word order)
  Nǐ zuótiān zài nóngmào shìchǎng mǎide nà sānge xīguā

  B 那三个你昨天在农贸市场买的西瓜
  nà sānge nǐ zuótiān zài nóngmào shìchǎng mǎide xīguā

G. The use of prepositions (called "coverbs" or "postverbs" in Chinese—see Chapter 11)

1. Unlike in English, Chinese "prepositions" are not a distinct group of words that only serve as prepositions. Chinese words that are used as prepositions in certain contexts are also used as verbs in other contexts. For example, the word 在 **zài** can be used as a preposition meaning *at* or *in* or as a verb meaning *to exist.*

♦ *He has worked in Beijing for three years.*
他在北京工作了两年。(in, at) **Tā zài Běijīng gōngzuòle liǎngnián.**

♦ *That restaurant no longer exists…it closed two months ago.*
那个餐馆已经不在了…两个月前关门了。(to exist)
Nèige cānguǎn yǐjīng bú zài le…liǎngge yuè qián guānmén le.

♦ *I've wanted to be a teacher since I was young.*
我从小就想当老师。(from a young age) **Wǒ cóngxiǎo jiù xiǎng dāng lǎoshī.**

---

[4] Incorrect expressions are indicated by ✗ throughout this book. Usually, the incorrect rendering will be given first in order to highlight the pitfall. In all cases, the correct rendering will be provided.

◆ *It was only later that I decided to make a career in education.*
我后来才决定从事教育。(engage in the profession of…)
Wǒ hòulái cái juédìng cóngshì jiàoyù.

To realign the English speaker's mindset with the Chinese mindset, many textbooks use the term **coverb** instead of **preposition**. Indeed, to think more like a native Chinese speaker on this point means replacing the notion of a prepositional phrase with that of an auxiliary verbal phrase.

2. Just as prepositions in English can appear before or after the main verb, coverbs in Chinese may also appear after the main verb, in which case they are called **postverbs** (see Chapter 11).

3. In Chinese, "locative prepositions" that indicate a relative location (e.g. *on, in, below, above*) are bifurcated into two parts that bracket the noun they apply to, as in 在…上 **zài…shàng**; 在…里 **zài…lǐ**; 在…下 **zài…xià**, etc." (see Chapter 9).

H. Chinese vs English interrogatives

1. To the Chinese way of thinking, English grammar makes interrogatives more complicated than they need to be, in two ways: (a) question words (*who, when, how, …*) are normally positioned at the front of a sentence (*When will you …?*), and (b) the subject-verb order is reversed (*Do you have any…?*). Neither of these complications exists in Chinese. And although questions in Chinese are much simpler to form, the English linguistic mindset can nevertheless often be a hindrance.

2. In Chinese, there are two ways of asking questions that don't exist in English: (a) adding a question particle at the end of the sentence, i.e. 吗 **ma**, 呢 **ne**; and (b) interposing positive and negative forms of a verb to indicate "whether or not…" (see Chapter 3)

3. Question words in Chinese and English are very similar, but in Chinese sentences these do not need to move up to the beginning (see Chapter 3.5).

I. Time expressions in Chinese

The Chinese mindset makes a clear distinction between "point in time" (e.g. *3 weeks ago*) and "duration of time" (e.g. *a period of 3 weeks*). These two concepts of time are reflected in different word orders in Chinese. While there is greater flexibility in the word order of time expressions in English, the distinction between the two concepts is not reflected in a difference in word order. Hence, thinking in English while expressing time in Chinese can be a pitfall (see Chapter 10).

J. Common function verbs in Chinese

Many common function verbs in English become **verb + object** compounds when translated into Chinese:

to speak: 说话 **shuōhuà**	*to study:* 读书 **dúshū**	*to cook:* 做饭 **zuòfàn**
to sing: 唱歌 **chànggē**	*to teach:* 教书 **jiāoshū**	*to move:* 搬家 **bānjiā**

This is a manifestation of the tendency for words in Chinese to be bisyllabic. When no particular object of the verb is mentioned, a generic word is added to a verb as a second syllable. For example:

to speak 说话 **shuōhuà** (= *to speak speech*); *to study* 读书 **dúshū** (= *to study a book*); *to eat* 吃饭 **chīfàn** (= *to eat rice*); *to sing* 唱歌 **chànggē** (= *to sing a song*).

While the first syllable or simple verb in the **verb + object** compound has an independent meaning, it cannot be used as a stand-alone word without an object and must be used as a kind of morpheme building block in combination with other morphemes.

K. Verb "tenses" expressed as verb "aspects" in Chinese

In the Chinese linguistic mindset, there are no tenses such as present, past, or future, and Chinese verbs are not conjugated. Instead, other morphemes or **aspect markers** are added to indicate ideas like *completion, in the process of, sustained state*, etc.(see Chapters 7 and 8). The English system of tense takes the present as the main point of reference. The Chinese system of **verb aspects** takes each event/action on its own and the speaker shifts the point of reference to the time of that event or action. The visual parallel to these two types of time perspective can be illustrated by a Western painting with single-point perspective and a Chinese scroll painting where the viewer moves his eyes along the scroll as it is unrolled. Adopting the Chinese **verb aspect** mindset—i.e. thinking like a Chinese speaker—is the key to expressing verbal concepts with ease and confidence in Chinese.

ADDENDUM: Exercises for Improving Your Chinese Tones and Rhythm

1. Fill in a blank tonal pairs table like the one in 1.1 with your own set of words. Say them out loud, using a tutor as your sounding board.

2. Do an oral "reverse-order sentence build-up" exercise with the two sentences below. Begin each sentence with the last word or phrase, then add the word/phrase preceding it, etc., until you can say the entire sentence fluently. Repeat each sentence fragment until you can pronounce it accurately and fluently before adding the preceding segment. Example:

我有很多中国朋友 **Wǒ yǒu hěn duō Zhōngguó péngyou**
(*I have many Chinese friends*):

朋友 **péngyou**

中国朋友 **Zhōngguó péngyou**

很多中国朋友 **hěn duō Zhōngguó péngyou**

我有很多中国朋友。 **Wǒ yǒu hěn duō Zhōngguó péngyou.**

- 在过去的两个星期，我的汉语进步了不少。
  Zài guòqùde liǎngge xīngqī, wǒde Hànyǔ jìnbùle bùshǎo.
  (*In the past two weeks, my Chinese improved quite a bit.*)
- 用成语来练习四声发音是个一举两得的好方法。
  Yòng chéngyǔ lái liànxí sìshēng fāyīn shì ge yìjǔ-liǎngdéde hǎo fāngfǎ.
  (*Using set phrases to practice the four tones is a good method that kills two birds with one stone.*)

3. Make a blank table with 3-syllable tone sequences (e.g. 1-1-1, 1-1-2, 1-1-3; 1-2-1, 1-2-2, etc.). There should be 64 (4x4x4) slots. Fill in the slots with 3-syllable phrases. Typically, 3-syllable phrases can be parsed into 1-syllable+2-syllables (e.g. 高-医生 **Gāo yīshēng** *Dr. Gao*, 吃-中饭 **chī zhōngfàn** *to eat lunch*) or 2-syllables+1-syllable (e.g. 中国-人 **Zhōngguórén** *Chinese people*, 非常-快 **fēicháng kuài** *extremely fast*). Fill in the table with phrases in both of these formats. If you are stymied, you may take any 2-syllable word in the above table (exclude those in the column that end in the neutral tone) and add a 1-syllable word at either the front or the end. For example, 医生 **yīshēng** *doctor*: 李医生 **Lǐ yīshēng** *Dr. Li*, 医生忙 **yīshēng máng** *the doctor is busy*, 医生好 **yīshēng hǎo** *the doctor is good*, 看医生 **kàn yīshēng** *to see a doctor*. Practice saying the 3-syllable phrases in your chart out loud and have a teacher critique your pronunciation.

4. A fun way to practice 4-syllable tone sequences is to memorize some 成语 **chéngyǔ** (set phrases, or idioms) Begin creating your personal collection of favorite set phrases by googling "Chinese idioms" on the internet. To get you started, here are three useful websites (active as of 2/19/2018). If some of these have vanished, you can no doubt find others.

   - https://chinaculturecorner.com/2014/12/06/learn-chinese-idioms-when-working-at-a-chinese-company/
   - https://www.fluentu.com/blog/chinese/2013/12/26/chinese-idioms-chengyu/
   - https://www.saporedicina.com/english/list-chengyu/

   Organize the idioms you have collected into a chart with slots for the 256 (4x4x4x4) possible combinations. You may never be able to fill all 256 slots with idioms, so go ahead and fill some of the slots with ordinary 4-syllable phrases. For example, for the tonal sequences 1111, 1112, 1113, 1114, you may use 他吃西瓜 **tā chī xīguā** (*he eats watermelon*), 风中之烛 **fēng-zhōng-zhī-zhú** (*candle in the wind*, i.e. *precarious*), 惊弓之鸟 **jīng-gōng-zhī-niǎo** (*bird in fear of the bow*, i.e. *an easily frightened person*), 交通工具 **jiāotōng gōngjù** (*transportation apparatus*). Practice saying the phrases in your chart out loud and have a teacher critique your pronunciation. Incorporate these idioms in your Chinese conversations at every opportunity and watch your Chinese friends be amazed by your quantum leap.

2 Common Pitfalls in Basic Vocabulary Usage

People who are fortunate enough to be bilingual often find it difficult, even impossible, to translate certain expressions from one language to the other. When speaking in one language, they may switch in midstream to the other language for just one word or phrase. This phenomenon illustrates the fact that different cultures conceptualize the world of ideas differently, and many concepts simply have no exact equivalents in two languages, especially two that are as divergent as English and Chinese. Even when the conceptualization of an idea is the same, the vocabulary used for expressing it may not correspond due to grammatical differences. As a teacher, I am delighted when a student is stymied in trying to translate a phrase with the proper nuance, or resorts to the other language to express a subtle idea, because this is a sign that the student is wearing the thinking cap of the target language. In this chapter, we will discuss twelve types of faulty vocabulary usage, most of which can be attributed to thinking in English while speaking in Chinese.

2.1 Single English words corresponding to multiple words in Chinese

When a single English word corresponds to two or more different Chinese words, the corresponding Chinese words are often mistaken as "synonyms." While the distinctions among the corresponding Chinese words may seem subtle to the English speaker, they are very clear and significant to the native Chinese speaker. Therefore, the corresponding Chinese words cannot simply be used interchangeably. The most common cases are the following ones.

1. Translations of "can" ("to be able"): 会 huì, 可以 kěyǐ, 能 néng, and 可能 kěnéng

The common Chinese verbs 会 huì, 可以 kěyǐ, 能 néng, 可能 kěnéng can all be translated into English as *can*, and they are all auxiliary verbs, but to a native Chinese these four words have distinct meanings and cannot be used interchangeably.

a. The correct usage of 会 huì

会 huì, as auxiliary verb (not as the noun meaning "meeting"), has two meanings: 1) it implies an acquired ability, a learned skill (e.g. swimming, driving, speaking a foreign language, etc.); 2) meaning "will, would" indicating prediction (with certainty or at least high probability). It is the first of these two meanings that corresponds to the word *can* in English.

a. 会 **huì** implying learned ability:

◆ *That child <u>can</u> walk now.* 那个孩子会走路了。 **Nèige háizi huì zǒulù le.**

b. 会 **huì** in the sense of "will":

◆ *<u>Will</u> you be coming tomorrow?* 你明天会来吗？ **Nǐ míngtiān huì lái ma?**

b. The correct usage of 可以 kěyǐ

可以 **kěyǐ** implies that external circumstances (rules and regulations, weather conditions, etc.) make it possible to do something. The auxiliary verb *may* is a synonym of *can* in this sense.

◆ *One <u>cannot</u> turn left at this intersection.*
在这个路口不可以左拐。 **Zài zhèige lùkǒu bù kěyǐ zuǒguǎi.**

◆ *In the U.S., tap water is drinkable (<u>can</u> be drunk).*
在美国，自来水是可以喝的。 **Zài Měiguó, zìláishuǐ shì kěyǐ hēde.**

c. The correct usage of 能 néng

能 **néng** also implies that circumstances permit something to be done, but it's more inclusive than 可以 **kěyǐ** in that the circumstances may be "internal" (property of the person, e.g. his health, work schedule, etc.) as well as external.

◆ *I'm too busy these few days, so I <u>can't</u> come see you.*
这几天我太忙，不能来看你了。 **Zhèi jǐtiān wǒ tài máng, bùnéng lái kàn nǐ le.**

◆ *I <u>can't</u> tell you right now whether or not it <u>will</u> rain tomorrow.*
我现在还不能告诉你明天会不会下雨。
Wǒ xiànzài hái bùnéng gàosu nǐ míngtiān huì-buhuì xiàyǔ.

d. The correct usage of 可能 kěnéng

可能 **kěnéng** implies that there is the possibility of something occurring. It is more commonly translated into English as *could* or *might*, but it can also be translated as *can*.

◆ *The weather in Canada is hard to predict, it can snow even in June.*
加拿大的天气很难预测，六月都可能会下雪。
Jiānádàde tiānqì hěn nán yùcè, liùyuè dōu kěnéng huì xiàxuě.

◆ *He didn't come to class, he might be ill.*
他没来上课，可能是病了。 **Tā méi lái shàngkè, kěnéng shì bìngle.**

◆ *Over vacation, I could go home, or I could travel, I haven't decided yet.*
放假的时候，我可能回家，也可能去旅遊，现在还没决定。
Fàngjiàde shíhou, wǒ kěnéng huíjiā, yě kěnéng qù lǚyóu, xiànzài hái méi juédìng.

EXERCISES:

Translate the following sentences into Chinese:

1. The teacher will tell us.
2. At this Chinese language center, students may not speak English.
3. The teacher is sick, (and therefore) cannot come to class.
4. After drinking (liquor), one may not drive!
5. I can speak a little Chinese, but I cannot read Chinese.
6. I'm too busy today, so I cannot come see you.
7. In China, can a sixteen-year-old drive a car?
8. It won't rain today, will it?
9. According to the weather forecast, it can (might) snow tomorrow.
10. Any vocabulary the teacher taught this semester may appear on the final exam.

ANSWERS:

1. 老师会告诉我们的。 **Lǎoshī huì gàosu wǒmen de.**
2. 在这个汉语中心，学生不可以/能说英语。
   Zài zhèige Hànyǔ zhōngxīn, xuésheng bù kěyǐ/néng shuō Yīngyǔ.
3. 老师病了，不能来上课。 **Lǎoshī bìngle, bùnéng lái shàngkè.**
4. 喝了酒就不可以/能开车了！ **Hēle jiǔ jiù bù kěyǐ/néng kāichē le!**
5. 我会说一点中文，可是不会看中文书。
   Wǒ huì shuō yìdiǎn Zhōngwén, kěshì búhuì kàn Zhōngwén shū.
6. 我今天太忙了，不能来看你。 **Wǒ jīntiān tài máng le, bùnéng lái kàn nǐ.**
7. 在中国，十六岁就可以/能开车了吗？
   Zài Zhōngguó, shíliùsuì jiù kěyǐ/néng kāichē le ma?
8. 今天不会下雨吧？ **Jīntiān búhuì xiàyǔ ba?**
9. 按照天气预报，明天可能会下雪。 **Ànzhào tiānqì yùbào, míngtiān kěnéng huì xiàxuě.**
10. 老师这个学期教过的生词都可能出现在大考上。
    Lǎoshī zhèige xuéqī jiāoguode shēngcí dōu kěnéng chūxiàn-zài dàkǎo-shang.

2. Translations of "to know": 知道 zhīdao vs 认识 rènshi

知道 **zhīdao** implies knowing certain facts; 认识 **rènshi** means being acquainted with or having familiarity with (someone, some place, some Chinese character, etc.).

a. The correct usage of 知道 zhīdao:

● *You'll <u>know</u> what classes you'll be in only after taking the placement test.*
  考了入学考试以后才知道要上什么课。
  Kǎole rùxué kǎoshì yǐhòu cái zhīdao yào shàng shénme kè.

b. The correct usage of 认识 rènshi:

● *You don't <u>know</u> him? No matter, I can introduce you.*

你不认识他吗？没关系，我可以给你们介绍。
Nǐ bú rènshi tā ma? Méi guānxi, wǒ kěyǐ gěi nǐmen jièshào.

♦ *The people in Taiwan often don't know simplified characters, but they can learn them very quickly.*
在台湾的人通常不认识简体字，不过他们很快就能学会了。
Zài Táiwānde rén tōngcháng bú rènshi jiǎntǐzì, búguò tāmen hěn kuài jiù néng xuéhuìle.

EXERCISES:

Translate the following sentences into Chinese:

1. I like this dish very much, but I don't know what it's called.
2. If you don't know that place, you can look at the map.
3. I know who he is, but I don't know him (personally).

ANSWERS:

1. 我很喜欢这个菜，可是不知道叫什么名字。
   Wǒ hěn xǐhuan zhèige cài, kěshì bù zhīdao jiào shénme míngzi.

2. 如果你不认识那个地方，可以看地图。**Rúguǒ nǐ bú rènshi nèige dìfang, kěyǐ kàn dìtú.**

3. 我知道他是谁，可是不认识他。**Wǒ zhīdao tā shì shéi, kěshì bú rènshi tā.**

3. Translations of "to ask": 请 qǐng, 问 wèn, 请问 qǐngwèn

问 **wèn** means to ask a question; 请 **qǐng** means to ask for (a favor), to request someone to do something (often translated as *please…*), or to invite someone (to an event). 请 **qǐng** and 问 **wèn** together (i.e. 请问 **qǐngwèn**) means *"please may I ask."* "请⋯问⋯ **qǐng…wèn…**" means *"ask so-and-so to ask…"* (see the last example below).

a. The correct usage of 问 wèn:

♦ *He asked me many questions.* 他问了我很多问题。**Tā wènle wǒ hěn duō wèntí.**

b. The correct usage of 请 qǐng:

♦ *Please sit down!* 请坐！**Qǐng zuò!**

♦ *Please don't smoke here.* 请别在这里抽烟。**Qǐng bié zài zhèlǐ chōuyān.**

♦ *Their family often invite guests (for dinner).*
他们家常常请客。**Tāmen jiā chángcháng qǐngkè.**

c. The correct usage of 请问 qǐngwèn:

♦ *May I ask, does this town have a liquor store?*
请问，这个城里有没有卖酒的商店？
Qǐngwèn, zhèige chénglǐ yǒu méiyǒu mài jiǔde shāngdiàn?

● *Please ask the doctor how long I'll have to stay in the hospital.*
请你问医生我得在医院住多久。
Qǐng nǐ wèn yīshēng wǒ děi zài yīyuàn zhù duōjiǔ.

EXERCISES:

Translate the following sentences into Chinese:

1. What did the teacher ask you?

2. May I ask, where's the restroom?

3. Ask him not to smoke in the room.

4. Please tell me your Chinese name.

5. Anything you don't understand, you may ask the teacher.

6. Please introduce me to some good Chinese books.

7. Teacher Wang wants to invite us to dinner.

8. Please ask him when he can come.

ANSWERS:

1. 老师问了你什么? **Lǎoshī wènle nǐ shénme?**

2. 请问，厕所在哪儿? **Qǐngwèn, cèsuǒ zài nǎr.**

3. 请他别在屋子里抽烟。**Qǐng tā bié zài wūzilǐ chōuyān.**

4. 请你告诉我你的中文名字。**Qǐng nǐ gàosu wǒ nǐde Zhōngwén míngzi.**

5. 有什么你不懂的，都可以问老师。**Yǒu shénme nǐ bùdǒngde, dōu kěyǐ wèn lǎoshī.**

6. 请你给我介绍几本好的中文书。**Qǐng nǐ gěi wǒ jièshào jǐběn hǎode Zhōngwén shū.**

7. 王老师要请我们吃饭。**Wáng Lǎoshī yào qǐng wǒmen chīfàn.**

8. 请问他什么时候能来。**Qǐng wèn tā shénme shíhou néng lái.**

4. Translations of "other, others, the other (one)": 别的 biéde, 别人 biérén, 另外那 lìngwài nèi + M

a. The correct usage of 别的 biéde

别的 **biéde** refers to all the others aside from the one in question or mentioned previously. It may be followed by a noun (e.g. 别的东西 **biéde dōngxi**, 别的国家 **biéde guójiā**), or be left dangling without a noun if that noun is understood (see 1.3, sec. 2). If the following noun is monosyllable (e.g. 人 **rén**, 国 **guó**), 的 **de** is omitted to preserve the bisyllabic rhythm.

● *Aside from English, he also knows <u>other</u> foreign languages.*
除了英文以外，他还会很多别的外语。
Chúle Yīngwén yǐwài, tā hái huì hěn duō biéde wàiyǔ.

● *You cannot ask other people to help you take exams.*
不能请别人帮你考试。 **Bùnéng qǐng biérén bāng nǐ kǎoshì.**

- *He has never been abroad, and doesn't have foreign friends, how can he understand the cultures of other countries?*
  他没出过国，也没有外国朋友，怎么能了解别国的文化呢?
  Tā méi chūguo guó, yě méiyǒu wàiguó péngyou, zěnme néng liǎojiě biéguóde wénhuà ne?

Note the use of 都 **dōu** in some of the above sentences to add emphasis to the idea of ALL the others.

b. The correct usage of 别 bié

别 **bié** also functions as an auxiliary verb, meaning *don't*.

- *It would be best if you didn't meddle in <u>other people's</u> affairs.*
  别人的事情，你最好别管。 **Biérénde shìqing, nǐ zuìhǎo bié guǎn.**

c. The correct usage of 另外那 lìngwài nèi + M

另外那 **lìngwài nèi** + M refers to "the other one" in talking about two entities in juxtaposition.

- *The other man is not a teacher at our center.*
  另外那位先生不是我们中心的老师。
  Lìngwài nèiwèi xiānsheng búshì wǒmen zhōngxīnde lǎoshī.

In everyday speech, the word 另外 **lìngwài** may be omitted in context, leaving just 那 **nèi** + M to carry the meaning *the other one*.

- *We have two kids, this one is our birth child, the other is adopted.*
  我们有两个孩子，这个是我们亲生的，(另外)那个是领养的。
  Wǒmen yǒu liǎngge háizi, zhèige shì wǒmen qīnshēngde, (lìngwài) nèige shì lǐngyǎngde.

- *These two seem to be the same, but only this one is real, the other one is a fake.*
  这两个好像一样，不过这个才是真的，那个是假的。
  Zhèi liǎngge hǎoxiàng yíyàng, búguò zhèige cái shì zhēnde, nèige shì jiǎde.

EXERCISES:

Translate the following sentences into Chinese:

1. I can come only on Sunday, I'm very busy all the other days.
2. No one else knows about this matter. (Other people don't know about this matter.)
3. Please don't eat in class!
4. Have you finished reading that other book?
5. I only want this one, not any of the others.
6. These two kids aren't both mine. The older one (the big one) is mine, the other one is my younger sister's.

ANSWERS:

1. 我只有星期天能来，别的日子我都很忙。
   Wǒ zhǐyǒu xīngqītiān néng lái, biéde rìzi wǒ dōu hěn máng.

2. 别人都不知道这件事。**Biérén dōu bù zhīdao zhèijiàn shì.**

3. 请别在课上吃东西。**Qǐng bié zài kèshang chī dōngxi.**

4. 你看完了另外那本书了吗？**Nǐ kànwánle lìngwài nèiběn shū le ma?**

5. 我只要这个，别的我都不要。**Wǒ zhǐ yào zhèige, biéde wǒ dōu bú yào.**

6. 这两个孩子不都是我的。大的是我的，另外那个是我妹妹的。
   Zhèi liǎngge háizi bù dōu shì wǒde. Dàde shì wǒde, lìngwài nèige shì wǒ mèimeide.

5. Translations of "to hear" and "to see": 听 tīng vs 听见 tīngjiàn; 看 kàn vs 看见 kànjian

The difference between 听 **tīng** vs 听见 **tīngjiàn** is equivalent to *to listen* vs *to hear*; and 看 **kàn** vs 看见 **kànjian** is equivalent to *to look* vs *to see*. The verbs 听 **tīng** and 看 **kàn** refer to "deploying" one's auditory or visual faculty to receive sensory input, but they do not necessarily result in receiving the sounds or images.

- *Listening to recordings is very useful.* 听录音很有用。 **Tīng lùyīn hěn yǒuyòng.**

- *I've listened to it, but didn't understand it.*
  我听了，可是没听懂。**Wǒ tīngle, kěshì méi tīngdǒng.**

- *What are you looking at?* 你在看什么？ **Nǐ zài kàn shénme?**

- *He's sick, so I'd like to go see him.*
  他病了，所以我想去看看他。 **Tā bìngle, suǒyǐ wǒ xiǎng qù kànkan tā.**

- *No one has seen him, perhaps he didn't come.*
  大家都没看见他，也许他没来。 **Dàjiā dōu méi kànjian tā, yěxǔ tā méi lái.**

- *When the air quality is good, one can see the West Hill from here.*
  空气好的时候，从这里可以看见西山。
  Kōngqì hǎode shíhou, cóng zhèlǐ kěyǐ kànjian Xīshān.

EXERCISES:

Translate the following sentences into Chinese:

1. I've read that book, but I didn't understand it.

2. We should listen to the news every day.

3. Your voice is too faint (small), I cannot hear it.

4. It's too far, I can't see it.

5. Have you seen him today?

ANSWERS:

1. 我看了那本书，可是没看懂。**Wǒ kànle nèiběn shū, kěshì méi kàndǒng.**
2. 我们每天都应该听新闻。**Wǒmen měitiān dōu yīnggāi tīng xīnwén.**
3. 你的声音太小了，我听不见。**Nǐde shēngyīn tài xiǎo le, wǒ tīng-bú-jiàn.**
4. 太远了，我看不见。**Tài yuǎn le, wǒ kàn-bú-jiàn.**
5. 你今天看见他了吗？**Nǐ jīntiān kànjiàn tā le ma?**

6. Translations of "year": 年 nián vs 岁 suì

The word 年 **nián** refers to a specific year or a certain number of years, whereas 岁 **suì** refers to years of age.

◆ *Children normally begin to speak at two years of age.*
小孩子平常两岁就开始说话了。
Xiǎoháizi píngcháng liǎngsuì jiù kāishǐ shuōhuàle.

◆ *My dog is only six years old, it should live another six years.*
我的狗才六岁，应该能再活六年。
Wǒde gǒu cái liùsuì, yīnggāi néng zài huó liùnián.

EXERCISES:

Translate the following sentences into Chinese:

1. He was born in 1990, so he's 28 this year.
2. It was three years ago that he died, at the time he was only 60 years old.

ANSWERS:

1. 他是一九九零年出生的，所以今年二十八岁了。
   Tā shì yī-jiǔ-jiǔ-líng-nián chūshēng de, suǒyǐ jīnnián èrshíbā-suì le.
2. 他是三年以前去世的。那时才六十岁。
   Tā shì sānnián yǐqián qùshì de. Nà shí cái liùshí-suì.

7. Translations of "almost": 差不多 chàbuduō, 差一点儿 chàyìdiǎnr, 差一点儿没 chàyìdiǎnr méi

a. The correct usage of 差不多 chàbuduō

The phrase 差不多 **chàbuduō** has two meanings: 1) *approximately* (*quantitative*) and 2) *to have almost – but not quite – reached an end point.*

◆ *Approximately 60% of the graduate students in this department are foreign students.*
这个系的研究生<u>差不多</u>百分之六十是国际学生。
Zhèige xìde yánjiūshēng chàbuduō bǎifēn-zhī-liùshí shì guójì xuésheng.

◆ *I'm <u>almost</u> done reading that book, I should be able to return it to you tomorrow.*
那本书我差不多看完了，明天就可以还给你了。
Nèiběn shū wǒ chàbuduō kànwánle, míngtiān jiù kěyǐ huángěi nǐ le.

b. The correct usage of 差一点儿 chàyìdiǎnr

The phrase 差一点儿 **chàyìdiǎnr** implies that *in retrospect,* an event almost occurred, or an endpoint was almost reached, *but not quite.* So actually, the event did not occur or the endpoint was not reached.

♦ *He almost (but not quite) rammed into the truck coming toward him.*
他差一点儿撞到前面来的货车。
Tā chàyìdiǎnr zhuàngdào qiánmiàn láide huòchē.

♦ *He almost (but not quite) passed the college entrance exam last year. With some hard work reviewing this year, he will surely be able to pass it.*
他去年差一点儿考上了大学。今年再努力复习一下，肯定能考上。
Tā qùnián chàyìdiǎnr kǎoshangle dàxué. Jīnnián zài nǔlì fùxí yíxià, kěndìng néng kǎoshang.

c. The correct usage of 差一点儿没 chàyìdiǎnr méi

The phrase 差一点儿没 **chàyìdiǎnr méi** has two meanings:

1. 差一点儿 **chàyìdiǎnr** (same meaning as above) + 没 **méi** added to the verb: *almost didn't*

♦ *Last night as I was driving home, it was too dark, I almost didn't see the bicyclist in front of me (but I did see him after all).*
昨天晚上我开车回家的时候，天太黑了，我差一点儿没看见前面骑车的人。**Zuótiān wǎnshang wǒ kāichē huíjiāde shíhou, tiān tài hēile, wǒ chàyìdiǎnr méi kànjian qiánmian qíchēde rén.**

2. There is an odd and confusing usage of 差一点儿没 **chàyìdiǎnr méi** that native speakers sometimes use in colloquial speech. This one is especially difficult for non-natives to emulate, but we introduce it here so that readers would at least understand it when they hear it used. 差一点儿没 **chàyìdiǎnr méi** can mean *almost, but not quite,* which makes it synonymous with 差一点儿 **chàyìdiǎnr,** and the opposite of the first meaning of 差一点儿没 **chàyìdiǎnr méi** above.

♦ *Last year he was gravely ill and almost died. Later he gradually got well.*
去年他病得很厉害，差一点儿没死。后来慢慢儿就好了。
Qùnián tā bìngde hěn lìhai, chàyìdiǎnr méi sǐ, hòulái mànmānr jiù hǎole.

♦ *It snowed hard last night. Driving home I had a close call. I should count myself lucky!*
昨天晚上下大雪，我开车回家差一点儿没出事，算是很幸运！
Zuótiān wǎnshang xià dàxuě, wǒ kāichē huíjiā chàyìdiǎnr méi chūshì, suànshì hěn xìngyùn!

EXERCISES:

Translate the following sentences into Chinese:

1. It's almost 6:00. Let's go to dinner! Wait a bit, I'm almost done.

2. I almost forgot! Today is a holiday, we don't have to go to school!

3. I almost didn't bring enough money! (The money I brought was almost not enough.)

4. It was about three years ago that I saw him.

5. He has almost recovered from illness. (His illness is almost well.)

6. Fifty years ago, almost all doctors in America were men.

7. I was almost late today, tomorrow I must start out a little earlier!

8. He almost didn't pass the college entrance exam (i.e. he did in fact pass, but barely).

ANSWERS:

1. 差不多六点了，我们去吃饭吧！等一等，我差不多做完了。
   Chàbuduō liùdiǎn le, wǒmen qù chīfàn ba! Děng-yīděng, wǒ chàbuduō zuòwánle.

2. 我差一点儿忘了！今天放假，我们不必上学！
   Wǒ chàyìdiǎnr wàngle! Jīntiān fàngjià, wǒmen búbì shàngxué!

3. 我带的钱差一点儿不够！ **Wǒ dàide qián chàyìdiǎnr bú gòu!**

4. 我是差不多三年以前见到他的。 **Wǒ shì chàbuduō sānnián yǐqián jiàndào tā de.**

5. 他的病差不多好了。 **Tāde bìng chàbuduō hǎo le.**

6. 五十年以前，在美国的医生差不多都是男的。
   Wǔshí-nián yǐqián, zài Měiguóde yīshēng chàbuduō dōu shì nánde.

7. 我今天差一点儿迟到了，明天我一定要早一点儿出发。
   Wǒ jīntiān chàyìdiǎnr chídào le, míngtiān wǒ yídìng yào zǎo yìdiǎnr chūfā.

8. 他差一点儿没考上大学。 **Tā chàyìdiǎnr méi kǎoshang dàxué.**

---

8. Translations of "a little": 一点儿 yìdiǎnr vs 有一点儿 yǒu yìdiǎnr[1]

a. The correct usage of 一点儿 yìdiǎnr

The phrase 一点儿 **yìdiǎnr** occurs in two contexts; the first one is easy, but the second one requires putting on the Chinese thinking cap.

1. 一点儿 **yìdiǎnr** followed by a noun (*a little bit of…*)

♦ *In drinking coffee, some like to add a bit of sugar, some like to add a bit of milk.*
喝咖啡，有人喜欢放一点儿糖，有人喜欢放一点儿牛奶。
Hē kāfēi, yǒurén xǐhuan fàng yìdiǎnr táng, yǒurén xǐhuan fàng yìdiǎnr niúnǎi.

♦ *Yours is not enough, I'll give you a little bit.* 你的不够，我给你一点儿吧。
(the noun after 一点儿 is understood and omitted)
Nǐde búgòu, wǒ gěi nǐ yìdiǎnr ba.

A favorite Chinese sentence pattern that incorporates 一点儿 **yìdiǎnr** is "连一点儿…都不/没 **lián yìdiǎnr…dōu bù/méi…**", and it is used to convey the idea "*not even the least bit of…*" In this pattern, 连 **lián** may be omitted without change in meaning. (see also part II, 124 and 191)

---

[1] 一点儿 **yìdiǎnr** and 有一点儿 **yǒu yìdiǎn** may be abbreviated to 点儿 **diǎnr** and 有点儿 **yǒudiǎnr** respectively in actual speech. This is consistent with the deletion of 一 **yī** in situations where it is understood, e.g. 我有个哥哥 **wǒ yǒu ge gēge** "I have an older brother."

◆ *I don't put any sugar in my coffee.*
我喝咖啡(连)一点儿糖都不放。 **Wǒ hē kāfēi (lián) yìdiǎnr táng dōu búfàng.**

◆ *Although I had studied Chinese for two years in the U.S. before I went to China, the day I arrived, I couldn't understand anything the local people said.*
虽然我去中国以前在美国学过两年的中文，可是刚到的那天，当地人说的话我一点儿都听不懂！
Suīrán wǒ qù Zhōngguó yǐqián zài Měiguó xuéguo liǎngniánde Zhōngwén, kěshì gāng dàode nèitiān, dāngdì-rén shuōde huà wǒ yìdiǎnr dōu tīng-bù-dǒng.

2. An adjective or adverb followed by 一点儿 **yìdiǎnr** (*a little more…*).
In a statement, when 一点儿 **yìdiǎnr** follows an adjective or adverb, it describes something/someone or some action as *being a little more in a certain way*. If used in a request or command, it means the speaker wants the action to be done in a certain way a bit more.

Statements:

◆ *She's a bit taller than I.* 她比我高一点儿。 **Tā bǐ wǒ gāo yìdiǎnr.**

◆ *This way of doing it is a bit faster.* 这个做法快一点儿。
Zhèige zuòfǎ kuài yìdiǎnr.

◆ *He's a bit better today.* 他今天好一点儿了。 **Tā jīntiān hǎo yìdiǎnr le.**

Requests:

◆ *Please speak a little more slowly.* 请说慢一点儿。 **Qǐng shuō màn yìdiǎnr.**

◆ *Can you come a bit earlier?* 你能不能来早一点儿?
Nǐ néng-bunéng lái zǎo yìdiǎnr?

◆ *Please speak a little louder.* 请大声一点儿说。 **Qǐng dàshēng yìdiǎnr shuō.**

b. The correct usage of 有一点儿 **yǒu yìdiǎnr**

The phrase 有一点儿 **yǒu yìdiǎnr** deserves special mention because it does not necessarily mean *have a little bit*. More often, it is used before an adjective with a negative connotation, to convey a lament, complaint or criticism. The word 太 **tài** may precede the adjective to reinforce the negativity. but the usage of the diminutive 一点儿 **yìdiǎnr** softens the tone.

◆ *This matter makes me feel a bit embarrassed. (vs This is really embarrassing to me.)*
这件事让我有一点儿不好意思。
Zhèijiàn shì ràng wǒ yǒu yìdiǎnr bùhǎo-yìsi.

◆ *His attitude is really a bit too much! (vs His attitude is truly overboard!)*
他的态度真是有一点儿太过分了!
Tāde tàidù zhēnshì yǒu yìdiǎnr tài guòfèn le.

Note that when the adjective is positive, the pattern "adj. + 一点儿 **yìdiǎnr…**" introduced at the beginning of this section is used instead of the "有一点儿 **yǒu yìdiǎnr** + adj." pattern discussed above.

◆ *I'm feeling a bit better today.*

   ✗ 今天我有一点儿舒服了。 **Jīntiān wǒ yǒu yìdiǎnr shūfu le.**

   ✓ 我今天舒服一点儿了。 **Wǒ jīntiān shūfu yìdiǎnr le.**

   ✓ 我今天好一点儿了。 **Wǒ jīntiān hǎo yìdiǎnr le.**

Finally, 有一点儿 **yǒu yìdiǎnr** can be interpreted as 有 + 一点儿 **yǒu + yìdiǎnr** (something), meaning *to have a little bit of … .*

◆ *Do you have a bit of time today?*
你今天有一点儿时间吗？ **Nǐ jīntiān yǒu yìdiǎnr shíjiān ma?**

◆ *There's a bit of a problem in your way of thinking.*
你的想法有一点儿问题。 **Nǐde xiǎngfǎ yǒu yìdiǎnr wèntí.**

EXERCISES:

Translate the following sentences into Chinese:

1. Please speak a little more clearly.
2. Do you have a little time today? I'd like to come chat with you.
3. These few days I don't have any free time. Can you wait until the weekend?
4. When the Chinese eat *jiaozi*, they like to use a little vinegar.
5. Although I can speak Chinese, I don't understand a bit of Sichuanese.
6. The train is a little faster than the bus.
7. That restaurant is a bit too expensive, but it's very classy.
8. I like this apartment, but it's a bit too far from my school.
9. This course is a little difficult for me.
10. I'm a bit under the weather today.

ANSWERS:

1. 请你说大声一点儿。 **Qǐng nǐ shuō dàshēng yìdiǎnr.**
2. 你今天有一点儿时间吗？我想来跟你谈谈。
   Nǐ jīntiān yǒu yìdiǎnr shíjiān ma? Wǒ xiǎng lái gēn nǐ tántan.
3. 这几天我一点儿空都没有，你能不能等到周末？
   Zhè jǐtiān wǒ yìdiǎnr kòng dōu méiyǒu, nǐ néng-bùnéng děngdào zhōumò?
4. 中国人吃饺子喜欢用一点醋。 **Zhōngguórén chī jiǎozi xǐhuan yòng yìdiǎnr cù.**
5. 虽然我会说普通话，我一点儿四川话都不懂。
   Suīrán wǒ huì shuō pǔtōnghuà, wǒ yìdiǎnr Sìchuān-huà dōu bù dǒng.
6. 火车比公交车快一点儿。 **Huǒchē bǐ gōngjiāochē kuài yìdiǎnr.**
7. 那个餐馆有一点儿贵，可是很高级。 **Nèige cānguǎn yǒuyìdiǎnr guì, kěshì hěn gāojí.**

8. 我喜欢这个公寓，可是离我的学校有一点儿太远了。
   Wǒ xǐhuan zhèige gōngyù, kěshì lí wǒde xuéxiào yǒuyìdiǎnr tài yuǎn le.

9. 这门课对我有一点儿难。**Zhèimén kè duì wǒ yǒuyìdiǎnr nán.**

10. 我今天有一点儿不舒服。**Wǒ jīntiān yǒuyìdiǎnr bùshūfu.**

9. Translations of "just": 刚 gāng, 刚刚 gānggāng, 刚才 gāngcái

The three Chinese words above can all be translated as *just* to convey the brevity of time lapse since some pertinent event, but there are differences in their usage, especially with 刚才 gāngcái.

a. The correct usage of 刚 gāng and 刚刚 gānggāng

The word 刚 **gāng** indicates that an event has just occurred, but the time of the event can be relative to the past, the present, or even the future. 刚刚 **gānggāng** is a more intense form of 刚 **gāng**, conveying even shorter time lapse since the event than 刚 **gāng**. 刚刚 **gānggāng** is generally not used when the time of the event is relative to the future.

● *The students have just arrived in Beijing, how can they immediately take an exam?* (present)
  学生刚到北京，怎么能马上就考试呢？
  Xuésheng gāng dào Běijīng, zěnme néng mǎshàng jiù kǎoshì ne?

● *When he just arrived in Beijing, he couldn't speak any Chinese.* (past)
  他刚到北京的时候，一点儿汉语都不会说。
  Tā gāng dào Běijīngde shíhou, yìdiǎnr Hànyǔ dōu búhuì shuō.

● *I will arrive in Hong Kong the day after tomorrow. The first few days after just arriving will be very busy, perhaps I won't be able to write you until a week after that.* (future)
  我后天到香港，刚到的头几天肯定会很忙，可能一个星期以后才能给你写信。**Wǒ hòutiān dào Xiānggǎng, gāng dàode tóujǐtiān kěndìng huì hěn máng, kěnéng yíge xīngqī yǐhòu cái néng gěi nǐ xiěxìn.**

● *He just got home, [he] hasn't even taken off his coat.* (present)
  他刚刚到家，还没脱外套呢。**Tā gānggāng dào jiā, hái méi tuō wàitào ne.**

● *This morning, just after he went out, someone called looking for him.* (past)
  今天早上他刚刚出门就有人来电话找他了。
  Jīntiān zǎoshang tā gānggāng chūmén jiù yǒurén lái diànhuà zhǎo tā le.

● *You're just graduating, and have no work experience, so it would be best to do a year of internship first.* (present)
  你刚毕业，没有什么工作经验，所以最好先做一年的实习。
  Nǐ gāng bìyè, méiyǒu shénme gōngzuò jīngyàn, suǒyǐ zuìhǎo xiān zuò yìniánde shíxí.

b. The correct usage of 刚才 gāngcái

The word 刚才 gāngcái contrasts with 刚 gāng and 刚刚 gānggāng in two ways: 1) the timing of the event is relative only to the present, so 刚才 gāngcái means more precisely "just a moment ago, just now." 2) 刚才 gāngcái is a movable adverb (i.e., it can occur before or after the subject of the sentence, as long as it is before the verb), whereas 刚 gāng and 刚刚 gānggāng are adverbs that occur only before the verb. The preferred position for 刚才 gāngcái is at the beginning of the sentence before the subject.

◆ *Just now didn't you say you can help me? How come now you say you can't.*
刚才你不是说你能帮我吗？怎么现在又说不行了？
Gāngcái nǐ búshì shuō nǐ néng bāng wǒ ma? Zěnme xiànzài yòu shuō bùxíng le?

Also acceptable: 你刚才不是说··· **Nǐ gāngcái búshì shuō...**

EXERCISES:

Translate the following sentences into Chinese:

1. He's just arrived.
2. Did you understand what he said just now?
3. We just finished studying Lesson Five today.
4. Just now someone called you; I told him that you had just left.
5. We just started school, so everyone is very busy.
6. Last year when she just arrived in the U.S., she could not speak any English.
7. When I just moved here, I didn't know anyone, but soon I made many new friends.
8. Thanks! I just had lunch, so I'm not hungry yet.
9. What did you say just now? I didn't hear you clearly.
10. I just heard a piece of good news.

ANSWERS:
1. 他刚到了。 **Tā gāng dàole.**
2. 他刚才说的话，你听懂了吗？ **Tā gāngcái shuōde huà, nǐ tīngdǒngle ma?**
3. 我们今天刚读完第五课。 **Wǒmen jīntiān gāng dúwán dìwǔkè.**
4. 刚才有人打电话给你，我告诉他你刚走了。
   Gāngcái yǒurén dǎ diànhuà gěi nǐ, wǒ gàosu tā nǐ gāng zǒule.
5. 我们刚开学，所以大家都很忙。 **Wǒmen gāng kāixué, suǒyǐ dàjiā dōu hěn máng.**
6. 去年她刚到美国的时候，一点儿英文都不会说。
   Qùnián tā gāng dào Měiguóde shíhou, yìdiǎnr Yīngwén dōu búhuì shuō.
7. 我刚搬来的时候，一个人都不认识，可是我很快就认识了很多新的朋友了。
   Wǒ gāng bānláide shíhou, yíge rén dōu bú rènshi, kěshì wǒ hěn kuài jiù rènshile hěn duō xīnde péngyou le.
8. 谢谢！我刚刚吃完中饭，现在还不饿。
   Xièxie! Wǒ gānggāng chīwán zhōngfàn, xiànzài hái bú è.

9. 你刚才说什么？我没听清楚。**Nǐ gāngcái shuō shénme? Wǒ méi tīng-qīngchǔ.**
10. 我刚刚听到一个好消息。**Wǒ gānggāng tīngdào yíge hǎo xiāoxi.**

10. Translations of "or": 还是 háishi vs 或是 huòshì

a. The correct usage of 还是 háishi

The word 还是 **háishi** is used in "choice type" questions, in which one of the given options/possibilities is selected in the answer to the question.

- *Would you like to have coffee <u>or</u> tea?*
  你要喝咖啡<u>还是</u>喝茶？**Nǐ yào hē kāfēi háishi hē chá?**

- *Are imported cars <u>or</u> domestic cars better?*
  汽车是进口的<u>还是</u>国产的好？**Qìchē shì jìnkǒude háishi guóchǎnde hǎo?**

b. The correct usage of 或是 huòshì

In contrast to 还是 **háishi**, 或是 **huòshì** is used in statements in which two or more options are acceptable/possible.

- *Coffee <u>or</u> tea are both fine. Whatever's more convenient, I'll take that.*
  咖啡<u>或</u>是茶都可以。什么方便，我就喝什么。
  Kāfēi huòshì chá dōu kěyǐ. Shénme fāngbiàn, wǒ jiù hē shénme.

- *This restaurant has lots of customers at lunch, it would be best if you come before 11:30 <u>or</u> after 1:30.*
  这个餐馆中午客人特别多，你最好十一点半之前<u>或是</u>一点半之后来。
  Zhèige cānguǎn zhōngwǔ kèrén tèbié duō, nǐ zuìhǎo 11:30 zhīqián huòshì 1:30 zhīhòu lái.

Sometimes, a sentence containing 还是 **háishi** is not a question per se, but deeper analysis would reveal that there exists within it an "embedded question." This point will be revisited in 3.7, within the chapter on asking questions.

- *I don't know if he is Chinese or Japanese.* (Embedded question: Is he Chinese or Japanese?)
  我不知道他是中国人还是日本人。
  Wǒ bù zhīdao tā shì Zhōngguórén háishi Rìběnrén.

- *Now there's a way to know if an unborn child is male or female.* (Embedded question: …is male or female?)
  现在有法子知道未出生的孩子是男的还是女的了。
  Xiànzài yǒu fázi zhīdao wèi-chūshēngde háizi shì nánde háishi nǚde le.

EXERCISES:

Translate the following sentences into Chinese:

1. Is it faster to go by train or by car?

2. I'd like to study in North America. The U.S. or Canada are both not bad (implying it doesn't matter which, as long as it's North America).

3. After graduation, do you want to stay in the U.S. or return to China?

4. Staying in the U.S. or returning to China are both OK, it depends on where I can find a good job.

5. Please ask him if he would prefer tea or coffee.

6. He hasn't told me yet whether he's coming this week or next week.

ANSWERS:

1. 是坐火车还是开车比较快？ **Shì zuò huǒchē háishi kāichē bǐjiào kuài?**

2. 我想去北美留学。美国或是加拿大都不错。
   Wǒ xiǎng qù Běi-Měi liúxué, Měiguó huòshì Jiānádà dōu búcuò.

3. 毕业以后，你想留在美国还是回中国？
   Bìyè yǐhòu, nǐ xiǎng liúzài Měiguó háishi huí Zhōngguó?

4. 留在美国或是回中国都行，就看我在哪儿能找到好的工作。
   Liúzài Měiguó huòshì huí Zhōngguó dōu xíng, jiù kàn wǒ zài nǎr néng zhǎodào hǎode gōngzuò.

5. 请问他想喝茶还是咖啡。 **Qǐng wèn tā xiǎng hē chá háishi kāfēi.**

6. 他还没告诉我他是这个星期还是下个星期来。
   Tā hái méi gàosu wǒ tā shì zhèige xīngqī háishì xiàge xīngqī lái.

11. Translations of "afraid of/to" vs "afraid that": 怕 pà vs 恐怕 kǒngpà

a. The correct usage of 怕 pà

The verb 怕 **pà** is most commonly used as a transitive verb, i.e. a verb that has an object. It is translated into English as either *afraid of (something)* or *afraid to (do something).*

♦ *Chinese students generally are afraid of the college entrance exam.*
中国学生一般都很怕高考。 **Zhōngguó xuésheng yìbān dōu hěn pà gāokǎo.**

♦ *I'm afraid to go see the dentist.* 我很怕去看牙医。 **Wǒ hěn pà qù kàn yáyī.**

♦ *He's not afraid of anyone, except his wife.*
他谁都不怕，就怕他太太。 **Tā shéi dōu bú pà, jiù pà tā tàitai.**

怕 **pà** can also function as an adjective, meaning *afraid, scared,* in which case it is synonymous with the more commonly used adjective 害怕 **hàipà**.

♦ *Having you with me makes me unafraid.*
有你和我在一起，我就不怕/害怕了。
Yǒu nǐ hé wǒ zài yìqǐ, wǒ jiù bú pà/hàipà le.

♦ *(Dentist to the patient) Don't be afraid, this won't hurt much, besides it will soon be over.*
别怕/害怕，这个不会很疼，而且很快就完了。
Bié pà/hàipà, zhèige búhuì hěn téng, érqiě hěn kuài jiù wán le.

b. The correct usage of 恐怕 kǒngpà

The adverb 恐怕 kǒngpà is an adverb that can be placed interchangeably before or after the subject of a sentence, and it literally means *afraid that … .* But just like the English phrase *I'm afraid that…*, it often indicates the *possibility* (of something undesirable) rather than real *fear* (of something), in which case it is a near synonym of *perhaps*. In the first two examples here, note that the subject "I" does not appear in the Chinese translation.

● *I'm afraid he won't be able to pass the college entrance exam.*
他恐怕考不上大学。　　　　or:　恐怕他考不上大学。
Tā kǒngpà kǎo-bu-shàng dàxué.　　**Kǒngpà tā kǎo-bu-shàng dàxué.**

● *I'm afraid his wife might really be fierce.*
恐怕他太太真的很厉害。　　or:　他太太恐怕真的很厉害。
Kǒngpà tā tàitai zhēnde hěn lìhai.　　**Tā tàitai kǒngpà zhēnde hěn lìhai.**

● *I keep feeling tired lately, perhaps I'm not getting enough sleep.*
我最近老觉得很累，恐怕是睡得不够。
Wǒ zuìjìn lǎo juéde hěn lèi, kǒngpà shì shuìde búgòu.

EXERCISES:

Translate the following sentences into Chinese:

1. It's already so late, I'm afraid all the restaurants are closed.
2. My mother is afraid to take a plane, so she has never gone abroad.

> **ANSWERS:**
> 1. 已经太晚了，恐怕餐馆都关门了。**Yǐjīng tài wǎn le, kǒngpà cānguǎn dōu guānmén le.**
> 2. 我妈妈很怕坐飞机，所以她从来没出过国。
> **Wǒ māma hěn pà zuò fēijī, suǒyǐ tā cónglái méi chū-guo-guó.**

12. Translations of "from": 从 cóng vs 离 lí

The word 从 **cóng** indicates a starting point (a place or a time), whereas 离 **lí** means *distance from.* These two concepts are totally different, even though they share the word *from* in English.

● *Are all these students <u>from</u> the U.S.?* 这些学生都是<u>从</u>美国来的吗？
Zhèixiē xuésheng dōushì cóng Měiguó láide ma?

● *How many hours does it take to fly <u>from</u> the U.S. to China?*
<u>从</u>美国坐飞机来中国要几个钟头？
Cóng Měiguó zuò fēijī lái Zhōngguó yào jǐge zhōngtou?

● *<u>From</u> today on, I will not smoke anymore.*
<u>从</u>今天起，我不再抽烟了。**Cóng jīntiān qǐ, wǒ búzài chōuyānle.**

◆ *The U.S. is too far from Australia.*
美国离澳大利亚太远了。 **Měiguó lí Àodàlìyà tài yuǎn le.**

◆ *We're still four hours from our arrival in Beijing.*
现在离到达北京的时间还有四个小时呢。
Xiànzài lí dàodá Běijīngde shíjiān háiyǒu sìge xiǎoshí ne.

◆ *I feel it's best to be as far from smokers as possible.*
我觉得离抽烟的人越远越好。 **Wǒ juéde lí chōuyānde rén yuèyuǎn-yuèhǎo.**

In the above examples, 从 **cóng** and 离 **lí** function as coverbs (see Chapter 11), but they also occur as components in bisyllabic words, in which case they can also function as verbs meaning *follow* and *depart* respectively, e.g. 从事 **cóngshì** (follow a career), 从命 **cóngmìng** (follow order), 服从 **fúcóng** (obey), 离开 **líkāi** (leave), 离婚 **líhūn** (divorce), 离职 **lízhí** (leave a job).

EXERCISES: ▶

Translate the following sentences into Chinese.

1. Shenzhen is a new city. The people here have all come from elsewhere.
2. From the time I was 18 years old, I have not lived with my parents.
3. I'd like to find an apartment that's not far from the school.
4. Final exams are only a month away (It's only a month from final exams), you should start preparing for them!

> **ANSWERS:**
> 1. 深圳是个新的城市。这里的人都是从别的地方来的。
>   **Shēnzhèn shì ge xīnde chéngshì. Zhèlǐde rén dōu shì cóng biéde dìfang lái de.**
> 2. 我从十八岁就没有跟我父母住在一起了。
>   **Wǒ cóng shíbāsuì jiù méiyǒu gēn wǒ fùmǔ zhùzài yìqǐ le.**
> 3. 我想找一个离学校不远的公寓。 **Wǒ xiǎng zhǎo yíge lí xuéxiào bùyuǎnde gōngyù.**
> 4. 离大考只有一个月了，你应该开始准备了吧！
>   **Lí dàkǎo zhǐyǒu yíge yuè le, nǐ yīnggāi kāishǐ zhǔnbèi le ba!**

13. Translations of "if": 如果 **rúguǒ**, 要是 **yàoshi** (synonyms, but 要是 **yàoshi** is more colloquial)

The *if* in English, aside from the primary meaning that we all know, can mean *whether... or...*, as in "*I don't know if I can come tomorrow.*" and "*Do you know if this is a fruit or a vegetable?*" This quirky usage of *if* gets lost in direct translation into Chinese. In Chinese, the idea of *whether...or...* is conveyed by an embedded interrogative phrase eliciting a choice between two options (either "*yes or no*" or "*A or B*"). These two forms are detailed in Chapter 3.7 (parts 2 and 3), but a few examples below should be sufficient to make them clear.

- *I don't know if it will rain today.*
  ✗ 我不知道今天如果会下雨。 **Wǒ bù zhīdao jīntiān rúguǒ huì xiàyǔ.**
  ✓ 我不知道今天会不会下雨。 **Wǒ bù zhīdao jīntiān huì-buhuì xiàyǔ.**

- *Do you know if he can speak Chinese?*
  ✗ 你知道不知道如果他会说普通话？
  Nǐ zhīdao-bùzhīdao rúguǒ tā huì shuō pǔtōnghuà?
  ✓ 他会不会说普通话，你知道吗？
  Tā huì-buhuì shuō pǔtōnghuà, nǐ zhīdao ma?
  or 你知道不知道他会不会说普通话？
  Nǐ zhīdao-bùzhīdao tā huì-buhuì shuō pǔtōnghuà?

This may seem like a simple point, but a surprising number of students trip over this pitfall. By putting on your Chinese thinking cap, you should be able to correctly translate the following sentences into Chinese.

EXERCISES:

Translate the following sentences into Chinese:

1. If you don't have enough money, I can lend you some.
2. Do you know (can you tell) if he's Chinese or Japanese?
3. I don't know if he likes spicy foods, so it would be best if you don't make it too spicy.

> **ANSWERS:**
> 1. 如果你的钱不够，我可以借一点给你。
>   **Rúguǒ nǐde qián bú gòu, wǒ kěyǐ jiè yìdiǎn gěi nǐ.**
> 2. 他是中国人还是日本人？你看得出来吗？
>   **Tā shì Zhōngguórén háishi Rìběnrén? Nǐ kàn-de-chūlai ma?**
> 3. 我不知道他喜欢不喜欢吃辣的，所以你最好别做得太辣。
>   **Wǒ bù zhīdao tā xǐhuan-bùxǐhuan chī làde, suǒyǐ nǐ zuì hǎo bié zuòde tài là.**

14. Translations of "some": 一些 yìxiē, 一点儿 yìdiǎnr, 几 jǐ..., 有些 yǒuxiē, 有人 yǒurén, 有些人 yǒuxiē rén, 有的 yǒude

The English word *some* is imprecise and covers multifarious meanings. The correct rendering of *some* into Chinese requires the native English speaker to make some unaccustomed distinctions.

a. The correct usage of 一些 yìxiē, 一点儿 yìdiǎnr, 几 jǐ...

Some meaning "a small amount, a few": 一些 yìxiē, 一点儿 yìdiǎnr, 几 jǐ...

- *Before coming to China, I had learned some Chinese.*
  来中国之前我学过一些中文。 **Lái Zhōngguó zhīqián wǒ xuéguo yìxiē Zhōngwén.**

- *This dish would be tastier by adding some wine.*
  这个菜要放一点儿酒才好吃。 **Zhèige cài yào fàng yìdiǎnr jiǔ cái hǎochī.**

- *His friends have introduced some ladies to him, but he feels none of them are suitable.*
  他的朋友给他介绍过几位女朋友，可是他觉得都不合适。
  Tāde péngyou gěi tā jièshàoguo jǐwèi nǔpéngyou, kěshì tā juéde dōu bù héshì.

At a slightly more literary level of Chinese, *a small amount, a certain number of…* may be expressed by two other terms which are synonyms to 一些 **yìxiē**/一点儿 **yìdiǎnr** and 几 **jǐ…**:

少许 **shǎoxǔ** *a small amount*: may replace 一点儿 **yìdiǎnr** in the second example above.

- *She only carried a small amount of money on her.*
  她身上仅带了少许的钱。 **Tā shēnshang jǐn dàile shǎoxǔde qián.**

若干 **ruògān** *a certain number of…*: may replace 几 **jǐ** in the third example above.

- *After a certain number of years, that lake totally dried up.*
  若干年之后，那个湖就完全枯干了。
  Ruògān nián zhīhòu, nèige hú jiù wánquán kūgānle.

Similarly, the common term 很多 **hěnduō** has the idiomatic synonym 不少 **bùshǎo** (frequently used by native Chinese) and the slightly more literary term 大量 的 **dàliàngde**.

- *I learn a large amount of vocabulary daily, but I also forget quite a lot!*
  我每天都学大量的生词，可是忘记的也不少。
  Wǒ měitiān dōu xué dàliàngde shēngcí, kěshì wàngjìde yě bùshǎo.

b. The correct usage of 有些 **yǒuxiē**, 有人 **yǒurén**, 有些人 **yǒuxiē rén…**

Some referring to unspecified person(s) or entity(ies) (singular or plural), *a certain…*, *certain ones…*: 有些 **yǒuxiē**, 有人 **yǒurén**, 有些人 **yǒuxiē rén**, etc., or simply "一 **yī** + M." A simple measure word (either alone or with 一 **yī**) can convey the idea of a certain someone or something. But when a sentence begins with the indefinite thing or person, 有 **yǒu** is added, making it literally *there is a (certain person or thing)*.

- *Some friends tried to persuade them not to divorce, but it was too late.*
  有些朋友劝他们别离婚，可是已经太晚了。
  Yǒuxiē péngyou quàn tāmen bié líhūn, kěshì yǐjīng tài wǎn le.

- *I only know that he is teaching at some high school, but I don't know which one.*
  我只知道他在(某)一个中学教书，可是不知道是哪个。
  Wǒ zhǐ zhīdao tā zài (mǒu) yíge zhōngxué jiāoshū, kěshì bù zhīdao shì něige.

- *These days some restaurants no longer use MSG.*
  现在有些餐馆已经不用味精了。
  Xiànzài yǒuxiē cānguǎn yǐjīng bú yòng wèijīng le.

c. The correct usage of 有的 yǒude

Some in the sense of *some of…*: 有的 **yǒude** (which may or may not be followed by a noun)

♦ *I like some of these CDs, some of them I don't care for.*
这些光盘，有的我喜欢，有的我不喜欢。
Zhèixiē guāngpán, yǒude wǒ xǐhuan, yǒude wǒ bùxǐhuan.

♦ *Some of the dishes in this restaurant are pretty good, some are just so-so.*
这家餐馆的菜，有的不错，有的不怎么样。
Zhèijiā cānguǎnde cài, yǒude búcuò, yǒude bù zěnmeyàng.

♦ *Some universities are private, some are public.*
有的大学是私立的，有的是公立的。
Yǒude dàxué shì sīlìde, yǒude shì gōnglìde.

有的 **yǒude** (+ noun) conveys the notion of a "subset" of a group of things, and it must be the subject or topic of a clause. Thus, it would be incorrect to translate the first example above as:

✗ 这些光盘，我喜欢有的，不喜欢有的。
Zhèixiē guāngpán, wǒ xǐhuan yǒude, wǒ bùxǐhuan yǒude.

The "group" of which the subset is a part may be—but not necessarily—pre-stated at the beginning of the sentence as the "topic," as in the first two examples.

EXERCISES:

Translate the following sentences into Chinese:

1. You drank some (liquor) today; it would be best not to drive.
2. I already gave him some, but he said it's not enough.
3. I've asked some teachers, their explanations are all different.
4. Someone said that Mr. Wang has already got his Ph.D.
5. Someday, you will succeed!
6. She didn't say on the phone who she is, but she seems like some company's salesperson.
7. I can speak some Chinese, but not a bit of Sichuanese.
8. We bought some fruits; some are inexpensive, some are expensive.
9. Someone told me that Leshan (乐山) is a fun place.
10. Some Sichuan people can't speak Chinese.

ANSWERS:

1. 你今天喝了一点酒，最好别开车。**Nǐ jīntiān hēle yìdiǎn jiǔ, zuì hǎo bié kāichē.**
2. 我已经给了他一点儿，可是他说不够。**Wǒ yǐjīng gěile tā yìdiǎnr, kěshì tā shuō búgòu.**

3. 我问了几位老师，他们的解释都不一样。
   Wǒ wènle jǐwèi lǎoshī, tāmende jiěshì dōu bù yíyàng.

4. 有人说王先生已经得到博士了。 **Yǒurén shuō Wáng Xiānsheng yǐjīng dédào bóshì le.**

5. 有一天，你会成功的！ **Yǒu yìtiān, nǐ huì chénggōng de!**

6. 她在电话上没说她是谁，可是好像是一个公司的推销员。
   Tā zài diànhuà-shang méi shuō tā shì shéi, kěshì hǎoxiàng shì yíge gōngsīde tuīxiāo-yuán.

7. 我会说一点儿普通话，可是一点儿四川话都不会。
   Wǒ huì shuō yìdiǎnr pǔtōnghuà, kěshì yìdiǎnr Sìchuān-huà dōu búhuì.

8. 我们买了一些水果，有的便宜，有的贵。
   Wǒmen mǎile yìxiē shuǐguǒ, yǒude piányi, yǒude guì.

9. 有人告诉我乐山是个好玩儿的地方。 **Yǒurén gàosu wǒ Lèshān shì ge hǎowánrde dìfang.**

10. 有的四川人不会说普通话。 **Yǒude Sìchuān-rén búhuì shuō pǔtōnghuà.**

15. Translations of "even, even though (although), even if...": 连···也 lián...yě..., 虽然 suīrán, 就是···也 jiùshi...yě..., 即使···也 jíshǐ...yě...

The three concepts conveyed by the terms *even, even though,* and *even if,* are sufficiently distinct in the minds of the native English speakers, so that they tend not to be mixed up in actual usage. However, because the three terms share the same first word *even*, native English speakers tend to think of the word 连 **lián** when they intend to express any of the three concepts in Chinese. If this pitfall applies to you, then practice using the patterns 虽然 **suīrán**, 就是···也 **jiùshi...yě...**, 即使···也 **jíshǐ...yě...** to engrave them in your mind.

a. The correct usage of 连···也 **lián...yě...:**

◆ *The college library is open every day; even on Sundays, it doesn't close.*
  大学的图书馆每天都开，<u>连</u>星期天<u>也</u>不关门。
  Dàxuéde túshūguǎn měitiān dōu kāi, lián xīngqītiān yě bù guānmén.

b. The correct usage of 虽然 **suírán:**

◆ *Even though the tickets are all sold out, there are still lots of people waiting at the window (ticket counter).*
  <u>虽然</u>票都卖光了，还有很多人在窗口等。
  Suīrán piào dōu màiguāngle, háiyǒu hěnduō rén zài chuāngkǒu děng.

c. The correct usage of 就是···也 **jiùshi...yě...** or 即使···也 **jíshǐ...yě...** (both mean "even if...," but 即使 **jíshǐ** is more formal than 就是 **jiùshi**):

◆ *Even if it's windy and raining I will come. I won't be able to come only if it snows hard.*
  <u>就是</u>下雨刮风我<u>也</u>会来，只有下大雪我就不能来了。
  Jiùshi xiàyǔ guāfēng wǒ yě huì lái, zhǐyǒu xià dàxuě wǒ jiù bùnéng lái le.

♦ *Even if I live in China for 20 years, my Chinese would not be as good as a native's.*
即使我在中国生活二十年，我的中文也不可能跟中国人的一样好。
Jíshǐ wǒ zài Zhōngguó shēnghuó èrshí-nián, wǒde Zhōngwén yě bù kěnéng gēn Zhōngguórénde yíyàng hǎo.

EXERCISES:

Translate the following sentences into Chinese:

1. He has to go to work even on Sundays.
2. Even though his parents are from China, he cannot speak even a bit of Chinese.
3. Even if I had the time, I wouldn't go see that meaningless movie.
4. Even if she can pass the college entrance exam, she still must stay at home to help her parents.

ANSWERS:

1. 连星期天他也得上班。**Lián xīngqītiān tā yě děi shàngbān.**
2. 虽然他父母是从中国来的，他连一点儿中国话都不会说。
   Suīrán tā fùmǔ shì cóng Zhōngguó lái de, tā lián yìdiǎnr Zhōngguóhuà dōu búhuì shuō.
3. 我就是有时间也不会去看那个没有意思的电影。or 即使我有时间…
   Wǒ jiùshì yǒu shíjiān yě búhuì qù kàn nèige méiyǒu yìside diànyǐng. or Jíshǐ wǒ yǒu shíjiān…
4. 即使她能考上大学也得留在家里帮助她父母。
   Jíshǐ tā néng kǎoshang dàxué yě děi liúzài jiālǐ bāngzhù tā fùmǔ.

---

16. Translations of "again": 又 yòu vs 再 zài

The English word *again* is simple, but it translates into two non-interchangeable terms in Chinese: 又 **yòu** or 再 **zài**. 又 **yòu** applies to events that have occurred, 再 **zài** applies to the future.

♦ *Darn, I forgot your name again!*
糟糕，我又忘了你的名字了！ **Zāogāo, wǒ yòu wàngle nǐde míngzi le!**

♦ *If you forget my name again, I won't tell you anymore.*
如果你再忘记我的名字，我就不再告诉你了。
Rúguǒ nǐ zài wàngjì wǒde míngzi, wǒ jiù búzài gàosu nǐ le.

There is a lot more to the usage of 又 **yòu** and 再 **zài** that warrants discussion. Fuller coverage of these two words will be included in the chapter on adverbs (see 5.1, sections 5 and 6).

EXERCISES:

Translate the following sentences into Chinese:

1. It rained again today, and I hear it will rain again tomorrow.
2. Darn, I caught a cold again!
3. Will you be coming again tomorrow?

4. I won't be coming again this week. Goodbye!

> **ANSWERS:**
> 1. 今天又下雨了，我听说明天还会下雨。
>   **Jīntiān yòu xiàyǔ le, wǒ tīngshuō míngtiān hái huì xiàyǔ.**
> 2. 糟糕，我又感冒了！ **Zāogāo, wǒ yòu gǎnmào le!**
> 3. 你明天会再来吗？ **Nǐ míngtiān huì zài lái ma?**
> 4. 这个星期我不会再来了，再见！ **Zhèige xīngqī wǒ búhuì zài lái le, zàijiàn!**

17. Translations of "then": 然后 ránhòu, 就 jiù, 才 cái

The word *then* in English is used to signal a sequential relationship between two clauses. The relationship could be either a temporal sequence or a conditional relationship. When translated into Chinese, the different meanings covered by the single English word "then" are conveyed by three different words: 然后 **ránhòu**, 就 **jiù**, and 才 **cái**. To the native English speaker, the differences may be very subtle, but to the native Chinese, they are quite distinct.

a. The correct usage of 然后 ránhòu

然后 **ránhòu** is the most clear-cut of the three words mentioned above. It signals a temporal sequence and functions like a conjunction between two clauses.

◆ *There are too many people in the restaurant now. We had better go see the movie first, then have dinner afterwards.*
现在餐馆的人太多了，我们最好先去看电影，<u>然后</u>去吃饭。
Xiànzài cāiguǎnde rén tài duō le, wǒmen zuìhǎo xiān qù kàn diànyǐng, ránhòu qù chīfàn.

b. The correct usage of 就 jiù and 才 cái

就 **jiù** and 才 **cái** both signal a conditional relationship, i.e. the first clause states the condition that leads to the effect stated in the second clause. But 才 **cái** indicates that the condition is absolute, i.e. it means *then and only then*....

◆ *I'm planning to begin working after I graduate.*
我打算毕业以后<u>就</u>开始工作了。 **Wǒ dǎsuàn bìyè yǐhòu jiù kāishǐ gōngzuòle.**

◆ *Rest a couple of days, then you'll be well.*
你休息两三天就会好了。 **Nǐ xiūxi liǎng-sān tiān jiù huì hǎole.**

◆ *You must stay in the hospital a couple of days, then you may go home.*
你得在医院住两三天才能回家。
Nǐ děi zài yīyuàn zhù liǎng-sān tiān cái néng huíjiā.

There is a lot more to the usage of 就 **jiù** and 才 **cái** that warrants discussion. Fuller coverage of these two words will be included in the chapter on adverbs (see 5.1, sections 4 and 7).

▶ **EXERCISES:**

Translate the following sentences into Chinese:

1. After taking this medicine, you will soon be well.
2. You must take this medicine for three days, and only then will you recover.
3. After studying this book, your Chinese will be greatly improved.
4. In learning Chinese, we first learned by using *pinyin* for one semester, then we began learning Chinese characters.

ANSWERS:
1. 吃了药以后，你很快就会好的。 **Chīle yào yǐhòu, nǐ hěn kuài jiù huì hǎo de.**
2. 这个药你得吃三天才会好。 **Zhèige yào nǐ děi chī sāntiān cái huì hǎo.**
3. 读完这本书，你的中文就会有很大的进步。
   Dúwán zhèiběn shū, nǐde Zhōngwén jiù huì yǒu hěn dàde jìnbù.
4. 我们学中文，先用拼音学了一个学期，然后才开始学汉字。
   Wǒmen xué Zhōngwén, xiān yòng pīnyīn xuéle yíge xīngqī, ránhòu cái kāishǐ xué Hànzì.

18. Translations of "later on": 以后 yǐhòu, 后来 hòulái, 然后 ránhòu

然后 **ránhòu** was already discussed in the preceding section and is not a difficult word to master. 以后 **yǐhòu** and 后来 **hòulái**, however, are sometimes confused in the mind of the native English speaker.

a. The correct usage of 以后 yǐhòu

以后 **yǐhòu** means *after (a certain event or time)*, and that event or time can be explicit or implicit.

♦ *After they divorced, they have not seen each other again.*
  他们离了婚以后就没再见面了。(the divorce is explicitly stated before 以后)
  Tāmen lí-le-hūn yǐhòu jiù méi zài jiànmiàn le.

♦ *…. Thereafter, they have not seen each other again.*
  …。以后他们就没再见面了。(a preceding event is implicit in the ellipsis)
  …. Yǐhòu tāmen jiù méi zài jiànmiàn le.

以后 **yǐhòu** can apply to future as well as past events.

♦ *After you go abroad, you'll still come home often to see your parents, won't you?*
  你出国以后，还会常常回家看父母吧?
  Nǐ chūguó yǐhòu, hái huì chángchang huíjiā kàn fùmǔ ba?

♦ *After he went abroad, he hasn't come home to see his parents again.*
  他出国以后，就没再回家看父母了。
  Tā chūguó yǐhòu, jiù méi zài huíjiā kàn fùmǔ le.

◆ *He went abroad ten years ago. Thereafter, he has not come home to see his parents again.*
他十年前出国了，以后就没再回家看父母了。
Tā shínián qián chūguó le, yǐhòu jiù méi zài huíjiā kàn fùmǔ le.

b. The correct usage of 后来 hòulái

后来 hòulái applies only to the past, and is not linked directly to a specific event or time, although it does imply a loose connection with a past event, e.g.

◆ *Shenzhen was formerly a place that no one had heard of. Later on, it developed into a big city.*
深圳原来是个没有人听过的地方。后来发展成了一个大都市。
Shēnzhèn yuánlái shì ge méiyǒu rén tīngguode dìfang, hòulái fāzhǎn chéngle yíge dà dūshì.

EXERCISES:

Translate the following sentences into Chinese:

1. My home was originally in the countryside. Later on, we moved to the city.
2. After we moved to the city, I have not returned to my old home.
3. We will first learn to speak a little Chinese, and then we will begin learning some Chinese characters.
4. It was only after I came to the U.S. that I began to learn English.

> **ANSWERS:**
> 1. 我家原来是在乡下，后来我们搬到城里去了。
>   **Wǒ jiā yuánlái shì zài xiāngxia, hòulái wǒmen bāndào chénglǐ qùle.**
> 2. 我们搬到城里去以后，我就没回过老家了。
>   **Wǒmen bāndào chénglǐ qù yǐhòu, wǒ jiù méi huíguo lǎojiā le.**
> 3. 我们先学说一点中国话，然后就开始学一些汉字。
>   **Wǒmen xiān xué shuō yìdiǎn Zhōngguóhuà, ránhòu jiù kāishǐ xué yìxiē Hànzì.**
> 4. 我是来了美国以后才开始学英文的。
>   **Wǒ shì láile Měiguó yǐhòu cái kāishǐ xué Yīngwén de.**

2.2 Single Chinese words corresponding to multiple words in English

The converse of the phenomenon described in 2.1 is the case of Chinese words that translate into several different words in English, depending on the context. Such cases are generally much easier for the non-native speaker to master than the reverse situation. All one needs to do is to learn the various different meanings of the Chinese words. In some cases, just as in English, these are in fact familiar Chinese words with relatively unfamiliar or uncommon secondary meanings. Here are just a few examples.

1. The word 算 **suàn** (basic meaning: *calculate*) has the additional meanings of *to reckon as* or *to consider* and *to forget about it* (or *count it as done*):

♦ *¥20 cannot be <u>considered</u> (counted as) too expensive.* ¥20不算太贵。 **¥20 búsuàn tàiguì.**

♦ *Forget about it! Don't argue with him anymore!*
算了吧！ 别跟他吵了！ **Suànle ba! Bié gēn tā chǎo le!**

2. The word 数 **shǔ** (basic meaning: *count*) has the additional meaning of *to count as, to rank as*:

♦ *Peking University and Tsinghua University rank as the top two universities in China.*
北大和清华是中国数一数二的大学。
Běi Dà hé Qīnghuá shì Zhōngguó shǔyī-shǔèrde dàxué.

♦ *Among the four kids, we can count him as the smartest.*
四个孩子里头，数他最聪明。
Sìge háizi lǐtou, shǔ tā zuì cōngming.

In the above usages, 算 **suàn** and 数 **shǔ** seem to be synonyms. There is actually this difference between them: 数 **shǔ** must imply comparison within a group, whereas 算 **suàn** does not necessarily imply comparison.

3. The word 打 **dǎ** (basic meaning: *to hit*) has the following additional meanings:

• *to play (a sport or game): to play Mahjong* 打麻将 **dǎ májiàng**; *to play basketball* 打篮球 **dǎ lánqiú**
• *to fetch (colloquial): to fetch water* 打水 **dǎ shuǐ**; *to fetch/get/buy oil* 打油 **dǎ yóu**
• *from (very colloquial): from tomorrow on* 打明儿起 **dǎ míngr qǐ**;
• *coming from where?* 打哪儿来 **dǎ nǎr lái**
• *to make a phone call* 打电话 **dǎ diànhuà**
• *a dozen (pronounced dá): a dozen eggs* 一打鸡蛋 **yìdá jīdàn**; *a dozen socks* 一打袜子 **yìdá wàzi**

2.3 English and Chinese words with similar meanings that function as different parts of speech

When corresponding Chinese and English words carry the same meaning but are grammatically different, direct translation from English into Chinese can lead to some wacky utterances. Here are three common examples:

1. Chinese 都 **dōu** (adverb) vs English "*all*" (adjective):[2]

---

[2] We discuss the adverb 都 **dōu** as a vocabulary issue in this chapter. A full discussion on 都 **dōu** as an adverb will be given in 5.1.1.

- *Not all Americans can speak English.*
  - ✗ 不都美国人会说英语。**Bù dōu Měiguórén huì shuō Yīngyǔ.**
  - ✓ 美国人不都会说英语。**Měiguórén bù dōu huì shuō Yīngyǔ.**

- *He can understand everything the teacher says.*
  - ✗ 他能听懂都老师说的话。**Tā néng tīngdǒng dōu lǎoshī shuōde huà.**
  - ✗ 他都能听懂老师说的话。**Tā dōu néng tīngdǒng lǎoshī shuōde huà.**
  - ✓ 老师说的话他都能听懂。**Lǎoshī shuōde huà, tā dōu néng tīngdǒng.**

- *I like to eat all Chinese foods.*
  - ✗ 我喜欢吃都中国菜。**Wǒ xǐhuan chī dōu Zhōngguó cài.**
  - ✓ 中国菜我都喜欢吃。**Zhōngguó cài, wǒ dōu xǐhuan chī.**

- *All Chinese can speak Chinese, but not all of them can speak it well.*
  - ✗ 都中国人会说普通话，可是不都他们说得很好。
    Dōu Zhōngguórén huì shuō pǔtōnghuà, kěshì bù dōu tāmen shuōde hěn hǎo.
  - ✓ 中国人都会说普通话，可是他们不都说得很好。
    Zhōngguórén dōu huì shuō pǔtōnghuà, kěshì tāmen bù dōu shuōde hěn hǎo.

2. Chinese 多 / 少 **duō/shǎo** (adverbs) vs English "*more/less*" (indicators of quantities):

- *You should work more and talk less.*
  - ✗ 应该做多事，说少话。**Yīnggāi zuò duō shì, shuō shǎo huà.**
  - ✓ 应该多做事，少说话。**Yīnggāi duō zuòshì, shǎo shuōhuà.**

- *It would be best for you to meddle less in others' affairs.*
  - ✗ 你最好管别人的事少些。**Nǐ zuìhǎo guǎn biérénde shì shǎo xiē.**
  - ✓ 你最好少管别人的事。**Nǐ zuìhǎo shǎo guǎn biérénde shì.**

多 **duō** and 少 **shǎo** can also function as adjectives, as will be discussed in 2.4.

3. 多少 **duōshǎo** has two meanings:

a. As an interrogative meaning *how much*:

- *How much does it cost to study in China for a year?*
  去中国留学一年需要多少钱？
  Qù Zhōngguó liúxué yìnián xūyào duōshǎo qián?

b. As adverb, it means *to some extent, more or less*:

- *All Chinese college students more or less know some English.*
  中国的大学生多少都会一点儿英语。
  Zhōngguóde dàxuésheng duōshǎo dōu huì yìdiǎnr Yīngyǔ.

EXERCISES: ▶

Translate the following sentences into Chinese:

1. Not all Americans are rich.
2. None of them have money.
3. All of my students will be English teachers in the future.
4. You should eat more vegetables and less meat.
5. Mom, I'm bringing a friend home for dinner tonight; please make two more dishes.
6. His parents are from China, so to some extent he should be able to speak a bit of Chinese.
7. You haven't recovered from your illness yet; (you) should rest more.

ANSWERS:

1. 美国人不都有钱。**Měiguórén bù dōu yǒuqián.**
2. 他们都没有钱。**Tāmen dōu méiyǒu qián.**
3. 我的学生将来都会当英语老师。**Wǒde xuésheng jiānglái dōu huì dāng Yīngyǔ lǎoshī.**
4. 你应该多吃蔬菜，少吃肉。**Nǐ yīnggāi duō chī shūcài, shǎo chī ròu.**
5. 妈，今天晚上我要带一个朋友回家，请多做两个菜。
   Mā, jīntiān wǎnshang wǒ yào dài yíge péngyou huíjiā, qǐng duō zuò liàngge cài.
6. 他父母是从中国来的，所以他应该多少能说一点儿中文吧?
   Tā fùmǔ shì cóng Zhōngguó lái de, suǒyǐ tā yīnggāi duōshǎo néng shuō yìdiǎnr Zhōngwén ba?
7. 你的病还没好，应该多休息。**Nǐde bìng hái méi hǎo, yīnggāi duō xiūxi.**

2.4 Three Chinese single-syllable adjectives that cannot be used in front of a noun: 够 gòu *enough*; 多 duō *much*; 少 shǎo *little*

In English, adjectives appear in two locations: before a noun and in the predicate. E.g. *Good food is expensive*; *expensive food is not necessarily good*. Adjectives in Chinese generally function the same way, but there are at least three single-syllable ones—*enough* 够 **gòu**, *much* 多 **duō**, *little* 少 **shǎo**—that can only be used in the predicate and not in front of a noun.

- *I don't have enough money.*
   ✗ 我没有够的钱。**Wǒ méiyǒu gòude qián.**
   ✓ 我的钱不够。**Wǒde qián búgòu.**

- *I don't have much money.*
   ✗ 我没有多的钱。**Wǒ méiyǒu duōde qián.**
   ✓ 我的钱不多。**Wǒde qián bùduō.**
   ✓ 我没有很多的钱。**Wǒ méiyǒu hěnduōde qián.**
   (很多 **hěnduō** can be used as a noun modifier, but not 多 **duō** alone.)

◆ *I only have a little bit of money.*

　✗ 我只有少的钱。 **Wǒ zhǐyǒu shǎode qián.**

　✓ 我只有一点儿钱。 **Wǒ zhǐyǒu yìdiǎnr qián.**

　✓ 我的钱很少。 **Wǒde qián hěnshǎo.**

EXERCISES:

Translate the following sentences into Chinese:

1. There is not enough time today. How about tomorrow?

2. There are too many cars in the city!

3. This teacher does not give us a lot of homework, but she often gives us tests!

> **ANSWERS:**
> 1. 今天时间不够，明天怎么样？ **Jīntiān shíjiān bú gòu, míngtiān zěnmeyàng?**
> 2. 城里的车太多了！ **Chénglǐde chē tài duō le!**
> 3. 这位老师给我们的功课不多，可是她常常给我们考试。
>   **Zhèiwèi lǎoshī gěi wǒmende gōngkè bù duō, kěshì tā chángchang gěi wǒmen kǎoshì.**

2.5 Some Chinese single-syllable "word components" that cannot stand alone

Certain English words are translated into Chinese single-syllable "word components" (i.e. "morphemes") that cannot stand alone as words and can be used only in combination with other word components. Examples of these word components include: *male/female* 男 / 女 **nán/nǚ**, *much/little* 多 / 少 **duō/shǎo**, *same* 同 **tóng**, and all word components denoting colors. Linguists call these "bound forms" because they are bound to some other components to form whole words, e.g. 男人 **nánrén** *man*, 女士 **nǚshì** *professional woman*, 男生 **nánshēng** *male student*. In this sense, they are like affixes in English, and we may see them as another manifestation of the bisyllabic rhythm of spoken Chinese. Aside from being combined with other word components to form whole words, "bound forms" can be made into "whole words" by the addition of preceding or succeeding elements like 很- **hěn**, 不- **bu**, -的 **de**.

◆ *Her three children are all girls.*

　✗ 她的三个孩子都是女。 **Tāde sānge háizi dōu shì nǚ.**

　✓ 她的三个孩子都是女的。 **Tāde sānge háizi dōu shì nǚde.**

◆ *My favorite color is red.*

　✗ 我最喜欢的颜色是红。 **Wǒ zuì xǐhuande yánsè shì hóng.**

　✓ 我最喜欢的颜色是红色。 **Wǒ zuì xǐhuande yánsè shì hóngsè.**

◆ *These two dishes taste exactly the same.*

　✗ 这两道菜的味道完全同。 **Zhèi liǎngdào càide wèidao wánquán tóng.**

　✓ 这两道菜的味道完全一样。 **Zhèi liǎngdào càide wèidao wánquán yíyàng.**

　✓ 这两道菜的味道完全相同。 **Zhèi liǎngdào càide wèidao wánquán xiāngtóng.**

◆ *There are many foreign students at Peking University.*

✗ 北大有多外国学生。 **Běi Dà yǒu duō wàiguó xuésheng.**

✓ 北大有很多外国学生。 **Běi Dà yǒu hěnduō wàiguó xuésheng.**

EXERCISES: ▶

Translate the following sentences into Chinese:

1. In the past, when it wasn't raining, the sky was always blue. But now, the sky is always gray.

2. In many colleges, dormitories are not segregated by men and women. That is to say, men and women live in the same dorm.

3. Many Americans have learned a bit of Chinese, but those who can speak it well are few.

ANSWERS:

1. 从前不下雨的时候天总是蓝的，现在天总是灰色的了。
   Cóngqián bú xiàyǔde shíhou tiān zǒngshì lánde, xiànzài tiān zǒngshì huīsède le.

2. 在很多大学，宿舍不分男女。也就是说，男的跟女的住在同一个宿舍楼里。
   Zài hěnduō dàxué, sùshè bù fēn nán-nǚ. Yě jiùshì shuō, nánde gēn nǚde zhùzài tóng yíge sùshè-lóulǐ.

3. 很多美国人学过一点中文，可是能说得好的不多。
   Hěnduō Měiguórén xuéguo yìdiǎn Zhōngwén, kěshì néng shuōde hǎode bùduō.

"Localizers" are also "bound forms." These include: *inside/outside* 里／外 **lǐ/wài**, *front/back* 前／后 **qián/hòu**, *up/down* 上／下 **shàng/xià**, *center* 中 **zhōng**, *right/left* 左／右 **zuǒ/yòu**, *east/south/west/north* 东／南／西／北 **dōng/nán/xī/běi**. This group will be discussed in Chapter 9 on "locations."

2.6 Certain Chinese single-syllable verbs are "bound"

The phenomenon of "bound" word components described in the preceding section also occurs with certain single-syllable verbs in Chinese. That is, they do not stand alone like their English counterparts, but are always followed by an object attached to them. When there is no specific object, a generic object is added to make the single-syllable verb "whole." Four common examples are: *to eat* 吃 **chī**, *to teach* 教 **jiāo**, *to walk* 走 **zǒu**, and *to test* 考 **kǎo**. All these verbs must have an object attached to them and cannot be used alone.

The verb 吃 **chī** in the sense of *to eat a meal* always needs an object, e.g.:

◆ *When do we eat?*

✗ 我们什么时候吃？ **Wǒmen shénme shíhou chī?**

✓ 我们什么时候吃饭？ **Wǒmen shénme shíhou chīfàn?**

The generic object *rice* **fàn** or other objects can be added: *to eat a meal* 吃饭 **chīfàn**, *to eat snack* 吃点心 **chī diǎnxīn**, *to eat Western food* 吃西餐 **chī Xīcān**.

The verb 教 **jiāo** *to teach* similarly must have an object.

- *She's gone into business, and is no longer teaching.*
  - ✗ 她现在做生意了，不教了。**Tā xiànzài zuò shēngyì le, bù jiāo le.**
  - ✓ 她现在做生意了，不教书了。**Tā xiànzài zuò shēngyì le, bù jiāoshū le.**

Various objects can be added to complement the single verb: 教书 **jiāoshū**, *to teach Chinese* 教汉语 **jiāo Hànyǔ**, *to teach math* 教数学 **jiāo shùxué**, *to teach high school* 教高中 **jiāo gāozhōng**.

The verb 走 **zǒu** in the sense of *to walk* is translated as 走路 **zǒulù** (走 **zǒu** alone means *to leave*).

- *Americans are too lazy, they don't like to walk.*
  - ✗ 美国人太懒了，不喜欢走。**Měiguórén tài lǎn le, bùxǐhuan zǒu.**
  - ✓ 美国人太懒了，不喜欢走路。**Měiguórén tài lǎn le, bùxǐhuan zǒulù.**

The verb 考 **kǎo** in the sense of *to take an exam* must be translated as 考试 **kǎoshì**. Other objects can be added as well, for example: *to take a college entrance exam* 考大学 **kǎo dàxué**, *to take an English exam* 考英语 **kǎo Yīngyǔ**.

- *No one likes to take exams.*
  - ✗ 没有人喜欢考。**Méiyǒu rén xǐhuan kǎo.**
  - ✓ 没有人喜欢考试。**Méiyǒu rén xǐhuan kǎoshì.**

EXERCISES:

Translate the following sentences into Chinese:

1. I love to read. What kind of books do you like to read?
2. What is your line of work? I teach at a university.
3. The children in this village all have to walk to school.

ANSWERS:

1. 我很喜欢看书。你喜欢看什么书？ **Wǒ hěn xǐhuan kànshū. Nǐ xǐhuan kàn shénme shū?**
2. 你做什么事？我在大学里教书。 **Nǐ zuò shénme shì? Wǒ zài dàxuélǐ jiāoshū.**
3. 这个农村里的孩子们都得走路上学。
   Zhèige nóngcūnlǐde háizimen dōu děi zǒulù shàngxué.

2.7 *To think, to feel, to consider,* and *to believe* in the negative

"Cognitive verbs" such as *to think* 想 **xiǎng**, *to feel* 觉得 **juéde**, *to consider* 认为 **rènwéi**, and *to believe* 相信 **xiāngxìn**, when used in the negative, involve a difference in "logic" between Chinese and English. In English, the verb is usually negated but in Chinese, the phrase that follows the cognitive verb is usually negated (which logically makes more sense).

- *I don't think Chinese is too difficult to learn.*
    - ✗ 我不想中文太难学。 **Wǒ bù xiǎng Zhōngwén tài nánxué.**
    - ✓ 我想中文不太难学。 **Wǒ xiǎng Zhōngwén bú tài nánxué.**

- *He doesn't feel very well today.*
    - ✗ 他今天不觉得很舒服。 **Tā jīntiān bù juéde hěn shūfu.**
    - ✓ 他今天觉得不很舒服。 **Tā jīntiān juéde bù hěn shūfu.**
    - ✓ 他今天觉得很不舒服。 **Tā jīntiān juéde hěn bùshūfu.**
    (The last sentence is also correct, but it means "He is feeling very ill today.")

- *I don't feel that he really likes me.* (the negative applies to the cognitive verb "feel")
    - ✓ 我不觉得他真的喜欢我。 **Wǒ bù juéde tā zhēnde xǐhuan wǒ.**

There are two other word orders that convey differences in nuance:

I sense that he doesn't really like me. (only pretending to like me)
我觉得他不是真的喜欢我。 **Wǒ juéde tā búshì zhēnde xǐhuan wǒ.**

I sense that he really dislikes me.
我觉得他真的不喜欢我。 **Wǒ juéde tā zhēnde bù xǐhuan wǒ.**

- *I don't consider money to be of prime importance.*
    - ✓ 我不认为钱是最重要的。 **Wǒ bú rènwéi qián shì zuì zhòngyàode.**
    - ✓ 我认为钱不是最重要的。 **Wǒ rènwéi qián bú shì zuì zhòngyàode.**
    Both the above Chinese sentences are correct, but there is a difference in nuance between them. The second rendering indicates that the speaker feels even more strongly that money is not that important.

- *As long as you don't give up, I believe you won't fail.*
    - ✗ 你只要不放弃，我一定不相信你会失败。
      Nǐ zhǐyào bú fàngqì, wǒ yídìng bù xiāngxìn nǐ huì shībài.
    - ✓ 你只要不放弃，我相信你一定不会失败。
      Nǐ zhǐyào bú fàngqì, wǒ xiāngxìn nǐ yídìng búhuì shībài.

EXERCISES:

Translate the following sentences into Chinese:

1. I don't think he understood what you meant.

2. He's not feeling very well today, so he didn't come to class.

3. I don't think he can finish (that job) in one week.

4. I don't feel money is as important as health.

5. I originally didn't believe that Trump would be elected President, but in the end he did in fact become President!

6. I don't think he would ever come back, you'd better not think about him anymore.

7. Nowadays women no longer consider marriage to be the most important thing in life.

ANSWERS:

1. 我想他不明白你的意思。**Wǒ xiǎng tā bù míngbái nǐde yìsi.**

2. 他今天不太舒服，所以没来上课。**Tā jīntiān bú tài shūfu, suǒyǐ méi lái shàngkè.**

3. 我想他一个星期做不完。**Wǒ xiǎng tā yíge xīngqī zuò-bu-wán.**

4. 我不觉得金钱有健康那么重要。or 我觉得金钱没有健康那么重要。**Wǒ bù juéde jīnqián yǒu jiànkāng nàme zhòngyào.** or **Wǒ juéde jīnqián méiyǒu jiànkāng nàme zhòngyào.**

5. 我本来不相信特郎普会被选上总统，结果他居然当上总统了。 **Wǒ běnlái bù xiāngxìn Tèlángpǔ huì bèi xuǎnshang zǒngtǒng, jiéguǒ tā jūrán dāngshang zǒngtǒng le.**

6. 我想他永远不会回来了，你最好别再想他了。 **Wǒ xiǎng tā yǒngyuǎn búhuì huílái le, nǐ zuì hǎo bié zài xiǎng tā le.**

7. 现在妇女不再认为婚姻是人生中最重要的事了。 **Xiànzài fùnǚ búzài rènwéi hūnyīn shì rénshēng-zhōng zuì zhòngyàode shì le.**

2.8 Differences between English *to have* and Chinese 有 yǒu

The word 有 **yǒu** in Chinese does not necessarily have the same meaning as the English *to have*. In 2.1, section 8, in our discussion of 有一点儿 **yǒu yìdiǎnr** (see p. 35), we saw an example of 有 **yǒu** that does not translate into *to have* in English. In 9.9, we will see the usage of 有 **yǒu** in expressing the existence of something at a particular place. In this section, we will discuss two other differences between 有 **yǒu** in Chinese and *to have* in English.

有 **yǒu** is a key word used in stating measurements of things, such as height, depth, weight, volume, area, age, etc. The corresponding English expressions use "to be," instead of "to have." In Chinese, the verb 是 **shì** "to be" is generally not used in this type of sentences, although there are exceptions (see last example below).

- *Taishan is over 5,000 feet high.*
  泰山有五千多英尺高。**Tàishān yǒu wǔqiānduō yīngchǐ gāo.**

- *This big watermelon weighs three kilos.*
  这个大西瓜有三公斤(重)。**Zhèige dà xīgua yǒu sān gōngjīn (zhòng).**

- *By the way she looks, my guess is that she weighs less than 100 pounds.*
  看她的样子，我猜她没有一百磅。**Kàn tāde yàngzi, wǒ cāi tā méiyǒu yìbǎi bàng.**

- *Children must be six years old before they can enter first grade.*
  孩子必须有六岁才能上一年级。 **Háizi bìxū yǒu liùsuì cái néng shàng yìniánjí.**

- *Is this room as large as 15 square meters?*
  这间屋子有没有十五平方米? **Zhèijiān wūzi yǒu-méiyǒu shíwǔ píngfāngmǐ?**

- *Does it get as hot as 100 degrees in the summer around here?*
  这一带夏天的气温会不会有100度?
  Zhè yídài xiàtiānde qìwēn huì-búhuì yǒu yìbǎidù?
  这一带夏天的气温会不会高到100度?
  Zhè yídài xiàtiānde qìwēn huì-búhuì gāodào yìbǎidù?

- *The high temperature today will be 100 degrees.*
  今天最高气温有100度。 or 今天最高气温是100度。
  Jīntiān zuì gāo qìwēn yǒu yìbǎidù. or **Jīntiān zuì gāo qìwēn shì yìbǎidù.**

The idea of "possession" as expressed in English by the verb *to have* or by possessive pronouns is usually omitted when it is considered implicit by Chinese speakers. Look at the correct and incorrect sentences below. Can you figure out the Chinese logic in each case? What is wrong with the incorrect sentences?

- *Do all Chinese people have black hair?*
  ✗ 中国人都有黑头发吗? **Zhōngguórén dōu yǒu hēi tóufa ma?**
  ✓ 中国人的头发都是黑的吗? **Zhōngguórénde tóufa dōu shì hēide ma?**
  (The fact that all people have hair is assumed, so possession is not the issue. The relevant issue is the color of their hair.)

- *Hurry up and go wash your face and brush your teeth!*
  ✗ 快去洗你的脸、刷你的牙! **Kuài qù xǐ nǐde liǎn, shuā nǐde yá.**
  ✓ 快去洗脸刷牙! **Kuài qù xǐliǎn shuāyá.**
  (Since people usually wash their own face and brush their own teeth, it is not necessary to mention "your.")

- *I must finish my homework before I can go to bed.*
  (acceptable) 我得做完我的功课才能睡觉。
  Wǒ děi zuòwán wǒde gōngkè cái néng shuìjiào.
  ✓ (preferred) 我得做完功课才能睡觉。
  Wǒ děi zuòwán gōngkè cái néng shuìjiào.
  (Same logic as the preceding sentence. The first sentence is not incorrect, but it is less likely to be said than the second one.)

- *Did you drive your car here, or did you walk?*
  ✗ 你是开你的车来的, 还是走路来的?
  Nǐ shì kāi nǐde chē lái de, háishi zǒulù lái de?

✓ 你是开车来的，还是走路来的？ **Nǐ shì kāichē lái de, háishi zǒulù lái de?** (The issue is whether the person arrived by car or on foot, so ownership of the car is not the main issue and therefore need not be mentioned.)

EXERCISES:

Translate the following sentences into Chinese

1. How tall is Yao Ming? He is (as tall as) 7'3"!
2. How far is the bus stop? From here, it's only half a mile.
3. Do all Chinese people have black eyes?
4. No, some Chinese people have brown eyes.
5. Have you taken your medicines today?

ANSWERS:

1. 姚明有多高？他有七尺三寸那么高！ **Yáo Míng yǒu duō gāo? Tā yǒu qīchǐ sāncùn nàme gāo.**
2. 公车站有多远？离这里只有半英里。
   Gōngchē-zhàn yǒu duō yuǎn? Lí zhèlǐ zhǐyǒu bàn yīnglǐ.
3. 中国人的眼睛都是黑的吗？ **Zhōngguórénde yǎnjing dōu shì hēide ma?**
4. 不，有的中国人的眼睛是棕色的。 **Bù, yǒude Zhōngguórénde yǎnjing shì zōngsède.**
5. 你今天吃了药没有？ **Nǐ jīntiān chīle yào méiyǒu?**

2.9 Chinese word order in directional expressions

The word order in directional expressions like "northeast" and "southwest" is reversed. In Chinese, east and west always precede north and south. *North-south* is translated as 南北 **nán-běi** (literally "south-north") in Chinese.

English	incorrect	correct	Examples
northeast	*北东 **běidōng**	东北 **dōngběi**	*The Northeast was occupied by Japan at one time.* 东北曾经被日本占领了。 **Dōngběi céngjīng bèi Rìběn zhànlǐngle.**
southeast	*南东 **nándōng**	东南 **dōngnán**	*The southeast region of China developed especially fast.* 中国的东南部发展得特别快。 **Zhōngguóde dōngnán-bù fāzhǎndé tèbié kuài.**
northwest	*北西 **běixī**	西北 **xīběi**	*There are quite a few minority peoples in the Northwest and the Southwest.*
southwest	*南西 **nánxī**	西南 **xī'nán**	西北、西南都有不少的少数民族。 **Xīběi, xī'nán dōu yǒu bùshǎode shǎoshǔ-mínzú.**
north-south	*北南 **běi-nán**	南北 **nán-běi**	*The war between the North and the South in the U.S. was a huge civil war.* 美国的南北战争是一场非常大的内战。 **Měiguóde Nánběi zhànzhēng shì yìchǎng fēicháng dàde nèizhàn.**

EXERCISES:

Translate the following sentences into Chinese:

1. Kunming is in southwestern China.

2. The ethnic groups in Northwestern China were originally not the Han people.

3. Peking University and Tsinghua University are both located in the northwestern part of Beijing.

ANSWERS:

1. 昆明在中国的西南部。 **Kūnmíng zài Zhōngguóde xī'nánbù.**

2. 中国西北部的民族原来不是汉族。 **Zhōngguó xīběibù de mínzú yuánlái búshì Hànzú.**

3. 北大和清华都在北京的西北部。 **Běi-Dà hé Qīnghuá dōu zài Běijīngde xīběibù.**

2.10 The use of reduplication in spoken Chinese

An aspect of spoken Chinese that infuses vibrancy into the language is the use of reduplication, and nothing like it exists in English. Reduplication in Chinese occurs with verbs, adjectives, adverbs, measure words and in onomatopoeic expressions. Foreign learners should try to incorporate these expressions into their Chinese speech, but doing so entails mastering the formulas that apply to reduplication of different parts of speech.

1. Reduplicated verbs

Single-syllable as well as bisyllabic function verbs may be reduplicated to convey the sense of doing something lightly or briefly (i.e. less intensely). The second syllable in the reduplication is always unstressed. Examples: *to take a look* 看看 **kànkan**; *to give it a try* 试试 **shìshi**; *to try it* and *see* 试试看 **shìshi kàn**. Reduplicated bisyllabic verb takes the ABAB form. Examples: *to rest a bit* 休息休息 **xiūxi-xiūxi**; *to clean up a bit* 打扫打扫 **dǎsǎo-dǎsǎo** (NOT 休休息息 **xiūxiūxixi**; 打打扫扫 **dǎdǎsǎosǎo**).

The second syllable in a bisyllabic verb, even when not reduplicated, is usually unstressed.

Reduplicated **verb + object** compounds take the V-V-O form. Examples: *to read a bit* 看看书 **kànkanshū**; *to chat a bit* 聊聊天 **liáoliaotiān**. (NOT 看书看书 **kànshū kànshū**; 聊天聊天 **liáotiān liáotiān**.)

2. Reduplicated adjectives

Reduplicating an adjective has the effect of intensifying the adjective, whereas reduplicating a verb reduces its intensity. And unlike reduplicated verbs, reduplicated adjectives take the form AABB. Examples: *so-so* 马马虎虎 **mǎmahūhū**; *slovenly* 邋邋遢遢 **lālātāta**; *white and plump* 白白胖胖 **báibáipàngpàng**.

3. Reduplicated adverbs

Adverbs may be derived by reduplicating adjectives with the addition of the "suffix" 地 **de** (e.g. *nicely* 好好儿地 **hǎohāorde**; *slowly* 慢慢儿地 **mànmānrde**, *lightly* 轻轻地 **qīngqīngde**). When the adjective being reduplicated consists of just one syllable, the tone of the second syllable becomes the first tone if it is not already a first tone— as in the first two examples above. In the Beijing dialect, an 儿-r is often tagged on. When the adjective being reduplicated into an adverb is bisyllabic, the resulting adverb takes the form AABB 地 (e.g. *happily* 高高兴兴地 **gāogāoxìngxìngde**; *casually* 随随便便地 **suísuíbiànbiànde**; *frankly/straightforwardly* 老老实实地 **lǎolaoshíshíde**; *earnestly* 认认真真地 **rènrenzhēnzhēnde**), just like the reduplicated adjectives introduced in the last paragraph.

4. Reduplicated measure words

Any measure word can be reduplicated to convey the meaning of *every…*, e.g. *every volume* (of a group of books) 本本 **běnběn**; *every one* 个个 **gège**; *every day* 天天 **tiāntiān**.

5. Reduplicated Nouns

A very limited number of common nouns also may be reduplicated to convey the meaning of *every*. For example: *every person* 人人 **rénrén**, *every family* 家家 **jiājiā**, *everything* 事事 **shìshì**; and even the bisyllabic noun *aspect* 方面 **fāngmiàn** can be reduplicated (*every aspect* 方方面面 **fāngfāngmiànmiàn**). But these examples of noun reduplication are exceptions rather than a pattern that can be applied generally.

6. Onomatopoeia (including "visual onomatopoeia") is created by reduplication

If the expression imitates a sound, the reduplication can take either the ABAB or the AABB form, depending on the sound being imitated. Examples:

ABAB: 喀喳喀喳 **kāchākāchā** (sound of machine wheels turning)
　　　扑通扑通 **pūtōngpūtōng** (sound of frogs jumping into the pond)
AABB: 唧唧喳喳 **jījīzhāzhā** (sound of birds chirping)

There are also alliterative terms like 辟里啪啦 **pīlipālā** (sound of fire crackers), which can be considered partial reduplications.

Finally, reduplication can be used to intensify a visual image. We can call this "visual onomatopoeia" for lack of a better term. This kind of reduplication takes on the form ABB or ABCC:

ABB: 红通通 **hóng-tōngtōng** *red throughout*
　　　胖嘟嘟 **pàng-dūdū** *plump in a cute way, as in a baby*
　　　脏兮兮 **zāng-xīxī** *filthy, yucky*
　　　黑漆漆 **hēi-qīqī**; 黑黝黝 **hēi-yōuyōu**; 黑矇矇 **hēi-méngméng**
　　　(all three intensify blackness, but are used to create different mental images)

ABCC: 可怜兮兮 **kělián-xīxī** (intensifying the word *pitifulness*)
白雪皑皑 **báixuě-áiái** (intensifying an expanse of white snow)

EXERCISES:

Translate the following passage into Chinese, incorporating as many reduplicated forms as you can:

Everyone told me that Chinese is too difficult to learn. But I still wanted to try it and see. Every day, aside from earnestly doing my homework, I also chatted a bit with my Chinese friends. I went on this way for three years, and happily mastered Chinese!

ANSWERS:

人人都说中文太难学，可是我还是想试试看。我除了天天努力做功课以外，也跟中国朋友聊聊天。这样过了三年，我就高高兴兴地学会了中文。

Rénrén dōu shuō Zhōngwén tài nán xué, kěshì wǒ háishi xiǎng shìshi-kàn. Wǒ chúle tiāntiān nǔlì zuò gōngkè yǐwài, yě gēn Zhōngguó péngyou liáoliáotiān. Zhèyàng guòle sānnián, wǒ jiù gāogāoxìngxìngde xuéhuìle Zhōngwén.

2.11 Chinese abbreviations for long compound nouns

Chinese abbreviations are similar to acronyms in English. There is a strong tendency in the Chinese language to abbreviate long compound nouns—especially names of institutions—while at the same time preserving the strong bisyllabic rhythm of the language. Typically, a four-syllable term formed of two bisyllabic terms will be abbreviated by using the <u>key component</u> from each bisyllabic term. The key component is usually—but not always—the first syllable. The majority of abbreviated terms are proper nouns.

Term in English	Abbreviated term	Full term
Peking University	北大 **Běi Dà**	北京大学 **Běijīng Dàxué**
Tsinghua University	清华 **Qīnghuá** (not 清大 **Qīng Dà**)	清华大学 **Qīnghuá Dàxué**
Beijing Language and Culture University	北语 **Běi Yǔ**	北京语言文化大学 **Běijīng Yǔyán Wénhuà Dàxué**
People's University	人大 **Rén Dà**	人民大学 **Rénmín Dàxué**
People's Congress	also 人大 **Rén Dà** (same as above)	全国人民代表大会 **Quánguó Rénmín Dàibiǎo Dàhuì**
Education Commission	教委 **Jiào Wěi**	教育委员会 **Jiàoyù Wěiyuánhuì**
Bank of China	中行 **Zhōng Háng** (not 中银 **Zhōng Yín**)	中国银行 **Zhōngguó Yínháng**

Term in English	Abbreviated term	Full term
civil aviation (vs military aviation)	民航 **mín háng** (not 人航 **rén háng**)	人民航空 **rénmín hángkōng**
World Trade Center	国贸 **Guó Mào**	国际贸易中心 **Guójì Màoyì Zhōngxīn**
state-run	国营 **guóyíng**	国家经营 **guójiā jīngyíng**
remote control	遥控 **yáokòng**	遥远控制 **yáoyuǎn kòngzhì**

Recognizing abbreviated terms requires knowledge of the full terms (i.e. requisite vocabulary) and an ability to pick out the key components.

The strong bisyllabic nature of Chinese is manifested in yet another way that is the opposite of abbreviations, which is the expansion of single-syllable words into bisyllabic synonyms in formal speech, e.g.: *to use* 用／使用 **yòng/shǐyòng**; *book* 书／书籍 **shū/shūjí**; *boat* 船／船只 **chuán/chuánzhī**;, *paper* 纸／纸张 **zhǐ/zhǐzhāng**.

EXERCISES: ▶

Translate the following terms into English:

1. 民营 **mínyíng**
2. 中旅 **Zhōng Lǚ**
3. 台大 **Tái Dà**
4. 高铁 **gāotiě**

> **ANSWERS:**
> 1. run by civilians (non-government)
> 2. China Travel Agency
> 3. Taiwan University
> 4. high-speed train

2.12 Common Chinese words with surprising alternate meanings

Common words in Chinese sometimes pop up with surprising alternate meanings. This occurs more often in formal speech and writing than in colloquial speech, and this is due to a different usage and meaning of the word in Classical Chinese that is different from the meaning in modern Chinese. Students who have reached the advanced or intermediate level in Chinese should be alert to this phenomenon when they encounter a puzzling usage of a familiar word. Sometimes, a familiar single-syllable word becomes a component in a compound, and takes on a new meaning in that context. Examples:

word	classical meaning	contemporary usage
自 **zì**	*from*	来自 **láizì**: *come from* 自古英雄难过美人关 **zì gǔ yīngxióng nán guò měirén guān**: *Since ancient times, heroes have had difficulty getting past the trap of beauties (heroes have a weakness for the charms of beautiful women).*

起 qǐ	measure word for incidents	两起车祸 liǎngqǐ chēhuò: two auto accidents
纸 zhǐ	a measure word for formal documents	一纸法令 yìzhǐ fǎlìng: a decree
从 cóng	to follow	服从 fúcóng: to obey (submit and follow) 从事 cóngshì: to pursue (follow) a career (e.g. military, business)
他 tā	others	其他 qítā: all the others (other than the one already mentioned) 异国他乡 yìguó tāxiāng: foreign nations and other regions
就 jiù	to approach, to take up	就业 jiùyè: to take up a profession, employment 就这个问题进行了很详细的调查 jiù zhèige wèntí jìnxíngle hěn xiángxìde diàochá: On this issue, (we) have conducted detailed investigation.
张 zhāng	to expand, to stretch	夸张 kuāzhāng: to exaggerate 领土扩张 lǐngtǔ kuòzhāng: territorial expansion

EXERCISES:

An exercise to demonstrate the frequent occurrence of classical meanings in contemporary Chinese vocabulary: For each of the following single characters, first look up the meaning of each of the compounds, then surmise the meaning(s) of the single character:

1. 应 yīng/yìng: 应该 yīnggāi; 应招 yìngzhāo; 应对 yìngduì; 应变 yìngbiàn
2. 故 gù: 故事 gùshi, 故乡 gùxiāng; 缘故 yuángù; 无故 wúgù; 故意 gùyì
3. 所 suǒ: 所以 suǒyǐ; 所得 suǒdé; 所有 suǒyǒu; 厕所 cèsuǒ; 研究所 yánjiūsuǒ; 答非所问 dá-fēi-suǒ-wèn
4. 足 zú: 满足 mǎnzú; 足以 zúyǐ; 知足常乐 zhī-zú-cháng-lè; 足球 zúqiú,; 立足 lìzú
5. 革 gé: 革命 gémìng; 改革 gǎigé; 人造革 rénzào-gé

> **ANSWERS:**
>
> 1. should, to respond: should; to respond to recruitment; to react; to adapt to change
> 2. cause, old/original: story, old home; reason; without reason; intentionally
> 3. that which, place: therefore; that which was gained; all; lavatory; research institute/graduate school; irrelevant answer (answer that doesn't fit the question)
> 4. sufficient, foot: to satisfy, sufficient to; he who knows satisfaction will always be happy; soccer; to stand on one's feet (established)
> 5. to expel, leather: revolution; reform; leatherette

3 Asking Questions in Chinese

As in English, there are many different ways of asking questions in Chinese. However, these are often quite different from their English equivalents. Here is an overview of the various ways that questions are formed in Chinese.

3.1 Questions seeking a yes/no answer

This type of question takes two forms in Chinese—both totally different from the English equivalent. The first one is very simple; the second is a bit more complicated, but quite logical and therefore easy to grasp.

1. Adding the question particle 吗 ma

The first yes/no question form involves adding the question particle 吗 **ma** at the end of a statement.

- *Can you speak Chinese?* 你会说汉语吗？ **Nǐ huì shuō Hànyǔ ma?**

- *Do you still remember the characters you learned 20 years ago?*
  二十年前学过的汉字，你还记得吗？
  Èrshí-nián qián xuéguode Hànzì, nǐ hái jìde ma?

2. The positive/negative choice form

The second form can be called the **positive/negative choice** form, in that the verb (or adjective) is repeated in both the positive and the negative form.

- *Is Chinese <u>easy</u> to learn (or not easy)? Is learning Chinese <u>easy</u> (or not easy)?*
  学中文容易不容易？ **Xué Zhōngwén róngyì bùróngyì?**
  (the adjective 容易 **róngyì** *easy* is repeated in the positive and negative)

- *Do you normally <u>read</u> the newspaper?*
  你平常<u>看</u>报<u>不看</u>？ **Nǐ píngcháng kànbào búkàn?**
  你平常<u>看不看</u>报？ **Nǐ píngcháng kàn-bukàn bào?**
  Note: The object 报 **bào** *newspaper* may be placed after either the positive or the negative form of the verb.

- *Do you like to sing?* (all three sentences below are correct)
  你喜欢唱歌不喜欢？ **Nǐ xǐhuan chànggē bùxǐhuan?**
  你喜欢不喜欢唱歌？ **Nǐ xǐhuan bùxǐhuan chànggē?**
  你喜不喜欢唱歌？ **Nǐ xǐ-buxǐhuan chànggē?**

◆ *Have you heard about that incident?* (see 7.1 regarding the Chinese counter-part to the present perfect tense in English)

你听说了那件事没有？ **Nǐ tīngshuōle nèijiàn shì méiyǒu?**

你有没有听说那件事？ **Nǐ yǒu-méiyǒu tīngshuō nèijiàn shì?**

Many learners have the tendency to use only the first form above because it is "safe," and do not attempt the second form. But if you aspire to sound like a native speaker, you should get out of your comfort zone and challenge yourself to use the "positive/negative choice" form as much as possible. Soon, it will become second nature!

EXERCISES:

Restate the following questions using the second form:

1. 这个商店星期天开门吗？ **Zhèige shāngdiàn xīngqītiān kāimén ma?**
2. 他们今天晚上能回到家吗？ **Tāmen jīntiān wǎnshang néng huídào jiā ma?**
3. 你大学毕业了吗？ **Nǐ dàxué bìyèle ma?**
4. 美国人去中国需要签证吗？ **Měiguórén qù Zhōngguó xūyào qiānzhèng ma?**
5. 学校餐厅的东西好吃吗？ **Xuéxiào cāntīngde dōngxi hǎochī ma?**

ANSWERS:

1. 这个商店星期天开不开门？ **Zhèige shāngdiàn xīngqītiān kāi-bu-kāimén?**
2. 他们今天晚上能不能回到家？ **Tāmen jīntiān wǎnshang néng-bunéng huí-dào-jiā?**
3. 你大学毕业了没有？ **Nǐ dàxué bìyèle méiyǒu?**
4. 美国人去中国需要不需要签证？ **Měiguórén qù Zhōngguó xūyào-bù-xūyào qiānzhèng?**
   (需要不需要 **xūyào-bù-xūyào** may be abbreviated as 需不需要 **xū-bù-xūyào**)
5. 学校餐厅的东西好不好吃？ **Xuéxiào cāntīngde dōngxi hǎo-bù-hǎochī?**

Translate the following questions into Chinese, using the second form:

1. Will it rain tomorrow?
2. Do you believe that all humankind originated from Africa?
3. Have you seen him since he returned from China?

ANSWERS:

1. 明天会不会下雨？ **Míngtiān huì-búhuì xiàyǔ?**
2. 你相信不相信人类都是从非洲来的？ **Nǐ xiāngxìn-bù-xiāngxìn rénlèi dōu shì cōng Fēizhōu lái de?** (相信不相信 **xiāngxìn-bù-xiāngxìn** may be abbreviated as 相不相信 **xiāng-bù-xiāngxìn**.)
3. 他从中国回来以后，你有没有见到他？
   Tā cóng Zhōngguó huílái yǐhòu, nǐ yǒu-méiyǒu jiàndào ta?

3.2 A or B "choice" questions

The pattern "**A 还是 háishi B?**" is used in questions where the answer sought is the correct option out of the two (or more) choices given. Hence, these questions are called "choice" questions (see p. 40 for a comparison of 还是 **háishi** and 或是 **huòshì**).

♦ *Is he an Englishman or an American?*
他是英国人还是美国人? **Tā shì Yīngguórén háishi Měiguórén?**

♦ *Is it better to start grad school right away or to work for a couple of years first?*
(是)马上开始上研究所好，还是先工作两年好?
(Shì) mǎshàng kāishǐ shàng yánjiūsuǒ hǎo, háishi xiān gōngzuò liǎngnián hǎo?
哪个办法比较好? 马上开始上研究所，还是先工作两年?
Něige bànfǎ bǐjiào hǎo? Mǎshàng kāishǐ shàng yánjiūsuǒ, háishi xiān gōngzuò liǎngnián?

EXERCISES:

Translate the following sentences into Chinese:

1. Do you prefer Chinese food or Western food?
2. Is it better to learn to read and speak at the same time, or to learn to speak first?

> **ANSWERS:**
> 1. 你喜欢中餐还是西餐? **Nǐ xǐhuan Zhōngcān háishi Xīcān?**
> 2. 是同时学说话跟看书好呢，还是先学说话好?
> **Shì tóngshí xué shuōhuà gēn kànshū hǎo ne, háishi xiān xué shuōhuà hǎo?**

3.3 Tagged-on questions: "..., and what about X?"

A tagged-on question follows a presumed fact which may either be understood or something that was already stated in a previous statement. The tagged-on question—"*What about X?*"—is conveyed simply by adding the particle 呢 **ne?** at the end of the sentence.

♦ *There are four persons in our family, what about yours?*
我们家有四口人，你们(家)呢? **Wǒmen jiā yǒu sìkǒu rén, nǐmen (jiā) ne?**

♦ *His Dad is Chinese, what about his Mom?*
他爸爸是中国人，(那)他妈妈呢? **Tā bàba shì Zhōngguórén, (nà) tā māma ne?**

♦ *You finally finished your homework from last week, then what about this week's homework?*
你终于把上个星期的功课做完了，(那)这个星期的(功课)呢?
Nǐ zhōngyú bǎ shàngge xīngqīde gōngkè zuòwánle, (nà) zhèige xīngqīde (gōngkè) ne?

♦ *(Dialogue between a candidate for a position and a prospective employer)*
Candidate: I've taught American and European history...
Employer: What about Asian history? Can you teach that as well?

A: 我教过美国和欧洲历史… **Wǒ jiāoguo Měiguó hé Ōuzhōu lìshǐ...**

B: 亚洲历史呢？你也能教吗？ **Yàzhōu lìshǐ ne? Nǐ yě néng jiāo ma?**

Note: The previous statement referred to by the "tagged-on question" may be spoken by a different person; and the topic of the tagged-on question may parallel the object in the prior statement (e.g. "Asian history" parallels "American and European history" in the previous statement).

Aside from the "tagged-on question" usage of 呢 **ne**, this sentence-ending particle has several other usages, each of which is reflected by a different intonation. These usages will be discussed below in 3.11.

EXERCISES:

Translate the following sentences into Chinese:

1. You said you're busy today. What about tomorrow?

2. This school offers courses in Spanish and French, what about Chinese and Japanese?

3. A: Those two houses are both too expensive, I can't afford them.
    B: Then what about this one?

ANSWERS:

1. 你说你今天很忙，明天呢？ **Nǐ shuō nǐ jīntiān hěn máng, míngtiān ne?**

2. 这个学校有西班牙文和法文课，那中文和日文呢？
   Zhèige xuéxiào yǒu Xībānyá-wén hé Fǎwén kè, nà Zhōngwén hé Rìwén ne?

3. 那两个房子都太贵，我买不起。那么这个呢？
   Nèi liǎngge fángzi dōu tài guì, wǒ mǎi-bu-qǐ. Nàme zhèige ne?

3.4 Rhetorical questions

In this type of question, the speaker is not posing a question per se, but seeking confirmation of an assumption, and this is done by adding the particle 吧 **ba**—spoken with a rising intonation—at the end of the sentence.

*   *The boss will come too, won't he?* 老板也会一起来吧？ **Lǎobǎn yě huì yìqǐ lái ba?**

*   *I'm allergic to MSG. They don't use MSG at this restaurant, do they?*
    我对味精过敏，这个餐馆不用味精吧？
    Wǒ duì wèijīng guòmǐn, zhèige cānguǎn bú yòng wèijīng ba?

*   *College is so expensive these days, you have to work every summer, don't you?*
    现在大学那么贵，你每年夏天都得工作吧？
    Xiànzài dàxué nàme guì, nǐ měinián xiàtiān dōu děi gōngzuò ba?

Aside from the "rhetorical question" usage of 吧 **ba**, this sentence-ending particle has several other usages, each of which is pronounced with a different intonation. These usages will be discussed below in 3.12.

EXERCISES:

Translate the following sentences into Chinese:

1. All Americans can speak English, can't they?
2. You can understand my spoken Chinese, can't you?
3. You'll call me when you arrive, won't you?

> **ANSWERS:**
> 1. 美国人都会说英语吧？ **Měiguórén dōu huì shuō Yīngyǔ ba?**
> 2. 你能听懂我说的中国话吧？ **Nǐ néng tīngdǒng wǒ shuōde Zhōngguóhuà ba?**
> 3. 你到了就会给我打个电话吧？ **Nǐ dàole jiù huì gěi wǒ dǎ ge diànhuà ba?**

The interrogative forms involving 呢 **ne** and 吧 **ba** discussed above tend to be avoided by native-English speakers, perhaps because comparable patterns are not found in the English language. However, these two forms are pervasive in the speech of native Chinese speakers. So if you aspire to sound like a native speaker, you should practice using them actively.

3.5 Questions seeking information using "who, what, when, why," etc.

Questions seeking information are posed by using interrogative pronouns (e.g. *who*, *what*, *when*, *why*, etc.) in English, and the typical answer "fills in the blank." Interrogative pronouns in English have their Chinese equivalents in what Chinese linguists call 疑问词 **yíwèncí** or question words (QW for short), as follows:

Interrogative pronouns	Equivalent Chinese QW's
what	什么 **shénme**
when	什么时候 **shénme shíhou**
who, whom	1) 谁 **shéi**; 2) 什么人 **shénme rén**
where	1) 哪儿 **nǎr** or 哪里 **nǎli**; 2) 什么地方 **shénme dìfang**
why	为什么 **wèishénme**
which (one)	哪个 **něige** (or another measure word)
how (to do something)	怎么 **zěnme**
how (to what extent) e.g. how far, how tall	多么 **duōme** or 多 **duō** (followed by an adjective, e.g. 高 **gāo**, 贵 **guì**, 远 **yuǎn**, 漂亮 **piàoliang**)
how much	多少 **duōshǎo**
how many	几个 **jǐge** (or another measure word)

Grammatically, this type of question is simpler in Chinese than in English because the QW is not transposed to the beginning of the sentence as it is in English. In Chinese, the question follows the same word order as a corresponding statement (see the first example below).

♦ *Where can I buy the best and least expensive clothes?*
（我)在什么地方能买到最好最便宜的衣服？
(Wǒ) zài shénme dìfang néng mǎidào zuì hǎo zuì piányide yīfu?

You can buy the best and least expensive clothes online.
你在网上能买到最好最便宜的衣服。
Nǐ zài wǎngshang néng mǎidào zuì hǎo zuì piányide yīfu.

♦ *Why did you decide to come to a university in the U.S.?*
你为什么决定来美国留学？ **Nǐ wèishénme juédìng lái Měiguó liúxué?**

♦ *Who knows who the first president of the U.S. was? Please raise your hand.*
谁知道美国第一位总统是谁？请举手。
Shéi zhīdao Měiguó dìyīwèi zǒngtǒng shì shéi, qǐng jǔshǒu.

This type of question—involving the use of QWs—may have the particle 呢 **ne** tagged on at the end for a "softening" effect. This phenomenon will be discussed at the end of 3.11 along with various other usages of 呢 **ne**.

EXERCISES:

A. What's wrong with the following sentences? How would you fix them?

1. ✗ 你长大以后，什么你要做？ **Nǐ zhǎngdà yǐhòu, shénme nǐ yào zuò?**
2. ✗ 老师，几个生字我们每天要学？ **Lǎoshī, jǐge shēngzì wǒmen měitiān yào xué?**
3. ✗ 什么菜你最喜欢吃？ **Shénme cài nǐ zuì xǐhuan chī?**
4. ✗ 几点钟你到北京？ **Jǐdiǎn zhōng nǐ dào Běijīng?**
5. ✗ 哪儿是厕所？ **Nǎr shì cèsuǒ?**

> **ANSWERS:**
> 1. 你长大以后要做什么？ **Nǐ zhǎngdà yǐhòu yào zuò shénme?**
> 2. 老师，我们每天要学几个生字？ **Lǎoshī, wǒmen měitiān yào xué jǐge shēngzì?**
> 3. 你最喜欢吃什么菜？ **Nǐ zuì xǐhuan chī shénme cài?**
> 4. 你几点钟到北京？ **Nǐ jǐdiǎn zhōng dào Běijīng?**
> 5. 厕所在哪儿？ **Cèsuǒ zài nǎr?**

B. Translate the following sentences into Chinese:

1. What is the meaning of this Chinese set phrase?
2. Where in China is the air quality the best?
3. Which day next week would be most convenient for you?

4. Why do you always wait until Sunday night before preparing for Monday's class?

5. If you can only bring one friend with you, whom would you choose?

ANSWERS:

1. 这个中国成语是什么意思？ **Zhèige Zhōngguó chéngyǔ shì shénme yìsi?**

2. 中国什么地方的空气最好？ **Zhōngguó shénme dìfangde kōngqì zuì hǎo?**

3. 下个星期哪天对你最方便？ **Xiàge xīngqī něitiān duì nǐ zuì fāngbiàn?**

4. 你为什么老是等到星期天晚上才预备星期一的功课呢？
   Nǐ wèishénme lǎoshi děngdào xīngqītiān wǎnshang cái yùbèi xīngqīyīde gōngkè ne?

5. 如果你只能带一个朋友，你会选谁呢？
   Rúguǒ nǐ zhǐ néng dài yíge péngyou, nǐ huì xuǎn shéi ne?

3.6 The rhetorical use of question words

In English, we hear sentences like "*Who cares?!*" or "*How should I know?!*" These are not actual questions, but rhetorical expressions spoken using a special tone of voice. The same phenomenon occurs in Chinese. Aside from seeking information, QWs may be used rhetorically to strengthen the speaker's point. The implication is that, while the idea in the speaker's mind could have been expressed by a normal declarative sentence, he chooses to use a rhetorical QW-type "question" to empha-size his expression. Compare the following pairs:

◆ *No one knows.*   vs   *Who knows!?*
  没有人知道。   谁知道(呢)?
  Méiyǒu rén zhīdao.   **Shéi zhīdao (ne)?**
  (see 3.11 for the usage of 呢 to nudge a point)

◆ *Don't ask me, I don't know.*   vs   *Don't ask me, how should I know?*
  别问我，我不知道。   别问我，我哪儿知道！
  Bié wèn wǒ, wǒ bù zhīdao.   **Bié wèn wǒ, wǒ nǎr zhīdao?**
  Note: The rhetorical *how* is not expressed by 怎么 **zěnme**, but by 哪儿 **nǎr**.

◆ *He wouldn't understand*   vs   *What does he know (understand)?*
  (no use discussing it with him)
  他不懂(跟他谈没用)。   他懂什么？
  Tā bù dǒng (gēn tā tán méiyòng).   **Tā dǒng shénme?**

EXERCISES:

Translate the following sentences into Chinese:

1. That teacher never gives any A's. Who would want to take her course?!

2. So much homework! How can I possibly finish?! (see note in the second example above)

3.7 Questions embedded within a longer sentence

There are three interrogative sentence patterns that occur within longer sentences. They deserve a special place in this book because native English speakers tend to avoid this type of sentence when speaking Chinese, perhaps because they assume these sentences are too complicated. The three sentence patterns are actually quite straightforward once you put on a Chinese thinking cap.

In all three cases, the embedded question is a noun phrase, and it is inserted into the longer sentence without any alteration. The longer sentence in which a question is embedded may be a statement (as in the first two examples) or a question in itself (as in the last example). What gives English-speaking learners of Chinese the impression that this sort of sentence is complicated is that they ARE complicated if translated word for word from English into Chinese, resulting in an incorrect sentence. The three types of question that can be embedded in longer sentences are as follows:

1. Embedded questions involving QWs:

◆ *I really don't understand <u>what he is saying</u>.*
   我真不明白<u>他在说什么</u>。 **Wǒ zhēn bù míngbái tā zài shuō shénme.**

◆ *Please ask her <u>what she would like to drink</u>.*
   请你问她<u>要什么饮料</u>。 **Qǐng nǐ wèn tā yào shénme yǐnliào.**

◆ *Can you tell me <u>where the restroom is</u>?*
   你能不能告诉我<u>厕所在哪儿</u>? **Nǐ néng-bunéng gàosu wǒ cèsuǒ zài nǎr?**

2. The "positive/negative choice" type of question that seeks a yes/no answer (e.g. 是不是 **shì-bushì**...? see 3.1.2). Note: Questions seeking yes/no answers using the sentence-ending particle 吗 **ma** (described in 3.1.1) do not occur as embedded questions in statements.

As you read the examples below, pay special attention to the incorrect Chinese sentences and figure out what's wrong with them.

◆ *I don't know at this point <u>if I will have time this weekend</u>.*
   我现在还不知道<u>这个周末会不会有空</u>。
   Wǒ xiànzài hái bù zhīdào zhèige zhōumò huì-buhuì yǒukòng.

   ✗ 我现在还不知道如果我这个周末有没有空。
   Wǒ xiànzài hái bù zhīdao rúguǒ wǒ zhèige zhōumò yǒu-méiyǒu kòng.

♦ *Did the doctor say whether I will be able to leave the hospital tomorrow?*
医生有没有说我明天能不能出院? (A question embedded within a question)
Yīshēng yǒu-méiyǒu shuō wǒ míngtiān néng-bunéng chūyuàn.

✗ 医生有没有说如果我明天能不能出院?
  Yīshēng yǒu-méiyǒu shuō rúguǒ wǒ míngtiān néng-bunéng chūyuàn.

♦ *I should know by Friday afternoon if I will have time this weekend.*
我星期五下午就应该知道这个周末会不会有空了。
Wǒ xīngqīwǔ xiàwǔ jiù yīnggāi zhīdao zhèige zhōumò huì-buhuì yǒukòng le.

3. The "choice-type" question discussed in 3.2 using A 还是 **háishi** B?. What's wrong with the sentences marked as incorrect below?

♦ *Please ask him if he wants tea or coffee.*
请问他要喝咖啡还是茶。 **Qǐng wèn tā yào hē kāfēi háishi chá.**

✗ 请问他如果要喝咖啡还是茶。 **Qǐng wèn tā rúguǒ yào hē kāfēi háishi chá.**

♦ *I don't know if he is an Englishman or an American.* (The question regarding his nationality is embedded in this statement.)
我不知道他是英国人还是美国人。
Wǒ bù zhīdao tā shì Yīngguórén háishi Měiguórén.

✗ 我不知道如果他是英国人还是美国人。
  Wǒ bù zhīdao rúguǒ tā shì Yīngguórén háishi Měiguórén.

♦ *Have you decided whether you will go to study in Taiwan or China?* (A choice-type question embedded within a question)
你有没有决定要去台湾还是中国留学?
Nǐ yǒu-méiyǒu juédìng yào qù Táiwān háishi Zhōngguó liúxué?

Due to a quirk in the English language, the second and third types of embedded questions described above can trip up a student if he thinks in English while speaking Chinese. The quirk is the English usage of the word *if* in the sense of *whether*. This point was discussed in 2.1.13. The notion of *whether…or* is not translatable into Chinese word for word, but rather by using one of the two choice-type questions in Chinese ("yes or no" and "A or B").

EXERCISES:

Translate the following sentences into Chinese:

1. The teacher should let us know on the first day of the semester when we will have exams.

2. In China, students must decide what they want to study when they take the college entrance exam.

3. Regardless of whether or not you can succeed, you should give it a try!

4. When you invite friends for a meal, it would be best to ask them if they are vegetarians.

5. She is so young, I cannot tell if she is a student or a professor.

ANSWERS:

1. 老师应该在学期的头一天就告诉我们什么时候有考试。
   Lǎoshī yīnggāi zài xuéqīde tóu yìtiān jiù gàosu wǒmen shénme shíhou yǒu kǎoshì.

2. 在中国，学生在高考的时候就必须决定要学什么了。
   Zài Zhōngguó, xuésheng zài gāo-kǎode shíhou jiù bìxū juédìng yào xué shénme le.

3. 不管你能不能成功都应该试一试。
   Bùguǎn nǐ néng-bunéng chénggōng dōu yīnggāi shìyíshì.

4. 请朋友吃饭的时候，最好问问他们是不是吃素。
   Qǐng péngyou chīfànde shíhou, zuì hǎo wènwen tāmen shì-bushì chīsù.

5. 她那么年轻，我看不出来她是学生还是教授。
   Tā nàme niánqīng, wǒ kàn-bu-chūlai tā shì xuésheng háishi jiàoshòu.

3.8 Non-interrogative uses of question words

In both English and Chinese, QWs serve other non-interrogative functions. One example in English is the usage of QWs as relative pronouns (e.g. "*Thomas Jefferson, who drafted the Declaration of Independence, served as the third U.S. president.*") In the next three sections, we will discuss several ways in which Chinese QWs can have non-interrogative functions.

1. The first of these concerns the usage of QWs coupled with 都 **dōu** to convey all-inclusiveness.

● *Everything in this restaurant is delicious.*
   这个餐馆什么菜都好吃。**Zhèige cānguǎn shénme cài dōu hǎochī.**

● *These days everywhere in the city there are too many cars!*
   现在城里头哪儿都有太多的车了！
   Xiànzài chéng-lǐtou nǎr dōu yǒu tài duōde chē le.

● *I'm free any time, you're welcome to come any time.*
   我什么时候都有空，欢迎你随时来。
   Wǒ shénme shíhou dōu yǒukòng, huānyíng nǐ suíshí lái.

2. In this *all-inclusive* usage of QWs, if a verb is in the negative, the adverb 都 **dōu** may be replaced by 也 **yě**. Moreover, if the all-inclusiveness applies to the object of the verb, the object is normally stated first as the topic of the sentence (see 1.3.1 for discussion on the **topic + comment** sentence pattern).

● *I don't understand any of these sentences!*
   这些句子，我哪句都/也不懂！**Zhèixiē jùzi, wǒ něijù dōu/yě bùdǒng.**

   ✗ 这些句子，我都/也不懂哪句！**Zhèixiē jùzi, wǒ dōu/yě bùdǒng něijù.**

   ✗ 我都/也不懂这些句子！**Wǒ dōu/yě bùdǒng zhèixiē jùzi.**

● *I don't like any of these dresses.*
这些衣服，我哪件都/也不喜欢。
Zhèixiē yīfu, wǒ něijiàn dōu/yě bùxǐhuan.

● *Before college, I have not studied any foreign language.*
上大学之前，我什么外语都/也没学过。
Shàng dàxué zhīqián, wǒ shénme wàiyǔ dōu/yě méi xuéguo.

● *Every day next week won't work (No day next week will work), can you wait until the week after next?* (see next paragraph)
下个星期哪天都不行，你能不能等到下下个星期？
Xiàge xīngqī něitiān dōu bùxíng, nǐ néng-bunéng děngdào xiàxiàge xīngqī?

3. In the last example above, the first part of the sentence can be stated in two different ways in English—but the first way is quite awkward. In fact, this exemplifies a key difference between English and Chinese in the location of negation. In sentences that convey *all-inclusiveness*, negation is more likely to be located with the subject in English, whereas it is just as likely to be located with the verb in Chinese. Here are some further examples:

● <u>*No one*</u> *knows where they have gone.*
谁都/也<u>不</u>知道他们到哪儿去了。 **Shéi dōu/yě bù zhīdao tāmen dào nǎr qùle.**
<u>没有人</u>知道他们到哪儿去了。 **Méiyǒu rén zhīdao tāmen dào nǎr qùle.**
(not as strong as the preceding)

● *As long as you have self-confidence,* <u>*nothing*</u> *is too difficult.*
只要你有信心，<u>什么</u>事都<u>不</u>会太难。
Zhǐyào nǐ yǒu xìnxīn, shénme shì dōu búhuì tài nán.

EXERCISES:

Translate the following sentences using QWs to convey the notion of all-inclusiveness:

1. If you have <u>any</u> questions, you can go ask him.
2. There are Chinese people <u>everywhere</u> in the world.
3. That supermarket is open 24 hours, you can go <u>any time</u>.
4. I did not go <u>anywhere</u> yesterday.
5. He's not afraid of <u>anything</u>.
6. <u>No one</u> knows why he is so mad.

ANSWERS:
1. 你有什么问题都可以去问他。**Nǐ yǒu shénme wèntí dōu kěyǐ qù wèn tā.**
2. 世界上哪儿都有中国人。**Shìjiè-shang nǎr dōu yǒu Zhōngguórén.**
3. 那个超市24小时都开门，什么时候都可以去。
   Nèige chāoshì èrshísì xiǎoshí dōu kāimén, shénme shíhou dōu kěyǐ qù.

4. 我昨天哪儿都没去。 **Wǒ zuótiān nǎr dōu méi qù.**
5. 他什么都不怕。 **Tā shénme dōu bú pà.**
6. 谁都/也不知道他为什么那么生气。 **Shēi dōu/yě bù zhīdao tā wèishénme nàme shēngqì.**

3.9 Question words coupled with negatives to indicate something "indefinite"

Using question words coupled with a negative to indicate "indefinites" (e.g. "*I didn't go anywhere (in particular), just went for a walk.*")

In contrast to the usage of QWs coupled with 都 **dōu** that we discussed in the preceding section, QWs coupled with a negative but without 都 **dōu** convey the notion of something that is *indefinite* or *not particular*, rather than the notion of *all-inclusiveness*. The difficulty in mastering this pattern in Chinese lies in a concept that can be clearly conveyed in Chinese, but it is conveyed only optionally and indistinctly in English by intonation. One might even say that the concept of "indefiniteness" exists naturally in the Chinese mindset, but is one that native English speakers need to acquire. In the first two examples below, each English sentence actually has two possible meanings, and their difference is clearly brought out by the two different Chinese translations. The first translation is in fact the *all-inclusive* form used with a negative verb discussed in the preceding section.

♦ *I didn't go anywhere yesterday.*
  A 我昨天什么地方都没去。 **Wǒ zuótiān shénme dìfang dōu méiqù.**
  (implying that I absolutely didn't go anywhere, didn't even step out of the house.)
  B 我昨天没去什么地方。 **Wǒ zuótiān méi qù shénme dìfang.**
  (implying that I didn't go anywhere in particular, but I could have gone out for a stroll.)

♦ *In four years of college, I didn't learn anything.*
  A 在大学四年里，我什么都没学到。
    Zài dàxué sìnián-lǐ, wǒ shénme dōu méi xuédào.
  (implying that my four years of colleges was a total waste as I learned nothing.)
  B 在大学四年里，我没学到什么。 **Zài dàxué sìnián-lǐ, wǒ méi xuédào shénme.**
  (implying that I didn't learn anything in particular, or anything much, but I probably did learn a few things.)

♦ *How much money do you have? I don't have much money (anymore).*
  你有多少钱? 我没有多少钱了。
  Nǐ yǒu duōshǎo qián? Wǒ méiyǒu duōshǎo qián le.

♦ *He took me to look at a lot of houses, but I didn't see anything I liked.*
  他带我去看了很多房子，可是我没看到什么喜欢的。
  Tā dài wǒ qù kànle hěnduō fángzi, kěshì wǒ méi kàndào shénme xǐhuande.

EXERCISES:

Translate the following sentences into Chinese:

1. I just came to this place, so I don't know anyone (not a soul).

2. Although I've been here for a year now, I still don't know anyone (in particular).

3. I went to the party, but didn't see anyone in particular.

4. She searched for a long time, but didn't find anything (of particular interest).

5. In China before 1980, stores didn't carry any luxury goods.

ANSWERS:

1. 我刚到这个地方，所以谁也不认识。**Wǒ gāng dào zhèige dìfang, suǒyǐ shéi yě bú rènshi.**

2. 虽然我来了一年了，可是还是不认识什么人。
   Suīrán wǒ láile yìnián le, kěshì háishi bú rènshi shénme ren.

3. 那个晚会我去了，可是没有看见谁。**Nèige wǎnhuì wǒ qùle, kěshì méiyǒu kànjian shéi.**

4. 她找了很久，可是没找到什么。**Tā zhǎole hěn jiǔ, kěshì méi zhǎodao shénme.**

5. 中国在一九八零年以前，商店里没有什么奢侈品。
   Zhōngguó zài yī-jiǔ-bā-líng-nián yǐqián, shāngdiànlǐ méiyǒu shénme shēchǐpǐn.

3.10 Expressing "wherever, whatever, whoever," etc. using a QW

The notion of *wherever, whatever, whoever,* etc. can be expressed with a QW in a very idomatic way using the sentence pattern QW... 就 **jiù** QW....

● *Just go whenever it's convenient for you.*
什么时候对你方便就什么时候去吧。
Shénme shíhou duì nǐ fāngbiàn jiù shénme shíhou qù ba.

● *Whoever arrives first will be able to get the best seat.*
谁先到，谁就可以占到最好的位子。
Shéi xiān dào, shéi jiù kěyǐ zhàndào zuìhǎode wèizi.
(The QW happens to be the subject of the sentence, therefore it precedes the adverb 就 **jiù**.)

● *In the Maoist era, jobs were allocated by the government. People could not do whatever job they wanted.*
在毛泽东时代，工作是政府分配的。人们不是想做什么，就能做什么。
Zài Máo Zédōng shídài, gōngzuò shì zhèngfǔ fēnpèide, rénmen búshì xiǎng zuò shénme jiù néng zuò shénme.

The same ideas, stated in other less idiomatic ways will sound lame and awkward in Chinese. The following expressions have the same meanings as the three examples above, but do not sound nearly as forceful and natural as the sentences given above.

● *You may go when it's convenient for you.*
你可以在(对你)方便的时候去。**Nǐ kěyǐ zài (duì nǐ) fāngbiànde shíhou qù.**

● *The person who arrives first may take the best seat.*
先到的人可以占到最好的位子。**Xiān dàode rén kěyǐ zhàndào zuìhǎode wèizi.**

● *In the Maoist era, ... People didn't necessarily end up in jobs that they wanted.*
在毛泽东时代，……人们不一定能做他们想做的工作。
Zài Máo Zédōng shídài, ...rénmen bùyídìng néng zuò tāmen xiǎng zuòde gōngzuò.

EXERCISES:

Translate the following sentences into Chinese:

1. At buffet restaurants (自助餐厅 **zìzhù cāntīng**), you may eat however much you want.

2. In American movie theaters, you may sit wherever you like. Is it that way in China too?

3. Before 1980, Chinese people could have as many children as they wished; there were no restrictions.

ANSWERS:

1. 在自助餐厅，你要吃多少就吃多少。**Zài zìzhù cāntīng, nǐ yào chī duōshǎo jiù chī duōshǎo.**

2. 在美国的电影院，你要坐哪儿就坐哪儿。在中国也是这样吗？
Zài Měiguóde diànyǐngyuàn, nǐ yào zuò nǎr jiù zuò nǎr. Zài Zhōngguó yě shì zhèyàng ma?

3. 一九八零年以前，中国人要生几个孩子就生几个，没有限制。
Yī-jiǔ-bā-líng-nián yǐqián, Zhōngguórén yào shēng jǐge háizi jiù shēng jǐge, méiyǒu xiànzhì.

3.11 The sentence-ending particle 呢 ne

Including the tagged-on question form using the particle 呢 **ne?** already discussed in 3.3 above, this versatile particle has four distinct usages. The first two are interrogatives and therefore carry a rising intonation. The other two carry a low-level intonation to impart weight to the expression.

1. 呢 ne tagged on to form a question (already presented in 3.3 above)

● *Tickets are sold out for today and tomorrow. How about the day after tomorrow?*
今天跟明天的票都卖光了。后天的呢？
Jīntiān gēn míngtiānde piào dōu màiguāngle. Hòutiānde ne?

● *Your daughter is married. What about your son?*
你的女儿已经结婚了，儿子呢？ **Nǐde nǚ'ér yǐjīng jiéhūn le, érzi ne?**

2. 呢 ne tagged onto a question to impart a "softening" effect.

When a question has an accusatory or challenging tone (e.g. "*Why are you late for class?*" "*Teacher, how many new words do you want us to memorize each day?*"), the tone of voice can be softened a bit by added the particle 呢 **ne** (spoken with the rising interrogative tone of voice) at the end. This usage is favored by women, although it's perfectly fine for men to use it as well. However, regardless of one's gender, over-using this form gives the speaker a softer non-assertive image.

♦ *Teacher, how many new words do we have to learn each day? (I heard she assigns a huge load of vocabulary for students to memorize every day.)*
老师，我们每天要学几个生词呢？
Lǎoshī, wǒmen měitiān yào xué jǐge shēngcí ne?

♦ *Why do so many Chinese college students want to study abroad these days? (Aren't Chinese universities good enough?)*
为什么那么多中国大学生都要出国留学呢？
Wèishémme nàme duō Zhōngguó dàxuésheng dōu yào chūguó liúxué ne?

♦ *What would you like to eat today?*
今天你想吃什么菜呢？ **Jīntiān nǐ xiǎng chī shémme cài ne?**

♦ *Your son is already married. How come your daughter hasn't gotten married yet?*
你的儿子已经结婚了，那为什么女儿还没结婚呢？
Nǐde érzi yǐjīng jiéhūn le, nà wèishénme nǚ'ér hái méi jiéhūn ne?

In the last two examples, 呢 **ne** also makes reference to an understood antecedent. In "What would you like to eat today?" the speaker (waitperson) is subtly referring to the dishes the patron has ordered in past visits to the restaurant. In the last example, the antecedent—the married son—is explicitly stated.

3. 呢 ne coupled with 还 hái

This construction reinforces the notion that an action or situation is continuing. Adding the word 还 **hái** *still* alone is sufficient, but 呢 **ne** is often added at the end of the sentence to strengthen the idea. In short, the usage of 呢 **ne** in this type of sentence is optional and stylistic rather than mandatory.

♦ *He still hasn't gotten out of bed.* 他还没起床呢。 **Tā hái méi qǐchuáng ne.**

♦ *Everyone is still eating, why don't you wait a bit.*
大家还在吃饭呢，你等一等吧。 **Dàjiā hái zài chīfàn ne, nǐ děngyìděng ba.**

4. 呢 ne used to reinforce a point

This is to reinforce a point, often in contradiction to a view held by someone else. There is nothing quite like this in English, but a rough approximation would be the colloquial phrase "you know" tagged on to statements in English.

♦ *I certainly don't want to go!* (contrary to what you might think)
我才不要去呢！ **Wǒ cái búyào qù ne!**

* *You say he's very smart, but I feel he's a bit stupid.*
  你说他很聪明，我倒觉得他有点笨呢。
  Nǐ shuō tā hěn cōngming, wǒ dào juéde tā yǒudiǎn bèn ne.

* *Your oldest son is a professor, what about your second son?*
  He's a used car salesman, but he makes more money, you know.
  你的老大是教授，那老二呢？他是卖二手车的，可是挣的钱更多
  呢！**Nǐde lǎodà shì jiàoshòu, nà lǎo'èr ne? Tā shì mài èrshǒuchēde, kěshì zhèngde qián gèng duō ne!**
  (Note the two different usages of 呢 **ne** in the above example.)

EXERCISES:

Translate the following sentences into Chinese:

1. How come you are tardy again today?
2. Which university in the U.S. are you thinking of attending?
3. They've been together for five years already, but they still haven't gotten married.
4. Nowadays, young people aren't that concerned about marriage; they are all busy with professional development, you know.
5. I know you don't eat meat. Then what about fish?

ANSWERS:
1. 你怎么又迟到了呢？ **Nǐ zěnme yòu chídào le ne?**
2. 你想上美国的哪个大学呢？ **Nǐ xiǎng shàng Měiguóde něige dàxué ne?**
3. 他们在一起已经五年了，可是还没结婚呢。
   Tāmen zài yìqǐ yǐjīng wǔnián le, kěshì hái méi jiéhūn ne.
4. 现在年轻人并不那么在乎成家／结婚，他们都忙着发展事业呢。
   Xiànzài niánqīngrén bìng bú nàme zàihu chéngjiā/jiéhūn, tāmen dōu mángzhe fāzhǎn shìyè ne.
5. 我知道你不吃肉，那么鱼呢？ **Wǒ zhīdao nǐ bù chī ròu, nàme yú ne?**

3.12 The sentence-ending particle 吧 ba

Including the rhetorical usage of 吧 **ba** already discussed in 3.4 above, this versatile particle has four distinct usages, each one spoken with a different intonation.

1. 吧 ba in a rhetorical question (with rising intonation)

This was already presented in 3.4 above.

* *You understood what I said, didn't you?*
  我说的话，你听懂了吧？ **Wǒ shuōde huà, nǐ tīngdǒngle ba?**

* *They have already gotten married, I presume?*
  他们已经结婚了吧？ **Tāmen yǐjīng jiéhūnle ba?**

2. 吧 **ba in a suggestion or mild command** (mid-falling intonation)

- *It's started raining, why don't you wait until tomorrow to go.*
  下雨了，等明天再去吧！ **Xiàyǔle, děng míngtiān zài qù ba!**

- *Let's give a little face to this old colleague of ours! (i.e. don't embarrass him).*
  给我们这个老同事一点儿面子吧！
  Gěi wǒmen zhèige lǎo tóngshì yìdiǎnr miànzi ba!

3. 吧 **ba used to convey assent** (mid-falling intonation)

- *OK! In that case, we'll go together!*
  好吧！那我们就一起去吧！ **Hǎo ba! Nà wǒmen jiù yìqǐ qù ba!**

- *In that case, we'll do as you say!*
  那就按照你说的做吧！ **Nà jiù ànzhào nǐ shuōde zuò ba!**

4. 吧 **ba used to convey suspicion, skepticism or doubt** (low-level intonation)

- *It's only 8:00, the restaurant wouldn't be closed already, would it?*
  才八点，饭馆不会已经关门了吧。
  Cái bādiǎn, fànguǎn búhuì yǐjīng guānménle ba.

- *You won't forget the appointment tonight, will you?*
  你不会忘了今天晚上的约会吧。
  Nǐ búhuì wàngle jīntiān wǎnshangde yuēhuì ba.

- *Such a tense U.S.-China relationship couldn't last too long, could it?*
  这么紧张的中美关系不可能持续太久吧。
  Zhème jǐnzhāngde Zhōng-Měi guānxi bù kěnéng chíxù tài jiǔ ba.

Note: The above sentences can also be spoken with 吧 **ba** in the rising intonation (see section 1 above), in which case they would be rhetorical questions. The difference in meaning conveyed by the two intonations is quite distinct in Chinese. The same applies to the English translations. Try reading out loud the example sentences in section 1 and 4 with different intonations to convey the two different nuances.

EXERCISES:

Translate the following sentences into Chinese:

1. Your car is broken down? No problem, just borrow mine!

2. Forget it! If you're not willing to help, I'll go find someone else! (see 2.2, example for 算 **suàn**)

3. You're well prepared for the test tomorrow, I presume?

4. Tomorrow's final exam won't be too difficult, will it? (actually suspecting that it will be quite difficult)

5. He has been in the U.S. for 20 years already, his English should be pretty good, no? (wondering if his English is in fact good)

ANSWERS:

1. 你的车坏了吗？没问题，借我的吧！ **Nǐde chē huàile ma? Méi wèntí, jiè wǒde ba!**

2. 算了吧！如果你不愿意帮忙，我就去找别人吧！
    Suànle ba! Rúguǒ nǐ bú yuànyi bāngmáng, wǒ jiù qù zhǎo biérén ba!

3. 明天的考试，你预备好了吧？ **Míngtiānde kǎoshì, nǐ yùbèi-hǎo le ba?**

4. 明天的大考不会太难吧。(low-level intonation) **Míngtiānde dàkǎo búhuì tài nán ba.**

5. 他来美国已经二十年了，他的英语应该不错了吧。(low-level intonation)
    Tā lái Měiguó yǐjīng èrshí-nián le, tāde Yīngyǔ yīnggāi búcuò le ba.

4 Measures, Numbers and Units

4.1 "Measure words" in Chinese do not necessarily indicate quantities

Units of measure are used in every language for quantifying things—mostly concrete things, but some abstract things as well. Words referring to weights and measures, time, temperature, etc. can be translated straightforwardly from one language to another. This usage of measure is for the purpose of conveying quantitative information, and it is a necessary aspect of all languages. However, measures in Chinese have an additional grammatical usage that does not convey additional information, and this usage does not exist in most Western languages. In English, it exists only in a few exceptional cases, and these cases can help you understand the concept of grammatical measures in Chinese. In general, the grammatical usage of measures in Chinese does not come naturally to an English speaker, and therefore needs to be inculcated.

To illustrate the grammatical usage of measures in Chinese, we will use a few special cases of "quasi measures" in English (i.e. words that fall into a gray area between nouns and measures) that parallel this general phenomenon in Chinese.

two <u>slices</u> of pizza   a <u>batch</u> of mail   a <u>school</u> of fish
a <u>loaf</u> of bread   a dozen <u>heads</u> of cabbage   five <u>head</u> of cattle[1]

All the underlined words in the above examples are nouns, but grammatically they occupy the position of measure words. In the first three examples, the underlined words can also be construed as measures, even though they are not as precise as the units of measure mentioned in the first paragraph. In the last three examples, it's hard to justify calling "loaf" and "head(s)" measure words. In other words, "loaf" and "head(s)" serve only a grammatical function in this context. Such "grammatical measures" are exceptional in English, but they are obligatory in Chinese.

In Chinese, whenever something is quantified and/or specified (by a number and/or a specifier),[2] a "measure word" must be inserted, regardless of whether it conveys any meaning not already covered by the number and/or specifier. Conceptually, this grammatical function of measure words in Chinese is not difficult to grasp. But what takes a bit of memory work is the list of measure words corresponding to the different nouns, especially where there is minimal meaning to hang the measure words on. The analogy in English is remembering that "loaf" goes with bread and "head" goes with cabbage and cattle.

---

[1] The singular "head" may seem odd, but it is correct. In this context, it is similar to "herd" in "a herd of buffalo."

[2] As we will see later in this chapter, that "something" being quantified or specified is not necessarily an object; it could be something abstract or even an action. "Number" in this context also includes 几 **jǐ** (*several, how many*). "Specifier" includes 这 **zhè**, 那 **nà**, 哪 **nǎ**, and 每 **měi** (*this/these, that/those, which, each*).

The most commonly-used measure word in Chinese is 个 **ge**, followed closely by 本 **běn**, 张 **zhāng**, 只 **zhī**, and 条 **tiáo**, which should all be familiar to most readers of this book. To sound like a native speaker, however, you also need to incorporate some less common measure words listed in the final section of this chapter into your day-to-day repertoire.

As mentioned above, a measure word is mandatory whenever a noun is quantified and/or specified. In fact, the grammatical need for the measure word to be stated is even greater than for the noun itself to be stated. When the noun is understood, it can often be omitted, but the corresponding measure word has to be stated, almost as a stand-in for the omitted noun.

- *I went to the library today looking for several books, but I only found <u>one</u>.* *("book" is understood after "one")*

    ✓ 我今天去图书馆找几本书，可是只找到<u>一本</u>。
    （书 **shū** is understood after 一本 **yìběn**.）
    Wǒ jīntiān qù túshūguǎn zhǎo jǐběn shū, kěshì zhǐ zhǎodào yìběn.

    ✗ ……，可是只找到一。 ..., **kěshì zhǐ zhǎodào yī.** (measure word lacking)

    ✗ ……，可是只找到一本书。
    ..., kěshì zhǐ zhǎodào yìběn shū. (书 too is redundant)

- *Our college originally had only one Chinese professor. This year suddenly two more came, so now there are three.*

    ✓ 我们的大学本来只有一位中国教授，今年突然来了<u>两位</u>，所以现在有<u>三位</u>了。
    Wǒmende dàxué běnlái zhǐyǒu yíwèi Zhōngguó jiàoshòu, jīnnián tūrán láile liǎngwèi, suǒyǐ xiànzài yǒu sānwèi le.

    ✗ ···，今年突然来了<u>两</u>，所以现在有<u>三</u>了。
    ..., jīnnián tūrán láile liǎng, suǒyǐ xiànzài yǒu sān le.
    (measure word lacking after 两 **liǎng** and 三 **sān**)

4.2 Various categories of measure words

Measure words can be grouped into nine different categories. For convenience, each category is labeled below, but it is not important for you to learn the labels as long as you understand the underlying concepts.

1. Measure words that act as classifiers

The most common measure words are those that "more or less" express the shape, or some other physical property of their associated nouns—hence they are often referred to as "classifiers." The following table presents only a dozen of the most common ones. A more comprehensive list is presented in 4.15. As you can see from this table, the relationship between the nouns and their corresponding measure words is not always logical, i.e. the "classification" is often arbitrary. For example, both 双

shuāng and 对 **duì** mean *pair*, but the two are not interchangeable, and 只 **zhī** generally is used with animals, but it is also the measure word for 船 **chuán** *boat*.

measure word	characteristics of associated nouns	examples of associated nouns
本 **běn**	volumes	书 **shū** *book*
张 **zhāng**	sheets; flat surfaces	照片 **zhàopiàn** *photo*, 票 **piào** *ticket*, 地图 **dìtú** *map*, 桌子 **zhuōzi** *table*, 嘴 **zuǐ** *mouth*
枝 **zhī**	stick-like things	毛笔 **máobǐ** *writing brush*, 铅笔 **qiānbǐ** *pencil*, 香烟 **xiāngyān** *cigarette*, 花 **huā** *flower with its stem*
只 **zhī**	certain animals; one of something that comes in pairs	猫 **māo** *cat*, 狗 **gǒu** *dog*, 老虎 **lǎohǔ** *tiger*, 船 **chuán** *boat*, 筷子 **kuàizi** *chopsticks*, 袜子 **wàzi** *socks*, 鞋 **xié** *shoes*, 眼睛 **yǎnjīng** *eyes*
条 **tiáo**	line, belt-like objects	鱼 **yú** *fish*, 路 **lù** *road*, 河 **hé** *river*, 船 **chuán** *boat*, 消息 **xiāoxi** *news*, 头条新闻 **tóutiáo xīnwén** *headline news*
套 **tào**	sets of things	书 **shū** *books*, 餐具 **cānjù** *tableware*, 家具 **jiājù** *(furniture*, 衣服 **yīfu** *suit of clothing*, 房子 **fángzi** *suite of rooms*
双 **shuāng**	matching pairs	筷子 **kuàizi** *chopsticks*, 袜子 **wàzi** *socks*, 鞋 **xié** *shoes*, 眼睛 **yǎnjīng** *eyes*
对 **duì**	couples	夫妻 **fūqī** *husband and wife*, 枕头 **zhěntóu** *matching pillows*
位 **wèi**	honorable persons	教授 **jiàoshòu** *professor*, 客人 **kèrén** *guest*, 专家 **zhuānjiā** *expert*
场 **chǎng**	sessions	电影 **diànyǐng** *movie*, 演讲比赛 **yǎnjiǎng bǐsài** *speech contest*, 雨 **yǔ** *rain*, 病 **bìng** *bout of illness*, 战争 **zhànzhēng** *war*
串 **chuàn**	strings; series	钥匙 **yàoshi** *keys*, 珍珠 **zhēnzhū** *pearls*, 一串羊肉 **yíchuàn yángròu** *a skewer of lamb*, 一串问题 **yíchuàn wèntí** *a series of questions*, 一串笑声 **yíchuàn xiàoshēng** *a peal of laughter*
件 **jiàn**	items; articles	衬衫 **chènshān** *shirt*, 礼物 **lǐwù** *gift*, 一件事 **yíjiàn shì** *a matter, an incident*

Normally, each noun uses only one measure word, but there are exceptions, such as 船 **chuán** *boat*, which uses both 只 **zhī** and 条 **tiáo**, and there is no difference in meaning between the two. However, if a word has different meanings in different contexts, or different nuances, the use of a different measure word helps to signal which meaning is intended. In other words, using a different measure word with the same noun conveys a difference in the meaning/nuance of the noun that is intended. Examples:

- 门 **mén** *door*: 一道门 **yídào mén** *a doorway*; 一扇门 **yíshàn mén** *a door itself*
- 课 **kè** *class, course*: 一门课 **yìmén kè** *a course*; 一节课 **yìjié kè** *a class session*
- 心 **xīn** *heart*, in the abstract sense; in contrast to 心脏 **xīnzàng** *the heart organ*: 一颗心 **yìkē xīn** *heart, emotions*; 一片好心 **yípiàn hǎoxīn** *purely good intentions*; 一条心 **yìtiáo xīn** *aspiration, desire, will*, e.g. 全体一条心 **quántǐ yìtiáo xīn** *entire group united in aspiration*

2. Measure words that act as quantifiers (units of measure)

These can be considered the truest measure words since they actually measure round length, weight, distance, temperature, etc. These words have parallels in other languages. The noun logically associated with this type of measure word is usually left unstated, because it is already implicit from the measure word itself. Examples:

- 八十英里 **bāshí yīnglǐ** *80 miles* (the implicit noun is *distance*)
- 三十六度 **sānshíliù dù** *36 degrees* (the implicit noun is *temperature*)
- The **number + measure word** combination is frequently followed by an adjective indicating the feature being measured. Examples:
- 两米高 **liǎng mǐ gāo**   *two meters high*
- 五十斤重 **wǔshí jīn zhòng**   *50 kilo in weight*
- 三英尺长 **sān yīngchǐ cháng**   *3 feet in length*

Note: In the above examples, the adjectives 高 **gāo** *high*, 长 **cháng** *long*, 重 **zhòng** *heavy* actually function like nouns, meaning "in height, in length, in weight."

An important point for native-English speakers to remember is that in Chinese, statements about the size, height, weight, etc., of something always use the verb 有 **yǒu** *to have* rather than 是 **shì** *to be*. Examples:

- *He is over 6' tall.*
  - ✓ 他有六英尺多(高)。 **Tā yǒu liù yīngchǐ duō (gāo).**
  - ✗ 他是六英尺多(高)。 **Tā shì liù yīngchǐ duō (gāo).**

- *I hope this luggage is not more than 35 pounds.*
  - ✓ 我希望这件行李没有/不到 (not reach) 35 磅。
    Wǒ xīwàng zhèijiàn xínglǐ méiyǒu/búdào 35 bàng.
  - ✗ 我希望这件行李不是35磅多。 **Wǒ xīwàng zhèijiàn xínglǐ búshì 35 bàng duō.**

- *Today's temperature will be a high of only 10 degrees.*
  - ✓ 今天的气温最高只有十度。 **Jīntiānde qìwēn zuìgāo zhǐyǒu shí dù.**
  - ✗ 今天的气温最高只是十度。 **Jīntiānde qìwēn zuìgāo zhǐshì shí dù.**

3. Numerical measure words

These numerical measure words are actually the large round numbers above 100, e.g. 百 **bǎi** *hundred,* 千 **qiān** *thousand,* 万 **wàn** *ten thousand,* 亿 **yì** *one hundred thousand,* but they have certain similarities to measure words, as follows:

a. The use of 二 **èr vs** 两 **liǎng before large numbers**

The English *two* is translated as 二 **èr**, except when it is followed by a measure word, in which case it becomes 两 **liǎng**. Large round numbers behave like measure words in this regard: when the number *two* precedes a large round number above 100, 两 **liǎng** is used rather than 二 **èr**. However, for very large round numbers, this rule becomes more flexible, and 二 **èr** or 两 **liǎng** may be used. For example:

Two represented by 二 **èr**:

- *20 people*: 二十个人 **èrshíge rén**
- *the year 2012*: 二零一二年 **èr-líng-yī-èr nián**
- *352-234-8226*: 三五二-二三四-八二二六 **sān-wǔ-èr-èr-sān-sì-bā-èr-èr-liù**
- *200,000 persons*: 二十万人 **èrshíwàn rén**
  - ✗ 两十万个人 **liǎngshíwànge rén** (the digit to which 2 is attached is 十, so 两 would be incorrect)

Two represented by 两 **liǎng**:

- *2 persons*: 两个人 **liǎngge rén**
- *two Chinese restaurants*: 两家中国餐馆 **liǎngjiā Zhōngguó cānguǎn**
- *2,500 years ago*: 两千五百年以前 **liǎngqiān-wǔbǎi-nián yǐqián**

Two represented by 两 **liǎng**, but 二 **èr** is also acceptable:

- *¥2,000,000*: 两百万元 **liǎngbǎiwàn yuán** or 二百万元 **èrbǎiwàn yuán**
- *12,000*: 一万两千 **yíwàn liǎngqiān** or 一万二千 **yíwàn èrqiān**
- *1,200 persons*: 一千两 (or 二) 百个人 **yìqiān-liǎng/èrbǎige rén**
- (but *200 persons* can only be 两百个人 **liǎngbǎige rén**, not 二百 **èrbǎi...**)

b. 百 **bǎi** *hundred,* 千 **qiān** *thousand,* **etc. when referring to people**

Normally, a measure word is mandatory when a noun is quantified or specified. But when numbers above 100 are used to quantify nouns referring to people, e.g. 人 **rén** *persons;* 学生 **xuésheng** *students;* 士兵 **shìbīng** *soldiers,* the use of the measure word 个 **ge** is optional. This indicates that this requirement is already fulfilled by the large round number, which functions as both a number and a measure word. Examples:

- *300 people* 三百(个)人 **sānbǎi(ge) rén**
- *5,000 students* 五千(个)学生 **wǔqiān(ge) xuésheng**
- *200,000 soldiers* 二十万士兵 **èrshíwàn shìbīng**

Note: In expressing a large quantity (above 100), the last unit of measure is often omitted in colloquial speech. A few examples will make this point clear:

- *150*: 一百五十 yìbǎi-wǔshí = 一百五 yìbǎiwǔ
- *1,500*: 一千五百 yìqiān-wǔbǎi = 一千五 yìqiān wǔ
- *1,005*: 一千零五 yìqiān-líng-wǔ
- *1,050*: 一千零五十 yìqiān-líng-wǔshí (十 shí is not optional because it is not the next unit down from 千 qiān)
- *The rent is $3,500 per month.* 房租一个月要三千五(百)(元)。**Fángzū yíge yuè yào sānqiān-wǔ(bǎi)(yuán).** (元 yuán may be omitted first, then 百 bǎi may be omitted)
- *The movie ticket is $8.50 each.* 电影票八块五(毛)一张。**Diànyǐngpiào bākuài-wǔ(máo) yìzhāng.**
- *Body height of 1.8 meters* 身高一米八(十)(公分) **shēn'gāo yìmǐ-bā(shí) (gōngfēn)** (公分 gōngfēn may be omitted first, then 十 shí may be omitted)

4. Container measure words

Like the quantifiers and numerical measures, container measures actually measure things, and are usually 3-dimensional, but can also be 2-dimensional. Some textbooks call these "temporary measures" because they are nouns that are "borrowed" to serve as measure words. When these words function as normal nouns, they usually carry the suffix 子 zi, e.g. 两杯水 liǎngbēi shuǐ (*two cups of water*) vs 两个杯子 liǎngge bēizi (*two cups*). Examples of container measures:

- *three suitcases of old clothes* 三箱旧衣服 **sānxiāng jiù yīfu**
- *a bag of apples* 一袋苹果 **yídài píngguǒ**
- *a set of bedding* 一床被窝 **yìchuáng bèiwō**
- *a set banquet* (with many courses served to one tableful of guests) 一桌菜 **yìzhuō cài**

5. Group measure words

These measure words indicate some kind of aggregation or grouping, and they have parallels in English. A few of the "classifiers" mentioned in section 1—套 tào *set*, 双 shuāng *pair*, 对 duì *pair*, 串 chuàn *string/series*—can also be called group measures.

- *a row of poplars* 一排杨树 **yìpái yángshù**
- *a kind of plants* 一种植物 **yìzhǒng zhíwù**
- *a batch of merchandise* 一批货 **yìpī huò**
- *a gang of vagabonds* 一帮流氓 **yìbāng liúmáng** (note unusual meaning of 帮)
- *a pair of twins* 一对双胞胎 **yíduì shuāngbāotāi**

Note: The word *pair* is translated into Chinese using different measure words, depending on the noun it applies to:

- *a married couple* 一对夫妻 **yíduì fūqī**
- *a pair of glasses* 一副眼镜 **yífù yǎnjìng**
- *a pair of shoes* 一双鞋子 **yìshuāng xiézi**
- *a pair of trousers* 一条裤子 **yìtiáo kùzi** (Chinese don't think of trousers as pairs).

6. Partitive measure words

Conceptually, these measures are the opposites of group measures, in that they refer to a part of a larger entity or grouping.

- *that subgroup of people* 那部分人 **nèi bùfen rén**
- *this paragraph* (within an article) 这段文字 **zhèi duàn wénzì**
- *a drop of water* 一滴水 **yìdī shuǐ**
- *a slice of bread* 一片面包 **yípiàn miànbāo**

A special partitive measure word is 些 **xiē** *some*, which can refer to both an indefinite quantity as well as a subset of a larger set. 些 **xiē** is also generic in that it does not correspond to particular nouns.

- *these magazines* (some particular ones among a pile) 这些杂志 **zhèixiē zázhì**
- *in those days* 在那些日子里 **zài nèixiē rìzi li**
- *have some time* 有一些时间 **yǒu yìxiē shíjiān**

7. Temporary measure words

Like the "container measures" discussed in section 4 above, these are also nouns temporarily "borrowed" to function grammatically as measure words. They are not actual containers, but words used figuratively to imply *all over, filled up with... .* Unlike other measure words, temporary measures can be two syllables because they are actually nouns in their own right. This kind of measure can be preceded by 一 **yī** *whole/all*, as in 一天到晚 **yìtiān-dào-wǎn** *all day until night*, 满 **mǎn** *full*, or a specifier 这 **zhè** *this* or 那 **nà** *that*. Many phrases that contain a temporary measure words are idioms.

- *full of trash* (on the ground) 一地垃圾 **yídì lājī**
- *table covered with waste paper:* 一桌子废纸 **yìzhuōzi fèizhǐ**
- *yard full of fallen leaves:* 一院子落叶 **yíyuànzi luòyè**
- *hair all white:* 一头白发 **yìtóu báifà**
- *a bellyful of anger:* 一肚子气 **yídùzi qì**
- *full of passion:* 满腔热情 **mǎnqiāng rèqíng**
- *full of debt* (re a person): 一身债 **yìshēn zhài**
- *a nose-ful of dust* (i.e. a run-in with obstacles): 一鼻子灰 **yìbízi huī**

8. Measure words that act as classifiers for "verb+object" compounds

These differ from the noun classifiers in section 1, in that the measure word is associated with both the verb and its object, and the measure word has meaning of its own. Examples:

- 说一句英语 **shuō yíjù Yīngyǔ** *to utter an English sentence*
- 说一口漂亮的英语 **shuō yìkǒu piàoliangde Yīngyǔ** *to speak English beautifully*
- 说了一大通话 **shuōle yídàtōng huà** *uttered a long-winded pile of stuff*
- 说了一番真心话 **shuōle yìfān zhēnxīnhuà** *uttered a bunch of heartfelt things*
- 能写一手好字 **néng xiě yìshǒu hǎozì** *able to write a bunch of nice characters* (i.e., has beautiful writing skills)
- 当两任总统 **dāng liǎngrèn zǒngtǒng** *to be president for two terms*
- 打了三局球 **dǎle sānjú qiú** *played three innings of ball*

9. Verbal measure words

The use of measure words with **verb + object** compounds above demonstrates that actions can also be quantified through the use of measures. With verbal measure words, the grammatical function of measure words is extended to actions that are thought of as nouns. In the following examples, some of the verb phrases have a noun after the measure word while others do not. But even when a noun is added, what the measure word really measures is the verb phrase and not the noun that follows it. Examples (measure word underlined):

- 看一眼 **kàn yìyǎn** *to take one look*
- 叫一声"奶奶" **jiào yìshēng "nǎinai"** *to call "grandma" once*
- 劝了一番 **quànle yìfān** *gave (someone) a round of persuasion*
- 谈一下功课 **tán yíxià gōngkè** *to chat a bit about school work*
- 去了几趟日本 **qùle jǐtàng Rìběn** *went to Japan several times*

4.3 Common errors made by English speakers when using measure words

Given the fundamental differences between English and Chinese in the use of measure words, it is only natural that students of Chinese are likely to stumble at certain points. Knowing where these points lie will help you avoid them.

1. Forgetting to use the measure word

Students at the very basic level may forget to insert a measure word where it is required, especially in cases where the measure word is devoid of meaning and only fulfills a grammatical requirement. The first category of measure words described in 4.2—the "classifiers"—are prone to this pitfall. But beyond the basic level, students usually learn quickly to use them and no longer make this error.

2. Overusing the generic measure word 个 ge

At the intermediate level and beyond, students tend to fall back on the "generic" measure word 个 ge when they don't know or cannot recall the correct measure word that corresponds to a particular noun. Overusing 个 ge does not usually lead to a misunderstanding, but it is a dead giveaway that a non-native speaker of Chinese does not know the language very well. Examples:

The correct measure word for *bicycle* 自行车 zìxíngchē

- *those three bicycles*
  那三辆自行车 nèi sānliàng zìxíngchē or 那三部自行车 nèi sānbù zìxíngchē
  (那三个自行车 nèi sānge zìxíngchē is acceptable, but does not sound natural.)

The measure word for *class* 课 kè
The two meanings of "class"—*a session of a class* and *a course*—are distinguished by using different measure words 节 jié for *session* and 门 mén for *course*. So using the generic measure 个 ge can lead to ambiguity as to which one you are referring to.

- *I have three classes on Mondays.*
  星期一我有三节课。 **Xīngqīyī wǒ yǒu sānjié kè.**

- *I want to take a Chinese class this year.*
  今年我要上一门中文课。 **Jīnnián wǒ yào shàng yìmén Zhōngwén kè.**

3. Measure words for abstract nouns

Associating the correct measure word with each noun becomes more sophisticated at a more abstract level, where words are used figuratively. At this level, measure words often add subtle meanings or nuances to the associated nouns, and the correspondence between the noun and the measure word is often by convention rather than logic. It is best to simply memorize these **measure word+noun** combinations as idiomatic expressions. Idioms often lack precise translations, so they are best learned as Chinese set phrases. Because of this, the English glosses in the examples below are only approximate.

- 一番话 **yìfān huà** *a load of talk*
- 一席话 **yìxí huà** *a round of discourse* (formal)
- 一条心 **yìtiáo xīn** *a "line" of heart* (resolute or united)
- 一片好心 **yípiàn hǎoxīn** *a "slice" of good heart* (pure good intentions)

4. Adding unnecessary measure words

When quantifiers (units of measure) and large round numbers (above 100) are misconstrued as nouns, it can lead a student to over-apply the "mandatory measure word" rule and to add extraneous measure words. Examples:

Quantifiers:

- 三英里 **sān yīnglǐ** (* 三个英里 **sānge yīnglǐ**) *3 miles*
- 五公斤 **wǔ gōngjīn** (* 五个公斤 **wǔge gōngjīn**) *5 kilograms*
- 两尺高 **liǎngchǐ gāo** (* 两个尺高 **liǎngge chǐ gāo**) *2 feet tall*

Numerical measures:

- 两万 **liǎngwàn** (* 两个万 **liǎngge wàn**) *20,000*
- 一亿 **yíyì** (* 一个亿 **yíge yì**, but see exception below) *100,000,000*

Note: There is one idiomatic instance where the numerical measure 亿 **yì** does not take an additional measure word. To emphasize the enormity of a number, the generic measure word 个 **ge** may be added to highlight the nuance of "a large round number," but it is not mandatory. This nuance may be conveyed in English by the phrase "the sum of…"

- *By 1980, China's population already exceeded one billion.*
  到了1980 年，中国的人口已经超过了十个亿。
  Dàole 1980 nián, Zhōngguóde rénkǒu yǐjīng chāoguòle shíge yì.

- *He invested a sum of $5,000,000,000 within just one year.*
  他一年内就投资了五十个亿。 **Tā yìnián-nèi jiù tóuzīle wǔshíge yì.**

5. Overuse of measure words

Certain nouns in English are translated into measure words in Chinese. These have the meaning of English nouns, but in Chinese they function grammatically as measure words. For convenience, we will call them "quasi measures" here. In the last section, we discussed how students may over-apply the mandatory measure word rule to quantifiers and numerical measures. This occurs with quasi-measures as well. Because these nouns are already themselves measure words, it is incorrect to add another measure word in front of them.

Examples of quasi measures:
年 **nián** *year*, 岁 **suì** *year (in age)*, 等 **děng** *class*,
代 **dài** *generation*, 天 **tiān** *day*, 处 **chù** *place/location*,
课 **kè** *lesson*

- *How old is your child?* 你的孩子几岁? **Nǐde háizi jǐsuì?**
  ✗ 你的孩子几个岁? **Nǐde háizi jǐge suì?**

- *I can't afford to go by first class (on a plane or ship).*
  我坐不起头等舱。 **Wǒ zuò-bu-qǐ tóuděng cāng.**

- *four generations under one roof.* 四代同堂 **sìdài tóngtáng**
  ✗ 四个代同堂 **sìge dài tóngtáng**

◆ *He made his decision that very day.*
他当天就决定了。 **Tā dāngtiān jiù juédìngle.**

◆ *There are refugees in various countries in the world.*
世界各国都有难民。 **Shìjiè gèguó dōu yǒu nànmín.**

◆ *This book contains 15 lessons.* (**Note:** 课 also means *class* and *course*.)
这本书有十五课。 **Zhèiběn shū yǒu shíwǔ kè.**
✗ 这本书有十五个课。 **Zhèiběn shū yǒu shíwǔ ge kè.**

6. Nouns vs measure words

Words referring to periods of time are inconsistent. Grammatically, some of them function as regular nouns and some as measure words in Chinese, even though their English equivalents are all nouns.

a) Nouns: 月 **yuè** *month*, 星期/礼拜 **xīngqī/lǐbài** *week*, 学期 **xuéqī** *semester*, 钟头 **zhōngtou** *hour*
The measure word used with the above nouns is 个 **ge**.

b) Measure words: 年 **nián** *year*, 周 **zhōu** *week*, 天 **tiān** *day*
A specific and/or number is used directly with these words without another intervening measure words

- 三年(以)前 **sānnián (yǐ)qián** *3 years ago*
- 前四天 **qián sìtiān** *the previous 4 days*
- 病了两个星期/两周 **bìngle liǎngge xīngqī/liǎng zhōu** *ill for 2 weeks*

◆ *There are only four months in a semester.*
一个学期只有四个月。 **Yíge xuéqī zhǐyǒu sìge yuè.**

◆ *I've waited here for 3 hours!*
我在这里等了三(个)小时了! **Wǒ zài zhèlǐ děngle sān(ge) xiǎoshí le.**

Note: The word 小时 **xiǎoshí** *hour* can function as either a noun or a measure word (see the last example above), which means the addition of 个 **ge** is optional.

EXERCISES:

Translate the following sentences into Chinese:

1. That classroom has four tables and twenty chairs.
2. These apples are $2 per pound, or $5 for three pounds.
3. Obama was American President for two terms.
4. Our family has two children, one dog, two cats, and three goldfish.
5. We don't have a car, only two bicycles.
6. Every year we have a three-month summer vacation and a two-week winter vacation.

ANSWERS:

1. 那个教室有四张桌子、二十把椅子。 Nèige jiàoshì yǒu sìzhāng zhuōzi, èrshíbǎ yǐzi.
2. 这些苹果两块钱一磅，五块钱三磅。
   Zhèixiē píngguǒ liǎngkuài qián yíbàng, wǔkuài qian sānbàng.
3. 奥巴马当了两任美国总统。 Àobāmǎ dāngle liǎngrèn Měiguó zǒngtǒng.
4. 我们家有两个孩子、一只狗、两只猫和三条金鱼。
   Wǒmen jiā yǒu liǎngge háizi, yìzhī gǒu, liǎngzhī māo hé sāntiáo jīnyú.
5. 我们没有汽车，只有两辆自行车。 Wǒmen méiyǒu qìchē, zhǐyǒu liǎngliàng zìxíngchē.
6. 我们每年有三个月的暑假跟两个星期的寒假。
   Wǒmen měinián yǒu sānge yuède shǔjià gēn liǎngge xīngqīde hánjià.

4.4 Cardinal vs ordinal numbers

The cardinal numbers are 1, 2, 3, etc., and the ordinal numbers are 1st, 2nd, 3rd, etc. In Chinese, cardinal numbers are turned into ordinal numbers simply by adding 第 **dì**. This is all very straightforward. However, there are a few differences between English and Chinese in the usages of these two kinds of numbers:

1. When referring to a lesson or chapter in a book, or a particular page

Cardinal numbers are used in English while ordinal numbers are used in Chinese.

* 第三课 dìsānkè *Lesson three*
* 第十章, 第四十页 dìshí zhāng, dìsìshí yè *Chapter 10, page 40*
* 三课 sān kè *3 lessons*; 十章 shí zhāng *10 chapters*; 四十页 sìshí yè *40 pages*

2. Grades or years in school

Ordinal numbers are used in English to refer to particular grades, whereas the cardinal numbers are used in Chinese.

* *second grade in elementary school* 小学二年级 xiǎoxué èrniánjí
* *third year in high school* 高中三年级 gāozhōng sānniánjí or 高三 gāo sān
* *fourth year in college (senior)* 大学四年级 dàxué sìniánjí or 大四 dà sì

3. Centuries

When referring to a particular century, ordinal numbers are always used in English. The situation is more complicated in Chinese. From the 1st century through the 10th century, ordinal numbers are used. From the 11th century onward, cardinal numbers are used. When referring to several centuries as a span of time, the word 世纪 shìjì becomes a noun and the measure word 个 ge is added.

* *21st century* 二十一世纪 èrshíyī shìjì
* *from the 1st through the 3rd century* 从第一到第三世纪
  cóng dìyī dào dìsān shìjì

- *3 centuries* 三个世纪 **sānge shìjì**
- *12th century* 十二世纪 **shí'èr shìjì**
- *12 centuries* 十二个世纪 **shí'èrge shìjì**

EXERCISES:

Translate the following sentences into Chinese:

1. Someone said that the 20th century was the American century, and the 21st century will be China's. I disagree! I believe the 21st century will be the global century.

2. Twenty years ago, most students who studied Chinese did not begin until the first year of college. Now many begin in the first year of high school, some even begin in elementary school.

3. The teacher said that before we begin studying Lesson 13, we will have a summary exam on the first 12 lessons!

4. China's final dynasty, the Qing dynasty, was from 1644 to 1911, so it lasted less than three centuries.

ANSWERS:

1. 有人说二十世纪是美国的世纪，二十一世纪是中国的世纪。我不同意！
我相信二十一世纪将会是全球的世纪。**Yǒurén shuō èrshí shìjì shì Měiguóde shìjì, èrshíyī shìjì shì Zhōngguóde shìjì. Wǒ bù tóngyì! Wǒ xiāngxìn èrshíyī shìjì jiāng huì shì quánqiúde shìjì.**

2. 二十年前，学中文的学生多半是在大学一年级才开始学的。现在很多是在高中一年级就开始了，有的甚至于在小学就开始了。**Èrshí-nián qián, xué Zhōngwénde xuésheng duōbàn shì zài dàxué yìniánjí cái kāishǐ xué de. Xiànzài hěnduō shì zài gāozhōng yìniánjí jiù kāishǐ le, yǒude shènzhìyú zài xiǎoxué jiù kāishǐ le.**

3. 老师说我们开始读第十三课之前，要有一个总结头十二课的考试！**Lǎoshī shuō wǒmen kāishǐ dú dìshísān-kè zhīqián, yào yǒu yíge zǒngjié tóu shí'èrkède kǎoshì!**

4. 中国最后的朝代清朝是从1644年到1911年，所以持续了不到三个世纪。**Zhōngguó zuìhòude cháodài Qīng-cháo shì cóng 1644 nián dào 1911 nián, suǒyǐ chíxùle búdào sānge shìjì.**

4.5 The difference between 二 **èr** and 两 **liǎng** when translating the number 2

Knowing when to use 二 **èr** and when to use 两 **liǎng** seems easy enough, but some idiomatic usages can complicate the situation.

1. The rule of thumb is that 两 **liǎng** is used only before a measure word and only when it refers to the cardinal number "2" (i.e., not as part of a larger number like 102, 20, 12, etc.), and never when it refers to the ordinal number "2nd"), and 二 **èr** is used in all other contexts.

- *(phone number)* 243-422-5272 二四三－四二二－五二七二
èrsìsān-sì'èrèr-wǔ'èrqī'èr

- *$2* 两块 **liǎng kuài** but *$12* 十二块 **shí'èr kuài**

- $20 二十块 **èrshí kuài** but $200 两百块 **liǎngbǎi kuài** or 二百块 **èrbǎi kuài**

- *our second year in the U.S.*
  我们在美国的第二年 **wǒmen zài Měiguóde dì'èr nián**

- *We lived in the U.S. for two or three years.*
  我们在美国住了两三年。 **Wǒmen zài Měiguó zhùle liǎng-sān-nián.**

2. 两 **liǎng** is also used with large numerical measures (digits larger than 100), but with very high numbers, especially in formal situations, 二 **èr** may be used in place of 两 **liǎng** (see 4.2, section 3).

- *¥2200* 两千两百元 **liǎngqiān-liǎngbǎi yuán** or 二千二百元 **èrqiān èrbǎi yuán** (formal)

- *25,000 students* 两万/二万五千个学生 **liǎngwàn/èrwàn-wǔqiānge xuésheng**

- *250,000 students* 二十五万个学生 **èrshíwǔwànge xuésheng**

3. Either 二 **èr** or 两 **liǎng** may be used with units of measure (called "quantifiers" in 4.2, section 2) which measure weight, length, distance, etc., with 两 **liǎng** being more colloquial.

- *2.8 meters* 二/两米八 **èr/liǎng mǐ bā**
- *2 kms* 二/两公里 **èr/liǎng gōnglǐ**
- *2 inches* 二/两英寸 **èr/liǎng yīngcùn**
- *2 kilograms* 二/两公斤 **èr/liǎng gōngjīn**
- *2 pounds* 两磅 **liǎng bàng** (but not 二磅 **èr bàng**; native speakers simply don't say this)

4. Some points to note with regard to 二 **èr** vs 两 **liǎng** when referring to money:

   a. The basic monetary unit called "dollar" in English translates into one of two words in Chinese: the colloquial 块 **kuài** and the slightly more formal 元 **yuán** (which is the written form). 两 **liǎng** is used with 块 **kuài** and 二 **èr** is used with 元 **yuán**. For the units 毛 **máo** (*10 cents*) and 分 **fēn** (*cent*), either 二 **èr** or 两 **liǎng** may be used.

      - *$2* 两块 **liǎngkuài**/二元 **èryuán**
      - *20 cents* 两/二毛 **liǎng/èrmáo** (not 二十分 **èrshífēn**!)
      - *2 cents* 两/二分 **liǎng/èrfēn**

   b. In monetary amounts involving several levels of units (dollars, cents, etc.), the unit at the end is usually understood and omitted, just as in English. This is the same principle that applies to a "tiered quantity" discussed in a note in 4.2, section 3, and it also appears in *2.8 meters* (the first example in section 3 above).

- *$1.20* 一块两／二毛 **yíkuài liǎng/èrmáo** or 一块二 **yíkuài-èr**
  ✗ 一块两 **yíkuài-liǎng** (this is incorrect because 两 **liǎng** must be followed by a measure word)
- *$1.22* 一块两／二毛二 **yíkuài liǎng/èrmáo-èr**

5. In some situations, as discussed above, 二 **èr** and 两 **liǎng** are both correct, but 二 **èr** is more formal than 两 **liǎng**. This difference traces back to classical Chinese, where 二 **èr** was the primary word for *two*, and the usage of measure words was very limited. In modern Chinese, the word 二 **èr** pops up in formal polite speech and in certain set phrases, echoing the classical usage.

For example, 二位 **èrwèi** is a very polite way to address two guests. It can be used alone or with an honorific term like 先生 **xiānsheng**. By contrast, 两位 **liǎngwèi** is not an especially polite expression, nor is it used to directly address someone.

◆ (addressing two guests) *Please come in and sit a bit.*
二位请进来坐坐。 **Èrwèi qǐng jìnlai zuòzuo.**

◆ *These two English teachers are both Americans.*
这两位英语老师都是美国人。 **Zhèi liǎngwèi Yīngyǔ lǎoshī dōushì Měiguórén.**

Another example of the formal usage of 二 **èr** is in the couplet 二人同心，黄土变金 **èrrén tóngxīn, huángtǔ biànjīn** *when two are united in their hearts, even the brown earth can turn to gold.* In this classical aphorism, the modern phrase 两个人 **liǎngge rén** becomes 二人 **èrrén**, i.e. 两 **liǎng** is replaced by 二 **èr**, and no measure word is used.

EXERCISES:

Translate the following passage into Chinese:

I like to say that I have two native languages. It's like this: When my American family adopted me from China, I was only two years old. In the following year (second year), English became my second native language, and my first language was almost totally forgotten. Then, when I was 12, my parents had an opportunity to go work in China for two years. I very quickly relearned my first language. Now I use both languages every day, so I will never forget them.

ANSWERS:
我喜欢说我有两个母语。是这样的：我的美国家庭从中国领养我的时候，我才两岁。第二年，英语就变成我的母语了。我的第一个母语差不多都忘了。然后，我十二岁的时候，我父母得到一个去中国工作两年的机会。很快地，我又学会了我的第一个母语。现在我每天都用这两种语言，这样我就永远不会忘记这两种语言了。 **Wǒ xǐhuan shuō wǒ yǒu liǎngge mǔyǔ. Shì zhèyàngde: Wǒde Měiguó jiātíng cóng Zhōngguó lǐngyǎng wǒde shíhou, wǒ cái liǎngsuì. Dì'èrnián, Yīngyǔ jiù biànchéng wǒde mǔyǔ le. Wǒde dìyīge mǔyǔ chàbuduō dōu wàngle. Ránhòu, wǒ shí'èrsuìde shíhou, wǒ fùmǔ dédào yíge qù Zhōngguó gōngzuò liǎngniánde jīhuì. Hěn kuàide, wǒ yòu xuéhuìle wǒde dìyīge mǔyǔ. Xiànzài wǒ měitiān dōu yòng zhè liǎngzhǒng yǔyán, zhèyàng wǒ jiù yǒngyuǎn búhuì wàngjì zhè liǎngzhǒng yǔyán le.**

4.6 Numbers having four digits and above

Large English numbers are organized as multiples of three digits, i.e. thousand, million, billion, trillion. This system derived from the Arabic numeral system, where every group of three digits is marked by a comma (i.e. 1,000, 1,000,000, etc.). The equivalent Chinese numbers are organized by multiples of four digits, i.e. 万 **wàn** *10,000*, 亿 **yì** *100,000,000*, and 兆 **zhào** *1,000,000,000,000*. Translating these high digit numbers requires considerable mental gymnastics. Even linguists who are totally bilingual often find it necessary to write out the numbers in order to get it right. So, don't worry if you first find it difficult to translate these very large numbers (in either direction)—you are not alone!.

EXERCISES:

Answer the following questions in Chinese.

1. 美国的人口是多少？中国呢？ **Měiguóde rénkǒu shì duōshǎo? Zhōngguó ne?**

2. 上哈佛大学，一年要六万七千五百八十美元 (2018-19 数据)。那是多少人民币啊？ **Shàng Hāfó Dàxué, yìnián yào liùwàn-qīqiān-wǔbǎi-bāshí Měiyuán (2018-19 shùjù). Nà shì duōshǎo rénmínbì a?**

> **ANSWERS:**
> 1. 美国的人口是差不多三亿两千六百万，而中国的人口是差不多十三亿九千万。**Měiguóde rénkǒu shì chàbuduō sānyì-liǎngqiān-liùbǎi-wàn, ér Zhōngguóde rénkǒu shì chàbuduō shísānyì-jiǔqiān-wàn.**
> 2. 目前的兑换率是差不多1:7，所以六万七千五百八十美元就是差不多四十七万三千元人民币。
> **Mùqiánde duìhuàn-lǜ shì chàbuduō yī-duì-qī, suǒyǐ liùwàn-qīqiān-wǔbǎi-bāshí Měiyuán jiùshì chàbuduō sìshíqīwàn-sānqiān-yuán rénmínbì.**

4.7 The use of 几 jǐ vs 多少 duōshǎo in referring to quantities

Both 几 **jǐ** and 多少 **duōshǎo** are used to ask questions about quantities of things, but generally 几 **jǐ** applies to countable entities (discrete things that can be counted), whereas 多少 **duōshǎo** applies to non-countable entities (called "mass nouns"). This subchapter is about how they differ in terms of their grammatical usage.

The word 几 **jǐ** actually has two meanings: *several* and *how many*, but here we are concerned with only the meaning *how many*. Context usually makes it clear which of the two meanings is intended. Grammatically, 几 **jǐ** is a number (albeit an unspecified number), and when it means *how many*, it is also a question word. 多少 **duōshǎo** is also a question word, but with the basic meaning of *how much*. It can also mean *how many*, but the number in question is likely to be large and a precise count is not pertinent, i.e. the things being quantified are discrete, but are conceptualized as a "group," such as the number of students in a school, or soldiers in a military unit. When the number in question is small, 几 **jǐ** is used instead of 多少 **duōshǎo**.

Grammatically, the "mandatory measure word" rule applies to 几 **jǐ** but not to 多少 **duōshǎo**. This means 几 **jǐ** (a specified number) is always followed by a measure word, even when the noun is understood and omitted. 多少 **duōshǎo** is generally followed directly by a noun (with no measure word added), unless the noun itself is understood and omitted. A measure word may also be used after 多少 **duōshǎo**; however, this sounds a bit redundant.

- 几位客人？ **jǐwèi kèrén?** *how many guests?*
- 第几页？ **dìjǐ yè?** *which (what number) page*
- 上几门课？ **shàng jǐmén kè?** *take how many courses?*
- 放多少糖？ **fàng duōshǎo táng?** *put in how much sugar?*
- 多少人口？ **duōshǎo rénkǒu?** *what is the population size?*
- 多少时间？ **duōshǎo shíjiān?** *how much time?*

◆ *I have many chairs here. How many do you want?*
我这里有很多椅子，你要几把？
Wǒ zhèlǐ yǒu hěnduō yǐzi, nǐ yào jǐbǎ?

◆ *If you don't have enough money, I can lend you some. How much do you want?*
如果你的钱不够，我可以借你一点，你要多少？
Rúguǒ nǐde qián búgòu, wǒ kěyǐ jiè nǐ yìdiǎn, nǐ yào duōshǎo?
(**Note**: In the last two examples, the noun is unstated at the end because it is understood.)

◆ *How many international students are there at Peking U.? Probably around 300–400.*
北大有多少国际学生？大概三四百吧。(多少个 **duōshǎoge** is acceptable, but sounds redundant)
Běi Dà yǒu duōshǎo guójì xuésheng? Dàgài sān-sìbǎi ba.

In the answers to questions asked with 几 **jǐ** and 多少 **duōshǎo**, measure words are generally used, but they differ in one regard. The answer to a question involving 几 **jǐ** always assumes the same measure word used in the question, whereas the measure word in the answer to a question involving 多少 **duōshǎo** varies. Note the underlined measure words in the following examples.

◆ 你等了几个小时？ **Nǐ děngle jǐge xiǎoshí?** *How many hours did you wait?*
半个小时 **bànge xiǎoshí** *half an hour*   三个小时 **sānge xiǎoshí** *three hours*

◆ 你等了多长时间？ **Nǐ děngle duōcháng shíjiān?** *How long did you wait?*
半天！ **bàntiān!** *half a day (a long time)!*
很久 **hěnjiǔ** *very long*
半(个)小时 **bàn(ge) xiǎoshí** *half an hour*
好几天呢！ **hǎojǐtiān ne!** *quite a few days!*

- 你买了几<u>个</u>苹果？ **Nǐ mǎile jǐge píngguǒ?** *How many apples did you buy?*
  六<u>个</u> **liùge** *six*

- 你买了多少糖果？ **Nǐ mǎile duōshǎo tángguǒ?** *How much candy did you buy?*
  三磅 **sān bàng** *3 pounds*　　　　两公斤 **liǎng gōngjīn** *2 kilos*
  一大堆 **yí dà duī** *a big pile*　　　三袋 **sān dài** *3 bags*

- 今晚来了几位客人？ **Jīnwǎn láile jǐwèi kèrén?** *How many guests came tonight?*
  二十多位 **èrshíduō wei** *twenty-some*

- 今晚来了多少客人？ **Jīnwǎn láile duōshǎo kèrén?** *How many guests came tonight?*
  二十多<u>位</u> **èrshíduō wèi** *or* 二十多<u>个</u> **èrshíduō ge** *twenty-some*

The word 多少 **duōshǎo** has an additional usage totally unrelated to questions. 多少 **duōshǎo** in itself and also in its reduplicated form 多多少少 **duōduōshǎoshǎo** can be used as an adverb, meaning *more or less, to some extent.*

- *Chinese college students more or less all know a bit of English.*
  中国的大学生多多少少都会一点儿英语。
  Zhōngguóde dàxuésheng duōduōshǎoshǎo dōu huì yìdiǎnr Yīngyǔ.

- *Between parents and children, there is always a generation gap to some extent.*
  父母和孩子之间多少会有一点儿代沟。
  Fùmǔ hé háizi zhījiān duōshǎo huì yǒu yìdiǎnr dàigōu.

EXERCISES:

Translate the following sentences into Chinese:

1. How many children do you have? And how old are they?

2. How much money do professors in China make each month? ¥8000 at the low end, ¥20,000 at the high end.

3. People in their 80s all have memory problems to some extent.

ANSWERS:
1. 你有几个孩子？他们几岁了？ **Nǐ yǒu jǐge háizi? Tāmen jǐsuì le?**
2. 在中国，教授的月薪是多少？少的八千元，多的两万元。
   Zài Zhōngguó, jiàoshòude yuè-xīn shì duōshǎo? Shǎode bāqiān-yuán, duōde liǎngwàn-yuán.
3. 八十多岁的人多少都有一点记忆问题。
   Bāshíduō-suìde rén duōshǎo dōu yǒu yìdiǎn jìyì wèntí.

4.8 Larger units precede smaller units in dates, times, addresses, etc.

In stating things involving several levels of units, the English word order tends to go from the small to the large, while the Chinese word order is the opposite, i.e. from the large to the small. The English word order reflects a vision of the world that begins from the most "local" point, and extends outward. In this mode, the individual precedes the whole. The Chinese word order reflects a perspective that begins from the outer layer and "peels" inward, progressing from the whole to the individual. The prime example of this difference in mindset is the way personal names are stated. In English, the given name precedes the family name, whereas in Chinese the family name precedes the given name.

- *Date of birth: April 9, 1975*
  出生日期：1975 年 4 月 9 日 **chūshēng rìqī: 1975 nián 4 yuè 9 rì**

- *Address: 32 Lane 58, East Green Lake Rd., Kunming, Yunnan, China*
  地址：中国 云南省 昆明市 翠湖东路 58 巷 32 号
  dìzhǐ: Zhōngguó Yúnnán-shěng Kūnmíng-shì Cuìhú Dōng Lù, 58 xiàng 32 hào

- *He is a professor in the Foreign Languages Department at Peking University.*
  他是北大外语系的教授。**Tā shì Běi Dà wàiyǔxìde jiàoshòu.**

EXERCISES:

Translate the following sentences into Chinese:

1. July 4, 1776; October 1, 1949

2. He invited us to dinner at 6:00 p.m. next Friday evening.

3. His hometown is Bai Family Village (白家庄 **Báijiāzhuāng**), Clearwater County (清水县 **Qīngshuǐ Xiàn**), Henan Province (河南 **Hénán**).

ANSWERS:
1. 1776年7月4日；1949年10月1日
   yī-qī-qī-liù-nián qī-yuè sì-rì; yī-jiǔ-sì-jiǔ-nián shí-yuè yī-rì
2. 他请我们下星期五晚上六点钟吃饭。
   Tā qǐng wǒmen xià-xīngqīwǔ wǎnshang liùdiǎn zhōng chīfàn.
3. 他的老家在河南，清水县，白家庄。
   Tāde lǎojiā zài Hénán, Qīngshuǐ-xiàn, Báijiā-zhuāng.

4.9 Conceptulizing dates relative to the present

Native English speakers often confuse 前 **qián** *in front of, before* and 后 **hòu** *behind, later* when referring to dates. Understanding the reasons for this may help you avoid this error. The Chinese vocabulary for dates is based on an "objective" timeline rather than from the speaker's time perspective. Therefore, what comes earlier in the timeline is expressed using the words 前 **qián** *in front of, before* or 上 **shàng** *on / at top / above*, respectively. as shown by the two tables below. The usage of 上 **shàng** in the second table reflects the Chinese conceptualization of time as a vertical line, comparable to falling rain or traditional Chinese writing, which runs from top to bottom. To native English speakers, whose main point of reference is the speaker's present, it seems more logical to associate a date that lies in the future (in front of the speaker) with the word 前 **qián**, and a date that is in the past (behind the present) with the word 后 **hòu**. This is exactly what causes the confusion.

The words 天 **tiān** *day* and 年 **nián** *year* are both grammatical measure words, and they follow a parallel pattern, with the exception of 昨天 **zuótiān** vs 去年 **qùnián**:

3 days ago	the day before yesterday	yesterday	today	tomorrow	day after tomorrow	3 days from today
大前天 **dàqiántiān**	前天 **qiántiān**	昨天 **zuótiān**	今天 **jīntiān**	明天 **míngtiān**	后天 **hòutiān**	大后天 **dàhòutiān**
3 years ago	the year before last	last year	this year	next year	year after next	3 yrs from now
大前年 **dàqiánnián**	前年 **qiánnián**	去年 **qùnián**	今年 **jīnnián**	明年 **míngnián**	后年 **hòunián**	大后年 **dàhòunián**

The words 星期 **xīngqī** / 礼拜 **lǐbài** *week* and 月 **yuè** *month* follow the same pattern. Since both are nouns, the measure word 个 **ge** is added.

month before last	last month	this month	next month	month after next
上上个月 **shàngshàngge yuè**	上个月 **shàngge yuè**	这个月 **zhèige yuè**	下个月 **xiàge yuè**	下下个月 **xiàxiàge yuè**

week before last	last week	this week	next week	week after next
上上个星期 **shàngshàngge xīngqī**	上个星期 **shàngge xīngqī**	这个星期 **zhèige xīngqī**	下个星期 **xiàge xīngqī**	下下个星期 **xiàxiàge xīngqī**

A more succinct and formal alternative word for 星期 **xīngqī** is 周 **zhōu**. 周 **zhōu** is grammatically a measure word (like 天 **tiān** and 年 **nián**), so 个 **ge** is not used with it. It basically follows the same pattern as 月 **yuè**, except for this month, in which 这个 **zhèige** is replaced with the more classical 本 **běn**.

上上周 **shàngshàngzhōu**	上周 **shàngzhōu**	本周 **běnzhōu**	下周 **xiàzhōu**	下下周 **xiàxiàzhōu**

If you are prone to mixing up 前 **qián** with 后 **hòu**, or 上 **shàng** with 下 **xià**, memorizing the following sentences may help.

♦ *Don't forget,* 前天 **qiántiān** *is two days ago,* 后天 **hòutiān** *is two days hence. From today onward (after today), I will not mistake these two words.*
别忘了，前天就是两天以前，后天就是两天以后。今后我不会再弄错这两个词了。
Bié wàngle, qiántiān jiùshì liǎngtiān yǐqián, hòutiān jiùshì liǎngtiān yǐhòu. Jīnhòu wǒ búhuì zài nòngcuò zhèiliǎngge cí le.

♦ *Counting time is like reading old books, always from top to bottom, i.e.* 上 **shàng** *comes before* 下 **xià.**
算时间跟看古文书一样，总是从上往下，也就是说，"上"是先，"下"是后。 **Suàn shíjiān gēn kàn gǔwénshū yíyàng, zǒngshì cóng shàng wǎng xià, yě jiùshì shuō, shàng shì xiān, xià shì hòu.**

▶ **EXERCISES:**

Translate the following sentences into Chinese:

1. She began attending college last year, so she should graduate the year after next.
2. My car broke down the week before last, it's still in repair.
3. I'm too busy tomorrow; would the day after tomorrow be OK?
4. I mailed it out day before yesterday, so it should arrive today.

> **ANSWERS:**
> 1. 她去年开始上大学，所以后年就应该毕业了。
>   **Tā qùnián kāishǐ shàng dàxué, suǒyǐ hòunián jiù yīnggāi bìyè le.**
> 2. 我的车上上个星期坏了，现在还在修理。
>   **Wǒde chē shàngshàngge xīngqī huàile, xiànzài hái zài xiūlǐ.**
> 3. 我明天太忙，后天行不行？ **Wǒ míngtiān tài máng, hòutiān xíng-buxíng?**
> 4. 我是前天寄出去的，所以今天应该到了。
>   **Wǒ shì qiántiān jì-chūqu de, suǒyǐ jīntiān yīnggāi dào le.**

4.10 The correct word order for 半 bàn "half" and 多 duō "and then some"

Expressing a quantity that is not an even whole number necessitates the use of 半 **bàn** …*and a half* or ⋯ 多 **duō** …*and then some*. In this case, the mandatory measure word always comes before 半 **bàn** or 多 **duō**. In other words, the Chinese word order follows the pattern of "two pounds and a half" rather than "two and a half pounds." In the following examples, note that 半 **bàn** or 多 **duō** always follows the measure words (underlined):

- 一点半 **yìdiǎnbàn** *1:30*
- 一个半小时 **yígebàn xiǎoshí** *an hour and a half*
- 三天半的时间 **sāntiānbànde shíjiān** *three and a half days (of time)*
- 两块多（钱） **liǎngkuàiduō (qián)** *over $2*
- 三斤多的苹果 **sānjīnduōde píngguǒ** *over three kilos of apples*
- *This child is only a bit over 9 months old, and can already walk!*
  这个孩子才九个多月，已经会走路了！(*九多个月 **jiǔduōge yuè** is incorrect)
  Zhèige háizi cái jiǔgeduō yuè, yǐjīng huì zǒulù le!

- *A 2.5 year old child should be able to talk a bit, right?*
  两岁半的孩子应该能说几句话了吧？（*两半岁 **liǎngbàn suì** is incorrect）
  Liǎngsuìbànde háizi yīnggāi néng shuō jǐjù huà le ba?

- *I've waited here for over an hour!*
  我在这儿等了一个多钟头了！ **Wǒ zài zhèr děngle yígeduō zhōngtóu le!**
  （*一多个钟头 **yìduōge zhōngtóu** and *一个钟头多 **yíge zhōngtóu duō** are incorrect）

- *Movie tickets cost only $2 and some last year, this year it's gone up to $3.50!*
  电影票去年只要两块多，今年就要三块半了！
  Diànyǐngpiào qùnián zhǐyào liǎngkuàiduō, jīnnián jiù yào sānkuàibàn le!

When numerical measures (see 4.2, section 3)—i.e. ten, hundred, thousand, etc. (十 **shí**, 百 **bǎi**, 千 **qiān**)—are followed by 半 **bàn** or 多 **duō**, to indicate a portion of a numerical unit, they function like normal measure words. Here are some examples:

- *She looks to be a 20-something, but she's actually over 40 years old!*
  她看上去好像只有二十几岁，其实她已经四十多岁了！
  Tā kàn-shàngqu hǎoxiàng zhǐyǒu èrshíjǐ suì, qíshí tā yǐjīng sìshíduō le!

- *Rent for a house like this is probably over $3,000 a month.*
  租这样的房子一个月大概要三千多块。
  Zū zhèyàngde fángzi yíge yuè dàgài yào sānqiānduō kuài.

- *She's been ill for a week and a half!*
  她病了一个半星期了！ **Tā bìngle yígebàn xīngqī le!**

- *They've been married for over 50 years!*
  他们结婚已经五十多/几年了！ **Tāmen jiéhūn yǐjīng wǔshí-duō/jǐ-nián le!**

- *He's studied Chinese for only a year and a half, but already speaks it very well!*
  他学中文才学了一年半，已经说得很好了！
  Tā xué Zhōngwén cái xuéle yìnián-bàn, yǐjīng shuōde hěn hǎo le!

EXERCISES:

Translate the following sentences into Chinese:

1. He left home when he was in his teens.
2. A pound of apples costs a dollar and a half, grapes cost over $2.
3. How can you marry him? You've only known him for a little over a week!
4. We invited over twenty guests.

4.11 Expressing approximate quantities

There are three different terms for expressing approximation, and all of them have different grammatical usages:

1. The phrase 差不多 **chàbuduō** itself has two different meanings: *approximately, about* and *almost (but not quite)* (see 2.1, section 7). In both meanings, 差不多 **chàbuduō** functions just like its English counterparts, and it precedes the quantifying number.

- 差不多三个小时 **chàbuduō sānge xiǎoshí** *about 3 hours*
- 差不多五十万元 **chàbuduō wǔshíwàn yuán** *about ¥500,000*

When 差不多 **chàbuduō** is used in the sense of *almost but not quite*, it is not necessarily followed by a number, and the word 了 **le** is added at the end of the sentence to indicate that something is still progressing toward a "targeted" completion.

- *She was ill for <u>about</u> three days, and is <u>almost</u> well now.*
  她病了差不多三天，现在差不多好了。
  Tā bìngle chàbuduō sāntiān, xiànzài chàbuduō hǎole.

- *The American population is about 325,000,000; or we can say, it is almost 330,000,000.*
  美国人口是差不多三点二五亿，也可以说，是差不多三点三亿了。
  Měiguó rénkǒu shì chàbuduō sāndiǎn-èrwǔ yì, yě kěyǐ shuō, shì chàbuduō sāndiǎnsān yì le.

2. The word 左右 **zuǒyòu**, used in the sense of *approximately*, is usually—but not always—used with round numbers, and it follows the measure word. When an expression has no measure word apart from a numerical measure (10, 100, 1,000, etc.), then it follows that measure. 左右 **zuǒyòu** is usually NOT followed by a noun, since the noun is understood.

- *How many students are in your program? A: about 30.*
  你们的项目有多少学生？三十个左右 or 三十左右 but not: *三十左右个
  Nǐmende xiàngmù yǒu duōshǎo xuésheng? Sānshíge zuǒyòu or **sānshí zuǒyòu**, but not: *****sānshí zuǒyòu ge**

◆ *Every five years or so, there's a major typhoon here.*
每五年左右，这里会有一次大的台风。
Měi wǔnián zuǒyòu, zhèlǐ huì yǒu yícì dàde táifēng.

3. 来 **lái** is a more colloquial way to express an approximate number than either 差不多 **chàbuduō** or 左右 **zuǒyòu**. It is used only with round numbers. In contrast to both 差不多 **chàbuduō** and 左右 **zuǒyòu**, 来 **lái** follows the number and precedes the measure word.

◆ *There are about 30 students in my Chinese class.*
   ✓ 我的中文班上有差不多三十个学生。
      Wǒde Zhōngwén bānshang yǒu chàbuduō sānshíge xuésheng.
   ✓ 上我的中文课的学生，有三十个左右。
      Shàng wǒde Zhōngwénkède xuésheng, yǒu sānshíge zuǒyòu.
   ✗ 我的中文班上有三十个左右学生。
      Wǒde Zhōngwén bān-shang yǒu sānshíge zuǒyòu xuésheng.
   ✓ 我的中文班上有三十来个学生。
      Wǒde Zhōngwén bān-shang yǒu sānshí-lái ge xuésheng.
   ✗ 我的中文班上有三十个来学生。
      Wǒde Zhōngwén bānshang yǒu sānshí ge lái xuésheng.

◆ *He's been sick for about 10 days already!*
   ✓ 他已经病了十来天了！   ✗ 他已经病了十天来了！
      Tā yǐjīng bìngle shí-lái tiān le!   **Tā yǐjīng bìngle shí tiān lái le!**

The word 来 **lái** has another totally different function in quantifying time, which can be easily confused with the above usage. When 来 **lái** follows a time period, it means *in the past (up to now)*, and is a shortened form of ⋯以来 ...**yǐlái**. In this usage, 来 **lái** follows the measure word associated with the amount of time. In contrast, when 来 **lái** indicates an approximation, it precedes the measure word. The following pairs make the distinction clear:

A 三十天来 **sānshí tiān lái** *for the past 30 days*
B 三十来天 **sānshí-lái tiān** *approximately 30 days*

A 一百年来 **yìbǎi-nián lái** *for the past 100 years*
B 一百来年 **yìbǎi-lái nián** *around 100 years*
(**Note:** For the meaning *about 100 years*, the pattern ⋯左右 **zuǒyòu** or 差不多 **chàbuduō**... is more likely to be used.)

A 十个星期来 **shíge xīngqī lái** *for the last 10 weeks* vs
B 十来个星期 **shí-lái ge xīngqī** *approximately 10 weeks*

A In the past ten weeks, my Chinese has improved a lot.
   这<u>十个星期来</u>，我的汉语有了很大的进步。
   Zhèi shíge xīngqī lái, wǒde Hànyǔ yǒule hěn dàde jìnbù.

B   In those 10 weeks or so, my Chinese improved a lot. (re a summer program)
在那<u>十来个星期里</u>，我的汉语有了很大的进步。
Zài nà shí-lái ge xīngqīlǐ, wǒde Hànyǔ yǒule hěn dàde jìnbù.

EXERCISES:

Translate the following sentences using 差不多 **chàbuduō**, 左右 **zuǒyòu** and 来 **lái**:

1. Almost all the students in this class will continue to study Chinese next year.
2. Of the students in this class, about half will not continue to study Chinese next year.
3. In these past 10 years, the population of this town has not grown, and has remained around 20,000.

> **ANSWERS:**
> 1. 这班学生，差不多全部都要明年继续学中文。
>   **Zhèibān xuésheng, chàbuduō quánbù dōu yào míngnián jìxù xué Zhōngwén.**
> 2. 这班学生，差不多一半明年不继续学中文了。
>   **Zhèibān xuésheng, chàbuduō yíbàn míngnián bú jìxù xué Zhōngwén le.**
> 3. (过去)十年来，这个小城的人口没有增加，一直是两万左右。
>   **(Guòqu) shínián lái, zhèige xiǎo chéngde rénkǒu méiyǒu zēngjiā, yìzhí shì liǎngwàn zuǒyòu.**

4.12 Expressing multiples with 倍 bèi

There are two patterns that compare two things (A and B) in terms of multiples.

1.   A is X times B (X being a number): A 是 shì B 的 de X 倍 bèi

◆   *My daughter is 27, I'm 54; my age is twice that of my daughter.*
我的女儿二十七岁，我五十四岁。 我的岁数是她的两倍。
Wǒde nǚ'ér èrshíqī suì, wǒ wǔshísì suì. Wǒde suìshù shì tāde liǎngbèi.

◆   *China's population is four times that of the U.S.!*
中国的人口是美国的四倍！ **Zhōngguóde rénkǒu shì Měiguóde sìbèi.**

2.   A is X times more...than B: A 比 bǐ B + adjective X 倍 bèi

To compare two things qualitatively and quantitatively, the word 比 **bǐ** is used with an adjective followed by a number and 倍 **bèi**. This is only one of several usages of 比 **bǐ** that will be detailed in Chapter 14; here we only discuss how 比 **bǐ** is used in tandem with 倍 **bèi**.

◆   *This one is three times as expensive as that one; the price of this one is four times higher.*
这个比那个贵三倍。 也就是说，这个的价钱是那个的四倍。
Zhèige bǐ nèige guì sānbèi. Yě jiùshì shuō, zhèigede jiàqián shì nèigede sìbèi.

- *College tuition has doubled in the last 10 years.*
  大学的学费比十年前高了一倍。**Dàxuéde xuéfèi bǐ shínián-qián gāole yíbèi.**

Neither of the above two patterns is equivalent to the familiar English pattern "*A is X times as… as B*" (e.g. *I am twice as old as you*). Hence, native English speakers are prone to equate the second Chinese pattern with the most common pattern in English, which leads to missing the "number of times" by one. To avoid this pitfall requires replacing the English-speaking mindset with the Chinese one.

- *This room is twice as large as that one.*
  ✗ 这个房间比那个大两倍。**Zhèige fángjiān bǐ nèige dà liǎngbèi.**
  　(This would mean the room is three times as large.)
  ✓ 这个房间比那个大一倍。**Zhèige fángjiān bǐ nèige dà yíbèi.**
  ✓ 这个房间是那个的两倍。**Zhèige fángjiān shì nèigede liǎngbèi.**

- *There are four times as many students studying Chinese as 50 years ago.*
  ✗ 现在学中文的学生比五十年前多了四倍。
  　Xiànzài xué Zhōngwénde xuésheng bǐ wǔshí-nián-qián duōle sìbèi.
  (This would mean there are five times as many students learning Chinese now.)
  ✓ 现在学中文的学生比五十年前多了三倍。
  　Xiànzài xué Zhōngwénde xuésheng bǐ wǔshí-nián-qián duōle sānbèi.

When expressing a half or some portion of a multiple, 倍 **bèi** functions like other measure words, and the words 半 **bàn** and 多 **duō** come after it. (see 4.11)

- *This tree grew by two and a half times in just one year!*
  这棵树在一年中就长高了两倍半！
  Zhèikē shù zài yìnián-zhōng jiù zhǎnggāole liǎngbèibàn!

- *The daughter is only 80 pounds, but her Mom is 170 pounds. So the Mom is more than twice as heavy as the daughter.*
  女儿只有80磅，可是妈妈有170磅。妈妈比女儿重一倍多。
  Nǚ'ér zhǐ yǒu bāshí-bàng, kěshì Māma yǒu yìbǎi-qīshí-bàng. Māma bǐ nǚ'ér zhòng yíbèiduō.

- *China's current population is more than twice as much as in 1949.*
  中国现在的人口是1949年的两倍多。
  Zhōngguó xiànzàide rénkǒu shì 1949 niánde liǎngbèiduō.

EXERCISES:

Translate the following sentences into Chinese:

1. This cell phone is twice as expensive as that one. I can't afford it!

2. At this university, the average income of a professor is one fold more than that of a lecturer.

ANSWERS:
1. 这部手机的价格是那部的两倍，我买不起。
   Zhèibù shǒujīde jiàgé shì nèibùde liǎngbèi, wǒ mǎi-bu-qǐ.
2. 在这所大学，教授的平均收入比讲师的多一倍。
   Zài zhèisuǒ dàxué, jiàoshòude píngjūn shōurù bǐ jiǎngshīde duō yíbèi.

4.13 Expressing fractions and percentages

Fractions and percentages in Chinese both follow the pattern "X 分之 **fēn-zhī** Y" in which X is the denominator and Y is the numerator. In percentages, the denominator is 百 **bǎi** *hundred*. The pattern "X 分之 **fēn-zhī** Y" means *Y out of a total of X*, but note that the word order in English is the opposite of Chinese—the numerator is stated before the denominator, and the word *percent* is added after the percentage. This is another example of the Chinese tendency to state larger units before smaller units (see 4.9). In fractions and percentages, this means stating the whole before the part. Native English speakers need to adapt to this new mindset when expressing fractions and percentages in Chinese.

- *3/4* 四分之三 **sìfēn-zhī-sān**
- *1/2* 二分之一 **èrfēn-zhī-yī** (not 两分之一 **liǎngfēn-zhī-yī**) or 一半 **yíbàn**

- *Some say that 99% of the news is fake.*
  有人说，百分之九十九的新闻是假的。
  Yǒurén shuō, bǎifēn-zhī-jiǔshíjiǔde xīnwén shì jiǎde.

- *In a society, an unemployment rate that exceeds 10% is quite serious.*
  在一个社会里，失业率超过百分之十就相当严重了。
  Zài yíge shèhuìlǐ, shīyè-lǜ chāoguò bǎifēn-zhī-shí jiù xiāngdāng yánzhòng le.

- *We can simplify 3/15 to 1/5 or 20%.*
  我们可以把十五分之三简化为五分之一或百分之二十。
  Wǒmen kěyǐ bǎ shíwǔfēn-zhī-sān jiǎnhuà wéi wǔfēn-zhī-yī huò bǎifēn-zhī-èrshí.

To express a fraction or percentage <u>of a particular thing</u>, two different word orders are possible:

A. fraction/percentage + 的 **de** + noun   B. noun + 的 **de** + fraction/percentage

- *1/3 of the students in this university are foreigners.*
  A 在这所大学，三分之一的学生是外国人。
    Zài zhèisuǒ dàxué, sānfēn-zhī-yī de xuésheng shì wàiguórén.
  B 在这所大学，学生的三分之一是外国人。
    Zài zhèisuǒ dàxué, xuéshengde sānfēn-zhī-yī shì wàiguórén.

- 8.41% of China's population are minorities.

  A 百分之八点四一的中国人口是少数民族。

  Băifēn-zhī-bādiǎnsìyīde Zhōngguó rénkǒu shì shǎoshù mínzú.

  B 中国人口的百分之八点四一是少数民族。

  Zhōngguó rénkǒude băifēn-zhī-bādiǎnsìyī shì shǎoshù mínzú.

- Less than 10% of China's population are minorities.

  A 不到百分之十的中国人口是少数民族。

  Búdào băifēn-zhī-shí de Zhōngguó rénkǒu shì shǎoshù mínzú.

  B 中国人口，不到百分之十是少数民族。

  Zhōngguó rénkǒu, búdào băifēn-zhī-shí shì shǎoshù mínzú.

Of the two correct word orders given above, the first is more commonly used. However, when the relevant "thing" is a long noun phrase, a third alternative—the **topic+comment** pattern—is preferred (see 1.3, section 1). In this pattern, the relevant "thing" is stated upfront as the topic of the sentence, and the fraction or percentage is in the "comment."

- Six percent of the American adult population are illiterate.

  美国的成人人口，（有）百分之六不识字。

  Měiguóde chéngrén rénkǒu, (yǒu) băifēn-zhī-liù bù shízì.

- One third of the graduate students who studied in China married Chinese spouses.

  去中国留学的研究生，三分之一跟中国人结婚了。

  Qù Zhōngguó liúxuéde yánjiūshēng, sānfēn-zhī-yī gēn Zhōngguórén jiéhūnle.

EXERCISES:

Translate the following sentences into Chinese:

1. Compared with last year, the number of students increased by 150%.

2. That is to say, this year's students are one and a half times more than last year's.

3. At this university, the football coach's salary is higher than that of the president by 3/4!

ANSWERS:

1. 比起去年，学生人数增加了百分之一百五十。
   Bǐqǐ qùnián, xuésheng rénshù zēngjiāle băifēn-zhī-yìbăi-wŭshí.

2. 也就是说，学生人数比去年多了一倍半。
   Yě jiùshì shuō, xuésheng rénshù bǐ qùnián duōle yíbèi-bàn.

3. 在这所大学，美式足球教练的薪水比校长的高四分之三！
   Zài zhèisuǒ dàxué, Měi-shì zúqiú jiàoliànde xīnshuǐ bǐ xiàozhăngde gāo sìfēn-zhī-sān!

Addendum: Common Measure Words and their Associated Nouns

The most common measure words, including those covered in 4.2, are familiar to students who have completed a basic level of study. There are many references for measure words available on the Internet these days. One of the most user-friendly websites found by this author is www.archchinese.com/chinese_measure_words. html. It lists 232 measure words, and is quite comprehensive.

The list below covers the most common measure words that immediate students need to learn in order to sound more like native Chinese speakers. This list is not exhaustive. Now and again you will hear a measure word that you don't recognize or that is rarely used. But based on your knowledge of Chinese grammar, at least you will be able to recognize it as a measure word immediately!

noun measures	usage	examples
笔 **bǐ**	sums of money or transactions	一笔钱 **yìbǐ qián** *a sum of money*
部 **bù**	reference books; machines; films	一部电影 **yíbù diànyǐng** *a movie* 一部小说 **yíbù xiǎoshuō** *a novel* 一部电脑 **yíbù diànnǎo** *a computer*
场 **chǎng**	events; shows	一场雨 **yìchǎng yǔ** *a spell of rain, a shower* 一场病 **yìchǎng bìng** *a bout of illness* 一场战争 **yìchǎng zhànzhēng** *a war* 一场灾难 **yìchǎng zāinàn** *a disaster* 一场演出 **yìchǎng yǎnchū** *a performance* 一场电影 **yìchǎng diànyǐng** *a film showing* 一场比赛 **yìchǎng bǐsài** *a competition*
串 **chuàn**	things strung together or in clusters	一串钥匙 **yíchuàn yàoshi** *a string of keys* 一串珍珠 **yíchuàn zhēnzhū** *a string of pearls* 一串羊肉 **yíchuàn yángròu** *a skewer of lamb* 一串铃声 **yíchuàn língshēng** *ringing of bells* 一串问题 **yíchuàn wèntí** *a series of questions* 一串笑声 **yíchuàn xiàoshēng** *a peal of laughter*
道 **dào**	long things (concrete and abstract)	一道光 **yídào guāng** *a stream of light* 一道皱纹 **yídào zhòuwén** *a line of wrinkles* 一道门 **yídào mén** *a doorway* 一道题 **yídào tí** *a question (in an exam)* 一道手续 **yídào shòuxù** *a procedure* 一道命令 **yídào mìnglìng** *an order*
滴 **dī**	drops	一滴水 **yìdī shuǐ** *a drop of water*
堆 **duī**	piles or stacks	一堆土 **yìduī tǔ** *a pile of dirt* 一堆雪 **yìduī xuě** *a pile of snow* 一堆垃圾 **yìduī lājī** *a pile of trash* 一堆文件 **yìduī wénjiàn** *a stack of documents*

noun measures	usage	examples
对 **duì**	pairs	一对枕头 **yíduì zhěntóu** *a pair of pillows* 一对夫妻 **yíduì fūqī** *a married couple* 一对新人 **yíduì xīnrén** *a pair of newlyweds*
顿 **dùn**	meals; a bout of...	一顿饭 **yídùn fàn** *a meal* 一顿批评 **yídùn pīpíng** *a round of criticism*
份 **fèn**	an item of... (a measure for a variety of different things)	一份快餐 **yífèn kuàicān** *a fast food meal for one* 一份礼物 **yífèn lǐwù** *a gift* 一份材料 **yífèn cáiliào** *a set of data* 一份杂志 **yífèn zázhì** *a copy of magazine* 一份工作 **yífèn gōngzuò** *a job* 一份心意 **yífèn xīnyì** *an intention*
幅 **fú**	paintings or textiles	一幅画 **yìfú huà** *a painting*
副 **fù**	sets of things; facial expression	一副手套 **yífù shǒutào** *a pair of gloves* 一副眼镜 **yífù yǎnjìng** *a pair of glasses* 一副牌 **yífù pái** *a deck of cards* 一副冷面孔 **yífù lěng miànkǒng** *a cold face (expression)* 一副笑脸 **yífù xiàoliǎn** *a smiling face*
架 **jià**	large vehicles; piano	一架飞机 **yíjià fēijī** *an airplane* 一架钢琴 **yíjià gāngqín** *a piano*
件 **jiàn**	an item of...(a variety of things both concrete and abstract)	一件衬衫 **yíjiàn chènshān** *a shirt* 一件礼物 **yíjiàn lǐwù** *a gift* 一件事儿 **yíjiàn shìr** *a matter* 一件行李 **yíjiàn xíngli** *a piece of luggage*
届 **jiè**	periodic events; meetings; terms of office	第五届会议 **dìwǔjiè huìyì** *fifth annual meeting* 这届领导 **zhèijiè lǐngdǎo** *this term of leadership* 首届毕业生 **shǒujiè bìyèshēng** *first group of graduates*
卷 **juǎn**	things in rolls	一卷画儿 **yìjuǎn huàr** *a painting scroll* 一卷手纸 **yìjuǎn shǒuzhǐ** *a roll of toilet paper* 一卷电线 **yìjuǎn diànxiàn** *a spool of electrical wire*
类 **lèi**	categories	这类问题 **zhèilèi wèntí** *this type of question* 这类人物 **zhèilèi rénwù** *this type of people* 这类事情 **zhèilèi shìqing** *this kind of affairs*
缕 **lǚ**	hair; hemp; smoke	一缕头髮 **yìlǚ tóufa** *a strand of hair*

noun measures	usage	examples
枚 **méi**	coins; badges; medals	一枚铜钱 **yìméi tóngqián** *a coin* 一枚勋章 **yìméi xūnzhāng** *a medal*
排 **pái**	things in rows	一排柳树 **yìpái liǔshù** *a row of willow trees* 一排警察 **yìpái jǐngchá** *a row of policemen* 一排宿舍 **yìpái sùshè** *a row of dormitories*
批 **pī**	batches of things	一批工人 **yìpī gōngrén** *a contingent of workers* 一批产品 **yìpī chǎnpǐn** *a batch of products* 一批货 **yìpī huò** *a batch of merchandise*
篇 **piān**	written works	一篇作文 **yìpiān zuòwén** *an essay* 一篇论文 **yìpiān lùnwén** *a thesis* 一篇故事 **yìpiān gùshi** *a written story*
群 **qún**	groups (mostly people or animals)	一群人 **yìqún rén** *a group of people* 一群羊 **yìqún yáng** *a flock of sheep* 一群孩子 **yìqún háizi** *a group of children* 一群海岛 **yìqún hǎidǎo** *an archipelago* 一群动物 **yìqún dòngwù** *a group of animals*
束 **shù**	bunches or bundles	一束鲜花 **yíshù xiānhuā** *a bunch of fresh flowers* 一束信件 **yíshù xìnjiàn** *a bundle of mail*
双 **shuāng**	pairs	一双筷子 **yìshuāng kuàizi** *a pair of chopsticks* 一双袜子 **yìshuāng wàzi** *a pair of socks* 一双鞋 **yìshuāng xié** *a pair of shoes* 一双眼睛 **yìshuāng yǎnjīng** *a pair of eyes*
滩 **tān**	puddle; pool	一滩泥 **yìtān ní** *a puddle of mud* 一滩血 **yìtān xiě** *a pool of blood*
摊 **tān**	business in need of attention	一摊工作 **yìtān gōngzuò** *a pile of work* 一摊事 **yìtān shì** *a pile of issues*
套 **tào**	sets and collections	一套房子 **yítào fángzi** *a suite of rooms* 一套家具 **yítào jiājù** *a set of furniture*
条 **tiáo**	long thin objects (including abstract things)	一条领带 **yìtiáo lǐngdài** *a necktie* 一条路 **yìtiáo lù** *a road* 一条船 **yìtiáo chuán** *a boat* 一条新闻 **yìtiáo xīnwén** *a piece of news* 一条要求 **yìtiáo yāoqiú** *a request* 一条说明 **yìtiáo shuōmíng** *a note of explanation*

noun measures	usage	examples
团 **tuán**	things in a ball or joined together	一团毛线 **yìtuán máoxiàn** *a ball of yarn* 一团面 **yìtuán miàn** *a lump of dough* 一团火 **yìtuán huǒ** *a ball of fire*
位 **wèi**	people (polite)	一位客人 **yíwèi kèren** *a guest*
项 **xiàng**	items; tasks; projects	一项内容 **yíxiàng nèiróng** *a content item* 一项声明 **yíxiàng shēngmíng** *an announcement* 一项工作 **yíxiàng gōngzuò** *a project* 一项任务 **yíxiàng rènwù** *a task*
盏 **zhǎn**	lamps (limited usage)	一盏灯 **yìzhǎn déng** *a lamp*
张 **zhāng**	flat sheet-like objects or things that spread out	一张票 **yìzhāng piào** *a ticket* 一张煎饼 **yìzhāng jiānbǐng** *a grilled pancake* 一张嘴 **yìzhāng zuǐ** *a mouth* 一张脸 **yìzhāng liǎn** *a face* 一张网 **yìzhāng wǎng** *a net*
阵 **zhèn**	events of short duration	一阵风 **yízhèn fēng** *a gust of wind* 一阵掌声 **yízhèn zhǎngshēng** *a round of applause* 一阵雨 **yízhèn yǔ** *a shower*
桩 **zhuāng**	major events or business transactions (limited usage)	一桩事情 **yìzhuāng shìqing** *an incident*

verb measures	usage	examples
顿 **dùn**	bout or round of some action	骂一顿 **mà yídùn** *to mete out a round of scolding* 批评一顿 **pīpíng yídùn** *to conduct a round of criticism*
番 **fān**	actions done thoroughly	讨论一番 **tǎolùn yìfān** *to hold a round of discussion* 表示一番 **biǎoshì yìfān** *to express one's stance fully* 整理一番 **zhěnglǐ yìfān** *to do a round of neatening up*
趟 **tàng**	coming/going	来一趟 **lái yítàng** *to come once* 跑一趟 **pǎo yítàng** *to make a run (to do something)* 买一趟东西 **mǎi yítàng dōngxi** *to make a shopping trip* 去一趟厕所 **qù yítàng cèsuǒ** *to make a trip to the restroom*
下 **xià**	action done briefly	来一下 **lái yíxià** *to come for a minute* 找一下 **zhǎo yíxià** *to search a bit* 介绍一下 **jieshào yíxià** *to make an introduction*

5 Adverbs in Chinese

Adverbs and adverbials are an assorted class of linguistic elements that add something to the verb in sentences. An adverb can modify a verb, an adjective, or another adverb. Rather than describe all the different types of adverbial elements used in Chinese, we will only focus on the types that English speakers have difficulty with. In this chapter, we will discuss the two types of Chinese adverbs that are most closely linked to the verb in a sentence: single-syllable adverbs that immediately precede the verb, and two-syllable adverbs that precede the verb, sometimes with the subject in-between.

Several other types of adverbials will be covered in other chapters of this book. In Chapter 6, we will discuss adverbials of manner, which describe the manner in which something is done. In English, the majority of these are derived by adding the suffix "-ly" to an adjective (e.g. *beautifully, definitely, rapidly, electronically*, etc.), although some adverbs of manner are not formed that way (e.g. *fast, well*). In modern Chinese, word inflections do not exist, and "the manner in which something is done" is expressed by certain grammatical patterns. Two other categories of adverbials are place elements and time elements, which range from single words (e.g. *here, there, now, previously*) to prepositional phrases (e.g. *behind the church, during the Cold War*). These two categories, also expressed by certain grammatical patterns in Chinese, will be covered in Chapters 9 and 10 respectively.

5.1 Single-syllable adverbs that precede verbs

The most important single-syllable adverbs in Chinese are: 都 **dōu**, 也 **yě**, 还 **hái**, 就 **jiù**, 再 **zài**, 又 **yòu**, 才 **cái**, 并 **bìng**. To native Chinese speakers, these terms are extremely straightforward. Because natives have intuitive mastery of these words, they may not even realize how significant these adverbs are in conveying certain nuances in their speech. To non-native students, they can be deceptively simple. The following Chinese proverb, howeever, is truly pertinent here: 会者不难、难者不会 **Huìzhě bùnán, nánzhě búhuì**. *What you know is not difficult; it is what you don't know that is difficult.* The apparent simplicity in usage for all these single-syllable adverbs is due to their word order. They are always located immediately before the verb, and after the subject if the sentence has a subject. The factors that make them not so simple are the following:

a. Certain adverbs in Chinese do not coincide with English equivalents, because the English words with equivalent meanings are often not adverbs, and/or may not be used in the same word order.

b. Each of these adverbs has a primary meaning, but most have secondary meanings as well, and it's the secondary meanings that tend to be subtle to non-natives.

c. Some single-syllable adverbs have no counterparts in English, and the same ideas are conveyed by more complicated constructions in English.

d. In some cases, the distinction between two Chinese adverbs is not obvious to English speakers and they are therefore prone to be confused. Examples are 再 **zài** and 又 **yòu**, both translated into English as *again*, but differ in usage and meaning.

Now we are ready to get down to the specific single-syllable adverbs.

1. The adverb 都 dōu = "all"

The word *all* in English is an adjective and a pronoun—not an adverb. As an adjective, it may modify either the subject or the object of a sentence. In Chinese, 都 **dōu** may refer to either the subject or the object of the sentence, but being an adverb, its position is always immediately before the verb. When the object of the sentence is being totalized by 都 **dōu**, it is prestated as the topic of the sentence, before the subject (see the second example below).

◆ *All my Chinese friends can speak English.*
   我的中国朋友都会说英语。 **Wǒde Zhōngguó péngyou dōu huì shuō Yīngyǔ.**

◆ *I like all these dishes.*
   ✓ 这些菜我都喜欢。 **Zhèixiē cài, wǒ dōu xǐhuan.**
   ✗ 我都喜欢这些菜。 **Wǒ dōu xǐhuan zhèixiē cài.**

◆ *Not all Chinese people can speak Chinese.*
   中国人不都会说普通话。 **Zhōngguórén bùdōu huì shuō pǔtōnghuà.**

◆ *We all love to eat Chinese food.*
   我们都爱吃中国菜。 **Wǒmen dōu ài chī Zhōngguó cài.**

◆ *I love to eat all Chinese dishes.*
   中国菜，我都爱吃。 **Zhōngguó cài, wǒ dōu ài chī.**

◆ *I found all the books that I need for this semester.*
   我这个学期需要的书都找到了。 **Wǒ zhèige xuéqī xūyàode shū dōu zhǎodàole.**

◆ *I didn't find any of the books that I was looking for!*
   我要找的书都没找到！ **Wǒ yào zhǎode shū dōu méi zhǎodào!**

◆ *She knows everything about the neighbors, so people call her "private eye."*
   邻居的什么事她都知道，所以人们叫她"包打听"。
   Línjūde shénme shì tā dōu zhīdao, suǒyǐ rénmen jiào tā "bāo dǎtīng."

A secondary meaning of 都 **dōu** is *already*. In this usage, it is a colloquial synonym of 已经 **yǐjīng**. It carries a subtle tone of disapproval or annoyance, and therefore should be used in this sense with caution. When the meaning of *already* is applied to a time, the sentence in Chinese may not require a verb, in which case 都 **dōu** precedes the time expression without an intervening verb (see the last example below).

♦ *It's already dark, why haven't they come home yet?*
天都黑了，他们怎么还没回家呢？
Tiān dōu hēile, tāmen zěnme hái méi huíjiā ne?

♦ *Others are already almost finished, he is only now starting.*
人家都快做完了，他现在才开始。
Rénjiā dōu kuài zuòwánle, tā xiànzài cái kāishǐ.

♦ *It's already almost noon, and he still hasn't gotten out of bed!*
都快中午了，他还没起床呢！ **Dōu kuài zhōngwǔ le, tā hái méi qǐchuáng ne!**

EXERCISES:

Translate the following sentences into colloquial Chinese:

1. The things sold in this store are all made in China.
2. Not everything in this store is made in China.
3. Have you finished all your homework?
4. Everyone has arrived. Let's begin!
5. Her son is already 30, but still lives with her.

ANSWERS:
1. 这个商店卖的东西都是中国制造的。
   Zhèige shāngdiàn màide dōngxi dōu shì Zhōngguó zhìzàode.
2. 这个商店卖的东西不都是中国制造的。
   Zhèige shāngdiàn màide dōngxi bù dōu shì Zhōngguó zhìzàode.
3. 你的功课都做完了吗？ **Nǐde gōngkè dōu zuòwánle ma?**
4. 大家都到了，我们开始吧！ **Dàjiā dōu dàole, wǒmen kāishǐ ba!**
5. 她儿子都/已经三十岁了，还跟她住在一起呢。
   Tā érzi dōu/yǐjīng sānshí-suì le, hái gēn tā zhùzài yìqǐ ne.

2. The adverb 也 yě = "also"

The adverb *also* in English may be positioned at the beginning of a sentence or before the verb, depending on whether it refers to the sentence as a whole, or only to the verb. In Chinese, 也 **yě** is always located immediately before the verb, regardless of what it refers to.

- *My friend also participated in the speech contest.*
  我的朋友也参加了那个演讲比赛。
  Wǒde péngyou yě cānjiāle nèige yǎnjiǎng bǐsài.

- *She is talented in languages, and is also a fine musician.*
  她是个语言天才，也是个很棒的音乐家。
  Tā shì ge yǔyán tiāncái, yě shì ge hěn bàngde yīnyuèjiā.

- *I don't want to go, because I'm too busy, also the weather is not too good.*
  我不想去，因为太忙了，(而且)天气也不太好。
  Wǒ bùxiǎng qù, yīnwèi tài máng le, (érqiě) tiānqì yě bú tài hǎo.

A secondary usage of 也 **yě** is to reinforce the notion of all-inclusiveness in a negative sentence. This point was discussed in a previous chapter (see 3.8), where we saw interrogative pronouns (i.e. "question words" or QWs, such as 谁 **shéi** and 什么 **shénme**) coupled with 都 **dōu** to convey all-inclusiveness. When a sentence of this type is in the negative, 也 **yě** may be used in place of 都 **dōu**, and in fact 也 **yě** is a bit stronger and more colloquial.

- *This guy is very stubborn, nobody can persuade him!*
  他这个人很固执，谁也没法子劝他！
  Tā zhèige rén hěn gùzhi, shéi yě méi fázi quàn tā!

- *Housing here is too expensive. If you don't have a million dollars, you won't be able to buy any house here.*
  这个地方的房子太贵了，如果没有一百万，什么房子也买不到。
  Zhèige dìfangde fángzi tài guì le, rúguǒ méiyǒu yìbǎiwàn, shénme fángzi yě mǎi-bu-dào.

- *He got drunk last night, so no matter how, he cannot recall what happened.*
  他昨晚喝醉了，发生了什么事情他怎么想也想不起来了。
  Tā zuówǎn hēzuìle, fāshēngle shénme shìqing tā zěnme xiǎng yě xiǎng-bu-qǐlaile.

Another pattern in which 也 **yě** is used to convey the notion of all-inclusiveness is 连 **lián**…也 **yě** … (*even…*). As in the pattern above, 都 **dōu** and 也 **yě** are interchangeable here as well. This pattern was mentioned in 2.1, sec. 15, and will be revisited in Part II of this book. Here is just one example to serve as a reminder:

- *The entire family, adults and kids, all attended the party. Even their dog went along.*
  他们全家大人小孩儿都参加了晚会，连他们的狗也去了。
  Tāmen quánjiā dàrén xiǎoháir dōu cānjiāle wǎnhuì, lián tāmende gǒu yě qùle.

EXERCISES:

Translate the following sentences into Chinese:

1. He can speak Japanese, and also a bit of Chinese.
2. Buses don't come to this area. Also, housing is too expensive here.

3. The adverb 还 hái = "still"

This single-syllable adverb is equivalent to the English adverb *still* in meaning, but its position in a sentence is always before the verb or the "stative verb" (i.e., the adjectival predicate; see "adjectives" in 1.5, sec. A). In Chinese, no equivalent of the English copula *to be* is used between the subject and the stative verb, but the stative verb is typically modified by 很 **hěn**, which technically means *very*, but is actually just a "filler." The first two sentences below exemplify this point.

⬥ *These days, folks who are in their sixties are still considered to be quite young.*
现在六十多岁的人<u>还</u>算很年轻。
Xiànzài liùshíduō suìde rén hái suàn hěn niánqīng.

⬥ *This fish was bought this morning, it's still fresh.*
这条鱼是今天早上买的，<u>还</u>很新鲜。
Zhèi tiáo yú shì jīntiān zǎoshang mǎide, hái hěn xīnxiān.

⬥ *Everyone has gone off work; only he is still working.*
大家都下班了，只有他<u>还</u>在工作。
Dàjiā dōu xiàbānle, zhǐyǒu tā hái zài gōngzuò.

The adverb 还 **hái** also has a secondary meaning of *passably, not quite but still....* In this usage, the word 算 **suàn** *to count as...* is often added to reinforce the idea of *barely, passably.* An expression of this type typically begins with a deprecatory remark, followed by 可是 **kěshì....** In everyday conversation, phrases like 还不错 **hái búcuò** *not bad* and 还好 **hái hǎo** *pretty good* are often used to express faint praise.

⬥ *This is not the best, but it will do.*
这个不是最好的，可是还行。**Zhèige búshì zuì hǎode, kěshì hái xíng.**

⬥ *This hotel is not very high class, but it's clean enough.*
这个旅馆不怎么高级，可是还算干净。
Zhèige lǚguǎn bùzěnme gāojí, kěshì hái suàn gānjìng.

⬥ *Their income is not high, but still enough to get by.*
他们的收入不高，可是还过得去。
Tāmende shōurù bù gāo, kěshì hái guò-de-qù.

The syllable 还 **hái** occurs in two other words that have nothing to do with the notion of *still*: 还是 **háishi** *or* and 还有 **háiyǒu** *moreover*.

♦ *She is very young. No one can tell whether she is a professor or a student.*
她很年轻，没有人能看出她是教授还是学生。
Tā hěn niánqīng, méiyǒu rén néng kànchū tā shì jiǎoshòu háishi xuésheng.

♦ *Furthermore, quite a few male students would like to be her friend.*
还有，有不少男学生想要跟她做朋友。
Háiyǒu, yǒu bùshǎo nánxuésheng xiǎngyào gēn tā zuò péngyou.

Finally, the character 还, pronounced differently as **huán**, means *to return (something)*. It is best to think of this as a totally different word sharing the same character.

♦ *This library book must be returned by tomorrow.*
这本图书馆的书，最晚明天一定要还。
Zhèiběn túshūguǎnde shū, zuìwǎn míngtiān yídìng yào huán.

EXERCISES:

Translate the following sentences into Chinese:

1. He's already 80, but <u>still</u> not retired.
2. What do you think of this restaurant? It's OK.

ANSWERS:
1. 他已经八十岁了，还没退休呢。**Tā yǐjing bāshí-suì le, hái méi tuìxiū ne.**
2. 你觉得这个餐馆怎么样？还行。**Nǐ juéde zhèige cānguǎn zěnmeyàng? Hái xíng.**

4. The adverb 就 jiù

This is a multi-purpose adverb that defies simple translation into English, so we will discuss each of its various meanings and usages individually.

a. 就 jiù in the sense of "then"

The word 就 **jiù** can mean *then* when in a sequential order or as a consequence:

♦ *We are planning to have dinner first, and then go see the movie.* (sequential order)
我们打算先吃饭，（然后)就去看电影。
Wǒmen dǎsuàn xiān chīfàn, (ránhòu) jiù qù kàn diànyǐng.

♦ *After you take the medicine, you will get well.* (consequence)
吃了药就会好了。**Chīle yào jiù huì hǎole.**

♦ *When you grow up, you'll understand.* (sequential order and consequence, both)
你长大了就会明白了。**Nǐ zhǎngdàle jiù huì míngbáile.**

When used to indicate *then* in a sequential order, 就 **jiù** is used when the sentence is a statement. When it is a suggestion or command for something to be done in the future, 再 **zài** is used instead. (See the next section under 再 **zài** *then*.)

◆ *Wait until he arrives, then we'll decide.*

   ✗ 等他到了我们就决定吧。 **Děng tā dàole wǒmen jiù juédìng ba.**

   ✓ 等他到了我们再决定吧。 **Děng tā dàole wǒmen zài juédìng ba.**

◆ *I couldn't tell on the phone whether he's Chinese; we'll know when he arrives.*
在电话上我听不出来他是不是中国人。他到了以后我们就知道了。
Zài diànhuà-shang wǒ tīng-bu-chūlai tā shì-bushì Zhōngguóren. Tā dàole yǐhòu wǒmen jiù zhīdaole.

b. 就 **jiù** to convey a sense of "imminence" or "immediacy"

The word 就 **jiù** can convey imminence, temporal brevity/immediacy, or *sooner or faster than expected or is typical*. Notice that in all the English sentences below, the sense expressed by 就 **jiù** (imminence, urgency, brevity, etc.) in the Chinese version is only inferred. This is why students often neglect this usage of 就 **jiù** when speaking Chinese. Because this usage has no English equivalent, mastery by a native English speaker requires some practice.

◆ *Final exams will be next week, how come you're still not preparing for them?*
下个星期就大考了，你怎么还不准备呢？
Xiàge xīngqī jiù dàkǎole, nǐ zěnme hái bù zhǔnbèi ne?

◆ *If you study English at Berlitz, you'll be functional in less than three months.*
在贝立兹学英文，不到三个月就能学会。
Zài Bèilìzī xué Yīngwén, búdào sānge yuè jiù néng xuéhuì.

◆ *How come he left the movie when he had watched only half of it.*
他怎么电影看到一半就走了呢？
Tā zěnme diànyǐng kàndào yíbàn jiù zǒule ne?

c. 就 **jiù** in the sense of "sufficiency"

The word 就 **jiù** can convey *sufficiency with a small quantity (less than normal or expected)*. Like the preceding usage, this one also has no English equivalent.

◆ *He's not that smart. If he can learn five characters in a day, that's pretty good.*
他不那么聪明，一天能学会五个字就不错了。
Tā bú nàme cōngming, yìtiān néng xuéhuì wǔge zì jiù búcuòle.

◆ *Camels don't need to drink water often; once every three days is enough.*
骆驼不需要常常喝水，三天一次就够了。
Luòtuo bù xūyào chángchang hēshuǐ, sāntiān yícì jiù gòule.

d. 就 **jiù** in the sense of "only"

The word 就 **jiù** can convey the sense of *only, merely*. In this usage, it is synonymous with 只 **zhǐ**, but there are regional differences in preference for 就 **jiù** or 只 **zhǐ**.

- *Hurry! Everyone is waiting just for you.*
  快来啊！ 大家<u>就</u>等你一个人了。 **Kuài lái a! Dàjiā jiù děng nǐ yíge rén le.**

- *These days each family has only one child, naturally they become "little emperors"!*
  现在每家<u>就</u>有一个孩子，这些孩子自然地<u>就</u>会变成小皇帝啦！
  Xiànzài měijiā jiù yǒu yíge háizi, zhèixiē háizi zìránde jiù huì biànchéng xiǎo huángdì la!
  (就 **jiù** appears twice in this sentence, with different meanings.)

Used in the sense of *only*, 就 **jiù** is an exception among single-syllable adverbs in that it can be used at the beginning of a sentence rather than adhering to the verb. In this sense, it is synonymous with 只有 **zhǐyǒu**:

- *There is only me at home, everyone else has gone out.*
  就我一个人在家，大家都出去了。 **Jiù wǒ yíge rén zài jiā, dàjiā dōu chūqule.**

- *There's only this bit of food, how can it be enough to eat?*
  就这么一点饭菜，怎么够吃呢？ **Jiù zhème yìdiǎn fàn-cài, zěnme gòu chī ne?**

就 **jiù** is used in the construction "一···就 **yí...jiù**" to mean *as soon as...(then)...*

- *He's really smart, as soon as he learns something, he has mastered it.*
  他真聪明，一学就会。 **Tā zhēn cōngming, yì xué jiù huì.**

- *In former times, quite a few women college students get married as soon as they graduate.*
  从前有不少女大学生一毕业就结婚了。
  Cóngqián yǒu bùshǎo nǚ dàxuésheng yí bìyè jiù jiéhūn le.

- *Foreign students studying in China all go traveling as soon as vacation begins.*
  在中国的留学生，一放假就都去旅游了。
  Zài Zhōngguóde liúxuésheng, yí fàngjià jiù dōu qù lǚyóu le.

就是 **jiùshì** means *precisely, none other than* (more emphatic than just 是 **shì**):

- *To a teacher, there is no greater joy than seeing progress in students.*
  看到学生进步就是老师最大的快乐。
  Kàndào xuésheng jìnbù jiùshì lǎoshī zuì dàde kuàilè.

- *They decided to stay in the U.S. for the sake of their kids. (emphasizing "for no reason other than...)*
  他们决定留在美国就是为了孩子。
  Tāmen juédìng liúzài Měiguó jiùshì wèile háizi.

e. Other uses of 就 **jiù**

Aside from the abverbial usages of 就 **jiù**, it can also function as a preposition (also called "coverb" by Chinese linguists), meaning *on the issue of, in reference to*. This usage is rather formal, therefore it appears only in speeches and formal writing.

♦ *The government has conducted investigation into the issue of traffic safety in this area.*
政府就这个地区的交通安全问题进行了调查。
Zhèngfǔ jiù zhèige dìqūde jiāotōng ānquán wèntí jìnxíngle diàochá.

♦ *On the issue of global climate change, the UN has already held many conferences.*
就全球气候变化这个问题，联合国已经举行过很多次会议了。
Jiù quánqiú qìhòu biànhuà zhèige wèntí, Liánhéguó yǐjīng jǔxíngguo hěnduō cì huìyì le.

就 **jiù** also has the classical meaning of *to engage in, approach*; and in this meaning, appears in certain **verb+object** compounds in modern Chinese. These terms, like all classical Chinese expressions, tend to be very succinct when compared with English and modern Chinese.

- *to attend school* 就学 **jiùxué**
- *to engage in a profession* 就业 **jiùyè**
- *to seek medical treatment* 就医 **jiùyī**
- *to go (somewhere) for a meal* 就餐 **jiùcān**
- *to study in situ* 就地实学 **jiùdì shíxué** (useful phrase for Chinese language students)

♦ *High school graduates don't have many job opportunities.*
中学毕业生没有太多的就业机会。
Zhōngxué bìyèshēng méiyǒu tài duōde jiùyè jīhuì.

♦ *Please everyone take your seats, the meeting is about to begin.*
请大家就坐，会议就要开始了。 **Qǐng dàjiā jiùzuò, huìyì jiùyào kāishǐ le.**

▶ EXERCISES:

Translate the following sentences into Chinese:

1. After you introduced us last year, we got married soon thereafter.
2. If you take classes every summer, you can graduate in just three years.
3. Things here are relatively inexpensive. $300 per month for one person should be enough.
4. Please give me a call <u>as soon as</u> you arrive.
5. I want to learn Chinese <u>precisely because</u> there are too few people in America who really understand China.
6. Everyone had a long discussion <u>on the issue of</u> unemployment.
7. When a foreign student gets sick in China, where should he <u>go for</u> medical treatment?

ANSWERS:
1. 你去年介绍我们认识了以后，我们很快就结婚了。
Nǐ qùnián jièshào wǒmen rènshile yǐyòu, wǒmen hěn kuài jiù jiéhūn le.

2. 如果(你)每年夏天都上课，(那)三年就能毕业了。
   Rúguǒ (nǐ) měinián xiàtiān dōu shàngkè, (nà) sānnián jiù néng bìyè le.

3. 这里东西比较便宜，一个人一个月三百块就够了。
   Zhèlǐ dōngxi bǐjiào piányi, yíge rén yíge yuè sānbǎikuài jiù gòule.

4. 请你一到就给我来个电话。**Qǐng nǐ yí dào jiù gěi wǒ lái ge diànhuà.**

5. 我想学中文就是因为在美国真正了解中国的人太少了。
   Wǒ xiǎng xué Zhōngwén jiùshì yīnwèi zài Měiguó zhēnzhèng liǎojiě Zhōngguóde rén tài shǎo le.

6. 大家就失业的问题讨论了很久。**Dàjiā jiù shīyède wèntí tǎolùnle hěn jiǔ.**

7. 留学生在中国生病的话，应该到哪儿去就医呢？
   Liúxuésheng zài Zhōngguó shēngbìng dehuà, yīnggāi dào nǎr qù jiùyī ne?

5. The adverb 再 zài = "again"

The primary meaning of this adverb is *again*. Like most single-syllable adverbs, 再 **zài** also has several secondary usages, and some of them do not have simple English translations.

a. 再 zài in the sense of "again" (**Note:** Some constraints to be discussed in the next section 6 on 又 **yòu**)

● *Goodbye (see you again)* 再见！ **Zàijiàn!**

● *Please say it again.* 请再说一次。 **Qǐng zài shuō yícì.**

● *He will not come again.* 他不会再来了。 **Tā búhuì zài lái le.**

● *Youth once gone will not return again.*
   青春一去不再回。 **Qīngchūn yí qù bú zài huí.**

● *When I went again, it was already too late.*
   我再去的时候，已经太晚了。 **Wǒ zài qùde shíhou, yǐjīng tài wǎn le.**

b. 再 zài in the sense of "in addition, furthermore"

● *Three drinks should be quite enough! In my opinion, you can't drink anymore!*
   三杯酒该够了吧！我看你不能再喝了！
   Sānbēi jiǔ gāi gòule ba! Wǒ kàn nǐ bùnéng zài hēle!

● *She has a lovely daughter already, but her mother-in-law hopes that she will have another child.*
   她已经有一个很可爱的女儿了，可是她婆婆希望她再生一个孩子。
   Tā yǐjīng yǒu yíge hěn kě'àide nǚ'ér le, kěshì tā pópo xīwàng tā zài shēng yíge háizi.

● *The burden of raising one child is enough; furthermore, I'm over 40 already.*
   养一个孩子的负担已经够重了，再说，我也已经四十多岁了。
   Yǎng yíge háizide fùdān yǐjīng gòu zhòng le, zàishuō, wǒ yě yǐjīng sìshíduō suì le.

c. 再 zài in the sense of deferring an action

The adverb 再 **zài** can be used in a sentence that requests or suggests that someone defer an action until a certain time. As suggestions, these sentences typically end in the sentence particle 吧 **ba** (see 3.12, sec. 2). Because this usage of 再 **zài** has no English equivalent, a Chinese sentence of this type can be translated into English only in a complicated roundabout way. In the following examples, notice how much simpler the Chinese is as compared with the English; therefore, with a bit of practice, it should be relatively easy to master this usage of 再 **zài**. For a native Chinese speaker to master the English equivalent is much more difficult!

♦ *It's raining too hard now, why don't you wait until the rain stops before going out.*
现在雨下得太大了。你等雨停了再出去吧。
Xiànzài yǔ xiàde tài dà le. Nǐ děng yǔ tíngle zài chūqu ba.

♦ *I'm too busy right now, I'll get in touch with you in a few days.*
我现在太忙了，过几天再跟你联系吧。
Wǒ xiànzài tài máng le, guò jǐtiān zài gēn nǐ liánxì ba.

♦ *She's in a bad mood today; let's wait until she's better before raising this matter with her.*
她今天心情不好，我们等她好了再跟她提这个问题吧。
Tā jīntiān xīnqíng bù hǎo, wǒmen děng tā hǎole zài gēn tā tí zhèige wèntí ba.

d. 再 zài used in a negative sense to mean "no longer"

The adverb 再 **zài** occurs in four negative patterns that carry the meaning *no longer, no more*:

a) 不再⋯了 **búzài…le**: refers to either a present situation or a situation with no particular time reference.

b) 再也不⋯了 **zài yě bù…le**: an even stronger version of 不再⋯了 **búzài…le**. (i.e. "never…again!")

c) 没再⋯了 **méi zài…le**: refers to a situation that began sometime in the past and continues to the present.

d) 再也没⋯了 **zài yě méi…le**: an even stronger version of 没再⋯了 **méi zài…le**. (i.e. *have never…again!*)

The most ordinary way to express the idea of *no longer* (indicating a change from before) is the pattern 不⋯了 **bú…le** (see 7.2, sec. 1). Pattern a above, with 再 **zài** added, is stronger and more poignant. Pattern b takes the emphasis to an even higher level. In the first example below, note how the same sentence in English is translated into three Chinese versions with increasing intensity.

♦ *We have broken up. She is no longer my girlfriend.*
我们已经分手了，她不是我的女朋友了。
Wǒmen yǐjīng fēnshǒule, tā búshì wǒde nǚpéngyou le.

我们已经分手了，她不再是我的女朋友了。(stronger and more poignant)
Wǒmen yǐjīng fēnshǒule, tā búzài shì wǒde nǚpéngyou le.

我们已经分手了，她再也不是我的女朋友了。(tone of lament is very
strong) **Wǒmen yǐjīng fēnshǒule, tā zài yě bú shì wǒde nǚpéngyou le.**

♦ *Children when they grow up no longer listen to their parents.*
孩子大了就不再听父母的话了。**Háizi dàle jiù búzài tīng fùmǔde huà le.**

孩子大了就再也不听父母的话了。(stronger than the preceding sentence)
Háizi dàle jiù zài yě bù tīng fùmǔde huà le.

♦ *We will never again believe him!*
我们再也不相信他了！ **Wǒmen zài yě bù xiāngxìn tā le.**

♦ *Ever since I began eating an apple a day, I have never gotten sick again.*
自从我每天都吃一个苹果以后，就没再生病了。
Zìcóng wǒ měitiān dōu chī yíge píngguǒ yǐhòu, jiù méi zài shēngbìng le.

♦ *After getting food poisoning that time, I have never gone to that restaurant again!*
那次食物中毒以后，我再也没去过那个餐馆了！
Nèicì shíwù zhòngdú yǐhòu, wǒ zài yě méi qùguo nèige cānguǎn le.

EXERCISES:

Translate the following sentences into colloquial Chinese:

1. I believe you can do it. Try again and see.
2. After I graduated, I have never been back to my alma mater.
3. Since that car accident, I have <u>never again</u> driven after drinking.
4. Three is not enough, you need to buy two <u>more</u>.
5. He would like to retire this year, but he must work for two <u>more</u> years before he will have social security.
6. Don't rush, wait until you've thought it through clearly and <u>then</u> decide.
7. Let's wait until you are done with your exam and <u>then</u> we'll meet, OK?
8. After we had that fight (verbal), I never saw him again.

> **ANSWERS:**
> 1. 我相信你能做到，再试试看。**Wǒ xiāngxìn nǐ néng zuòdào, zài shìshi-kàn.**
> 2. 我毕业以后，就没再回过我的母校了。
>   **Wǒ bìyè yǐhòu, jiù méi zài huíguo wǒde mǔxiào le.**
> 3. 自从那次车祸以后，我就再也没酒后开车了。
>   **Zìcóng nèicì chēhuò yǐhòu, wǒ jiù zài yě méi jiǔ-hòu kāichē le.**

4. 三个不够，你得再买两个。**Sānge bú gòu, nǐ děi zài mǎi liǎngge.**

5. 他想今年退休，可是必须再工作两年才能有社会保险。
Tā xiǎng jīnnián tuìxiū, kěshì bìxū zài gōngzuò liǎngnián cái néng yǒu shèhuì bǎoxiǎn.

6. 别急，等你想清楚了再决定吧。**Bié jí, děng nǐ xiǎng-qīngchǔ le zài juédìng ba.**

7. 等你考完试我们再见面吧。**Děng nǐ kǎo-wán-shì wǒmen zài jiànmiàn ba.**

8. 我们那次吵了架以后，我就没再见到他了。
Wǒmen nèicì chǎo-le-jià yǐhòu, wǒ jiù méi zài jiàndào tā le.

6. The adverb 又 yòu = "again"

The primary meaning of this adverb is also *again*, but its usage and meanings are different from those of 再 **zài**. 又 **yòu** refers to a recurrence of actions or events that have already occurred in the past, whereas 再 **zài** refers to actions or events in the future, or seen as being in the future as compared to an event mentioned before in the sentence. Like other single-syllable adverbs, 又 **yòu** also has several secondary meanings.

a. Using 再 zài vs 又 yòu in the sense of "again"

First, we will compare 再 **zài** with 又 **yòu** when they are used to convey the notion of *again*.

● *He was sick again yesterday.* (past event)
昨天他又生病了。**Zuótiān tā yòu shēngbìng le.**

● *If you get a shot, you will not be sick again.* (future prediction)
打了针就不再生病了。**Dǎ-le-zhēn jiù búzài shēngbìng le.**

● *You said you would never smoke again, so how come you've started smoking again?*
你说你再也不抽烟了，怎么又抽烟了呢？
Nǐ shuō nǐ zài yě bù chōuyānle, zěnme yòu chōuyānle ne?

● *That movie is wonderful, a lot of people have seen it again and again.* (past action)
那部电影太好了，不少人看了又看。
Nèibù diànyǐng tài hǎo le, bùshǎo rén kànle yòu kàn.

As an exception to the usage of 又 **yòu** in referring to past events, the pattern 又要…了 **yòu yào...le** (*about to*) refers to an imminent action or event in the near future.

● *He is about to go the U.S. again next year.* (implying that he often goes to the U.S., and is about to again in the near future)
明年他又要去美国了。**Míngnián tā yòu yào qù Měiguó le.**

Compare the above with:

● *If he has the chance, he would like to go to the U.S. again.* (implying that he has been to the U.S. at least once in the past)
他希望将来有机会再去美国。**Tā xīwàng jiānglái yǒu jīhuì zài qù Měiguó.**

♦ *It rains a lot here in the spring, today it is about to rain again.*
这儿春天常下雨，今天又要下了。
Zhèr chūntiān cháng xiàyǔ, jīntiān yòu yào xiàle.

b. 又 yòu in the sense of "moreover, furthermore"

In this usage, 又 **yòu** is synonymous with 也 **yě**.

♦ *She treats people very well, and is also very capable, so everyone likes her.*
她对人特别好，又非常能干，所以大家都喜欢她。
Tā duì rén tèbié hǎo, yòu fēicháng nénggàn, suǒyǐ dàjiā dōu xǐhuan tā.

♦ *We just finished our exams today, and it's also Friday; let's go out to play!*
今天刚考完试，又是星期五，我们出去玩儿吧!
Jīntiān gāng kǎowán shì, yòu shì xīngqīwǔ, wǒmen chūqu wánr ba!

c. 又 yòu used for emphasis or to drive home a point

Along this line, in a negative statement that contradicts someone's assumption, 又 **yòu** may be used to add a bit more punch. This usage of 又 **yòu** is often coupled with a rhetorical question, which is also used to drive home a point.

All of the examples below would be grammatically correct without the adverb 又 **yòu**, but they would sound rather lame.

♦ *What good is there to doing it this way?* (implying that there is nothing good about it)
这样做又有什么好处呢? **Zhèyàng zuò yòu yǒu shénme hǎochù ne?**

♦ *This isn't my fault, why blame me?* (contradicting the assumption that it's my fault)
又不是我的错，干嘛怪我呢? **Yòu búshì wǒde cuò, gànmá guài wǒ ne?**

♦ *You're not a child anymore, why must you always listen to your mother?*
你又不是小孩子了，为什么老是要听你妈的呢?
Nǐ yòu búshì xiǎoháizi le, wèishénme lǎoshì yào tīng nǐ māde ne?

♦ *So what if he has an American Ph.D.? We still have to see what he can actually do.*
有个美国的博士学位又怎么样? 我们还得看他到底能做什么。
Yǒu ge Měiguóde bóshì xuéwèi yòu zěnmeyàng? Wǒmen hái děi kàn tā dàodǐ néng zuò shénme.

d. 又 yòu reduplicated to mean "both...and..."

The word 又 **yòu** is often reduplicated in the commonly used pattern 又…又… **yòu...yòu...** (*both...and...*) to state two co-existing qualities or conditions that lead to a certain conclusion or inference. This pattern can be extended to three reduplications of 又 **yòu**, but more than three is rare.

◆ *You can't speak English, and you have no friends there. How can you live there?*
你又不会说英语，在那儿又没有朋友，怎么能在那儿生活呢？
Nǐ yòu búhuì shuō Yīngyǔ, zài nàr yòu méiyǒu péngyou, zěnme néng zài nàr shēnghuó ne?

◆ *He is tall and handsome, and is also rich. So people call him "tall-rich-handsome."*
他长得又高又帅，又有钱，所以人们叫他"高富帅"。
Tā zhǎngde yòu gāo yòu shuài, yòu yǒuqián, suǒyǐ rénmen jiào tā "gāo-fù-shuài."

◆ *His speech had depth and was also humorous, all who heard it felt they reaped a great deal.*
他的演讲又有深度又幽默，大家听了都觉得很有收获。
Tāde yǎnjiǎng yòu yǒu-shēndù yòu yōumò, dàjiā tīngle dōu juéde hěn yǒu shōuhuò.

◆ *A child who is both smart and loves learning is bound to be very accomplished in the future.*
一个又聪明又好学的孩子将来肯定会很有成就。
Yíge yòu cōngming yòu hàoxuéde háizi jiānglái kěndìng huì hěn yǒu-chéngjiù.
(special meaning of 好 **hào** (fourth tone): love to…)

The above examples demonstrate that 又…又… **yòu…yòu…** may be used with function verbs and adjectives (also called "stative verbs"). A synonymous pattern is 也…也… **yě…yě…**, but it can only be used with function verbs (not adjectives).

✓ 你也不会说英语，在那儿也没有朋友，怎么能在那儿生活呢？
Nǐ yě búhuì shuō Yīngyǔ, zài nàr yě méiyǒu péngyou, zěnme néng zài nàr shēnghuó ne?
(equivalent to first example in the previous group)

✗ 一个也聪明也好学的孩子将来肯定会很有成就。
Yíge yě cōngming yě hàoxuéde háizi jiānglái kěndìng huì hěn yǒu chéngjiù.
(incorrect substitute for the last example in the previous group)

EXERCISES:

Translate the following sentences into Chinese:

1. I've only seen it once, but if I have the chance, I will certainly see it <u>again</u>. (future action)

2. You are late to work <u>again</u> today! If you are <u>again</u> late tomorrow, you won't need to come to work anymore.

3. Tuition fee is about to go up <u>again</u>; it would be best if you can graduate earlier.

4. He hasn't gone to college, <u>moreover</u> he can't speak English; so it's very difficult (for him) to find a job.

5. I didn't say it's your fault, so don't get mad. (stress "didn't")

6. Hot and sour soup is <u>both</u> sour <u>and</u> spicy-hot. Was it invented in America?

7. I love coming to this restaurant, because the dishes here are <u>both</u> inexpensive and delicious.

8. She can <u>both</u> sing and dance, but she doesn't like to perform.

ANSWERS:

1. 我只看过一次；如果有机会，我一定会再看一次。
   Wǒ zhǐ kànguo yícì; rúguǒ yǒu jīhuì, wǒ yídìng huì zài kàn yícì.

2. 你今天上班又迟到了！如果你明天再迟到，就不必再来上班了。
   Nǐ jīntiān shàngbān yòu chídào le! Rúguǒ nǐ míngtiān zài chídào, jiù búbì zài lái shàngbān le.

3. 学费又要涨了，你最好早一点毕业。**Xuéfèi yòu yào zhǎng le, nǐ zuì hǎo zǎo yìdiǎn bìyè.**

4. 他没上过大学，又不会英语，所以很难找到工作。
   Tā méi shàngguo dàxué, yòu búhuì Yīngyǔ, suǒyǐ hén nán zhǎodào gōngzuò.

5. 我又没说是你的错，别生气。**Wǒ yòu méi shuō shì nǐde cuò, bié shēngqì.**

6. 酸辣汤又酸又辣，是在美国发明的吗？
   Suānlà-tāng yòu suān yòu là, shì zài Měiguó fāmíng de ma?

7. 我很喜欢来这个餐馆，因为这里的菜又便宜又好吃。
   Wǒ hěn xǐhuan lái zhèige cānguǎn, yīnwèi zhèlǐde cài yòu piányi yòu hǎochī.

8. 她又会唱歌又会跳舞，可是不喜欢表演。
   Tā yòu huì chànggē yòu huì tiàowǔ, kěshì bù xǐhuan biǎoyǎn.

---

7. The adverb 才 cái = "only then"

More so than any other single-syllable adverb, the meaning of 才 **cái** runs counter to the normal mindset of English speakers. In itself, 才 **cái** is very simple, but the same concept expressed in English would strike a Chinese as a linguistic detour. Once you abandon the English mindset and think directly in Chinese, you will appreciate 才 **cái** as a simple elegant adverb that can accomplish so much with so little. By memorizing a few favorite sentences that use it, you will carve this Chinese linguistic groove in your mind, and will never again think along the lines of that English detour. Aside from the primary usage of 才 **cái**, there are several other common usages, which are easier for English-speaking students to master than the primary usage.

a. 才 cái in the sense of a condition to be fulfilled before something can happen

The primary usage of 才 **cái** is to place a focus on a necessary time or condition in order for something to occur. Putting it conversely, without meeting that necessary condition or before that particular time, something cannot occur.

◆ *It's the same in China and America, one must finish college in order to get a good job.*
中国跟美国一样，一定要读完大学才能找到好的工作。
Zhōngguó gēn Měiguó yíyàng, yídìng yào dúwán dàxué cái néng zhǎodào hǎode gōngzuò.

◆ *It will probably be next year before I can finish my Ph.D. dissertation.*
我大概明年才能写完我的博士论文。
Wǒ dàgài míngnián cái néng xiěwán wǒde bóshì lùnwén.

◆ *Must one know English before one can become an American citizen?*
必须会说英语才能当美国公民吗？
Bìxū huì shuō Yīngyǔ cái néng dāng Měiguó gōngmín ma?

In conjunction with the above usage, 才 **cái** can convey the additional sense that a required condition or time is more than what one would expect.

- *Last night I studied until 1:00 a.m. before going to bed.*
  (implying that I normally go to bed earlier)
  昨天晚上我学习到一点钟才睡觉。
  Zuótiān wǎnshang wǒ xuéxí dào yìdiǎnzhōng cái shuìjiào.

- *$5 certainly will not be enough, I think you will need $10.*
  (you may have thought $5 would be enough)
  五块钱肯定不够，我想要十块钱才够。
  Wǔkuài qián kěndìng búgòu, wǒ xiǎng yào shíkuài qián cái gòu.

- *My girlfriend says that I must have a house before her parents will let me marry her!*
  (This condition, coming from a Chinese girlfriend, is a bit of a shock to this hapless foreign man.)
  我的女朋友说我必须有房子她的父母才会让她跟我结婚！
  Wǒde nǚpéngyou shuō wǒ bìxū yǒu fángzi tāde fùmǔ cái huì ràng tā gēn wǒ jiéhūn!

The above use of 才 **cái** contrasts with a usage of 就 **jiù** in which 就 **jiù** conveys the sense of *sufficiency with a small quantity (less than normal or expected)*. Compare the first two pairs of sentences below:

- *This child could not walk until he was two years old.*
  这个孩子两岁才会走路。 **Zhèige háizi liǎngsuì cái huì zǒulù.**

- *This child could walk when he was only nine months old!*
  这个孩子九个月就会走路了！ **Zhèige háizi jiǔge yuè jiù huì zǒulù le.**

- *Last night I didn't go to bed until 1. a.m.*
  昨天晚上我一点钟才睡觉。 **Zuótiān wǎnshang wǒ yìdiǎnzhōng cái shuìjiào.**

- *Last night she went to bed when it was only 9 p.m.*
  昨天晚上她九点钟就睡觉了。 **Zuótiān wǎnshang tā jiǔdiǎnzhōng jiù shuìjiào le.**

- *In the past, divorce required the approval of a judge, now mutual agreement is sufficient.*
  从前要离婚必须法官批准才行，现在双方同意就行了。
  Cóngqián yào líhūn bìxū fǎguān pīzhǔn cái xíng, xiànzài shuāngfāng tóngyì jiù xíngle.

- *In that era, women were allowed to marry when they were only 20, but men had to be 25 before they could marry.*
  在那个年代，女方二十岁就可以结婚了，男方要二十五岁才能结婚。
  Zài nèige niándài, nǚfāng èrshí-suì jiù kěyǐ jiéhūnle, nánfāng yào èrshíwǔ-suì cái néng jiéhūn.

- *Don't think that I'm satisfied with just being able to communicate with Chinese people. I want Chinese people to be unable to tell that I'm a foreigner before I am satisfied.*

  别以为我能跟中国人沟通<u>就</u>满意了，我要中国人听不出我是个老外<u>才</u>满意。

  Bié yǐwéi wǒ néng gēn Zhōngguórén gōutōng jiù mǎnyì le, wǒ yào Zhōngguórén tīng-bu-chū wǒ shì ge lǎowài cái mǎnyì.

b. Secondary meanings of 才 cái

A secondary usage of 才 **cái** is to indicate the meaning *just, only.* In this usage, it is often followed by a quantity, either immediately or following the verb.

- *It's only eight o'clock, still early!*

  现在<u>才</u>八点，还早呢！ **Xiànzài cái bādiǎn, hái zǎo ne!**

- *This dress sells for only $30, it's too cheap!*

  这件衣服<u>才</u>卖三十块，太便宜了！

  (只 **zhǐ** or 就 **jiù** may be used in lieu of 才 **cái** here)

  Zhèijiàn yīfu cái mài sānshíkuài, tài piányi le!

- *I arrived just yesterday. (It was only yesterday that I arrived.)*

  我是昨天<u>才</u>到的。 **Wǒ shì zuótiān cái dào de.**

Another secondary usage of 才 **cái** is for emphasizing contradiction against an overt or implied assumption. In this usage, the verb is usually—but not necessarily—in the negative.

- *Don't just see him as a peasant, he's NOT stupid! (he's no country bumpkin!)*

  别看他是个农民，他<u>才</u>不笨呢！ **Bié kàn tā shì ge nóngmín, tā cái búbèn ne!**

- *Driving too slowly on an expressway is actually unsafe.*

  在高速公路上，开车开得太慢<u>才</u>不安全呢。

  Zài gāosù gōnglù-shang, kāichē kāide tài màn cái bù ānquán ne.

- *That salesman thinks I would believe anything he says, but I certainly don't believe him!*

  那个售货员以为他说什么我都会相信，我<u>才</u>不相信他呢！

  Nèige shòuhuòyuán yǐwéi tā shuō shénme wǒ dōu huì xiāngxìn, wǒ cái bù xiāngxìn tā ne!

In this usage of 才 **cái**, there is usually a preceding clause stating the situation or notion that is being contradicted by the 才 **cái** clause. That preceding clause may be implicit rather than overtly stated. On page 130, we learned that 又 **yòu** can also be used for emphasis. The difference between the two is this: Whereas the 才 **cái** clause functions as a follow-up, the 又 **yòu** clause either stands alone or precedes a clause that states a result or conclusion.

♦ *He treats me so badly, I certainly won't be his friend.*
他对我那么不好，我**才**不做他的朋友呢。
Tā duì wǒ nàme bù hǎo, wǒ cái bú zuò tāde péngyou ne.

♦ *He's NOT my friend, why should I lend him money?*
他**又**不是我的朋友，我何必要借钱给他呢?
Tā yòu búshì wǒde péngyou, wǒ hébì yào jiè qián gěi tā ne?

EXERCISES:

Translate the following sentences into Chinese:

1. This child started talking when he was only a year and a half, but he could not read until he was ten.

2. Don't think that speaking fluently is enough. One must be able to speak accurately before one can speak fluently.

3. I'm sorry, I've studied Chinese for only two years, so my Chinese is not very good.

4. You've studied Chinese for only two years? Wow! You speak it beautifully!

5. Things in farmers' markets in the U.S. are certainly not cheap! (contrary to what the Chinese might assume)

6. Talent is of course helpful, but it's diligence that's most important. (contradicting the assumption that talent will naturally lead to success)

ANSWERS:
1. 这个孩子一岁半就会说话了，可是他十岁才会看书。
   Zhèige háizi yísuì-bàn jiù huì shuōhuà le, kěshì tā shísuì cái huì kànshū.
2. 别以为说得流利就够了，必得先说得准确才能说得流利。
   Bié yǐwéi shuōde liúlì jiù gòule, bìděi xiān shuōde zhǔnquè cái néng shuōde liúlì.
3. 对不起，我才学了两年的中文，所以我的中文不太好。
   Duì-bu-qǐ, wǒ cái xuéle liǎngniánde Zhōngwén, suǒyǐ wǒde Zhōngwén bú tài hǎo.
4. 你才学了两年的中文?! 哇! 你说得太漂亮了。
   Nǐ cái xuéle liǎngniánde Zhōngwén? Wa! Nǐ shuōde tài piàoliang le!
5. 美国农贸市场的东西才不便宜呢。
   Měiguó nóngmào shìchǎngde dōngxi cái bù piányi ne.
6. 天赋当然很有帮助，可是努力才是最重要的。
   Tiānfù dángrán hěn yǒu bāngzhù, kěshì nǔlì cái shì zuì zhòngyàode.

8. The adverb 并 bìng = "by no means"

The adverb 并 **bìng** is a synonym of 才 **cái** in emphasizing opposition to a belief or assumption. It is also typically used with the negative 不 **bù** or 没 **méi**, but is less colloquial than 才 **cái**, and the sense of contradiction is less strong. A 并 **bìng** sentence also does not usually follow a preceding clause. The meaning of 并 **bìng** comes close to the phrase *by no means* in English.

◆ *I don't think this medicine does me any good.*
我并不认为这种药对我有好处。
Wǒ bìng bú rènwéi zhèizhǒng yào duì wǒ yǒu hǎochù.

我才不认为这种药对我有好处呢。
Wǒ cái bú rènwéi zhèizhǒng yào duì wǒ yǒu hǎochù ne.

(The second version is more expressive and conveys a greater sense of contradiction.)

◆ *She knew this long ago, but she did not inform me (as I expected her to).*
她老早就知道了，但并没有告诉我。
Tā lǎozǎo jiù zhīdaole, dàn bìng méiyǒu gàosu wǒ.

◆ *This was by no means the first time that he got into a car accident.*
这并不是他第一次出车祸了。 **Zhè bìng búshì tā dìyīcì chū chēhuò le.**

EXERCISES:

Translate the following sentences into Chinese:

1. He went through four years of college, but is <u>by no means</u> a true scholar.
2. I don't believe <u>by any means</u> that Western medicine is more effective than Chinese medicine.

> **ANSWERS:**
> 1. 他上了四年大学，但并不是一个真正有学问的人。
>   **Tā shàngle sìnián dàxué, dàn bìng búshì yíge zhēnzhèng yǒu-xuéwènde rén.**
> 2. 我并不相信西药比中药有效。 **Wǒ bìng bù xiāngxìn Xī-yào bǐ Zhōng-yào yǒuxiào.**

5.2 Adverb pairs that are frequently confused with one another

In this chapter, we have discussed the usages of various single-syllable adverbs. Until all these usages become intuitive, the distinctions between some of them may be unclear. In this section, we will juxtapose three pairs of adverbs that can be confusing to students.

A. 就 jiù vs 才 cái = "only"

There is no simple English translation for these two adverbs. 就 (see also 2.1, section 17) conveys shortness of time or the minimum conditions for something to occur; 才 **cái** conveys length of time and the full extent of conditions required for something to occur.

◆ *This prodigy of a kid was able to read at age three!*
这个天才儿童三岁<u>就</u>会看书了！ **Zhèige tiāncái értóng sānsuì jiù huì kànshū le!**

◆ *Her older brother couldn't read until he was seven.*
她的哥哥七岁<u>才</u>会看书呢！ **Tāde gēge qīsuì cái huì kànshū ne!**

◆ *I thought I could get home by 4:00, but because my car broke down, I didn't get home until midnight.*
我以为四点钟就能到家。可是因为汽车坏了，我半夜才到家。
Wǒ yǐwéi sìdiǎnzhōng jiù néng dàojiā. Kěshì yīnwèi qìchē huàile, wǒ bànyè cái dàojiā.

B. 才 cái vs 再 zài = "not until"

Both can be used in the sense of *not until a certain time.* 才 **cái** is used in statements of fact; 再 **zài** is used in suggestions or requests (see page 127).

◆ *We waited until the rain stopped before we went out, so we were late.*
我们等雨停了才出门，所以迟到了。
Wǒmen děng yǔ tíngle cái chūmén, suǒyǐ chídàole.

◆ *It's raining too hard right now, wait until it stops before going out.*
现在雨下得太大了，等停了再出门吧。
Xiànzài yǔ xiàde tài dà le, déng tíngle zài chūmén ba.

◆ *It's not enough to finish one's Ph.D. dissertation, one has to pass the oral defense and only then is one all done.*
博士论文写完还不够，要通过答辩才行。
Bóshì lùnwén xiěwán hái búgòu, yào tōngguò dábiàn cái xíng.

C. 再 zài vs 又 yòu = "again"

In the sense of *again, further, …more,* 再 **zài** is used with contemplated or future events. 又 **yòu** is used with events that have already occurred (see also 2.1, section 16).

◆ *Teacher, please teach that set phrase to me again. I forgot it again!*
老师，请你再教我一次那个成语，我又忘了！
Lǎoshī, qǐng nǐ zài jiāo wǒ yícì nèige chéngyǔ, wǒ yòu wàngle!

◆ *OK, this is the last time. If you forget it again, I won't teach it to you again.*
好，这是最后一次啦！如果你再忘了，我就不再教你了。
Hǎo, zhè shì zuìhòu yícì la! Rúguǒ nǐ zài wàngle, wǒ jiù búzài jiāo nǐ le.

◆ *We walked for another ten minutes, but still didn't find that restaurant.*
我们又走了十分钟，可是还是没找到那个餐馆。
Wǒmen yòu zǒule shífēnzhōng, kěshì háishi méi zhǎodào nèige cānguǎn.

◆ *Walk ahead for another five minutes, and you'll be there (you'll arrive there).*
再往前走五分钟，你就到了。**Zài wǎng qián zǒu wǔfēnzhōng, nǐ jiù dàole.**

◆ *Another shooting incidence occurred this week. What can we do to prevent this kind of thing from happening again?*
这个星期又发生了一次枪击事件。我们有什么办法避免这种事情再发生呢？ **Zhèige xīngqī yòu fāshēngle yícì qiāngjī shìjiàn. Wǒmen yǒu shénme bànfǎ bìmiǎn zhèizhǒng shìqing zài fāshēng ne?**

EXERCISES:

Translate the following sentences into Chinese:

1. In the U.S., a 16-years-old is old enough to drive, but one <u>cannot</u> purchase liquor <u>until</u> age 21.

2. You can leave the hospital <u>as early as</u> tomorrow, but you'll need to rest a month <u>before</u> you can return to normal.

3. You should see which college gives you a scholarship <u>before</u> deciding which college to attend.

4. They did not get married <u>until</u> they already had two children.

5. She gave birth to a pair of twins just six months ago, now she is expecting <u>again</u>!

6. You've already had three drinks tonight, you shouldn't drink <u>anymore</u>!

7. I'll wait <u>another</u> five minutes. If she <u>still</u> doesn't come, I'll leave!

8. He won <u>again</u>! If he wins <u>again</u> next year, he will break the world record!

ANSWERS:

1. 在美国，十六岁就可以开车了，可是二十一岁才可以买酒。
   Zài Měiguó, shíliù-suì jiù kěyǐ kāichē le, kěshì èrshíyī-suì cái kěyǐ mǎi jiǔ.

2. 你明天就可以出院了，可是得休息一个月才能恢复正常状态。
   Nǐ míngtiān jiù kěyǐ chūyuàn le, kěshì děi xiūxi yíge yuè cái néng huīfù zhèngcháng zhuàngtài.

3. 你应该先看看哪所大学给你奖学金再决定上哪所大学。
   Nǐ yīnggāi xiān kànkan něisuǒ dàxué gěi nǐ jiǎngxuéjīn zài juédìng shàng něisuǒ dàxué.

4. 他们有了两个孩子以后才结婚的。Tāmen yǒule liǎngge háizi yǐhòu cái jiéhūn de.

5. 她六个月前才生了一对双胞胎，现在又怀孕了！
   Tā liùge yuè qián cái shēngle yíduì shuāngbāotāi, xiànzài yòu huáiyùn le.

6. 你今晚已经喝了三杯酒了，不应该再喝了！
   Nǐ jīnwǎn yǐjing hēle sānbēi jiǔ le, bù yīnggāi zài hē le!

7. 我再等五分钟。如果她还不来，我就走了！
   Wǒ zài děng wǔfēn zhōng. Rúguǒ tā hái bù lái, wǒ jiù zǒu le!

8. 他又赢了！如果他明年再赢，就打破世界纪录了！
   Tā yòu yíngle! Rúguǒ tā míngnián zài yíng, jiù dǎpò shìjiè jìlù le!

5.3 Two-syllable adverbs that modify verbs or entire sentences

There are two categories of two-syllable adverbs: 1) Those that occur in a simple sentence to modify the verb or an entire sentence; 2) Those that come in pairs linking two clauses to form a complex sentence. This second group are also called conjunctions (连词 liáncí "linking words" in Chinese), or more accurately "adverbial conjunctions,." These will be discussed in the next section 5.4.

The first group of two-syllable adverbs, those that occur in simple sentences, convey information about the timing or the speaker's "attitude." (The latter may seem murky, but the second group of examples below will make it clear.) Here are some of the most common two-syllable adverbs:

A. Adverbs related to timing:

1. 从来 **cónglái** = *always* (can be used with a negative to mean *never*)

♦ *I am never late to class.* 我上课从来不迟到。 **Wǒ shàngkè cónglái bù chídào.**

2. 已经 **yǐjīng** = *already*

♦ *We already studied to lesson four.*
我们已经上到第四课了。 **Wǒmen yǐjīng shàngdào dìsìkè le.**

3. 立刻 **lìkè** or 马上 **mǎshàng** (synonyms) = *immediately* (usually coupled with 就 **jiù**)

♦ *Don't be anxious, we'll be there immediately!*
别着急，我们马上就到了！ **Bié zhāojí, wǒmen mǎshàng jiù dàole.**

4. 正在 **zhèngzài** = *in the midst of, on the point of*

♦ *I am in the midst of driving, so I can't receive a call.*
我正在开车，所以不能接电话！ **Wǒ zhèngzài kāichē, suǒyǐ bùnéng jiē diànhuà!**

5. 刚才 **gāngcái** = *just now, few moments ago* (see 2.1, sec. 9, re 刚 **gāng** vs 刚才 **gāngcái**)

♦ *What did you say just now? I didn't hear you clearly.*
你刚才说什么？我没听清楚。 **Nǐ gāngcái shuō shénme? Wǒ méi tīng-qīngchǔ.**

6. 将来 **jiānglái** = *in the future*

♦ *We may adopt a Chinese child in the future.*
我们可能将来会领养一个中国孩子。
Wǒmen kěnéng jiānglái huì lǐngyǎng yíge Zhōngguó háizi.

7. 前天 **qiántiān** = *the day before yesterday*

♦ *My dog disappeared the day before yesterday, today it returned by itself!*
我的狗前天失踪了，今天它自己回来了！
Wǒde gǒu qiántiān shīzōng le, jīntiān tā zìjǐ huílaile!

8. 去年 **qùnián** = *last year*

♦ *He studied in China last year, and made quite a few Chinese friends.*
他去年在中国留学，认识了不少中国朋友。
Tā qùnián zài Zhōngguó liúxué, rènshile bùshǎo Zhōngguó péngyou.

B. Adverbs conveying an "attitude" toward the substance of the sentence

9. 也许 **yěxǔ** = *perhaps*

♦ *The teacher may be able to tell you the meaning of this poem.*
老师也许能告诉你这首诗的意思。
Lǎoshī yěxǔ néng gàosu nǐ zhèishǒu shīde yìsi.

10. 当然 **dāngrán** = *of course*

◆ *This one is too small? Then we can of course exchange it for you.*
这件太小了吗？那我们当然可以给您换一件。
Zhèijiàn tài xiǎo le ma? Nà wǒmen dāngrán kěyǐ gěi nín huàn yíjiàn.

11. 好像 **hǎoxiàng** = *seems to, must be*

◆ *She seems to be especially interested in you.*
她好像对你特别感兴趣。 **Tā hǎoxiàng duì nǐ tèbié gǎn-xìngqù.**

12. 显然 **xiǎnrán** = *obviously*

◆ *She obviously doesn't love me anymore.*
她显然不爱我了。 **Tā xiǎnrán bú ài wǒ le.**

In all the examples above, the adverbs are located right before the verb. However, unlike the single-syllable adverbs discussed earlier in this chapter, some two-syllable adverbs relating to time (#5–8) and all of those relating to "attitude" may be located at the beginning of the sentence (i.e. before the subject or topic). Adverbs with two possible locations are called "movable adverbs." Whether a movable adverb is placed at the beginning of a sentence or after the subject depends on the speaker and the difference is only one of nuance. See if you can feel the differences in each of these pairs of sentences (in both the English and Chinese versions):

◆ *My dog disappeared the day before yesterday.*
我的狗前天失踪了。 **Wǒde gǒu qiántiān shīzōng le.**

vs

◆ *The day before yesterday, my dog disappeared.*
前天我的狗失踪了。 **Qiántiān wǒde gǒu shīzōng le.**

◆ *She obviously doesn't love me anymore.*   vs   *Obviously, she no longer loves me.*
她显然不爱我了。   显然她不爱我了。
Tā xiǎnrán bú ài wǒ le.   **Xiǎnrán tā bú ài wǒ le.**

From the above, you may draw the conclusion that, when in doubt, it is always best to just locate an adverb after the subject. With this strategy, you will always be grammatically correct.

C. Three-syllable adverbs

There are also two three-syllable adverbs that function just like the two-syllable adverbs described in this section: 差不多 **chàbuduō** and 差一点儿 **chàyìdiǎnr**. Both are translated as *almost* and are non-movable. These two are prone to be confused by English speakers and were already discussed in 2.1, sec. 7. We will not delve into them again, except to point out that they are examples of the few adverbs that exceed two syllables.

EXERCISES:

Translate the following sentences into Chinese:

1. <u>Just now</u> he told the doctor he <u>never</u> smokes. But I saw him smoking yesterday.

2. My car broke down, <u>so perhaps</u> we won't be able to go (implying a change in plan).

ANSWERS:

1. 他刚才告诉医生他从来不抽烟，可是我昨天看见他抽烟了。
   Tā gāngcái gàosu yīshēng tā cónglái bù chōuyān, kěshì wǒ zuótiān kànjian tā chōuyān le.

2. 我的车坏了，我们恐怕不能去了。
   Wǒde chē huàile, wǒmen kǒngpà bùnéng qù le.

5.4 Adverbs that function as conjunctions

For clarity, we will call this group of adverbs "adverbial conjunctions." They are used in conjoining two or more clauses to form a complex sentence. Such complex sentences exist in English; however in English, a single adverb is usually sufficient to signal the linkage. In Chinese, most typically, both clauses contain an adverb, and the two adverbs form a pair, with at least one of them being two syllables. Compare the usage of adverbs between the English and Chinese sentences below:

a. *<u>Because</u> it's snowing, we cancelled the trip.*

b. *It's snowing, <u>therefore</u> we cancelled the trip.*

c. *<u>Because</u> it is snowing, <u>therefore</u> we have cancelled the trip.*

(In all three versions, the second clause is the result of the first, but the first two versions contain only one linking word. The third version is strictly speaking not proper English. It contains a linking word in each clause, which is redundant.) In Chinese however, linking words are commonly used in both clauses:

> <u>因为</u>下雪，<u>所以</u>我们取消了这次旅行。
> **Yīnwèi xiàxuě, suǒyǐ wǒmen qǔxiāole zhècì lǚxíng.**
> (This is the most typical Chinese rendition, although the sentence would be correct even without 所以 **suǒyǐ**.)

When beginning to learn Chinese, students are introduced to a few basic adverbial conjunctions that come in pairs. The following examples may be already familiar to you:

- 因为···，所以··· **yīnwèi…, suǒyǐ…:**
  Because they could not have a child, they decided to adopt one from China.
  因为他们没有法子生孩子，所以决定从中国领养一个。
  Yīnwèi tāmen méiyǒu fázi shēng háizi, suǒyǐ juédìng cóng Zhōngguó lǐngyǎng yíge.

- 如果···, 就··· **rúguǒ..., jiù...**:
  If it snows too hard, today's classes will be cancelled!
  如果雪下得太大，今天的课就取消了！
  Rúguǒ xuě xiàde tài dà, jīntiānde kè jiù qǔxiāo le.

- 好像···, 可是··· **hǎoxiàng..., kěshì...**:
  She seems to be unhappy (about something), but she's unwilling to tell us why.
  她好像不太高兴，可是不愿意告诉我们为什么。
  Tā hǎoxiàng bú tài gāoxìng, kěshì bú yuànyi gàosu wǒmen wèishénme.

As a caveat to the point that complex sentences in Chinese often contain an adverbial conjunction in each clause, there are cases where only one clause contains an adverb. These adverbs strongly imply linkage to another clause, so that the sentence will be incomplete without the other clause.

- 其实 **qíshí** *actually*:
  People think I'm Chinese, actually I am an American of Chinese descent.
  人们以为我是中国人，其实我是个美籍华人。
  Rénmen yǐwéi wǒ shì Zhōngguórén, qíshí wǒ shì ge Měijí Huárén.

- 要不然 **yàoburán** *otherwise*:
  I work every summer vacation, otherwise, I would not have money to pay tuition.
  我每年暑假都工作，要不然，我就没有钱付学费了。
  Wǒ měinián shǔjià dōu gōngzuò, yàoburán, wǒ jiù méiyǒu qián fù xuéfèi le.

Because paired adverbial conjunctions are used to form complex sentences, they appear more frequently in sophisticated discourse, and are therefore an important component of the vocabulary for intermediate and advanced level speakers of Chinese. We have provided a few examples of paired adverbial conjunctions here to familiarize you with the concept, but a longer list of examples will appear in Chapter 16, and a more extended repertoire will be included in Part II of this book.

EXERCISES:

Translate the following sentences into Chinese:

1. Chinese seems difficult to learn, but actually learning to speak Chinese is not that difficult.

2. Driver, can you go faster? Otherwise, I'll be late!

ANSWERS:
1. 中文好像很难学，其实学说中国话并不那么难。
   Zhōngwén hǎoxiàng hěn nán xué, qíshí xué shuō Zhōngguóhuà bìng bú nàme nán.
2. 师傅，你能不能开快一点? 要不然，我就迟到了。
   Shīfu, nǐ néng-bunéng kāi kuài yìdiǎn? Yànburán, wǒ jiù chídào le.

6 Describing the Manner of an Action

The "manner" of an action is distinguished from the "result" in that it describes the process rather than the consequence. Both kinds of descriptions—the process and the result—are expressed by the same type of sentence pattern in Chinese: **verb +** 得 **de + description**. In this pattern, the "description" can take on a variety of different forms. For convenience and clarity, we will use the grammatical term *verb complement* to refer to all these various forms, although only the simplest *verb complement*—the adjective—will appear in the examples that follow below.

The following pair of sentences contrasts "process" and "result:"

- *He runs very fast.* (describing the process)
  他跑得很快。 **Tā pǎode hěnkuài.**

- *He washed (it) very clean.* (describing the result)
  他洗得很干净。 **Tā xǐde hěn gānjìng.**

Sometimes, it is difficult to tell exactly whether a description refers to the process or the result, or both. For example:

- *He explained it very clearly.*
  (He clearly explained it. and *The result was clarification.)*
  他解释得很清楚。 **Tā jiěshìde hěn qīngchǔ.**

- *We chatted happily.*
  (We were happy as we chatted. and *We became happy as we chatted.)*
  我们谈得很高兴。 **Wǒmen tánde hěn gāoxìng.**

In the pattern **verb +** 得 **de +** *verb complement*, if the verb has an object, the object is not simply tagged onto the verb. Instead, the **verb + object** pair or the object alone must be before the **verb+** 得 **de +** *verb complement* construction:

> Correct: a. **verb + object + verb +** 得 **de +** *verb complement*
> b. **object + verb +** 得 **de +** *verb complement*
> c. the object may also be preposed before the subject, as the topic of the
>   sentence

Incorrect: **verb + object +** 得 **de +** *verb complement*

Examples:

- *He speaks Chinese beautifully.*
  a) ✓ 他说中文说得很漂亮。**Tā shuō Zhōngwén shuōde hěn piàoliang.**
  b) ✓ 他中文说得很漂亮。**Tā Zhōngwén shuōde hěn piàoliang.**
  c) ✓ 中文，他说得很漂亮。**Zhōngwén, tā shuōde hěn piàoliang.** (less common)
  ✗ 他说中文得很漂亮。**Tā shuō Zhōngwén de hěn piàoliang.**

- *This book explains grammar very clearly.*
  a) ✓ 这本书解释语法解释得很清楚。
     Zhèiběn shū jiěshì yǔfǎ jiěshì de hěn qīngchǔ.
  b) ✓ 这本书语法解释得很清楚。**Zhèiběn shū yǔfǎ jiěshì de hěn qīngchǔ.**
  c) ✓ 语法，这本书解释得很清楚。
     Yǔfǎ, zhèiběn shū jiěshì de hěn qīngchǔ. (less common)
  ✗ 这本书解释语法得很清楚。**Zhèiběn shū jiěshì yǔfǎ de hěn qīngchǔ.**

- *He speaks Chinese beautifully, but he's terrible with Japanese.*
  他中文说得很漂亮，可是日文说得很糟糕。（日文 is preposed as sentence topic）
  Tā Zhōngwén shuōde hěn piàoliang, kěshì Rìwén shuōde hěn zāogāo.

A note of caution: Because many verbs in English are translated into **verb + object** compounds in Chinese (see 2.6), English speakers sometimes mistakenly treat **verb + object** compounds in Chinese as bisyllabic verbs, leading to flawed sentences like this one:

- *Teacher, you speak too fast, I can't understand you.*
  ✗ 老师，你说话得太快了，我听不懂。
     Lǎoshī, nǐ shuōhuà de tài kuài le, wǒ tīng-bu-dǒng.

  ✓ 老师，你说话说得太快了，我听不懂。
     Lǎoshī, nǐ shuōhuà shuōde tài kuài le, wǒ tīng-bu-dǒng.

- *Teacher: I don't speak too fast. It's you who hears Chinese too slowly, isn't it?*
  ✓ 老师：我说话说得不太快，是你听中文听得太慢了吧？ (or 是你中文听得太慢了吧？)。
     Lǎoshī: Wǒ shuōhuà shuōde bú tài kuài, shì nǐ tīng Zhōngwén tīngde tài màn le ba? (or shì nǐ Zhōngwén tīngde tài màn le ba?)

- *She sings superbly, but she doesn't sing well in Chinese.*
  她唱歌唱得很棒，可是中文歌她唱得不好。
  （中文歌 **Zhōngwén-gē** is preposed as sentence topic）
  Tā chànggē chàngde hěn bàng, kěshì Zhōngwén-gē tā chàngde bù hǎo.

A **verb+object** compound in which the object is "generic" (as described in 2.6) usually appears as a unit (i.e. both parts are necessary), except when the **verb+object** has just appeared in a preceding sentence or question, in which case the object part of the **verb+object** compound is omitted (see the second and third examples below).

- *He reads very slowly.* 他看书看得很慢。 **Tā kànshū kànde hěn màn.**
  Q: *How does he read?* A: *He reads very slowly.*
  他看书看得怎么样? 他看得很慢。
  (the object 书 **shū** is omitted in the reply)
  Tā kànshū kànde zěnmeyàng? Tā kànde hěn màn.
  (The reply 他看书看得很慢 **Tā kànshū kànde hěn màn** is also correct, but it sounds redundant.)

- *Her older brother sings well, but she doesn't.*
  她哥哥唱歌唱得很棒, 可是她唱得不好。
  (the object 歌 **gē** is omitted in the second phrase)
  Tā gēge chànggē chàngde hěn bàng, kěshì tā chàngde bù hǎo.

- *He reads quite fast, but when it comes to Chinese, he reads very slowly.*
  他看书看得很快, 可是中文他看得很慢。
  Tā kànshū kànde hěn kuài, kěshì Zhōngwén tā kànde hěn màn.

- Q: *How does he speak Chinese?* 他汉语说得怎么样?
  Tā Hànyǔ shuōde zěnmeyàng?
  A: *He speaks Chinese very slowly, but his grammar is quite accurate.*
  他汉语说得很慢, 可是他的语法相当准确。
  Tā Hànyǔ shuōde hěn màn, kěshì tāde yǔfǎ xiāngdāng zhǔnquè.

The above examples all describe the manner of actions. The same pattern also applies to descriptions of the result of actions. Examples:

- *They do a great job with the laundry. (They wash clothes really clean.)*
  他们洗衣服洗得很干净。 **Tāmen xǐ yīfu xǐde hěn gānjìng.**

- Q: *How is their laundry service?* A: *They do a great job.*
  他们洗衣服洗得怎么样? 他们洗得很干净。
  (the object 衣服 **yīfu** is omitted in the reply)
  Tāmen xǐ yīfu xǐde zěnmeyàng? Tāmen xǐde hěn gānjìng.

- *This professor lectures very clearly. (clearly describes both the manner and the result)*
  ✓ 这位教授讲课讲得很清楚。 **Zhèiwèi jiàoshòu jiǎngkè jiǎngde hěn qīngchǔ.**
  ✗ 这位教授讲课得很清楚。 **Zhèiwèi jiàoshòu jiǎngkè de hěn qīngchǔ.**

- Q: *How well does this professor lecture?* A: *He lectures quite clearly.*
  这位教授讲课讲得怎么样? 他讲得相当清楚。
  Zhèiwèi jiàoshòu jiǎngkè jiǎngde zěnmeyàng? Tā jiǎngde xiāngdāng qīngchǔ.

The description of manner or result can apply to a general/habitual situation, or to a specific occasion.

♦ *He's old now, so he walks very slowly.* (habitual)
  ✓ 他老了，所以走路走得很慢。 **Tā lǎole, suǒyǐ zǒulù zǒude hěn màn.**
  ✗ 他老了，所以走路得很慢。 **Tā lǎole, suǒyǐ zǒulù de hěn màn.**

♦ *He's not feeling well today, so he's walking slowly.* (specific circumstance)
  他今天不舒服，所以走路走得很慢。
  Tā jīntiān bùshūfu, suǒyǐ zǒulù zǒude hěn màn.

♦ *How is your Mom's cooking?*
  Normally, she doesn't cook too well, but we have guests tonight, so she cooked especially well. (In the reply, the first part describes a habitual situation, the second part describes a special occasion)
  你妈妈做菜做得怎么样？ **Nǐ māma zuòcài zuòde zěnmeyàng?**
  平常她做得不太好，可是今晚请客，所以她做得特别好。
  Píngcháng tā zuòde bú tài hǎo, kěshì jīnwǎn qǐngkè, suǒyǐ tā zuòde tèbié hǎo.

6.2 Describing the manner of an action using the *adverbial* form ···地 de

The *adverbial* form is the closest thing in Chinese to English adverbs formed by adding the suffix -*ly* to adjectives. In this pattern, 地 **de** is added to an adjective to form an *adverbial* which describes the manner of an action.

1. Comparing the *adverbial* and *verb complement* forms

Structurally, the two forms differ in their position within a sentence: the *verb complement* comes *after* the verb, whereas the *adverbial* comes *before* the verb. The difference in meaning between these two patterns is in the focus of the sentence, as illustrated by the following pair of examples:

♦ *Prof. Li lectured very clearly today.* (focus is on *how* Prof. Li lectured today)
  李教授今天讲课讲得很清楚。
  Lǐ Jiàoshòu jīntiān jiǎngkè jiǎngde hěn qīngchǔ.
  (*verb complement* used to describe the manner of action)

♦ *Prof. Li very clearly explained the vocabulary in this lesson today.*
  李教授今天很清楚地讲了这一课的生词。
  Lǐ Jiàoshòu jīntiān hěn qīngchǔde jiǎngle zhèiyíkède shēngcí.
  (focus is on *what* Prof. Li taught today; adverbial 很清楚地 **hěn qīngchǔde** describes how Prof. Li did what he did)

The first sentence focuses on the "manner," and tells how the teacher conducted his lecture today. The second sentence doesn't focus on the manner, but tells what the teacher did today (he lectured on the vocabulary of this lesson), and (incidentally) he did it very clearly. The first sentence is a likely reply to the question "How did Prof. Li do in his lecture today?" The second sentence is a likely reply to "What did Prof. Li do today?"

The two sentences focus on different aspects, but both describe a specific instance. As noted in the preceding section, the *verb complement* pattern may be used to describe a habitual situation as well as a specific instance. However, the *adverbial* pattern may be used only to describe a specific action (i.e. it is not used to describe habitual situations).

- *Prof. Li very clearly explained the vocabulary in this lesson today.*
  李教授今天很清楚地讲了这一课的生词。
  Lǐ Jiàoshòu jīntiān hěn qīngchǔde jiǎngle zhèiyíkède shēngcí.

  (specific instance, using adverbial form)

- *Prof. Li lectures very clearly.* (habitual situation)
  ✓ 李教授讲课讲得很清楚。 (habitual situation, using *verb complement*)
    Lǐ Jiàoshòu jiǎngkè jiǎngde hěn qīngchǔ.
  ✗ 李教授很清楚地讲课。
    Lǐ Jiàoshòu hěn qīngchǔde jiǎngkè.

  (adverbial pattern may not be applied to a habitual situation)

Here are some additional examples of adverbial constructions describing specific actions:

- *How did your day of play go yesterday? We had a good time yesterday.*
  你们昨天玩儿得怎么样? 昨天我们玩儿得很高兴。
  Nǐmen zuótiān wánrde zěnmeyàng? Zuótiān wǒmen wánrde hěn gāoxìng.
  (*verb complement* used to describe both the manner and the result of the action)

- *What did you all do yesterday? We had great fun playing all day long.*
  你们昨天做了什么? 昨天我们高高兴兴地玩儿了一天。
  Nǐmen zuótiān zuòle shénme? Zuótiān wǒmen gāogāoxìngxìngde wánrle yìtiān.
  (focus is on what they did, *adverbial* used to describe how they did it)

- *What are you going to do tomorrow? We want to have fun playing all day long.*
  ✓ 你们明天要做什么? 我们明天要高高兴兴地去玩儿一天。
    Nǐmen míngtiān yào zuò shénme? Wǒmen míngtiān yào gāogāoxìngxìngde qù wánr yìtiān.
  (adverbial used)
  ✗ 我们明天要玩儿得很高兴。 **Wǒmen míngtian yào wánrde hěn gāoxìng.**
  (This is a faulty attempt to use a verb complement to describe the manner of a future action. While this sentence is not outright wrong, this pattern is not commonly applied to future actions, because the pattern is used to describe the manner in which an action is "actually" performed, not the "intention" of how it is to be performed.)

Another difference between the *verb complement* and *adverbial* form is that the *verb complement* can be applied to both the manner and the result of an action, whereas the *adverbial* form may be applied to only the manner—not the result—of an action .

verb complement form	adverbial form
She explained that matter thoroughly. 她把那件事讲得很详细。 **Tā bǎ nèijiàn shì jiǎngde hěn xiángxì.**	*She thoroughly explained that matter to me.* 她详细地告诉了我那件事。 **Tā xiángxìde gàosule wǒ nèijiàn shì.**
He told that story in a very vivid way! 那个故事，他讲得太生动了。 **Nèige gùshi, tā jiǎngde tài shēngdòng le.**	*He vividly told that story.* 他很生动地讲了那个故事。 **Tā hěn shēngdòngde jiǎngle nèige gùshi.**
They wash clothes very clean. (a good laundry) 他们洗衣服洗得很干净。 **Tāmen xǐ yīfu xǐde hěn gānjìng.**	No counterpart for 2 reasons: Adverbial form not used with habitual case; *clean* is the result, not manner, of the action
You write characters very beautifully. 你写字写得真漂亮！ **Nǐ xiězì xiěde zhēn piàoliang.**	No counterpart for the same reasons as above.

EXERCISES:

Translate the following sentences using either the *verb complement* or *adverbial* form to convey the proper nuance:

1. After he arrived, he quickly wrote a letter to his family.
2. He not only cooks really fast, but also very well too.
3. She speaks Chinese quite fluently, but her grammar is terrible.
4. On the first day of class, the teacher clearly stated that students must shut off their cellphones in class.
5. He is usually slow in doing his homework. But because there's a party tonight, he quickly finished his homework in the afternoon.

ANSWERS:

1. 他到了以后，很快地就给家里写了一封信。
   Tā dàole yǐhòu, hěn kuàide jiù gěi jiālǐ xiěle yìfēng xìn.
2. 他做饭做得不但很快，而且做得很好。
   Tā zuòfàn zuòde búdàn hěn kuài, érqiě zuòde hěn hǎo.
3. 她中文说得很流利，可是她的语法很糟糕。
   Tā Zhōngwén shuōde hěn liúlì, kěshì tāde yǔfǎ hěn zāogāo.
4. 上课的第一天，老师很清楚地申明了上课时学生必须关上手机。
   Shàngkède dìyītiān, lǎoshī hěn qīngchǔde shēnmíngle shàngkè shí xuésheng bìxū guānshang shǒujī.
5. 他平常做功课做得很慢。可是因为今晚有个晚会，他下午很快地就把功课做完了。**Tā píngcháng zuò gōngkè zuòde hěn màn. Kěshì yīnwèi jīnwǎn yǒu ge wǎnhuì, tā xiàwǔ hěn kuàide jiù bǎ gōngkè zuòwánle.**

2. How adverbials are formed from adjectives

The *adverbial* form in Chinese is similar to English adverbs in that they are derived from adjectives by adding *-ly*. A fundamental difference between them is that Chinese adverbials are always positioned before the verb, whereas adverbs in English may be positioned before or after the verb.

Adverbials in Chinese are formed by adding 地 (pronounced **de**, unstressed) to adjectives. Most of the adjectives used to create adverbials are bisyllabic. If an adjective consists of only one syllable, then it is reduplicated to form an adverbial. Here are some adverbials derived from bisyllabic adjectives:

紧张地 **jǐnzhāngde** *anxiously*	*As soon as she got the bad news, she immediately ran over and anxiously notified everyone.* 她一听到这个坏消息，就马上跑来紧张地通告了大家。 **Tā yì tīngdào zhèige huài xiāoxi, jiù mǎshàng pǎolai jǐnzhāngde tōnggàole dàjiā.**
高兴地 **gāoxìngde** *happily*	*As soon as she got the good news, she immediately ran over to announce it to everyone.* 她一听到这个好消息，就马上跑来高兴地通知了大家。 **Tā yì tīngdào zhèige hǎo xiāoxi, jiù mǎshàng pǎolai gāoxìngde tōngzhīle dàjiā.**
苦闷地 **kǔmènde** *dejectedly*	*After his wife left him, he often dejectedly thought about his mistakes.* 妻子离开了他以后，他经常苦闷地思考他的过错。 **Qīzi líkāile tā yǐhòu, tā jīngcháng kǔmènde sīkǎo tāde guòcuò.**
沉默地 **chénmòde** *silently*	*He silently considered a long while, and finally agreed.* 他沉默地考虑了半天，终于答应了。 **Tā chénmòde kǎolùle bàntiān, zhōngyú dāyìngle.**
平静地 **píngjìngde** *calmly*	*That frozen lake is calmly waiting for the arrival of spring.* 那片结了冰的湖面平静地等待着春天的到来。 **Nèipiàn jié-le-bīngde húmiàn píngjìngde děngdàizhe chūntiānde dàolái.**

When *adverbials* are derived from monosyllabic adjectives by reduplication, their pronunciation is often changed in the following ways: 1) - 儿 **-r** is added to the second syllable; 2) the second syllable is changed to the first tone (if it is not originally in the first tone). Both of these transformations occur only with very common *adverbials*, and only in the standard Chinese dialect spoken in Beijing, i.e. these rules are not universally followed in other regions of China. Below are a few common and not-so-common *adverbials* formed from monosyllabic adjectives.

好好儿地 **hǎohāorde** *nicely*	*We can discuss this nicely, don't get mad.* 我们应该好好儿地商量，别生气。 **Wǒmen yīnggāi hǎohāorde shāngliang, bié shēngqì.**

快快儿地 **kuàikuārde** *quickly*	*As soon as the class was over, he quickly finished his homework, then went to work.* 一下课，他快快儿地做完了功课，就去打工了。 **Yí xiàkè, tā kuàikuārde zuòwánle gōngkè, jiù qù dǎgōngle.**
慢慢儿地 **mànmārde** *slowly*	*Relax, think slowly about where you could have left your cellphone.* 别着急，慢慢儿地想一想，你把手机落在哪儿了。 **Bié zhāojí, mànmārde xiǎngyìxiǎng, nǐ bǎ shōujī làzài nǎr le.**
静静地 **jìngjìngde** *quietly*	*The dog lay quietly by the door waiting for its master.* 狗静静地躺在门前等着它的主人。 **Gǒu jìngjìngde tǎngzài ménqián děngzhe tāde zhǔrén.**
悄悄地 **qiāoqiāode** *quietly, stealthily*	*As soon as the teacher turned her head, he stealthily slipped out.* 老师一转头，他就悄悄地溜出去了。 **Lǎoshī yì zhuǎntóu, tā jiù qiāoqiāode liū-chūqule.**
偷偷地 **tōutōude** *stealthily, secretly*	*For those 20 years, he secretly kept a mistress.* 在那二十年里，他偷偷地养了一个二奶。 **Zài nà èrshí-niánlǐ, tā tōutōude yǎngle yíge èrnǎi.**

Note: In some reduplicated *adverbials* that follow the above pattern (i.e. XX 地 **de**), X may sometimes not be an adjective, e.g. 偷偷地 **tōutōude** is actually derived from the verb 偷 **tōu** *to steal*, and the word 悄 **qiāo** in 悄悄地 **qiāoqiāode** is not an independent adjective (it only appears in idiomatic combinations like this one).

In idiomatic Chinese speech, adverbials formed from bisyllabic adjectives can also be reduplicated, for an intensifying or colorful effect.

◆ *We happily cooperated for a year.*
我们快乐地合作了一年。**Wǒmen kuàilède hézuòle yìnián.**
我们快快乐乐地合作了一年。**Wǒmen kuàikuàilèlède hézuòle yìnián.**
(more intense and vivid than the preceding)

◆ *She long-windedly explained it over and over, and still didn't explain it clearly.*
她啰啰嗦嗦地讲了又讲。还是没讲清楚。
Tā luōluōsuōsuōde jiǎngle yòu jiǎng, háishi méi jiǎng-qīngchǔ.

◆ *In all things, one must be open and upfront, one should not do things furtively.*
凡事应该光明正大；不能偷偷摸摸地做事。
Fánshì yīnggāi guāngmíng zhèngdà, bùnéng tōutōumōmōde zuòshì.
(偷偷摸摸地 **tōutōumōmōde** only appears in this reduplicated form, i.e. 偷摸地 **tōumōde** is never used)

EXERCISES:

Compose sentences using the following adverbials (you may need to look up some of them):

1. 兴奋地 **xīngfènde**
2. 干脆地 **gāncuìde**
3. 详细地 **xiángxìde**
4. 马马虎虎地 **mǎmahūhūde**
5. 唠唠叨叨地 **láolaodāodāode**
6. 平平安安地 **píngpíng'ān'ānde**

ANSWERS:

1. 小明兴奋地告诉大家他考上大学了。
   Xiǎo Míng xīngfènde gàosu dàjiā tā kǎoshang dàxué le.
2. 对方干脆地接受了所有的条件。**Duìfāng gāncuìde jiēshòule suǒyǒude tiáojiàn.**
3. 老师很详细地解释了这个语法点。**Lǎoshī hěn xiángxìde jiěshìle zhèige yǔfǎ-diǎn.**
4. 看你那样马马虎虎地打扫房间，怎么能打扫干净呢?
   Kàn nǐ nàyàng mǎmahūhūde dǎsǎo fángjiān, zěnme néng dǎsǎo gānjìng ne?
5. 妈妈每天唠唠叨叨地劝小明努力学习，可是一点用都没有。
   Māma měitiān láolaodāodāode quàn Xiǎo Míng nǔlì xuéxí, kěshì yìdiǎn yòng dōu méiyǒu.
6. 我的期望不高，平平安安地过日子就好了。
   Wǒde qīwàng bù gāo, píngpíng'ān'ānde guò rìzi jiù hǎo le.

6.3 Describing the manner of an action in the negative

The principle discussed here applies to both the *verb complement* and the *adverbial* form. When describing actions or events in the negative, it is the manner in which the action takes place that is negated, not the action itself. And so the negative 不 **bù** or 没 **méi** are associated with the *verb complement* or the *adverbial* and not with the verb. This principle may seem self-evident, and yet non-native Chinese speakers often make grammatical errors by placing the negatives in the wrong place in the sentence, due to interference from their native language. Note how the negative in the English examples is placed on the verb and not on the adverb phrase.

♦ *He doesn't sing well. (✗ He sings not well)*
   ✓ 他唱歌唱得不好听。 **Tā chànggē chàngde bù hǎotīng.**
   ✗ 他唱歌不唱得好听。 **Tā chànggē bú chàngde hǎotīng.**
   ✗ 他不唱歌得好听。 **Tā bú chànggēde hǎotīng.**

♦ *That teacher doesn't teach in an interesting way. (✗ That teacher teaches uninterestingly.)*
   ✓ 那位老师讲课讲得没有意思。 **Nèiwèi lǎoshī jiǎngkè jiǎngde méiyǒu yìsi.**
   ✗ 那位老师不讲课讲得有意思。 **Nèiwèi lǎoshī bù jiǎngkè jiǎngde yǒuyìsi.**
   ✗ 那位老师不讲课得有意思。 **Nèiwèi lǎoshī bù jiǎngkède yǒuyìsi.**

◆ *If you don't sit quietly, the usher will make you go out.*

✓ 如果你不静静地坐着，带座员就会叫你出去了。

　Rúguǒ nǐ bú jìngjìngde zuòzhe, dàizuò-yuán jiù huì jiào nǐ chūqule.

✗ 如果你不坐着静静地，⋯。**Rúguǒ nǐ bú zuòzhe jìngjìngde, ...**

By putting on your Chinese thinking cap, you can easily avoid the above errors.

EXERCISES:

Translate the following sentences into Chinese:

1. After he left the hospital, he did not rest nicely, so he got sick again.

2. That professor doesn't speak too fast, and what he says is always very interesting.

3. The teacher doesn't explain things thoroughly enough in class, so we must read the textbook.

4. I didn't prepare well, so I did not do well on the exam.

ANSWERS:

1. 他出院以后没有好好儿地休息，所以又病了。
   Tā chūyuàn yǐhòu méiyǒu hǎohāorde xiūxi, suǒyǐ yòu bìngle.

2. 那位教授说话说得不太快，而且他说的总是非常有意思。
   Nèiwèi jiàoshòu shuōhuà shuōde bú tài kuài, érqiě tā shuōde zǒngshì fēicháng yǒuyìsi.

3. 老师在课上解释得不够详细，所以我们必须看课本。
   Lǎoshī zài kèshang jiěshìde búgòu xiángxì, suǒyǐ wǒmen bìxū kàn kèběn.

4. 我没有预备好，所以考试考得不好。 or ⋯，所以考试没考好。
   Wǒ méiyǒu yùbèi hǎo, suǒyǐ kǎoshì kǎode bù hǎo. or ... suǒyǐ kǎoshì méi kǎo hǎo.

6.4 Using *verb complements* to describe the *degree* of an adjective

In a sentence that uses an adjective to describe the subject, the adjective may in turn be modified by a *complement of degree*, such as *very*, *extremely*, etc. As discussed in 1.5, sec. A, adjectives in Chinese function much like verbs, and are therefore called "stative verbs" by Chinese grammarians. Thus, the *verb complement* form introduced in 6.1 may be applied to adjectives to indicate *degree*. This is a variant of the *verb complement* that we call *complement of degree*. The pattern of the complete sentence becomes:

Subj. + adjective 得 de + *complement of degree*

The *complement of degree* comes in a wide variety of forms, making this pattern highly versatile. Here are some examples:

- *busy to the degree of…*: 忙得 + *degree* ... **mángde** + *degree*

  very busy　　　　　　　　　　　忙得很 **mángde hěn**

  extremely busy　　　　　　　　　忙得不得了 **mángde bùdéliǎo**

inextricably busy	忙得不可开交 **mángde bùkě kāijiāo**
so busy that I can't stand it anymore	忙得我受不了了 **mángde wǒ shòu-bù-liǎo le**
so busy that there's not even time to eat	忙得连吃饭的时间都没有 **mángde lián chīfànde shíjiān dōu méiyǒu**

- *expensive to the degree of…*: 贵得 + *degree*… **guìde** + *degree*

very expensive	贵得很 **guìde hěn**
extremely expensive	贵得不得了 **guìde bùdéliǎo**
frightfully busy	贵得可怕 **guìde kěpà**
so expensive that no one can afford it	贵得没人买得起 **guìde méi rén mǎi-de-qǐ**
indescribably expensive	贵得无法形容 **guìde wúfǎ xíngróng**
so expensive that it cannot be paid off even in 30 years	贵得连三十年都付不完 **guìde lián sānshí-nián dōu fù-bù-wán**

The *complement of degree* in the last example in each group above involves the idiomatic sentence pattern "even… also … not …":

连…也…不/没…　　**lián…yě…bù/méi…**

More examples of this pattern are given in Part II of this book (#124).

EXERCISES:

Translate the following sentences into Chinese:

1. She is so happy that she started to cry.
2. I am so tired that I cannot even eat.

> **ANSWERS:**
> 1. 她高兴得哭起来了。**Tā gāoxìngde kū-qǐlai le.**
> 2. 我累得连饭都吃不下了。**Wǒ lèide lián fàn dōu chī-bu-xià le.**

6.5 Adding *degrees* to a *verb complement*

The *verb complement* form, which describes the manner or the result of an action, can be further modified by having a *complement of degree* added at the end of it. The entire sentence then becomes:

Subj. + verb 得 **de +** *verb complement* 得 **de +** *complement of degree*

If the verb takes an object, then the front part of the sentence becomes:

Subj. + (verb) + object + verb 得 **de +** *verb complement* 得 **de +** *complement of degree*

♦ *The teacher speaks fast.*
老师说话说得很快。**Lǎoshī shuōhuà shuōde hěn kuài.**
(*verb complement* describing the manner of an action)

♦ *The teacher speaks extremely fast.*
老师说话说得快得不得了。 or 老师说话说得快极了。
Lǎoshī shuōhuà shuōde kuàide bùdéliǎo. or Lǎoshī shuōhuà shuōde kuài-jíle.
(*verb complement* with *complement of degree*)

♦ *The teacher speaks so fast that no one can keep up with her.*
老师说话说得快得没有人跟得上。
Lǎoshī shuōhuà shuōde kuàide méiyǒu rén gēn-de-shàng.
(*verb complement* with extended *complement of degree*)

♦ *He writes Chinese beautifully.*
他中文写得很漂亮。**Tā Zhōngwén xiěde hěn piàoliang.**
(*verb complement* describing the result of an action)

♦ *He writes Chinese so beautifully that everyone thinks he's Chinese.*
他中文写得漂亮得大家都以为他是中国人。
Tā Zhōngwén xiěde piàoliangde dàjiā dōu yǐwéi tā shì Zhōngguórén.
(*verb complement* with extended *complement of degree*)

♦ *He speaks Chinese just like a Chinese.*
他中文说得简直跟中国人一样。
Tā Zhōngwén shuōde jiǎnzhí gēn Zhōngguórén yíyàng.
(*verb complement* describing the manner of an action)

♦ *He speaks Chinese so well that he sounds just like a Chinese.*
他中文说得好得简直跟中国人一样。
Tā Zhōngwén shuōde hǎode jiǎnzhí gēn Zhōngguórén yíyàng.
(*verb complement* with *complement of degree*)

As you can imagine, extended *complements of degree* often make a sentence too long. To mitigate that, the sentence is often broken up into two segments, as follows:

Subj. + **(verb)** + **object** + **verb** 得 de + *verb complement*, **adjective** + 得 de + *complement of degree*

♦ *The teacher speaks very fast, so fast that no one can keep up with her.*
老师说话说得非常快，快得没有人跟得上。
Lǎoshī shuōhuà shuōde fēicháng kuài, kuàide méiyǒu rén gēn-de-shàng.

♦ *He speaks Chinese extremely well, so well that he sounds just like a Chinese.*
他中文说得好极了，(好得)简直跟中国人一样。
Tā Zhōngwén shuōde hǎo-jíle, (hǎode) jiǎnzhí gēn Zhōngguórén yíyàng.

◆ *She cleans very well, so well that not even a speck of dust is left.*
她打扫得很干净，干净得连一点儿灰尘都没有。
Tā dǎsǎode hěn gānjìng, gānjìngde lián yìdiǎnr huīchén dōu méiyǒu.

EXERCISES:

Translate the following sentences into colloquial Chinese:

1. That person, when he talks, is awfully long-winded. (express "awfully" as a *complement of degree*)
2. That person talks so long-windedly that no one can stand it!
3. He drives extremely fast, so fast that everyone is afraid to ride in his car.

ANSWERS:
1. 那个人说话(说得)啰嗦得不得了。**Nèige rén shuōhuà (shuōde) luōsuōde bùdéliǎo.**
2. 那个人说话(说得)啰嗦得没有人受了。 or …啰嗦得大家都受不了。
   Nèige rén shuōhuà (shuōde) luōsuōde méiyǒu rén shòu-de-liǎo. or luōsuōde dàjiā dōu shòu-bu-liǎo.
3. 他开车开得非常快，快得大家都怕坐他的车。
   Tā kāichē kāide fēicháng kuài, kuàide dàjiā dōu pà zuò tāde chē.

6.6 Requesting that something be done in a certain manner

The polite way to request someone to do something is to always begin with 请你…
Qǐng nǐ…. *Excuse me, may I ask you to* …. A less polite way to make the request is to turn it into a question using the formula 你能不能…? **Nǐ néng-bunéng…?** *Could you* …? If it's a request to do something in a certain manner, then the following pattern is used, with 一点儿 **yìdiǎnr** at the end:

请你 **qǐng nǐ** or 你能不能 **nǐ néng-bunéng** + **verb** + **adj. (manner)** + 一点儿 **yìdiǎnr**

When the manner describes a <u>process</u> (rather than a result), the position of the verb may be reversed with the "adjective + 一点儿 **yìdiǎnr**," placed before the verb as follows:

请你 **qǐng nǐ** or 你能不能 **nǐ néng-bunéng** + **adj. (manner)** + 一点儿 **yìdiǎnr** + **verb**

◆ *Please come earlier tomorrow.*
请你明天早一点儿来。or 请你明天来早一点儿。
Qǐng nǐ míngtiān zǎo yìdiǎnr lái. or Qǐng nǐ míngtiān lái zǎo yìdiǎnr.

◆ *Can you come an hour earlier tomorrow?*
你明天能不能早一个钟头来? or 你明天能不能早来一个钟头?
Nǐ míngtiān néng-bunéng zǎo yíge zhōngtóu lái? or … zǎo lái yíge zhōngtóu?

♦ *Teacher, please speak a little more slowly.*
老师，请您慢一点儿说。or 老师，请您说慢一点儿。
Lǎoshī, qǐng nín màn yìdiǎnr shuō. or ... shuō màn yìdiǎnr.
(note use of 您 **nín** for extra politeness)

♦ *I can't hear you; can you speak a little louder?*
我听不见，你能不能大声一点儿说？ or
我听不见，你能不能说大声一点儿？
Wǒ tīng-bu-jiàn, nǐ néng-bunéng dàshēng yìdiǎnr shuō? or ...shuō dàshēng yìdiǎnr?

When the "manner" describes the desired result of an <u>action</u> (rather than the process), then only the first pattern may be used, i.e. the verb must precede the description. This word order is perfectly logical, as action always precedes result.

♦ *Can you explain it a bit more clearly?*
  ✓ 你能不能讲清楚一点儿？ **Nǐ néng-bunéng jiǎng qīngchǔ yìdiǎnr?**
  ✗ 你能不能清楚一点儿讲？ **Nǐ néng-bunéng qīngchǔ yìdiǎnr jiǎng?**

♦ *Please wash it a bit cleaner next time.*
  ✓ 请你下次洗干净一点儿。 **Qǐng nǐ xiàcì xǐ gānjìng yìdiǎnr.**
  ✗ 请你下次干净一点儿洗。 **Qǐng nǐ xiàcì gānjìng yìdiǎnr xǐ.**

Another acceptable variation of the pattern in which the verb precedes the description of manner is to add the particle 得 **de** after the verb. Literally, the word 得 **de** means *to attain*, which makes sense in this context, even though it sounds a bit redundant in English. It is not necessary for you to practice using this pattern, but you may hear it from native speakers. The following are all acceptable variations of the examples in the two preceding groups.

• 请你明天来得早一点儿。 **Qǐng nǐ mìngtiān láide zǎo yìdiǎnr.**
• 老师，请您说得慢一点儿。 **Lǎoshī, qǐng nín shuōde màn yìdiǎnr.**
• 我听不见，你能不能说得大声一点儿。
  Wǒ tīng-bú-jiàn, nǐ néng-bunéng shuōde dàshēng yìdiǎnr?
• 你能不能讲得清楚一点儿。 **Nǐ néng-bunéng jiǎngde qīngchǔ yìdiǎnr?**
• 请你下次洗得干净一点儿。 **Qǐng nǐ xiàcì xǐde gānjìng yìdiǎnr.**

Finally, when requesting that something be done in a certain manner, if the verb is followed by an object (*verb+object*), then the description of manner usually precedes the *verb+object* compound. But the alternative word order may also be used in certain cases (see the last two examples below). When in doubt, use the more conventional pattern.

♦ *Please come a bit earlier tomorrow.*
请你明天早一点儿来。or 请你明天来早一点儿。
Qǐng nǐ mìngtiān zǎo yìdiǎnr lái.   or   Qǐng nǐ mìngtiān lái zǎo yìdiǎnr.
(no object involved, so both word orders acceptable)

♦ *Please come to school a bit earlier tomorrow.* ("come to school" is a *verb+object* compound)
✓ 请你明天早一点儿来学校。 **Qǐng nǐ mìngtiān zǎo yìdiǎnr lái xuéxiào.**
✗ 请你明天来早一点儿学校。 **Qǐng nǐ mìngtiān lái zǎo yìdiǎnr xuéxiào.**
✗ 请你明天来学校早一点儿。 **Qǐng nǐ mìngtiān lái xuéxiào zǎo yìdiǎnr.**

♦ *Can you drive a bit more slowly?* ("drive a car" is a *verb+object* compound)
你能不能慢一点儿开？ or 你能不能开慢一点儿？ (the object 车 **chē**
is understood.)
Nǐ néngbùnéng màn yìdiǎnr kāi?   or   Nǐ néng-bunéng kāi màn yìdiǎnr?
✓ 你能不能慢一点儿开车？ **Nǐ néng-bunéng màn yìdiǎnr kāichē?**
✗ 你能不能开慢一点儿车？ **Nǐ néng-bunéng kāi màn yìdiǎnr chē?**
✗ 你能不能开车慢一点儿？ **Nǐ néng-bunéng kāichē màn yìdiǎnr?**

♦ *When you're with grandma (with poor hearing), please speak more loudly.*
✓ 跟奶奶在一起的时候，请你大声一点儿说话。
Gēn Nǎinai zài yìqǐde shíhou, qǐng nǐ dàshēng yìdiǎnr shuōhuà.
✓ 跟奶奶在一起的时候，请你说话大声一点儿。
Gēn Nǎinai zài yìqǐde shíhou, qǐng nǐ shuōhuà dàshēng yìdiǎnr.

♦ *There's a school nearby, please drive more carefully.*
✓ 附近有学校，请你小心一点儿开车。
Fùjìn yǒu xuéxiào, qǐng nǐ xiǎoxīn yìdiǎnr kāichē.
✓ 附近有学校，请你开车小心一点儿。
Fùjìn yǒu xuéxiào, qǐng nǐ kāichē xiǎoxīn yìdiǎnr.

♦ *There's a school nearby, one must drive more carefully.*
(The same idea can be expressed in Chinese by the topic-comment sentence, in
which 开车 **kāichē** is the topic.)
附近有学校，开车要小心一点儿。
Fùjìn yǒu xuéxiào, kāichē yào xiǎoxīn yìdiǎnr.

EXERCISES: ▶

Translate the following sentences into Chinese:

1. We're in a library (i.e. it's the library here); please talk more softly.
2. We're expecting company tonight; can you come home a bit earlier?
3. This paragraph is especially important. Please read it more thoroughly.

4. When it snows, one should drive more carefully!

5. We are foreign students, please speak a little more clearly.

ANSWERS:

1. 这里是图书馆，请小声一点儿说话。 or …，请说话小声一点儿。
   Zhèlǐ shì túshūguǎn, qǐng xiǎoshēng yìdiǎnr shuōhuà. or … , qǐng shuōhuà xiǎoshēng yìdiǎnr.

2. 我们今晚有客人，你能不能早一点回家?
   Wǒmen jīnwǎn yǒu kèrén, nǐ néng-bunéng zǎo yìdiǎn huíjiā?

3. 这段特别重要，请看得仔细一点儿。 or …，请仔细一点儿看。
   Zhèiduàn tèbié zhòngyào, qǐng kànde zǐxì yìdiǎnr. or …, qǐng zǐxì yìdiǎnr kàn.

4. 下雪的时候，得小心一点儿开车。 or …，开车得小心一点儿。
   Xiàxuěde shíhou, děi xiǎoxīn yìdiǎnr kāichē. or …, kāichē děi xiǎoxīn yìdiǎnr.

5. 我们是外国学生，请说清楚一点儿。
   Wǒmen shì wàiguó xuésheng, qǐng shuō qīngchǔ yìdiǎnr.

7 Conceptualizing Time Using 了 le

The English system of verb tenses does not exist in Chinese. Words and phrases used for indicating time—e.g. *this afternoon, next year, when I was in China*—are easily translated into Chinese, but the grammar built into the verb follows different systems in the two languages. In the Chinese linguistics mindset, there are no tenses such as *present, past* and *future*, and verbs in Chinese are not conjugated. Instead, a number of time-related words called *aspect markers* are tagged onto verbs to indicate concepts such as *completion, in process, sustained state, future action*, etc.

To understand the concept of *verb aspects* in Chinese, let's look at English tenses for a moment. Verb tenses in English indicate two kinds of information: 1) time: *present, past*, or *future*; and 2) an *aspect* of the action: *simple* (no specific aspect), *perfect* (completed), *progressive* (continuous), and *subjunctive* (conditional). For example:

- *I will be studying in China next year.* (future progressive tense)
- *He had not studied any Chinese before he arrived.* (past perfect tense)

For the purpose of understanding *verb aspects* in Chinese, it is not necessary for you to know how English tenses work. The above examples are intended only to help you understand the basic concept of aspect in verbs. Chinese *verb aspects* do not equate with those in English anyway, so trying to translate them from English will be misleading. Grammatically, *aspect* in English is part of the verb tense indicated by a verb conjugation, whereas in Chinese, *verb aspects* are expressed by a special class of *particles* that are called *aspect markers*.

Now let's return to the absence of tenses in Chinese. The English system of tense takes the present time as the main point of reference—and anything which happens before or after it must be indicated by a verb tense. The Chinese system of *verb aspects* on the other hand takes each event or action on its own, and the speaker shifts the point of reference to the time of that event or action. The visual parallel to these two types of time perspective can be illustrated by a Western painting with single-point perspective and a Chinese scroll painting that is unrolled as the viewer moves along the scroll. In Chinese speech or writing, the *present, past* or *future* is usually clear from context, or it may be irrelevant to the point of the sentence. In any case, the speaker/writer always has the option of using words and phrases to indicate time if time or sequence is important. Thus, the absence of indication for *present, past*, or *future* is not a deficiency but an efficiency. Embracing the Chinese *verb aspects* mindset—i.e. thinking like a native Chinese—is the key to expressing temporal concepts with ease and confidence in Chinese.

This chapter will discuss the particle 了 **le**, the most versatile and ubiquitous of the three common aspect markers. The other two—过 **guo** and 着 **zhe**—will be discussed in the next chapter.[1]

The aspect marker 了 **le** in modern Chinese is derived from an ancient morpheme 了 (pronounced **liǎo**), meaning *to finish, to be settled*. Traces of its original meaning can still be found in the two most prominent contemporary usages of this particle, which are discussed in 7.1 and 7.2.[2]

7.1 Using 了 le after an action verb to signify a completed action

English speakers are prone to equate the "completion" aspect of Chinese verbs with the past tense in English, which can lead to errors as will be shown below. The completion particle 了 **le** is used only with action verbs, because logically, only actions can be completed. For non-action verbs like 是 **shì** *to be*, 有 **yǒu** *to have*, 在 **zài** *to be located at*, or verbs referring to a state of mind (e.g. 想 **xiǎng** *to think*, 觉得 **juéde** *to feel*, 希望 **xīwàng** *to hope* and 愿意 **yuànyi** *be willing to*), and auxiliary verbs (e.g. 会 **huì** *to know how to* and 可能 **kěnéng** *may, might*), the notion of completion is illogical, and therefore 了 **le** cannot be used. However, another usage of 了 **le** is to indicate change, and this usage—to be discussed in 7.2—can be applied to any of these categories of verbs. These two different usages of 了 **le** are easily confused. Thus, to avoid confusion between them, we will use the terms *verb-ending* 了 **le** and *sentence-ending* 了 **le** when appropriate.

To indicate the completion of an action, the marker 了 **le** is tagged onto the verb immediately, like a suffix. If the verb has an object, the object comes after 了 **le**. As you read the following examples, take special note of why the translations marked by an "✗" are incorrect.

◆ *The whole class went.* (past tense in English)
全班学生都去了。 **Quánbān xuésheng dōu qùle.**
("completion of action" pattern in Chinese)

---

[1] Note that all three aspect markers are pronounced in neutral tone in standard Chinese.

[2] This footnote is of interest to Cantonese speakers only. The Cantonese counterparts to the two most prominent usages of 了 **le** present us with a conundrum. In Cantonese, the marker tagged onto a verb to indicate "completion of action" and the one tagged onto the end of a sentence to indicate "change" are represented by two different morphemes.

    Chinese: 他休息了三天就好了。 **Tā xiūxile sāntiān jiù hǎo le.**
               (the first 了 **le** indicates completion; the second 了 **le** indicates change)
    Cantonese: 佢休息咗三日就好啦。 **Keoi5 jau1sik1zo2 saam1jat6 zau6 hou2 laa3.**
    Chinese: 他一口气把那个大西瓜吃了。 **Tā yìkǒuqì jiù bǎ nèige dà xīguā chīle.**
               (the "verb 了" and the "sentence 了." are merged in Chinese.)
    Cantonese: 佢一口气将嗰个大西瓜食咗啦。
           Keoi5 jat1hau2hei3 zoeng1 go2go3 daai6 sai1gwaa1 sik6zo2 laa3.
We don't have an answer to this conundrum, but Cantonese speakers can easily distinguish the "verb 了" from the "sentence 了," because all they have to do is to translate the sentence into Cantonese.

- *Our family bought a car.*
  我们家买了一辆车。**Wǒmen jiā mǎile yíliàng chē.**
  ✗ 我们家买一辆车了。**Wǒmen jiā mǎi yíliàng chē le.**
  (This Chinese sentence is incorrect, because 了 le must be tagged onto the verb rather than after the object to indicate completion of action. See first example sentence in 7.2 for another correct variation of this sentence.)

- *I read that book twice.* (past tense in English)
  那本书，我看了两次。**Nèiběn shū, wǒ kànle liǎngcì.**
  ("completion of action" pattern in Chinese)
  ✗ 我看那本书了两次。**Wǒ kàn nèiběn shū le liǎngcì.**
  (Incorrect, because 了 le must immediately follow the verb 看 **kàn**)

- *He drank a little liquor tonight.* 今晚他喝了一点酒。**Jīnwǎn tā hēle yìdiǎn jiǔ.**

- *I went to see him yesterday.* 我昨天去看了他。**Wǒ zuótiān qù kànle tā.**

- *When I went to see him yesterday, he was not home.* (both verbs in past tense)
  我昨天去看他的时候，他不在家。**Wǒ zuótiān qù kàn tāde shíhou, tā búzài jiā.**
  ✗ 我昨天去看了他的时候，他不在家。
    Wǒ zuótiān qù kànle tā de shíhou, tā búzài jiā.
  (The point of the sentence is not the completion of an action, 了 le should not be used, despite the use of the past tense in English.)

- *I used to know how to sing that song.* (past tense)
  我从前会唱那首歌。**Wǒ cóngqián huì chàng nèishǒu gē.**
  ✗ 我从前会了唱那首歌。　　　✗ 我从前会唱了那首歌。
    Wǒ cóngqián huìle chàng nèishǒu gē.　　**Wǒ cóngqián huì chàngle nèishǒu gē.**
  (会 **huì** is not an action verb, it cannot be "completed," so 了 le should not be used)

- *What did you learn at school today?*
  你今天在学校学了什么？**Nǐ jīntiān zài xuéxiào xuéle shénme?**

EXERCISES:

Translate the following sentences into Chinese:
1. I worked in China for five years. During that time, I learned Chinese.
2. Which foreign language did you study in high school?
3. I learned the vocabulary in this lesson, and also listened to the recordings. But the teacher says it's still not enough!

ANSWERS:
1. 我在中国工作了五年；那时候我学了中文。
   Wǒ zài Zhōngguó gōngzuòle wǔnián; nà shíhou wǒ xuéle Zhōngwén.
2. 你在中学学了哪种外语？**Nǐ zài zhōngxué xuéle něizhǒng wàiyǔ?**

3. 我学了这一课的生词，也听了录音，可是老师说还不够！
Wǒ xuéle zhèyíkède shēngcí, yě tīngle lùyīn, kěshì lǎoshī shuō hái búgòu!

1. The negative form of the *verb-ending* 了 le.

There are two negatives in Chinese: 不 **bù** and 没 **méi**. The negative form of a verb indicating an action not completed in the past (i.e. the negative form of the *verb-ending* 了 **le**) is 没 **méi**,[3] which is always placed just before the verb (and 了 **le** is not used). Compare the positive and negative examples below:

◆ *We bought clothes, but not shoes.*
我们买了衣服，没买鞋子。**Wǒmen mǎile yīfu, méi mǎi xiézi.**
✗ 我们买了衣服，没买了鞋子。**Wǒmen mǎile yīfu, méi mǎile xiézi.**
(the negative is indicated by 没 **méi** alone, without 了 **le**)

◆ *We went, but didn't see her.*
我们去了，可是没看见她。**Wǒmen qùle, kěshì méi kànjian tā.**

◆ *I did not buy that book, I borrowed the library's copy.*
我没买那本书，我借了图书馆的。
Wǒ méi mǎi nèiběn shū, wǒ jièle túshūguǎnde.

◆ *I haven't bought the textbook for this course yet.*
我还没买这门课的课本。**Wǒ hái méi mǎi zhèimén kède kèběn.**
这门课的课本，我还没买。**Zhèimén kède kèběn, wǒ hái méi mǎi.**
(object stated as the topic of the sentence, see 1.3, sec. 1)

◆ *Both of those programs accepted me, but I haven't decided which one to attend yet.*
那两个项目都录取了我，可是我还没决定去哪个。
Nèi liǎngge xiàngmù dōu lùqǔle wǒ, kěshì wǒ hái méi juédìng qù něige.

EXERCISES:

Translate the following sentences into Chinese:

1. We had dinner, but did not drink any wine.
2. I studied French in high school, not Chinese (didn't study Chinese).
3. The plane has already landed, but he hasn't gotten off the plane yet.

ANSWERS:
1. 我们吃了饭，但是没喝酒。**Wǒmen chīle fàn, dànshi méi hē jiǔ.**
2. 我在中学学了法语，没学中文。**Wǒ zài zhōngxué xuéle Fǎyǔ, méi xué Zhōngwén.**
3. 飞机已经降落了，可是他还没下飞机呢。**Fēijī yǐjing jiàngluòle, kěshì tā hái méi xià fēijī ne.**

---

[3] 没 **méi** is also the negative form used with 有 **yǒu** "to have." Thus, this parallels the use of "to have" in the present progressive tense in English. But this parallel only applies to the negative, and we should not make too much of this parallel anyway. As mentioned before, it is misleading to equate Chinese verb aspects with aspects in English verbs.

2. Interrogative forms of the *verb-ending* 了 le.

In Chapter 3, we saw the many forms that interrogative sentences can take. All of those may be used together with the *verb-ending* 了 le. The pattern introduced in 3.1, sec. 1—forming a yes/no questions by adding 吗 ma at the end—needs no further explanation. However, the "positive/negative choice" pattern introduced in 3.1, sec. 2 has three different versions when used in conjunction with the *verb-ending* 了 le. Learning to use all the patterns below may take you out of your comfort zone, but it will definitely make you sound more colloquial and native.

Pattern	*Has she arrived?*	*Have you done it?*
verb + 了吗? verb + **le ma**?	她到了吗? **Tā dàole ma?**	你做了吗? **Nǐ zuòle ma?**
verb + 了没有? verb + **le méiyǒu**?	她到了没有? **Tā dàole méiyǒu?**	你做了没有? **Nǐ zuòle méiyǒu?**
verb + 了没? verb + **le méi**?	她到了没? **Tā dàole méi?**	你做了没? **Nǐ zuòle méi?**
有没有 + verb? **yǒu méiyǒu** + verb? (prevalent in Taiwan)	她有没有到? **Tā yǒu-méiyǒu dào?**	你有没有做? **Nǐ yǒu-méiyǒu zuò?**

When the verb has an object, the interrogative sentence using the "positive/negative choice" form can take on even more variations. One commonly used strategy is to make the object the topic of the sentence and mention it first.

♦ *Have you done today's homework?*
　你做了今天的功课吗? **Nǐ zuòle jīntiānde gōngkè ma?**
　你做了今天的功课没有? **Nǐ zuòle jīntiānde gōngkè méiyǒu?**
　你做了今天的功课没? **Nǐ zuòle jīntiānde gōngkè méi?**
　你有没有做今天的功课? **Nǐ yǒu-méiyǒu zuò jīntiānde gōngkè?**

Preposing 今天的功课 **jīntiānde gōngkè** as the topic:
　今天的功课, 你做了吗? **Jīntiānde gōngkè, nǐ zuòle ma?**
　今天的功课, 你做了没有? **Jīntiānde gōngkè, nǐ zuòle méiyǒu?**
　今天的功课, 你做了没? **Jīntiānde gōngkè, nǐ zuòle méi?**
　今天的功课, 你有没有做? **Jīntiānde gōngkè, nǐ yǒu-méiyǒu zuò?**

> **EXERCISES:**

Translate the following (using a different form for each sentence):
1. Have you read today's news?
2. Have you bought the plane ticket already?
3. Before you came to the U.S., had you learned to drive a car?

4. You don't feel well? Have you seen a doctor?

5. Yesterday you said your dog disappeared. Has it returned?

ANSWERS:

1. 你看了今天的新闻没有？ **Nǐ kànle jīntiānde xīnwén méiyǒu?**

2. 你已经买了飞机票了吗？ **Nǐ yǐjing mǎile fēijī-piào le ma?**

3. 来美国以前，你有没有学开车？ **Lái Měiguó yǐqián, nǐ yǒu-méiyǒu xué kāichē?**

4. 你不舒服吗？有没有去看医生呢？ **Nǐ bùshūfu ma? Yǒu-méiyǒu qù kàn yīshēng ne?**

5. 昨天你说你的狗不见了。它回来了没？
   Zuótiān nǐ shuō nǐde gǒu bújiàn le. Tā huílaile méi?

7.2 Using 了 le at the end of a sentence to signify a change of status

For simplicity, when we talk about 了 **le** at the end of a sentence, we include the end of a clause within a complex sentence. Because 了 **le** has a variety of usages, it is important to pay attention to its position within a sentence. The last section focused on the *verb-ending* 了 **le**, used for indicating the completion of an action. In this and the next section, we will focus on the *sentence-ending* 了 **le**.

The most prominent use of the *sentence-ending* 了 **le** is for signaling a change in status or the onset of a new situation. In English, this signaling function is frequently served by the word *now* (implicitly contrasting with "previously") or by the use of *anymore* when a sentence is in the negative. Unlike the limitation of the *verb-ending* 了 **le** being used only with action verbs, the *sentence-ending* 了 **le** may be used with all kinds of verbs—and even with adjectives (*stative verbs*)—to signal a change in status.

- *After I went to college, I bought a car.*
  我上大学以后，就买了一辆车了。
  Wǒ shàng dàxué yǐhòu, jiù mǎile yíliàng chē le.
  (implying a change from not having had a car before)

- *Sigh, I've gotten old!* 哎，我老了！ **Ài! Wǒ lǎo le!**
  (onset of old age, a change from my youthful self)

- *She became a full professor recently.*
  她最近当上正教授了。 **Tā zuìjìn dāngshang zhèng-jiàoshòu le.**

- *She is no longer my girlfriend.*
  她不是我的女朋友了。 **Tā búshì wǒde nǚpéngyou le.**

- *How come you don't love me anymore?* 你怎么不爱我了？ **Nǐ zěnme bú ài wǒ le?**

- *Old Zhang doesn't smoke anymore.*
  老张不抽烟了。 **Lǎo Zhāng bù chōuyān le.**
  (implying a change from before)

● *After my son went to college, I don't have money anymore.*
我的儿子上了大学以后，我就没有钱了。
Wǒde érzi shàngle dàxué yǐhòu, wǒ jiù méiyǒu qián le.

● *She has recovered from her illness.* 她的病好了。 **Tāde bìng hǎole.**

● *Everything has become expensive, but computers are getting cheaper.*
东西都贵了，可是电脑越来越便宜了。
Dōngxi dōu guì le, kěshì diànnǎo yuèláiyuè piányi le.

● *As soon as he heard the bad news, he became anxious.*
他一听到那个坏消息，就着急了。 **Tā yì tīngdào nèige huài xiāoxi, jiù zhāojí le.**

● *As soon as she heard the good news, she stopped crying.*
她一听到那个好消息，就不哭了。 **Tā yì tīngdào nèige hǎo xiāoxi, jiù bù kū le.**

● *I got to know her at that party.*
我在那个晚会上认识了她。 **Wǒ zài nèige wǎnhuì-shang rènshile tā.**
(认识 **rènshi** in this context is an action verb, meaning "to become acquainted with." It is used with the *verb-ending* 了 **le** to indicate completion of action.)

● *After that party, we became good friends.*
那次晚会以后，我们就成了好朋友了。
Nèicì wǎnhuì yǐhòu, wǒmen jiù chéngle hǎo péngyou le.
(both the *verb-ending* 了 **le** and the *sentence-ending* 了 **le** appear in this sentence.)

● *My company moved to China last year. My wife was unwilling to move to China, so we got a divorce.*
我的公司去年搬到中国去了，我太太不愿意搬去中国，结果我们离婚了。 **Wǒde gōngsi qùnián bāndào Zhōngguó qùle, wǒ tàitai bú yuànyi bānqu Zhōngguó, jiéguǒ wǒmen líhūnle.**

EXERCISES: ▶

Translate the following sentences into Chinese:

1. He started attending college when he was only 16. (onset of a new situation at age 16)
2. The car broke down, so we can't go now.
3. My kids have all grown up, so I have more time now.
4. After he went abroad, he no longer called me often anymore.
5. I used to know how to sing that song, but I don't anymore.

ANSWERS:
1. 他十六岁就上大学了。 **Tā shíliù-suì jiù shàng dàxué le.**
2. 车坏了，我们不能去了。 **Chē huàile, wǒmen bùnéng qù le.**

3. 我的孩子都大了，所以现在我的时间多一些了。
   Wǒde háizi dōu dà le, suǒyǐ xiànzài wǒde shíjiān duō yìxiē le.
4. 他出国以后，就不常给我打电话了。 **Tā chūguó yǐhòu, jiù bù cháng gěi wǒ dǎ diànhuà le.**
5 我从前会唱那首歌，现在不会了。 **Wǒ cóngqián huì chàng nèishǒu gē, xiànzài bú huì le.**

In all of the examples above, the change of status or the onset of a new situation sig-naled by the *sentence-ending* 了 le is something that has already occurred. But this usage of the *sentence-ending* 了 le may also apply to imminent events or situations. The notion of imminence is made explicit by adding 快 **kuài** *soon*, 要 **yào** *will*, or 快 要 **kuàiyào** *soon will* before the verb. Without the addition of 快 **kuài**, 要 **yào**, or 快 要 **kuàiyào**, and without context, a sentence that ends with a *sentence-ending* 了 le could be ambiguous.

- 老师来了。 **Lǎoshī láile.**
  can mean *The teacher has come.* or *The teacher is about to come.*
- 我们家的孩子上学了。 **Wǒmen jiāde háizi shàngxuéle.**
  can mean *Our child has started school.* or *Our child is about to start school.*

However, given the context of everyday speech, the *sentence-ending* 了 le, even with-out the addition of 快 **kuài**, 要 **yào**, or 快要 **kuàiyào**, is often sufficient to signal imminent change.

- *It's about to rain! Don't go out now.* (a change in plan)
  下雨了！别出去了！ **Xiàyǔle! Bié chūqu le!**
  (快要 **kuàiyào** may be added in front of 下雨了 **xiàyǔle**, but given the context, it would be unnecessarily wordy)
- *Come, we're about to eat!* 来，吃饭了！ **Lái, chīfànle!**
- *The plane is about to land.* 飞机快要下降了！ **Fēijī kuàiyào xiàjiàngle.**

EXERCISES:

Translate the following sentences into Chinese:
1. The semester is about to end, summer vacation is about to start!
2. One look and you'd know that her child is about to be born.
3. Don't worry, we're almost there.
4. It's about to get dark, let's hurry on home.

ANSWERS:

1. 学期快要结束了，暑假快开始了/快放暑假了。
   Xuéqī kuàiyào jiéshù le, shǔjià kuài kāishǐ le / kuài fàng shǔjià le.
2. 一看她就知道她的孩子快要出生了。 **Yí kàn tā jiù zhīdao tāde háizi kuàiyào chūshēng le.**
3. 别着急，我们快到了。 **Bié zhāojí, wǒmen kuài dào le.**
4. 天快黑了，我们赶快回家吧。 **Tiān kuài hēi le, wǒmen gǎnkuài huíjiā ba.**

7.3 Using the *sentence-ending* 了 le to signify other situations

1. Time lapse since an event or change has occurred.

The *sentence-ending* 了 le tagged onto a time-span indicates the time lapse since a certain event or change has occurred.

- *They've been married for three years now, but they don't have a child yet.*
  他们结婚三年了，还没有孩子呢。
  Tāmen jiéhūn sānnián le, hái méiyǒu háizi ne.

- *It's been five months since I graduated from college, but I haven't found a job yet.*
  我大学毕业五个月了，可是还没找到工作。
  Wǒ dàxué bìyè wǔge yuè le, kěshì hái méi zhǎodào gōngzuò.

- *He has quit smoking for five years now; he probably won't ever smoke again.*
  他戒烟五年了，大概不会再抽烟了。
  Tā jièyān wǔnián le, dàgài búhuì zài chōuyān le.

EXERCISES:

Translate the following sentences into Chinese:

1. It's been two weeks since he left home; we still have no news of him.
2. It's been a week since we finished our exams, but we still don't know our grades.

> **ANSWERS:**
> 1. 他离开家两个星期了，我们还没有他的消息。
>   **Tā líkāi jiā liǎngge xīngqī le, wǒmen hái méiyǒu tāde xiāoxi.**
> 2. 我们考完试一个星期了，可是还不知道我们的成绩。
>   **Wǒmen kǎo-wán-shì yíge xīngqī le, kěshì hái bù zhīdao wǒmende chéngjì.**

In 7.4, sec. 3, we will encounter the "time lapse" usage of the sentence-ending 了 le in combination with another usage of the marker 了 le, making it a double 了 le sentence.

2. The notion of "excessively, overly, extremely"

There are many ways to express the notion of "excessively, overly, extremely" in Chinese. Three words commonly used are 太… **tài**... *too...*, …极了 *...jíle ex-tremely...*, and …死了 *...sǐle ...to death*. The last one is used with negative situations more than positive situations. All three expressions are reinforced by the indispensable *sentence-ending* 了 le.

太大了	太贵了	太棒了	太不讲道理了	太没良心了
tài dà le	**tài guì le**	**tài bàng le**	**tài bùjiǎng dàolǐ le**	**tài méi liángxīn le**
too big	*too expensive*	*fantastic*	*too unreasonable*	*too unconscionable*

好极了	高兴极了	贵极了	冷极了
hǎo-jíle	**gāoxìng-jíle**	**guì-jíle**	**lěng-jíle**
excellent	*extremely happy*	*extremely expensive*	*extremely cold*

难听死了	气死了	脏死了	饿死了	乐死了
nántīng-sǐle	**qì-sǐle**	**zāng-sǐle**	**è-sǐle**	**lè-sǐle**
too hard on the ear	*extremely angry*	*extremely filthy*	*famished*	*extremely happy*

In a given context, a 了 **le** tagged onto an adjective can mean *too...* even without the explicit use of one of the above additional words.

◆ *This dish needs a tiny bit of sugar, but if too much, it won't taste good.*
这个菜得放一点点糖，<u>多了</u>就不好吃了。
Zhèige cài děi fàng yìdiǎndiǎn táng, duō le jiù bù hǎochī le.

◆ *Will you sell it for $10? If it's too expensive (more expensive than $10), then I won't buy it.*
十块钱你卖不卖？<u>贵了</u>我就不买了。
Shíkuài qián nǐ mài-bumài?Guì le wǒ jiù bù mǎi le.

EXERCISES:

Translate the following sentences into Chinese:

1. The dishes you make are extremely tasty!
2. The teacher's expectations of us are way too high!
3. This dress is too ugly! No one would buy it.
4. The milk can be kept only a week. If it's too long, it will go bad.

> **ANSWERS:**
> 1. 你做的菜好吃极了。**Nǐ zuòde cài hǎochī-jíle.**
> 2. 老师对我们的期望太高了！**Lǎoshī duì wǒmende qīwàng tài gāo le.**
> 3. 这件衣服难看死了，没有人会买。**Zhèijiàn yīfu nánkàn-sǐle, méiyǒu rén huì mǎi.**
> 4. 牛奶只能保留一个星期；久了就会坏。
>   **Niúnǎi zhǐ néng bǎoliú yíge xīngqī, jiǔ le jiù huì huài.**

3. Conveying the nuance of time in progress

In the Chinese mindset, time is never at a standstill. A sentence or clause expressing age or time usually carries the *sentence-ending* 了 **le** to convey the nuance of "progression in time," which may sometimes be translated by the English word *already*. This nuance is so subtle however that a native speaker often will not be able to explain what that 了 **le** means, although he will know that the sentence sounds incomplete without it.

◆ *Q: What time is it now? A: It's 8:00 (already).*
现在几点了？（现在）八点了。 **Xiànzài jǐdiǎn le? (Xiànzài) bādiǎn le.**

◆ *Mrs. Lin is 80 this year (already), but she is still in very good health.*
林太太今年八十了，身体还很好呢。
Lín Tàitai jīnnián bāshí le, shēntǐ hái hěn hǎo ne.

◆ *It's already after 7:00, why is he not home yet?*
已经七点多了，怎么他还没回来？
Yǐjīng qīdiǎnduō le, zěnme tā hái méi huílai?

The notion of "the time has come to (do something)" is expressed by a sentence containing two clauses. The first one states the time or age, the second one states the event or action that should take place now. Both clauses end in a *sentence-ending* 了 **le**. In the first clause, 了 **le** indicates that the time or age has "reached a certain point in its progression." In the second clause, 了 **le** signals the onset of a new situation.

◆ *It's 11:00 p.m. now, we should go to bed.*
十一点了，该睡觉了。 **Shíyīdiǎn le, gāi shuìjiào le.**

◆ *The kid is big now, he should be helping his parents at home now.*
孩子大了，在家该帮帮父母了。 **Háizi dàle, zàijiā gāi bāngbāng fùmǔ le.**

EXERCISES:

Translate the following sentences into Chinese:

1. Your baby is almost two now, has he started to talk?
2. You've been together for five years now, you ought to get married.

> **ANSWERS:**
> 1. 你的宝宝差不多两岁了，他开始说话了吗？
>   **Nǐde bǎobao chàbuduō liǎngsuì le, tā kāishǐ shuōhuà le ma?**
> 2. 你们在一起已经五年了，该结婚了吧。
>   **Nǐmen zài yìqǐ yǐjīng wǔnián le, gāi jiéhūn le ba.**

7.4 Using the *verb-ending* and *sentence-ending* 了 le together

1. When the *verb-ending* 了 le and *sentence-ending* 了 le are merged into one

If the *marker* 了 **le** appears at the end of a sentence, and the word preceding it is a verb, it might be either the *verb-ending* 了 **le** indicating completion of action or the *sentence-ending* 了 **le** indicating a change of status, or both of them merged into one. Out of context, the sentence "她走了 **Tā zǒule.**" may be interpreted as:

She has left. (completion of action as well as change of status)

She is about to leave. (imminent change)

With more context, the meaning becomes clear. In everyday speech, the context is often implicit. In the following examples, the context is made explicit:

♦ *She stayed here for three days, and left this morning.*
她在这里住了三天，今天早上走了。
Tā zài zhèlǐ zhùle sāntiān, jīntiān zǎoshang zǒule.
(The 了 **le** in the first clause indicates completion of action, the final 了 **le** merges completion of action with change of status.[4])

♦ *She arrived only yesterday, and she's leaving already tomorrow.*
她昨天才到，明天就走了。 **Tā zuótiān cái dào, míngtiān jiù zǒule.**
(imminent change, reinforced by 明天 **míngtiān**)

♦ *1) I have read that book. 2) I have read that book now.* (change from not having read it before)
那本书我看了。 **Nèiběn shū wǒ kànle.**
(The two English sentences are translated into one Chinese sentence, thus indicating that the 了 **le** is the *verb-ending* 了 **le** indicating completion of action, and may also be the *sentence-ending* 了 **le** indicating change of status.)

♦ *I didn't used to read Chinese books, now I do.*
我从前不看中文书，现在看了。
Wǒ cóngqián bú kàn Zhōngwén shū, xiànzài kàn le. (change of status)

♦ *I didn't see a doctor, just rested a few days and got well.*
我没看医生，休息了几天就好了。
Wǒ méi kàn yīshēng, xiūxile jǐtiān jiù hǎo le.
(The first 了 **le** indicates completion of action; the second one indicates change.)

♦ *You don't need to see a doctor, just rest a few days and you'll be well.*
你不必看医生，休息几天就好了。 **Nǐ búbì kàn yīsheng, xiūxi jǐtiān jiù hǎo le.**
(了 **le** indicates expected change.)

> **EXERCISES:**

A. Translate the following sentences into English and compare their meanings. What is the function of 了 **le** in each case?

1. 到美国的第一个月，我就学会了开车。
   Dào Měiguóde dìyīge yuè, wǒ jiù xuéhuìle kāichē.

2. 你十六岁了，可以学开车了。 **Nǐ shíliù-suì le, kéyǐ xué kāichē le.**

3. 我的眼睛不行了，晚上不能开车了。
   Wǒde yǎnjīng bùxíngle, wǎnshang bùnéng kāichē le.

---

[4] For the benefit of Cantonese speakers, and as a rejoinder to footnote #2 in this chapter: Since the *verb-ending* 了 **le** and the *sentence-ending* 了 **le** translate into two different aspect markers in Cantonese, the two are not merged. In other word, in Cantonese, this sentence would end with two aspect markers 咗啦 **zo2 laa3**.

B. Translate the following sentences into Chinese:

1. When I found out (knew) about that matter, it was already too late.

2. We recently bought a house, so we have no money for travels now.

2. Quantifying the completed portion of an action which is still in progress

By now, you are familiar with the "completion of action" aspect indicated by the *verb-ending* 了 **le**. If a sentence refers to an action *in process*, and states the portion that has been completed *so far*, then both the *verb-ending* 了 **le** and the *sentence-ending* 了 **le** are used. The *verb-ending* 了 **le** indicates completion of the action *so far*, the *sentence-ending* 了 **le** indicates that continuing change is expected. By logic, in this kind of double 了 **le** sentence, the object of the *verb-ending* 了 **le** (the 1st one) is always a quantity. The object of the action is not placed after the verb, but before it as the topic of the sentence (see the last example below). Compare the following three sentences:

♦ *He wrote a book.*
  他写了一本书。 **Tā xiěle yìběn shū.** (completion of action only)

♦ *He has written 100 pages (of a book in progress).*
  他写了一百页了。 **Tā xiěle yìbǎiyè le.**
  (completion of action, plus continuing change expected)

♦ *He wrote 100 pages of that book, then he passed away.* (no continuation of action expected)
  那本书，他写了一百页就去世了。 **Nèiběn shu, tā xiěle yìbǎiyè jiù qùshì le.**
  (The object is preposed. The *verb-ending* 了 **le** indicates completion of action. The *sentence-ending* 了 **le** indicates a change in status.)

As you read the following examples, can you explain the function of each 了 **le**?

♦ *He studied Chinese for two years when he was in college.*
上大学期间，他学了两年的中文。
Shàng dàxué qījiān, tā xuéle liǎngniánde Zhōngwén.

or 上大学期间，他学中文学了两年。
Shàng dàxué qījiān, tā xué Zhōngwén xuéle liǎngnián.

♦ *He has been studying Chinese for two years already, but he still can't read a newspaper.*
他学中文学了两年了，可是还不会看报呢。
Tā xué Zhōngwén xuéle liǎngnián le, kěshì hái búhuì kàn bào ne.

♦ *He studied Chinese for a year in college, now he can't say even a single sentence!*
他在上大学期间学了一年中文，现在连一句话都说不出来了！
Tā zài shàng dàxué qījiān xuéle yìnián Zhōngwén, xiànzài lián yíjù huà dōu shuō-bù-chūlai le.

♦ *You've had two bowls of rice already, do you still want more?*
你已经吃了两碗饭了，还要吃吗？
Nǐ yǐjīng chīle liǎngwǎn fàn le, hái yào chī ma?

♦ *He has already written 200 pages of that book, so (he) should be finishing soon.*
那本书他已经写了两百页了，应该快写完了。
Nèiběn shū tā yǐjīng xiěle liǎngbǎiyè le, yīnggāi kuài xiěwánle.

EXERCISES:

Translate the following sentences into Chinese:

1. You've been wearing this shirt for three days already; you should wash it!
2. She has already given birth to five children; she shouldn't have any more!
3. That movie is not interesting. I saw half of it and then left.
4. He's been in grad school for 10 years now, so he should be getting his Ph.D. soon.

ANSWERS:

1. 这件衬衫你已经穿了三天了，该洗了吧！
Zhèijiàn chènshān nǐ yǐjing chuānle sāntiān le, gāi xǐ le ba!
2. 她已经生了五个孩子了，不应该再生了！
Tā yǐjing shēngle wǔge háizile, bù yīnggāi zài shēng le!
3. 那个电影没有意思，我看了一半就走了。
Nèige diànyǐng méiyǒu yìsi, wǒ kànle yíbàn jiù zǒule.
4. 他读研究所已经读了十年了，应该快拿到博士了吧。
Tā dú yánjiūsuǒ yǐjing dúle shínián le, yīnggāi kuài nádào bóshì le ba.

3. Time lapsed since a change in status or completion of an action

This type of sentence states the amount of time that has passed since an event or action has occurred. An example in English is: *It's been two years since my mother passed away.* The *marker* 了 **le** is used twice in this type of sentence in Chinese. The first one indicates the completion of an action or the onset of a new situation (a change). The second one—at the end of the sentence—is appended to an amount of time, and reflects the Chinese mindset that time is always moving on (see the first paragraph under 7.3, sec. 3).

♦ *The elevator has already been out of order for three days now.*
电梯已经坏了三天了。 **Diàntī yǐjīng huàile sāntiān le.**

♦ *It's been two years since they had a child, but they still have no plan to get married.*
他们的孩子已经两岁了，可是他们还没有计划结婚。
Tāmende háizi yǐjīng liǎngsuì le, kěshì tāmen hái méiyǒu jìhuà jiéhūn.

♦ *It's been three months since I bought that book, but I still haven't found time to read it.*
我买了那本书三个月了，可是还没有时间看呢！
Wǒ mǎile nèiběn shū sānge yuè le, kěshì hái méiyǒu shíjiān kàn ne!

EXERCISES:

Translate the following sentences into Chinese:

1. It's been a week since he arrived in Beijing, but he hasn't started work yet.
2. The kid has been sick for three days now; it's about time you take him to see a doctor!
3. I've been with this company for 10 years, and my salary is still the same as it was 10 years ago!

ANSWERS:
1. 他到北京一个星期了，还没开始上班呢。
   Tā dào Běijing yíge xīngqī le, hái méi kāishǐ shàngbān ne.
2. 孩子已经病了三天了，你该带他去看医生了吧？
   Háizi yǐjing bìngle sāntiān le, nǐ gāi dài tā qù kàn yīshēng le ba?
3. 我在这个公司已经十年了，我的薪水还是跟十年以前一样！
   Wǒ zài zhèige gōngsī yǐjing shínián le, wǒde xīnshuǐ háishi gēn shínián yǐqián yíyàng!

4. Amount of time during which a certain action or situation has NOT occurred

A sentence stating the amount of time lapsed without an action or situation occurring also has a *sentence-ending* 了 le, again reflecting the Chinese mindset that time is always advancing. The idea here is that a certain amount of time has passed *up to the present*, and the situation is continuing. The position of the amount of time lapsed in a negative sentence is different from a positive sentence. In the positive sentence, it follows the verb, whereas in a negative sentence, it precedes the verb. The negative word used in the sentence is always 没 **méi** (see 7.1, sec. 1).

♦ *We have not seen each other for twenty years now!*
我们二十年没见面了。 **Wǒmen èrshí-nián méi jiànmiàn le.**

◆ *I have not slept for three days now!*
我三天没睡觉了。 **Wǒ sāntiān méi shuìjiào le.**

If a sentence contains an amount of time, but the focus of the sentence is not on the time lapse, then the notion of time "in progress" is irrelevant, and the *sentence-ending* 了 **le** is not applied.

◆ *I don't get hungry even if I don't eat for a whole day.*
我一整天不吃东西也不会饿。 **Wǒ yìzhěngtiān bù chī dōngxi yě búhuì è.**

◆ *Camels can go a week without drinking water.*
骆驼一个星期不喝水也没关系。 **Luòtuo yíge xīngqī bù hēshuǐ yě méiguānxi.**

◆ *That dog hasn't seen its master for 10 years, but still has not forgotten him.*
那只狗十年没看见它的主人，但是还没忘记他。
Nèizhī gǒu shínián méi kànjian tāde zhǔrén, dànshì hái méi wàngjì tā.

The following examples have the *sentence-ending* 了 **le**, but this does not imply time "in progress," but rather a change or the onset of a new situation brought about by the clause that contains the time lapse, i.e., the usage discussed in 7.2.

◆ *He hasn't come to class all week, perhaps he has dropped the course.*
他整个星期都没来上课，也许他不上这门课了。
Tā zhěngge xīngqī dōu méi lái shàngkè, yéxǔ tā bú shàng zhèimén kè le.

◆ *If you AWOL from class for three days, you will be expelled from the course.*
如果你三天不来上课，你就不能再上这门课了。
Rúguǒ nǐ sāntiān bù lái shàngkè, nǐ jiù bùnéng zài shàng zhèimén kè le.

◆ *If we don't drink water for a week, we will die.*
人如果一个星期不喝水，就会死了。
Rén rúguǒ yíge xīngqī bù hēshuǐ, jiù huì sǐle.

EXERCISES:

Translate the following sentences into Chinese:

1. I haven't been back to Beijing for three years now. It must have changed a lot!
2. If you don't return to China for a couple of years, you will see a lot of changes.
3. It's been two years that I've been out of a job. I think I should return to school to learn some new skills now.

ANSWERS:

1. 我三年没回北京了，一定有了很大的变化。
   Wǒ sānnián méi huí Běijīng le, yídìng yǒule hěn dàde biànhuà.
2. 如果你两年不回中国，会看到很多的变化。
   Rúguǒ nǐ liǎngnián bù huí Zhōngguó, huì kàndao hěnduōde biànhuà.

3. 我失业已经两年了/我已经两年没工作了，我应该想办法学一些新的技能了。
   Wǒ shīyè yǐjing liǎngnián le/Wǒ yǐjing liǎngnián méi gōngzuò le, wǒ yīnggāi xiǎng bànfǎ xué yìxiē xīnde jìnéng le.

7.5 Idiomatic usages of 了 le

These are some usages of 了 le that do not fall under any grammatical category, and they are best treated as idioms. Here are five of the most common ones. The first two occur at the beginning of an utterance, the latter two at the end.

1. 算了 **suànle** *forget it!* (see top of 2.2)

◆ *Forget it, I won't argue with you anymore.*
   算了，我不跟你吵了。**Suànle, wǒ bù gēn nǐ chǎo le.**
   (with a tone of irritated resignation or compromise)

2. 得了 **déle** *okay, okay* (reluctantly accepting an unpleasant situation)

◆ *Okay, okay, don't harp on it anymore!*
   得了,别再说了! **Déle, bié zài shuō le!**

3. ……罢了! **bàle** *and that's the end of it* (grudging acceptance)

   The etymology of this expression is clear from the original meaning of 罢 **bà**. In pre-modern Chinese, 罢 **bà** meant *to cease, to quit*. In modern Chinese, 罢 **bà** occurs mostly in compounds, such as 罢工 **bàgōng** *to go on strike* and 罢课 **bàkè** *to boycott a class*.

◆ *It's no big deal, I just won't go, and that's that.*
   没什么，我不去(就)罢了! **Méi shénme, wǒ búqù (jiù) bàle!**

4. ……就是了! **jiùshìle** *and that's all there is to it* (grudging resolution)

◆ *Don't pay any attention to him, and let it go at that.*
   你别管他就是了。**Nǐ bié guǎn tā jiùshìle**

5. 算了吧 **suànle ba** (a variation of 算了 **suànle** that is used in advising someone) (see 3.12, sec. 2)

◆ *Forget it, don't argue with him anymore. We'll just manage our own affairs and let it go at that.*
   算了吧，别跟他吵了，我们管自己的事就是了。
   Suànle ba, bié gēn tā chǎo le, wǒmen guǎn zìjǐde shì jiùshìle.

EXERCISES:

Make up a sentence using each of the five expressions introduced in this section. These are all favorite colloquial phrases with native speakers, so mastering their usage will definitely put a feather in your Chinese cap! Answers are not posted here, but try out your sentences on your Chinese friends.

7.6 Another use of 了 (pronounced liǎo) as a *resultative complement*

In the introduction to this chapter (top of p. 160), we mentioned the origin of 了 (pronounced **liǎo**) as a morpheme with the meaning *to finish, to be settled*. This archaic meaning is alive and well in modern Chinese, but it has morphed into a *resultative complement*, the subject of Chapter 12. We will defer further discussion to that chapter, but provide a "preview of coming attraction" in the examples below:

♦ *If you listen to me, you definitely can't go wrong.*
你听我的话，绝对错不了。 **Nǐ tīng wǒde huà, juéduì cuò-bu-liǎo.**

♦ *I originally thought teaching Chinese to American students would be easy. But I discovered that I'm not capable of doing that job, so I quit.*
我本来以为教美国学生汉语很容易，后来发现这个工作我干不了，所以不干了。
Wǒ běnlái yǐwéi jiāo Měiguó xuésheng Hànyǔ hěn róngyì, hòulái fāxiàn zhèige gōngzuò wǒ gàn-bù-liǎo, suǒyǐ bú gàn le.

EXERCISES:

Summary translation exercise for Chapter 7:

1. Last night, he ate a lot of hot (spicy) foods, so he's not feeling so hot today.
2. He didn't feel well last night, but now he's OK. (change)
3. This dish is too hot! (overly…)
4. I said that sentence three times, but he still doesn't understand what I mean.
5. When the American President came to China, he first went to Xi'an.
6. He said he read that book, but he actually didn't.

ANSWERS:

1. 昨天晚上他吃了很多辣的东西，所以今天不太舒服。
   Zuótiān wǎnshang tā chīle hěn duō làde dōngxi, suǒyǐ jīntiān bú tài shūfu.
2. 他昨天晚上不太舒服，可是今天好了。
   Tā zuótiān wǎnshang bú tài shūfu, kěshì jīntiān hǎo le.
3. 这个菜太辣了! Zhèige cài tài là le.
4. 那个句子，我说了三次，可是他还是没听懂我的意思。
   Neige jùzi, wǒ shuōle sāncì, kěshì tā háishi méi tīngdǒng wǒde yìsi.
5. 美国总统来中国的时候，先去了西安。
   Měiguó zǒngtǒng lái Zhōngguóde shíhou, xiān qùle Xī'ān.
6. 他说他看了那本书，其实他没看。 Tā shuō tā kànle nèiběn shū, qíshí tā méi kàn.

8 Other Verb Aspect Markers

Before we delve into the usage of 过 **guo** (neutral tone) as a *aspect marker*, a word about its etymology is in order. The word 过 **guò** (4th tone) is originally a verb, meaning *to pass, to cross,* as in 过马路 **guò mǎlù** *to cross the street.* It can also form part of bisyllabic verbs, as in 通过安检 **tōngguò ānjiǎn** *to pass through security check.* This original meaning of 过 **guò** is carried over into its function as an aspect marker.

As an *aspect marker,* 过 **guo** signifies that a certain action or event has already occurred. It differs from the *verb-ending* 了 **le** in that 过 **guo** signifies *experience,* while 了 **le** signifies *completion.* Hence, 过 **guo** can be called an *experiential marker.* To a native-English speaker, the difference may be very subtle, but these two pairs of examples should make the distinction clearer:

- 我们去了长城。 **Wǒmen qùle Chángchéng.** *We went to the Great Wall.* (Statement of where we went)

- 我们去过长城。 **Wǒmen qùguo Chángchéng** *We've been to the Great Wall before.* (At some point in the past, we have gone there.)

- 她快四十岁了，还没结婚呢。 **Tā kuài sìshí-suì le, hái méi jiéhūn ne.** *She''ll soon be 40, but has not gotten married yet.*

- 她快四十岁了，还没结过婚呢。 **Tā kuài sìshí-suì le, hái méi jié-guo-hūn ne.** *She''ll soon be 40, and has never been married before.*

Aside from signaling the aspect of *experience,* the marker 过 **guo** can also refer to routine actions or events and signal whether they have transpired within their usual time frame (clarification will be provided below in 8.1, sec.2).

Grammatically, the aspect marker 过 **guo** is similar to the *verb-ending* 了 **le**. Both of them are used mainly with action verbs. Both are tagged to the verb. If the verb has an object, the object is located after 过 **guo** or 了 **le**.

1. Using 过 guo to signify an experience of having done something

We will illustrate the usage of 过 **guo** as an *experiential marker* through various examples in positive, negative and interrogative sentences. Note that the negative version of this pattern is formed by adding 没 **méi** or 没有 **méiyǒu** in front of the verb, as follows:

Subject + 没（有）**méi (yǒu)** + **verb** + 过 **guo** (+ **object**)

- *Of course I have been to the Great Wall.*
  我当然去过长城。 **Wǒ dāngrán qùguo Chángchéng.**

- *I have never been to the Great Wall.*
  我从来没(有)去过长城。 **Wǒ cónglái méi(yǒu) qùguo Chángchéng.**

- *None of them have been to the Great Wall.*
  他们都没(有)去过长城。 **Tāmen dōu méi(yǒu) qùguo Chángchéng.**

- *Not all of them have been to the Great Wall.*
  他们不都去过长城。 **Tāmen bùdōu qùguo Chángchéng.**
  (compare the use of 没 **méi** vs 不 **bù** in expressing *none* vs *not all*)

- *The students have all seen movies by Zhang Yimou.*
  学生都看过张艺谋拍的电影。
  Xuésheng dōu kànguo Zhāng Yìmóu pāide diànyǐng.

  or 张艺谋拍的电影，学生都看过。
  Zhāng Yìmóu pāide diànyǐng, xuésheng dōu kànguo.
  (Preposing the object as the topic of the sentence is a favored pattern with native speakers, see 1.3, sec. 1.)

- *They have all seen that movie; only I have never seen it.*
  他们都看过那部电影，就我没看过。
  Tāmen dōu kànguo nèibù diànyǐng, jiù wǒ méi kànguo.

- *Due to China's population policy, many women have had abortions.*
  由于中国的人口政策，很多妇女都做过人工流产。
  Yóuyú Zhōngguóde rénkǒu zhèngcè, hěnduō fùnǚ dōu zuòguo réngōng liúchǎn.

- *One must have "eaten bitterness" before one can truly know the joy of life.*
  人要吃过苦才真正知道人生的乐趣。
  Rén yào chī-guo-kǔ cái zhēnzhèng zhīdao rénshēngde lèqù.

- *I have never experienced any bitterness to speak of, but I do know the joy of life!*
  我没吃过什么苦，可是知道人生的乐趣啊！
  Wǒ méi chīguo shénme kǔ, kěshì zhīdao rénshēngde lèqù a!

Interrogative sentences with the aspect marker 过 **guo** parallel those that involve the *verb-ending* 了 **le**, which we have discussed in 7.1, sec. 2. To avoid redundancy, we will not repeat the list of applicable patterns here, but illustrate them with examples. In 7.1, sec. 2, we noted that the "有没有…? **yǒu-méiyǒu…?**" interrogative form is prevalent only in Taiwan when the *verb-ending* 了 **le** is involved. In contrast, when the *aspect marker* 过 **guo** is involved, the "有没有…? **yǒu-méiyǒu…?**" interrogative form is the one most commonly used throughout China as well as in Taiwan.

◆ *Have you ever been to the Great Wall?*

你去过长城吗？ **Nǐ qùguo Chángchéng ma?**

你去过长城没有？ **Nǐ qùguo Chángchéng méiyǒu?**

你去过长城没？ **Nǐ qùguo Chángchéng méi?**

你有没有去过长城？ **Nǐ yǒu-méiyǒu qùguo Chángchéng?**

◆ *Have you ever had Peking duck?*

你有没有吃过北京烤鸭？ **Nǐ yǒu-méiyǒu chīguo Běijīng kǎoyā?**

◆ *I'm a vegetarian, so of course I have never had Peking duck!*

我不吃肉，所以当然没吃过北京烤鸭！
Wǒ bù chīròu, suǒyǐ dāngrán méi chīguo Běijīng kǎoyā!

◆ *Have you ever told a lie?* 你有没有说过谎？ **Nǐ yǒu-méiyǒu shuō-guo-huǎng?**

◆ *Yes, but only once.* 有，可是只说过一次。 **Yǒu, kěshì zhǐ shuōguo yícì.**

◆ *Truth to tell, I have never told a lie!*

说真的，我从来没说过谎。 **Shuō zhēnde, wǒ cónglái méi shuō-guo-huǎng.**

◆ *Have you ever seen a Shakespearean play?*

你有没有看过莎士比亚的话剧？ **Nǐ yǒu-méiyǒu kànguo Shāshìbǐyà-de huàjù?**

◆ *I have read many Shakespearean plays, but I have never seen one on stage.*

莎士比亚写的话剧，我读过很多；可是台上演的，我从来没看过。
Shāshìbǐyà xiěde huàjù, wǒ dúguo hěnduō, kěshì táishang yǎnde, wǒ cónglái méi kànguo.
(Note usage of the preferred "topic-comment" pattern)

◆ *He's been married three times, and also divorced three times.*

他结过三次婚，也离过三次婚。 **Tā jiéguo sāncì hūn, yě líguo sāncì hūn.**

◆ *He has never been to China, how can he claim to be a China expert?*

他从来没去过中国，怎么能说自己是个中国通呢？
Tā cónglái méi qùguo Zhōngguó, zěnme néng shuō zìjǐ shì ge Zhōngguó-tōng ne?

EXERCISES:

Translate the following sentences into Chinese:

1. He has never formally taken any Chinese courses, but he speaks Chinese beautifully!

2. Have you ever heard a Cantonese speak Chinese? I heard that they have a strong accent.

3. Have you ever spanked your child? Never, but I have scolded him many times.

ANSWERS:

1. 他没正式上过中文课，可是他的中文说得很漂亮！
   Tā méi zhèngshì shàngguo Zhōngwén-kè, kěshì tāde Zhōngwén shuōde hěn piàoliang!

2. 你有没有听过广东人说普通话？听说他们有很重的口音。
   Nǐ yǒu-méiyǒu tīngguo Guǎngdōng-rén shuō pǔtōnghuà? Tīngshuō tāmen yǒu hěnzhòngde kǒuyīn.

3. 你有没有打过你的孩子？从来没有，可是我骂过他很多次。
   Nǐ yǒu-méiyǒu dǎguo nǐde háizi? Cónglái méiyǒu, kěshì wǒ màguo tā hěnduō cì.

2. Using 过 guo to signify having gone through a routine activity or event

When the aspect marker 过 guo is applied to an event or activity that occurs regularly at certain times—such as meals (daily), listening to recordings (with every lesson), arrival of mail (daily), and final exams (every semester)—it obviously does not indicate *experience* per se. What it does indicate is that a routine activity or event has occurred.

A word of caution: In the English speaker's mindset, there is a linguistic groove for the idea of *having had the <u>experience</u> of something before* (which is expressed by the *experiential* function of 过 guo), but there is no such groove for *having gone through a routine process*. So native-English speakers are prone to use the *verb-ending* 了 le where 过 guo would be more appropriate.

- *Have you eaten?* 你吃过了吗？ **Nǐ chīguole ma?**
  (A favorite Chinese greeting in the bad old days when regular meals were not taken for granted. This greeting seems to have fallen out of style.)

- *Has the mailman come today?*
  ✓ 今天邮差来过没有？ **Jīntiān yóuchāi láiguo méiyǒu?**
  ✗ 今天邮差来了没有？ **Jīntiān yóuchāi láile méiyǒu?**
  (Since the arrival of mail is a daily occurrence, 过 guo should be used rather than 了 le)

- *I have not read today's paper yet, please don't discard it.*
  今天的报纸我还没看(过)，请别扔掉哦！
  Jīntiānde bàozhǐ wǒ hái méi kàn(guo), qǐng bié rēngdiào ó!

- *He takes a walk every night after dinner.*
  他每天吃过晚饭都要出去散散步。
  Tā měitiān chī-guo-wǎnfàn dōu yào chūqu sànsànbù.

- *It's end of December already, and we still haven't had a snow yet this year.*
  已经十二月底了，今年还没下过雪呢。
  Yǐjīng shíèryuè-dǐ le, jīnnián hái méi xià-guo-xuě ne.

EXERCISES:

Translate the following sentences into Chinese:

1. We have not had any rain yet this month.
2. I have checked all the students' homework this week.
3. Have you read over the vocabulary and grammar in this lesson?

> **ANSWERS:**
> 1. 这个月还没下过雨。**Zhèige yuè hái méi xiàguo yǔ.**
> 2. 学生这个星期的作业，我都看过了。**Xuésheng zhèige xīngqīde zuòyè, wǒ dōu kànguo le.**
> 3. 这一课的生词和语法，你看过了吗？
>   **Zhèiyíkède shēngcí hé yǔfǎ, nǐ kànguo le ma?**

3. Combining two aspect markers—过 guo and 了 le—in the same sentence

When 过 **guo** and 了 **le** are both used after a verb, the idea of having gone through something (either as an *experience* or as a *routine*) is coupled with the idea of *completion*. This may seem redundant, but the marker 了 **le** conveys the nuance of having done something *thoroughly* (completely) rather than casually.

◆ *I have discussed that matter with my parents, but they didn't express any opinion.*
我和父母讨论过那件事，但是他们并没表示什么意见。
Wǒ hé fùmǔ tǎolùnguo nèijiàn shì, dànshì tāmen bìng méi biǎoshì shénme yìjiàn.
(The discussion with parents may have been casual or even perfunctory.)

◆ *After I had discussed that matter with my parents, I felt much better.*
我和父母讨论过了那件事，心里就舒服多了。
Wǒ hé fùmǔ tǎolùnguole nèijiàn shì, xīnlǐ jiù shūfu duōle.
(了 **le** in the first clause indicates that the discussion was thorough, and at the end of the sentence it indicates a change in status.)

◆ *Little Wang never discussed that matter with his parents, and just made the decision himself.*
小王没和他父母讨论过那件事就自己做了决定。
Xiǎo Wáng méi hé tā fùmǔ tǎolùnguo nèijiàn shì jiù zìjǐ zuòle juédìng.

◆ *I've read that book, but don't remember much of it anymore.*
我看过那本书，可是记不得多少了。
Wǒ kànguo nèiběn shū, kěshì jì-bu-de duōshǎo le.

◆ *It was only after I read that book that I came to have a little understanding about Tibet.*
我看过了那本书，才对西藏有了一点儿了解。
Wǒ kànguole nèiběn shū, cái duì Xīzàng yǒule yìdiǎnr liǎojiě.
(了 **le** in the first clause indicates that the reading was thorough. 有了 **yǒule** means *to have acquired*. 了解 **liǎojiě** means *to understand*.)

♦ *I told him about that matter, but he forgot.*

 1)我跟他说过那件事，可是他忘了。

 Wǒ gēn tā shuōguo nèijiàn shì, kěshì tā wàngle.

 (说过 **shuōguo** could just mean *to mention*, so it's not surprising that he forgot.)

 2)我跟他说过了那件事，可是他忘了。

 Wǒ gēn tā shuōguole nèijiàn shì, kěshì tā wàngle.

 (说过了 **shuōguole** means *talked through*, so it's regrettable that he forgot.)

When 过 **guo** and the *sentence-ending* 了 **le** are used in the same sentence, the idea of having gone through something (either as an *experience* or as a *routine*) is coupled with the idea of a change in status. This nuance conveyed by the *sentence-ending* 了 **le** may be very subtle, perhaps too subtle for non-native speakers, but the sentence without the 了 **le** would sound incomplete to a native-speaker.

♦ *You've already brushed your teeth tonight, so can't eat candy anymore!*

 你今晚已经刷过牙了，不能再吃糖了！

 Nǐ jīnwǎn yǐjīng shuā-guo-yá le, bùnéng zài chī táng le.

 (both occurrences of 了 **le** indicate change of status)

♦ *Are final exams over yet? If they are over, I'd like to ask you to come help me.*

 大考考过了吗？如果考过了，我想请你来帮忙。

 Dàkǎo kǎoguole ma? Rúguǒ kǎoguole, wǒ xiǎng qǐng nǐ lái bāngmáng.

 (both occurrences of 了 **le** indicate a change of status)

Another type of situation in which 过 **guo** is used in conjunction with the *sentence-ending* 了 **le** is to quantify a certain experience that may still be *in progress*, hinting that it may recur. This is parallel to the situation described in 7.4, sec. 2, in which the completed portion of an *action in progress* is being quantified.

♦ *He was divorced twice.* 他离过两次婚。 **Tā líguo liǎngcì hūn.**

 (simple statement of the number of divorces that he has gone through)

♦ *He has been divorced twice.*

 他已经离过两次婚了。 **Tā yǐjīng líguo liǎngcì hūn le.**

 (carries a slight hint that two divorces may not be the end of it)

♦ *I've gone twice, and have not been able to find him.*

 我去过两次，都没找到他。 **Wǒ qùguo liǎngcì, dōu méi zhǎodào tā.**

♦ *I've gone twice already, you want me to go again?*

 我去过两次了，你还要我再去吗？ **Wǒ qùguo liǎngcì le, nǐ hái yào wǒ zài qù ma?**

EXERCISES:

A. Translate the following sentences into English. As you read these sentences, try to figure out the nuances being conveyed by the aspect markers 了 **le** and 过 **guo**.

1. 别客气，我已经吃过晚饭了。 **Bié kèqi, wǒ yǐjīng chīguo wǎnfàn le.**

2. 他们结婚已经三十多年了，从来没吵过架。
   Tāmen jiéhūn yǐjīng sānshíduō-nián le, cónglái méi chǎoguo jià.

3. 他小时候在家里没做过家务事，后来结了婚才学会了。
   Tā xiǎo shíhou zài jiālǐ méi zuòguo jiāwùshì, hòulái jié-le-hūn cái xuéhuì le.

4. 在北京的人多半没去过台湾，可是他们很喜欢吃台湾菜。
   Zài Běijīngde rén duōbàn méi qùguo Táiwān, kěshì tāmen hěn xǐhuan chī Táiwān cài.

5. 我从前没考虑过童年对我的一生有什么影响，现在我才知道影响太大了。 **Wǒ cóngqián méi kǎolùguo tóngnián duì wǒde yìshēng yǒu shénme yǐngxiǎng, xiànzài wǒ cái zhīdao yǐngxiǎng tài dà le.**

6. 宝宝拉过大便了没有？没有，他三天没拉大便了！
   Bǎobao lāguo dàbiàn le méiyǒu? Méiyǒu, tā sāntiān méi lā dàbiàn le.

7. 在文革期间，他被下放到了新疆去劳改，真正吃过了很多苦。
   Zài Wén-Gé qījiān, tā bèi xiàfàng-dàole Xīnjiāng qù láogǎi, zhēnzhèng chīguole hěn duō kǔ.

8. 他这一辈子写过十几本书，教过几千个学生，却没恋爱过。
   Tā zhè yíbèizi xiěguo shíjǐběn shū, jiāoguo jǐqiānge xuésheng, què méi liàn'ài guo.

9. 他已经写过十几本小说了，但是肚子里还有不少没写出来的故事。
   Tā yǐjīng xiěguo shíjǐběn xiǎoshuō le, dànshì dùzi-li háiyǒu bùshǎo méi xiě-chūláide gùshi.

10. 医生已经试过了很多不同的药了，可是还没找到一种能治这种病的。
    Yīshēng yǐjīng shìguole hěn duō bùtóngde yào le, kěshì hái méi zhǎodào yìzhǒng néng zhì zhèizhǒng bìngde.

ANSWERS:

1. No need to be polite, I've already had dinner.

2. They've been married for over thirty years, and have never had a fight.

3. When he was young, he never did any housework at home, he learned only after he was married.

4. Most people in Beijing have never been to Taiwan, but they like Taiwanese food very much.

5. I had never before considered the influence my childhood had on my life. Only now did I realize how tremendous that influence was.

6. Has the baby had his bowel movement yet? No, he hasn't had one for three days now!

7. During the Cultural Revolution, he was sent to Xinjiang for labor reform, so he has truly experienced a great deal of hardship.

8. He has written over ten books in his life, and had taught several thousand students, but has never been in love.

9. He has already written over ten novels, but he has many more stories in his "belly" that he hasn't written yet.

10. The doctor has already tried many different medicines, but still hasn't found one that can cure this kind of illness.

B. Translate the following sentences into Chinese:

1. She has never been married, but she has had several boyfriends.
2. He has attended college for several years, but has not graduated.
3. He has done many different things in his life. He has been a teacher, a doctor, and a musician. Now he only wants to be a traveler.
4. She had never flown in an airplane before she was 80 years old.
5. Fifty years ago, few college students had gone abroad. Nowadays, almost all college students have studied abroad before graduation.

ANSWERS:
1. 她从来没结过婚，可是有过几个男朋友。
Tā cónglái méi jié-guo-hūn, kěshì yǒuguo jǐge nánpéngyou.
2. 他上过几年大学，可是还没有毕业。Tā shàngguo jǐnián dàxué, kěshì hái méiyǒu bìyè.
3. 他这一生做过很多不同的事，当过老师、医生和音乐家。现在他只想当一个旅行者。Tā zhè yìshēng zuòguo hěnduō bùtóngde shì, dāngguo lǎoshī, yīshēng, hé yīnyuè-jiā. Xiànzài tā zhǐ xiǎng dāng yíge lǚxíng-zhě.
4. 她八十岁以前没有坐过飞机。Tā bāshí-suì yǐqián méiyǒu zuòguo fēijī.
5. 五十年前，很少有大学生出过国。现在差不多所有的大学生在毕业以前都留过学。Wǔshí-nián qián, hěnshǎo yǒu dàxuésheng chū-guo-guó. Xiànzài chàbuduō suǒyǒude dàxuésheng zài bìyè yǐqián dōu liú-guo-xué.

8.2 Using the aspect marker 着 zhe to indicate an ongoing action

Some Chinese language textbooks call 着 **zhe** the "progressive aspect marker," which may mislead students into believing that it is equivalent to the progressive tense (*-ing*) in English. In reality, 着 **zhe** is applicable only in some of the situations that call for the progressive tense in English. We will start with some examples in this introduction, then analyze the various situations in which 着 **zhe** is used or not used. Note that in the first five examples that follow, the progressive tense in English is not translated using 着 **zhe** in Chinese.

♦ *We are in the midst of having dinner.*
我们正在吃饭。**Wǒmen zhèngzài chīfàn.**

♦ *The students are still taking an exam, please wait outside.*
学生还在考试，请你们在外头等着。
Xuésheng hái zài kǎoshì, qǐng nǐmen zài wàitou děngzhe.
(Note the use of 着 **zhe** in 等着 **děngzhe**, where the English equivalent is not in the progressive tense.)

- *It started _raining_ when we were _walking_ to school.*
  我们去学校的路上，开始下雨了(or 下起雨来了)。
  Wǒmen qù xuéxiàode lùshang, kāishǐ xiàyǔ le (or xià-qǐ-yǔ lái le).

- *I was still _studying_ in college when my mother passed away.*
  我还在读大学的时候，我母亲就去世了。
  Wǒ hái zài dú dàxuéde shíhou, wǒ mǔqin jiù qùshì le.

- *That painting is _hanging_ in the living room.*
  那幅画挂在客厅里。**Nèifú huà guàzài kètīnglǐ.**

- *Their family photo is _hanging_ on the wall of the living room.*
  (On the wall of the living room is _hanging_ their family photo.)
  客厅的墙上挂着他们全家的照片。
  Kètīngde qiángshang guàzhe tāmen quánjiāde zhàopiàn.

- *A photo of his kids is _sitting_ on the bookshelf.*
  书架上摆着他孩子的照片。**Shūjià-shang bǎizhe tā háizide zhàopiàn.**

- *He is _lying_ on the bed, as though he is _thinking_ about something.*
  他在床上躺着，好像在想(着)什么似的。
  Tā zài chuángshang tǎngzhe, hǎoxiàng zài xiǎng(zhe) shénme shìde.

- *We should be _standing_ when _singing_ the national anthem.*
  我们应该站着唱国歌。**Wǒmen yīnggāi zhànzhe chàng guógē.**

1. Using the aspect marker 着 zhe to signal an ongoing or "sustained" state

The aspect marker 着 **zhe** is used to call special attention to an ongoing or "sustained" state. When something is still "in progress," but its ongoing state is not the main focus of the sentence, the marker 着 **zhe** is *not* used. This is illustrated by the first five examples above. Below are examples of cases when the marker 着 **zhe** IS used to emphasize the ongoing nature of an action:

- *The restaurant is full, we have to wait outside.*
  餐馆里坐满了人，我们得在外头等着。
  Cānguǎnlǐ zuò-mǎnle rén, wǒmen děi zài wàitou děngzhe.
  (The point is, "waiting outside" may have to be sustained for a while.)

- *I was thinking and thinking, and unknowingly I fell asleep.*
  我想着想着，不知不觉地睡着了。
  Wǒ xiǎngzhe xiǎngzhe, bùzhī-bùjuéde shuìzháo le.

- *They are sitting in the coffee shop waiting for their friends.*
  他们在咖啡馆坐着等朋友。**Tāmen zài kāfēiguǎn zuòzhe děng péngyǒu.**

♦ *As we were waiting for her, she called to say she couldn't come today.*
我们在等(着)她的时候，她来电话说今天不能来了。
Wǒmen zài děng(zhe) tāde shíhou, tā lái diànhuà shuō jīntiān bùnéng lái le.
(着 **zhe** is optional in this sentence, depending on whether the speaker chooses to focus on the sustained state of waiting.)

The sustained state—expressed by 着 **zhe**—may be a state achieved as the *result* of an action rather than referring to the action itself.

♦ *A family photo is <u>hanging</u> on the wall.*
墙上挂着他们全家的照片。 **Qiángshang guàzhe tāmen quánjiāde zhàopiàn.**
(Hanging a photo is a one-time act, the *result* is an ongoing state of the photo hanging on the wall.)

♦ *I was <u>hanging</u> pictures in the living room, when a phone call came.*
我正在客厅挂画的时候，有人打电话来了。
Wǒ zhèngzài kètīng guà huàde shíhou, yǒurén dǎ diànhuà lái le.
(The above sentence is *not* about the sustained state of hanging pictures, therefore 着 **zhe** is not used). See 8.2, sec. 3 about the use of 正在 **zhèngzài**.)

♦ *The teacher couldn't come to class today, but the vocabulary and grammar to be practiced today are written on the board.*
老师今天不能来上课，可是黑板上写着今天要练习的生词和句型。
Lǎoshī jīntiān bùnéng lái shàngkè, kěshì hēibǎn-shang xiězhe jīntiān yào liànxíde shēngcí hé jùxíng.

EXERCISES:

A. Translate the following sentences into English, then explain the usage of 着 **zhe** in each sentence:

1. 请你在这儿等着，我去一下厕所，马上就回来。
   Qǐng nǐ zài zhèr děngzhe, wǒ qù yíxià cèsuǒ, mǎshàng jiù huílai.

2. 我在路上走着走着，忽然想起童年的事情来了。
   Wǒ zài lùshang zǒuzhe zǒuzhe, hūrán xiǎng-qǐ tóngniánde shìqing láile.

3. 你是看着他长大的，应该知道他童年的很多事情吧？
   Nǐ shì kànzhe tā zhǎngdà de, yīnggāi zhīdao tā tóngniánde hěn duō shìqing ba?

4. 我一个人在国外的时候，书桌上放着我家人的照片，那样我就不想家了。
   Wǒ yíge rén zài guówàide shíhou, shūzhuō-shang fàngzhe wǒ jiārénde zhàopiàn, nàyàng wǒ jiù bù xiǎngjiā le.

ANSWERS:
In all these cases, the aspect marker 着 **zhe** indicates a sustained state.
1. Please wait here, I'm going to the restroom and will be back shortly.

2. I was just walking along, and suddenly thought of things from my childhood.

3. You've watched him grow up, so you should know a lot about his childhood, right?

4. When I was abroad, I kept my family's photo on my desk, that way I avoided getting homesick.

B. Translate the following sentences into Chinese:

1. A Chinese painting is hanging on the wall.

2. At the airport, you must keep an eye on your luggage.

ANSWERS:
1. 墙上挂着一幅国画。 **Qiángshang guàzhe yìfú guóhuà.**
2. 在机场，你必得看着你的行李。 **Zài jīchǎng, nǐ bìděi kānzhe nǐde xínglǐ.**
   (**Note**: 看 is pronounced in the 1st tone when it means "watch over.")

---

2. Using 着 zhe in a sentence that involves two concurrent activities

When two activities of equal significance are going on concurrently, the pattern "一边…，一边… **yìbiān…, yìbiān…**" is used (see Part II, #190). However, if one of the activities is going on in the "background" while the main activity is proceeding, then the "background activity" is expressed as an ongoing state using the aspect marker 着 **zhe**. This is illustrated by the last two sentences in 8.2, just before section 1 on p. 185. Here are additional examples:

- *She is managing her family and working at the same time, so she is exhausted every day.* (The two activities are of equal importance.)
  她一边管家一边上班，所以每天都很累。
  Tā yìbiān guǎnjiā yìbiān shàngbān, suǒyǐ měitiān dōu hěn lèi.

- *He likes to listen to classical music while doing homework.*
  他喜欢一边听古典音乐，一边做功课。
  Tā xǐhuan yìbiān tīng gǔdiǎn yǐnyuè, yìbiān zuò gōngkè.
  他喜欢听着古典音乐做功课。 **Tā xǐhuan tīngzhe gǔdiǎn yǐnyuè zuò gōngkè.**
  (The first version implies that his focus is equally divided between the two activities. The second one implies that the music is going on in the background while he focuses on his homework.)

- *Prof. Zhang is not in good health, so he has to sit while lecturing.*
  张教授身体不好，所以得坐着讲课。
  Zhāng Jiàoshòu shēntǐ bù hǎo, suǒyǐ děi zuòzhe jiǎngkè.

- *Nowadays many families watch TV while they eat, thus they have lost an opportunity to communicate.*
  现在有不少家庭都看着电视吃饭，这样就失去了沟通的机会。
  Xiànzài yǒu bùshǎo jiātíng dōu kànzhe diànshì chīfàn, zhèyàng jiù shīqùle gōutōng-de jīhuì.

◆ *There's not enough time now, so let's talk about this as we walk.*
时间不够了，我们走着谈这件事吧。
Shíjiān búgòule, wǒmen zǒuzhe tán zhèijiàn shì ba.

EXERCISES:

Translate the following sentences into Chinese:

1. We are not busy right now, just sitting here chatting.
2. Don't read while lying down, it's bad for your eyes.
3. We should not be sitting down while singing the national anthem, we should be standing.

ANSWERS:

1. 我们现在不忙，就是在这里坐着聊天。
   Wǒmen xiànzài bù máng, jiùshì zài zhèlǐ zuòzhe liáotiān.
2. 别躺着看书，对眼睛不好。 **Bié tǎngzhe kànshū, duì yǎnjing bù hǎo.**
3. 我们不应该坐着唱国歌，应该站着。
   Wǒmen bù yīnggāi zuòzhe chàng guógē, yīnggāi zhànzhe.

3. Using 正在 zhèngzài or 在 zài + verb to express "in the midst of doing something"

The notion of being "in the midst of doing something" is conveyed by the adverb 在 **zài** or 正在 **zhèngzài**, and not by the *aspect marker* 着 **zhe**. This pattern conveys a sense of immediacy (*at this very moment*), especially when 正在 **zhèngzài** (rather than just 在 **zài**) is used. This is illustrated by the first sentence in the opening section to 8.2. Additional examples are the following:

◆ *I was driving when your call came, so I didn't answer it.*
你来电话的时候，我正在开车，所以没接。
Nǐ lái diànhuàde shíhou, wǒ zhèngzài kāichē, suǒyǐ méi jiē.

◆ *We're in the middle of class, you can't answer the phone right now.*
我们正在上课呢，现在不能接电话。
Wǒmen zhèngzài shàngkè ne, xiànzài bùnéng jiē diànhua.

◆ *The government is at this very moment trying to solve economic problems. What we need now is not criticism but cooperation.*
政府正在解决经济问题，现在需要的不是批评而是人民的合作。
Zhèngfǔ zhèngzài jiějué jīngjì wèntí, xiànzài xūyàode búshì pīpíng érshì rénmínde hézuò.

EXERCISES:

Translate the following sentences into Chinese:

1. They are still having dinner, let's wait a bit before going over.
2. We are discussing China's population problem.

3. The boss is taking a nap (just now), please come back after 3:00.

ANSWERS:

1. 他们还在吃饭呢，我们等一下再去吧。
   Tāmen hái zài chīfàn ne, wǒmen děng yíxià zài qù ba.

2. 我们正在讨论中国的人口问题。**Wǒmen zhèngzài tǎolùn Zhōngguóde rénkǒu wèntí.**

3. 老板正在睡午觉，请三点以后再来吧。
   Lǎobǎn zhèngzài shuì-wǔjiào, qǐng sāndiǎn yǐhòu zài lái ba.

---

4. Word order with 了 le, 过 guo or 着 zhe when the verb has an object

We have already discussed the position of objects when the aspect markers 了 **le** or 过 **guo** are involved. The same word order applies to the aspect marker 着 **zhe** as well. All three must immediately follow the verb, with the object—if any—following the aspect marker.

The only slight stumbling block here is that bisyllabic verbs and *verb+object* compounds often look very similar to non-native speakers, and many simple verbs in English translate into *verb+object* compounds in Chinese (see 1.5, sec. J). The word order in a sentence involving one of the aspect markers depends on whether the verb is a bisyllabic verb or a verb+object compound. The following pairs of examples illustrate the differences in word order.

- *I have helped him in the past.*
  我曾经帮助过他。 **Wǒ céngjīng bāngzhùguo tā.**
  我曾经帮过他的忙。 **Wǒ céngjīng bāngguo tāde máng.**
  (帮助 **bāngzhù** and 帮忙 **bāngmáng** both mean *to help*, but 帮助 **bāngzhù** is a bisyllabic verb whereas 帮忙 **bāngmáng** is a *verb+object* compound)

- *I felt better after I rested.*
  我休息了以后就好一点了。 **Wǒ xiūxile yǐhòu jiù hǎo yìdiǎn le.**
  I felt better after I slept.
  我睡了觉以后就好一点了。 **Wǒ shuì-le-jiào yǐhòu jiù hǎo yìdiǎn le.**
  (休息 **xiūxi** is a bisyllabic verb whereas 睡觉 **shuìjiào** is a *verb+object* compound)

- *I was just reading all by myself, when she patted me from the back and startled me.*
  我一个人正看<u>着</u>书，她从后面拍了我一下，吓了我一跳。
  Wǒ yígerén zhèng kànzhe shū, tā cóng hòumian pāile wǒ yíxià, xiàle wǒ yítiào.

- *I was just lying on the sofa resting, when suddenly I heard someone knocking on the door.*
  我正躺在沙发上休息着，突然听见有人敲门。
  Wǒ zhèng tǎngzài shāfā-shang xiūxizhe, tūrán tīngjiàn yǒurén qiāomén.

Additional examples of bisyllabic verbs used with an aspect marker are given here:

♦ *He has never been in love.* 他从来没有恋爱过。 **Tā cónglái méiyǒu liàn'ài guo.**

♦ *I've communicated with her, but it's of no use.*
我跟她沟通过，可是没有用。 **Wǒ gēn tā gōutōngguo, kěshì méiyǒu yòng.**

♦ *I practiced for a long time, but still cannot do it.*
我练习了半天，还是不会。 **Wǒ liánxíle bàntiān, háishi búhuì.**

♦ *They discussed it for a long time, and finally came to an agreement.*
他们讨论了很久，结果同意了。 **Tāmen tǎolùnle hěnjiǔ, jiéguǒ tóngyìle.**

♦ *Customs examined my baggage and didn't find any narcotics.*
海关检查了我的行李，没找到什么毒品。
Hǎiguān jiǎnchále wǒde xínglǐ, méi zhǎodào shénme dúpǐn.

Examples of *verb+object* compounds used with an aspect marker:

♦ *I've never had an accident driving.*
我开车从来没出过事。 **Wǒ kāichē cónglái méi chū-guo-shì.**

♦ *He gave me a big help last year. I will never forget it!*
去年他帮了我很大的忙，我永远不会忘记！
Qùnián tā bāngle wǒ hěn dàde máng, wǒ yǒngyuǎn búhuì wàngjì.

♦ *She has had two abortions in the past. Now she takes birth control pills.* (a change from before)
她做过两次人工流产，现在她吃避孕药了。
Tā zuòguo liǎngcì réngōng liúchǎn, xiànzài tā chī bìyùnyào le.

♦ *They have played (some kind of ball game) for two hours and should be tired now.* (implying that the game is not over)
他们打了两个小时的球了，应该累了吧。
Tāmen dǎle liǎngge xiǎoshíde qiú le, yīnggāi lèi le ba.

♦ *It's very dangerous to drive while talking on the phone.*
打着电话开车是很危险的事！ **Dǎzhe diànhuà kāichē shì hěn wēixiǎnde shì.**

To determine whether a two-syllable verb is a bisyllabic verb or a *verb+object* compound, the following tests may be used:

a. The second syllable of a bisyllabic verb is always a verb in itself. It also tends to be a synonym of the first syllable, e.g. 帮助 **bāngzhù**, 休息 **xiūxi**, 恋爱 **liàn'ài**.

b. The second syllable of a *verb+object* compound is a noun. Often it serves the grammatical function of a generic object in the absence of a specific object. Examples:

verb+generic object			verb+specific object	
to read	看书 **kànshū**		to read fiction	看小说 **kàn xiǎoshuō**
to teach	教书 **jiāoshū**		to teach Chinese	教汉语 **jiāo Hànyǔ**
to play (ball)	打球 **dǎqiú**		to play basketball	打篮球 **dǎ lánqiú**
to eat	吃饭 **chīfàn**		to eat Western food	吃西餐 **chī xīcān**

Some common bisyllabic verbs:

拜访 **bàifǎng**	to pay a visit		开始 **kāishǐ**	to begin
帮助 **bāngzhù**	to help		考察 **kǎochá**	to investigate
保证 **bǎozhèng**	to guarantee		面临 **miànlín**	to faced with
表示 **biǎoshì**	to express		培养 **péiyǎng**	to nurture
表演 **biǎoyǎn**	to perform		欺负 **qīfù**	to bully
参加 **cānjiā**	to participate		认识 **rènshi**	to become acquainted
打听 **dǎting**	to inquire		研究 **yánjiū**	to research
估计 **gūjì**	to estimate		招待 **zhāodài**	to treat (guests)
解释 **jiěshì**	to explain		支持 **zhīchí**	to support
举行 **jǔxíng**	to conduct, convene		主张 **zhǔzhāng**	to advocate

Some common *verb+object* compounds:

罢工 **bàgōng**	to strike		革命 **gémìng**	to have a revolution
保险 **bǎoxiǎn**	to insure		鼓掌 **gǔzhǎng**	to applaud
毕业 **bìyè**	to graduate		见面 **jiànmiàn**	to meet
唱歌 **chànggē**	to sing		讲价 **jiǎngjià**	to bargain
吃惊 **chījīng**	to be startled		结婚 **jiéhūn**	to get married
吃苦 **chīkǔ**	to eat bitterness		开刀 **kāidāo**	to have an operation
出事 **chūshì**	to have an accident		拼命 **pīngmìng**	to make utmost effort
辞职 **cízhí**	to resign		起床 **qǐchuáng**	to get out of bed
打架 **dǎjià**	to fight		生气 **shēngqì**	to get angry
道歉 **dàoqiàn**	to apologize		睡觉 **shuìjiào**	to sleep
丢脸 **diūliǎn**	to lose face		跳舞 **tiàowǔ**	to dance
读书 **dúshū**	to study		洗澡 **xǐzǎo**	to take a bath
罚款 **fákuǎn**	to fine		照相 **zhàoxiàng**	to photograph
分手 **fēnshǒu**	to part company		做饭 **zuòfàn**	to cook

8.3 Other verb aspects expressed by grammatical patterns

The grammatical concept of a *verb complement* will be the subject of Chapter 12. Here, we will introduce just two verb complements and explain how they are used to express verb aspects.

1. Verb + 起来 qǐlai meaning "to start to do something":

As a standalone verb, 起来 **qǐlái** means *to rise*. As a *verb complement*, it means *to get up and do something*, *to begin something*, and the tone on 来 **lái** becomes neutral (**lai**). This *verb complement* is usually applied to action verbs to indicate that the action is just getting started, but it can also be used with stative verbs or adjectives (see the second example below). A direct translation of *to begin* into Chinese is 开始 **kāishǐ**, but this sounds intentional and formal, while the *verb complement* 起来 **qǐlai** is more colloquial and spontaneous.

♦ *Everyone started laughing.* 大家都笑起来了。 **Dàjiā dōu xiào-qǐlai le.**

♦ *Things are getting expensive.* 东西贵起来了。 **Dōngxi guì-qǐlai le.**

♦ *He started to sing.* 他唱起歌来了。 **Tā chàng-qǐ-gē-lái le.**
(note the word order: the object 歌 **gē** is located in between 起 **qǐ** and 来 **lái**)
(To compare 开始 **kāishǐ** with 起来 **qǐlai**: 他开始唱歌了 **Tā kāishǐ chànggē le** indicates that his singing was planned in advance; whereas 他唱起歌来了 **Tā chàngqǐgē lái le** means it happened spontaneously, e.g. maybe after a few drinks.)

♦ *When did you start smoking?*
你什么时候抽起烟来了？ **Nǐ shénme shíhou chōu-qǐ-yān-lai le?**

♦ *It was after I started college that I started smoking.*
我上了大学以后就抽起烟来了。 **Wǒ shàngle dàxué yǐhòu, jiù chōu-qǐ-yān-lai le.**

The *verb complement* 起来 **qǐlai** can also mean *when it comes to (doing something), as for....*

♦ *When it comes to talking about it, it's easy, but when it comes to actually doing it, it is difficult.*
说起来容易，做起来难！ **Shuō-qǐlai róngyì, zuò-qǐlai nán!**

♦ *Looks like we won't be able to arrive before dark. (When it comes to looking at the situation...)*
看起来今天天黑以前我们到不了了。
Kàn-qǐlai jīntiān tiānhēi yǐqián wǒmen dào-bu-liǎo le.

2. Verb + 下去 xiàqu meaning "to continue to do something":

As a standalone verb, 下去 **xiàqu** means *to go down*. As a *verb complement*, it means *to continue doing something, to keep on doing something*. A direct translation of *to* *continue* in Chinese is 继续 **jìxù**, but it sounds intentional and formal, while the *verb complement* 下去 **xiàqu** is more colloquial and informal in tone.

● *Your story is really interesting, please continue (telling it).*
你的故事真有意思，请说下去! **Nǐde gùshi zhēn yǒuyìsi, qǐng shuō-xiàqu!**

● *This job is too tough, I can't go on doing it anymore.*
这个工作太难了，我干不下去了!
Zhèige gōngzuò tài nán le, wǒ gàn-bú-xiàqu le!

● *After his wife passed away, he felt that he couldn't go on living anymore.*
他妻子去世以后，他觉得自己也活不下去了。
Tā qīzi qùshì yǐhòu, tā juéde zìjǐ yě huó-bú-xiàqu le.

In the pattern involving the *verb complement* 下去 **xiàqu**, the object of the verb, if any, is usually placed at the beginning of the sentence as the topic (as in the second example above). In this regard, the word order is different from that used with the *verb complement* 起来 **qǐlai**, in which the object is inserted in between 起 **qǐ** and 来 **lái** (e.g. 他唱起歌来了 **Tā chàng-qǐ-gē-lái le**).

● *You cannot quit in mid stream, you've got to keep at it!*
这件事，你不能做到一半就不做了，必须做下去啊!
Zhèijiàn shì, nǐ bùnéng zuòdào yíbàn jiù búzuò le, bìxū zuò-xiàqu a!

  ✗ 你必须做下去这件事，不能做到一半就不做了。
  Nǐ bìxū zuò-xiàqu zhèijiàn shì, bùnéng zuòdào yíbàn jiù búzuò le.

  ✗ 你必须做下这件事去，不能做到一半就不做了。
  Nǐ bìxū zuò-xià-zhèijiàn-shì-qù, bùnéng zuòdào yíbàn jiù búzuòle.

3. The reduplication of action verbs

This was first introduced in 2.10. Reduplication is also a grammatical device used to convey an aspect of the verb. Its function is to indicate that something is done casually or on a trial basis.

● *Take a look, are any of them the guy who grabbed your purse?* (looking at some mug shots)
你看看，这里有没有抢了你的皮包的那个人?
Nǐ kànkan, zhèlǐ yǒu-méiyǒu qiǎngle nǐde píbāode nèige rén?

● *I hope you will give it a try and see. You don't need to finish it.*
我希望你试试看，你不一定要做完。
Wǒ xīwàng nǐ shìshi kàn, nǐ bù yídìng yào zuòwán.

● *Listen, what is that sound?*
你听听，那是什么声音? **Nǐ tīngtīng, nà shì shénme shēngyīn?**

EXERCISES:

Translate the following sentences into Chinese (the underlined words involve elements introduced in this chapter):

1. That old lady again <u>started telling</u> a story from the time she was young.

2. This book is too boring, I don't want to <u>go on</u> reading it anymore.

3. The year my high school started (opened up) Chinese courses, I wanted to <u>give it a try</u>. Very soon, I <u>started loving</u> it, and then I just <u>kept on</u> learning it!

ANSWERS:

1. 那个老太太又说起她年轻时候的故事来了。
   Nèige lǎotàitai yòu shuōqǐ tā niánqīng shíhoude gùshi lái le.

2. 这本书太没意思了，我不想看下去了。
   Zhèiběn shū tài méi yìsi le, wǒ bùxiǎng kàn-xiàqu le.

3. 我的高中开了中文课那年，我就想试试看。很快地，我就爱上学中文了，然后就一直学下去了。 **Wǒde gāozhōng kāile Zhōngwénkè nèinián, wǒ jiù xiǎng shìshi-kàn. Hěnkuàide, wǒ jiù àishang xué Zhōngwén le, ránhòu jiù yìzhí xué-xiàqu le.**

A "relative location" is a location relative to some other known or stated reference point. This concept is best explained through the use of the following three sets of examples. The grammar associated with the underlined Chinese words will be discussed below; for now, just take note of their meaning.

Locations with a proper place name (capitalized) as the *point of reference*:

south of the Yangtze River	长江以<u>南</u> Chángjiāng yǐ<u>nán</u>
outside the Capitol	国会大厦<u>外</u>头 Guóhuì Dàshà <u>wài</u>tou
southwest region of the U.S.	美国的<u>西南</u>部 Měiguóde <u>xī'nán</u>bù
bottom of the Grand Canyon	大峡谷<u>底下</u> Dàxiágǔ <u>dǐxia</u>
in Yellowstone Park	黄石公园<u>里</u>(头) Huángshí Gōngyuán <u>lǐ</u>(tou)

Locations with a "generic" place as *point of reference*:

outside the train station	火车站<u>外</u>头 huǒchēzhàn <u>wài</u>tou
in front of the library	图书馆<u>前</u>面 túshūguǎn <u>qián</u>mian
in the classroom	教室<u>里</u>(头) jiàoshì <u>lǐ</u>(tou)
southern edge of the lake	湖的<u>南</u>边 húde <u>nán</u>bian
on top of that building	那栋楼的<u>上</u>面 nèidòng lóude <u>shàng</u>mian

Locations with reference to persons or things (not places):

inside a box	盒子<u>里</u>(头) hézi <u>lǐ</u>(tou)
top of the table	桌子<u>上</u> zhuōzi<u>shang</u>
to the left of Prof. Li	李教授的<u>左</u>边 Lǐ Jiàoshòude <u>zuǒ</u>bian
behind the tree	树的<u>后</u>面 shùde <u>hòu</u>mian
bottom of this page	这一页的<u>下</u>面 zhèi yíyède <u>xià</u>mian

The above examples illustrate three points:

a. All three types of *points of reference* translate readily from English to Chinese. The differences in *points of reference* makes no difference to the *grammar* of the

Chinese location expressions. In other words, a *relative location* can be stated with reference to a specific or generic place, or even an entity which is not a place.

b. A phrase designating a *location* consists of two components: *relative <u>position</u>* and *point of reference*. The word order of these two components in Chinese is the opposite of English.

c. The *relative position* component in Chinese is grammatically quite different from English, and this will be discussed in sections 9.1–9.7.

9.1 Single-syllable *localizers*

In the table above, the underlined Chinese *morphemes* indicate *relative positions*. We refer to them as "morphemes[1]" rather than "words" because they carry meaning but are not standalone words. In actual usage, they are always affixed either before or after another *morpheme*[1] (or word). Grammatically, we called them *localizers*, because they indicate the *locations* of things. The most common *localizers* are listed in the table below.

Native speakers of English are prone to use *localizers* in Chinese as though they are equivalent to English words with the same meaning, forgetting that *localizers* in Chinese are not independent words. For any of the *localizers* in the table below to become a word, a suffix must be added. There are four common *localizer* suffixes:

头 **tou**   *head* (as a suffix, it has no particularly meaning)

面 **mian** *face*

边 **bian** *side*

部 **bù**   *part, section*

Each of these suffixes is a *morpheme*, in its own right, with an original meaning. When the first three—头 **tou**, 面 **mian**, 边 **bian**—are used as suffixes, their original meanings are diminished, and they are therefore pronounced without stress or tone. When the last one, 部 **bù**, is used as a suffix, however, it retains its original meaning of *section* and therefore it is spoken with stress and tone. A *localizer* may be used with more than one of these suffixes, but the usages are not random. In other words, certain *localizers* always take certain suffixes, as listed in the table below:

English	localizers	corresponding suffixes
in/out	里/外 **lǐ/wài**	头 **tou**, 面 **mian**, (边 **bian**)
before/after; front/back	前/后 **qián/hòu**	头 **tou**, 面 **mian**, (边 **bian**)
above/below	上/下 **shàng/xià**	头 **tou**, 面 **mian**

---

[1] See 1.2 for a discussion of *morphemes*. Essentially, a morpheme is the smallest linguistic unit that has meaning, but a *morpheme* may or may not be a standalone word.

English	localizers	corresponding suffixes
middle, center	中 zhōng	部 bù
left/right	左/右 zuǒ/yòu	边 bian
east/south/west/north	东/南/西/北 dōng/nán/xī/běi	边 bian, 部 bù

In the above table, the localizers in the first three rows can all be used with more than one suffix. There is no real difference in meaning between the suffixes 头 **tou** and 面 **mian**, although there may be regional, or even individual, preferences for one over the other. The suffix 边 **bian** may also be added to 里 **lǐ** or 外 **wài** and 前 **qián** or 后 **hòu**, but it is not as common as the other two suffixes.

The localizer 中 **zhōng** is a bit different from the others because it combines with two other morphemes to form the words meaning *middle*— 中间 **zhōngjiān** and 当中 **dāngzhōng**, but neither is formed by adding a suffix to 中 **zhōng**, so these terms are idiomatic. However, 部 **bù**—with its meaning of *section*—may be suffixed to 中 **zhōng** to mean *middle section*.

♦ *Kansas and Missouri are in the middle of the United States.*
堪萨斯州和密苏里州在美国的中部。
Kǎnsàsī-zhōu hé Mìsūlǐ-zhōu zài Měiguóde zhōngbù.

As for the suffixes 边 **bian** and 部 **bù** used with the four cardinal directions (last row in the table), there is a difference between the two. 部 **bù** implies a portion within the *point of reference* whereas 边 **bian** is more ambiguous. Strictly speaking, it refers to an area outside the *point of reference*, but it can also be used to refer to an area within the *point of reference*.

♦ *Inner Mongolia (a region of China) is in North China.*
✓ 内蒙古在中国的北部。 **Nèi Měnggǔ zài Zhōngguóde běibù.**
✓ 内蒙古在中国的北边。 **Nèi Měnggǔ zài Zhōngguóde běibian.** (acceptable)

♦ *Mongolia (a nation) is north of China.*
✓ 蒙古在中国的北边。 **Měnggǔ zài Zhōngguóde běibian.**
✗ 蒙古在中国的北部。 **Měnggǔ zài Zhōngguóde běibù.**

♦ *Canada is to the north of the United States.*
✓ 加拿大在美国的北边。 **Jiānádà zài Měiguóde běibian.**
✗ 加拿大在美国的北部。 **Jiānádà zài Měiguóde běibù.**

The suffixes in the last row of the above table apply to the intermediate directions (e.g. 东北 **dōngběi**, 西南 **xī'nán**, etc.) as well. That is, both 边 **bian** and 部 **bù** may be used with them.

♦ *Peking University and Tsinghua University are both in the northwestern part of Beijing.*
北大和清华都在北京的西北部/西北边。
Běi-Dà he Qīnghuá dōu zài Běijīngde xībĕibù/xībĕibian.

♦ *Yunnan Province is in southwestern China.*
云南在中国的西南边/西南部。 **Yúnnán zài Zhōngguóde xī'nánbian/xī'nánbù.**

♦ *Nepal is to the southwest of China.*
✓ 尼泊尔在中国的西南边。 **Níbó'ĕr zài Zhōngguóde xī'nánbian.**
✗ 尼泊尔在中国的西南部。 **Níbó'ĕr zài Zhōngguóde xī'nánbù.**
(Nepal is not a part of China, hence 部 **bù** is inappropriate.)

A note about the pronunciation of 面 **mian** and 边 **bian**: In the colloquial Chinese spoken around Beijing, many words get an extra -r ending, called "erization" by linguists. This phenomenon is not random, i.e. there are certain rules governing it, but erization is rigorously applied to the *localizer* suffixes 面 **mian** and 边 **bian** by Beijingers. People from other regions are less likely to follow suit, and some may even find it annoying. Foreigners with less than native proficiency in Chinese may sound affected when they apply erization to their speech, so use it at your discretion.

Below are some additional examples of *relative positions* and *relative locations* as used in sentences:

♦ *There is an empty seat in front.* 前面有个空位。 **Qiánmian yŏu ge kòngwèi.**

♦ *This house has two levels. The bedrooms are upstairs, the living room is downstairs.*
这个房子有两层楼。卧房在上面/楼上、客厅在下面/楼下。
（楼上/楼下: upstairs/downstairs）
Zhèige fángzi yŏu liǎngcéng lóu. Wòfáng zài shàngmian/lóushàng, kètīng zài xiàmian/lóuxià.

♦ *You can ask the person to your left.*
你可以问你左边的那个人。 **Nĭ kĕyĭ wèn nĭ zuŏbiande nèige rén.**
(**Note:** In 你左边 **nĭ zuŏbian**, the *point of reference* is a pronoun.)

♦ *Traditional Chinese courtyard houses are like this: rooms are on the east, west, and north sides; there is a courtyard in the middle; the front door is on the south side.*
中国传统的四合院是这样的：东边、西边、北边都是屋子，中间是个院子，前门在南边。
Zhōngguó chuántŏngde sìhéyuàn shì zhèyàngde: dōngbian, xībiān, bĕibiān dōushì wūzi, zhōngjiān shì ge yuànzi, qiánmén zài nánbian.

EXERCISES:

Translate the following sentences into Chinese:

1. Please come to the front.
2. Please come to the front of the classroom.

3. I work in the city, but I live outside of the city.

4. Originally there were no Han people north of the Great Wall.

5. The kid in the middle is my son. The ones to his left and right are his friends.

ANSWERS:

1. 请到前头来。**Qǐng dào qiántou lái.**

2. 请到教室前头来。**Qǐng dào jiàoshì qiántou lái.**

3. 我在城里工作，可是住在城外头。**Wǒ zài chénglǐ gōngzuò, kěshì zhùzài chéng-wàitou.**

4. 原来长城北边没有汉人。**Yuánlái Chángchéng běibian méiyǒu Hànrén.**

5. 中间的那个孩子是我的，他左边和右边的那两个是他的朋友。
   Zhōngjiānde nèige háizi shì wǒde, tā zuǒbian hé yòubiande nèi liǎngge shì tāde péngyou.

9.2 Using the "modifier particle" 的 de with a *localizer*

Looking back at the three sets of examples at the beginning of this chapter, we see that three of the location phrases include a 的 **de** between the *point of reference* and the *localizer*: 美国的西南部 **Měiguóde xī'nánbù**; 李教授的左边 **Lǐ Jiàoshòude zuǒbian**; 这一页的下面 **zhèi yíyède xiàmian**. The connector 的 **de** is called the "modifier particle" by some linguists, because it is used generally to connect a modifier with an entity being modified. It serves that same function in these three phrases indicating relative locations. To generalize, 的 **de** may be used—optionally—with any word indicating *relative position* (e.g. 里头 **lǐtou**, 上面 **shàngmian**, 左边 **zuǒbian**, 东边 **dōngbian**), but not with just a single *morpheme* without a suffix (e.g. 里 **lǐ**, 上 **shàng**, 左 **zuǒ**, 东 **dōng**).

- *in the room*   屋子里头 **wūzi lǐtou** or 屋子的里头 **wūzide lǐtou**
  but not: ×屋子的里 **wūzide lǐ**

- *northern Japan*   日本北边 **Rìběn běibian** or 日本的北边 **Rìběnde běibian**
  but not: ×日本的北 **Rìběnde běi**

While the use of 的 **de** is optional, its usage is heavily influenced by the tendency toward bisyllabic rhythm in Chinese. Therefore, there is a preference for the constructions given in the middle column below which preserve a bisyllabic rhythm:

	preferred version	acceptable but not preferred
to my left	我的左边 **wǒde zuǒbian**	我左边 **wǒ zuǒbian**
on the table	桌子上头 **zhuōzi shàngtou**	桌子的上头 **zhuōzide shàngtou**
to the east of the lake	湖的东边 **húde dōngbian**	湖东边 **hú dōngbian** (see note below)
to the east of West Lake	西湖东边 **Xīhú dōngbian**	西湖的东边 **Xīhúde dōngbian**

Note: The phrase 湖东边 **hú dōngbian** is not only not preferred, it even borders on unacceptable. This illustrates the following exception to the optional nature of 的

de: In a *relative location* where the *point of reference* is monosyllabic, and the *relative position* involve a cardinal direction (东/南/西/北 **dōng/nán/xī/běi** + 边/部 **bian/bù**) or is 中部 **zhōngbù**, the use of 的 **de** is mandatory. A few additional examples:

	with 的 de	without 的 de	
	correct	correct	incorrect
central part of the island	岛的中部 **dǎode zhōngbù**		✗岛中部 **dǎo zhōngbù**
central part of Taiwan	台湾的中部 **Táiwānde zhōngbù**	台湾中部 **Táiwān zhōngbù**	
to the east of the hill	山的东边 **shānde dōngbian**		✗山东边 **shān dōngbian**
to the east of West Hill	西山的东边 **Xīshānde dōngbian**	西山东边 **Xīshān dōngbian**	
south of the city (city: 城 **chéng**)	城的南边 **chéngde nánbian**		✗城南边 **chéng nánbian**
south of the city (city: 城市 **chéngshì**)	城市的南边 **chéngshìde nánbian**	城市南边 **chéngshì nánbian**	

The above constraint does not apply to other *relative positions* like 里 **lǐ**/外 **wài**/前 **qián**/后 **hòu**/上 **shàng**/下 **xià**/左 **zuǒ**/右 **yòu** + 头 **tou**/面 **mian**/边 **bian**, nor to 中间 **zhōngjiān** and 当中 **dāngzhōng**. That is to say, monosyllabic *points of reference* may be used directly with words designating a *relative position* without using the intermediary 的 **de**. Examples:

	both correct (with or without 的 de)	
to my left	我左边 **wǒ zuǒbian**	我的左边 **wǒde zuǒbian**
to our left	我们左边 **wǒmen zuǒbian**	我们的左边 **wǒmende zuǒbian**
outside of the city	城外头 **chéng wàitou**	城的外头 **chéngde wàitou**
outside of the city	城市外头 **chéngshì wàitou**	城市的外头 **chéngshìde wàitou**
in front of the tree	树前面 **shù qiánmian**	树的前面 **shùde qiánmian**
in front of the oak tree	橡树前面 **xiàngshù qiánmian**	橡树的前面 **xiàngshùde qiánmian**
under the bowl	碗下面 **wǎn xiàmian**	碗的下面 **wǎnde xiàmian**
under the plate	盘子下面 **pánzi xiàmian**	盘子的下面 **pánzide xiàmian**
in front of the school	学校前头 **xuéxiào qiántou**	学校的前头 **xuéxiàode qiántou**
on the bookshelf	书架上头 **shūjià shàngtou**	书架的上头 **shūjiàde shàngtou**

When the point of reference itself is bisyllabic, there is a slight preference for omitting 的 **de**, because adding 的 **de** will make the whole phrase five syllables, which sounds a bit wordy.

EXERCISES:

Translate the following phrases into Chinese:

1. in front of the store
2. in the restaurant
3. on the Great Wall
4. in the center of Tiananmen Square
5. east of the Mississippi River
6. under the apple tree
7. on top of the birthday cake
8. at the far right of this photo
9. behind the house
10. outside of the White House

ANSWERS:

1. 商店前面 **shāngdiàn qiánmian**
2. 餐馆里头 **cānguǎn lǐtou**
3. 长城上 **Chángchéng-shang**
4. 天安门的中间 **Tiān'ānménde zhōngjiān**
5. 密西西比河的东边 **Mìxīxībǐ Héde dōngbian**
6. 苹果树下 **píngguǒ shùxia**
7. 生日蛋糕上 **shēngrì dàngāo-shang**
8. 照片的最右边 **zhàopiànde zuì yòubian**
9. 房子后头 **fángzi hòutou**
10. 白宫外面 **Báigōng wàimian**

9.3 Tagging a *localizer* directly onto its point of reference

So far, we have learned that *localizers* are *morphemes* with meaning which cannot be used as standalone words. In actual usage, a *localizer* either has another morpheme suffixed to it, or is suffixed to another morpheme or word. We have discussed how suffixes (e.g. 头 **tou**, 面 **mian**, 边 **bian**) are added to *localizers* to create place words. In this section, we will see how certain *localizers* may be suffixed to a *point of reference* without a suffix. That is, rather than tagging something on it, the *localizer* itself is tagged to a preceding word. Here are some examples:

	point of reference (的 de) + localizer + 头 tou/面 mian/边 bian	point of reference + localizer (without a suffix)
in the house	房子(的)里头 fángzi(de) lǐtou	房子里 fángzilǐ
outside the school	学校(的)外头 xuéxiào(de) wàitou	校外 xiàowài
on the bookshelf	书架(的)上头 shūjià(de) shàngtou	书架上 shūjiàshang
on the bed	床(的)上面 chuáng(de) shàngmian	床上 chuángshang
on the wall	墙(的)上面 qiáng(de) shàngmian	墙上 qiángshang
in front of the door	门(的)前面 mén(de) qiánmian	门前 ménqián

	point of reference (的 de) + localizer + 头 tou/面 mian/边 bian	point of reference + localizer (without a suffix)
on the table	桌子(的)上面 zhuōzi(de) shàngmian	桌子上/桌上 zhuōzishang/ zhuōshang
in the room	屋子(的)里面 wūzi(de) lǐmian	屋子里/屋里 wūzilǐ/wūlǐ
in the hills	山里头 shān lǐtou	山里 shānlǐ, 山中 shānzhōng

The pattern illustrated in the third column above can be used with the *localizers* 里 lǐ/外 wài/上 shàng/下 xià/中 zhōng/前 qián/后 hòu. Actual usage in everyday speech is again influenced by the dominant bisyllabic rhythm in Chinese. Thus, the two-syllable terms in the third column are preferred over other alternatives. They also have the advantage of being succinct. In the middle column, the optional 的 de makes the phrase a bit too wordy and is therefore not preferred.

In contrast to the spatial *localizers* mentioned above, the directional *localizers* 左 zuǒ/右 yòu/东 dōng/南 nán/西 xī/北 běi cannot be used without a suffix (边 bian or 部 bù) in normal colloquial Chinese. In other words, these *localizers* cannot be directly attached to a location or thing in colloquial Chinese. Here are some examples to clarify this further:

	correct	incorrect
to the left of the teacher	老师(的)左边 lǎoshī(de) zuǒbian	✕ 老师左 lǎoshī zuǒ
eastern part of the U.S.	美国(的)东部 Měiguó(de) dōngbù	✕ 美国东 Měiguó dōng

Although the *localizers* 左 zuǒ/右 yòu/东 dōng/南 nán/西 xī/北 běi normally require a suffix (边 bian or 部 bù) in colloquial Chinese, there are two grammatical patterns from literary Chinese that contradict this. Both of these involve the use of "particles" (morphemes that serve a grammatical function) to provide a literary flavor or flair. These are commonly used only in written Chinese, not when speaking.

1. **Using 之 zhī to connect a *point of reference* with a *localizer*:**

- *to the left of the emperor* 皇帝之左 huángdì zhīzuǒ
  The empress is to the left of the emperor.
  皇后位于皇帝之左。 Huánghòu wèiyú huángdì zhīzuǒ.

- *southern Xinjiang* 新疆之南 Xīnjiāng zhīnán
  Southern Xinjiang is also called Nan-Jiang.
  新疆之南亦称南疆。 Xīnjiāng zhīnán yì chēng Nán-Jiāng.

- *west of Tiananmen Square* 天安门之西 Tiān'ānmén zhīxī
  The Great Hall of the People is on the west side of Tiananmen Square.
  人民大会堂位于天安门之西。 Rénmín Dàhuìtáng wèiyú Tiān'ānmén zhīxī.

2. **Using** 以 **yǐ to connect a *point of reference* with a *localizer*:**

- *south of the Yangtze River* 长江以南 **Chángjiāng yǐnán**
  The region south of the Yangtze River is abbreviated as Jiang-Nan.
  长江以南简称江南。 **Chángjiāng yǐnán jiǎnchēng Jiāngnán**

- *north of the 38th parallel* 北纬38度以北 **běiwěi 38 dù yǐběi**
  North of the 38th parallel is North Korea.
  北纬38度以北是朝鲜。 **Běiwěi 38 dù yǐběi shì Cháoxiǎn.**

- *south of the Heavenly Mountains* 天山以南 **Tiānshān yǐnán**
  Nan-Jiang designates the part of Xinjiang south of the Heavenly Mountains.
  南疆指新疆天山以南的部分。 **Nán-Jiāng zhǐ Xīnjiāng Tiānshān yǐnánde bùfen.**

The two above patterns differ from one another in two ways:

1. With 之 **zhī**, the location in question may be either within or outside of the point of reference, i.e., the point of reference may be either the encompassing area or the boundary. With 以 **yǐ**, the location in question is always just beyond the point of reference, i.e. the point of reference is the boundary and the *localizer* indicates an area outside of the boundary.

2. The ···之··· **...zhī...** pattern can be applied to 左 **zuǒ**/右 **yòu**, as well as to the four cardinal directions 东 **dōng**/南 **nán**/西 **xī**/北 **běi**, and the intermediate directions (e.g. 东北 **dōngběi**, 西南 **xī'nán**, etc.). The ···以··· **...yǐ...** pattern may be applied to the four cardinal directions only, not to 左 **zuǒ**/右 **yòu**, nor to the intermediate directions.

9.4 The cardinal directions 东 dōng/南 nán/西 xī/北 běi in geographic names

To anyone who has traveled in China or knows some Chinese geographic names, the tendency for the cardinal directions to appear in place names is striking. This phenomenon exists in other cultures as well, but nowhere is it as prevalent as it is in China. Another tendency of these names is that they are normally just two syllables, which makes them succinct, easy to remember, and perfectly suited to the dominant bisyllabic rhythm of Chinese.

Place names with cardinal directions follow two formats: 1) a cardinal direction following a point of reference; and 2) a cardinal direction preceding a point of reference, as though modifying it. Examples for each type will be given below. For both of these formats, the *localizer* 中 **zhōng** joins the ranks of the four cardinal directions as a possible component in place words.

a. A cardinal direction following a point of reference:

Provinces:

河南	Hénán	河北	Héběi
山西	Shānxī	山东	Shāndōng
湖南	Húnán	湖北	Húběi
广东	Guǎngdōng	广西	Guǎngxī
海南	Hǎinán	云南	Yúnnán

Other place names:

岭南	Lǐngnán	江西	Jiāngxī		
台北	Táiběi	台南	Táinán	台东	Táidōng

The above examples may all be familiar to you. Below are some others formed according to the same grammatical pattern, which may be unfamiliar to you. These are also bisyllabic place names, but the first syllable is an abridged term (often with a classical reference) for a place name. Every Chinese province has such an abridged form and it is used on license plates, even though many are not commonly known. Nevertheless, those that are used in familiar geographical names are commonly used by native speakers.

闽南 **Mǐnnán**: 福建的南部 **Fújiànde nánbù** (*southern Fujian province*)
(as in 闽南话 **Mǐnnán-huà**, the dialect spoken in southern Fujian and Taiwan)

赣南 **Gànnán**: 江西的南部 **Jiāngxīde nánbù** (*southern Jiangxi province*)

粤西 **Yuèxī**: 广东的西部 **Guǎngdōngde xībù** (*western Guangdong province*)

塞北 **Sàiběi**: 长城以北 **Chángchéng yǐběi** (*north of the Great Wall*)

浦东 **Pǔdōng**: 黄浦江以东 **Huángpǔjiāng yǐdōng** (*east of the Huangpu River, newly developed part of Shanghai*)

华东 **Huádōng**: 中国的东部 **Zhōngguóde dōngbù** (*East China*)

华中 **Huázhōng**: 中国的中部 **Zhōngguóde zhōngbù** (*Central China*)

关中 **Guānzhōng**: 陕西平原的中部 **Shǎnxī Píngyuánde zhōngbù** (*center of the Shaanxi Plains*)

b. A cardinal direction preceding a point of reference, as though modifying it:

南疆 **Nánjiāng** *southern Xinjiang*

北疆 **Běijiāng** *northern Xinjiang*

东京 **Dōngjīng** *Tokyo*

北京 **Běijīng** *Beijing*

南京 **Nánjīng** *Nanjing*

西湖 **Xī Hú** *West Lake*

北美 **Běi-Měi** *North America*

东欧 **Dōng-Ōu** *Eastern Europe*

北欧 **Běi-Ōu** *Northern Europe*

南非 **Nán-Fēi** *South Africa*

北韩(朝鲜) **Běi-Hán (Cháoxiǎn)** *North Korea*

中东 **Zhōngdōng** *Middle East*

中亚 **Zhōng-Yà** *Central Asia*

中欧 **Zhōng-Ōu** *Central Europe*

The differences between the two formats for place names above may seem clear, but the logic behind their placement is often not. Even native Chinese find it difficult to explain why Central China and East China are in the first format (华中 **Huāzhōng** and 华东 **Huádōng**), but North America, Eastern Europe, Central Asia, and Central Europe are in the second format, i.e. 北美 **Běi-Měi**, 东欧 **Dōng-Ōu**, 北欧 **Běi-Ōu**, 中亚 **Zhōng-Yà**, 中欧 **Zhōng-Ōu**. It is best to simply remember these terms rather than to try and figure out the logic behind them.

EXERCISES:

Translate the following into two-syllable Chinese place names:

1. North Carolina
2. Central African Republic
3. South America
4. East Germany

5. North China
6. northern part of Fujian province
7. eastern part of Guangdong province
8. South Korea

ANSWERS:

1. 北卡 **Běi-Kǎ**
2. 中非(共和国) **Zhōng-Fēi (Gònghéguó)**
3. 南美 **Nán-Měi**
4. 东德 **Dōng-Dé**

5. 华北 **Huáběi**
6. 闽北 **Mǐnběi**
7. 粤东 **Yuèdōng**
8. 南韩 **Nán-Hán**

9.5 Two special usages of 上 shàng

One usage of the *localizer* 上 **shàng** that is counter-intuitive to native English speakers is in referring to something on a printed page, e.g., a book or newspaper. The Chinese mind conceptualizes printed materials to be on the surface of a page and therefore uses 上 **shàng**; the English speaker conceptualizes something that opens up, and therefore uses *in*. When 上 **shàng** is tagged onto a *point of reference* or a noun, as though it is a suffix, it is often pronounced in a neutral tone (*shang*).

♦ *I read that piece of news in today's newspaper.*
我在今天的报纸上看到那条新闻了。
Wǒ zài jīntiānde bàozhǐshang kàndào nèitiáo xīnwén le.

♦ *There was no explanation in the book.*
　　书上没有说明。**Shūshang méiyǒu shuōmíng.**

Aside from indicating a physical location, 上 **shàng** may also be associated with certain abstract concepts. In this usage, it is translated into English variously as *in; in terms of...; from the point of view of....*

- 世界上 **shìjiè-shang** *in the world*
  There are Chinese people everywhere in the world.
  世界上到处都有华人。**Shìjiè-shang dàochù dōu yǒu Huárén.**

- 社会上 **shèhuì-shang** *in society*
  The status of farmers in society is gradually rising.
  农民在社会上的地位渐渐上升了。
  Nóngmín zài shèhuì-shangde dìwèi jiànjian shàngshēngle.

- 课上 **kèshang** *in class* (antonym: 课外 **kèwài** *outside of class, extracurricular*)
  We are not allowed to open our books in Chinese class.
  我们在中文课上不许打开书。**Wǒmen zài Zhōngwén kèshang bùxǔ dǎkāi shū.**

- 系上 **xìshang** *in the department* (academic)
  I have notified my department that I will be on maternity leave next semester.
  我已经通知了系上我下学期要休产假。
  Wǒ yǐjīng tōngzhīle xìshang wǒ xià xuéqī yào xiū chǎnjià.

- 道德上 **dàodé-shang** *from the point of view of morality*
  Although this is not illegal, morally speaking, it is unacceptable.
  虽然不算犯法，可是道德上说不过去。
  Suīrán búsuàn fànfǎ, kěshì dàodé-shang shuō-bú-guòqu.

- 实际上 **shíjì-shang** *in reality*
- 理论上 **lǐlùn-shang** *in theory*
  This should work in theory, but in reality, it doesn't.
  理论上应该行得通，可是实际上行不通。
  Lǐlùn-shang yīnggāi xíng-de-tōng, kěshì shíjì-shang xíng-bu-tōng.

- 原则上 **yuánzé-shang** *in principle*
  In principle, on all these matters we should seek approval from the leadership in advance.
  原则上这些事都应该事先争取领导的同意。
  Yuánzé-shang zhèixiē shì dōu yīnggāi shìxiān zhēngqǔ lǐngdǎode tóngyì.

EXERCISES:

Translate the following sentences into Chinese:

1. In principle, everyone should be equal before the law. But this ideal has never been realized in the world.

2. This method is workable in theory, but in reality it is difficult to put into practice.

> **ANSWERS:**
> 1. 原则上，在法律面前应该人人平等。可是这个理想在世界上从来没有
>   实现过。**Yuánzé-shang, zài fǎlǜ miànqián yīnggāi rénrén píngděng. Kěshì zhèige lǐxiǎng
>   zài shìjiè-shang cónglái méiyǒu shíxiànguo.**
> 2. 这个办法理论上行得通，实际上很难执行。
>   **Zhèige bànfǎ lǐlùn-shang xíng-de-tōng, shíjì-shang hěn nán zhíxíng.**

9.6 Using 以… yǐ … to signify relationships to reference points

In 9.3, we have already seen examples of "以… **yǐ…**" used with the four cardinal directions 东 **dōng**/南 **nán**/西 **xī**/北 **běi**. This pattern actually has a wide variety of applications beyond locations. In all these, the word order of the phrase using "以… **yǐ…**" within the sentence is the opposite of the order in English.

1. 以前 **yǐqián** (*before*) and 以后 **yǐhòu** (*after*):

♦ *That film portrays social conditions before the 20th century.*
  那部电影演的是二十世纪以前的社会情况。
  Nèibù diànyǐng yǎnde shì èrshí shìjì yǐqiánde shèhuì qíngkuàng.

♦ *Will you still have income after you retire?*
  你退休以后还会有收入吗？ **Nǐ tuìxiū yǐhòu hái huì yǒu shōurù ma?**

2. 以外 **yǐwài** (*beyond, outside of, aside from*) and 以内 **yǐnèi** (*within*)

♦ *I guarantee that I will finish that job within three days.*
  我保证三天以内把这件事做完。
  Wǒ bǎozhèng sāntiān yǐnèi bǎ zhèijiàn shì zuòwán.

♦ *Rent is very high here, one cannot find an apartment for under (within) $2000
  a month.*
  这里的房租很贵，找不到月租在 $2000 以内的公寓。
  Zhèlǐde fángzū hěn guì, zhǎo-bu-dào yuèzū zài $2000 yǐnèide gōngyù.

♦ *In ancient times, the area outside of the Great Wall was no longer Chinese territory.*
  在古代，长城以外就不是中国的领土了。
  Zài gǔdài, Chángchéng yǐwài jiù búshì Zhōngguóde lǐngtǔ le.

♦ *I just arrived not long ago, and haven't had the chance to get acquainted with
  colleagues outside of the department.*
  我刚来不久，还没有机会认识本系以外的同事。
  Wǒ gāng lái bùjiǔ, hái méiyǒu jīhuì rènshi běnxì yǐwàide tóngshì.

Note: 以外 **yǐwài** is also part of the sentence pattern "除了… 以外，…。 **chúle…
yǐwài, ….**" (see Part II, #39 & 40)

3. 以上 **yǐshàng** (*above, over*) and 以下 **yǐxià** (*below, under*)

♦ *People over 65 may ride public transportation free.*
65岁以上的人可以免费坐公车。
65 suì yǐshàngde rén kěyǐ miǎnfèi zuò gōngchē.

♦ *In the U.S. only people over 18 may vote.*
在美国十八岁以上才有资格投票。
Zài Měiguó shíbā-suì yǐshàng cái yǒu zīgé tóupiào.

♦ *Students with family annual income under $30,000 are exempt from paying tuition.*
家庭年收入在 $30,000 以下的学生可以免缴学费。
Jiātíng nián-shōurù zài $30,000 yǐxiàde xuésheng kěyǐ miǎn jiǎo xuéfèi.

♦ *Body temperature above 104 is very dangerous.*
体温如果在104度以上就很危险了！
Tǐwēn rúguǒ zài 104 dù yǐshàng jiù hěn wēixiǎn le.

EXERCISES:

Translate the following sentences into Chinese:

1. At this buffet restaurant, children under 5 are free, kids between 5 and 12 pay half price.

2. Originally, the population south of the Great Wall was Han, those north of the Great Wall were minorities. In the last half century, many Han people migrated to north of the Great Wall, so now over half of Inner Mongolia's population are also Han.

> **ANSWERS:**
> 1. 在这个自助餐厅，五岁以下的孩子免费，五岁到十二岁半价。
>   **Zài zhèige zìzhù cāntīng, wǔ-suì yǐxiàde háizi miǎnfèi, wǔ-suì dào shí'èr-suì bànjià.**
> 2. 原来长城以南的人口是汉人，长城以北的是少数民族。过去半个世纪，很多汉人迁移到长城以北去了，所以现在内蒙古的人口一半以上是汉人了。
>   **Yuánlái Chángchéng yǐnánde rénkǒu shì Hànrén, Chángchéng yǐběide shì shǎoshù mínzú. Guòqù bànge shìjì, hěnduō Hànrén qiānyídào Chángchéng yǐběi qùle, suǒyǐ xiànzài Nèi Ménggǔde rénkǒu yíbàn yǐshàng shì Hànrén le.**

9.7 Adding 这儿 zhèr or 那儿 nàr to indicate a location

The words 这儿 **zhèr**/那儿 **nàr** are place words in their own right, but they can also be added to other nouns or pronouns to indicate a location. In other words, nouns and pronouns that are not in themselves locations can become locational phrases when 这儿 **zhèr** or 那儿 **nàr** are tagged onto them.

♦ *He lived at my place for a few days when he first arrived.*
他刚到的时候，在我这儿住了几天。
Tā gāng dàode shíhou, zài wǒ zhèr zhùle jǐtiān.

♦ *Please go over there to the sofa to talk to Grandma (she's hard of hearing).*
请到沙发那儿去跟奶奶说话。(✗请到沙发去…)
Qǐng dào shāfā nàr qù gēn Nǎinai shuōhuà. (✗ qǐng dào shāfā qù)

这儿 **zhèr** or 那儿 **nàr** may also be optionally suffixed to words that are place words in their own right. This may sound redundant, but it has the effect of emphasizing the location, and indicating the speaker's location relative to the place in question.

♦ *The foreign students' dormitory (which is here) has a dining room.* (indicates that the speaker is in the dormitory)
留学生宿舍这儿就有个餐厅。 **Liúxuésheng sùshè zhèr jiù yǒu ge cāntīng.**

♦ *Her room is in Building Three (which is "over there")*
她的房间在三号楼那儿。 **Tāde fángjiān zài sānhào lóu nàr.**

♦ *The bank is over there by the front gate of the school.*
银行在校门外头那儿。 **Yínháng zài xiàomén wàitou nàr.**

EXERCISES:

Translate the following short paragraph into Chinese:

You're welcome to come stay with me, but I don't have internet at my place. You can get on the internet at the Starbucks across the way.

> **ANSWERS:**
> 欢迎你来住在我这儿，可是我家没有因特网。你可以到对面星巴克那儿去上网。 **Huānyíng nǐ lái zhùzài wǒ zhèr, kěshì wǒjiā méiyǒu yīntèwǎng. Nǐ kěyǐ dào duìmian Xīngbākè nàr qù shàngwǎng.**

9.8 Nouns modified by their locations

When a noun is modified by a word or phrase that indicates its location, the "location modifier"—no matter how simple or complex—always *precedes* the noun, and is linked to it using the particle 的 **de**. This is the same pattern used to link any other kind of modifier, so it should be easy. However, the Chinese word order is the opposite of English, and therefore can be a stumbling block for students. In English, a "location modifier" *follows* the entity being modified and typically begins with a preposition (e.g. *at, in, behind*) or a "relative pronoun" (e.g. *which, that*). In Chinese, a "location modifier" is just like any other kind of modifier, and therefore precedes the noun.

- *the books on top of the desk* 书桌上的书 **shūzhuō-shangde shū**
- *the restaurant outside the school's front gate*
  学校前门外的那个餐馆 **xuéxiào qiánmén-wàide nèige cānguǎn**
- relatives in mainland China 在大陆的亲戚 **zài dàlùde qīnqi**

◆ *Please refer to the explanation below.*
请参考以下的说明。 **Qǐng cānkǎo yǐxiàde shuōmíng.**

◆ *The restaurants near the university all have good business.*
学校附近的餐馆生意都很好。
Xuéxiào fùjìnde cānguǎn shēngyì dōu hěn hǎo.

◆ *In Japan, the staff in supermarkets and stores are all super polite to customers.*
在日本，超市里和商店里的服务员对顾客都非常客气。
Zài Rìběn, chāoshìlǐ hé shāngdiànlǐde fúwùyuán duì gùkè dōu fēicháng kèqi.

EXERCISES:

Translate the following sentences into Chinese:

1. Nowadays, college students prefer to buy books on the web. Many bookstores near the university have become coffee shops.

2. Apartments in the city are all very expensive, therefore people prefer to live in the suburbs.

3. My wife is an artist. The pictures hanging on the living wall are all her works.

ANSWERS:

1. 现在大学生比较喜欢上网买书了。大学附近的很多书店都变成咖啡馆了。
   Xiànzài dàxuéshēng bǐjiào xǐhuan shàngwǎng mǎi shū le. Dàxué fùjìnde hěnduō shūdiàn dōu biànchéng kāfēi-guǎn le.

2. 城里/市内的公寓都很贵，所以人们比较喜欢住在郊区。
   Chénglǐ/shìnèide gōngyù dōu hěn guì, suǒyǐ rénmen bǐjiào xǐhuan zhùzài jiāoqū.

3. 我太太是个画家。挂在客厅墙上的画都是她的作品。
   Wǒ tàitai shì ge huàjiā. Guàzài kètīng qiángshangde huà dōu shì tāde zuòpǐn.

9.9 Stating the location of something vs the existence of something

These two types of statements contain the same facts, but the focus—the point of the statement—is different. Sentences stating the location of something follow the same word order in English and Chinese, but the sentence pattern is different:

English: Subject + verb (*to be*) + preposition (*at/in/in front of...*, etc.) + location

Chinese: Subject + 在··· **zài...** + location + (localizer)

However, there are two differences between the Chinese and English versions. First, the copula verb *to be* in English is replaced by 在 **zài** in Chinese. Second, the preposition in English is often bifurcated when translated into Chinese, i.e. 在 **zài** alone is incomplete and a *localizer* is needed after the *point of reference*.

◆ *Professor Zhang is in the office building, but not in her office.*
张教授在办公楼里，可是不在她的办公室。
Zhāng Jiàoshòu zài bàngōnglóu-lǐ, kěshì búzài tāde bàngōngshì.
Note: 里 **lǐ** is used in the first clause, but not the second, because the first clause emphasizes that the professor is somewhere *inside* the building

◆ *The first rate universities in the U.S. are not all on the East Coast.*
美国的一流大学不都在东部。 **Měiguóde yīliú dàxué bùdōu zài dōngbù.**

◆ *The vagabonds in New York are mostly in subway stations.*
纽约的流浪汉多半在地铁站里。
Niǔyuēde liúlànghàn duōbàn zài dìtiě-zhàn-lǐ.

The second type of sentence, stating the existence of something at a certain location, follows quite different word orders in English and Chinese:

English: There are/is … + preposition (*at/in/in front of…*/etc.) + location
Chinese: (在 **zài**) location + 有／没有 **yǒu/méiyǒu…**

It may strike English speakers as odd that 有／没有 **yǒu/méiyǒu** is used to express the notion of existence of something at a particular place, but Chinese is not alone in conceptualizing existence in this way. In French, a statement about the existence of something begins with "Il y a…" To a native Chinese speaker, the parallel English sentence pattern seems convoluted and wordy. So we come back to the same refrain: Students of Chinese will do well to replace the English linguistic mindset with a Chinese one when speaking the language!

◆ *There's someone in the restroom, you have to wait a bit outside the door.*
厕所里有人，你得在门外头等一会儿。
Cèsuǒ-lǐ yǒu rén, nǐ děi zài mén wàitou děng yìhuǐr.

◆ *There are quite a few Chinese restaurants in New York. The best ones are all in Chinatown.*
纽约有很多中国餐馆，最好的都在中国城。
Niǔyuē yǒu hěnduō Zhōngguó cānguǎn, zuìhǎode dōu zài Zhōngguóchéng.

◆ *There's a salesperson at the door, but I'm not clear what he's selling. You go take a look, OK?*
门前有个推销员，我不清楚他要推销什么，你去看看吧。
Ménqián yǒu ge tuīxiāoyuán, wǒ bù qīngchǔ tā yào tuīxiāo shénme, nǐ qù kànkan ba.

EXERCISES:

Translate the following sentences into Chinese:

1. There are only fast food restaurants near the university. The good restaurants are all quite far.

2. There are bad people in every country in the world, but many of them in America have guns.

3. As I see it, the most interesting places are not located at favorite tourist sites.

ANSWERS:

1. 大学附近只有快餐店，好的餐馆都相当远。
   Dàxué fùjìn zhǐ yǒu kuàicān-diàn, hǎode cānguǎn dōu xiāngdāng yuǎn.

2. 世界上每个国家都有坏人，可是在美国的很多坏人都有枪。
   Shìjiè-shang měige guójiā dōu yǒu huàirén, kěshì zài Měiguóde hěnduō huàirén dōu yǒu qiāng.

3. 在我看来，最有意思的地方不是游客最喜欢去的地方。
   Zài wǒ kànlai, zuì yòuyìside dìfang bú shì yóukè zuì xǐhuan qùde dìfang.

9.10 Stating the location of an action

The following pairs of sentences share the same sentence pattern in English, but in Chinese, the "在… zài…" phrase is in a different position.

● *He is sitting on the sofa.* 他坐在沙发上。**Tā zuòzài shāfāshang.**

● *He is resting on the sofa.* 他在沙发上休息。**Tā zài shāfāshang xiūxi.**

● *He wrote a note on the door.*
  他写了一个便条在门上。**Tā xiěle yíge biàntiáo zài ménshang.**

● *He wrote a note in the hotel.*
  他在旅馆里写了一个便条。**Tā zài lǚguǎn-lǐ xiěle yíge biàntiáo.**

Notice that the phrase beginning with "在… zài…" precedes the verb in some cases but follows the verb in others. The difference lies in the grammatical function of 在 zài, which can serve as either a *coverb* or a *postverb*. This will be discussed in Chapter 11. For now and for the purpose of stating the location of an action, just remember the following rule of thumb: When the "在… zài…" phrase simply indicates the location of the action (and the focus is really on the action itself), then it precedes the verb, as though it is modifying the action. When the "在… zài…" phrase is central to the action, or if the action is <u>acted</u> upon the location, it follows the verb. In most cases, the correct word order is clear by using this rule of thumb, but some cases will remain ambiguous, so that both word orders are acceptable. We will start with some examples of clear-cut cases. In the first four examples below, the location is where the action takes place. In the last two examples, the action of writing is acted upon the location.

● *This summer I'll be studying Chinese in Beijing.*
  ✓ 今年夏天我在北京学习中文。
  Jīnnián xiàtiān wǒ zài Běijīng xuéxí Zhōngwén.
  ✗ …我学习中文在北京。**…wǒ xuéxí Zhōngwén zài Běijīng.**

● *That letter from him was written in a subway station.*
  ✓ 他那封信是在地铁站里写的。 **Tā nèifēng xìn shì zài dìtiě-zhàn-lǐ xiěde.**
  ✗ …是写在地铁站里的。 **… shì xiězài dìtiě-zhàn-lǐ de.**

● *Not all vagabonds in New York spend the night in subway stations.*
  ✓ 纽约的流浪汉不都在地铁站里过夜。
  Niǔyuēde liúlànghàn bùdōu zài dìtiě-zhàn-lǐ guòyè.
  ✗ …不都过夜在地铁站里。 **… bùdōu guòyè zài dìtiě-zhàn-lǐ.**

● *When I just arrived in America, I could only do odd jobs in restaurants.*
  ✓ 我刚到美国的时候，只能在餐馆打零工。
  Wǒ gāng dào Měiguóde shíhou, zhǐ néng zài cānguǎn dǎ línggōng.
  ✗ …，只能打零工在餐馆。 **… zhǐ néng dǎ línggōng zài cānguǎn.**

● *I don't have any paper, so I'll just write it on the envelope.*
  我没有纸，就写在信封上吧。 **Wǒ méiyǒu zhǐ, jiù xiězài xìnfēng-shang ba.**

● *This is a library book, if you have any comments, write it in a notebook, don't write it in the book.*
  这是图书馆的书，如果你有什么见解，写在笔记本上，别写在书上。
  Zhè shì túshūguǎnde shū, rúguǒ nǐ yǒu shénme jiànjiě, xiězài bǐjìběn-shang, bié xiězài shūshang.

Examples of ambiguous cases:

● *After I went to college, I no longer lived at home.*
  ✓ 我上大学以后，就不住在家里了。　or …，就不在家里住了。
  Wǒ shàng dàxué yǐhòu, jiù bú zhùzài jiālǐ le.　or **…, jiù búzài jiālǐ zhùle.**
  (ambiguity in whether the "act of living" is acted upon the home.)

● *Every year, there are some homeless people who freeze to death in the street.*
  ✓ 每年都有一些无家可归的人在街头冻死。or …冻死在街头。
  Měinián dōu yǒu yìxiē wú-jiā-kě-guīde rén zài jiētóu dòngsǐ. or **…dòngsǐ zài jiētóu.**
  (The street is where the "freezing to death" occurs. Obviously, it makes no sense to have the "freezing to death" acted upon the street. Going by the rule of thumb, the first option is the correct one. But the following paragraph explains why the second option is more than acceptable as well.)

Native Chinese speakers are clear about the usage of "在… **zài**…" in front of the verb, but even they are sometimes confused about the usage of "在… **zài**…" after the verb. Their sense of word order is intuitive, so they usually speak with correct word order, even if they cannot explain the distinction between the *coverbal* and the *postverbal* 在 **zài**. Another factor in this lack of clarity is that this distinction does not exist in literary Chinese. The literary Chinese equivalent of 在 **zài** is 于 **yú** which may either precede or follow the verb. As we noted earlier, elements of literary Chinese are ever-present in modern Chinese, especially in poetic things like song lyrics or highly formal speech. In a phrase like 冻死在街头 **dòngsǐ zài jiētóu**, using the less standard word order gives it a literary flavor and makes it more eloquent and dramatic.

EXERCISES:

Translate the following sentences into Chinese:

1. My eyes are poor, so I need to sit in the front.

2. He no longer works in the restaurant; he has found a real job now.

3. She is studying Chinese at Harvard now, but she heard the learning environment in Taiwan is very good, so she wants to go there to study next year.

ANSWERS:

1. 我的眼睛不好，所以我必须坐在前面。
   Wǒde yǎnjing bù hǎo, suǒyǐ wǒ bìxū zuòzài qiánmian.

2. 他不在餐馆打工了，因为他找到一个正式的工作了。
   Tā bú zài cānguǎn dǎgōng le, yīnwèi tā zhǎodào yíge zhèngshìde gōngzuò le.

3. 她现在在哈佛学中文，可是她听说台湾的学习环境很好，所以想明年到那儿去学习。
   Tā xiànzài zài Hāfó xué Zhōngwén, kěshì tā tīngshuō Táiwānde xuéxí huánjìng hěn hǎo, suǒyǐ xiǎng míngnián dào nàr qù xuéxí.

For English speakers who are learning Chinese, there are two key principles to remember when formulating Chinese sentences about time:

1. The distinction between "point in time" (i.e. *when something happens*) and "time duration" (i.e. *for how long something happens*) determines their order within a sentence. For convenience, we will call these two time concepts "time-when" and "time-span" in this chapter. The distinction between the two is clear in most cases, but as we will see below, there are cases where it is less than obvious.

2. Compared with English, Chinese word order for both kinds of time expressions is much less flexible. Therefore, the pitfall of "thinking in English" when forming Chinese sentences is especially hazardous when it comes to time expressions. The following two groups of sentences illustrate the range of possible word orders in English and Chinese, and some crucial differences.

> *Next year I'm going to Japan to study.*
> *I'm going to Japan <u>next year</u> to study.*
> *I'm going to Japan to study <u>next year</u>.*
> 我明年要去日本留学。 **Wǒ míngnián yào qù Rìběn liúxué.**
> 明年我要去日本留学。 **Míngnián wǒ yào qù Rìběn liúxué.**

In the example above, there are three possible word orders in English but only two in Chinese.

> *<u>For two years</u>, our family lived in the country.*
> *Our family lived in the country <u>for two years</u>.*
> *Our family lived <u>for two years</u> in the country.*
> 我们家在乡下住了两年。 **Wǒmen jiā zài xiāngxià zhùle liǎngnián.**

In the above example, there are three possible word orders in English but only one in Chinese.

If we add "During the Cultural Revolution" to the above sentence (add a *time-when* to the existing *time-span*), then the possible permutations in English increase to 7, while there is only one correct word order in Chinese:

> 在文革期间，我们家在乡下住了两年。
> **Zài Wén-Gé qījiān, wǒmen jiā zài xiāngxia zhùle liǎngnián.**

10.1 *Time-when* expressions

There are two correct positions for *time-when* expressions within a Chinese sentence: either before or after the subject, but always before the predicate.

(*time-when* expression) + subject + (*time-when* expression) + predicate

Both the subject and the predicate may be single words or complex phrases with one or more modifiers. In each of the following examples in English and Chinese, identify the *time-when* element and note its position within the sentence.

- *He will come today. (Today he will come.)*
    - ✓ 他今天会来。 **Tā jīntiān huì lái.**
    - ✓ 今天他会来。 **Jīntiān tā huì lái.**

- *Every year in November, we have a conference on Chinese language teaching.*
    我们每年十一月举行一次汉语教学研讨会。
    Wǒmen měinián shíyīyuè jǔxíng yícì Hànyǔ jiàoxué yántǎohuì.

    每年十一月我们举行一次汉语教学研讨会。
    Měinián shíyīyuè wǒmen jǔxíng yícì Hànyǔ jiàoxué yántǎohuì.

- *China did not yet have the "one child policy" in the 1970's.*
    中国在七十年代的时候还没有一胎化政策。
    Zhōngguó zài qīshí niándàide shíhou hái méiyǒu yìtāi-huà zhèngcè.

    在七十年代的时候中国还没有一胎化政策。
    Zài qīshí niándàide shíhou Zhōngguó hái méiyǒu yìtāi-huà zhèngcè.

- *The shoes that you ordered on the web were finally shipped out from the factory in China last week.*
    你在网上订购的鞋子上个星期终于从中国的工厂运出去了。
    Nǐ zài wǎngshang dìnggòude xiézi shàngge xīngqī zhōngyú cóng Zhōngguóde gōngchǎng yùn-chūqu le.

    (Can you identify the subject and predicate in the above sentence?)
    上个星期你在网上订购的鞋子终于从中国的工厂运出去了。
    Shàngge xīngqī nǐ zài wǎngshang dìnggòude xiézi zhōngyú cóng Zhōngguóde gōngchǎng yùn-chūqu le.

    (What event or action does 上个星期 **shàngge xīngqī** refer to? Is there any ambiguity?)

The two following examples also serve to illustrate the position of *time-when* expressions, but in addition, they review grammatical points discussed earlier.

- *I was not homesick the first few days after arriving in Beijing. In the second week, I started getting homesick.*
    刚到北京的那几天我不怎么想家，第二个星期我就开始想家了。
    Gāng dào Běijīngde nèijǐtiān wǒ bù zěnme xiǎngjiā, dì'èrge xīngqī wǒ jiù kāishǐ xiǎngjiā le.

    (What is the function of 了 **le** at the end of the sentence? See 7.2)

● *I was not homesick the first few days after arriving in Beijing. It was not until the second week that I started getting homesick.*

刚到北京的那几天我不怎么想家，第二个星期我才开始想家的。

Gāng dào Běijīngde nèijǐtiān wǒ bù zěnme xiǎngjiā, dì'èrge xīngqī wǒ cái kāishǐ xiǎngjiā de. (What is the difference in meaning between these two sentences? What is the key word in each sentence that resulted in the difference? See 5.2. For an explanation of 的 **de** at the end of the above sentence, see 15.5.)

10.2 *Time-span* expressions

Time-span expressions, as measures of duration of an event or action, always follow the verb. Thus, their position in the sentence is the opposite of *time-when* expressions, which always precede the verb. The event or action referred to can be in the past or future, or can be "neutral" (not related to any point in time).

Subject + verb + *time-span* expression

We normally think of verbs as words which indicate actions, but in Chinese the verb may also be an adjective (also called "stative verb") or a term that describes a state of mind, as we will demonstrate in the examples below. As you read the following sentences, identify the *time-span* as well as *time-when* expression in each one.

● *That International Women's Conference lasted three weeks.* (past event)

那个世界妇女大会举行了三个星期。

Nèige shìjiè fùnǚ dàhuì jǔxíngle sānge xīngqī.

● *The annual Chinese Language Conference only lasts three days.* (neutral time frame)

每年一次的那个汉语教学研讨会只举行三天。

Měinián yícìde nèige Hànyǔ jiàoxué yántǎohuì zhǐ jǔxíng sāntiān.

● *I lived in Taiwan for four years when I was a kid.*

我小时候在台湾住了四年。 **Wǒ xiǎoshíhou zài Táiwān zhùle sìnián.**

● *How long are you planning to stay in Japan this time?*

这次你预备在日本待多长时间？

Zhèicì nǐ yùbèi zài Rìběn dāi duō cháng shíjiān?

● *Employees of this company have two weeks of vacation each year.*

这个公司的员工每年可以休假两个星期。

Zhèige gōngsīde yuángōng měinián kěyǐ xiūjià liǎngge xīngqī.

● *After his wife left him, he was miserable for five years.*

他妻子离开了他以后，他难过了五年。（难过 **nánguò** is a state of mind）

Tā qīzi líkāile tā yǐhòu, tā nánguòle wǔnián.

- *For the sake of saving money for her child's college education, she endured over ten years of hardship.*
  为了省钱给孩子上大学，她辛苦了十几年。
  Wèile shéngqián gěi háizi shàng dàxué, tā xīngkǔle shíjǐ-nián.

A note of caution: *Time-when* expressions are not always just particular moments in time (*year, month, day, "when...,"* etc.). The designated *point in time* may be rather large, so it can sometimes be mistaken for a *time-span* expression. The definitive test is whether the time expression focuses on when something occurs or the length of time the event/action lasts. Compare the usage of 三十年 **sānshí-nián** (*thirty years*) in these two sentences.

- *This Chinese language center has been in operation for thirty years now.*
  这个汉语中心已经办了三十年了。
  Zhèige Hànyǔ zhōngxīn yǐjīng bànle sānshí-nián le.

- *In the past thirty years, this Chinese language center has trained about 2000 students.*
  在过去三十年里，这个汉语中心培训了差不多两千个学生。
  Zài guòqu sānshí-nián-lǐ, zhèige Hànyǔ zhōngxīn péixùnle chàbuduō liǎngqiānge xuésheng.
  (三十年 **sānshí-nián** is a *time-span* expression in the first example—because it addresses the question of *for how long*. In the second example it is a *time-when* expression—because it addresses the question of *when*.)

As you read the following examples, identify the time expressions, and determine whether they indicate *time-when* or *time-span*.

- *They lived in the countryside for decades, so of course they are not used to urban living.*
  他们在乡下住了几十年，当然不习惯都市的生活。
  Tāmen zài xiāngxia zhùle jǐshí-nián, dāngrán bù xíguàn dūshìde shēnghuó.

- *In the ten years that I was sent down to the countryside, I did all kinds of farm work.*
  我下乡的那十年，什么农活都干过。
  Wǒ xiàxiāngde nà shínián, shénme nónghuó dōu gànguo.

- *In summer school, I lived with a Chinese roommate for ten weeks.*
  在暑期班，我跟一个中国同屋一起住了十个星期。
  Zài shǔqī-bān, wǒ gēn yíge Zhōngguó tóngwū yìqǐ zhùle shíge xīngqī.

- *During those ten weeks, I didn't speak a word of English.*
  那十个星期，我一句英文都没说。
  Nà shíge xīngqī, wǒ yíjù Yīngwén dōu méi shuō.

- *When I married him 60 years ago, I decided to love him for a whole life time.*
  我六十年前跟他结婚的时候，就决定了要爱他一辈子。
  Wǒ liùshínián qián gēn tā jiéhūnde shíhou, jiù juédìngle yào ài tā yíbèizi.

♦ *That couple have never had a fight in their entire lives!*
那对夫妻一辈子都没吵过架。**Nèiduì fūqī yíbèizi dōu méi chǎo-guo-jià.**

In the last example sentence, it might be argued that 一辈子 **yíbèizi** indicates both *time-when* and *time-span*. Its position—before the verb phrase 都没吵过架 **dōu méi chǎo-guo-jià**—might indicate that it is a *time-when* expression, but even if it describes a *time-span*, the adverb 都 **dōu** pre-empts the normal position and re-positions it to precede 都 **dōu**. In 5.1, sec.1 we saw how the adverb 都 **dōu** always refers to something prestated, i.e. that "something" being *totalized* by 都 **dōu** must be placed before 都 **dōu**. This in effect creates an exception to the general word order for *time-span* expressions. The following pairs of examples state essentially the same facts, but there is a difference in nuance between them because of the addition of 都 **dōu**.

♦ *She was a professor at Harvard for 30 years.*
她在哈佛大学当教授当了30年。
Tā zài Hāfó Dàxué dāng jiàoshòu dāngle 30 nián.

♦ *She was a professor at Harvard for all those 30 years.*
她那30年都在哈佛大学当教授。
Tā nèi 30 nián dōu zài Hāfó Dàxué dāng jiàoshòu.

♦ *When I was in college, I worked in a Chinese restaurant for four years.*
我上大学期间，在中国餐馆打工打了四年。
Wǒ shàng dàxué qījiān, zài Zhōngguó cānguǎn dǎgōng dǎle sìnián.

♦ *I worked in a Chinese restaurant all four years that I was in college.*
我上大学的那四年，一直都在中国餐馆打工。
Wǒ shàng dàxuéde nèi sìnián, yìzhí dōu zài Zhōngguó cānguǎn dǎgōng.

EXERCISES: ▶

Translate the following sentences into Chinese:

1. He lived in Chengdu for five years.
2. During those five years, he taught at Sichuan Normal University.
3. I'm going to Kunming in three days.
4. We have a vacation next week; I want to go to Kunming for three days.
5. When my father first arrived in the U.S., he stayed on Angel Island for 3 months. During those 3 months, he got very homesick.
6. In the past, students from China did odd jobs every summer; nowadays, most of them go home for a three-month vacation!

ANSWERS:
1. 他在成都住了五年。**Tā zài Chéngdū zhùle wǔnián.**
2. 那五年，他在四川师范大学教书。**Nà wǔnián, tā zài Sìchuān Shīfàn Dàxué jiāoshū.**

3. 我三天以后到昆明去。or …去昆明。
   Wǒ sāntiān yǐhòu dào Kūnmíng qù or **…qù Kūnmíng.**

4. 我们下星期放假。我想去昆明三天。
   Wǒmen xià-xīngqī fàngjià. Wǒ xiǎng qù Kūnmíng sāntiān.

5. 我父亲刚到美国的时候，在天使岛呆了三个月。那三个月(中)，他非常想家。
   Wǒ fùqin gāng dào Měiguóde shíhou, zài Tiānshǐ Dǎo dāile sānge yuè. Nà sānge yuè (zhōng), tā fēicháng xiǎngjiā.

6. 从前来自中国的留学生每年夏天都打工；现在他们多半回家休假三个月！
   Cóngqián láizì Zhōngguóde liúxuésheng měinián xiàtiān dōu dǎgōng; xiànzài tāmen duōbàn huíjiā xiūjià sānge yuè!

10.3 *Time-span* expressions with verbs that have an object

In English, the position of a *time-span* phrase is not affected by whether or not the verb has an object. In Chinese, the basic sentence pattern discussed in the preceding section morphs into several variations depending on the type of object and whether the *aspect marker* 了 **le** is used after the verb (see Chapters 7 and 8).

First, we need to distinguish "direct objects" from "indirect objects." Direct objects are integral to the action of the verb, e.g. *to play basketball, to do homework, to teach Chinese.* Indirect objects are the persons or things to which an action is done, e.g. *to take care of children, to teach American students.*

- I do homework for 5 hours every day. (*homework* is direct object)
- My grandma took care of me for 10 years. (*me* is indirect object)
- Prof. Li taught Chinese for 10 years, and linguistics for 5 years. (both *Chinese* and *linguistics* are direct objects)
- Prof. Li taught me Chinese for only one year. (*me* is indirect object, *Chinese* is direct object)

Each of the above sentences may be translated into Chinese using two different patterns. As you read the Chinese translations, notice the word order of the direct and indirect objects, as well as the *time-span* expressions:

- *I do homework for 5 hours every day.* (*homework* is direct object)
  - ✓ 我每天做功课做五个小时。 **Wǒ měitiān zuò gōngkè zuò wǔge xiǎoshí.**
  - ✓ 我每天做五个小时的功课。 **Wǒ měitiān zuò wǔge xiǎoshíde gōngkè.**
  - ✗ 我每天做功课五个小时。 **Wǒ měitiān zuò gōngkè wǔge xiǎoshí.**

- *My grandma took care of me for 10 years.* (*me* is indirect object)
  - ✓ 我姥姥照顾我照顾了十年。 **Wǒ lǎolao zhàogù wǒ zhàogùle shínián.**
  - ✓ 我姥姥照顾了我十年。 **Wǒ lǎolao zhàogùle wǒ shínián.**
  - ✗ 我姥姥照顾了十年我。 **Wǒ lǎolao zhàogùle shínián wǒ.**

♦ *Prof. Li taught Chinese for 10 years, and linguistics for 5 years.* (both *Chinese* and *linguistics* are direct objects)

✓ 李教授教中文教了十年，（教)语言学教了五年。
  Lǐ Jiàoshòu jiāo Zhōngwén jiāole shínián, (jiāo) yǔyánxué jiāole wǔnián.

✓ 李教授教了十年中文，（教了)五年语言学。
  Lǐ Jiàoshòu jiāole shínián Zhōngwén, (jiāole) wǔnián yǔyánxué.

✗ 李教授教了中文十年，（教了）语言学五年。
  Lǐ Jiàoshòu jiāole Zhōngwén shínián, (jiāole) yǔyánxué wǔnián.

♦ *Prof. Li taught me Chinese for only one year.* (*me* is indirect object, *Chinese* is direct object)

✓ 李教授教我中文只教了一年。 **Lǐ Jiàoshòu jiāo wǒ Zhōngwén zhǐ jiāole yìnián.**

✓ 李教授只教了我一年(的)中文。 **Lǐ Jiàoshòu zhǐ jiāole wǒ yìnián(de) Zhōngwén.**

✗ 李教授只教了一年我中文。 **Lǐ Jiàoshòu zhǐ jiāole yìnián wǒ Zhōngwén.**

1. The first Chinese sentence in each of the four examples above exhibits the same pattern regardless of whether the object is direct or indirect. The verb and the object (indirect or direct, or both) are first linked, as though they become one item, then the verb is repeated, with the *time-span* expression following it to indicate the duration. If the action is already "complete," the *aspect marker* 了 **le** is suffixed to the verb.

> Subject + verbs + object (indirect or direct) +verb (了 **le**) + *time-span*

This is the most commonly used pattern when the *aspect marker* 了 **le** is used in a sentence. This pattern may sound a bit redundant however, and is not the preferred pattern when the verb does not carry the *aspect marker* 了 **le**. Thus, in the first of the four examples above, the second Chinese translation is the preferred version.

2. The second Chinese sentence in each of the four examples above exhibits two different word orders depending on whether the object is direct or indirect:

With direct object:
Subject + verb (了 **le**) + *time-span* (的 **de**) + direct object

With indirect object, and optional direct object:
Subject + verb (了 **le**) + indirect object + *time-span* (+ direct object)

In all four examples, the faulty Chinese translations given at the end are due to mismatching the sentence pattern with the nature of the object. These two patterns are more succinct than the one discussed in 1 above, but because the nature of the object creates a difference in word order, they present a challenge (some would say a pitfall) to non-native speakers. One mnemonic device that may help is this: Since a *time-span* measures the duration of an action, it can be construed as a *quantifier* of a direct object, but not of an indirect object. Therefore it must come before a direct object but after an indirect object. The "modifier particle" 的 **de** may be optionally tagged onto a *time-span* before a direct object, thus reinforcing the idea that it measures the direct object. The same cannot be done with an indirect object.

Even for students who think they have mastered the distinction between direct and indirect objects, the choice of which of the two above patterns to use can still be confusing, because in many cases, it is virtually impossible to tell whether an object is integral to the action (direct object) or the "thing" which is acted upon (indirect object). The following examples serve to illustrate this ambiguity.

♦ *Every Sunday, I spend three hours cleaning rooms.* (the object is *rooms*)

   ✓ 每个星期天我打扫房间打扫三个小时。
      Měige xīngqītiān wǒ dǎsǎo fángjiān dǎsǎo sānge xiǎoshí.

   ✓ 每个星期天我花三个小时打扫房间。
      Měige xīngqītiān wǒ huā sānge xiǎoshí dǎsǎo fángjiān.

   ✗ 每个星期天我打扫三个小时(的)房间。
      Měige xīngqītiān wǒ dǎsǎo sānge xiǎoshí(de) fángjiān.

♦ *We've been eating dinner for an hour.* (the object is *dinner*)

   ✓ 我们吃晚饭吃了一个小时了。 **Wǒmen chī wǎnfàn chīle yíge xiǎoshí le.**
   ✗ 我们吃了一个小时的晚饭了。 **Wǒmen chīle yíge xiǎoshí de wǎnfàn le.**

In each example, the object seems to be a direct object, although it is difficult to rationalize the *time-span* as a *quantifier* for that object. But the last Chinese translation for each example—using the pattern for direct objects—turns out not to be correct. In both cases, using the pattern presented in 1 above is correct. Native Chinese speakers have an intuitive sense of which pattern to use. Until you acquire that native intuition, it would be best, when in doubt, to use the pattern presented in 1, in which the verb is repeated.

In the preceding discussion, we have already included examples that include the *aspect marker* 了 **le**, either suffixed to a verb and/or at the end of the sentence. If you are still not clear about the various usages of this *aspect marker*, this would be a good time to review Chapter 7. We bring up this topic here only to reassure you that the addition of 了 **le** does not alter the word order of the sentence. As you read the example sentences below, think about the function of the marker 了 **le**, and explain why the sentences marked with an "✗" are incorrect.

♦ *He studied in college for four years, but did not graduate.*

   ✓ 他读了四年(的)大学，可是没毕业。
      Tā dúle sìnián(de) dàxué, kěshì méi bìyè.

   ✗ 他读了大学四年，⋯ **Tā dúle dàxué sìnián, ...**

♦ *I did three hours of homework tonight. Although I didn't finish, I'm going to bed.*

   ✓ 我今晚做了三个小时的功课，虽然没做完，我要去睡觉了。
      Wǒ jīnwǎn zuòle sānge xiǎoshíde gōngkè, suīrán méi zuòwán, wǒ yào qù shuìjiàole.

   ✗ 我今晚做了功课三个小时，⋯ **Wǒ jīnwǎn zuòle gōngkè sānge xiǎoshí, ...**

◆ *I've done three hours of homework already tonight. and I'm still not finished!*
(implying that he will continue to work on his homework until it is done)

   ✓ 我今晚已经做了三个小时的功课了，还没做完呢！
     Wǒ jīnwǎn yǐjīng zuòle sānge xiǎoshíde gōngkè le, hái méi zuòwán ne!

   ✓ 我今晚做功课已经做了三个小时了，···
     Wǒ jīnwǎn zuò gōngkè yǐjīng zuòle sānge xiǎoshí le, ...

   ✗ 我今晚已经做了功课三个小时了，···
     Wǒ jīnwǎn yǐjīng zuòle gōngkè sānge xiǎoshí le, ...

◆ *Kids need to sleep 10 hours each day.*

   ✓ 孩子每天需要睡十个小时。 **Háizi měitiān xūyào shuì shíge xiǎoshí.**

   ✓ 孩子每天需要睡十个小时的觉。 **Háizi měitiān xūyào shuì shíge xiǎoshíde jiào.**

   ✗ 孩子每天需要睡觉十个小时。 **Háizi měitiān xūyào shuìjiào shíge xiǎoshí.**

◆ *This kid has been sleeping for over 12 hours already* (implying that he is still asleep)

   ✓ 这个孩子已经睡了十二个小时了。
     Zhèige háizi yǐjīng shuìle shí'èrge xiǎoshí le.

   ✓ 这个孩子已经睡觉睡了十二个小时了。
     Zhèige háizi yǐjīng shuìjiào shuìle shí'èrge xiǎoshí le.

   ✗ 这个孩子已经睡觉十二个小时了。
     Zhèige háizi yǐjīng shuìjiào shí'èrge xiǎoshí le.

Aside from the sentence patterns presented in 1 and 2 above, native speakers use two other variations in which the object is placed before the verb for special emphasis. These variations are worth learning, at least to understand them.

Direct object + subject + verb (了 **le**) + *time-span*   (了 **le**)

Subject + direct object + verb (了 **le**) + *time-span*   (了 **le**)
(less commonly used than the preceding one)

◆ *I cannot rest even on Sundays, because I have to do housework for a whole day!*
我星期天也不能休息，因为家务就得做一整天！
Wǒ xīngqītiān yě bùnéng xiūxi, yīnwèi jiāwù jiù děi zuò yìzhěngtiān!
(家务 **jiāwù** is preposed for special emphasis)

◆ *Her major in college was English. At that time, she planned to teach English her whole life. Surprisingly, she ended up teaching English for only five years, but Chinese she taught for thirty years.*
她大学的专业是英语，当时她预备教一辈子英语。没想到，<u>英语</u>她只教了五年，<u>汉语</u>她倒是教了三十年。
Tā dàxuéde zhuānyè shì Yīngyǔ, dāngshí tā yùbèi jiāo yíbèizi Yīngyǔ. Méi xiǎng-dào, yīngyǔ tā zhǐ jiāole wǔnián, Hànyǔ tā dàoshi jiāole sānshí-nián.
(英语 **Yīngyǔ** and 汉语 **Hànyǔ** are preposed as the topic of the last two clauses in this sentence, thus juxtaposing them for extra emphasis.)

EXERCISES:

Translate the following sentences in Chinese:

1. She taught Chinese for forty years.

2. When you married him, how did you know that he would love you his whole life?

3. After I went abroad, I was awfully homesick the first six months.

4. How long does it take to go from Beijing to Shanghai by train?

5. We've been driving for ten hours already. How come we're not there yet?!

6. I loved him for twenty years, in the end he married someone else!

ANSWERS:

1. 他教中文教了四十年。 **Tā jiāo Zhōngwén jiāole sìshí-nián.**

2. 你跟他结婚的时候，怎么知道他会爱你一辈子呢？
   Nǐ gēn tā jiéhūnde shíhou, zěnme zhīdao tā huì ài nǐ yíbèizi ne?

3. 我出国以后，头六个月非常想家。 **Wǒ chūguó yǐhòu, tóu liùge yuè fēicháng xiǎngjiā.**

4. 从北京到上海，坐火车要多长时间？
   Cóng Běijīng dào Shànghǎi, zuò huǒchē yào duō cháng shíjiān?

5. 我们(开车)已经开了十个小时了，怎么还没到呢？
   Wǒmen (kāichē) yǐjing kāile shíge xiǎoshí le, zěnme hái méi dào ne?

6. 我爱了他二十年，最后他跟别人结婚了。
   Wǒ àile tā èrshí-nián, zuì hòu tā gēn biérén jiéhūn le.

10.4 Expressing time lapse

To indicate an amount of time that has passed since a particular event has occurred (e.g. since graduation from college, getting married, starting a job, death), or since a situation began (e.g. being ill, being married, becoming a vegetarian), a *time-span* expression is positioned at the end of the sentence. More often than not, the situation is ongoing (i.e. it is still continuing at present), in which case the *sentence-ending* 了 le is added as well (see 7.3, sec. 1).

First, let's compare the following two sentences to see the differences between an expression of *time-span* vs a expression of *time lapse*.

♦ *For how many years was he on drugs?*
(*time-span* indicating duration of an activity; implying that he is no longer on drugs.)
他吸了几年毒？ **Tā xīle jǐnián dú?** or 他吸毒吸了几年？ **Tā xīdú xīle jǐnián?**

♦ *How many years has it been since he started taking drugs?*
(*time lapse* since activity began, implying that he is still on drugs.)
他吸毒几年了？ **Tā xīdú jǐnián le?**

Additional examples of *time lapse*:

- *It's been three years since I left home, but I still get homesick every day.*
  我离开家三年了，可是还是每天都想家。
  Wǒ líkāi jiā sānnián le, kěshì háishi měitiān dōu xiǎngjiā.

- *It's been a month since we moved here, so we're used to everything now.*
  我们搬到这儿来一个月了，一切都习惯了。
  Wǒmen bāndào zhèr lái yíge yuè le, yíqiè dōu xíguànle.

- *They've been married for 20 years, and have had a good relationship all along. How come they suddenly want to get divorced?*
  他们结婚二十年了，关系一直很好，怎么突然要离婚了呢？
  Tāmen jiéhūn èrshí-nián le, guānxi yìzhí hěn hǎo, zěnme tūrán yào líhūn le ne?

- *They are planning to go to Canada for a few years first, then consider immigrating to the U.S.*
  他们打算先去加拿大几年，然后再考虑移民来美国。
  Tāmen dǎsuàn xiān qù Jiānádà jǐnián, ránhòu zài kǎolǜ yímín lái Měiguó.
  (In the first clause, the *time lapse* is contemplated for the foreseeable future, and does not refer to an event that has already occurred, hence no 了 **le** is used at the end of it.)

- *I've been a vegetarian for 10 years now. (It's been 10 years since I became vegetarian.)*
  我吃素十年了。 **Wǒ chīsù shínián le.** or
  我吃素吃了十年了。 **Wǒ chīsù chīle shínián le.**

EXERCISES:

Translate the following sentences into Chinese:

1. It's been 3 years since they got married. Aren't they thinking of having children?
2. It's been over five years since my doggie died, I still miss him every day!
3. He quit smoking for three years, then started up again! (quit smoking: 戒烟 **jièyān**)
4. Its been three years already since I quit smoking, I don't think I'll ever smoke again!

ANSWERS:

1. 他们结婚三年了。他们不想要孩子吗？
   Tāmen jiéhūn sānnián le. Tāmen bù xiǎng yào háizi ma?
2. 我的小狗死了五年多了，我还是每天都想它。
   Wǒde xiǎogǒu sǐle wǔnián-duō le, wǒ háishi měitiān dōu xiǎng tā.
3. 他戒烟戒了三年，然后又抽起烟来了！
   Tā jièyān jièle sānnián, ránhòu yòu chōu-qǐ-yān-lái le.
4. 我戒烟已经三年了，我想我再也不会抽烟了。
   Wǒ jièyān yǐjing sānnián le, wǒ xiǎng wǒ zài yě búhuì chōuyān le.

10.5 *Time-span* during which an action or event has NOT occurred

In contrast to all the *time-span* expressions we have discussed so far, *time-span* as measure of time lapse *without* a certain action or event occurring is positioned *before* the verb phrase. The negative used with the verb is either 没 **méi** or 不 **bù**, depending on whether the onset of the situation was in the past.

Subject + *time-span* + 不 **bù** or 没 **méi** + verb phrase + (了 **le**)

♦ *He is seriously ill, and hasn't eaten for three days now.*
他病得很厉害，三天没吃饭了。 **Tā bìngde hěn lìhai, sāntiān méi chīfàn le.**

♦ *If a person doesn't drink any liquid for three days, he won't be able to live anymore.*
人要是三天不喝水，就活不了了。
Rén yàoshi sāntiān bù hēshuǐ, jiù huó-bù-liǎo le.

♦ *Camels are OK without drinking water for three days.*
骆驼三天不喝水也没关系。 **Luòtuo sāntiān bù hēshuǐ yě méiguānxi.**

♦ *It hasn't rained here for three months already.*
这里已经三个月没下雨了。 **Zhèlǐ yǐjīng sānge yuè méi xiàyǔ le.**

♦ *I've been a vegetarian for 10 years already, in other words, I haven't eaten meat for ten years now.*
我吃素已经十年了，也就是说，我十年没吃肉了。
Wǒ chīsù yǐjīng shínián le, yě jiùshi shuō, wǒ shínián méi chī ròu le.

EXERCISES:

Translate the following sentences into Chinese:

1. We have had no news of him for twenty years now. Is he still alive?
2. Oh, it's been five years already since he passed away.
3. After you return to the U.S., if you don't speak Chinese for two years, you will forget it all!

ANSWERS:
1. 我们二十年没他的消息了，他还活着吗？
   Wǒmen èrshí-nián méi tāde xiāoxi le, tā hái huózhe ma?
2. 噢，他去世已经五年了。**Ō, tā qùshì yǐjing wǔnián le.**
3. 你回美国以后，如果两年不说中文，就会完全忘记了！
   Nǐ huí Měiguó yǐhòu, rúguǒ liǎngnián bù shuō Zhōngwén, jiù huì wánquán wàngjì le.

10.6 *Time-span* with 了 le to indicate an ongoing situation or action

This section is a summary of a grammatical point that has been touched upon before, so you may have a feeling of déjà-vu, but it is an important point that deserves to be reinforced. The *aspect marker* 了 le at the end of a sentence is just a single syllable, pronounced without stress or tone, so its significance is easy to overlook. In fact, it conveys the key information that the action or situation conveyed in the sentence is still continuing at present, and it may last indefinitely. The *time-span* in such a sentence indicates how long the action or situation has been going on. If the sentence has a 了 le after the verb but not at the end, it means the action or situation was concluded after the *time-span* referred to. If the sentence does not have either a *verb-ending* 了 le or the *sentence-ending* 了 le, then it is in a neutral time frame. In a sentence or clause that does not include a *time-span*, the *sentence-ending* 了 le indicates a change of status or onset of a new situation (see 7.2).

- *He had been on drugs for 10 years, this year he finally quit.*
  他吸毒吸了十年，今年终于戒了毒了。
  Tā xīdú xīle shínián, jīnnián zhōngyú jièle-dú le.
  (The *sentence-ending* 了 le in the second clause indicates a change from a previous situation.)

- *He has been on drugs for 10 years, and could never quit.*
  他吸毒吸了十年了，一直没法子戒(毒)。
  Tā xīdú xīle shíniánle, yìzhí méi fázi jiè(dú).
  (The *sentence-ending* 了 le in the first clause indicates an ongoing situation.)

- *There had been no rain here for three years, then a big rain this year caused a flood.*
  这里三年没下雨，今年一下就造成了水灾！
  Zhèlǐ sānnián méi xiàyǔ, jīnnián yí xià jiù zàochéngle shuǐzāi!

- *There has been no rain here for three years, so the farmers have to go find jobs in the city.*
  这里三年没下雨了，农民只好到城里打工去了。
  Zhèlǐ sānnián méi xiàyǔ le, nóngmín zhǐhǎo dào chénglǐ dǎgōng qù le.
  (The *sentence-ending* 了 le in the first clause indicates an ongoing situation; its use in the second clause indicates the onset of a new situation.)

- *Train tickets had not gone up in price in ten years, this time, it doubled in price in just one price increase!*
  火车票十年没涨价，这次一涨就涨了一倍！
  Huǒchēpiào shínián méi zhǎngjià, zhèicì yì zhǎng jiù zhǎngle yíbèi!
  (The *verb-ending* 了 le indicates "completion")

● *The boss hasn't given us a raise for three years now, so those of us who can find other jobs are quitting.*
老板三年没给我们加薪了，所以能找到别的工作的人都要辞职了。
Lǎobǎn sānnián méi gěi wǒmen jiāxīn le, suǒyǐ néng zhǎodào biéde gōngzuòde rén dōu yào cízhí le.
(The *sentence-ending* 了 le in the first clause indicates an ongoing situation; its use in the second clause indicates onset of a new situation.)

EXERCISES:

Translate the following sentences into Chinese:

1. After being unemployed for two years, I finally found a job.
2. He's been unemployed for over two years now, so he has decided he might as well stay home and be a househusband.
3. Since I started eating an apple a day, I have not been sick for two years now.

ANSWERS:
1. 我失业两年以后，终于找到工作了。
   Wǒ shíyè liǎngnián yǐhòu, zhōngyú zhǎodao gōngzuò le.
2. 他已经两年没工作了，所以决定干脆呆在家里当家庭主夫了。
   Tā yǐjīng liǎngnián méi gōngzuò le, suǒyǐ juédìng gāncuì dāizài jiālǐ dāng jiātíng zhǔfū le.
3. 自从我开始每天吃一个苹果以来，两年没生病了。
   Zìcóng wǒ kāishǐ měitiān chī yíge píngguǒ yǐlái, liǎngnián méi shēngbìng le.

10.7 *Time-when* and *time-span* expressions according to the clock

Time-when and *time-span* expressions that are measured by the clock follow the same word order within a sentence as described earlier in this chapter. Within a time expression having more than one type of units, the word order follows the general principle of larger before smaller (see 4.8). There is considerable overlap in the vocabulary used for *time-when* vs *time-span* expressions, but also some differences as well.

1. *Points in time* as measured by the clock

In everyday Chinese, the 12-hour format is used, just as in English. But in time schedules, the 24-hour format is standard.

Key vocabulary in referring to points in time:

点 **diǎn** *hour*	分 **fēn** *minute*	刻 **kè** *quarter hour*	秒 **miǎo** *second*
过 **guò** *past*	差 **chà** *short of, before*	零 **líng** *"zero" (filler)*	钟 **zhōng** *clock*
半 **bàn** *half*	多 **duō** *(and) more*	整 **zhěng** *exactly on the hour*	

The following examples illustrates the entire range of *points in time*. A parenthesis indicates that a word is optional, and in fact might be redundant, although it is used by some native speakers.

8:00	八点(钟) bādiǎn (zhōng); 八点(整) bādiǎn (zhěng)
8:00-9:00	八点多 bādiǎn-duō Technically, 多 duō can mean any time in the 8:00-9:00 range, but it is used more commonly to refer to a small amount of time after the hour.
8:02	八点(零)二分 bādiǎn (líng) èrfēn The optional 零 líng represents zero, and it is only used for times that are 1–9 minutes after the hour. Note that 二 èr is used before 分 fēn, but 两 liǎng is used before 点 diǎn (e.g. 2:02 两点零二分 liǎngdiǎn líng èrfēn). See 4.5 for an explanation of 二 èr vs 两 liǎng.
8:20	八点(过)二十(分) bādiǎn (guò) èrshí(fēn) 分 fēn is optional, but 过 guò is even more so. It is rarely used today. (Similarly, in English we rarely say "twenty minutes past eight," since "eight twenty" is shorter.)
8:15	八点(过)十五(分) bādiǎn (guò) shíwǔ(fēn); 八点(过)一刻 bādiǎn (guò) yíkè The 分 fēn and the 刻 kè formats are about equally common.
8:30	八点三十(分) bādiǎn sānshí(fēn); 八点半 bādiǎnbàn
8:45	八点四十五(分) bādiǎn sìshíwǔ(fēn); 八点三刻 bādiǎn sānkè; 九点差一刻 jiǔdiǎn chà yíkè; 差一刻九点 chà yíkè jiǔdiǎn Impressionistically, 八点三刻 bādiǎn sānkè seems more common because it is more succinct. There are two possible positions for the "差… chà..." expressions. Having the hour precede the "差… chà..." phrase conforms to the principle of the larger unit preceding the smaller one. But temporally, the notion of "差… chà..." precedes the hour. Thus, both are possible, and equally common.
8:50	八点五十(分) bādiǎn wǔshí(fēn); 九点差十分 jiǔdiǎn chà shífēn; 差十分九点 chà shífēn jiǔdiǎn

In English, the terms "a.m." and "p.m." divide the 24-hour day into two segments. In the Chinese mind, the day is divided into more than two segments, and they are represented by the following vocabulary:

凌晨 língchén *wee hours of the morning*
清晨 qīngchén *early morning* (starting around dawn)
早上 zǎoshang *morning*　　　　　上午 shàngwǔ *before noon*
下午 xiàwǔ *afternoon*　　　　　　晚上 wǎnshang *evening*

When any of the above are used with a specific point in time, it precedes the hour and the minute, which is consistent with the principle that larger units preceding smaller units. In addition, there are the two words— 中午 zhōngwǔ *noon* and 半夜 bànyè *midnight*—that may precede the hour of 12:00.

◆ *I did homework until 3:00 a.m. last night before going to bed!*
我昨天做功课做到凌晨三点才睡觉！
Wǒ zuótiān zuò gōngkè zuòdào língchén sāndiǎn cái shuìjiào!

◆ *To avoid traffic jam, he starts out at the early hour of 6:00 a.m. every day.*
为了避免塞车，他每天清晨六点(钟)就出门。
Wèile bìmiǎn sāichē, tā měitiān qīngchén liùdiǎn(zhōng) jiù chūmén.

◆ *The train should have arrived at 11:00 a.m. sharp. It's already a quarter to twelve, why has it not arrived yet?*
火车应该上午十一点整到站，现在已经差一刻十二点了，怎么还没到？ **Huǒchē yīnggāi shàngwǔ shíyīdiǎn-zhěng dàozhàn, xiànzài yǐjīng chàyíkè shí'èrdiǎn le, zěnme hái méi dào?**

In talking about the present, it may strike you as odd that the sentence always ends in a 了 **le**, whether it is a statement or a question. To the Western mind, the *sentence-ending* 了 **le** doesn't convey any meaning here, and doesn't serve a grammatical function either. However, as mentioned in 7.3, sec. 3, in the Chinese mindset, time is never at a standstill. A sentence or clause expressing age or time usually carries *sentence-ending* 了 **le** to convey the sense of "progression of time," even though native Chinese speakers may not be conscious of it.

◆ *What time is it now? It's 8:00.*
(现在)几点了？(现在)八点了。 **(Xiànzài) jǐdiǎn le? (Xiànzài) bādiǎn le.**
In everyday speech, 现在 **xiànzài** is often dispensed with because it is understood; but the *sentence-ending* 了 **le** is indispensable, and the sentence would sound abrupt and incomplete without it.

EXERCISES:

Translate the following into Chinese, using multiple formats if appropriate:

1. 9:30

2. a bit past 10:00 a.m.

3. 11:45 p.m.

4. 12:00 p.m. on the dot

5. Oh no, it's 2:05 already, I hope the train hasn't left yet!

ANSWERS:
1. 九点半、九点三十(分) **jiǔdiǎn-bàn, jiǔdiǎn sānshí(fēn)**
2. 上午十点多 **shàngwǔ shídiǎn-duō**
3. 晚上十一点三刻／四十五(分) **wǎnshang shíyīdiǎn sānkè/sìshíwǔ(fēn)**
4. 中午十二点(整) **zhōngwǔ shí'èrdiǎn (zhěng)**
5. 糟糕，已经两点(过)五分了，我希望火车还没走！
   Zāogāo, yǐjīng liǎngdiǎn (guò) wǔfēn le, wǒ xīwàng huǒchē hái méi zǒu!

2. *Time-spans* as measured by the clock

The methods of quantifying time are the same as quantifying anything else, and therefore most of the rules presented in Chapter 4 apply to *time-spans* as well. However, there is an anomaly in the grammar of 分 **fēn** and 刻 **kè** that deserves special mention. Just as 月 **yuè** and 星期 **xīngqī** function like nouns, whereas 年 **nián** and 天 **tiān** function like measure words (see 4.3, section 6), 钟头 **zhōngtóu** and 小时 **xiǎoshí** function like nouns, whereas 刻 **kè** and 分 **fēn** function like measure words.

time units	usage of time unit in *time-span* phrases (set pattern: number + measure + noun)
hour 钟头 **zhōngtóu**/ 小时 **xiǎoshí** (noun) 钟头 **zhōngtóu** and 小时 **xiǎoshí** are exact synonyms and are interchangeable.	*How many hours?* 几个小时? **jǐge xiǎoshí?** *20 hours* 二十个钟头 **èrshíge zhōngtóu** *half an hour* 半个小时 **bànge xiǎoshí** (半 **bàn** = "half" functions like other numbers in this context) *3 and a half hours* 三个半小时 **sānge-bàn xiǎoshí** *over 3 hours* 三个多小时 **sānge-duō xiǎoshí**

钟头 **zhōngtóu** and 小时 **xiǎoshí** are nouns, therefore a measure word (个 **ge**) must be used when they are quantified.

The position of 半 **bàn** and 多 **duō** in the last two examples follows the pattern for stating a quantity between two whole number (see 4.10), i.e. it follows the measure word.

a quarter of an hour 刻 **kè** (measure word)	*¾ of an hour* 三刻钟 **sānkè zhōng**

The meaning of ¼ hour is conveyed by 刻 **kè**, but because 刻 **kè** is grammatically a measure word and not a noun, a "dummy" noun (钟 **zhōng** meaning "clock") is added to complete the phrase. The same applies to 分 **fēn** in the next row.

minute 分 (measure word)	*20 minutes* 二十分钟 **èrshífēn zhōng**
a *time span* containing two or more levels of units	四个钟头(零)十五分(钟) **sìge zhōngtóu (líng) shíwǔfēn (zhōng)** 四个钟头(零)一刻(钟) **sìge zhōngtóu (líng) yíkè (zhōng)**

When a *time-span* involves an hour unit plus some fraction thereof, the noun 钟 **zhōng** after 分 **fēn** or 刻 **kè** becomes optional, and is in fact usually omitted. The word 零 **líng**, while optional, is usually added. 零 **líng** doesn't have any particular meaning in this context, but adds a sense of rhythm to the phrase. In this regard, it is similar to the word "and" in "four hours *and* fifteen minutes."

a *time span* shorter than a whole hour	四个小时差十五分 **sìge xiǎoshí chà shíwǔfēn** 四个小时差一刻 **sìge xiǎoshí chà yíkè** 差十五分四个小时 **chà shíwǔfēn sìge xiǎoshí** 差一刻四个小时 **chà yíkè sìge xiǎoshí**

The position of " 差··· **chà...**" parallels its usage in *points in time*, i.e. it can precede or follow the hour.

EXERCISES:

Translate the following sentences into Chinese:

1. I have three classes daily. Each class is 50 minutes, with 10 minutes in between. The time I spend in class each day comes to a total of two and a half hours.

2. Monday through Friday, I must get up before 7, so I often don't get enough sleep. On weekends, I can sleep until noon, so sometime I sleep for more than 10 hours!

3. We should have been home by 9:00 p.m., but the plane was delayed by two and a half hours, so we didn't get home until almost midnight!

ANSWERS:

1. 我每天有三节课。每节课是五十分钟，课间休息十分钟。我每天上课的时间是两个半小时。or 我每天上两个半小时的课。**Wǒ měitiān yǒu sānjié kè. Měijié kè shì wǔshífēn zhōng, kèjiān xiūxi shífēn zhōng. Wǒ měitiān shàngkède shíjiān shì liǎngge-bàn xiǎoshí.** or **Wǒ měitiān shàng liǎngge-bàn xiǎoshíde kè.**

2. 星期一到星期五我七点以前就得起床，所以我常常睡得不够。周末我可以睡到中午，所以有时候我睡十多个小时！**Xīngqīyī dào xīngqīwǔ wǒ qīdiǎn yǐqián jiù děi qǐchuáng, suǒyǐ wǒ chángchang shuìde búgòu. Zhōumò wǒ kěyǐ shuìdào zhōngwǔ, suǒyǐ yǒu shíhou wǒ shuì shí-duō-ge xiǎoshí!**

3. 我们本来九点就应该到家了，可是飞机晚了两个半小时，所以我们差不多夜里十二点(整)才到家！**Wǒmen běnlái jiǔdiǎn jiù yīnggāi dàojiā le, kěshì fēijī wǎnle liǎngge-bàn xiǎoshí, suǒyǐ wǒmen chàbuduō yèli shí'èrdiǎn (zhěng) cái dào jiā!**

10.8 Words to express relative time frames

We use the word "relative" when time frames being discussed are indicated in relation to other events, either explicitly or implicitly. Relative time frames come in two forms: those that are explicitly tied to a particular event and those that are not. The latter are expressed using one word, in both English and Chinese. In English, these words typically come at the beginning of a sentence, setting the entire sentence into a particular time frame. In Chinese, they can be placed either before or after the subject, but always before the verb phrase (see 10.1), like a *time-when* expression.

The most frequently used relative time words in this category are 从前 **cóngqián**, 以前 **yǐqián**, 后来 **hòulái**, 以后 **yǐhòu**, 然后 **ránhòu**. Because 从前 **cóngqián** and 以前 **yǐqián** are synonyms, as are 后来 **hòulái**, 以后 **yǐhòu** and 然后 **ránhòu**, students need to learn the grammatical distinctions between them in order to use them correctly.

1. 从前 cóngqián *vs* 以前 yǐqián = *formerly, before*

The two words 从前 **cóngqián** and 以前 **yǐqián**, when they function as detached words (not referenced to an event), are interchangeable. But only 以前 **yǐqián** is used in a relative time clause (e.g. 我来美国以前 **wǒ lái Měiguó yǐqián** *before I came to the U.S.*). (See next section)

2. 后来 hòulái = *later on, subsequently*

The word 后来 **hòulái** always refers to the past. On the surface, 后来 **hòulái** and 以后 **yǐhòu** (see below) may seem parallel to 从前 **cóngqián** and 以前 **yǐqián**, but 后来 **hòulái** and 以后 **yǐhòu** are not interchangeable even though they are synonyms.

3. 以后 yǐhòu = *thereafter, henceforth*

The first difference between 后来 **hòulái** and 以后 **yǐhòu** is that only 以后 **yǐhòu** may be used in a relative time clause (e.g. 我到了中国以后 **wǒ dàole Zhōngguó yǐhòu**). In this case, it is the mirror image of 以前 **yǐqián**. In contrast to both 后来 **hòulái** and 以前 **yǐqián**, 以后 **yǐhòu** implies a linkage to another event, even when it is not in a relative clause. 以后 **yǐhòu** can refer to the past or the future, whereas 后来 **hòulái** always refers to the past.

4. 然后 ránhòu = *..., and then*

The word 然后 **ránhòu** presumes an antecedent, usually stated in an immediately preceding sentence or clause. 然后 **ránhòu** is used to indicate a consequence as well as a time relationship between two occurrences, whereas 后来 **hòulái** and 以后 **yǐhòu** indicate only a time relationship. The event introduced by 然后 **ránhòu** is presumed to occur immediately or soon after a preceding event, whereas the time lapse in a sentence introduced by 后来 **hòulái** or 以后 **yǐhòu** can be longer.

As you read the following examples, think about the choice of relative time words and why their synonyms would not be correct.

♦ *I used to like only pop music; later on, I learned to appreciate classical music.*
我从前/以前只喜欢流行音乐。后来，我也学会欣赏古典音乐了。
Wǒ cóngqián/yǐqián zhǐ xǐhuan liúxíng yīnyuè. Hòulái, wǒ yě xuéhuì xīnshǎng gǔdiǎn yīnyuè le.

♦ *Three years ago, she fell in love with a classical musician, thereafter she no longer liked rock 'n roll.*
她三年前爱上了一位古典音乐家，那以后她就不再喜欢摇滚音乐了。
Tā sānnián-qián àishangle yíwèi gǔdiǎn yīnyuèjiā, nà yǐhòu tā jiù búzài xǐhuan yáogǔn yīnyuè le.

♦ *He went into a drug rehab center, then very soon he quit taking drug.*
他进了戒毒所，然后很快就戒毒了。
Tā jìnle jièdúsuǒ, ránhòu hěn kuài jiù jièdúle.

♦ *He quit drugs last year and left the drug rehab center. I don't know what happened later on.*
他去年戒了毒，出了戒毒所。后来怎么样，我就不知道了。
Tā qùnián jiè-le-dú, chūle jièdúsuǒ. Hòulái zěnmeyàng, wǒ jiù bù zhīdaole.
(以后 **yǐhòu** is also acceptable in this context. Can you explain why?)

- *She left the work environment that discriminated against women, and then opened her own company.*
  她离开了那个歧视妇女的工作环境，然后就自己开了一家公司。
  Tā líkāile nèige qíshì fùnǚde gōngzuò huánjìng, ránhòu jiù zìjǐ kāile yìjiā gōngsī.

- *She wants to leave the bad work environment, but she doesn't know how she should develop her career after that.*
  她要离开那个不好的工作环境，可是不知道以后该怎么发展自己的事业。
  Tā yào líkāi nèige bùhǎode gōngzuò huánjìng, kěshì bù zhīdao yǐhòu gāi zěnme fāzhǎn zìjǐde shìyè.

The second form of relative time frames are those explicitly tied to specific events. Many different terms can be used to "frame" the events to create a relationship. Some of the more frequently used ones are: ··· 以前 **...yǐqián**, ··· 以后 **...yǐhòu**, ··· 的时候 **...de shíhou**, ··· 的那天 **...de nèitiān**. When using these "time framing terms," the principle for students to remember is that their word order is usually the opposite of English. In the Chinese mindset, the "framing term" is the key word, and the event being framed is a modifier, thus the event comes first, followed by the time frame word, which accords with normal rules of Chinese noun modification (see 1.5, sec. F)

- *Before I went to college, I only liked popular music.*
  我上大学以前，只喜欢摇滚音乐。
  Wǒ shàng dàxué yǐqián, zhǐ xǐhuan yáogǔn yīnyuè.

- *After I took a course on music appreciation, I became interested in all kinds of music.*
  上过一门音乐欣赏课以后，我就对什么音乐都感兴趣了。
  Shàngguo yìmén yīnyuè xīnshǎng kè yǐhòu, wǒ jiù duì shénme yīnyuè dōu gǎn- xìngqù le.

- *When I'm in a bad mood, I like to listen to Beethoven's 9th Symphony.*
  我心情不好的时候，就会想听一听贝多芬的第九交响曲。
  Wǒ xīnqíng bùhǎode shíhou, jiù huì xiǎng tīng-yitīng Bèiduōfēnde dìjiǔ jiāoxiǎngqǔ.

- *The day he was fired, he immediately found a better job!*
  他被解雇的那天，马上就找到了一个更好的工作。
  Tā bèi jiěgùde nèitiān, mǎshàng jiù zhǎodàole yíge gèng hǎode gōngzuò.

The time frames in the above examples are all related to specific events. But ··· 以前 **...yǐqián** and ··· 以后 **...yǐhòu** can also be used to frame *time-spans*.

- *He got cancer two years ago, but is currently still alive.*
  他两年以前得了癌症，现在还活着。
  Tā liǎngnián yǐqián déle áizhèng, xiànzài hái huózhe.

♦ *She started chemotherapy immediately upon being diagnosed with cancer. Nine months later, she was completely cured.*
她被诊断患了癌症以后就立刻开始化疗，九个月<u>以后</u>，就完全好了。
Tā bèi zhěnduàn huànle áizhèng yǐhòu jiù lìkè kāishǐ huàliáo, jiǔge yuè yǐhòu, jiù wánquán hǎo le.

♦ *It was not until 3 hours after arriving in the emergency room that he got to see a doctor!*
他到了急诊三个小时<u>以后</u>才看到了医生！
Tā dàole jízhěn sānge xiǎoshí yǐhòu cái kàndàole yīshēng!

EXERCISES:

Translate the following sentences into Chinese:

1. We used to have a lot of social activities. Later on, we had kids, and life changed completely!

2. Are you planning to return to China after graduation?

3. After graduation, I'd like to do one year of internship first, and then decide whether I want to return to China.

4. In the past, whenever it snowed too hard, classes were cancelled. Starting this year, when it snows hard, the teacher can use the internet to hold class for us!

ANSWERS:

1. 我们从前有很多社交活动。后来有了孩子，我们的生活就完全变了！
Wǒmen cóngqián yǒu hěnduō shèjiāo huódòng. Hòulái yǒule háizi, wǒmende shēnghuó jiù wánquán biànle!

2. 你毕业以后预备回中国吗？ **Nǐ bìyè yǐhòu yùbèi huí Zhōngguó ma?**

3. 毕业以后我想先做一年实习，然后再决定要不要回中国。
Bìyè yǐhòu wǒ xiǎng xiān zuò yìnián shíxí, ránhòu zài juédìng yào-buyào huí Zhōngguó.

4. 从前，雪下得太大的时候，我们的课就被取消了。从今年起，下大雪的话，老师就可以利用因特网给我们上课了！
Cóngqián, xuě xiàde tài dàde shíhou wǒmende kè jiù bèi qǔxiāo le. Cóng jīnnián qǐ, xià dàxuě dehuà, lǎoshī jiù kěyǐ lìyòng yīntèwǎng gěi wǒmen shàngkè le!

10.9 Multiple occurrences vs one specific occurrence

The patterns used to state multiple occurrences of an event or action parallel those for *time-spans*; and the patterns used to state specific occurrences parallel those for *time-when*. If you have understood the points discussed above in 10.1–10.3, then all you need to do now is transfer these patterns to expressions about occurrences of events or actions.

The English word *time* (in the sense of "occasion") has three equivalents in Chinese: 次 **cì**, 遍 **biàn**, and 趟 **tàng**. The word 次 **cì** is the most generic of these, and may be used in all situations, while the other two can be used in two types of situations. The word 遍 **biàn** applies to an act that involves going through something from beginning to end, such as reading and explaining something. The word 趟 **tàng** applies to trips specifically, as hinted by the use of the radical 走 **zǒu** in the character.

Examples referring to a number of occurrences:

- *I called her three times, but she didn't answer.*
  我给她打了三次电话，她都没接。**Wǒ gěi tā dǎle sāncì diànhuà, tā dōu méi jiē.**
  我给她打电话打了三次，⋯ **Wǒ gěi tā dǎ diànhuà dǎle sāncì, …**
  ✗ 我给她打了电话三次，⋯ **Wǒ gěi tā dǎle diànhuà sāncì, …**

- *I've gone to look for him a number of times, but he was never home.*
  我去找了他好几趟了，可是他都不在家。
  Wǒ qù zhǎole tā hǎojǐtàng le, kěshì tā dōu bú zài jiā.

- *I listen to the recording of each lesson twice.*
  每一课的录音，我都听两次。**Měi yíkède lùyīn, wǒ dōu tīng liǎngcì.**
  ✗ 我听每一课的录音两次。**Wǒ tīng měi yíkède lùyīn liǎngcì.**

- *The teacher has explained it three times already, how come I still don't understand?*
  老师已经解释了三遍了，我怎么还不明白呢？
  Lǎoshī yǐjīng jiěshìle sānbiànle, wǒ zěnme hái bù míngbái ne?

- *He took the college entrance exam three times, and succeeded only on the third try.*
  他考大学考了三次才考上。**Tā kǎo dàxué kǎole sāncì cái kǎoshang.**

- *For the sake of developing her career, she moved many times.*
  为了发展事业，她搬过好几次家。**Wèile fāzhǎn shìyè, tā bānguo hǎojǐcì jiā.**

Examples referring to one specific occurrence:

- *The first time he came to China was for studying.*
  他第一次来中国是为了留学。**Tā dìyīcì lái Zhōngguó shì wèile liúxué.**

- *This time, coming to China is for developing his career.*
  他这次来中国是为了发展他的事业。
  Tā zhèicì lái Zhōngguó shì wèile fāzhǎn tāde shìyè.

- *Next time we have class, let's talk about our own childhoods.*
  我们下次上课的时候，请大家谈谈自己的童年。
  Wǒmen xiàcì shàngkède shíhou, qǐng dàjiā tántan zìjǐde tóngnián.

- *There is always a first time for everything.*
  任何事情都有第一次。**Rènhé shìqing dōu yǒu dìyīcì.**

In 10.2, we gave some examples of how *time-when* expressions can sometimes be mistaken for *time-span* expressions. A parallel pitfall exists with occurrences. The point made by an expression of plural occurrences may be about specific occurrence(s) rather than about the number of occurrences. The true test of whether an expression refers to specific occurrence(s) is the question "which occurrence(s) are we talking about?"

♦ *I was not home both times that he came.*
他(那)两次来，我都不在家。**Tā (nèi) liǎngcì lái, wō dōu bú zài jiā.**
(两次 **liǎngcì** refers to two specific occurrences. In colloquial speech, 那 **nèi** may be omitted, which may make 两次 **liǎngcì** appear to be an expression about the number of occurrences. Compare this sentence with the following one, and see if you can detect the difference in focus.)

♦ *He has been here twice, but I was not home either time.*
他来过两次，可是我都不在家。**Tā láiguo liǎngcì, kěshì wō dōu bú zàijiā.**

♦ *The first two times he came to China, it was with his parents. This time was the first time that he came by himself.*
他头两次来中国，都是跟着父母来的，这次是他第一次自己一个人来。**Tā tóu liǎngcì lái Zhōngguó, dōu shì gēnzhe fùmǔ láide, zhèicì lái shì tā dìyīcì zìjǐ yígerén lái.**
(次 **cì** is used three times, and each time it refers to one or more specific occurrences.)

As you read the following examples, identify which expressions refer to specific occurrences and which ones refer to the number of occurrences.

♦ *The first two times you're caught for speeding, you are fined. The third time, you must appear in court.*
开车超速被警察抓到，头两次罚款，第三次就必得上法庭了。
Kāichē chāosù bèi jǐngchá zhuādào, tóu liǎngcì fákuǎn, dìsāncì jiù bìděi shàng fǎtíng le.

♦ *The several times they fought were all due to disagreement over child-rearing methods.*
他们好几次争吵，都是因为教育孩子的方法不同。
Tāmen hǎojǐcì zhēngchǎo, dōu shì yīnwèi jiàoyù háizide fāngfǎ bùtóng.

♦ *My old computer broke down three times this month, each time it cost a lot of money to repair. Next time it breaks down, I think I should buy a new one.*
这个月我的旧电脑坏过三次，每次都花了很多钱修理。下次再坏，我想应该买一个新的了。
Zhèige yuè wǒde jiù diànnǎo huàiguo sāncì, měicì dōu huāle hěn duō qián xiūlǐ. Xiàcì zài huài, wǒ xiǎng yīnggāi mǎi yíge xīnde le.

EXERCISES:

Translate the following sentences into Chinese:

1. That movie is wonderful! Seeing it once was not enough, I must see it a second time.

2. The third time I saw that movie, I still saw something new in it.

3. The first three times that I had "mapo doufu," I felt it was too hot! Later on, I got used to it. Now every time we go to a Chinese restaurant, I order "mapo doufu."

4. He was caught speeding twice. The first time, he was fined $100. The second time, it was $200! Next time he goes over the speed limit, he will have to go to court.

5. We have had five meetings about this issue already. I don't think this problem can be resolved by meetings, so next time we have another meeting I'm not going anymore.

ANSWERS:

1. 那个电影太棒了！看一次还不够，我得再看一次。
   Nèige diànyǐng tài bàng le! Kàn yícì hái búgòu, wǒ děi zài kàn yícì.

2. 那个电影，我第三次看的时侯，还看到一些新的东西。
   Nèige diànyǐng, wǒ dìsāncì kànde shíhou, hái kàndào yìxiē xīnde dōngxi.

3. 我头三次吃麻婆豆腐，都觉得太辣！后来我就习惯了。现在我每次去中国餐馆，都点麻婆豆腐。**Wǒ tóu sāncì chī mápó dòufu, dōu juéde tài là! Hòulái wǒ jiù xíguàn le. Xiànzài wǒ měicì qù Zhōngguó cānguǎn, dōu diǎn mápó dòufu.**

4. 他超速被抓过两次。第一次被罚了一百块，第二次是两百块。下次再超速他就得上法庭了。**Tā chāosù bèi zhuāguo liǎngcì. Dìyīcì bèi fále yìbǎi kuài, dì'èrcì shì liǎngbǎi kuài. Xiàcì zài chāosù jiù děi shàng fǎtíng le.**

5. 关于这个问题，我们已经开过五次会了。我不觉得这个问题是开会能解决的，所以下次再开会我就不去了。**Guānyú zhèige wèntí, wǒmen yǐjing kāiguo wǔcì huì le. Wǒ bù juéde zhèige wèntí shì kāihuì néng jiějué de, suǒyǐ xiàcì zài kāihuì wǒ jiù bú qù le.**

To native speakers of English, prepositions are an unambiguous class of words. They belong to a distinct part of speech that create relationships in a sentence and associate the various elements to one another. Prepositions often carry an object, and in fact, that object is the essential element. A prepositional phrase may be associated with a verb (e.g. *to come <u>with</u> so-and-so*) or a noun (e.g. *animals <u>in</u> the zoo*), or with the entire sentence (e.g. <u>*Without*</u> *a cell phone, they were lost.*)

If we apply the term "prepositions" to the various types of words serving similar functions in Chinese, students will tend to gloss over their grammatical differences. Therefore, at the outset, it is best for students to abandon their English mindset and adopt a Chinese one.[1]

Because the words which function like prepositions in Chinese are originally derived from verbs, and because they are used to introduce other verbal phrases that co-exist with the main verb, Chinese linguists call them "coverbs." In most cases, the adjunct verbal phrase introduced by the coverb precedes the main verb, but sometimes it may also follow the main verb, in which case the term "postverb" is used. Unlike English prepositions, Chinese coverbs can often function as verbs also, and it is their function within a sentence that determines whether it is a verb, coverb, or postverb.[2] In the three sentences below, the same word 在 **zài** functions as a verb, a coverb, and a postverb respectively:

♦ *His home is in the U.S., but he is often not there.*
他家在美国，可是他常常不在那儿。(The verb in both clauses is 在 **zài**)
Tā jiā zài Měiguó, kěshì tā chángchang bú zài nàr.

♦ *He is working in an international company.*
他在一个国际公司工作。(The main verb is 工作 **gōngzuò**, 在 **zài** is a coverb)
Tā zài yíge guójì gōngsī gōngzuò.

♦ *We are living in a globalized environment.*
我们生活在一个全球化的环境中。
Wǒmen shēnghuó zài yíge quánqiú-huàde huánjìng-zhōng.
(The main verb is 生活 **shēnghuó**, 在 **zài** is a postverb)

---

[1] In Chapter 1 (1.5, sec. G), we did use the term "prepositions" as an expediency, but we put it in quotation marks to note a caveat.

[2] Only a few coverbs—such as 从 **cóng** and 被 **bèi**—do not function as verbs in modern Chinese, but even those are historically derived from verbs. Thus, there is ample justification for treating *coverbs* and *postverbs* as types of verbs.

In sum, *coverbs* and *postverbs* in Chinese are not a distinct class of words like prepositions in English, but are derived from verbs and serve the function of introducing additional elements in sentences. Aside from this, they differ from English prepositions in three other ways:

1. In English, prepositions mostly follow the verb; their counterparts in Chinese are mostly coverbs that precede the verb, and only sometimes postverbs that follow the verb.

2. One main function of prepositional phrases in English is to modify nouns (e.g. *the constitution of the United States, the ships in the harbor.* This type of noun modification, when translated into Chinese, uses the standard pattern for modifying nouns, i.e. "modifier + 的 **de** + noun."

3. Aside from the above, other prepositional phrases in English do not necessarily translate into coverbal or postverbal phrases in Chinese, and vice versa. As you read examples in this chapter, take note of the various cases.

11.2 Frequently used coverbs in Chinese

The list of coverbs discussed in this section is by no means exhaustive, but they will give you a foundation from which you will be able to recognize the less common ones when you encounter them. A few of the frequently-used ones—对 **duì**, 连 **lián**, and 使 **shǐ**—function in set patterns, and discussion of these will be deferred to Part II of this book.

In this section, we divide the most frequently-used coverbs in colloquial Chinese into four categories:

1. Those used exclusively as coverbs in modern Chinese (i.e. not as verbs): 从 **cóng**, 被 **bèi**, and 往 **wǎng**. These may also be used as components in bisyllabic verbs.

2. Words used primarily as coverbs but sometimes as verbs: 跟 **gēn**, 对 **duì**, 替 **tì**, 把 **bǎ**, 离 **lí**.

3. Words used as both verbs and coverbs: 在 **zài**, 到 **dào**, 靠 **kào**.

4. Words used primarily as verbs and only occasionally as coverbs: 给 **gěi**, 用 **yòng**, 叫 **jiào**, 让 **ràng**.

All the coverbs in the above list with the exception of 被 **bèi** are derived from verbs. The meaning of each coverb can be traced to the inherent meaning of the verb that it developed from. In other words, the meanings of coverbs for the most part are quite transparent, which is not the case with prepositions in English. This is why it is easier for an English-speaking student to understand the meaning of coverbs in Chinese than vice versa. As you read the sentences below, take note of the meaning of each coverb as it relates to its inherent verbal meaning.

1. Words used exclusively as coverbs in modern colloquial Chinese:

	inherent meaning	coverbal meaning	other usages in bisyllabic words
从 **cóng**	*to follow;* *to obey*	*from*	从事 **cóngshì** *to engage in, to follow a profession* 服从 **fúcóng** *to obey*

♦ *All the merchandise in this store is from China.*
这个店的商品都是从中国来的。**Zhèige diàn de shāngpǐn dōushì cóng Zhōngguó láide.**

被 **bèi**	(noun) *cover, quilt*	(passive marker) *by*	被迫 **bèipò** *to be forced (to do something)* 被辱 **bèirǔ** *to be insulted*

♦ *This child is often scolded by his parents for doing poorly in school.*
这个孩子学习成绩不好, 常常被父母责备。
Zhèige háizi xuéxí chéngjì bù hǎo, chángchang bèi fùmǔ zébèi.

♦ *The restaurant's business was not good, so he got laid off.*
餐馆的生意不好, 所以他被解雇了。**Cānguǎnde shēngyì bù hǎo, suǒyǐ tā bèi jiěgùle.**
(**Note:** As an exception to the rule that coverbs always have objects, 被 **bèi** may be used without an object when the object is either understood or unknown.)

♦ *He was elected class president.* 他被选上了班长。**Tā bèi xuǎnshangle bānzhǎng.**
(**Note:** Traditionally, 被 **bèi** was used in negative contexts only. Recently, it has come to be used to indicate the passive voice in positive contexts as well, although this usage is still uncommon.)

往 **wǎng**	*to go toward*	*toward*	往返 **wǎngfǎn** *round-trip, "going and returning"* 往年 **wǎngnián** *past years*

♦ *Walk in that direction for five minutes and you'll be there.*
往那个方向走五分钟就到了。**Wǎng nèige fāngxiàng zǒu wǔfēn zhōng jiù dàole.**

♦ *You should look ahead, don't dwell on those past painful experiences anymore.*
你现在应该往前看, 别再回忆过去痛苦的经历了。
Nǐ xiànzài yīnggāi wǎng qián kàn, bié zài huíyì guòqù tòngkǔde jīnglì le.

2. Words used primarily as coverbs and only sometimes as verbs:

	inherent meaning	coverbal meaning	other usages in modern vocabulary
跟 **gēn**	(noun) *heel;* (verb) *to follow*	*with, follow-ing behind*	跟踪 **gēnzōng** *to follow the track of* 高跟鞋 **gāogēn-xié** *high heel shoes*

♦ *Children should become independent when they grow up, and shouldn't always be sticking close to their parents.*
孩子长大了就应该独立, 不应该老跟着父母。(跟 **gēn** used as verb)
Háizi zhǎngdàle jiù yīnggāi dúlì, bù yīnggāi lǎo gēnzhe fùmǔ.

- *Please say it after me.* 请跟着我说。**Qǐng gēnzhe wǒ shuō.**

- *His Chinese is excellent, but still it cannot be compared with a Chinese.*
  他的中文非常好，可是还是不能跟中国人比。
  Tāde Zhōngwén fēicháng hǎo, kěshì háishi bùnéng gēn Zhōngguórén bǐ.

对 **duì**	to face; to match	to, for, on, vis-a-vis	面对 **miànduì** to face; 对不起 **duì-bu-qǐ** "unable to face," sorry; 对比 **duìbǐ** to compare; 对方 **duìfāng** counterpart

- *Please line up these two rows of numbers and check and see if there are any errors.*
  请你对一下这两排数字，看看有没有错。(对 **duì** used as verb)
  Qǐng nǐ duì yíxià zhèi liǎngpái shùzì, kànkan yǒu-méiyǒu cuò.

- *Chinese parents often hold unrealistic expectations of their children.*
  中国的父母对自己的孩子经常抱不实际的期望。
  Zhōngguóde fùmǔ duì zìjǐde háizi jīngcháng bào bùshíjìde qīwàng.

替 **tì**	to substitute, to take the place of	for	代替 **dàitì** to take the place of 替换 **tìhuàn** to replace

- *Take a rest, I'll take over for you.* 你休息一会儿吧，我来替你。(替 **tì** used as verb)
  Nǐ xiūxi yìhuǐr ba, wǒ lái tì nǐ.

- *How can you hire someone to take the exam for you?!*
  你怎么能请人替你考试呢？！ **Nǐ zěnme néng qǐng rén tì nǐ kǎoshì ne?!**

把 **bǎ**	to grasp, to hold	(see 11.6)	把关 **bǎguān** to guard a pass 有把握 **yǒu bǎwò** to have assurance, to have "a firm hold"

- *We must hold on to this precious opportunity.* (把握 **bǎwò** used as verb)
  我们必须把握住这个难得的机会。**Wǒmen bìxū bǎwòzhù zhèige nándéde jīhuì.**

- *Class is about to begin. Please turn off your cell phones.*
  要上课了，请把手机关上。**Yào shàngkè le, qǐng bǎ shǒujī guānshang.**

离 **lí**	to leave; to part from	distance from	离开 **líkāi** to leave, to separate from 离婚 **líhūn** to divorce

- *That pair of lovers are never apart by even an inch.*
  那对情人寸步不离。**Nèiduì qíngrén cùnbù-bùlí.** (离 **lí** used as verb)

- *This college is not bad, but it's a bit too close to my parent's house.*
  这所大学不错，就是离我父母家太近了。
  Zhèisuǒ dàxué búcuò, jiùshì lí wǒ fùmǔ jiā tài jìn le.

3. Words used equally frequently as verbs and coverbs:

	inherent meaning	coverbal meaning	usage in modern vocabulary
在 **zài**	to be at, to exist	at, in, etc.	存在 **cúnzài** to exist; 在世 **zàishì** to be living; 自在 **zìzài** at ease with oneself

- *He's no longer with this company. We heard he was fired.*
  他不在这家公司了，听说他被解雇了。(在 **zài** used as verb)
  Tā bú zài zhèijiā gōngsī le, tīngshuō tā bèi jiěgù le.

- *He found a new job, now he can work from home.*
  他找到了一个新的工作，现在他可以在家里上班了。
  Tā zhǎodàole yíge xīnde gōngzuò, xiànzài tā kěyǐ zài jiālǐ shàngbān le.

到 **dào**	to arrive	to	到底 **dàodǐ** after all; 达到 **dádào** to achieve, to attain

- *After a three-day trek in the desert, they finally arrived.*
  在沙漠里走了三天以后，他们终于到了。(到 **dào** used as verb)
  Zài shāmòli zǒule sāntiān yǐhòu, tāmen zhōngyú dàole.

- *He went to Shanghai to see his girlfriend.*
  他到上海去看他的女朋友去了。**Tā dào Shànghǎi qù kàn tāde nǚpéngyou qùle.**

靠 **kào**	to lean on, to depend on	to depend on	可靠 **kěkào** reliable; 依靠 **yīkào** to lean on

- *You have graduated from college already, how can you still lean on your parents?!*
  你已经大学毕业了，怎么能还靠着父母呢?! (靠 **kào** used as verb)
  Nǐ yǐjīng dàxué bìyèle, zěnme néng hái kàozhe fùmǔ ne?!

- *Can one live on just social security after retirement?*
  退了休以后能只靠社会保险金生活吗?
  Tuì-le-xiū yǐhòu néng zhǐ kào shèhuì bǎoxiǎnjīn shēnghuó ma?

4. Words used primarily as verbs and also secondarily as coverbs:

	inherent meaning	coverbal meaning	usage in modern vocabulary
给 **gěi**	to give	to, for	发给 **fāgěi** to distribute to; 交给 **jiāogěi** to hand over to

- *Don't give the kid so much candy.*
  别给孩子那么多糖。**Bié gěi háizi nàme duō táng.** (给 **gěi** used as verb)

- *May I trouble you to buy a bottle of milk for me while you're at it?*
  麻烦你顺便给我买一瓶牛奶。**Máfan nǐ shùnbiàn gěi wǒ mǎi yìpíng niúnǎi.**
  (给 **gěi** implies doing a favor for someone, rather than giving the milk to the person. Compare with usage of 给 **gěi** as a postverb in 11.5.)

- *When you arrive, please give me a call right away.*
  你到了以后，请马上给我打电话。**Nǐ dàole yǐhòu, qǐng mǎshàng gěi wǒ dǎ diànhuà.**

| 用
yòng | to use | "with" | 作用 zuòyong *effect;*
用功 yònggōng *hard working* |

♦ *Do you know how to use chopsticks?*
你会用筷子吗? **Nǐ huì yòng kuàizi ma?** (用 **yòng** used as verb)

♦ *I heard that in China, left-handed people have to learn to write with their right hands.*
我听说在中国左撇子也得学会用右手写字。
Wǒ tīngshuō zài Zhōngguó zuǒpiězi yě děi xuéhuì yòng yòushǒu xiězì.

♦ *These days most Chinese use WeChat to communicate with friends.*
现在多半的中国人都用微信跟朋友联系了。
Xiànzài duōbànde Zhōngguórén dōu yòng Wēixìn gēn péngyou liánxì le.

| 让
ràng | to yield,
to allow | to allow, to cause (some-
one to do something) | 割让 gēràng *to cede (territory);*
让座 ràngzuò *to yield one's seat to someone* |

♦ *According to traffic regulations, vehicles should yield to pedestrians.*
按照交通规则, 汽车应该让行人。(让 **ràng** used as verb)
Ànzhào jiāotōng guīzé, qìchē yīnggāi ràng xíngrén.

♦ *When I was in high school, my parents didn't allow me to have a boyfriend.*
我在中学的时候, 父母不让我交男朋友。
Wǒ zài zhōngxuéde shíhou, fùmǔ búràng wǒ jiāo nánpéngyou.

| 叫 jiào | to call
out | to make or cause (some-
one to do something) | 叫菜 jiàocài *to order dishes (in restaurant);*
叫醒 jiàoxǐng *to awaken (someone)* |

♦ *Last night in a dream he gave out a big yell!*
昨天夜里他在梦中大叫了一声。(叫 **jiào** used as verb)
Zuótiān yèli tā zài mèngzhōng dàjiàole yìshēng.

♦ *No matter what, the mother can't make her kid do homework.*
妈妈怎么也没法子叫孩子做功课。
Māma zěnme yě méi fázi jiào háizi zuò gōngkè.

♦ *That kid was scolded by his Mom, but is still unwilling to study.*
那个孩子叫妈妈给骂了, 可还是不愿意学习。
Nèige háizi jiào māma gěi màle, kě háishi bú yuànyi xuéxí.
(A very colloquial alternative to "叫⋯ **jiào...**" is "叫⋯给⋯ **jiào...gěi...**" More on this in 11.7.)

EXERCISES:

Translate the following sentences into Chinese:

1. Grandma is practicing taichi in the park.
2. To go from here to the train station, you have to go east.
3. Your teacher is sick. I'm teaching her classes for her today.
4. He's not home this week. He has gone to New York.
5. After our Dad died, the whole family depended on his life insurance for our livelihood.

6. Do Chinese students still learn to write with the writing brush? No! They all write with computers now.

7. Yale rejected him (did not accept him), but he was accepted by Harvard.

8. My son is really good to me. He remembered my birthday and made a birthday cake for me.

9. This boss often makes his employees work overtime. Sometimes even on weekends he won't let them rest.

10. There's a Chinese saying, "people go toward the high places, while water flows toward the low places."

ANSWERS:

1. 奶奶在公园里打太极拳。**Nǎinai zài gōngyuánlǐ dǎ tàijíquán.**

2. 从这里去火车站，你得往东走。**Cóng zhèlǐ qù huǒchēzhàn, nǐ děi wǎng dōng zǒu.**

3. 你们的老师病了；今天我替/代她上课。
   Nǐmende lǎoshī bìngle; jīntiān wǒ tì/dài tā shàngkè.

4. 他这个星期不在家；他到纽约去了。**Tā zhèige xīngqī bú zài jiā; tā dào Niǔyuē qùle.**

5. 父亲去世以后，我们全家就靠他的人寿保险过日子了。
   Fùqin qùshì yǐhòu, wǒmen quánjiā jiù kào tāde rénshòu bǎoxiǎn guò rìzi le.

6. 中国学生还学用毛笔写字吗？不，他们都用电脑打字了！
   Zhōngguó xuésheng hái xué yòng máobǐ xiězì ma? Bù, tāmen dōu yòng diànnǎo dǎzì le.

7. 耶鲁没录取他，而他却被哈佛录取了。
   Yélǔ méi lùqǔ tā, ér tā què bèi Hāfó lùqǔle.

8. 我儿子对我真好。他记得我的生日，又给我做了生日蛋糕。
   Wǒ érzi duì wǒ zhēn hǎo. Tā jìde wǒde shēngrì, yòu gěi wǒ zuòle shēngrì dàngāo.

9. 这个老板常常叫他的员工加班。有时候周末也不让他们休息。**Zhèige lǎobǎn chángchang jiào tāde yuángōng jiābān. Yǒu shíhou zhōumò yě búràng tāmen xiūxi.**

10. 中国人有句话说："人往高处走，水往低处流。"
    Zhōngguórén yǒu jù huà shuō: "Rén wǎng gāochù zǒu, shuǐ wǎng dīchù liú."

11.3 Nouns modified by prepositional phrases

A common use of prepositional phrases in English is to modify nouns (e.g. *relatives on my Dad's side of the family, the cost of living in rural areas, commodities imported from China*). These same concepts are often expressed in Chinese using the pattern "modifier + 的 **de** + noun," without the use of a coverb. Even when a coverb is used, it is not used to modify the noun directly, but rather in a "coverb + object + verb + 的 **de**" phrase. By definition, "coverbs" must co-exist with main verbs in a sentence, so a verb is always needed in the modifying phrase. This is not true in English when prepositional phrases are used without any verbs.

In the following examples, the nouns are modified by prepositional phrases in English. However, they are not modified by coverbial phrases in Chinese, but by phrases using 的 **de**.

- *relatives on my dad's side of the family*
  我父亲那边的亲戚 **wǒ fùqin nèibiānde qīnqi**

- *the cost of living in the rural areas*
  在乡下生活的费用 **zài xiāngxia shēnghuóde fèiyong**

- *foreign students from around the world*
  来自世界各地的留学生 **láizì shìjiè gèdìde liúxuésheng**
  从世界各地来的留学生 **cóng shìjiè gèdì láide liúxuésheng**
  ✗ 从世界各地的留学生 **cóng shìjiè gèdìde liúxuésheng**
  (**Note:** The last sentence is incorrect because the verb is lacking. The second sentence is correct because the verb 来 **lái**—which is not used in the English version—is added in the Chinese equivalent.)

- *the friends with you today*
  今天跟你在一起的那些朋友 **jīntiān gēn nǐ zài yìqǐde nèixiē péngyou**
  今天跟你一起来的那些朋友 **jīntiān gēn nǐ yìqǐ láide nèixiē péngyou**
  ✗ 今天跟你的那些朋友 **jīntiān gēn nǐde nèixiē péngyou**
  (**Note:** The last phrase is incorrect because the verb is lacking. The first two versions are correct because a verb—which is not necessary in the English version—is added in the Chinese phrase.)

Noun modification expressed in English by the "verb + prepositional phrase" pattern has a close parallel in the Chinese usage of coverb phrases. The equivalent pattern is the structure "coverb + object + verb + 的 **de**." There is one pitfall to avoid however: the word order in Chinese is the opposite of English. In Chinese, the modifying phrase always precedes the noun being modified. In English, the noun being modified comes before the modifying phrase.

- *merchandise imported from China*
  从中国进口的商品 **cóng Zhōngguó jìnkǒude shāngpǐn**
  ✗ 从中国的商品
    cóng Zhōngguóde shāngpǐn (a verb is lacking in this version)

- *characters written with a writing brush*
  用毛笔写的那些字 **yòng máobǐ xiěde nèixiē zì**

- *the teacher subbing for Teacher Wang*
  替王老师上课的那位老师 **tì Wáng Lǎoshī shàngkède nèiwèi lǎoshī**

- *the children adopted from China*
  从中国领养的孩子 **cóng Zhōngguó lǐngyǎngde háizi**

- *the textbooks written by Prof. Li*
  李教授写的教科书 **Lǐ Jiàoshòu xiěde jiàokēshū**

EXERCISES:

Translate the following sentences into Chinese:

1. The shoes you bought for me are too small!
2. The teacher who subbed for Prof. Li was very nice to us.
3. I really like that friend who came with you yesterday!
4. Beijing University has students from all over the world.
5. According to a report in Forbes (福布斯 **Fúbùsī**), the cost of living in Singapore is the highest in the world.

ANSWERS:

1. 你给我买的鞋子太小了！ **Nǐ gěi wǒ mǎide xiézi tài xiǎo le.**
2. 替李教授上课的那位老师对我们很好。
   Tì Lǐ Jiàoshòu shàngkède nèiwèi lǎoshī duì wǒmen hěn hǎo.
3. 我真喜欢昨天跟你一起来的那个朋友。
   Wǒ zhēn xǐhuan zuótiān gēn nǐ yìqǐ láide nèige péngyou.
4. 北京大学有来自世界各国的学生。 or ⋯有从世界各国来的学生。
   Běijīng Dàxué yǒu láizì shìjiè gèguóde xuésheng. or **…yǒu cóng shìjiè gèguó láide xuésheng.**
5. 按照福布斯的一篇报导，在新加坡的生活费用是世界上最高的。
   Ànzhào Fúbùsīde yìpiān bàodǎo, zài Xīnjiāpōde shēnghuó fèiyòng shì shìjiè-shang zuì gāo de.

11.4 Some less colloquial coverbs

Aside from the common coverbs used in colloquial Chinese, there are some "formal" coverbs that appear mainly in written Chinese and formal speech. Learners who aspire to interact with Chinese professionals or with well-educated Chinese friends should be aware of these. Unlike colloquial coverbs, which tend to move freely between their verbal and coverbal functions, "formal" coverbs tend to function exclusively or primarily as coverbs, even though they too have inherent verbal meanings. Of the eleven examples listed below, the first three (the 为 **wèi** in 因为 **yīnwèi**, the 以 **yǐ** in 所以 **suǒyǐ**, and 就 **jiù**) may surprise you because they form part of the basic Chinese vocabulary familiar to you, but here they are used at a higher level that may be new to you.

	coverbal meaning	other usages in modern vocabulary
为 **wèi**	*for, for the sake of*	为己 **wèijǐ** *egotistical*; 为何 **wèihé** *for what* (The character 为, pronounced in the second tone **wéi**, means *to do*, and there are many more compounds with this meaning of the character.)

- *serve the people (favorite Maoist slogan)* 为人民服务 **wèi rénmín fúwù**
- *Chinese parents are all anxious about their children taking the college entrance exam.* 中国的父母都为子女的高考着急。 **Zhōngguóde fùmǔ dōu wèi zǐnǚde gāokǎo zhāojí.**

以 yǐ	*by means of, in order to*	以便 **yǐbiàn** *in order to* (do something conveniently) 难以 **nányǐ** *hard to*

- *Parents should serve as role models by their own actions*
  父母应该以身作则。**Fùmǔ yīnggāi yǐshēn-zuòzé.**
- *I suggest that we respond to the myriad changes with calmness.*
  我建议大家以冷静应万变。**Wǒ jiànyì dàjiā yǐ lěngjìng yìng wànbiàn.**

就 jiù	*on (the question/issue of)*	就业 **jiùyè** *to start a job, take up employment* 高就 **gāojiù** *moving to a higher professional position*

- *Both sides hereupon announce the cessation of civil war.*
  双方就此宣布停止内战。**Shuāngfāng jiùcǐ xuānbù tíngzhǐ nèizhàn.**
- *Morally speaking, his conduct is unacceptable.*
  就道德而言，他的行为是不能接受的。**Jiù dàodé ér yán, tāde xíngwéi shì bùnéng jiēshòu de.**

由 yóu	*from, by*	自由 **zìyóu** *freedom;* 由来 **yóulái** *origin, derivation*

- *From this, we can see that diligence is the foundation of success.*
  由此看来，勤奋是成功的基础。**Yóu cǐ kànlai, qínfèn shì chénggōngde jīchǔ.**
- *In modern society, marriage is decided by oneself.*
  在现代的社会，婚姻是由自己决定的。**Zài xiàndàide shèhuì, hūnyīn shì yóu zìjǐ juédìng de.**

向 xiàng	*toward, to, in the direction of* (synonym of 往 **wǎng**)	方向 **fāngxiàng** *direction* 倾向 **qīngxiàng** *tendency*

- *What I said was "look forward," not "look to the money"!*
  我说的是"向前看"，不是"向钱看"！**Wǒ shuōde shì "xiàng qián kan", búshì "xiàng qián kàn"!**
- *We should report to our leader about the difficulties we encountered.*
  我们应该向领导报告我们遇到的困难。
  Wǒmen yīnggāi xiàng lǐngdǎo bàogào wǒmen yùdàode kùnnan.

朝 cháo	*toward, facing*	朝阳 **cháoyáng** *to face the sun* 朝圣 **cháoshèng** *to go on a pilgrimage*

(The original meaning of 朝 **cháo** was *court, dynasty*. In addition, the same character 朝, pronounced **zhāo**, means *morning*. There are many other compounds using these two meanings of the character 朝 **cháo**.)

- *He escaped in that direction.* 他朝那个方向逃走了。**Tā cháo nèige fāngxiàng táozǒule.**
- *Chinese people prefer houses with windows and doors facing south.*
  中国人比较喜欢门窗朝南的房子。**Zhōngguórén bǐjiào xǐhuan ménchuāng cháo nánde fángzi.**

按 **àn**	*according to*	按照 **ànzhào** *according to;* 按序 **ànxù** *in proper sequence*

- *In olden times, Chinese dictionaries were arranged by radicals.*
  从前中文字典是按部首排的。**Cóngqián Zhōngwén zìdiǎn shì àn bùshǒu pái de.**

- *The city government developed some housing where the rent is pegged to the renter's income.*
  市政府开发了一些按收入付房租的住房。
  Shì-zhèngfǔ kāifāle yìxiē àn shōurù fù fángzūde zhùfáng.

与 **yǔ**	*with, to*	参与 **cānyù** *to participate* (note 4th tone on 与 **yù**) 授与 **shòuyǔ** *to confer upon*

- *What do our affairs have to do with him?*
  我们的事与他有什么关系? **Wǒmende shì yǔ tā yǒu shénme guānxi?**

- *He is simply different from others.*
  他这个人就是与众不同。**Tā zhèige rén jiùshi yǔ zhòng bùtóng.**

于 **yú**	*to, at, in,* (formal synonym of 在 **zài**)	关于 **guānyú** *concerning;* 终于 **zhōngyú** *finally;* 由于 **yóuyú** *due to*

- *No one is willing to accept conditions that are not beneficial to himself.*
  没有人愿意接受于自己不利的条件。**Méiyǒu rén yuànyi jiēshòu yú zìjǐ búlìde tiáojiàn.**

- *We need to think of a way that would be beneficial to both sides.*
  我们必须想出一个于双方都有益的方法。
  Wǒmen bìxū xiǎngchū yíge yú shuāngfāng dōu yǒuyìde fāngfǎ.

将 **jiāng**	*to take,* formal synonym of 把 **bǎ** (将 **jiāng** is dominant in South China)	将来 **jiānglái** *future* 将近 **jiāngjìn** *nearly, close by*

- *Old people often leave their unrealized dreams to the next generation.*
  老年人经常将自己尚未实现的梦想寄托给下一辈。
  Lǎonián-rén jīngcháng jiāng zìjǐ shàngwèi shíxiànde mèngxiǎng jìtuō gěi xià yíbèi.

- *Seeing his expression, I could only swallow the words that I was about to say.*
  看到他的表情, 我只好将我要说的话吞回去了。
  Kàndào tāde biǎoqíng, wǒ zhǐhǎo jiāng wǒ yào shuōde huà tūn-huíqu-le.

凭 **píng**	*on the basis of*	文凭 **wénpíng** *diploma;* 凭空 **píngkōng** *on basis of nothing, baseless*

- *If the clothes you buy don't fit, you may get a refund with your receipt.*
  如果你买的衣服不合身, 可以凭收据退货。
  Rúguǒ nǐ mǎide yīfu bù héshēn, kěyǐ píng shōujù tuìhuò.

- *Speaking from my conscience, I did not live up to my parents' hopes when I was young.*
  凭良心说, 我年轻的时候辜负了我父母的期望。
  Píng liángxīn shuō, wǒ niánqīngde shíhou gūfùle wǒ fùmǔde qīwàng.

EXERCISES:

Translate the following sentences into Chinese:

1. This matter has nothing to do with you.
2. Actually, the President is not really elected by the people.
3. On what basis are you saying that gender inequality still exists in our company?
4. I am learning Chinese for the sake of career development in the future.
5. We can see the Bell Tower by looking southward from the living room window.

ANSWERS:

1. 这件事与你无关。**Zhèijiàn shì yǔ nǐ wúguān.**
2. 其实总统不是真的由人民选出来的。
   Qíshí Zǒngtǒng búshì zhēnde yóu rénmín xuǎn-chūlai de.
3. 你凭什么说我们公司还存在着男女不平等的现象?
   Nǐ píng shénme shuō wǒmen gōngsī hái cúnzàizhe nán-nǚ bù píngděngde xiànxiàng?
4. 我学中文是为了将来的事业发展。**Wǒ xué Zhōngwén shì wèile jiānglái de shìyè fāzhǎn.**
5. 我们从客厅的窗户朝南望过去就能看见钟楼了。
   Wǒmen cóng kètīngde chuānghu cháo nán wàng-guòqu jiù néng kànjian Zhōng Lóu le.

11.5   Coverbs that also function as postverbs

Of the twenty-six coverbs that we have discussed in this chapter, seven also function as postverbs. We have already had a glimpse of these two related functions in 9.11, as illustrated by 在 zài. Here, let's take a look at examples of all seven coverbs that function in both capacities:

	functioning as coverb: *coverb + object + verb*		
	functioning as postverb: *verb + (object1) + postverb + object2*		
在 **zài** *at, in, on*	• *to write (one's) diary on the computer* 在电脑上写日记 **zài diànnǎo-shang xiě rìjì**		
	• *lived abroad for half one's life* 在国外生活了半辈子 **zài guówài shēnghuóle bàn bèizi**		
	• *to write one's thoughts in the diary* 把心得写在日记里 **bǎ xīndé xiězài rìjìlǐ**		
	• *lying on the bed resting* 躺在床上休息 **tǎngzài chuángshang xiūxi**		

	functioning as coverb: *coverb + object + verb*		
	functioning as postverb: *verb + (object1) + postverb + object2*		
到 **dào** *to*	• *to go to Shanghai to see a friend* 到上海去看朋友 dào Shànghǎi qù kàn péngyou		
	• *To enjoy an unpolluted environment, one has to go to a faraway place.* 如果要享受没有污染的环境，得到边远的地方去。 **Rúguǒ yào xiǎngshòu méiyǒu wūrǎnde huánjìng, děi dào biānyuǎnde dìfang qù.**		
	• *For convenience of going to work, he moved into the city.* 为了上班方便，他搬到城里去了。 **Wèile shāngbān fāngbiàn, tā bāndào chénglǐ qule.**		
	• *When traveling, I often think of things that I normally can't think of.* 旅游的时候我常会想到一些平常想不到的事情。 **Lǚyóude shíhou wǒ cháng huì xiǎngdào yìxiē píngchang xiǎng-bu-dàode shìqing.**		
往 **wǎng** *toward*	• *Go east for one kilometer and you'll be there.* 往东走一公里就到了。**Wǎng dōng zǒu yìgōnglǐ jiù dàole.**		
	• *Flying from here to India, going westward and eastward take about the same amount of time.* 从这里去印度，往西飞和往东飞都要差不多一样的时间。**Cóng zhèlǐ qù Yìndù, wǎng xī fēi hé wǎng dōng fēi dōu yào chàbuduō yíyàngde shíjiān.**		
	• *Canada geese fly south every fall.* 加拿大雁每年秋天都飞往南方。 **Jiānádà yàn měinián qiūtiān dōu fēiwǎng nánfāng.**		
	• *The train bound for Xi'an is about to depart.* 开往西安的火车将要出发了。**Kāiwǎng Xī'ānde huǒchē jiāngyào chūfā le.**		
给 **gěi** *for, to*	• *to write a letter to a friend* 给朋友写一封信 **gěi péngyou xiě yìfēng xìn** (postverb position also correct: 写一封信给朋友 **xiě yìfēng xìn gěi péngyou**)		
	• *to buy a new dress for her (either giving it to her or helping her buy it)* 给她买一件新衣服 **gěi tā mǎi yíjiàn xīn yīfu**		
	• *I'm going to the library today, I can return that book for you while I'm at it.* 我今天去图书馆，可以顺便给你还那本书。 **Wǒ jīntiān qù túshūguǎn, kěyǐ shùnbiàn gěi nǐ huán nèiběn shū.**		
	• *to buy a new dress for her (giving it to her)* (compare with coverb position) 买一件新衣服给她 **mǎi yíjiàn xīn yīfu gěi tā** 买给她一件新衣服 **mǎi gěi tā yíjiàn xīn yīfu**		
	• *I don't need this book anymore, I can lend it to you.* 我不需要这本书了，可以借给你。 **Wǒ bù xūyào zhèiběn shū le, kěyǐ jiègěi nǐ.**		

functioning as coverb: *coverb + object + verb*
functioning as postverb: *verb + (object1) + postverb + object2*

向 **xiàng** *toward*	• *(car, bus, or train) to drive/go toward Tianjin* 向天津开 **xiàng Tiānjīn kāi** (向 **xiàng** as postverb is also correct: 开向天津 **kāixiàng Tiānjīn**) • *As soon as spring arrives, the Canada geese fly back to the north.* 春天一到, 加拿大雁又飞向北方了。 **Chūntiān yí dào, Jiānádà yàn yòu fēixiàng běifāng le.** • *For the sake of seeking freedom, she left her old home.* 为了奔向自由, 她离开了故乡。**Wèile bēnxiàng zìyóu, tā líkāile gùxiāng.**
以 **yǐ** *take...,* *by way* *of, in* *order to*	• *to take family to be the primary thing* 以家庭为主 **yǐ jiātíng wéi zhǔ** (以⋯为⋯ **yǐ...wéi...** is a commonly-used set pattern, see Part II, #197) • *to make a living by prostitution* 以卖淫谋生 **yǐ màiyín móushēng** • *to inform (someone) by sending a telegram* 去电报以告之 **qù diànbào yǐ gào zhī** • *to present a bouquet (to someone)* 赠以鲜花 **zèng yǐ xiānhuā**
于 **yú** *to, in,* *at, etc.*	• *Economic development is often detrimental to animals in the wild.* 经济发展往往于野生动物不利。**Jīngjì fāzhǎn wǎngwǎng yú yěshēng dòngwù búlì.** • *What you said resonated in my heart.* 你说的话, 于我心中产生了共鸣。 **Nǐ shuōde huà, yú wǒ xīnzhōng chǎnshēngle gòngmíng.** • *China's marble comes from Yunnan.* 中国的大理石出于云南。 **Zhōngguóde dàlǐshí chūyú Yúnnán.** • *The World Trade Center is situated in the center of the city.* 国贸位于市中心。**Guó-Mào wèiyú shì-zhōngxīn.** • *Health problems mostly lie in life habits.* 健康问题多半在于生活习惯。 **Jiànkāng wèntí duōbàn zàiyú shēnghuó xíguàn.** • *All people in the world are enthusiastic about soccer.* 全世界的人都热衷于足球。**Quán-shìjiède rén dōu rèzhōngyú zúqiú.** • *The problem is not in material insufficiency, but in the disparity between the rich and the poor!* 问题不在于物资不足, 而在于贫富不均! **Wèntí bú zàiyú wùzī bùzú, ér zàiyú pínfù bùjūn!**

The following key characteristics of postverbs may be observed from the examples:

1. Postverbs always carry an object (which is the same for all coverbs except 被 **bèi**).

2. Postverbs are generally more closely tied to their associated verbs. The object of a postverb can be considered the object of the combined verb+ postverb phrase.

3. For 在 **zài** and 给 **gěi**, the distinction between coverb and postverb is quite fuzzy, and even native speakers who have an intuitive sense of when to use a coverb vs a postverb may use them interchangeably. But in general terms, the coverb 在 **zài** indicates the location where something occurs, whereas the postverb 在 **zài** indicates that the verb in the sentence directly involves the object. The coverb 给 **gěi** implies an action done on someone's behalf, rather than something *given* to someone. Sometimes, this distinction is made using *for* and *to* in English (e.g. 给你借 **gěi nǐ jiè** *borrow it <u>for</u> you* vs 借给你 **jiè gěi nǐ** *lend it <u>to</u> you*). Consider the above described distinction just a rule of thumb, but don't be too surprised when you hear the rule broken by a native speaker.

4. For 往 **wǎng** and 向 **xiàng**, the line between coverb and postverb is even more vague. Their meaning is the same in either position, but the postverb usage is more succinct and formal, and carries the flavor of literary Chinese. 往 **wǎng** is more colloquial than 向 **xiàng**, and is therefore used as a coverb more often than 向 **xiàng**.

5. 给 **gěi** as postverb is often separated from its associated verb, in which case the verb has its own direct object, and 给 **gěi** has the indirect object. (see discussion of direct and indirect objects in 10.3)

6. 到 **dào**, in its function as postverb, can be considered a complement of the main verb that precedes it. As a verb complement, it has four possible conjugations, e.g. 想到了 **xiǎngdàole**, 没想到 **méi xiǎngdào**, 想得到 **xiǎng-de-dào**, 想不到 **xiǎng-bu-dào**. Verb complements will be the topic of the next chapter. The point here is that 到 **dào**, through its role as a *verb complement*, is a very prolific post-verb.

7. The three postverbs 向 **xiàng**, 以 **yǐ**, and 于 **yú** are used in formal expressions, which often contain elements of literary Chinese. While there is some flexibility in their use as a coverb or postverb, the postverbal form is preferred.

8. The coverbs 以 **yǐ** and 于 **yú** have very strong ties to their classical Chinese roots, and are the most prolific postverbs in modern formal Chinese. Like 往 **wǎng** and 向 **xiàng** mentioned above, 以 **yǐ** and 于 **yú** move freely between the coverb and postverb positions, but the postverb position is favored, due to its succinctness and its alignment with literary Chinese. In fact, some "verb + 以 **yǐ**" and "verb + 于 **yú**" combinations appear as frequently-used vocabulary in modern Chinese, and native Chinese treat them simply as words rather than as compounds. Here are a few of the possible examples: 可以 **kěyǐ**, 得以 **déyǐ**, 难以 **nányǐ**, 加以 **jiāyǐ**, 足以 **zúyǐ**, 何以 **héyǐ**, 关于 **guānyú**, 对于 **duìyú**, 至于 **zhìyú**, 由于 **yóuyú**, 属于 **shǔyú**, 等于 **děngyú**, 过于 **guòyú**, 限于 **xiànyú**, 处于 **chǔyú**. Many of these will resurface in the sentence patterns in Part II of this book.

EXERCISES:

Translate the following sentences into Chinese, using 在 **zài**, 到 **dào**, and 给 **gěi** as coverbs and postverbs:

1. American college students usually don't live at home, but at school.
2. It's too noisy in the dorm; students cannot study there, so they study in the library.
3. How much will it cost to mail this book to the U.S.?
4. You want to mail this to the U.S.? You must go to the big post office to mail it.
5. I cannot give this book to you, but I can lend it to you for a week.
6. I can also go to the library to borrow that book for you.

ANSWERS:
1. 美国大学生通常不住在家里而住在学校。
   Měiguó dàxuésheng tōngcháng bú zhùzài jiālǐ ér zhùzài xuéxiào.
2. 宿舍里太吵了，学生不能在那儿读书，所以他们在图书馆读书。
   Sùshèlǐ tài chǎo le, xuésheng bùnéng zài nàr dúshū, suǒyǐ tāmen zài túshūguǎn dúshū.
3. 这本书寄到美国去，要多少钱？ Zhèiběn shū jìdào Měiguó qù, yào duōshǎo qián?
4. 你要把这本书寄到美国去吗？那你得到那个大的邮局去寄。
   Nǐ yào bǎ zhèiběn shū jìdào Měiguó qù ma? Nà nǐ děi dào nèige dàde yóujú qù jì.
5. 我不能把这本书送给你，可是可以借给你一个星期。
   Wǒ bùnéng bǎ zhèiběn shū sòng-gěi nǐ, kěshì kěyǐ jiè-gěi nǐ yíge xīngqī.
6. 我也可以到图书馆去替你借那本书。 Wǒ yě kěyǐ dào túshūguǎn qù tì nǐ jiè nèiběn shū.

11.6 The coverb 把 bǎ

While 把 **bǎ** is one of the coverbs most frequently used by native speakers, it is one of the two trickiest (along with 被 **bèi**) for students to master. This section aims to provide you with the ability to use it correctly once and for all.

Grammatically, coverbs are mechanisms by which additional elements are associated with the main verb that follows. The coverb 把 **bǎ** is no different in this regard, but in terms of meaning, the "把 **bǎ** + object" phrase brings the focus of the sentence to the object of 把 **bǎ**. In other words, from the perspective of meaning, the object of 把 **bǎ** is not a secondary element in the sentence, but rather the main element.[3] There is no equivalent mechanism in English, except perhaps the use of intonation, which makes 把 **bǎ** sentences in Chinese difficult to translate into English. Compare the following two sentences:

---

[3] The coverb 把 **bǎ** is not the only mechanism for bringing focus to the object. Another favorite way to accomplish this is the "topic+comment" pattern (see 1.3, section 1). Neither pattern has an equivalent in English, thus it is important for students to develop this Chinese linguistics groove in their minds.

◆ 我做完了功课了。
   Wǒ zuòwánle gōngkè le. *I finished doing my homework.*
   (standard statement about what I did)

◆ 我把功课做完了。 **Wǒ bǎ gōngkè zuòwánle.**
   I took my homework and finished it.
   (focus on what I did with the homework)

Chinese speakers are much more likely to use the second sentence than the first, and to them, there is a significant difference between the two sentences even though the meaning is the same. The focus of the 把 **bǎ** sentence is on the homework and what happened to it, rather than on who did it. Students tend to have no difficulty comprehending 把 **bǎ** sentences, but because they do not have a linguistic groove for this type of construction, they tend to stick to the English form rather than the more expressive pattern using 把 **bǎ** favored by native Chinese speakers.

Another reason why students tend to avoid the 把 **bǎ** pattern is that they often made mistakes when trying to use it. Well-intentioned Chinese friends can tell them whether a sentence is correct or not, but often cannot explain why. Over time, with enough experience using 把 **bǎ** sentences and correcting one's errors, the persevering student does eventually attain the native speaker's sense (语感 **yǔgǎn**) of the usage of this coverb, but we hope this section will help you get there more quickly.

There are three rules of thumb governing the use of 把 **bǎ**, which we will delve into below. As a preview, however, let's look at some correct 把 **bǎ** sentences and some incorrect ones. As you read these examples, you may not be able to explain why the sentences marked by "✗" are incorrect. Give it a try though, and check your answers with those in the answer box, then read the explanations further on.

1. *I must learn this sentence pattern.*
   ✓ 我一定要把这个句型学会。 **Wǒ yídìng yào bǎ zhèige jùxíng xuéhuì.**
   ✗ 我一定要把这个句型学。 **Wǒ yídìng yào bǎ zhèige jùxíng xué.**
   ✓ 我一定要学会这个句型。 **Wǒ yídìng yào xuéhuì zhèige jùxíng.**

2. *Mom, please tell me the story of how you and Dad got married.*
   ✓ 妈妈，你能不能把你和爸爸结婚的故事讲给我听?
      Māma, nǐ néngbunéng bǎ nǐ hé bàba jiéhūnde gùshi jiǎnggěi wǒ tīng?

   Mom, please tell me a story.
   ✗ 妈妈，你能不能把一个故事讲给我听?
      Māma, nǐ néngbunéng bǎ yíge gùshi jiǎnggěi wǒ tīng?
   ✓ 妈妈，你能不能给我讲一个故事?
      Māma, nǐ néngbunéng gěi wǒ jiǎng yíge gùshi?
   ✓ 妈妈，你能不能讲一个故事给我听?
      Māma, nǐ néngbunéng jiǎng yíge gùshi gěi wǒ tīng?

3. *He wants to buy that Mercedes Benz.*

   ✓ 他要把那辆奔驰买下来。 **Tā yào bǎ nèiliàng Bēnchí mǎi-xiàlai.**

   ✗ 他要把那辆奔驰买。 **Tā yào bǎ nèiliàng Bēnchí mǎi.**

   ✓ 他要买那辆奔驰。 **Tā yào mǎi nèiliàng Bēnchí.**

4. *He wants to buy a Mercedes Benz for his wife.*

   ✓ 他要把那辆奔驰买给他妻子。 **Tā yào bǎ nèiliàng Bēnchí mǎigěi tā qīzi.**

   ✗ 他要把一辆奔驰买给他妻子。 **Tā yào bǎ yíliàng Bēnchí mǎigěi tā qīzi.**

5. *She buys a new car every five years.*

   ✗ 她每五年把一辆新汽车买。 **Tā měi wǔnián bǎ yíliàng xīn qìchē mǎi.**

   ✓ 她每五年买一辆新汽车。 **Tā měi wǔnián mǎi yíliàng xīn qìchē.**

6. *She explained this matter very clearly.*

   ✓ 她把这件事情解释得很清楚。 **Tā bǎ zhèijiàn shìqing jiěshìde hěn qīngchǔ.**

   I know the ins and outs of this matter (have clear knowledge of it).

   ✗ 我把这件事情知道得很清楚。 **Wǒ bǎ zhèijiàn shìqing zhīdaode hěn qīngchǔ.**

   ✓ 这件事情，我知道得很清楚。 **Zhèijiàn shìqing, wǒ zhīdaode hěn qīngchǔ.**

Why are the sentences marked with an "✗" incorrect?

- 1, 3: The verb lacks a complement. (3rd condition below not met)
- 2, 4, 5: The object of the verb is not some specific item(s), but just any specimen(s) of a class of things. (1st condition below not met)
- 6: The verb 知道 **zhīdao** is not a "functive" verb, i.e. it does not signify an action that affects the object 这件事情 **zhèijiàn shìqing**. (2nd condition below not met)

Now, read the following three rules of thumb about the usage of the 把 **bǎ** coverb, then return to the above examples and see if you can identify the error in each of the sentences marked with an "✗." Refer to the answer box again to check yourself.

1. The object of 把 bǎ must be specific items

The object of 把 **bǎ** must be a specific item or collection of items. It cannot be just *any* specimen or non-specific collection of things. Some examples:

Specific items: *that book, my homework, the family dog, the houses on Mott St., the dress that she wore at her wedding, things that happened in my childhood.* **Note:** These items may be concrete or abstract (e.g. *homework*), and may be singular or plural.

Non-specific items: *three tigers* (any three), *500 international students from China* (any 500 students), *foreign languages* (in general).

In English, nouns preceded by "the, this, that, those" as well as possessives are specific, whereas those preceded by "a/an" or a number are non-specific. Those without any of the above require some further analysis. Moreover, the markers for specificity that exist in English are often absent in Chinese, thus "specificity" is often implied rather than explicit. A case in point is 功课 **gōngkè** in 我把功课做完了 **wǒ bǎ gōngkè zuòwánle**. In English translation, 功课 **gōngkè** is made explicit by the addition of "my" or "the."

This rule of thumb is linked to the inherent meaning of 把 **bǎ** *to take hold of (something)*, which presumes that the "something" is known and is a specific thing.

2. 把 bǎ must be used with a "functive" verb

The verb that follows the 把 **bǎ** phrase must be a "functive" verb, which signifies that an action affects the object of 把 **bǎ** in some way. Thus, the 把 **bǎ** sentence pattern "Subject + 把 **bǎ** + object + verb phrase" means "so-and-so takes up something and does something to it." One class of *non-functive* verbs are *cognitive* verbs (such as 觉得 **juéde** *to feel*, 知道 **zhīdao** *to know something*, 认识 **rènshi** *to know someone*), and these are not compatible with the sense of the 把 **bǎ** pattern. Interestingly, the verb 想 **xiǎng** is conceptualized as a "functive" verb in Chinese, i.e., one can take something and think it over.

◆ 我得好好儿地把你提出的这个问题想一想。
   Wǒ děi hǎohāorde bǎ nǐ tíchūde zhèige wèntí xiǎng-yixiǎng.
   I should give this question you raised some thought.

3. The main verb used with 把 bǎ must have a complement

The verb that follows the 把 **bǎ** phrase must have a *complement*, i.e. it cannot be left dangling by itself. Therefore, in the above-mentioned sentence pattern ("Subject + 把 + object + verb phrase"), the verb phrase consists of something more than just a verb. The *complement* to the verb may be as simple as the *aspect marker* 了 **le**, or a reduplication of the verb itself (see 2.10):

◆ 我一个人把那个大西瓜吃了！ (verb complement is 了 **le**)
   Wǒ yígerén bǎ nèige dà xīgua chīle!
   I ate up that big watermelon all by myself!

◆ 你得把从垃圾堆里找来的那双鞋子洗洗。 (the verb 洗 **xǐ** is reduplicated)
   Nǐ děi bǎ cóng lājīduīli zhǎolaide nèishuāng xiézi xǐxǐ.
   You have to wash those shoes that you found in the trash pile.

In other words, if a 把 **bǎ** sentence ends with just a verb, it is too abrupt. Even when no verb complement is necessary for the meaning to be clear, a minimal complement must be tagged on to make the sentence grammatically complete.

The complement to the verb may also be something rather complex:

♦ 我把那双鞋子洗干净了。 **Wǒ bǎ nèishuāng xiézi xǐ-gānjìng le.**
I took that pair of shoes and washed them clean.
(verb complement is the "resultative" 干净 **gānjìng**)

♦ 我打算把那双鞋子送给那个没有鞋子的孩子。 (verb complement is
the postverbal phrase 给那个没有鞋子的孩子 **gěi nèige méiyǒu xiézi de háizi**)
Wǒ dǎsuàn bǎ nèishuāng xiézi sònggěi nèige méiyǒu xiézide háizi.
I'm planning to take that pair of shoes and give them to that child who has no shoes.

The following examples are all correct. As you read each of them, can you explain why the 把 **bǎ** pattern is or is not used? (Answers given below.)

a. *During my college years, I wrote a letter to my parents every week.*
读大学期间，我每个星期都给父母写一封信。
Dú dàxué qījiān, wǒ měige xīngqī dōu gěi fùmǔ xiě yìfēng xìn.

b. *My parents kept all the letters I wrote them.*
我父母把我写给他们的信都保留下来了。
Wǒ fùmǔ bǎ wǒ xiěgěi tāmende xìn dōu bǎoliú-xiàlai le.

c. *The four of us ordered three dishes and one soup.*
我们四个人点了三个菜，一个汤。 **Wǒmen sìge rén diǎnle sānge cài, yíge tāng.**

d. *The four of us ate up all the food that we ordered.*
我们四个人把(所有的)菜都吃光了。
Wǒmen sìge ren bǎ (suǒyǒude) cài dōu chīguāngle.

e. *Please move that table into the living room.*
请你把那张桌子搬到客厅去。 **Qǐng nǐ bǎ nèizhāng zhuōzi bāndào kètīng qù.**

f. *After we move, we will need to buy some new furniture.*
我们搬家以后必须买一些新的家具。
Wǒmen bānjiā yǐhòu bìxū mǎi yìxiē xīnde jiājù.

g. *I hope you can introduce that Chinese tutor to me.*
我希望你能把那位中文家教介绍给我。
Wǒ xīwàng nǐ néng bǎ nèiwèi Zhōngwén jiājiào jièshào gěi wǒ.

h. *I hope you can introduce some Chinese friends to me.*
我希望你能给我介绍几位中国朋友。
Wǒ xīwàng nǐ néng gěi wǒ jièshào jǐwèi Zhōngguó péngyou.

i. *I have considered all your suggestions, but I still feel that my way is best.*
我把你的建议都考虑过了，不过还是觉得我的做法最好。
Wǒ bǎ nǐde jiànyì dōu kǎolùguòle, búguò háishi juéde wǒde zuòfǎ zuì hǎo.

j. *We must solve this problem within two days. Otherwise, it will be too late.*
我们必需在两天内解决这个问题，要不然就太晚了。
Wǒmen bìxū zài liǎngtiān-nèi jiějué zhèige wèntí, yàoburán jiù tài wǎn le.

k. *Have you returned that library book yet?*
你把那本图书馆的书还了吗？ **Nǐ bǎ nèiběn túshūguǎnde shū huánle ma?**

l. *Before we start out, we should get a clear idea of the situation over there.*
我们出发之前，应该把那边的情况弄清楚。
Wǒmen chūfā zhīqián, yīnggāi bǎ nèibiānde qíngkuàng nòng-qīngchǔ.

ANSWERS:
- Examples b, d, e, g, i, k, l meet all 3 conditions of the 把 **bǎ** pattern.
- In examples a, c, f, h, the objects of the verb are not specific items, but any unspecified items, therefore 把 **bǎ** cannot be used.
- In example j, the verb 解决 **jiějué** lacks a complement. (3rd condition not met).

EXERCISES:

Translate the following sentences into Chinese (use the 把 **bǎ** pattern if applicable):

1. We learned thirty new characters in Chinese class every week.
2. Aiya! This week, I forgot all those thirty characters that I had learned the previous week!
3. I have to spend about $2,000 each month.
4. Every month, he uses up all the money that he makes.
5. Please don't tell other people about our family matters.

ANSWERS:
1. 在中文课上，我们每星期学三十个生字。
    Zài Zhōngwén kè-shang, wǒmen měi xīngqī xué sānshíge shēngzì.
2. 哎呀！这个星期我把上个星期学的那三十个生字都忘了。
    Aiya! Zhèige xīngqī wǒ bǎ shàngge xīngqī xuéde nèi sānshíge shēngzì dōu wàngle.
3. 我每个月得用两千块左右。 **Wǒ měige yuè děi yòng liǎngqiān-kuài zuǒyòu.**
4. 他每个月都把赚的钱全部花光。 **Tā měige yuè dōu bǎ zhuànde qián quánbù huāguāng.**
5. 请别把我们家的事告诉别人。 **Qǐng bié bǎ wǒmen jiāde shì gàosu biérén.**

11.7 The coverb 被 bèi

The sentence pattern formed using the coverb 被 **bèi** is the counterpart to the one using 把 **bǎ**. Whereas 把 **bǎ** brings the focus of the sentence to the object of the action, 被 **bèi** brings the focus to the agent or perpetrator of the action. We use the word "perpetrator" since the 被 **bèi** pattern was originally used with unfortunate or undesirable events, and it is still used mostly with such events today.[4] The subject of a 被 **bèi** sentence is the "recipient" of the action. In the following examples, the two sentence patterns are juxtaposed:

把 **bǎ pattern**:   Subject (agent) + 把 **bǎ**+object + verb phrase (action)

被 **bèi pattern**:   Subject (recipient of action) + 被 **bèi**+agent/perpetrator + verb phrase (action)

Compare the following pairs of sentences:

- *The police arrested the drug dealer.*
  警察把那个卖毒品的人抓去了。 **Jǐngchá bǎ nèige mài dúpǐnde rén zhuāqule.**

- *The drug dealer was arrested by the police.*
  那个卖毒品的人被警察抓去了。 **Nèige mài dúpǐnde rén bèi jǐngchá zhuāqule.**

- *Later on, the judge sent him to a drug rehab center.*
  后来法官把他送到戒毒所去了。 **Hòulái fǎguān bǎ tā sòngdào jièdúsuǒ qùle.**

- *Later on, he was sent to a drug rehab center.*
  后来他被送到戒毒所去了。 **Hòulái tā bèi sòngdào jièdúsuǒ qùle.**
  (**Note:** As noted in 11.2, 被 **bèi** is exceptional among coverbs in that its object may be implied or omitted when it is irrelevant to the point of the sentence. The logical object of 被 **bèi** here is 法官 **fǎguān**, but that is hardly relevant to the point of this sentence.)

- *An overload of homework has taken up all the children's play time.*
  过多的功课把孩子们玩乐的时间都占用了。
  Guòduōde gōngkè bǎ háizimen wánlède shíjiān dōu zhànyòngle.

- *The children's play time has all been taken up by an overload of homework.*
  孩子们玩乐的时间都被过多的功课占用了。
  Háizimen wánlède shíjiān dōu bèi guòduōde gōngkè zhànyòngle.

EXERCISES:

Rework the following sentences with a different focus using the coverb 被 **bèi**:

1. The result of the experiment disproved my hypothesis.
   实验的结果把我的假设否定了。 **Shíyànde jiéguǒ bǎ wǒde jiǎshè fǒudìngle.**

2. The new building in front of our house has damaged our fengshui.
   新盖在我们家门前的楼把我们的风水破坏了！
   Xīn gàizài wǒmen jiā ménqiánde lóu bǎ wǒmende fēngshuǐ pòhuàile.

---

[4] In the 1980s, when China re-opened to the Western world, an influx of Western culture into China began, including translations from English. Since the English passive voice indicated with the preposition "by" has no inclusive equivalent in the Chinese language, the usage of 被 **bèi** was extended beyond its original negative meaning to situations that are positive or neutral. See the examples at the end of this section.

3. After the government agency discovered that she abused her child, they sent the child to the Child Welfare Center.

政府发现她虐待自己的孩子以后，就把孩子送到儿童福利院去了。

Zhèngfǔ fāxiàn tā nüèdài zìjǐde háizi yǐhòu, jiù bǎ háizi sòngdào értóng fúlìyuàn qùle.

4. The commercial sector has bought off (bribed) all the candidates, what meaning is there left to the election?

商界已经把候选人都买通了，那选举还有什么意义呢？

Shāngjiè yǐjīng bǎ hòuxuǎn-rén dōu mǎitōngle, nà xuǎnjǔ háiyǒu shénme yìyì ne?

ANSWERS:

1. 我的假设被实验的结果否定了。Wǒde jiǎshè bèi shíyànde jiéguǒ fǒudìngle.
2. 我们的风水被新盖在我们家门前的楼破坏了！
   Wǒmende fēngshuǐ bèi xīn gài-zài wǒmen jiā ménqiánde lóu pòhuàile!
3. 她被政府发现虐待自己的孩子以后，她的孩子就被送到儿童福利院去了。
   Tā bèi zhèngfǔ fāxiàn nüèdài zìjǐde háizi yǐhòu, tāde háizi jiù bèi sòngdào értóng fúlìyuàn qùle.
4. 候选人都已经被商界买通了，那选举还有什么意义呢？
   Hòuxuǎnrén dōu yǐjīng bèi shāngjiè mǎitōngle, nà xuǎnjǔ hái yǒu shénme yìyì ne?

While the 被 **bèi** pattern is most often used with unfortunate or undesirable events, it may also be used with positive events (see footnote 4), as illustrated by these two examples.

◆ *That young accomplished candidate was elected mayor.*

那个年轻有为的候选人被选上市长了。

Nèige niánqīng yǒuwéide hòuxuǎnrén bèi xuǎnshang shìzhǎng le.

◆ *She has been accepted by three top-ranked universities; the final choice will depend on which one gives her the most scholarship.*

她被三所一流大学录取了，最后的选择得看哪所给她的奖学金最多。

Tā bèi sānsuǒ yīliú dàxué lùqǔle, zuìhòude xuǎnzé děi kàn něisuǒ gěi tāde jiǎngxué-jīn zuì duō.

The coverb 被 **bèi** is not the only one used to mark the agent of an action in a passive sense. In colloquial Chinese, 叫 **jiào** and 让 **ràng** are used in the same way, and their usage in positive passive sentences has also crept into the language in recent years. But 被 **bèi** differs from 叫 **jiào** and 让 **ràng** in several respects:

a. 叫 **jiào** and 让 **ràng** are colloquial, so they generally occur only in spoken form. 被 **bèi** may be used in a wide range of situations, from colloquial speech to formal writing.

b. 被 **bèi**—as a single syllable—only has a coverbal function, whereas 叫 **jiào** and 让 **ràng** have other verbal functions (see next section).

c. With 被 **bèi**, the object of the coverb, i.e. the agent or perpetrator, may be omitted, leaving 被 **bèi** "dangling" without an object. With 叫 **jiào** and 让 **ràng**, the agent must always be explicitly stated.

In most passive sentences in which 叫 **jiào** or 让 **ràng** are used to introduce an agent of action, an optional 给 **gěi** may be added immediately before the main verb to impart a more colloquial flavor to the sentence. This is illustrated in the first and last examples below.

Examples of 叫 **jiào** and 让 **ràng** used as coverbs:

● *My newly-bought car was wrecked by my son in the first week!*
我新买的汽车在头一个星期就让我儿子给撞坏了！
Wǒ xīnmǎide qìchē zài tóuyíge xīngqī jiù ràng wǒ érzi gěi zhuànghuàile.

● *He cheated on an exam and was reported by a classmate.*
他考试作弊叫同学告了。 **Tā kǎoshì zuòbì jiào tóngxué gàole.**

● *His mistress was discovered by his wife, as a result he lost everything!*
他的情妇叫妻子发现了，结果他失去了一切！
Tāde qíngfù jiào qīzi fāxiànle, jiéguǒ tā shīqùle yíqiè!

● *Their home management has been kept in perfect order by the mother-in-law, so the young couple can devote themselves to developing their careers without a care!*
他们的家务都让婆婆给弄得有条有理，夫妻俩可以完全放心地去发展他们的事业。
Tāmende jiāwù dōu ràng pópo gěi nòngde yǒutiáo yǒulǐ, fūqī liǎ kěyǐ wánquán fàngxīnde qù fāzhǎn tāmende shìyè.

EXERCISES:

Translate the following sentences into Chinese:

1. My new car was stolen within the first week!

2. Due to unequal pay for male and female employees, this company was sued.

3. Their "extra child" (a birth that exceeds the quota: 超生儿 **chāoshēng'ér**) was discovered by the government. As a result, they were fined.

ANSWERS:

1. 我的新车在第一个星期就被偷了。 **Wǒde xīn chē zài dìyīge xīngqī jiù bèi tōule.**

2. 这家公司由于男女员工的待遇不公而被告了。
Zhèijiā gōngsī yóuyú nán-nǚ yuángōngde dàiyù bùgōng ér bèi gàole.

3. 他们的超生儿被政府发现了，结果他们被罚款了。
Tāmende chāoshēng'ér bèi zhèngfǔ fāxiànle, jiéguǒ tāmen bèi fákuǎnle.

11.8   Four important coverbs: 被 **bèi,** 让 **ràng,** 叫 **jiào and** 由 **yóu**

These four words are all translated into English by the preposition *by*; therefore students are prone to mistake them as synonyms. In the Chinese mind, they are quite distinct from each other, and may not be used interchangeably.

The usage of 让 **ràng** and 叫 **jiào** as coverbs has already been covered in the preceding section. In this section, we will elaborate on a characteristic of these two words that sets them apart from 被 **bèi**, namely their usage as main verbs introducing a clause in a sentence. As main verbs, 让 **ràng** and 叫 **jiào** mean *to allow, to cause (someone to do something)*. In this function, they are called "causative verbs."[5] The object of a "causative verb" is typically the person who does the action indicated by the verb phrase. In a nutshell, the sentence pattern involving a *causative verb* is the following:

Subject + 让 **ràng/**叫 **jiào** + so-and-so + verb phrase

♦ *When I was young, my Mom did not allow me to take the subway by myself.*
小时候，我妈不让我一个人坐地铁。
Xiǎo shíhou, wǒ mā bú ràng wǒ yígerén zuò dìtiě.

♦ *My teacher insists that I join the speech competition.*
我的老师一定要让我参加演讲比赛。
Wǒde lǎoshī yídìng yào ràng wǒ cānjiā yǎnjiǎng bǐsài.

♦ *So many people are making me join the competition, making it hard for me to refuse.*
那么多人让我参加比赛，叫我难以拒绝。
Nàme duō rén ràng wǒ cānjiā bǐsài, jiào wǒ nányǐ jùjué.

♦ *Before I left home, my Mom told me to write her every week.*
我离开家之前，母亲叫我每个星期都给她写一封信。
Wǒ líkāi jiā zhīqián, mǔqin jiào wǒ měige xīngqī dōu gěi tā xiě yìfēng xìn.

♦ *Don't let students look at their book in class, and of course, don't let them speak English!*
别让学生在课上看书，当然更不能让他们说英语。
Bié ràng xuésheng zài kèshang kànshū, dāngrán gèng bùnéng ràng tāmen shuō Yīngyǔ.

Apart from being coverbs, and on an underlying level, 让 **ràng** and 叫 **jiào** function as transitive verbs that take objects. As such 让 **ràng** means *to yield to someone or something* and 叫 **jiào** means *to call (someone or something), to be called, to order (a dish)*.

---

[5] Another important *causative verb* that deserves mention here is 使 **shǐ**. It is not included in this discussion because its meaning and function are another level removed from the coverb 被 **bèi**, but it will be covered in three different sentence patterns in Part II of this book.

♦ *According to Western etiquette, gentlemen should yield to ladies.*
按照西方人的规矩，男人得<u>让</u>女人。
Ànzhào xīfāng-rénde guīju, nánrén děi ràng nǚrén.

♦ *The ambulance is coming, please everyone make way!*
救护车来了，请大家<u>让</u>路！ **Jiùhùchē láile, qǐng dàjiā ràng lù!**

♦ *People feel that this little boy will grow up to be tall and handsome, so they call him "little tall and handsome."*
人们觉得这个小男孩将来会长得又高又帅，所以<u>叫</u>他"小高帅"。
Rénmen juéde zhèige xiǎo nánhái jiānglái huì zhǎngde yòu gāo yòu shuài, suǒyǐ jiào tā "xiǎo gāo shuài."

♦ *We are old friends, calling me "Mr. Wang" is awkward, so just call me "Old Wang."*
我们是老朋友了，<u>叫</u>我王先生挺别扭的，<u>叫</u>我老王就好了。
Wǒmen shì lǎopéngyou le, jiào wǒ Wáng Xiānsheng tǐng bièniǔ de, jiào wǒ Lǎo Wáng jiù hǎole.

♦ *Let's each order one dish, then order a soup, how about that?*
我们各人<u>叫</u>一个菜，再<u>叫</u>一个汤，怎么样？
Wǒmen gèrén jiào yíge cài, zài jiào yíge tāng, zěnmeyàng?

Finally, we come to the coverb 由 **yóu**, which is usually introduced at an advanced level because it is used mainly in formal Chinese. While 由 **yóu** and 被 **bèi** are both translated into English as *by*, there is a world of difference in meaning between them. 被 **bèi** focuses attention on the agent or perpetrator of an action, whereas 由 **yóu** (with its inherent meaning of *from*) indicates the agent who has (or who takes) responsibility for the action.

♦ *The classes for the grammar part of the course are conducted by Prof. Ling.*
✓ 这门课的语法部分是<u>由</u>凌老师来讲的。
Zhèimén kède yǔfǎ bùfen shì yóu Líng Lǎoshī lái jiǎng de.
✗ 这门课的语法部分是被凌老师来讲的。
Zhèimén kède yǔfǎ bùfen shì bèi Líng Lǎoshī lái jiǎng de.

♦ *The year she was six, she was sent off to the Wang family as a child bride.*
她六岁那年就<u>被</u>家里送给王家当童养媳了。
Tā liùsuì nèinián jiù bèi jiālǐ sòng gěi Wáng jiā dāng tóngyǎngxí le.

♦ *Her marriage was totally decided by her parents.*
她的婚事是由父母决定的。 **Tāde hūnshì shì yóu fùmǔ juédìng de.**
她的婚事被父母包办了。 **Tāde hūnshì bèi fùmǔ bāobànle.**
(**Note:** Both sentences are correct, but there is a difference in sentiment. The first one is a straightforward statement about who was responsible for arranging the marriage. The second is a lament about parents having total control in a situation that mostly impacts the poor daughter.)

♦ *The books on the windowsill got wet from the rain.*

✓ 放在窗台上的那些书被雨水淋湿了。

    Fàngzài chuāngtáishangde nèixiē shū bèi yǔshuǐ línshī le.

✗ 放在窗台上的那些书由雨水淋湿了。

    Fàngzài chuāngtáishangde nèixiē shū yóu yǔshuǐ línshī le.

♦ *The class president is appointed by the teacher and not elected by classmates.*

班长是由老师指定的，而不是由同学们选出来的。

Bānzhǎng shì yóu lǎoshī zhǐdìng de, ér búshì yóu tóngxuémen xuǎn-chūlai de.

♦ *He became class president by being elected by his classmates.*

他被同学们选出来当上了班长。(被 **bèi** used in its less common positive sense here.) **Tā bèi tóngxuémen xuǎn-chūlai dāngshangle bānzhǎng.**

他是由全班同学投票选出来当班长的。

Tā shì yóu quánbān tóngxué tóupiào xuǎn-chūlai dāng bānzhǎng de.

Since the function of 由 **yóu** is to indicate the agent responsible for the action, the time element in the sentence is flexible. It could apply to an event in the past, a general situation, or a hypothetical situation in the future.

♦ *My mother's marriage was arranged by her parents.* (event in the past)

我母亲的婚姻是由她父母安排的。

Wǒ mǔqinde hūnyīn shì yóu tā fùmǔ ānpái de.

♦ *In modern society, marriage is decided by oneself.* (general situation)

在现代的社会，婚姻是由自己决定的。

Zài xiàndàide shèhuì, hūnyīn shì yóu zìjǐ juédìng de.

♦ *In China, which university a student ends up in is determined by the results of his college entrance exam.* (general situation)

在中国，上哪所大学是由高考成绩决定的。

Zài Zhōngguó, shàng něisuǒ dàxué shì yóu gāokǎo chéngjì juédìng de.

Like 由 **yóu**, 被 **bèi** may also apply to an event in the past, a general situation, or a hypothetical situation.

♦ *Today "Little Stubborn" was again criticized by the teacher in front of the class.* (past event)

今天小犟又被老师在全班同学面前批评了。

Jīntiān Xiǎo Jiàng yòu bèi lǎoshī zài quánbān tóngxué miànqián pīpíngle.

♦ *In China, students who don't work hard are often criticized by teachers.* (general situation)

在中国不努力的学生常被老师批评。

Zài Zhōngguó bù nǔlìde xuésheng cháng bèi lǎoshī pīpíng.

- *If you don't prepare for class, you'll be criticized by the teacher.* (hypothetical situation).

如果不准备功课，会被老师批评。

Rúguǒ bù zhǔnbèi gōngkè, huì bèi lǎoshī pīpíng.

EXERCISES:

Translate the following sentences into Chinese:

1. During the Maoist era, housing was allocated by one's work unit.

2. She was abandoned at birth, but was later adopted by an American family.

3. My parents went to the city to find work, so I was raised by my grandmother.

ANSWERS:

1. 在毛泽东时代，房子是由工作单位分配的。
   Zài Máo Zédōng shídài, fángzi shì yóu gōngzuò dānwèi fēnpèi de.

2. 她在出生的时候被抛弃了，后来让一个美国家庭领养了。
   Tā zài chūshēngde shíhou bèi pāoqìle, hòulái ràng yíge Měiguó jiātíng lǐngyǎngle.

3. 我父母到城里打工去了，所以我是(让)姥姥带大的。
   (让 **ràng** may be omitted here.)
   Wǒ fùmǔ dào chénglǐ dǎgōng qùle, suǒyǐ wǒ shì (ràng) lǎolao dài-dà de.

11.9 Preview of related topics

There are two other coverbs— 比 **bǐ** *to compare* and 离 **lí** *to depart*—which have the same grammatical characteristics as other coverbs covered in this lesson. But because their usages are specialized and important, a separate chapter in this book (Chapter 13) is devoted to them.

In addition to the usage of coverbs and postverbs discussed in this lesson, another mechanism for introducing elements that are associated with the main verb of the sentence is the usage of two-syllable conjunctions, e.g. 对于 **duìyú**, 关于 **guānyú**, 由于 **yóuyú**, 至于 **zhìyú**. These conjunctions typically come at the beginning of a sentence to provide some additional background to the main point of the sentence. They will be discussed as a group in Chapter 16, and treated individually as sentence patterns in Part II of this book.

The "Verb + Complement" Structure

The *verb + resultative complement* is one of the most frequently-used structures in colloquial Chinese.[1] For students of Chinese, a hallmark of reaching near-native speaking level is the ability to use this structure spontaneously and idiomatically. This structure has no parallel in English, so a new linguistic groove needs to be carved into the learner's mind. The challenge is not in comprehending these expressions—for they are in fact quite simple—but in using them actively, in place of the more cumbersome expressions that seem like translations from English.

The beauty of this structure lies in its simplicity. The central concept behind it can be illustrated by the Chinese translations of three common English words: *to see, to find, to break.* Each of these is rendered into Chinese using two components: the first indicating a process and the second indicating a result:

to see: 看 **kàn** *to look* + 见 **jiàn** *to catch sight of* = 看见 **kànjian**

to find: 找 **zhǎo** *to search* + 到 **dào** *to arrive/attain* = 找到 **zhǎodào**

to break: 打 **dǎ** *to hit* + 破 **pò** *broken* = 打破 **dǎpò**

The three examples are given here *not* because they represent how most Chinese verbs are formed, but to illustrate the linguistic mindset behind the *verb + resultative complement* structure that has produced so many manifestations. The two-part structure is simple, and it embodies grammatical as well as semantic agility.

Grammatical agility is manifested in the four variations that can be created by adding just one more syllable to the basic form.

basic form	positive actual	negative actual	positive capability	negative capability
verb + complement	verb + complement + 了 **le**	没 **méi** + verb + complement	verb + 得 **de** + complement	verb + 不 **bu** + complement
看见 **kànjian** *to see*	看见了 **kànjianle** *saw*	没看见 **méi kànjian** *didn't see*	看得见 **kàn-de-jiàn** *can see*	看不见 **kàn-bu-jiàn** *can't see*
找到 **zhǎodào** *to find*	找到了 **zhǎodàole** *found*	没找到 **méi zhǎodào** *didn't find*	找得到 **zhǎo-de-dào** *can find*	找不到 **zhǎo-bu-dào** *can't find*

---

[1] We begin this chapter by calling this structure the "verb + resultative complement" because that is the term used in most Chinese language textbooks, but for reasons to be explained shortly, the word "resultative" will be dropped before the end of the introduction.

basic form	positive actual	negative actual	positive capability	negative capability
打破 **dǎpò** *to break*	打破了 **dǎpòle** *broke*	没打破 **méi dǎpò** *didn't break*	打得破 **dǎ-de-pò** *can break*	打不破 **dǎ-bu-pò** *can't break*

As for semantic flexibility, the three Chinese compounds 看见 **kànjian**, 找到 **zhǎodào** and 打破 **dǎpò** are not the only translations for *to see, to find, to break*. Different nuances of these three simple words in English can be conveyed by changing either the verb or the complement, e.g. 看穿 **kànchuān** (*to see through*), 找出 **zhǎochū** (*to find out*) and 弄破 **nòngpò** (*to cause to break*). This semantic flexibility is even more evident in the different meanings conveyed by various complements used with the verb 买 **mǎi** *to buy*:

买不起 **mǎi-bu-qǐ** *cannot afford to buy*

买不到 **mǎi-bu-dào** *unable to buy because it's unavailable*

买不得 **mǎi-bu-de** *inadvisable to buy (due to quality, etc.)*

All three expressions can be translated into English as "cannot buy," but to convey their full meanings in English requires a bit of elaboration.

Because the vast majority of *verb + complement* compounds are bisyllabic, a wide range of expressions can be created with just three syllables, making them very succinct and expressive. No wonder this is a favorite form of expression among Chinese speakers. In fact, the *resultative complement* is such a well-oiled linguistic device that the Chinese have extended its usage well beyond its archetypal function of stating an action and its result. To reflect the broader use of this structure, we will henceforth drop the word *resultative* in front of *complement* wherever appropriate. To illustrate the extended usage of this grammatical structure, here is an example that has nothing to do with an action and its result.

够得上 **gòu-de-shàng** *to qualify for* (lit. "sufficient attain up")

◆ *He doesn't have a Ph.D., but on the basis of his experience and knowledge, he is fully qualified to be a professor.*
他没有博士学位，但以他的经历和知识，完全够得上当教授了。
Tā méiyǒu bóshì xuéwèi, dàn yǐ tāde jīnglì hé zhīshi, wánquán gòu-de-shàng dāng jiàoshòu le.
(Alternative translation: ⋯，完全够资格当教授了。 **..., wánquán gòu zīgé dāng jiàoshòu le.**)

The archetypal usages of the *verb + complement* are relatively easy to master, because their meanings are transparent from the components. It is the extended usages of these expressions—especially those that become figurative and idiomatic—that require a bit of "immersion" before they become intuitive for non-native speakers.

12.1 The classic *verb + complement* form

The most straightforward version of the *verb + complement* structure is an action verb combined with a complement describing the result of that action. The "result" is often expressed by an adjective (aka a *stative verb*), but it can also be some other part of speech. As you read each of the following examples, note the underlined *verb + complement* in the sentence. Also, take note of which of the five forms (the basic form and the four variations listed in the table in the previous pages) is represented.

- *Teacher, are you sure I can learn Chinese?*
  老师，你觉得我一定能学会中文吗？
  Lǎoshī, nǐ juéde wǒ yídìng néng xuéhuì Zhōngwén ma?

- *My computer cannot be repaired, I can only buy a new one.*
  我的电脑修不好了，只好买一部新的。
  Wǒde diànnǎo xiū-bu-hǎo le, zhǐhǎo mǎi yíbù xīnde.

- *The dishwasher did not wash these glasses clean!*
  洗碗机没把这些杯子洗干净！ **Xǐwǎnjī méi bǎ zhèixiē bēizi xǐgānjìng!**

- *I heard everything the teacher said, but I hardly understood any of it.*
  老师说的我都听见了，可是差不多都没听懂。
  Lǎoshī shuōde wǒ dōu tīngjiànle, kěshì chàbuduō dōu méi tīngdǒng.

- *So much homework, I'm afraid I won't be able to finish it.*
  那么多的功课，我恐怕做不完了。
  Nàme duōde gōngkè, wǒ kǒngpà zuò-bu-wán le.

- *Thanks, that's enough, I'm full.*
  谢谢，够了，我吃饱了。 **Xièxie, gòule, wǒ chībǎo le.**

- *In speaking a foreign language, making mistakes is unavoidable, but it doesn't matter.*
  说外语免不了常常会说错，不过没关系！
  Shuō wàiyǔ miǎn-bu-liǎo chángcháng huì shuōcuò, búguò méi guānxi!

- *I just straightened up the house today, and my kid messed it all up again!*
  我今天刚收拾好房子，又被我的孩子弄乱了！
  Wǒ jīntiān gāng shōushihǎo fángzi, yòu bèi wǒde háizi nòngluàn le.

- *You guessed right! I was born in the U.S.*
  你猜对了！我是在美国出生的。 **Nǐ cāiduìle! Wǒ shì zài Měiguó chūshēngde.**

- *He broke the record again in this race.*
  这次赛跑他又打破了纪录。 **Zhèicì sàipǎo tā yòu dǎpòle jìlù.**

Combine each of the verbs below with two combinable complements, then give the meaning of each *verb + complement*. Use all four permutations. Due to the meaning of the paired function verbs and complements, some permutations do not exist because they simply don't make sense.

function verbs: 看 **kàn**   做 **zuò**   买 **mǎi**   卖 **mài**   写 **xiě**

说 **shuō**   教 **jiāo**   弄 **nòng**   打 **dǎ**   长 **zhǎng**

complements: 对 **duì**   错 **cuò**   完 **wán**   好 **hǎo**   脏 **zāng**

死 **sǐ**   高 **gāo**   胖 **pàng**   坏 **huài**   懂 **dǒng**

SAMPLE ANSWERS:

1. 看不完 **kàn-bu-wán** cannot finish reading
2. 看得懂 **kàn-de-dǒng** able to understand by reading
3. 做错了 **zuòcuòle** made a mistake in doing something
4. 做不完 **zuò-bu-wán** unable to finish doing
5. 买错了 **mǎicuòle** bought the wrong thing
6. 没买对 **méi mǎiduì** did not buy the right thing
7. 卖不完 **mài-bu-wán** cannot finish selling
8. 卖完了 **màiwánle** sold out
9. 没写对 **méi xiěduì** did not write correctly
10. 写不完 **xiě-bu-wán** unable to finish writing
11. 说得好 **shuō-de-hǎo** said it well
12. 说错了 **shuōcuòle** said it incorrectly
13. 没教完 **méi jiāowán** did not finish teaching
14. 教错了 **jiāocuòle** taught it wrong
15. 弄脏了 **nòngzāngle** made (something) dirty
16. 弄坏了 **nònghuàile** ruined (something)
17. 打死了 **dǎsǐle** killed by hitting
18. 打完了 **dǎwánle** finished making a phone call (e.g. 打完了电话 **dǎwánle diànhuà**)
19. 长高了 **zhǎnggāole** grew tall
20. 没长胖 **méi zhǎngpàng** did not grow fat

12.2 Extending the *verb + complement* to *stative verbs*

The term *stative verb* as another term for *adjectives* was introduced in 1.4. One way in which a *stative verb* functions grammatically like a *function verb* is in its usage in the *verb + complement* structure. A *stative verb + complement* phrase has the same structure as those in the last section, but its meaning has nothing to do with an action and its result. These phrases tend to have an idiomatic flavor, and are not randomly created. Even more so than the classic *verb + resultative complement* combinations, only certain variations of the *stative verb + complement* combinations are used by native speakers; the others either don't make sense or sound contrived. The examples below are idiomatic expressions frequently heard in colloquial speech.

stative verb	complement	four permutations: SV + 了 le; 没 méi + SV + complement; SV + 得 de + complement; SV + 不 bu + complement
累 **lèi** *tired*	坏 **huài** *to break*	累坏了 **lèihuàile** *exhausted to breaking point* (other three permutations are not heard)
饿 **è** *hungry*	死 **sǐ** *to die*	饿死了 **èsǐle** *hungry "to death"*; 没饿死 **méi èsǐ** *did not die from hunger*; 饿不死 **è-bu-sǐ** *can't die from hunger* (饿得死 **è-de-sǐ** makes no sense)
错 **cuò** *wrong*	了 **liǎo** *to end*	错不了 **cuò-bu-liǎo** *can't go wrong* (the other 3 permutations don't exist) (note pronunciation of 了 when it is used as a complement)
难 **nán** *difficult*	倒 **dǎo** *to topple*	难倒了 **nándǎole** *to be stumped ("toppled" by difficulty)*; 没难倒 **méi nándǎo** *was not stumped*; 难不倒 **nán-bu-dǎo** *can't be stumped* (难得倒 **nán-de-dǎo** is simply not used)
富 **fù** *wealthy*	起来 **qǐlai** *to get up, become*	富起来了 **fù-qǐlaile** *to have become rich*; 没富起来 **méi fù-qǐlai** *did not become rich*; 富不起来 **fù-bu-qǐlai** *unable to become rich* (富得起来 **fù-de-qǐlai** sounds odd)

You may have noticed that the meanings of 了 **liǎo**, 倒 **dǎo** and 起来 **qǐlai** as complements in the context of composite phrases have morphed quite a bit from their inherent meanings. Moreover, these meanings are often figurative rather than literal (e.g. 累死了 **lèi-sǐle** = *dead tired*). This is a common phenomenon with complements used in this structure. Often the complete phrases are easier to translate into English than the individual complements. Once you are familiar with the frequently-used phrases containing these complements, you will have a clear *sense* of their meaning. This is more effective than memorizing the list of complements.

As you read each of the sentences below, identify the *stative verb + complement* phrase and take note of the sense conveyed by the complement. For each occurrence of the character 了, figure out why it is pronounced **le** or **liǎo**.

♦ *Grandma is old, you should help her more, and not let her get too tired.*
 奶奶老了，你应该多帮她的忙，别让她累坏了。
 Nǎinai lǎo le, nǐ yīnggāi duō bāng tāde máng, bié ràng tā lèihuàile.

♦ *Organic milk has a longer shelf life; it can be kept in the refrigerator for a month without going bad.*
 有机牛奶比较耐久，放在冰箱里一个月也坏不了。
 Yǒujī niúnǎi bǐjiào nàijiǔ, fàngzài bīngxiānglǐ yíge yuè yě huài-bu-liǎo.

- *The reason why this region cannot become affluent is that transportation is inconvenient.*
  这个地区富不起来是因为交通不方便。
  Zhèige dìqū fù-bu-qǐlai shì yīnwèi jiāotōng bù fāngbiàn.

- *Old Zhang is very experienced, surely we can't go wrong if we do it according to his directions.*
  老张很有经验，按照他的说明去做肯定错不了。
  Lǎo Zhāng hěn yǒu jīngyàn, ànzhào tāde shuōmíng qù zuò kěndìng cuò-bu-liǎo.

- *This dog is already 15 years old. He probably can't recover from this illness, let's just euthanize him.*
  这只狗已经十五岁了，这次得病恐怕好不了了，我们就让它安乐死吧。 **Zhèizhī gǒu yǐjīng shíwǔsuì le, zhèicì débìng kǒngpà hǎo-bu-liǎo le, wǒmen jiù ràng tā ānlèsǐ ba.**

- *That child prodigy was finally defeated by a computer-generated problem in a math competition.*
  那个神童在一场数学比赛上终于被一个电脑出的题目难倒了。
  Nèige shéntóng zài yìchǎng shùxué bǐsài-shang zhōngyú bèi yíge diànnǎo chūde tímù nán-dǎole.

- *The pay for a teacher in such a poor area is enough to keep me from starving, but definitely will never make me rich.*
  在这个贫困地区当教师，我的工资让我饿不死，可也绝对富不起来。
  Zài zhèige pínkùn dìqū dāng jiàoshī, wǒde gōngzī ràng wǒ è-bu-sǐ, kě yě juéduì fù-bu-qǐlai.

EXERCISES:

Choose three *verb + complement* phrases from the third column of the table in 12.2 and put them in the context of sentences. Use different permutations from those that have already appeared in the above example sentences.

12.3 Parts of speech that can function as complements

While *function verbs* and *stative verbs* are the two types of verbals that can be *complemented*, there are many other parts of speech that can fill the slot of the complement in this structure. Words in Chinese tend to be grammatically fluid (see 1.4); thus in the table below, the assignment of words to parts of speech is somewhat arbitrary. As you study the following table, link the meaning of each phrase in the right column with the inherent meaning of the corresponding complement in the second column. As you will see, the further down the list you go, the more the complements have morphed in meaning.

types of complements	inherent meanings[2]	example "verb + complement" phrases
stative verbs	好 **hǎo** *good*	修不好 **xiū-bu-hǎo** *cannot be repaired;* 做好了 **zuòhǎole** *finished making (something)*
	高 **gāo** *tall*	长不高 **zhǎng-bu-gāo** *cannot grow tall*
	错 **cuò** *incorrect*	看错了 **kàncuòle** *mistaken in seeing;* 没弄错 **méi nòngcuò** *did not get mixed up*
	对 **duì** *correct*	没猜对 **méi cāiduì** *did not guess correctly;* 答对了 **dáduìle** *answered correctly*
	脏 **zāng** *dirty*	弄脏了 **nòngzāngle** *made (something) dirty*
	清楚 **qīngchǔ** *clear*	没说清楚 **méi shuō-qīngchǔ** *did not say it clearly;* 看不清楚 **kàn-bu-qīngchǔ** *unable to see clearly*
	满 **mǎn** *full*	放满 **fàngmǎn** *to fill (a space);* 铺满 **pūmǎn** *to fill (a flat surface);* 填满 **tiánmǎn** *to fill (a form);* 坐满 **zuòmǎn** *seats all taken*
	死 **sǐ** *dead*	累死了 **lèi-sǐle** *dead tired;* 难看死了 **nánkàn-sǐle** *extremely ugly;* 乐死了 **lè-sǐle** *extremely happy*
function verbs (general)	开 **kāi** *to open*	打开了 **dǎkāile** *opened up;* 离不开 **lí-bu-kāi** *cannot be away from;* 分不开 **fēn-bu-kāi** *cannot distinguish;* 看开了 **kàn-kāile** *to come around to accepting an unpleasant situation;* 想开了 **xiǎng-kāile** *thought through an impasse, resigned to a misfortune;* 吃得开 **chī-de-kāi** *in an advantageous human environment, to have privileged status*
	动 **dòng** *to move*	搬得动 **bān-de-dòng** *can move (not too heavy);* 走不动 **zǒu-bu-dòng** *unable to walk;* 带动 **dài-dòng** *to spur, to bring along;* 发动 **fā-dòng** *to mobilize, to initiate*
	到 **dào** *to arrive*	没看到 **méi kàndào** *did not see;* 想不到 **xiǎng-bu-dào** *unexpectedly;* 没感到 **méi gǎndào** *did not feel;* 遇到了 **yùdàole** *encountered;* 办不到 **bàn-bu-dào** *cannot do it*

[2] A word about the use of neutral tone in verb complements: There is no strict standard in the usage of the neutral tone in verb complements among native speakers, but northerners tend to use it more than southerners. The context as well as speed of speech also affect the usage. The neutral tone tends to be used most often with the high-frequency verb complements: 来 **lai**, 去 **qu**, 上 **shang**, 得 **de**, and 见 **jian**. In this book, we will observe the standard Chinese pronunciation, but do not be surprised when you hear native Chinese deviate from this rather flexible standard.

types of complements	inherent meanings[2]	example "verb + complement" phrases
	住 **zhù** to dwell	拴住 **shuānzhù** to tie up; 记不住 **jì-bu-zhù** can't remember; 坐不住 **zuò-bu-zhù** can't sit still; 留不住 **liú-bu-zhù** can't retain (e.g. a friend or employee); 忍不住 **rěn-bu-zhù** can't resist (doing something)
	懂 **dǒng** to understand	听不懂 **tīng-bu-dǒng** can't understand by listening; 没看懂 **mei kàndǒng** didn't understand by reading
	见 **jiàn** to see, to perceive	听见 **tīngjian** to hear; 碰见 **pèngjian** to encounter
	走 **zǒu** to walk, to go away	飞走 **fēizǒu** to fly away; 逃走 **táozǒu** to escape; 赶走 **gǎnzǒu** to drive out; 拐走 **guǎizǒu** to abduct; 带不走 **dài-bu-zǒu** cannot take along/away
	消 **xiāo** to dissipate	打消 **dǎxiāo** to give up, to dispel; 吃不消 **chī-bu-xiāo** unable to take
	通 **tōng** to go through, to penetrate	打通 **dǎtōng** to get through (on the phone); 走不通 **zǒu-bu-tōng** can't go through, impractical; 买通 **mǎitōng** to buy off, to bribe; 想不通 **xiǎng-bu-tōng** can't understand, can't see the reason; 说不通 **shuō-bu-tōng** doesn't make sense
	掉 **diào** to lose, to fall	扔掉 **rēngdiào** to throw out; 拔掉 **bádiào** to pull out; 冲掉 **chōngdiào** to wash out; 省掉 **shěngdiào** to save, to spare; 辞掉 **cídiào** to resign (from job); 扣掉 **kòudiào** to deduct; 开掉 **kāidiào** to fire (from job)
来 **lai**/去 **qu** (function verbs with special characteristics when used as complements)	来 **lái** to come	送来了 **sònglaile** delivered; 回不来 **huí-bu-lái** can't return; 起来了 **qǐlaile** got up (from bed); 惹来 **rě-lái** to incur (trouble); 做得来 **zuò-de-lái** up to doing something; 谈不来 **tán-bu-lái** incompatible (don't have much in common); 处得来 **chǔ-de-lái** can get along; 吃不来 **chī-bu-lái** unable to eat (due to one's taste); 合不来 **hé-bu-lái** incompatible; 划不来 **huá-bu-lái** not worthwhile
	去 **qù** to go	没寄去 **méi jìqu** didn't mail (out); 进得去 **jìn-de-qù** can enter; 刨去 **páoqu** to shave off, excluding; 过得去 **guò-de-qù** can get by; 过不去 **guò-bu-qù** can't get past, to feel bad (about something)

types of complements	inherent meanings[2]	example "verb + complement" phrases
directional verbs (a special subgroup of function verbs)	上 **shàng** *to move up*	赶得上 **gǎn-de-shàng** *able to make it in time*; 看不上 **kàn-bu-shàng** *to find something unappealing*; 爱上 **àishang** *to fall in love with*; 染上 **rǎnshàng** *infested with*; 没考上 **méi kǎoshang** *did not pass an exam (e.g. for college)*; 穿不上 **chuān-bu-shàng** *cannot put on (clothing, shoes)*; 谈不上 **tán-bu-shàng** *be out of the question*; 说不上 **shuō-bu-shàng** *not up to being called*; 顾不上 **gù-bu-shàng** *unable to attend to*; 配得上 **pèi-de-shàng** *be able to match, good enough for*
	下 **xià** *to move down*	留下 **liúxià** *to leave behind*; 剩下 **shèngxià** *to be left, remained*; 收下 **shōuxià** *to accept (e.g. a gift), take in*; 吃不下 **chī-bu-xià** *can't eat (too full)*; 装得下 **zhuāng-de-xià** *can fit in (a container)*; 住得下 **zhù-de-xià** *can accommodate (re housing)*; 穿不下 **chuān-bu-xià** *cannot wear because it's too small* (compare with 穿不上 **chuān-bu-shàng** in box above)
	出 **chū** *to exit*	挑出 **tiāochū** *to pick out*; 想出 **xiǎngchū** *to think of*; 猜出 **cāichū** *to guess correctly*; 找出 **zhǎochū** *to find (e.g. solution, issue, etc.)* (compare with 找到 **zhǎodào**, which applies to finding an object, place, person, etc.)
	起 **qǐ** *to rise*	住得起 **zhǔ-de-qǐ** *can afford (housing)*; 看不起 **kàn-bu-qǐ** *to look down on, to disdain*; 对不起 **duì-bu-qǐ** *sorry, to have let someone down*; 了不起 **liǎo-bu-qǐ** *outstanding, extraordinary*
	过 **guò** *to pass, across*	渡过 **dùguò** *to tide over, to pull through*; 超过了 **chāoguòle** *to have exceeded*; 熬不过 **áo-bu-guò** *unable to endure*; 胜得过 **shèng-de-guò** *can win over*; 比不过 **bǐ-bu-guò** *can't compare with, not up to*; 信不过 **xìn-bu-guò** *cannot trust*
	进 **jìn** *to enter*	没考进 **méi kǎojìn** *did not pass admission exam*
directional verb + 来 **lái**/ 去 **qù** (combination of above two groups)	回 **huí** + 来 **lai**/ 去 **qu** *to return (come/go)*	寄回去 **jì-huíqu** *to mail back*; 带回来 **dài-huílai** *to bring back*; 找回来 **zhǎo-huílai** *to retrieve*; 走不回去了 **zǒu-bù-huíqule** *cannot walk back* (literal or figurative)
	进 **jìn** + 来 **lai**/ 去 **qu** *to enter (come/go)*	搬不进来 **bān-bú-jìnlai** *cannot move in*; 开进去 **kāi-jìnqu** *to drive into*; 闯进来了 **chuǎng-jìnlaile** *crashed in*; 听不进去 **tīng-bú-jìnqu** *can't stand listening to (advice, etc.)*

types of complements	inherent meanings[2]	example "verb + complement" phrases
出来 chūlai to exit (come)		放出来 fàng-chūlai to release; 算出来 suàn-chūlai to calculate, to figure out; 拿不出来 ná-bù-chūlai cannot take out; 看不出来 kàn-bù-chūlai can't tell by looking; 说不出来 shuō-bù-chūlai cannot say; 想不出来 xiǎng-bù-chūlai can't think of; 蹦出来 bèng-chūlai to crop up
出去 chūqu to exit (go)		卖不出去 mài-bù-chūqu can't sell; 溜出去 liū-chūqu to slip out; 豁出去 huō-chūqu to go for broke, to take out all the stops
上来 shànglai to come up		开不上来 kāi-bú-shànglai unable to drive up (a hill); 答不上来 dá-bú-shànglai unable to come up with an answer; 交上来 jiāo-shànglai to submit, to hand in (to person in higher position)
上去 shàngqu to go up		爬不上去 pá-bú-shàngqu can't climb up; 挤上去 jǐ-shàngqu to squeeze onto (e.g. a bus); 弄上去 nòng-shàngqu to get something to go up; 看上去 kàn-shàngqu by the looks of it, seems like
下来 xiàlai to come down		摔下来 shuāi-xiàlai to fall down; 记下来 jì-xiàlai to note down; 留下来 liú-xiàlai to stay behind; 定下来 dìng-xiàlai to decide, to settle on; 活下来 huó-xiàlai to survive; 冷静下来 lěngjìng-xiàlai to calm down; 答应下来 dāyìng-xiàlai to promise; 批下来 pī-xiàlai to approve (from above); 停不下来 tíng-bú-xiàlai unable to stop (e.g. an energetic person)
下去 xiàqu to go down		扔下去 rēng-xiàqu to toss down; 呆下去 dāi-xiàqu to continue at a certain place; 混下去 hùn-xiàqu to continue to muddle through; 活下去 huó-xiàqu to live on (compare with 活下来 huó-xiàlai to survive)
起来 qǐlai to rise (起去 qǐqu does not exist)		堆起来 duī-qǐlai to pile up, 捆起来 kǔn-qǐlai to tie up; 锁起来 suǒ-qǐlai to lock up; 加起来 jiāqǐlai to add up; 躲起来 duǒ-qǐlai to hide; 想不起来 xiǎng-bù-qǐlai cannot recall; 看起来 kàn-qǐlai the way things look; 说起来 shuō-qǐlai when it comes to talking about it
过 guò + 来 lai/ 去 qu to cross (come/go)		递过来 dì-guòlai to hand over; 搬过去 bān-guòqu to move over (there); 翻过来 fān-guòlai to turn over; 改过来了 gǎi-guòlaile corrected; 晕过去 yūn-guòqu to pass out, to faint; 醒过来 xǐng-guòlai to awaken, to regain consciousness; 明白过来 míngbái-guòlai to suddenly have a clear understanding; 看得过去 kàn-de-guòqu passably presentable; 说不过去 shuō-bú-guòqu can't be justified or explained away

types of complements	inherent meanings[2]	example "verb + complement" phrases
Other verbals derived from verbs, but not used independently as verbs in modern colloquial Chinese	会 **huì** *to be able, to know how to*	学会了 **xuéhuìle** *learned*
	得 **de** *to attain*	舍不得 **shě-bu-de** *can't bear to part with;* 看不得 **kàn-bu-de** *unfit for the eye (e.g. R-rated film for the underaged);* 穿不得 **chuān-bu-de** *unfit to wear (e.g. too risqué);* 怪不得 **guài-bu-de** *no wonder;* 要不得 **yào-bu-de** *dreadful, unacceptable*
	着 **zháo** *to catch on*[3]	找着了 **zhǎozháole** *to have found (synonym of* 找到了 **zhǎodàole***);* 睡不着 **shuì-bu-zháo** *unable to sleep;* 猜着了 **cāizháole** *guessed correctly*
	及 **jí** *to reach*	来得及 **lái-de-jí** *can make it in time;* 来不及 **lái-bu-jí** *can't make it in time;* 等不及 **děng-bu-jí** *too impatient to wait;* 赶得及 **gǎn-de-jí** *able to make it by hurrying*
	了 **liǎo** *to end* This is one of the most prolific complements in colloquial Chinese. Most of the phrases are in the "negative capability" form (···不了 **bùliǎo**) and are idiomatic.	吃不了 **chī-bu-liǎo** *cannot finish eating;* 免不了 **miǎn-bu-liǎo** *unavoidable (synonym of* 免不得 **miǎn-bude***);* 吃得了 **chī-de-liǎo** *can finish eating;* 大不了 **dà-bu-liǎo** *at the worst, at most;* 少不了 **shǎo-bu-liǎo** *indispensable;* 长不了 **cháng-bu-liǎo** *can't last long;* 错不了 **cuò-bu-liǎo** *can't go wrong;* 管不了 **guǎn-bu-liǎo** *can't be bothered with, out of one's authority;* 等不了 **děng-bu-liǎo** *can't wait any longer;* 受不了 **shòu-bu-liǎo** *can't bear;* 死不了 **sǐ-bu-liǎo** *non-fatal*

As you may have noticed, the words in the second column are all basic vocabulary that are very familiar to you, but their meanings as verb complements are often not obvious. The verbs with the complements 来 **lái**/去 **qù** and directional verbs fall into the less obvious category, because more often than not, they are used figuratively. These figurative uses illustrate an aspect of the Chinese linguistic mindset that's not so prevalent in English, i.e. an underlying sense of "directional movement," even in abstract things. From the second example onward, take note of the differences in the phrases 想起来 **xiǎng-qǐlai**, 想出来 **xiǎng-chūlai** and 想到 **xiǎngdào**.

♦ *He will be returning next week.*
他下个星期就回来了 or ···回去了
Tā xiàge xīngqī jiù huílái le or **...huíqu le.**

---

[3] 着 **zháo**, in its function as a verb, occurs in the compounds 着凉 **zháoliáng** "catch a cold," 着火 **zháohuǒ** "catch on fire," and 着急 **zháojí** "be anxious." The same character 着, pronounced **zhe**, is an aspect marker (see 8.1).

(Without 来 **lái** or 去 **qù**, the sentence would be incomplete. The notion of movement toward or away from the speaker is inherent in the speaker's mind.)

- *This person looks very familiar, but I thought and thought, and still couldn't think of who he is.*
  这个人我很面熟，可是他是谁，我想来想去也想不起来了。
  Zhèige rén wǒ hěn miànshú, kěshì tā shì shéi, wǒ xiǎnglái-xiǎngqù yě xiǎng-bu-qǐlai le.

- *I often have to spend a lot of time before I can think of interesting example sentences.*
  我常常得花很多时间才能想出有趣的例句来。
  Wǒ chángcháng děi huā hěn duō shíjiān cái néng xiǎngchū yǒuqùde lìjù lái.

- *I thought he was just my teacher, I never thought he would fall in love with me!*
  我以为他就是我的老师，根本没想到他会爱上我！
  Wǒ yǐwéi tā jiùshi wǒde lǎoshī, gēnběn méi xiǎngdào tā huì àishang wǒ!

The English word *to think* in the last three sentences is rendered into Chinese using different complements, and their meanings are quite distinct to Chinese speakers. All three complements have a sense of "directional movement."

In the above table, we gave the inherent meanings for the complements (the 2nd column), but not their meanings when used as complements. You may be annoyed that we are telling you what you already know but not what you need to know, but we did this for several reasons. Some of the verb complements have more than one figurative meaning; the figurative meanings are generally "lost in translation" from one language to another; and most importantly, the best way for students to grasp the nuances of these phrases is to immerse themselves in their natural usage by native speakers. Because the *verb + complement* structure is such a popular "way of saying things" in Chinese, once you begin keeping an ear out for them, you will notice that they are ubiquitous, and soon you will come to appreciate their wit and expressiveness.

12.4 Using *verb + complement* phrases figuratively and idiomatically

Immersing yourself in a Chinese speaking environment in order to master the *verb + complement* structure is of course a long process, but we will provide some shortcuts here, with examples of frequently-used figurative and idiomatic phrases. English translations of these sentences are provided only as a convenience. You will acquire a more nuanced understanding of these by approaching them directly from the Chinese rather than through the translations.

The following figurative and idiomatic *verb + complement* expressions are from the table in the preceding section. Space in this chapter only allows for 20 example sentences, which will serve as a start in bringing these phrases to life. Refer to the online "Appendix: Figurative and Idiomatic Expressions" for additional examples.

1. 死 sǐ: 累死了 lèi-sǐle *to be dead tired*

   为了写这篇文章，我三天都没睡觉，现在快累死了！

   Wèile xiě zhèipiān wénzhāng, wǒ sāntiān dōu méi shuìjiào, xiànzài kuài lèi-sǐle!

   To write this article, I didn't sleep for three days, and now I'm dead tired!

2. 开 kāi: 吃得开 chī-de-kāi *in an advantageous position, to have a privileged status*

   他的智商不低，情商更高，所以走到哪里都很吃得开。

   Tāde zhìshāng bùdī, qíngshāng gèng gāo, suǒyǐ zǒudào nǎli dōu hěn chī-de-kāi.

   He has a good IQ, and his EQ is even higher, so he can do well wherever he goes.

3. 住 zhù: 留不住 liú-bu-zhù *can't retain (e.g. a friend or employee)*

   像这种不死不活的公司根本留不住优秀人才！

   Xiàng zhèizhǒng bùsǐ-bùhuóde gōngsī gēnběn liú-bu-zhù yōuxiù réncái!

   There's no way a half-dead (barely limping along) company like this can keep first-rate talent!

4. 消 xiāo: 吃不消 chī-bu-xiāo *unable to take it*

   连续一个多星期的高温天气让很多人感觉吃不消了，尤其是老年人。

   Liánxù yígeduō xīngqīde gāowēn tiānqì ràng hěn duō rén gǎnjué chī-bu-xiāole, yóuqíshì lǎonián-rén.

   High temperatures continuing for more than a week made a lot of people feel that they couldn't take it anymore, especially old people.

5. 通 tōng: 买通 mǎitōng *to buy off, to bribe*

   黑帮组织买通了警察局长，此后贩毒就一路畅通无阻了。

   Hēibāng zǔzhī mǎitōngle jǐngchá júzhǎng, cǐhòu fàndú jiù yílù chàngtōng wúzǔ le.

   A criminal gang bribed the chief of police, and after that, dope dealers had a free rein and there was no stopping them.

6. 掉 diào: 开掉 kāidiào *to be fired (from job)*

   他上班总是迟到，做事情又不认真，不到半年就被公司开掉了。

   Tā shàngbān zǒngshì chídào, zuò shìqíng yòu bú rènzhēn, búdào bànnián jiù bèi gōngsī kāidiàole.

   He was always late for work, and he was not serious about his work; in less than half a year he was fired by the company.

7. 来 lái: 吃不来 chī-bu-lái *unable to eat (due to the taste)*

   榴莲这种水果，有的人很爱吃，有的人一点儿也吃不来。

   Liúlián zhèizhǒng shuǐguǒ, yǒude rén hěn ài chī, yǒude rén yìdiǎnr yě chī-bu-lái.

   This fruit called durian, some people love it, while other people can't stand it at all.

8. 来 lái: 划不来 huá-bu-lái *not worthwhile*

他父母花了一百多万元送他去美国留学，毕业后回国只能找到月
薪3000多元的工作，实在有点儿划不来。

Tā fùmǔ huāle yìbǎiduō-wàn yuán sòng tā qù Měiguó liúxué, bìyè hòu huíguó zhǐ néng zhǎodào yuèxīn 3000-duō-yuánde gōngzuò, shízài yǒudiǎnr huá-bu-lái.

His parents spent more than a million yuan (RMB) to send him to America to study, and after he graduated and returned to China he was only able to find a job that paid a bit over three thousand yuan per month; that was really not quite worth it.

9. 去 qù: 过不去 guò-bu-qù *not able to get past, to feel bad (about something)*

虽然她原谅了老公出轨的事情，但心里总有点儿过不去。

Suīrán tā yuánliàngle lǎogōng chūguǐde shìqing, dàn xīnlǐ zǒng yǒudiǎnr guò-bu-qù.

Although she forgave her husband for going "off track," she still can't get over her feelings of resentment.

10. 上 shàng: 谈不上 tán-bu-shàng *to be out of the question*

他现在的成绩都不一定上得了普通的大学，更谈不上名牌大学了。

Tā xiànzàide chéngjì dōu bù yídìng shàng-de-liǎo pǔtōngde dàxué, gèng tán-bu-shàng míngpái dàxué le.

Given his present grades, he might not even be able to get into a run-of-the-mill college, not to mention a renowned university.

11. 起 qǐ: 了不起 liǎo-bu-qǐ *outstanding, extraordinary*

她真是一位了不起的大法官，85岁还是停不下来！(Re Ruth Bader Ginsburg)

Tā zhēn shì yíwèi liǎo-bu-qǐde dà fǎguān, 85 suì háishi tíng-bu-xiàlai!

She is really an extraordinary judge. 85 years old and she still can't stop working!

12. 上来 shànglai: 答不上来 dá-bu-shànglai *unable to come up with an answer*

我面试的时候太紧张了，脑子里一片空白，好多问题都没答上来。

Wǒ miànshìde shíhou tài jǐnzhāng le, nǎozi-li yípiàn kòngbái, hǎo duō wèntí dōu méi dá-shànglai.

When I was in the interview I was too nervous. My mind was a blank. There were many questions that I couldn't answer.

13. 下来 xiàlai: 活下来 huó-xiàlai *to survive*

熊猫美香一共生过五只小熊猫，只有三只活下来了。

Xióngmāo Měixiāng yígòng shēngguo wǔzhī xiǎo xióngmāo, zhǐ yǒu sānzhī huó-xiàlaile.

The panda Meixiang has altogether given birth to five baby pandas, but only three survived.

14. 下去 **xiàqu**: 活下去 **huó-xiàqu** *to live on*

医生给了我第二次生命，我一定要好好活下去！
Yīshēng gěile wǒ dì'èrcì shēngmìng, wǒ yídìng yào hǎohāor huó-xiàqu!
The doctor has given me a second life; I definitely want to do my best to go on living!

15. 起来 **qǐlai**: 想不起来 **xiǎng-bu-qǐlai** *cannot recall*

他看上去好面熟，但是真想不起来他叫什么名字了。
Tā kàn-shàngqu hǎo miànshú, dànshì zhēn xiǎng-bu-qǐlai tā jiào shénme míngzi le.
He looks very familiar, but I really can't recall his name.

16. 过 **guò**+ 来 **lai**/去 **qu**: 改得过来 **gǎi-de-guòlai** *can be corrected*

老师，你看我的四声问题改得过来吗？
Lǎoshī, nǐ kàn wǒde sìshēng wèntí gǎi-de-guòlai ma?
Teacher, do you think my tone problem can be corrected?

17. 得 **dé**: 怪不得 **guài-bu-de** *no wonder*

怪不得她希望毕业以后到北京去工作，原来她男朋友在那里。
Guài-bu-de tā xīwàng bìyè yǐhòu dào Běijīng qù gōngzuò, yuánlái tā nánpéngyou zài nàli.
No wonder she wants to go to Beijing to work after she graduates; her boyfriend is there.

18. 及 **jí**: 来得及 **lái-de-jí** *can make it in time*; 来不及 **lái-bu-jí** *can't make it in time*

我下个月要去美国，现在申请签证来不来得及？
Wǒ xiàge yuè yào qù Měiguó, xiànzài shēnqǐng qiānzhèng lái-bu-lái-de-jí?
I want to go to the U.S. next month. If I apply for a visa now, will I get it in time?

19. 了 **liǎo**: 少不了 **shǎo-bu-liǎo** *indispensable*

老同学从国外回来，大家少不了要聚一聚，吃吃饭聊聊天。
Lǎotóngxué cóng guówài huílai, dàjiā shǎo-bu-liǎo yào jùyíjù, chīchīfàn liáoliáotiān.
When old classmates return from abroad, everybody has to get together to eat and chat.

20. 了 **liǎo**: 受不了 **shòu-bu-liǎo** *can't bear it*

像你这样动不动就发火，谁都受不了！
Xiàng nǐ zhèiyàng dòngbudòng jiù fāhuǒ, shéi dōu shòu-bu-liǎo!
Someone like you who gets angry at the slightest touch, nobody can stand it.

EXERCISES:

Choose ten *verb + complement* phrases from the table in 12.3 and create sentences using them. Use different variations from the phrases on the list (e.g. 睡不着 **shuì-bu-zháo** → 没睡着 **méi shuìzháo**). Make your sentences as interesting as you can, as this will help to etch these idiomatic phrases in your mind.

12.5 When a *verb + complement* has an object

There are three possible ways to introduce an object of a *verb + complement* phrase.:

1. When the *verb + complement* is in the *actual* form (either positive or negative), adding the object within a 把 **bǎ** + *object* coverbal phrase is the most natural and obvious way. In fact, if you go to the section on the coverb 把 **bǎ** (11.6), you will find that about half of the sentences illustrating the usage of 把 **bǎ** involve the coupling of 把 **bǎ** + *object* with a *verb + complement* phrase. This aligns with the notion that "把 **bǎ** + *object* + *verb* phrase" means taking something and doing something with it. As an exercise, turn to 11.6 and identify *verb + complement* phrases in the sentences there.

Three of the variations of the *verb + complement* structure may be coupled with 把 **bǎ** + *object* phrases: the basic form, and the positive and negative *actual* forms (refer to the table at the introduction to this chapter). The *capability* forms (positive and negative) do not use the coverb 把 **bǎ** to state an object, but rather two other ways discussed in the next two sections.

♦ *We'll be starting out tomorrow, so must get the car fixed today.*
我们明天就出发了，所以必须今天就把这部车修好。
Wǒmen míngtiān jiù chūfā le, suǒyǐ bìxū jīntiān jiù bǎ zhèibù chē xiūhǎo.
(修好 **xiūhǎo** is in the basic *verb + complement* form)

♦ *We have fixed your car, but if you are taking a long trip, you should change the four tires.*
我们把你的汽车修好了。不过要长途旅行的话，还得把四个轮胎换掉。 **Wǒmen bǎ nǐde qìchē xiūhǎo le. Búguò yào chángtú lǚxíng dehuà, hái děi bǎ sìge lúntāi huàndiào.**
(修好了 **xiūhǎole** is in the *positive actual* form; 换掉 **huàndiào** is in the *basic* form)

♦ *They said it's fixed, took $500, but actually it's not fixed!*
他们说修好了，要了我五百块，其实没修好！
Tāmen shuō xiūhǎole, yàole wǒ wǔbǎi kuài, qíshí méi xiūhǎo!
(没修好 **méi xiūhǎo** is in the *negative actual* form)

♦ *This car is too old to be fixed satisfactorily.*
这部车太旧了，修不好了。 **Zhèibù chē tài jiù le, xiū-bu-hǎo le.**
(修不好 **xiū-bu-hǎo** is in the *negative capability* form; the object cannot be stated using 把 **bǎ**)

♦ *They said this car is still fixable, but it would cost $2,000!*
他们说这部车还修得好，可是要两千块！
Tāmen shuō zhèibù chē hái xiū-de-hǎo, kěshì yào liǎngqiānkuài!
(alternative: ⋯这部车还是能修好，⋯ **...zhèibù chē háishi néng xiūhǎo, ...**)
(修得好 **xiū-de-hǎo** is in the *positive capability* form; the object cannot be stated using 把 **bǎ**)

2. The second way to state the object of a *stative verb + complement* phrase is to position it as the topic of a *topic + comment* sentence (see 1.3, section 1). The last two examples in the above group have already illustrated this. In contrast to the 把 **bǎ** pattern, the *topic + comment* format is unrestricted, i.e. it may be used for any of the various *verb + complement* permutations.

♦ *I must remember the students' names.*
  ✓ 学生们的名字，我一定要记住。
    (*basic* form used in *topic + comment* pattern)
    Xuéshengmende míngzi, wǒ yídìng yào jìzhù.
  ✓ 我一定要把学生的名字记住。(*basic* form used with 把 **bǎ**)
    Wǒ yídìng yào bǎ xuéshengde míngzi jìzhù.

♦ *I remembered all the students' names on the first day of the semester.*
  ✓ 学生们的名字，我在开学的头一天就记住了。
    Xuéshengmende míngzi, wǒ zài kāixuéde tóuyìtiān jiù jìzhùle.
    (*positive actual* form used in *topic + comment* pattern)
  ✓ 我在开学的头一天就把学生们的名字都记住了。
    Wǒ zài kāixuéde tóuyìtiān jiù bǎ xuéshengmende míngzi dōu jìzhùle.
    (*positive actual* form used with 把 **bǎ**)

♦ *Some professors don't remember students' names even by the end of the semester.*
  ✓ 学生们的名字，有些教授到学期末都还没记住。
    Xuéshengmende míngzi, yǒuxiē jiàoshòu dào xuéqī-mò dōu hái méi jìzhù.
    (*negative actual* form used in *topic + comment* pattern)
  ✓ 有些教授到学期末都还没把学生们的名字记住。
    Yǒuxiē jiàoshòu dào xuéqī-mò dōu hái méi bǎ xuéshengmende míngzi jìzhù.
    (*Negative actual* form used with 把 **bǎ**; but note that 没 **méi** is placed before the coverb 把 **bǎ**, which is consistent with the rule that the negative 不 **bù** or 没 **méi** comes before the coverb rather than the main verb in a sentence)

♦ *Can you recall that student's name?*
  ✓ 那个学生的名字，你想得起来吗？
    Nèige xuéshengde míngzi, nǐ xiǎng-de-qǐlai ma?
    (*positive capability* form used in *topic + comment* pattern)
  ✗ 你把那个学生的名字想得起来吗？
    (*capability* form cannot be used with 把 **bǎ**)
    Nǐ bǎ nèige xuéshengde míngzi xiǎng-de-qǐlai ma?

♦ *I cannot recall that student's name anymore!*
  ✓ 那个学生的名字，我想不起来了。
    Nèige xuéshengde míngzi, wǒ xiǎng-bu-qǐlai le.
    (*negative capability* form used in *topic + comment* pattern)

✗ 我把那个学生的名字想不起来了。
(capability form cannot be used with 把 **bǎ**)
Wǒ bǎ nèige xuéshengde míngzi xiǎng-bu-qǐlai le.

3. The third position for an object with a *verb + complement* expression is after the *complement*. Thus, the examples in the preceding section may all be restated as follows:

♦ *I must remember the students' names.*
我一定要记住学生们的名字。 **Wǒ yídìng yào jìzhù xuéshengmende míngzi.**

♦ *I remembered all the students' names on the first day of the semester.*
我在学期的头一天就记住了学生们的名字了。
Wǒ zài xuéqīde tóuyìtiān jiù jìzhùle xuéshengmende míngzi le.

♦ *Some professors don't remember students' names even by the end of the semester.*
有些教授到学期末都还没记住学生们的名字。
Yǒuxiē jiàoshòu dào xuéqī-mò dōu hái méi jìzhù xuéshengmende míngzi.

♦ *Can you recall that student's name?*
你想得起那个学生的名字吗？ **Nǐ xiǎng-de-qǐ nèige xuéshengde míngzi ma?**

♦ *I cannot recall that student's name anymore!*
我想不起那个学生的名字了。 **Wǒ xiǎng-bu-qǐ nèige xuéshengde míngzi le.**

This format for stating the object of a *verb + comment* phrase may align more closely with English, but it is not as frequently used by native Chinese speakers, especially when the object is a long phrase. Chinese speakers have a tendency to get long objects "out of the way" by moving them to the front of the sentence either as the topic or as the object with the coverb 把 **bǎ**.

With two-syllable complements where the second syllable is 来 **lái** or 去 **qù** (起来 **qǐlai**, 上来 **shànglai**, 下去 **xiàqu**, etc.), if the object is not prestated as the topic or as an object with 把 **bǎ**, then it is generally placed in between the two syllables of the complement, and may also come at the end after 来 **lái** or 去 **qù**, but cannot be placed in between the verb and the complement.

♦ *Ah, I remember that student's name now!*
✓ 啊，我想起那个学生的名字来了。
À, wǒ xiǎng-qǐ nèige xuéshengde míngzi lái le!
✓ 啊，我想起来那个学生的名字了。 (less likely choice by natives)
À, wǒ xiǎng-qǐlai nèige xuéshēngde míngzi le.
✗ 啊，我想那个学生的名字起来了。
À, wǒ xiǎng nèige xuéshengde míngzi qǐlai le.

EXERCISES:

Add an object to each of the *verb + complement* phrases below and use it in a sentence. The phrases below are in their basic form. Use all of the other forms at least once in your sentences.

1. 卖完 màiwán
2. 说错 shuōcuò
3. 看懂 kàndǒng
4. 收拾好 shōushihǎo

5. 带回去 dài-huíqu
6. 写下来 xiě-xiàlai
7. 算出来 suàn-chūlai
8. 锁起来 suǒ-qǐlai

SAMPLE ANSWERS:

1. 我们到电影院的时候，票都卖完了！
   Wǒmen dào diànyǐng-yuànde shíhou, piào dōu màiwánle!
   When we arrived at the theater, the tickets were sold out!

2. 说话要特别小心，因为说错了话再后悔就太晚了。
   Shuōhuà yào tèbié xiǎoxīn, yīnwèi shuōcuòle-huà zài hòuhuǐ jiù tài wǎn le.
   One must be especially careful when speaking, because if one says something wrong, regretting it will be too late.

3. 外国学生一般看不懂草书。 **Wàiguó xuésheng yìbān kàn-bu-dǒng cǎoshū.**
   Foreign students generally cannot understand cursive Chinese writing.

4. 我们马上要出发了，你怎么还没把你的行李收拾好呢？
   Wǒmen mǎshang yào chūfā le, nǐ zěnme hái méi bǎ nǐde xínglǐ shōushi-hǎo ne?
   We are about to leave, how come you still haven't finished packing your baggage?

5. 在餐馆吃不完的东西，可以带回家去。 **Zài cānguǎn chī-bu-wánde dōngxi, kěyǐ dài huíjiā qù.** Whatever you can't finish at a restaurant can be taken home.

6. 请你把我的电话号码写下来，有事随时跟我联系。
   Qǐng nǐ bǎ wǒde diànhuà hàomǎ xiě-xiàlai, yǒushì suíshí gēn wǒ liánxì.
   Please write down my phone number; call me anytime if something comes up.

7. 我们下个月去旅行的费用，你算得出来吗？
   Wǒmen xiàge yuè qù lǚxíngde fèiyòng, nǐ suàn-de-chūlai ma?
   Are you able to calculate the expenses for our trip next month?

8. 昨天下班的时候，她忘了把柜子锁起来，结果那些机密的文件被偷了。
   Zuótiān xiàbānde shíhou, tā wàngle bǎ guìzi suǒ-qǐlai, jiéguǒ nèixiē jīmìde wénjiàn bèi tōule.
   Yesterday, she forgot to lock up the cabinet when she left work; as a result, those top-secret documents were stolen.

12.6 Using *verb + complement* phrases in questions

All the interrogative sentence patterns introduced in Chapter 3 may be used with *verb + complement* expressions. The following examples illustrate the full range of interrogatives that may be used with *verb + complement* phrases. As you read each example, take note of which interrogative pattern is used and the function or meaning of the underlined words.

♦ *Can you see that road sign ahead?*
你看得见前面那个路牌吗？ **Nǐ kàn-de-jiàn qiánmiàn nèige lùpái <u>ma</u>?**
前面那个路牌，你看得见看不见？
Qiánmiàn nèige lùpái, nǐ <u>kàn-de-jiàn kànbujiàn</u>?

♦ *Can you see that road sign ahead clearly?*
前面那个路牌，你看得清楚<u>吗</u>？
Qiánmiàn nèige lùpái, nǐ kàn-de-qīngchǔ <u>ma</u>?
前面那个路牌，你<u>看不看得清楚</u>？
Qiánmiàn nèige lùpái, nǐ <u>kàn-bu-kànde-qīngchǔ</u>?
前面那个路牌，你<u>看得清楚看不清楚</u>？
Qiánmiàn nèige lùpái, nǐ <u>kàn-de-qīngchǔ kàn-bu-qīngchǔ</u>?
(due to its wordiness, this pattern is less likely to be used by a native speaker than the preceding two.)

♦ *You ran a red light just now, didn't you see it?*
刚才你闯了红灯，你没看见吗？
Gāngcái nǐ chuǎngle hóngdēng, nǐ méi kànjian <u>ma</u>?
刚才你闯了红灯，你是不是没看见？
Gāngcái nǐ chuǎngle hóngdēng, nǐ <u>shì-bushì</u> méi kànjian?

♦ *When at the earliest can you get my car fixed?*
你们最快什么时候能把我的车修好？
Nǐmen zuì kuài <u>shénme shíhou</u> néng bǎ wǒde chē xiūhǎo?

♦ *We can get it fixed by noon, do you want to change the four tires as well?*
我们今天中午就能修好，你要不要把四个轮胎也换掉？
Wǒmen jīntiān zhōngwǔ jiù néng xiūhǎo, nǐ <u>yào-buyào</u> bǎ sìge lúntāi yě huàndiào?

♦ *Do you think it would be better to sell this old car or to repair it?*
我的这部旧车，你看最好是卖掉还是修一修？
Wǒde zhèibù jiù chē, nǐ kàn zuì hǎo <u>shì</u> màidiào <u>háishi</u> xiū-yìxiū?

♦ *This old car wouldn't sell for much, so I think you're better off repairing it after all.*
这部旧车卖不了多少钱，我看你还是把它修好吧！
Zhèibù jiù chē mài-bu-liǎo duōshǎo qián, wǒ kàn nǐ háishi bǎ tā xiūhǎo <u>ba</u>!

♦ *Your daughter has done so well scholastically, she should be able to test into the best universities in China, don't you think?*
你的女儿成绩那么优秀，应该考得上国内最好的大学吧？
Nǐde nǚ'ér chéngjì nàme yōuxiù, yīnggāi kǎo-de-shàng guónèi zuì hǎode dàxué <u>ba</u>?
(What is the difference in the meaning of 吧 **ba** in this sentence vs the preceding one?)

♦ *Which university are you hoping your daughter will test into?*
你希望女儿考上哪所大学呢？ **Nǐ xīwàng nǚ'ér kǎoshang <u>něisuǒ</u> dàxué <u>ne</u>?**

● *She plans to go to the U.S. to attend college, so it's not a question which university her test scores allow her to get into, but how much scholarship she can get.*

她预备去美国留学，所以<u>考上哪所</u>大学不是问题，问题是<u>能申请到多少</u>奖学金。

Tā yùbèi qù Měiguó liúxué, suǒyǐ <u>kǎoshang něisuǒ</u> dàxué búshì wèntí, wèntí shì <u>néng shēnqǐngdào duōshǎo</u> jiǎngxuéjīn.

EXERCISES:

Translate the following sentences into Chinese:

1. Teacher: Did you hear clearly what I said just now?

2. Student: I heard it clearly, but I don't know if I understood it.

3. Teacher: Which part didn't you understand? I can say it more clearly.

ANSWERS:

1. 我刚才说的，你听清楚了吗？ **Wǒ gāngcái shuōde, nǐ tīng-qīngchǔle ma?**

2. 我听清楚了，可是不知道我是不是听懂了。
   Wǒ tīng-qīngchǔle, kěshì bù zhīdao wǒ shì-bushì tīngdǒngle.

3. 你没听懂哪部分？我可以说得更清楚一点。
   Nǐ méi tīngdǒng něi bùfen? Wǒ kěyǐ shuōde gèng qīngchǔ yìdiǎn.

12.7 Thinking and speaking like a Chinese

Students tend to comprehend the *verb + complement* structure fairly easily, but using it actively in their everyday speech is a skill that takes practice. The basic facts about the structure are simple, but the devil is in the details. As a summary, this section will discuss the three main stumbling blocks for non-native speakers, thereby helping you to overcome them.

1. Non-native speakers tend to avoid the *capability* form (both positive and negative) of the *verb + complement* structure (the two right-hand columns in the table at the beginning of this chapter), and fall back on the "能 **néng**/不能 **bùnéng**" pattern, because it aligns with the English equivalent of "can/cannot." However, the *verb + complement* pattern is not only more colloquial and expressive, but also conveys more information through the usage of different complements. Every time you wish to express the notion of "can/cannot," stop for a second to think if there is a *verb + complement* phrase that can be used instead. However, this is only an interim strategy, because your ultimate goal is to have the *capability* form of the *verb + complement* in your subconscious so that it will rise to the fore spontaneously.

2. In 12.3, we saw the prevalence of 来 **lái** and 去 **qù** used as complements to verbs, either independently or in combination with another *directional complement* (e.g. 上 **shàng**, 下 **xià**, 起 **qǐ**). Because this notion of "directional movement" does not exist in the minds of English speakers, they are prone to omit 来 **lái**/去 **qù** even in

expressions involving movement. Again, every time you wish to express something that involves movement, stop for a second to think whether 来 **lái** or 去 **qù** is needed. This applies even to abstract notions unrelated to the movement of physical objects.

● *He ran down.*
  他跑下去了。 **Tā pǎo-xiàqu le.** (speaker is up above) or
  他跑下来了。 **Tā pǎo-xiàlai le.** (speaker is down below)
  ✗ 他跑下了。 **Tā pǎoxià le.** (来 **lai**/去 **qu** may not be omitted)

● *He ran up the stairs.*
  他跑上楼去了。 **Tā pǎo-shàng-lóu-qù le.**
  他跑上楼了。 **Tā pǎo-shàng-lóu le.**
  (acceptable, but less likely said than the preceding one)

● *When he was running up the stairs, he fell down.*
  他跑上楼(去)的时候，不小心摔倒了。
  Tā pǎo-shàng-lóu-(qù)de shíhou, bù xiǎoxīn shuāidǎole.
  (去 **qù** is optional in this case; in fact, the phrase would be more succinct without 去 **qù**)

● *Tomorrow, we will deliver the bed that you bought today.*
  你今天买的床，我们明天就送去。
  Nǐ jīntiān mǎide chuáng, wǒmen míngtiān jiù sòngqu.
  ✗ ……，我们明天就送。 **wǒmen míngtiān jiù sòng.**
  (送 **sòng** without the complement 去 **qu** is incorrect.)

Mastering the figurative uses of *verb + complement* phrases discussed in 12.4 takes time. But as the saying goes, 学中文犹如吃美食，得一口一口地吃。 **Xué Zhōngwén yóurú chī měishí, děi yìkǒu-yìkǒude chī.** *Learning Chinese is like eating gourmet food; you must eat it one mouthful at a time.* Some deliberate counter-intuitive thinking before speaking may be a shortcut to ultimate mastery, though in the short run, it will slow down your speech and make you less fluent. One phenomenon that deserves extra attention is that certain synonyms actually need to be distinguished in order to express yourself accurately. Namely:

• 想得起来 **xiǎng-de-qǐlai** *to be able to recall*
• 想得出来 **xiǎng-de-chūlai** *to be able to think of*
• 想得到 **xiǎng-de-dào** *to be able to anticipate*
• 想得开 **xiǎng-de-kāi** *to be able to come to terms with something unhappy*
• 想得通 **xiǎng-de-tōng** *to be able to think through something difficult*

Eloquent speakers in any language are fond of metaphors, and this seems to apply especially to the Chinese. Note the usage of 吃不饱 **chī-bu-bǎo** in this context:

♦ *These students are so eager to learn Chinese that I'm afraid my course is not enough to satisfy them. So I must create a lot of supplementary teaching materials.*

这些学生对学中文那么热心，我怕这门课他们会<u>吃不饱</u>，所以我得编很多补充教材。

Zhèixiē xuésheng duì xué Zhōngwén nàme rèxīn, wǒ pà zhèimén kè tāmen huì chī-bu-bǎo, suǒyǐ wǒ děi biān hěn duō bǔchōng jiàocái.

EXERCISES:

Translate the following sentences into Chinese:

1. Will I be able to buy traditional Chinese medicine abroad?

2. Some yes, and some no. But even if it can be bought abroad (i.e. available), it's much more expensive than in China.

3. If you want a refund, you must bring your receipt.

4. When you leave the hospital, you may not walk out yourself; they take you out in a wheelchair. This is because they are afraid you might fall.

ANSWERS:

1. 我在国外也买得到（or 能买到）中药吗？ **Wǒ zài guówài yě mǎi-de-dào (or néng mǎidào) Zhōng-yào ma?**

2. 有的买得到，有的买不到。不过即使买得到，也比在国内贵多了。 **Yǒude mǎi-de-dào, yǒude mǎi-bu-dào. Búguò jíshǐ mǎi-de-dào, yě bǐ zài guónèi guì duōle.**

3. 如果要退款，你必须把收据带来。 **Rúguǒ yào tuìkuǎn, nǐ bìxū bǎ shōujù dàilai.**

4. 你出院的时候，不能自己走出去。他们会用轮椅把你送出去。这是因为他们怕你会摔跤。 **Nǐ chūyuànde shíhou, bùnéng zìjǐ zǒu-chūqu. Tāmen huì yòng lúnyǐ bǎ nǐ sòng-chūqu. Zhè shì yīnwèi tāmen pà nǐ huì shuāijiāo.**

13 Talking about Travel

Expressions about traveling from one point to another involve five key elements: point of origin (*from...*); destination (*to...*); mode of transportation (*by means of...*); purpose (*to do...*); and timing of the trip. The grammatical structures for expressing these elements have been discussed previously, in the chapter on *coverbs* and *post-verbs* (Chapter 11) and in the chapter on time expressions (Chapter 10). What remains to be covered in this chapter is the correct word order for incorporating these various elements in sentences.

In general, the word order in Chinese expressions about travel follows a logical time sequence, with one exception. The *point of origin* and *destination* are expressed using *coverbal phrases* which must precede the main verb, and the main verb in these expressions is always 来 **lái** or 去 **qù**. Temporally, phrases using the *coverbal* "到··· **dào...**" indicating a *point of arrival* should follow 来 **lái** or 去 **qù**, but grammatically, they must be placed before the main verb, just like all other *coverbal phrases*.

Comparable expressions in English also use *go* or *come*, but the first four elements listed above are expressed by prepositional phrases *after* the main verb, and the last element—the timing—can be positioned flexibly. In sum, word order in Chinese expressions about travel is much stricter than English, so this is another area that requires putting on your Chinese thinking cap!

13.1 Point of origin (*from ...*); destination (*to ...*); and mode of transportation

In an expression about travel that includes only a point of origin and/or a destination, there are two possible patterns. In both cases, the point of origin comes first, which is logical. The difference between the two patterns is in how the destination is expressed.

> Standard pattern: Subject + 从 **cóng** + point of origin + 到 **dào** + destination + 来 **lái** or 去 **qù**
>
> Alternate pattern: Subject + 从 **cóng** + point of origin + 来 **lái** or 去 **qù** + destination

The standard pattern is used in North China, and is the one presented in Chinese textbooks. The alternative pattern is favored by southerners because it aligns with the southern dialects. Non-native speakers may choose to switch between the two depending on where they are; but if they learn just one pattern, the choice should be the standard one.

Compare the following pairs of sentences:

♦ *This elderly couple's children have all gone to the U.S.*
这对老夫妻的子女都到美国去了。
Zhèiduì lǎo-fūqīde zǐnǚ dōu dào Měiguó qùle.
这对老夫妻的子女都去了美国。
Zhèiduì lǎo-fūqīde zǐnǚ dōu qùle Měiguó. (alternative)

♦ *At present, they still have no plans to go to America.*
他们目前还没有计划到美国去。
Tāmen mùqián hái méiyǒu jìhuà dào Měiguó qù.
他们目前还没有计划去美国。
Tāmen mùqián hái méiyǒu jìhuà qù Měiguó. (alternative)

♦ *Their whole family came to the U.S. in 2001.*
他们全家在2001年就到美国来了。
Tāmen quánjiā zài 2001 nián jiù dào Měiguó láile.
他们全家在2001年就来了美国。
Tāmen quánjiā zài 2001 nián jiù láile Měiguó. (alternative)

♦ *Do all young people in China want to go to the U.S.?*
中国的年轻人都想到美国去吗？
Zhōngguóde niánqīng-rén dōu xiǎng dào Měiguó qù ma?
中国的年轻人都想去美国吗？
Zhōngguóde niánqīng-rén dōu xiǎng qù Měiguó ma? (alternative)

♦ *Not necessarily, some would like to go to Europe or Australia.*
不一定，有的想到欧洲或澳大利亚去。
Bù yídìng, yǒude xiǎng dào Ōuzhōu huò Àodàlìyà qù.
不一定，有的想去欧洲或澳大利亚。(alternative)
Bù yídìng, yǒude xiǎng qù Ōuzhōu huò Àodàlìyà.

In longer and more complex sentences, the alternate pattern is more likely to be used—even by northerners—because it is a bit simpler.

♦ *I plan to first go to Canada, and then go to the U.S. from Canada.*
我预备先去加拿大，然后从加拿大去美国。(preferred)
Wǒ yùbèi xiān qù Jiānádà, ránhòu cóng Jiānádà qù Měiguó.
我预备先到加拿大去，然后从加拿大到美国去。(standard pattern)
Wǒ yùbèi xiān dào Jiānádà qù, ránhòu cóng Jiānádà dào Měiguó qù.

When the mode of transportation is added to the above patterns, it is considered to be "simultaneous" with the point of origin, so following temporal logic, it may be positioned either before or after the 从 **cóng** + *point of origin* phrase, but always before the 到 **dào** + *destination* phrase:

Subject + mode of transport + 从 **cóng** + point of origin + 到 **dào** + destination + 来 **lái** or 去 **qù**; or

Subject + 从 **cóng** + point of origin + mode of transport + 到 **dào** + destination + 来 **lái** or 去 **qù**

♦ *I'm planning to take the fast train from Beijing to Shanghai tomorrow.*
我预备明天坐高铁从北京到上海去。
Wǒ yùbèi míngtiān zuò gāotiě cóng Běijīng dào Shànghǎi qù.
我预备明天从北京坐高铁到上海去。
Wǒ yùbèi míngtiān cóng Běijīng zuò gāotiě dào Shànghǎi qù.

Alternatively, following the basic pattern preferred by southerners, the above patterns become:

Subject + mode of transport + 从 **cóng** + point of origin + 来 **lái**/ or 去 **qù** + destination; or

Subject + 从 **cóng** + point of origin + mode of transport + 来 **lái** or 去 **qù** + destination

♦ *I'm planning to take the fast train from Beijing to Shanghai tomorrow.*
我预备明天坐高铁从北京去上海。
Wǒ yùbèi míngtiān zuò gāotiě cóng Běijīng qù Shànghǎi.
我预备明天从北京坐高铁去上海。
Wǒ yùbèi míngtiān cóng Běijīng zuò gāotiě qù Shànghǎi.

Additional examples:

♦ *In his youth he once walked from Jiayuguan to Shanhaiguan (one end of the Great Wall to the other).*
他年轻的时候曾经从嘉峪关走到山海关去。
Tā niánqīngde shíhou céngjīng cóng Jiāyùguān zǒudào Shānhǎiguān qù.

♦ *There were no planes in those days. We could only take a ship to go from Hong Kong to San Francisco.*
那个时候没有飞机。我们只能坐船从香港到旧金山去。
Nèige shíhou méiyǒu fēijī, wǒmen zhǐ néng zuò chuán cóng Xiānggǎng dào Jiùjīnshān qù.

♦ *Going to work from home, I have to first walk 10 minutes to a bus stop, then take a bus to a subway station, then take the subway to downtown, and finally walk another 10 minutes to reach the office.*
我上班得先从家里走十分钟到公车站，从那儿坐公车到地铁站，再坐地铁到市中心，最后走十分钟才到办公室。
Wǒ shàngbān děi xiān cóng jiālǐ zǒu shífēnzhōng dào gōngchēzhàn, cóng nàr zuò gōngchē dào dìtiězhàn, zài zuò dìtiě dào shìzhōngxīn, zuìhòu zǒu shífēnzhōng cái dào bàngōngshì.
(**Note**: This sentence is about the process of going to the office. The main verb in all four clauses is not 来 **lái** or 去 **qù**, but 到 **dào** *to arrive*. 到 **dào** is in fact very versatile; in different contexts, it may be a main verb, a coverb or a postverb, see 11.5.)

EXERCISES:

Answer the following questions in Chinese in detail:

1. Explain in Chinese how you go from home to work or school every day.

2. Tell where you would like to travel in the foreseeable future by completing the sentence "我希望··· **Wǒ xīwàng...**"

> **ANSWERS:**
>
> 1. 我每天都骑自行车上下班，从家里到办公室只要二十分钟。如果下大雨或下雪，我就得坐公车。坐公车平常要半个小时；塞车的话，可能要一个小时，所以很不方便。
>
>   **Wǒ měitiān dōu qí zìxíngchē shàng-xiàbān, cóng jiālǐ dào bàngōngshì zhǐyào èrshífēn zhōng. Rúguǒ xià dàyǔ huò xiàxuě, wǒ jiù děi zuò gōngchē. Zuò gōngchē píngcháng yào bànge xiǎoshí; sāichē dehuà, kěnéng yào yíge xiǎoshí, suǒyǐ hěn bù fāngbiàn.**
>
>   I ride my bike to and from work every day. From home to the office takes only 20 minutes. If it's raining hard or snowing, then I have to take the bus. The bus normally takes half an hour, but if traffic is heavy, it could take an hour, so it's very inconvenient.
>
> 2. 我希望明年夏天跟我的男朋友到欧洲去旅行一个月。我们想先坐飞机到伦敦，在英国旅游一个星期，然后坐火车穿过海底隧道到法国去。在欧洲买欧铁通票就可以去很多地方，又方便又省钱。
>
>   **Wǒ xīwàng míngnián xiàtiān gēn wǒde nánpéngyou dào Ōuzhōu qù lǚxíng yíge yuè. Wǒmen xiǎng xiān zuò fēijī dào Lúndūn, zài Yīngguó lǚyóu yíge xīngqī, ránhòu zuò huǒchē chuānguò hǎidǐ suìdào dào Fǎguó qù. Zài Ōuzhōu mǎi Ōu-Tiě tōngpiào jiù kěyǐ qù hěn duō dìfang, yòu fāngbiàn yòu shěngqián.**
>
>   I hope to travel in Europe for a month with my boyfriend next summer. We are thinking of flying to London first, spend a week in England, than take the Chunnel train to France. In Europe, we will buy Eurail passes, which will allow us to go to many places. It's convenient and economical.

13.2 Expressing the timing of a trip

There is some flexibility in the word order to express the timing of a trip, although the flexibility is not nearly as great as it is in English. In Chinese, time may be expressed at the beginning of a sentence or after the subject, but always before the other elements. In this regard, it is no different from other *time-when* expressions discussed in 10.1. If you go back to the preceding section and check where the *time-when* expressions are located, you will discovered that almost all of them are positioned right after the subject. This is in fact the preferred position, unless the speaker intends to focus on the time of the event, or if the time expression is long and convoluted.

♦ *On your business trip tomorrow, are you planning to take the train or the plane from New York to Washington?*

明天出差，你预备坐火车还是坐飞机从纽约到华盛顿去？

Míngtiān chūchāi, nǐ yùbèi zuò huǒchē háishi zuò fēijī cóng Niǔyuē dào Huáshèngdùn qù?

◆ *After China's Reform and Opening, many scholars emigrated abroad from China's universities.*
中国改革开放以后，很多学者从国内的高校移民到国外去了。
Zhōngguó gǎigé-kāifàng yǐhòu, hěnduō xuézhě cóng guónèide gāoxiào yímín dào guówài qùle.

◆ *At the same time, more and more foreign students have come to China from abroad.*
同时越来越多的留学生也从国外到中国来了。
Tóngshí yuèláiyuè duōde liúxuésheng yě cóng guówài dào Zhōngguó láile.

In the next section, we will see an even clearer way to put focus on timing and other elements in sentences concerning traveling.

13.3　Focusing on a particular element of a journey

In discussing travel, the basic sentence pattern introduced in 13.1 can only be the beginning of the conversation. We often wish to go a bit deeper and make a point about a certain aspect of the trip, such as the *point of origin*, the *mode of transportation*, or the *timing*. Focusing on a certain aspect is sometimes done for the purpose of comparison or contradicting an assumption, whether it be explicit or implicit. The most frequently used grammatical mechanism for doing this is the 是···的 **shì...de** pattern. In the examples below, the element emphasized in each English sentence is underlined. Take note of the position of the 是···的 **shì...de** *frame* in each of the corresponding Chinese sentences.

◆ *It was <u>in 1492</u> that Columbus came from Europe to America.* (focus on time)
哥伦布是1492年从欧洲到美洲来的。
Gēlúnbù shì 1492 nián cóng Ōuzhōu dào Měizhōu lái de.

◆ *Columbus wasn't headed <u>for America</u>, he thought he was headed <u>for Asia</u>!* (focus on destination, and comparing Columbus' intention with the actual outcome.)
哥伦布不是要到美洲去，其实他以为他是到亚洲去。
Gēlúnbù búshì yào dào Měizhōu qù, qíshí tā yǐwéi tā shì dào Yàzhōu qù.
(**Note:** A corollary of the 是···的 **shì...de** pattern, without the 的 **de** part is used here. We will discussed the difference between 是···的 **shì...de** and 是··· **shì...** when we take up these patterns in greater detail in 15.4 and 15.5.)

◆ *I <u>did not come from China</u> to the U.S. I <u>was born in the U.S.</u>* (focus on point of origin, contradicting a common assumption.)
我不是从中国来美国的，我是在美国出生的。
Wǒ búshì cóng Zhōngguó lái Měiguó de, wǒ shì zài Měiguó chūshēng de.

● *We did not come directly to the U.S. from China, we actually* <u>*first went from China to*</u> <u>*Canada, then came to the U.S.*</u> (emphasizing 2-step process for coming to the U.S.)
我们不是直接从中国到美国来的，是先从中国到加拿大去，然后才到美国来的。**Wǒmen búshì zhíjiē cóng Zhōngguó dào Měiguó lái de, shì xiān cóng Zhōngguó dào Jiānádà qù, ránhòu cái dào Měiguó lái de.**

● *19th century immigrants from Europe and Asia to the U.S. all came* <u>*by ship*</u>. (focus on mode of transportation)
十九世纪来自欧洲和亚洲的移民都是坐船来的。
Shíjiǔ shìjì láizì Ōuzhōu hé Yàzhōude yímín dōu shì zuò chuán lái de.

● *When my family came from Hong Kong to San Francisco in 1955, we also came* <u>*by ship*</u>. (focus on mode of transportation)
✓ 我们家在1955年也是坐船从香港到旧金山来的。
　Wǒmen jiā zài 1955 nián yě shì zuò chuán cóng Xiānggǎng dào Jiùjīnshān lái de.
✓ 我们家在1955年从香港到旧金山(来)，也是坐船来的。
　Wǒmen jiā zài 1955 nián cóng Xiānggǎng dào Jiùjīnshān (lái), yě shì zuò chuán lái de.
✗ ……，也是坐船的。**…, yě shì zuò chuán de.**
(坐船 **zuòchuán** is a *coverbal phrase*, thus the verb 来 **lái** is indispensable.)

● *When I returned to Hong Kong in 1970, I went* <u>*by plane*</u>. (focus on *mode of transportation*, implicitly comparing with the 1955 trip in the preceding sentence.)
我1970年回香港的时候，是坐飞机去的。
Wǒ 1970 nián huí Xiānggǎngde shíhou, shì zuò fēijī qù de.
(As above, the verb 去 **qù** is indispensable.)

● *We went to Iceland for summer vacation last year.* (a statement without emphasis on the destination; compare this with the following example)
我们去年暑假旅游到冰岛去了。**Wǒmen qùnián shǔjià lǚyóu dào Bīngdǎo qùle.**
我们去年暑假旅游去了冰岛。**Wǒmen qùnián shǔjià lǚyóu qùle Bīngdǎo.**

● *Our vacation trip last summer was* <u>*to Iceland*</u>. (emphasis on the destination)
我们去年暑假旅游是去的冰岛。**Wǒmen qùnián shǔjià lǚyóu shì qùde Bīngdǎo.**
我们去年暑假旅游去的是冰岛。**Wǒmen qùnián shǔjià lǚyóu qùde shì Bīngdǎo.**

As you may have noticed, all the examples above pertain to past events. This is a constraint of the 是…的 **shì...de** pattern, which we will discuss in detail in 15.4 and 15.5.

EXERCISES:

Translate the following sentences into Chinese:

1. We did not come from England, we came from Australia!

2. It was before 1949 that my family immigrated to the U.S.

3. There were no planes in those days, so of course we came by ship.

ANSWERS:

1. 我们不是从英国来的，是从澳大利亚来的。
   Wǒmen bú shì cóng Yīngguó láide, shì cóng Àodàlìyà lái de.

2. 我们家是一九四九年以前移民到美国来的。
   Wǒmen jiā shì yī-jiǔ-sì-jiǔ-nián yǐqián yímín-dào Měiguó lái de.

3. 那时候没有飞机，所以我们当然是坐船来的。
   Nà shíhou méiyǒu fēijī, suǒyǐ wǒmen dāngrán shì zuò chuán lái de.

13.4 Stating the purpose of coming or going somewhere

The most straightforward way to state the purpose of a trip is to tag it onto 来 lái or 去 qù, and this applies to the both basic patterns stated at the beginning of 13.1.

> Subject + 从 cóng + point of origin + 到 dào + destination + 来 lái or 去 qù + purpose

> Subject 从 cóng + point of origin + 来 lái/去 qù + destination + purpose

* *I'm planning to go to Beijing to study next year.*
  我预备明年到北京去留学。 Wǒ yùbèi míngnián dào Běijīng qù liúxué.
  我预备明年去北京留学。 Wǒ yùbèi míngnián qù Běijīng liúxué.

* *He wants to return to China to find himself a wife.*
  他要回中国去找一个妻子。 Tā yào huí Zhōngguó qù zhǎo yíge qīzi.

In addition, native speakers use another pattern that places 来 lái or 去 qù at the end of the sentence.

> Subject + 从 cóng + point of origin + 到 dào + destination + (来 lái or 去 qù) + purpose + 来 lái or 去 qù

Notice here that 来 lái or 去 qù may be optionally stated before the purpose, in addition to the 来 lái or 去 qù after the purpose, which sounds redundant, but we just have to accept it as an idiomatic Chinese "way of speaking." Using this pattern the above examples become:

我预备明年到北京(去)留学去。 Wǒ yùbèi míngnián dào Běijīng (qù) liúxué qù.
他要回中国(去)找妻子去。 Tā yào huí Zhōngguó (qù) zhǎo qīzi qù.

You may prefer to use only the straightforward pattern, but there are situations when you have no choice but to use the less straightforward one. When talking about an event that has already occurred (rather than being *in prospect*), only the less straightforward pattern may be used, because to indicate *completion*, the *marker* 了 le needs to be suffixed to 来 lái or 去 qù at the end of the sentence. Notice the change in the word order of the *purpose phrase* when the two sentences given above refer to events in the past:

- *I went to Beijing to study last year.*
  我去年到北京(去)留学去了。 **Wǒ qùnián dào Běijīng (qù) liúxué qùle.**

- *He returned to China last month to find himself a wife.*
  他上个月回中国(去)找妻子去了。
  Tā shàngge yuè huí Zhōngguó (qù) zhǎo qīzi qùle.

Here are some additional examples:

- *After he graduated, he came to Shanghai to look for a job.*
  他毕业以后，就到上海(来)找工作来了。
  Tā bìyè yǐhòu, jiù dào Shànghǎi (lái) zhǎo gōngzuò láile.

- *He has gone to New York on business, and won't be back until Saturday.*
  他到纽约(去)出差去了，星期六才回来。
  Tā dào Niǔyuē (qù) chūchāi qùle, xīngqīliù cái huílǎi.

- *After he established himself professionally in the U.S., he returned to China to find himself a wife.*
  他在美国立业以后就回中国(去)找对象去了。
  Tā zài Měiguó lìyè yǐhòu jiù huí Zhōngguó (qù) zhǎo duìxiàng qùle.
  他是在美国立业以后才回中国去找对象的。
  Tā shì zài Měiguó lìyè yǐhòu cái huí Zhōngguó qù zhǎo duìxiàng de.
  (Same information restated with emphasis on the fact that he waited until he was established professionally before finding himself a wife. Note the use of the 是⋯的 **shì...de** pattern discussed in the previous section.)

From the above examples, it may seem as though the pattern with the 来 **lái** or 去 **qù** + 了 **le** at the end is used whenever the sentence is in the past tense. While this pattern usually correlates with past tense, it is not always so. One counter-example is the last Chinese sentence above, which is in the past tense in English but does not end in 来 **lái** or 去 **qù** + 了 **le**. Instead, the 是⋯的 **shì...de** pattern is used to focus on a certain point. Here is another counter-example:

- *In the past, when he went to New York on business, it was always with his boss.*
  他从前去纽约出差，都是跟他的老板一起去的。
  Tā cóngqián qù Niǔyuē chūchāi, dōu shì gēn tāde lǎobǎn yìqǐ qù de.

To explain when and when not to use 了 **le**, we return to the difference between the concept of *tense* in English and the concept of *verb aspects* in Chinese (see 7.1). This is why we use the phrase "an event that has occurred" rather than "past tense." The *aspect marker* 了 **le**, when suffixed to a verb, indicates the *completion aspect*, which most often but not always coincides with the past tense in English.

In the preceding section (13.3), we have already discussed the usage of the 是⋯的 **shì...de** pattern to focus on a certain aspect of travel. Here we will apply this to a certain purpose. In addition to this pattern, a coverbal phrase 为了⋯ **wèile...**

for the sake of may be used in conjunction. (Refer to Part II of this book for more examples of 为了··· **wèile…**). The first two examples below illustrate the difference between a statement about traveling and one that emphasizes the purpose.

♦ *We'd like to go to China to adopt a child.* (statement of purpose without special emphasis)

我们想到中国去领养一个孩子。

Wǒmen xiǎng dào Zhōngguó qù lǐngyǎng yíge háizi.

♦ *We came to China this time not for vacation travel, but to adopt a child.*

我们这次来中国不是为了旅游，是为了领养一个孩子。

Wǒmen zhèicì lái Zhōngguó búshì wèile lǚyóu, shì wèile lǐngyǎng yíge háizi.

♦ *It was for the purpose of making a living that a large rural population in China migrated to cities.*

中国大量的农村人口是为了谋生(而)流动到城市来的。

Zhōngguó dàliàngde nóngcūn rénkǒu shì wèile móushēng (ér) liúdòng dào chéngshì lái de.

中国大量的农村人口流动到城市来是为了谋生(而)来的。

Zhōngguó dàliàngde nóngcūn rénkǒu liúdòng dào chéngshì lái shì wèile móushēng (ér) lái de.

为了谋生，中国大量的农村人口流动到城市来了。

Wèile móushēng, Zhōngguó dàliàngde nóngcūn rénkǒu liúdòng dào chéngshì láile.

EXERCISES:

Translate the following sentences into Chinese:

1. I'm going to take the plane to Shanghai tomorrow.

2. To go abroad from his hometown, he has to go to Shanghai to take a plane.

3. My several previous trips to China were for studying; this time, I'm going there to work.

ANSWERS:

1. 我明天要坐飞机到上海去。 **Wǒ míngtiān yào zuò fēijī dào Shànghǎi qù.**

2. 从他的老家出国，他得到上海去坐飞机。
   Cóng tāde lǎojiā chūguó, tā děi dào Shànghǎi qù zuò fēijī.

3. 我前几次去中国都是为了留学，这次去是为了工作。
   or ···, 这次是为了去工作。
   Wǒ qián jǐcì qù Zhōngguó dōu shì wèile liúxué, zhèicì qù shì wèile gōngzuò.
   or **... zhèicì shì wèile qù gōngzuò.**

13.5 The *coverb* 往 wǎng = "toward, in the direction of"

The *coverb* 往 **wǎng** has already made an appearance in 11.2 and 11.5, but it warrants a more thorough discussion here. With its meaning of *toward, in the direction of*, 往 **wǎng** is naturally used in conjunction with travel. In a complete sentence about going from point A to point B, the word order of the 往··· **wǎng...** phrase follows temporal logic, as indicated by the two possible patterns below:

Subject + 从 **cóng** + point of origin + 往 **wǎng** + direction + 到 **dào** + destination + 来 **lái** or 去 **qù**

Subject + 从 **cóng** + point of origin + 往 **wǎng** + direction + 来 **lái** or 去 **qù** + destination

♦ *In the Middle Ages, there were already people sailing eastward from Europe to China.*
在中古时代，已经有人从欧洲往东航行到中国去了。
Zài Zhōnggǔ Shídài, yǐjīng yǒurén cóng Ōuzhōu wǎng dōng hángxíng dào Zhōngguó qùle.

♦ *In that era, to go from Europe to China, whether it be by land or sea, it was always eastward.*
在那个时代，要从欧洲去中国，无论是陆路还是水路，都是往东走的。
Zài nèige shídài, yào cóng Ōuzhōu qù Zhōngguó, wúlùn shì lùlù háishi shuǐlù, dōushì wǎng dōng zǒu de.

♦ *By the late 15th century, some seafaring explorers thought it was possible to sail westward from Europe to China.*
到了十五世纪末期，有航海探险家认为也可以从欧洲往西航行到中国去。
Dàole shíwǔ shìjì mòqī, yǒu hánghǎi tànxiǎn-jiā rènwéi yě kěyǐ cóng Ōuzhōu wǎng xī hángxíng dào Zhōngguó qù.

♦ *Later on they confirmed that it was possible to sail westward to reach China, but that path was much farther than traveling eastward!*
后来他们证实了真的可以往西航行到中国去，可是那条路比往东走远多了！
Hòulái tāmen zhèngshíle zhēnde kěyǐ wǎng xī hángxíng dào Zhōngguó qù, kěshì nèitiáo lù bǐ wǎng dōng zǒu yuǎn duōle.

Beyond discussions about traveling, there are other usages for the coverb 往 **wǎng**. In a 往··· **wǎng...** phrase, the object of 往 **wǎng** can be a direction (as in the above examples), a location, or even an abstract entity. When applied to traveling, the verb following the 往··· **wǎng...** phrase is typically a verb of movement (e.g. 来 **lái**, 去 **qù**, 走 **zǒu**, 飞 **fēi**, 开 **kāi** *to drive*); but when applied to other scenarios, the verb may be another type of function verb (e.g. 看 **kàn**, 想 **xiǎng**), especially when the object is an abstract entity.

- 往市中心走 **wǎng shì-zhōngxīn zǒu** *to walk toward downtown*
- 往纽约的世贸中心飞 **wǎng Niǔyuēde Shìmào Zhōngxīn fēi** *to fly toward the World Trade Center in New York*
- 往前看 **wǎng qián kàn** *to look forward, to look toward the future*

- 往好处想 **wǎng hǎochù xiǎng** *to think positively* (lit., "to think in the direction of good things")

Examples of 往 **wǎng** phrases in connection with traveling:

♦ *Go straight ahead from here, in less than five minutes, you'll see that restaurant.*
从这儿往前走，不到五分钟，你就会看见那家餐馆了。
Cóng zhèr wǎng qián zǒu, búdào wǔfēnzhōng, nǐ jiù huì kànjian nèijiā cānguǎn le.

♦ *Are there flights to Xi'an today?*
今天有没有往西安去的飞机？ **Jīntiān yǒu-méiyǒu wǎng Xī'ān qùde fēijī?**

Examples of 往 **wǎng** phrases in various other scenarios:

♦ *You should think more positively, don't always be thinking about those unsolvable problems anymore.*
你应该多往好处想，别老想那些解决不了的问题了。
Nǐ yīnggāi duō wǎng hǎochù xiǎng, bié lǎo xiǎng nèixiē jiějué-bù-liǎode wèntí le.

♦ *We often make overseas calls, that's why our phone bill is high every month.*
我们常常往国外打电话，所以每个月的电话费都很高。
Wǒmen chángchang wǎng guówài dǎ diànhuà, suǒyǐ měige yuède diànhuàfèi dōu hěn gāo.

♦ *Ancient Chinese culture developed from the North to the South.*
中国古代的文化是从北方往南方发展的。
Zhōngguó gǔdàide wénhuà shì cóng běifāng wǎng nánfāng fāzhǎn de.

♦ *Now the culture in every country in the world is developing in the direction of globalization.*
现在世界各国的文化都在往全球化这个方向发展。
Xiànzài shìjiè gèguóde wénhuà dōu zài wǎng quánqiú-huà zhèige fāngxiàng fāzhǎn.

♦ *Why do you keep stuffing the snacks in your own mouth? You should be encouraging our guests to eat more of them.*
你怎么老把点心往自己的嘴巴里塞呢？应该请客人多吃才对啊！
Nǐ zěnme lǎo bǎ diǎnxīn wǎng zìjǐde zuǐbali sāi ne? Yīnggāi qǐng kèrén duō chī cái duì a!

The coverb 往 **wǎng** may also function as a postverb, although this function is much more limited. Postverbal 往 **wǎng** is used in connection with travel only, and in this context there is no difference in meaning between the coverbal and postverbal usage. However, the postverbal usage is more succinct and formal; thus, it appears on posted schedules and announcements in airports and train stations.

♦ *The train going toward Guangzhou has just entered the station.* (i.e. it is at an intermediate station between the departure point and Guangzhou)
开往广州的火车已经进站了。
Kāiwǎng Guǎngzhōude huǒchē yǐjīng jìnzhàn le.

◆ *There are no more trains going to Shanghai tonight.*
今天晚上没有开往上海的火车了。
Jīntiān wǎnshang méiyǒu kāiwǎng Shànghǎide huǒchē le.

◆ *The weather is bad in Guangzhou, planes cannot land there, so we have no option but to fly toward Xiamen now.*
广州的天气不好，飞机不能在那儿降落，我们现在只好飞往厦门了。
Guǎngzhōude tiānqì bù hǎo, fēijī bùnéng zài nàr jiàngluò, wǒmen xiànzài zhǐhǎo fēiwǎng Xiàmén le.

◆ *There is a storm at sea today, all the planes headed for Japan are cancelled.*
今天海上有暴风雨，飞往日本的飞机都取消了。
Jīntiān hǎishàng yǒu bàofēngyǔ, fēiwǎng Rìběnde fēijī dōu qǔxiāo le.

The term 往下 **wǎng xià** warrants special mention. Aside from its literal mean of *downward*, it has a figurative meaning of *continuing on to…* . In this figurative usage, it is synonymous with the phrase *verb* + 下去 **xiàqu** (see 12.3).

◆ *You're afraid of heights? Just don't look down and you'll be OK!* (往下 **wǎng xià** is here used literally, in contrast with the examples below)
你怕高吗？别往下看就行了！ **Nǐ pà gāo ma? Bié wǎng xià kàn jiù xíngle.**

◆ *Read on a few more sentences and it will become clear.*
你再往下看几句就明白了。 **Nǐ zài wǎng xià kàn jǐjù jiù míngbái le.**

◆ *I'm not interested in your product, so you don't need to say anything more.*
我对你们的产品不感兴趣，你不必往下说了。
Wǒ duì nǐmende chǎnpǐn bù gǎn-xìngqù, nǐ búbì wǎng xià shuōle.

◆ *Given that the relationship between the two countries has already reached this impasse, is there any use in continuing with the talks?*
两国的关系既然已经到了这个地步，再往下谈会有用吗？
Liǎngguóde guānxi jìrán yǐjīng dàole zhèige dìbù, zài wǎng xià tán huì yǒuyòng ma?

EXERCISES:

Explain why the following sentences are incorrect, then revise them accordingly.
1. ✗台湾的公司都要发展往国外。 **Táiwānde gōngsi dōu yào fāzhǎn wǎng guówài.**
2. ✗改革开放以前，从中国打电话往国外非常贵。 **Gǎigé-kāifàng yǐqián, cóng Zhōngguó dǎ diànhuà wǎng guówài fēicháng guì.**

ANSWERS:
In both cases, 往 is a coverb, so it must precede the main verb.
1. 台湾的公司都要往国外发展。 **Táiwānde gōngsī dōu yào wǎng guówài fāzhǎn.**
2. 改革开放以前，从中国往国外打电话非常贵。
Gǎigé-kāifàng yǐqián, cóng Zhōngguó wǎng guówài dǎ diànhuà fēicháng guì.

EXERCISES:

Translate the following sentences into Chinese:

1. During the Cultural Revolution, there were no direct flights from China to the U.S.

2. "南辕北辙 **nán-yuán-běi-zhé**" means a person intending to go south actually ended up going north.

ANSWERS:

1. 在文化大革命时代，没有从中国直接飞往美国的班机。
   Zài Wénhuà Dàgémìng shídài, méiyǒu cóng Zhōngguó zhíjiē fēiwǎng Měiguóde bānjī.

2. 南辕北辙的意思是，一个人想往南走，可是他却往北走了。
   Nán-yuán-běi-zhé-de yìsi shì, yíge rén xiǎng wǎng nán zǒu, kěshì tā què wǎng běi zǒu le.

14 Expressing Comparisons and Distances in Chinese

One of the first things an English speaker thinks of when making comparisons is the use of comparative and superlative adjectives—such as *slow, slower, slowest*—or when the adjective has two or more syllables, the use of *more* and *most*, e.g. *interesting, more interesting*, and *most interesting*. Along with the use of these adjectives, the sentence pattern *A is…than B* comes to mind. The most obvious difference in the Chinese way of making comparisons is the lack of comparative and superlative adjectives. Secondarily, the function served by these adjectives in English is subsumed by grammatical patterns in Chinese.

The grammatical patterns for expressing comparisons and distances may seem varied at first glance, but actually they can all be boiled down to one formula. Once you grasp this formula, all the patterns fall into place. These sentences have four elements: the two entities being compared (or two locations), a *coverb* linking these two elements and stating the "relativity" between them, and an "assessment" of that "relativity." This "assessment" can take many forms, but generally involves a verb phrase (mostly an adjective, also called a *stative verb* in Chinese). As you study the grammatical patterns in this chapter, keep in mind the following underlying pattern:

A + "relativity" coverb + B + "assessment"

The following examples will illustrate the wide variety of comparisons that can be generated from this pattern by using different *relativity coverbs*.

"relativity" coverb	assessment
跟 **gēn** *and*	不一样 **bù yíyàng** *not the same*

• 你的母语跟我的(母语)不一样。**Nǐde mǔyǔ gēn wǒde (mǔyǔ) bù yíyàng.**
  Your native language and mine are not the same.

和 **hé** *and* (synonym of 跟 **gēn**)	不同 **bùtóng** *not the same*, 一样聪明 **yíyàng cōngming** *equally smart*, 一样能干 **yíyàng nénggàn** *equally capable*

• 女孩子和男孩子虽然不同，可是他们一样聪明、一样能干。
  (A and B are stated in the first clause, and merged into 他们 in the second clause.)
  Nǚháizi hé nánháizi suīrán bùtóng, kěshì tāmen yíyàng cōngming, yíyàng nénggàn.
  Although girls and boys are not the same, they are equally smart and capable.

有 **yǒu** *as, equal to or more*	高 **gāo** *high, tall*

• 台湾的玉山有日本的富士山高吗？**Táiwānde Yùshān yǒu Rìběnde Fùshìshān gāo ma?**
  Is Taiwan's Jade Mountain as high as Japan's Mt. Fuji?

"relativity" coverb	assessment
没有 **méiyǒu** *not as, less than*	那么难学 **nàme nánxué** *difficult to learn*

- 对西方人来说, 西班牙语没有中文那么难学。 **Duì Xīfāng-rén láishuō, Xībānyáyǔ méiyǒu Zhōngwén nàme nánxué.** *To Westerners, Spanish is not as difficult to learn as Chinese.*

不如 **bùrú** *not as, less than*	有精力 **yǒu jīnglì** *energetic* (lit., "have vim and vigor")

- 老年人不如年轻人有精力。 **Lǎonián-rén bùrú niánqīng-rén yǒu jīnglì.**
  Old folks are not as energetic as young people.
- 我的身体不如十年前了。 **Wǒde shēntǐ bùrú shínián-qián le.** (Without an explicit "assessment," 不如 **bùrú** implies "not as good" or some other relevant positive quality.)
  My health is not as good as ten years ago.

不像 **búxiàng** *not like, not as*	爱运动 **ài yùndòng** *to love athletics*

- 老二不像老大那么爱运动。 **Lǎo Èr búxiàng Lǎo Dà nàme ài yùndòng.**
  Son #2 is not as fond of athletics as son #1.

比 **bǐ** *to compare*	贵得多 **guì-de-duō** *much more expensive*

- 城里的房子比郊区的贵得多。 **Chénglǐde fángzi bǐ jiāoqūde guì-de-duō.**
  Housing in the city is much more expensive than in the suburbs.

In the following sections, we will delve into the various patterns in greater detail.

14.1 Comparing two entities

The basic pattern for expressing whether two entities are the same in some manner or quality is as follows. 跟 **gēn** and 和 **hé** are synonyms in this context.

positive: A + 跟 **gēn** or 和 **hé** + B + 一样··· **yíyàng**…
  A and B are the same; A and B are equally…

negative: A + 跟 **gēn** or 和 **hé** + B + 不一样··· **bù yíyàng**…
  A and B are not the same; A and B are not equally…

interrogative (2 options):
  A + 跟 **gēn** or 和 **hé** + B + 一样···吗? **yíyàng…ma?**
  or A + 跟 **gēn** or 和 **hé** + B + 一样不一样···? **yíyàng bù yíyàng…?**
  Are A and B the same? Are A and B equally…?

The sentence may end with 一样 **yíyàng** or 不一样 **bù yíyàng**, or it may be followed by a word or a more elaborate phrase indicating the manner or quality in which the two entities are equal or not equal. In the latter case, if the sentence is in the negative, there is no indication as to which one is greater.

♦ *Chinese characters and Japanese characters are not entirely the same.*
  中文字跟日文字不完全一样。 **Zhōngwénzì gēn Rìwénzì bù wánquán yíyàng.**

- *China's Southern dishes are very different from Northern dishes.*
  中国的南方菜和北方菜很不一样。
  Zhōngguóde nánfāng cài hé běifāng cài hěn bù yíyàng.

- *From the day they are born, boys and girls are not the same.*
  从出生的那一天起，男孩子就跟女孩子不一样。
  Cóng chūshēngde nèiyìtiān qǐ, nánháizi jiù gēn nǚháizi bù yíyàng.

- *Are Chinese and Arabic equally difficult to learn?*
  中文跟阿拉伯语一样难学吗？ **Zhōngwén gēn Ālābóyǔ yíyàng nánxué ma?**

- *The two of us are not equally tall.* 我们俩不一样高。 **Wǒmen liǎ bù yíyàng gāo.**

- *These several kinds of fruit are equally delicious.* (The entities being compared are aggregated.)
  这几种水果都一样好吃。 **Zhèi jǐzhǒng shuǐguǒ dōu yíyàng hǎochī.**

- *Adults and kids are equally fond of playing.*
  大人跟孩子一样爱玩儿。 **Dàrén gēn háizi yíyàng ài wánr.**

- *Do his two parents hold out equal hopes that he will become a musician in the future?*
  他的母亲和父亲一样希望他将来当音乐家吗？
  Tāde mǔqin hé fùqin yíyàng xīwàng tā jiānglái dāng yīnyuè-jiā ma?

EXERCISES:

Translate the following sentences into Chinese:

1. Chinese and Korean cultures are quite different.
2. Schools in the cities and rural areas are vastly different.
3. The English spoken by Australians is not entirely the same as that spoken by the British.
4. Of course apples and oranges are not the same, but I think they are equally delicious.
5. Kittens and puppies are equally cute, but they are not equally troublesome to raise.

ANSWERS:
1. 中国跟韩国的文化很不一样。 **Zhōngguó gēn Hánguóde wénhuà hěn bù yíyàng.**
2. 城里的学校跟乡下的非常不一样。 **Chénglǐde xuéxiào gēn xiāngxiade fēicháng bù yíyàng.**
3. 澳洲人说的英语和英国人说的不完全一样。
   Àozhōu-rén shuōde Yīngyǔ hé Yīngguó-rén shuōde bù wánquán yíyàng.
4. 苹果跟桔子当然不一样，可是我觉得都一样好吃。
   Píngguǒ gēn júzi dāngrán bù yíyàng, kěshì wǒ juéde dōu yíyàng hǎochī.
5. 小猫跟小狗一样可爱，可是养起来的麻烦不一样。
   Xiǎo māo gēn xiǎo gǒu yíyàng kě'ài, kěshì yǎng-qǐlaide máfan bù yíyàng.

14.2 Stating "A is not as...as B"

There are three ways to state that *A is not as...as B*, each using a different word to link A and B, but they all use the same grammatical formula. The three patterns are generally used in the negative sense (*A is not as...as B*), but there is one exception with the first pattern, as will be explained below.

1. The first pattern is used more frequently than the other two, and it is the only one with a positive option (*A is as....as B*).

    positive: A 有 **yǒu** B (这么 **zhème**/那么 **nàme**)... (see first example below; the positive version is not used nearly as frequently as the negative version)
    A is as...as B (A may be equally...as B, or more...than B)

    negative: A 没有 **méiyǒu** B (这么 **zhème**/那么 **nàme**)...
    A is not as...as B

    interrogative: A 有没有 **yǒu-méiyǒu** B (这么 **zhème**/那么 **nàme**)...
    or A 有 **yǒu** B (这么 **zhème**/那么 **nàme**)...吗 **ma**?
    Is A as...as B?

While 这么 **zhème** and 那么 **nàme** are optional, they place a bit more emphasis on the manner or quality in which the two entities are being compared, and native speakers are more likely to use them than not. The choice between 这么 **zhème** or 那么 **nàme** depends on whether B is closer to the speaker or to the present time. When neither one is closer, 那么 **nàme** is used. Note also that 有 **yǒu** in this pattern has nothing to do with the English word *to have*. (See 2.8 for a discussion of the difference between 有 **yǒu** in Chinese and *to have* in English.)

♦ *Japanese is as difficult to learn as Chinese.*
日文有中文那么难学。 **Rìwén yǒu Zhōngwén nàme nánxué.**
日文跟中文一样难学。 (preferred over the "A 有 **yǒu** B..." pattern)
Rìwén gēn Zhōngwén yíyàng nánxué.

♦ *Taiwan's Jade Mountain is as high as Japan's Mt. Fuji.*
台湾的玉山有日本的富士山那么高。
Táiwānde Yùshān yǒu Rìběnde Fùshìshān nàme gāo.

♦ *My memory is not as good as before.*
我的记性没有从前那么好了。 **Wǒde jìxìng méiyǒu cóngqián nàme hǎo le.**

♦ *Now that he's gotten old, Dad doesn't lose his temper as easily as before.*
爸爸老了，现在没有从前那么容易发脾气了。
Bàba lǎole, xiànzài méiyǒu cóngqián nàme róngyì fā-píqi le.

♦ *In the U.S., is soccer as popular (attractive to an audience) as baseball?*
在美国，足球有没有棒球那么吸引观众？
Zài Měiguó, zúqiú yǒu-méiyǒu bàngqiú nàme xīyǐn guānzhòng?

● *Life after retirement will not be as busy as now, will it?*
退了休以后的生活没有现在这么忙吧?
Tuì-le-xiū yǐhòude shēnghuó méiyǒu xiànzài zhème máng ba?

2. A second way to state *A is not as…as B* is to use 不像 **búxiàng** to link them.

A 不像 **búxiàng** B 这么 **zhème** or 那么 **nàme**…   *A is not so…as B*

This pattern differs from A 没有 **méiyǒu** B 这么 **zhème** or 那么 **nàme**… in that there is an underlying premise that the quality or manner that follow 这么 **zhème** or 那么 **nàme** is quite prominent in B. This difference is reflected in the English translation in this pattern (*A is not so…as B*). For the same reason, the manner or quality is always emphasized through the use of the non-optional 这么 **zhème** or 那么 **nàme**.

● *Many people say that girls are not as mischievous as boys.*
很多人说女孩子不像男孩子那么调皮。
Hěnduō rén shuō nǚháizi búxiàng nánháizi nàme tiáopí.

● *Throughout American history, there has never been a president as arrogant as Trump.*
美国历来的总统都不像特郎普这么骄傲。
Měiguó lìláide zǒngtǒng dōu búxiàng Tèlángpǔ zhème jiāoào.

● *Life in the country is not so rich as in the city, but it's also not so hectic as in the city.*
乡下的生活不像城里那么丰富，可是也不像城里那么忙碌。
Xiāngxiade shēnghuó búxiàng chénglǐ nàme fēngfù, kěshì yě búxiàng chénglǐ nàme mánglù.

● *Beijing's summers didn't used to be so hot as now, and the air pollution wasn't this serious either.*
从前北京的夏天不像现在这么热，空气污染也不像现在这么严重。
Cóngqián Běijīngde xiàtiān búxiàng xiànzài zhème rè, kōngqì wūrǎn yě búxiàng xiànzài zhème yánzhòng.

● *After my son went off to college, our home was no longer so chaotic as before.*
(implying that it had been very chaotic when the son was living at home)
我的儿子上了大学以后, 我们家里就不像从前那么乱七八糟了。
Wǒde érzi shàngle dàxué yǐhòu, wǒmen jiālǐ jiù búxiàng cóngqián nàme luàn-qī-bā-zāo le.

In all of the above examples, 不像 **búxiàng** can be replaced by 没有 **méiyǒu**, and the difference in meaning is one of nuance, with 不像 **búxiàng** implying that B is quite prominent in that certain quality or manner.

3. The third way to state *A is not as…as B* is to use 不如 **bùrú** to link A and B. This pattern differs from the other two in three ways:

a. Unlike the other two patterns, the word following 不如 **bùrú** to state the quality or manner compared is always positive, whereas the quality or manner compared using 没有 **méiyǒu** or 不像 **búxiàng** may be positive or negative. This is consistent with the fact that 不如 **bùrú** in itself means *not as good as*. In fact, a comparative sentence using 不如 **bùrú** does not necessarily require an assessment, as it is already implied:

- 奶奶的身体一天不如一天了！ **Nǎinaide shēntǐ yìtiān bùrú yìtiān le!**
  Grandma's health is getting worse by the day! (each day not as good as the last)

b. This pattern is a bit more formal, so it tends to be used in expressions that are more substantive.

c. 这么 **zhème** or 那么 **nàme** are optional in this pattern, and are used less often than in the other patterns. This is because the point of the sentence is to compare the two entities, rather than to emphasize the quality being compared.

As you read the following examples, note that the first four include some quality or manner in which the two entities are being compared, while the last three sentences leave it unstated.

- *I don't believe that country folks are not as smart as city folks.*
  我不相信乡下人不如城里人聪明。
  Wǒ bù xiāngxìn xiāngxia-rén bùrú chénglǐ-rén cōngming.

- *Actually, in many respects, I think city folks are not as capable as country folks.*
  其实，我认为在很多方面，城里人不如乡下人能干。
  Qíshí, wǒ rènwéi zài hěnduō fāngmiàn, chénglǐ-rén bùrú xiāngxia-rén nénggàn.

- *In disciplining young people, punishment is not as effective as rewards.*
  在管教青少年这方面，惩罚不如奖励那么有效。
  Zài guǎnjiào qīngshàonián zhè fāngmiàn, chéngfá bùrú jiǎnglì nàme yǒuxiào.

- *Some peasants still think that girls are not as useful as boys.*
  有些农民还是认为女孩子不如男孩子有用。
  Yǒuxiē nóngmín háishi rènwéi nǚháizi bùrú nánháizi yǒuyòng.

- *After his wife passed away, his mental state was not as good as before.*
  他妻子去世了以后，他的精神状况不如以前了。
  Tā qīzi qùshìle yǐhòu, tāde jīngshén zhuàngkuàng bùrú yǐqián le.

- *The environment throughout the world is not as good as fifty years ago.*
  世界上哪儿的环境都不如五十年以前了。
  Shìjiè-shang nǎrde huánjìng dōu bùrú wǔshí-nián yǐqián le.

- *How can you say that fake goods are as good as the real things? Of course, fake goods are not as good as the real things.*
  你怎么能说仿冒品跟真货一样好呢？仿冒品当然不如真货啦！
  Nǐ zěnme néng shuō fǎngmàopǐn gēn zhēnhuò yíyàng hǎo ne? Fǎngmàopǐn dāngrán bùrú zhēnhuò la!

EXERCISES:

Translation exercise: Make up one, two, or three versions, using all the possible ways of stating the sentence.

1. I'm not as smart as you.

2. In China, is classical music as popular as modern music?

3. After she grew up, she was not as chubby as she was when she was a young child.

4. Nowadays, are there as many women attending law school as men?

5. Clothing is not as important to men as it is to women.

6. The vegetables in farmers markets are just as good as those in supermarkets, yet they are not as expensive as those in supermarkets.

7. Public security in the U.S. is not nearly as good as in China.

ANSWERS:

1. 我没有/不如你聪明。 **Wǒ méiyòu/bùrú nǐ cōngming.**

2. 在中国，古典音乐有没有现代音乐那么受欢迎？ or …，古典音乐有现代音乐那么受欢迎吗？ **Zài Zhōngguó, gǔdiǎn yīnyuè yǒu-méiyǒu xiàndài yīnyuè nàme shòu huānyíng?** or …，**gǔdiǎn yīnyuè yǒu xiàndài yīnyuè nàme shòu huānyíng ma?**

3. 她长大以后就没有/不像小时候那么胖了。 **Tā zhǎngdà yǐhòu jiù méiyǒu/búxiàng xiǎo shíhou nàme pàng le.**

4. 现在上法学院的学生，女的有没有男的多？ or …，女的有男的那么多吗？ **Xiànzài shàng fǎxuéyuànde xuésheng, nǚde yǒu-méiyǒu nánde duō?** or …，**nǚde yǒu nánde nàme duō ma?**

5. 服装对男人没有/不像对女人那么重要。 **Fúzhuāng duì nánrén méiyǒu/búxiàng duì nǚrén nàme zhòngyào.**

6. 农贸市场的蔬菜跟超市的一样好，可是没有超市的那么贵。 **Nóngmào shìchǎngde shūcài gēn chāoshìde yíyàng hǎo, kěshì méiyǒu chāoshìde nàme guì.**

7. 美国的公共安全远不如中国的那么好。 **Měiguóde gōnggòng ānquán yuǎn bùrú Zhōngguóde nàme hǎo.**

14.3 Stating "A is more...than B" by using 比 bǐ

This is the basic pattern where the *coverb* 比 **bǐ** meaning *to compare* is used and this is the comparison pattern most frequently used by native speakers. The pattern itself is simple, but the *assessment* (called "quality or manner" in the above discussion) in this type of sentence is more versatile than in all the patterns discussed above. The most common *assessments* take the following forms:

a. an adjective (= *stative verb*), like 容易 **róngyì**, 便宜 **piányi**, 好听 **hǎotīng**, 聪明 **cōngming**, 常见 **chángjiàn**

b. an auxiliary verb + verb phrase, like 爱聊天 **ài liáotiān** *to love to chat*, 会说汉语 **huì shuō Hànyǔ** *to be able to speak Chinese*, 能侃大山 **néng kǎn dàshān** *able to shoot the breeze* (lit., "to boast the big mountain"), 喜欢跳舞 **xǐhuan tiàowǔ** *to like dancing*

c. a verb + object phrase, like 吸引观众 **xīyǐn guānzhòng** *to appeal to audience* (popular)

d. an adjective + a "degree of difference," like 快得多 **kuài-de-duō** *much faster*, 高三寸 **gāo sāncùn** *taller by 3 inches*

As you read the following examples, note the various ways in which this basic pattern can be embellished by the variety of forms A and B (the entities being compared) can take:

♦ *This sentence pattern is more common than the others.*
这个句型比其他的常见。 **Zhèige jùxíng bǐ qítāde chángjiàn.**

♦ *Japanese people seem to talk faster than Chinese people.*
日本人说话说得好像比中国人快。
Rìběnrén shuōhuà shuōde hǎoxiàng bǐ Zhōngguórén kuài.

♦ *To native English speakers, all European languages are easier to learn than Chinese.*
对英语为母语的人来说，欧洲的语言都比中文容易学。
Duì Yīngyǔ wéi mǔyǔde rén láishuō, Ōuzhōude yǔyán dōu bǐ Zhōngwén róngyì xué.

♦ *Almost all Chinese cities are more polluted than they were 20 years ago.*
中国城市里的空气污染差不多都比二十年前严重了。
Zhōngguó chéngshìlǐde kōngqì wūrǎn chàbuduō dōu bǐ èrshí-nián qián yánzhòng le.

♦ *Tonal languages sound better than non-tonal languages, but they are more difficult to learn.*
有声调的语言比没有声调的好听，可是也比较难学。
Yǒu shēngdiàode yǔyán bǐ méiyǒu shēngdiàode hǎotīng, kěshì yě bǐjiào nánxué.
(note the use of 比较 **bǐjiào** in the second clause to bypass the "A 比 B" pattern)

♦ *Women like to dance more than men.*
There are more women who like to dance than men.
女人比男人喜欢跳舞。 **Nǚrén bǐ nánrén xǐhuan tiàowǔ.**
喜欢跳舞的女人比男人多。 **Xǐhuan tiàowǔde nǚrén bǐ nánrén duō.**

♦ *In general, Asians like group activities more than Westerners.*
一般来说，亚洲人比西方人喜欢群体活动。
Yìbān láishuō, Yàzhōu-rén bǐ Xīfāng-rén xǐhuan qúntǐ huódòng.

♦ *Among the old folks who exercise in parks in the morning, there are many more who dance than those who do tai chi.*
早上在公园里运动的老人，跳舞的比打太极拳的多得多。
Zǎoshang zài gōngyuánlǐ yùndòngde lǎorén, tiàowǔde bǐ dǎ tàijíquánde duō-de-duō.

The first three *assessments* (a, b, c) listed above in the examples may also be modified by 更 **gèng** or 还要 **háiyào**, meaning *even more*, to intensify the comparison. The words 更 **gèng** or 还要 **háiyào** may also be used in dual-clause sentences comparing a third entity with the two compared in the first clause.

- *The second child is even more rambunctious than the first.* (implying that the first child is quite rambunctious already)
  老二比老大还要调皮。 **Lǎo Èr bǐ Lǎo Dà háiyào tiáopí.**

- *The second child is more rambunctious than the first, the third one is even more rambunctious! One can say, each one is more rambunctious than the last!*
  老二比老大调皮，老三比老二更调皮。可以说，他们一个比一个调皮！ **Lǎo Èr bǐ Lǎo Dà tiáopí, Lǎo Sān bǐ lǎo Èr gèng tiáopí, kěyǐ shuō, tāmen yíge bǐ yíge tiáopí.**

- *This summer was hotter than last summer; experts say that perhaps next summer will be even hotter than this one.*
  今年夏天比去年热，专家说恐怕明年夏天会比今年还要热！ **Jīnnián xiàtiān bǐ qùnián rè, zhuānjiā shuō kǒngpà míngnián xiàtiān huì bǐ jīnnián háiyào rè.**

- *Seafood is a bit better for health than meats, but a vegetarian diet is even healthier.*
  海鲜比肉类对身体好一点，可是素食比海鲜更健康。 **Hǎixiān bǐ ròulèi duì shēntǐ hǎo yìdiǎn, kěshì sùshí bǐ hǎixiān gèng jiànkāng.**

The negative counterpart to the *A* 比 **bǐ** *B…* pattern is *A* 不比 **bùbǐ** *B…* Note that the negative 不 **bù** is never positioned before the *assessment*. Think of 不 **bù** as an *adverb*, and it goes before the *coverb* 比 **bǐ**.

- *For a Chinese to learn English is not easier than for a Westerner to learn Chinese.*
  ✓ 中国人学英语不比西方人学中文容易。
  Zhōngguórén xué Yīngyǔ bùbǐ Xīfāng-rén xué Zhōngwén róngyì.
  ✗ 中国人学英语比西方人学中文不容易。
  Zhōngguórén xué Yīngyǔ bǐ Xīfāng-rén xué Zhōngwén bù róngyì.

- *I hope it will not be even hotter next summer than it has been this summer.*
  ✓ 我希望明年夏天不会比今年更热。
  Wǒ xīwàng míngnián xiàtiān bú huì bǐ jīnnián gèng rè.
  ✗ 我希望明年夏天比今年不会更热。
  Wǒ xīwàng míngnián xiàtiān bǐ jīnnián bú huì gèng rè.

- *Things at supermarkets are not better than at farmers markets, but they are more expensive.*
  超市的东西不比农贸市场的好，可是比较贵。
  Chāoshìde dōngxi bùbǐ nóngmào shìchǎngde hǎo, kěshì bǐjiào guì.

EXERCISES:

Translate the following sentences into Chinese:

1. Japanese is not more difficult to learn than Chinese.

2. In the past, vegetables were cheaper than meat, but now vegetables are more expensive than meat.

3. Fish is more easily digested than beef.

4. It's much easier for children than for adults to learn a second language.

5. Cantonese is even harder to learn than Chinese.

6. Normally Washington is hotter than Southern California in the summer, but this year Southern California is even hotter than Washington.

7. It's been two months since I came to China; now I am better at bargaining than when I first arrived.

8. Having lived here for two years, I have a little more understanding of Chinese society than before.

ANSWERS:

1. 日语不比中文难学。**Rìyǔ bùbǐ Zhōngwén nán xué.**

2. 从前蔬菜比肉便宜，可是现在蔬菜比肉贵了。
   Cóngqián shūcài bǐ ròu piányi, kěshì xiànzài shūcài bǐ ròu guì le.

3. 鱼比牛肉容易消化。**Yú bǐ niúròu róngyì xiāohuà.**

4. 小孩子学第二语言比大人容易多了。**Xiǎoháizi xué dì'èr yǔyán bǐ dàrén róngyì duōle.**

5. 广东话比普通话更难学。**Guǎngdōng-huà bǐ pǔtōnghuà gèng nán xué.**

6. 平常，在夏天，华盛顿比南加州热，可是今年南加州比华盛顿还要热。
   Píngcháng, zài xiàtiān, Huáshèngdùn bǐ Nán Jiāzhōu rè, kěshì jīnnián Nán Jiāzhōu bǐ Huáshèngdùn háiyào rè.

7. 我来中国两个月了，现在我比刚来的时候会讲价了。
   Wǒ lái Zhōngguó liǎngge yuè le, xiànzài wǒ bǐ gāng láide shíhou huì jiǎngjià le.

8. 我在这里住了两年了，对中国社会的了解比从前多了一点儿。
   Wǒ zài zhèlǐ zhùle liǎngnián le, duì Zhōngguó shèhuìde liǎojiě bǐ cóngqiān duōle yìdiǎnr.

14.4 Negative comparisons

In 14.2, we discussed several ways of stating *A is not as…as B*. How are these different from *A* 不比 **bùbǐ** *B*…? The three patterns in 14.2 all indicate that *B is more… than A*, so there is definitely a difference between A and B. In contrast, *A* 不比 **bùbǐ** *B*… does not mean that there is necessarily a difference between the two. That is, *B may be more…than A*, but more often than not, the implication is that there is no difference between the two.

♦ *When I first moved here, I was not as adjusted to life here as I am now.*
   我刚搬来的时候，没有现在那么适应这里的生活。
   Wǒ gāng bānlaide shíhou, méiyǒu xiànzài nàme shìyìng zhèlǐde shēnghuó.

(没有 **méiyǒu** may be replaced by 不像 **búxiàng** and 不如 **bùrú** with only slight difference in nuance.)

● *To tell the truth, I am not any more adjusted to life here than when I first arrived. I really don't like the environment here.*
说实话，我现在不比刚搬来的时候适应这里的生活。我真的不喜欢这里的环境。**Shuō shíhuà, wǒ xiànzài bùbǐ gāng bānlaide shíhou shìyìng zhèlǐde shēnghuó. Wǒ zhēnde bù xǐhuan zhèlǐde huánjìng.**

● *He is not as interested in Chinese culture now as he was when he first arrived.*
他现在没有刚到中国的时候对中国文化那么感兴趣了。
Tā xiànzài méiyǒu gāng dào Zhōngguóde shíhou duì Zhōngguó wénhuà nàme gǎn-xìngqù le.
(没有 **méiyǒu** may be replaced by 不像 **búxiàng** and 不如 **bùrú** with only slight difference in nuance.)

● *He has been living within a foreigners' circle all these years, so he doesn't understand Chinese culture any more than when he first arrived.*
这些年他一直生活在外国人的圈子里，所以现在不比刚来的时候对中国文化有更多的了解。
Zhèixiē nián tā yìzhí shēnghuó zài wàiguórénde quānzili, suǒyǐ xiànzài bùbǐ gāng láide shíhou duì Zhōngguó wénhuà yǒu gèngduōde liǎojiě.

EXERCISES:

Translate the following sentences into Chinese:

1. Our things are better than other stores', but our prices are not as high as theirs.

2. Our things are better than other stores', but our prices are not more expensive than theirs.

3. Their dishes are not as good as other restaurants', but their prices are by no means any cheaper. (See 并不 **bìngbù** in Part II. #7)

ANSWERS:
1. 我们的东西比别的商店的好，不过(我们的)价格没有他们的高。
Wǒmende dōngxi bǐ biéde shāngdiànde hǎo, búguò (wǒmende) jiàgé méiyǒu tāmende gāo.
2. 我们的东西比别的商店的好，不过(我们的)价钱不比他们的贵。
Wǒmende dōngxi bǐ biéde shāngdiànde hǎo, búguò (wǒmende) jiàqián bù bǐ tāmende guì.
3. 他们的菜不如别的餐馆，可是价钱并不更便宜。
Tāmende cài bùrú biéde cānguǎn, kěshì jiàqián bìng bú gèng piányi.

14.5 Stating the extent of a difference between A and B

The *A* 比 **bǐ** *B*… pattern is the only one that can be used to state the extent of difference between A and B, and this is done simply by adding it at the end of the phrase. As you read the following examples, take note of the various ways in which the difference can be stated.

- *Chinese is a little bit more difficult to learn than other foreign languages.*
  中文比其他的外语难学<u>一点儿</u>。 **Zhōngwén bǐ qítāde yǔyán nánxué <u>yìdiǎnr</u>.**

- *For a Westerner to learn Japanese is <u>much more difficult</u> than for a Chinese to do the same.*
  西方人学日语比中国人<u>难得多</u>。
  Xīfāng-rén xué Rìyǔ bǐ Zhōngguórén <u>nán-de-duō</u>.

- *The monthly rent for this apartment is <u>$200 more</u> than our present apartment. Do you think it's worth it?*
  这个公寓的月租比我们现在住的贵<u>两百元</u>。 你觉得值得吗？
  Zhèige gōngyùde yuèzū bǐ wǒmen xiànzài zhùde guì <u>liǎngbǎi yuán</u>. Nǐ juéde zhíde ma?

- *A real Rolex watch costs <u>several hundred times</u> more than a fake one.*
  真的劳力士手表比仿冒的贵<u>几百倍</u>。
  Zhēnde Láolìshì shǒubiǎo bǐ fǎngmàode guì <u>jǐbǎibèi</u>.

- *The enrollment in Chinese this year is <u>50% higher</u> than last year.*
  今年学中文的学生人数比去年多了<u>百分之五十</u>。
  Jīnnián xué Zhōngwénde xuésheng rénshù bǐ qùnián duōle <u>bǎifēn-zhī-wǔshí</u>.

EXERCISES:

Translate the following sentences into Chinese:

1. Your boyfriend is 20 years older than you, you should think carefully before you decide whether to marry him or not.
2. A vegetarian diet is much healthier than a carnivorous diet.
3. The tuition at private universities is twice as much as at state universities (one fold higher than at state universities).
4. The boss just announced that salaries next year will be 5% higher than this year.
5. Taking the high-speed train will costs ¥200 more than the regular train, but it will be faster by two hours.

ANSWERS:

1. 你的男朋友比你大二十岁，你应该好好地想一想再决定要不要跟他结婚。
   Nǐde nánpéngyou bǐ nǐ dà èrshí-suì, nǐ yīnggāi hǎohāorde xiǎng-yixiǎng zài juédìng yào-buyào gēn tā jiéhūn.
2. 吃素比吃肉健康得多。**Chī-sù bǐ chī-ròu jiànkāng-de-duō.**
3. 私立大学的学费比州立大学的贵一倍。**Sīlì dàxuéde xuéfèi bǐ zhōulì dàxuéde guì yíbèi.**
4. 老板刚宣布说明年的工资会比今年的高百分之五。
   Lǎobǎn gāng xuānbù shuō míngniánde gōngzī huì bǐ jīnniánde gāo bǎifēn-zhī-wǔ.
5. 坐高铁会比普通火车贵两百元，可是会快两个小时。
   Zuò gāo-tiě huì bǐ pǔtōng huǒchē guì liǎngbǎi-yuán, kěshì huì kuài liǎngge xiǎoshí.

14.6 Comparing how two people or "agents" do something

In most of the examples given in this chapter so far, the two entities being compared are noun phrases, as one would expect. But we have also seen a few examples of times (e.g. earlier vs now) or even verbal phrases (e.g. Westerners learning Japanese vs Chinese learning Japanese) being compared. In this section, we will provide more examples of comparing the way two "agents" do something. All the patterns we have introduced in this chapter may be adapted to this function simply by filling the A and B slots with a phrase indicating the "agent and action."

- *He speaks Chinese as well as a native Chinese.*
  他说中文说得跟中国人一样好。(A 跟 **gēn** B 一样… **yíyàng…**)
  Tā shuō Zhōngwén shuōde gēn Zhōngguórén yíyàng hǎo.

- *People who eat meat don't live as long as vegetarians.*
  吃肉的人活得没有吃素的人那么长。or 吃肉的人没有吃素的人
  活得长。(A 没有 **méiyǒu** B 那么 **nàme…**)
  Chīròude rén huóde méiyǒu chīsùde rén nàme cháng. or
  Chīròude rén méiyǒu chīsùde rén huóde cháng.

- *Although his Chinese is quite good, it's of course not as fluent as that of a native Chinese.*
  他的中文虽然不错，可是说得当然不像中国人那么流利。
  (A 不像 **búxiàng** B 那么 **nàme…**)
  Tāde Zhōngwén suīrán búcuò, kěshì shuōde dāngrán búxiàng Zhōngguórén nàme liúlì.

- *Although his Chinese is quite good, still he doesn't speak it as fluently as English.*
  他的中文虽然不错，可是说得当然不如英文说得流利。(A 不如
  bùrú B…)
  Tāde Zhōngwén suīrán búcuò, kěshì shuōde dāngrán bùrú Yīngwén shuōde liúlì.

- *Student A: You write (characters) faster than I, but I write better than you.*
  Student B: It's more important to write well than to write fast.
  *Student A: No, in an exam, of course it's more important to write fast than
  to write well.*
  Teacher: However, writing correctly is more important than anything else.
  学生甲：你写字写得比我快，可是我写得比你好。
  Xuésheng Jiǎ: Nǐ xiězì xiěde bǐ wǒ kuài, kěshì wǒ xiěde bǐ nǐ hǎo.
  学生乙：写得好比写得快重要。
  Xuésheng Yǐ: Xiěde hǎo bǐ xiěde kuài zhòngyào.
  学生甲：不，考试的时候，当然写得快比写得好重要。
  Xuésheng Jiǎ: Bù, kǎoshìde shíhou, dāngrán xiěde kuài bǐ xiěde hǎo zhòngyào.
  老师：不过，写得对更重要。or 不过，写得对比什么都重要。
  Lǎoshī: Búguò, xiěde duì gèng zhòngyào. or **Búguò, xiěde duì bǐ shénme dōu zhòngyào.**

♦ *Our shop sells clothes much faster than the one next door. This is because we sell our stuff much more cheaply than they.*
我们这个店卖衣服比旁边那个店卖得快得多，这是因为我们比他们便宜多了。
Wǒmen zhèige diàn mài yīfu bǐ pángbiān nèige diàn màide kuài-de-duō, zhè shì yīnwèi wǒmen bǐ tāmen piányi duōle.

♦ *Recently, internet stores have begun to sell even more cheaply than we do. Competition is too fierce! We had better hurry up and open an internet store ourselves!*
最近有些网上的商店开始卖得比我们还要便宜。竞争太激烈了！我们不如赶快也在网上开个商店吧！ **Zuìjìn yǒuxiē wǎngshàngde shāngdiàn kāishǐ màide bǐ wǒmen háiyào piányi. Jìngzhēng tài jīliè le! Wǒmen bùrú gǎnkuài yě zài wǎngshàng kāi ge shāngdiàn ba!**

EXERCISES:

Translate the following sentences into Chinese:

1. Americans spend more time working than Europeans. Young people in China spend even more time working than Americans.

2. Europeans focus more on quality of life than Americans; they are not as focused on income as Americans.

3. The highways in Europe are not as good as those in the U.S., that's why Europeans don't drive as fast as Americans.

4. It rains a lot more in Chengdu than in Beijing, so the climate there is not as nice as Beijing's.

ANSWERS:
1. 美国人工作的时间比欧洲人多。中国的年轻人比美国人工作的时间更多。
   Měiguórén gōngzuòde shíjiān bǐ Ōuzhōu-ren duō. Zhōngguóde niánqīng-rén bǐ Měiguórén gōngzuòde shíjiān gèng duō.
2. 欧洲人比美国人重视生活品质；他们没有美国人那么重视收入。
   Ōuzhōu-rén bǐ Měiguórén zhòngshì shēnghuó pǐnzhì; tāmen méiyǒu Měiguórén nàme zhòngshì shōurù.
3. 欧洲的公路没有美国的好，因此，欧洲人开车没有美国人那么快。
   Ōuzhōude gōnglù méiyǒu Měiguóde hǎo, yīncǐ, Ōuzhōu-rén kāichē méiyǒu Měiguórén nàme kuài.
4. 成都下雨下得比北京多得多，所以那里的气候没有北京的好。
   Chéngdū xiàyǔ xiàde bǐ Běijīng duōde duō, suǒyǐ nàlide qìhòu méiyǒu Běijīngde hǎo.

14.7 Expressing the distance between two points

The basic sentence pattern for comparing two entities presented in this chapter also can be used to state the distance between two points. In this case, A and B are the two points, and 离 **lí** = *distance away from* is the *relativity coverb*. What follows B is the *assessment* or distance, which can be either a descriptive phrase (e.g. *quite far*) or a specific measurement (e.g. *3 kilometers*).

A + 离 lí + B + assessment or distance

In the following examples, note that the English translation of 离 lí is *from*, which may mislead you into translating it using 从 cóng in Chinese. This is incorrect!

♦ *My home is not too far from where I work.*
我家离我上班的地方不太远。 **Wǒjiā lí wǒ shàngbānde dìfang bú tài yuǎn.**

♦ *My home is only half a mile from where I work.*
我家离我上班的地方只有半英里。
Wǒjiā lí wǒ shàngbānde dìfang zhǐyǒu bàn yīnglǐ.
(Note that 有 yǒu rather than 是 shì is the verb used to state a measurement of distance, consistent with statements of measurement for other things. See 2.8.)

♦ *How far is it from Beijing to Tokyo?*
北京离东京有多么远? **Běijīng lí Dōngjīng yǒu duōme yuǎn?**
(**Note**: 多么 duōme is an interrogative pronoun meaning *how, to what extent*. It is interchangeable with 多 duō. Either way, it must be followed by an adjective. See 3.5.)

♦ *Is it as far as thirty miles from your home to your office?*
你家离你的办公室有没有三十英里(那么远)? (see the following note)
Nǐjiā lí nǐde bàngōngshì yǒu-méiyǒu sānshí yīnglǐ (nàme yuǎn)?

In a statement or question giving a specific measurement, that measurement may be followed by 那么远 nàme yuǎn. The effect is to emphasize the greatness of the distance, similar to the usage of 这么 zhème/ 那么 nàme in the patterns in 14.2 above.

♦ *In that rural area, many children's homes are as far as three miles from their schools, so they walk a long way to and from school every day. (emphasizing that it really is far for those kids to walk to school)*
在那个乡下地方，很多孩子的家离他们的学校有三、四英里<u>那么</u>
<u>远</u>，所以他们每天上下学得走很远的路。
Zài nèige xiāngxia dìfang, hěnduō háizide jiā lí tāmende xuéxiào yǒu sān-sì yīnglǐ nàme yuǎn, suǒyǐ tāmen měitiān shàng-xiàxué děi zǒu hěnyuǎnde lù.

EXERCISES:

Translate the following sentences into Chinese:

1. My home is not far from campus; I can walk there.

2. How far is New York from Los Angeles?

3. I'm not too sure, probably about 3,000 miles.

4. Taipei is very near Xiamen in mainland China. A direct flight takes only half an hour.

ANSWERS:

1. 我家离校园不远，我可以走路去。Wǒ jiā lí xiàoyuán bù yuǎn, wǒ kěyǐ zǒulù qù.

2. 纽约离洛杉矶有多远？Niǔyuē lí Luòshānjī yǒu duō yuǎn?

3. 我不太清楚，大概三千英里左右吧。
   Wǒ bú tài qīngchǔ, dàgài sānqiān yīnglǐ zuǒyòu ba.

4. 台北离大陆的厦门很近。坐直达的航班只要半个小时。
   Táiběi lí Dàlùde Xiàmén hěn jìn. Zuò zhídáde hángbān zhǐ yào bànge xiǎoshí.

14.8 Comparing two distances

All the patterns presented in 14.1 through 14.5 may be used for comparisons of distance. In comparing the distance between two points with the distance between two other points, each of the two distances being compared is expressed as A 离 lí B.

- *The distance from my house to my office is about the same as the distance from your house to your college.*
  我家离我的办公室跟你家离你的大学差不多一样远。
  Wǒjiā lí wǒde bàngōngshì gēn nǐjiā lí nǐde dàxué chàbuduō yíyàng yuǎn.
  (**Note**: 远 yuǎn "far" is added after 一样 yíyàng, to mean "similarly *far*." If the distance is short, 远 yuǎn would be replaced by 近 jìn "near.")

- *The distance between Washington and New York is not as great as between Beijing and Shanghai.* 华盛顿离纽约没有北京离上海那么远。
  Huáshèngdùn lí Niǔyuē méiyǒu Běijīng lí Shànghǎi nàme yuǎn.

- *The distance from Beijing to Shanghai is much farther than from Washington to New York.* 北京离上海比华盛顿离纽约远得多。
  Běijīng lí Shànghǎi bǐ Huáshèngdùn lí Niǔyuē yuǎn-de-duō.

- *My new home from my office is 3 miles farther than my parents' house to my school.*
  我的新家离办公室比我父母家离学校远三英里。
  Wǒde xīnjiā lí bàngōngshì bǐ wǒ fùmǔ jiā lí xuéxiào yuǎn sān yīnglǐ.

- *Is the distance between New York and Los Angeles as much as that between Beijing and Hong Kong?* 纽约离洛杉矶有没有北京离香港那么远？
  Niǔyuē lí Luòshānjī yǒu-méiyǒu Běijīng lí Xiānggǎng nàme yuǎn?

- *The distance between New York and Los Angeles is several times farther than between Beijing and Shanghai.*
  纽约离洛杉矶比北京离上海远好几倍。
  Niǔyuē lí Luòshānjī bǐ Běijīng lí Shànghǎi yuǎn hǎojǐbèi.

As you read the above sentences, you may have noticed how much more succinct the Chinese sentences are in comparison to their English counterparts. This confirms the fact that the basic Chinese sentence pattern for expressing comparisons is truly a very "efficient" means of rendering these ideas.

14.9 Comparing the distances from two points to a third point

This section covers two situations: 1) comparing the distance from one point to two others points (from A to B and C); 2) comparing the distance from two points to a third point (from A and B to C). Again, all the comparison patterns presented in 14.1 through 14.5 may be applied here. If these sentences seem difficult to form, it is because conceptualizing these scenarios requires a bit of mental gymnastics, regardless of the language used. In real life, speakers will normally simplify these comparisons by omitting elements that are understood from the context.

Examples of comparing the distance from one point to two other points:

◆ *My home is about the same distance to this supermarket as that one.*
我家离这家超市跟那家差不多一样远。
Wǒjiā lí zhèijiā chāoshì gēn nèijiā chàbuduō yíyàng yuǎn.
(In context, this sentence may be reduced to 这两家超市(都)差不多一样远。 **Zhèi liǎngjiā chāoshì (dōu) chàbuduō yíyàng yuǎn.**)

◆ *Both the Chaoyang Hospital and the Xiehe Hospital have Emergency, but we're a bit closer to the Chaoyang Hospital than the Xiehe Hospital.*
朝阳医院跟协和医院都有急诊，不过这里离朝阳比(离)协和近一点。
Cháoyáng Yīyuàn gēn Xiéhé Yīyuàn dōu yǒu jízhěn, búguò zhèlǐ lí Cháoyáng bǐ (lí) Xiéhé jìn yìdiǎn.
(In context, the second clause may be reduced to 朝阳比协和近一点 **Cháoyáng bǐ Xiéhé jìn yìdiǎn.**)

◆ *Hong Kong is not as far from Taipei as it is from Beijing, is it?*
香港离台北没有离北京那么远吧？
Xiānggǎng lí Táiběi méiyǒu lí Běijīng nàme yuǎn ba?

Examples of comparing the distance from two points to a third point:

◆ *The metro station and the bus station are about the same distance from my house, but each one has its pluses and minuses.*
地铁站和公车站离我家的距离都差不多一样，不过各有利弊。
Dìtiězhàn hé gōngchēzhàn lí wǒjiāde jùlí dōu chàbuduō yíyàng, búguò gè yǒu lìbì.

◆ *The pizza shop is much farther from here than the **jiaozi** joint, it's really inconvenient to walk there. Let's just have **jiaozi** today.*
比萨店比饺子店离这里远得多，走路去真不方便，我们今天就吃饺子吧。
Bǐsàdiàn bǐ jiǎozidiàn lí zhèlǐ yuǎn-de-duō, zǒulù qù zhēn bù fāngbiàn, wǒmen jīntiān jiù chī jiǎozi ba.

♦ *The Chaoyang Hospital is not as close to here as the Xiehe Hospital. We'd better head for the Xiehe.*

朝阳医院离这里没有协和医院近，我们不如去协和。

Cháoyáng Yīyuàn lí zhèlǐ méiyǒu Xiéhé Yīyuàn jìn, wǒmen bùrú qù Xiéhé.

EXERCISES:

Translate the following sentences into Chinese. Simplify them if possible within the given context.

1. Do you want to go the zoo or the park? Both of them are about the same distance from here.

2. I'd like to travel over spring break. Is Xinjiang as far from Beijing as Yunnan? They are just about the same distance from Beijing.

3. Is Hong Kong closer to Singapore than it is to Taipei?

4. The distance between the U.S. East Coast and Europe is much less than that between the West Coast and Asia.

ANSWERS:

1. 你想去动物园还是公园？两个(离这儿)的距离都差不多一样。
   Nǐ xiǎng qù dòngwùyuán háishi gōngyuán? Liǎngge (lí zhèr) de jùlí dōu chàbuduō yíyàng.

2. 我想春假去旅游。新疆有没有云南离北京那么远？这两个地方离北京的距离都差不多一样。or ⋯，这两个地方(离北京)都差不多一样远。
   Wǒ xiǎng chūnjià qù lǚyóu. Xīnjiāng yǒu-méiyǒu Yúnnán lí Běijīng nàme yuǎn? Zhè liǎngge dìfang lí Běijīngde jùlí dōu chàbuduō yíyang. or Zhè liǎngge dìfang (lí Běijīng) dōu chàbuduō yíyang yuǎn.

3. 香港离新加坡比离台北近一点吗？ **Xiānggǎng lí Xīnjiāpō bǐ lí Táiběi jìn yìdiǎn ma?**

4. 美国东部离欧洲比西部离亚州近多了。
   Měiguó dōngbù lí Ōuzhōu bǐ xībù lí Yàzhōu jìn-duōle.

We provided an overview of the differences between Chinese and English sentences in 1.3, then delved into the grammar of the various sentence components in subsequent chapters. This chapter provides an overview of the order of the various sentence components and the ways of highlighting particular points. As you read it, you should already be familiar with most of the points, however, what is new is how these familiar points are tied together.

Chinese word order in a sentence in essence boils down to ordering the components within a *verb phrase* and a *noun phrase*. The "big picture" of the sentence in Chinese and English is the same, i.e. there is a subject followed by a predicate, except that in some cases in Chinese, the *topic-comment* concept is more apt (see 1.3, section 1). The position of conjunctions like 因为 **yīnwèi** *because*, 所以 **suǒyǐ** *therefore*, 虽然 **suīrán** *although*, 可是 **kěshì** *but* is also the same in both languages, except that in Chinese, there is another less common option of placing these after the subject. A greater flexibility in the positioning of *time-when* expressions in English was noted in the introduction to Chapter 10. Aside from these overall differences between Chinese and English word order, the remaining differences lie in the ordering of components within the verb phrases and noun phrases.

15.1 Extended verb phrases

A verb phrase may be a simple verb, a *stative verb* (equivalent to an adjective in English), or a long verbal phrase that includes other elements. Verb phrases in Chinese can be grouped into seven basic patterns, which have all been covered previously in this book. They are listed together below to show what they all have in common. Some of the patterns may seem complicated, but remember that the elements in parentheses are optional. In actual use, most sentences will include only one or two of these elements. As you read the sentences, identify each grammatical element within the underlined verb phrases.

1. (adverb) + stative verb or 是··· **shì...** (there may be one or more adverbs, here and below)

今天他好像很忙。 **Jīntiān tā <u>hǎoxiàng hěn máng</u>.**
or 他今天好像很忙。 **Tā jīntiān <u>hǎoxiàng hěn máng</u>.**
He seems to be very busy today.

退了休以后，每天都好像是星期天。
Tuìle-xiū yǐhòu, měitiān <u>dōu hǎoxiàng shì xīngqītiān</u>.
After retirement, every day is like a Sunday.

2. (adverb) + (auxiliary verb) + verb (object)

欧洲人<u>一般都会说几种语言</u>，多半的美国人<u>只会说一种</u>。
Ōuzhōu-rén <u>yìbān dōu huì shuō jǐzhǒng yǔyán</u>, duōbànde Měiguórén <u>zhǐ huì shuō yìzhǒng</u>.
Europeans generally can speak several languages, most Americans can only speak one.

3. (adverb) + (aux. v.) + coverb-object + verb (object)
   (there may be more than one "coverb-object," here and below)

因为他那么忙，所以我<u>总是想替他做点儿事</u>。
Yīnwèi tā nàme máng, suǒyǐ wǒ <u>zǒngshì xiǎng tì tā zuò diǎnr shì</u>.
Because he is so busy, I am always thinking of doing something for him.

4. (adverb) + (aux. v.) + (coverb-object) + verb + postverb-object or purpose

在全球化时代，很多年轻人<u>都想到国外去尝试一下异国的文化</u>。
Zài quánqiú-huà shídài, hěnduō niánqīng-rén <u>dōu xiǎng dào guówài qù chángshì</u> <u>yíxià yìguóde wénhuà</u>.
In the era of globalization, many young people want to go abroad to try out the cultures of other countries.

5. (adverb) + (aux. v.) + (coverb-object) + (verb-object) + verb-得 **de**-complement
   (see 6.1)

我<u>真希望在毕业之前能说中文说得很流利</u>。
Wǒ <u>zhēn xīwàng zài bìyè zhīqián néng shuō Zhōngwén shuōde hěn liúlì</u>.
I really hope that I can speak Chinese fluently by the time I graduate.

6. (adverb) + (aux. v.) + (coverb-object) + verb-complement (see Chapter 12)

我<u>打算在两年以内把我的博士论文写完</u>。
Wǒ <u>dǎsuàn zài liǎngnián yǐnèi bǎ wǒde bóshì lùnwén xiěwán</u>.
I am planning to complete my Ph.D. dissertation within two years.

7. (adverb) + (aux. v.) + (coverb-object) + (verb-object) + verb (了 **le** /过 **guo**) +
   (time-span or number of occurrences) (see 10.2 and 10.9)

他<u>去过好几次了</u>，<u>肯定不会走错路</u>，您放心吧！
Tā <u>qùguo hǎojǐcì le</u>, <u>kěndìng búhuì zǒu-cuò-lù</u>, nín fàngxīn ba!
He has been there several times, surely he would not take the wrong road, rest assured!

All of the above verb phrase patterns have negative and interrogative forms, which we will illustrate with a few examples below. As you read the examples, note the grammatical elements within the underlined verb phrases.

◆ 从中国领养来的孩子都真的是孤儿吗？
Cóng Zhōngguó lǐngyǎng láide háizi <u>dōu zhēnde shì gū'ér</u> ma?
Are all the children adopted from China really orphans?

◆ 来这个中心的学生，有的从来没学过中文，有的已经学过两三年了。**Lái zhèige zhōngxīnde xuésheng, yǒude <u>cónglái méi xuéguo Zhōngwén</u>, yǒude <u>yǐjīng xuéguo liǎng-sān-nián</u> le.**
Of the students who come to this center, some have never studied any Chinese, some have already studied it for two or three years.

◆ 你们什么时候<u>可以把我买的家具运到我家来</u>？
Nǐmen shénme shíhou <u>kěyǐ bǎ wǒ mǎide jiāju yùndào wǒjiā lái</u>?
When can you ship the furniture I bought to my house?

◆ 人工智能的发展<u>不可能把所有的职业都淘汰掉</u>吧？
Réngōng zhìnéngde fāzhǎn <u>bù kěnéng bǎ suǒyǒude zhíyè dōu táotài-diào</u> ba?
It isn't possible for artificial intelligence to make all professions obsolete, is it?

◆ 我们<u>已经去过那家餐馆太多次了</u>，以后出去吃饭，我<u>不想再去那家了</u>。**Wǒmen <u>yǐjīng qùguo nèijiā cānguǎn tài duō cì le</u>, yǐhòu chūqu chīfàn, wǒ <u>bùxiǎng zài qù nèijiā</u> le.**
We've already been to that restaurant too many times. When we go out to eat in the future, I don't want to go there again.

EXERCISES:

Create a sentence in Chinese for each of the verb phrase patterns below.

1. (adverb) + (aux. v.) + verb + (object)

2. (adverb) + (aux. v.) + (coverb-object) + verb-complement (or verb-得 **de**-complement)

3. A sentence that involves either a *time-when* or *time-span* expression

4. A sentence that involves the coverb 把 **bǎ** or 被 **bèi**

5. A sentence that involves using a postverb

ANSWERS:

1. 会说中文的外国人通常都喜欢看中国电影。
Huì shuō Zhōngwénde wàiguó-rén tōngcháng dōu xǐhuan kàn Zhōngguó diànyǐng.
Foreigners who can speak Chinese generally enjoy watching Chinese movies.

2. 一般的大学毕业生没有什么工作经验，所以不太可能在刚毕业的那年就找到一个理想的工作。**Yìbānde dàxuéshēng méiyǒu shénme gōngzuò jīngyàn, suǒyǐ bú tài kěnéng zài gāng bìyède nèinián jiù zhǎodào yíge lǐxiǎngde gōngzuò.** Most college graduates don't have much work experience, so it's not quite possible for them to find an ideal job the year they graduate.

3. 你预备什么时候回国去看你父母？这次回国，你大概会呆多长时间？
Nǐ yùbèi shénme shíhou huíguó qù kàn nǐ fùmǔ? Zhèicì huíguó, nǐ dàgài huì dāi duō cháng shíjiān?
When are you planning to return to your home country to see your parents? When you go home this time, about how long will you stay?

4. 为了吸引更多的观众，他想把这部话剧改编成电影剧本。
   Wèile xīyǐn gèng duōde guānzhòng, tā xiǎng bǎ zhèibù huàjù gǎibiān-chéng diànyǐng jùběn.
   In order to attract a larger audience, he would like to convert this play into a movie script.
   我们家门前的那棵树被台风吹倒了，幸亏没有砸到房子。
   Wǒmen jiā ménqiánde nèikē shù bèi táifēng chuīdǎo le, xìngkuī méiyǒu zádào fángzi.
   The tree in front of our house was blown over by the typhoon; fortunately it did not strike the house.

5. 他们全家都移民到美国去了。 **Tāmen quánjiā dōu yímín-dào Měiguó qùle.**
   Their whole family has emigrated to America.

15.2 Noun phrases with modifiers

A noun phrase may be anything from a single word or a proper name, to a long phrase with multiple modifiers ending with the main noun. Regardless of the type of modifier, all of them must precede the main noun in Chinese. The situation is more complicated in English: simpler modifiers may precede the main noun, whereas prepositional phrases and relative clauses follow the main noun. Therefore, in expressing noun phrases with multiple modifiers, one needs to steer away from the English version, and mentally get the ducks lined up in Chinese before speaking.

Noun modifiers come in a wide variety of forms, as shown in the following table. Note the position of the key noun at the end of each noun phrase, in contrast to the various different positions in English.

type of modifier	examples
stative verb	贵的东西 **guìde dōngxi** *expensive things* 便宜货 **piányi huò** *cheap goods* 漂亮的衣服 **piàoliangde yīfu** *a pretty dress* 白衬衫 **bái chènshān** *a white shirt*
another noun	公司的老板 **gōngsīde lǎobǎn** *the boss of the company* 人类的救星 **rénlèide jiùxīng** *the savior of mankind* 大学教授 **dàxué jiàoshòu** *a college professor*
a pronoun	我父母 **wǒ fùmǔ,** 我的父母 **wǒde fùmǔ** *my parents* 他们的家 **tāmende jiā** *their home*
time-when expression	今天的新闻 **jīntiānde xīnwén** *today's news* 明年的学费 **míngniánde xuéfèi** *next year's tuition*
time-span expression	一年的收入 **yìniánde shōurù** *one year's income* 八个小时的工作 **bāge xiǎoshíde gōngzuò** *eight hours of work*
a location	城里的公园 **chénglǐde gōngyuán** *the park in the city* 在非洲的野生动物 **zài Fēizhōude yěshēng dòngwù** *the wild animals in Africa*

type of modifier	examples
verb phrases	卖花的女孩子 **màihuāde nǚháizi** *the girl who sells flowers* 修理房子的费用 **xiūlǐ fángzide fèiyong** *the expense of repairing the house*
clauses	我在中国留学的那年 **wǒ zài Zhōngguó liúxuéde nèinián** *the year I was studying in China* 你去年买给我的那件外套 **nǐ qùnián mǎigěi wǒde nèijiàn wàitào** *that coat you bought for me last year*

As you may have noticed, the modifier is linked to the noun using the particle 的 **de** in most of the above examples but not always. This is not random, as there are some rules of thumb regarding the use of this particle.

1. There are two situations in which the particle 的 **de** cannot be used between the modifier and the noun:

a. When the modifier is integral to the noun in the Chinese linguistic mindset. This is similar to words like *blackbird*, *blackboard* and *mankind* in English. These integral modifiers tend to be single syllables, but not always.

nouns with integral modifiers (no 的 de)	counter examples with 的 de
男学生 **nán xuésheng** *male students*	男的服务员 **nánde fúwùyuán** *male waiters*
女朋友 **nǚpéngyou** *girlfriend*	女的婴儿 **nǚde yīng'ér** *female infants* (alternative abbreviated term is 女婴 **nǚyīng**)
我家 **wǒjiā** *my home*	我的家园 **wǒde jiāyuán** *my home (and garden)*
我母亲 **wǒ mǔqin** *my mother*, 国父 **guófù** *nation's founding father*	人类的救星 **rénlèide jiùxīng** *mankind's savior*
白衬衫 **bái chènshān** *white shirt*, 白领阶层 **báilǐng jiēcéng** *white-collar class*	蓝色的领带 **lánsède lǐngdài** *a blue tie*
乌云 **wūyún** *dark clouds*, 蓝天 **lántiān** *blue sky*	黄色的河水 **huángsède héshuǐ** *brown river water*
黄鱼 **huángyú** *yellow fish*, 白鹅 **bái'é** *white geese*	花白的狗 **huābáide gǒu** *a spotty gray dog*
博士论文 **bóshì lùnwén** *doctoral thesis*, 大学教授 **dàxué jiàoshòu** *college professor*	学生的文章 **xuéshengde wénzhāng** *students' essays*
卖国贼 **màiguózéi** *traitor* (lit. "sell nation thief")	卖旧货的摊子 **mài jiùhuòde tānzi** *a stall that sells second-hand goods*
流行歌曲 **liúxíng gēqǔ** *popular song*	动人的歌曲 **dòngrénde gēqǔ** *moving songs*

b. When the modified noun is used in a formal or literary context, as in the titles of books, movies or brand names. For example:

- 红衣少女 **Hóngyī Shàonǚ** *The Girl in Red* (an old film)
- 蓝带啤酒 **Lándài Píjiǔ** *Blue Ribbon Beer*
- 红色黄昏 **hóngsè huánghūn** *red dusk*

2. Conversely, there are certain situations in which the modifier and the noun *must* be connected by 的 **de**:

a. When the modifier is a verb phrase or a clause (the last two types in the table at the top of p. 325).

- 开公共汽车的司机 **kāi gōnggòng qìchēde sījī** (alternative 公车司机 **gōngchē sījī**) *drivers who drive buses*
- 卖保险的公司 **mài bǎoxiǎnde gōngsī** (alternative 保险公司 **bǎoxiǎn gōngsī**) *company that sells insurance*

Note: In the two above examples, the *verb phrase* modifier may be replaced by a noun modifier which is considered an integral part of the noun, in which case 的 **de** may be dispensed with.

- 打工的大学生 **dǎgōngde dàxuésheng** *college students who work (part-time)*
- 学汉语的留学生 **xué Hànyǔde liúxuésheng** *foreign students studying Chinese*
- 他在这两个月内认识的朋友 **tā zài zhèiliǎngge yuè nèi rènshide péngyou** *the friends he made in the last two months*
- 李老师教过我们的课本 **Lǐ Lǎoshī jiāoguo wǒmende kèběn** *the textbooks that Teacher Li has taught us*

b. When the modifier is another noun indicating possession

- 老王的妻子 **Lǎo Wángde qīzi** *Old Wang's wife*
- 王老师的办公室 **Wáng Lǎoshīde bàngōngshì** *Teacher Wang's office*
- 我们家的洗衣机 **wǒmen jiāde xǐyījī** *our family's washing machine*
- 学校的电脑 **xuéxiàode diànnǎo** *the school's computers*
- 学生的信箱 **xuéshengde xìnxiāng** *students' mailboxes*
- 国家的企业 **guójiāde qǐyè** *state-owned enterprises* (an alternative term is 国营企业 **guóyíng qǐyè**, in which 国营 **guóyíng** *state-run* is integral to the noun)

c. The same rule of thumb applies to pronouns as well, but with one exception. When the notion of "possession" actually indicates a close personal relationship, 的 **de** is optional if the pronoun is single syllable, and in exceptional cases, even if the pronoun is bisyllabic.

correct examples	incorrect parallel examples
他的妻子 **tāde qīzi** or 他妻子 **tā qīzi** his wife	✘老王妻子 **Lǎo Wáng qīzi** Old Wang's wife (老王 Lǎo Wáng is neither a pronoun nor monosyllabic)
他的母亲 **tāde mǔqin** or 他母亲 **tā mǔqin** his mother, 他们的母亲 **tāmende mǔqin** their mother	✘他们母亲 **tāmen mǔqin** (他们 **tāmen** is two syllables)
我家 **wǒjiā** or 我的家 **wǒde jiā** my home, 他们家 **tāmen jiā** or 他们的家 **tāmende jiā** their home	In contrast to 他们母亲 **tāmen mǔqin** in the "incorrect" box above, 他们家 **tāmen jiā** is acceptable. This is simply one of those irregularities in the language.
我的朋友 **wǒde péngyou** or 我朋友 **wǒ péngyou** my friend	✘我办公室 **wǒ bàngōngshì** my office (this phrase is not about a close personal relationship)

3. When a noun is modified by a *stative verb* (first type of modifiers listed in the table on p. 324), the usage of 的 **de** hinges on whether the *stative verb* has one or more syllables. With most single syllable *stative verbs*, 的 **de** is dispensed with. *Stative verbs* with two or more syllables generally require 的 **de**. But there are exceptions in both directions.

a. Monosyllabic *stative verbs* used with nouns (where 的 **de** is not used):

好人 **hǎorén** good person   新衣服 **xīn yīfu** new clothes
笨孩子 **bèn háizi** stupid kid   大苹果 **dà píngguǒ** big apple

Exceptions of monosyllabic modifiers linked to nouns using 的 **de**:

贵的书 **guìde shū** (✘贵书 **guìshū**) expensive books
对的答案 **duìde dá'àn** (✘对答案 **duì dá'àn**) correct answers

b. Stative verbs with two or more syllables modifying nouns using 的 **de**:

努力的学生 **nǔlìde xuésheng** diligent students
舒服的环境 **shūfude huánjìng** comfortable environment
有意思的问题 **yǒuyìside wèntí** interesting questions
便宜的东西 **piányide dōngxi** inexpensive things

Exception of a bisyllabic modifier linked to a noun without 的 **de**:

便宜货 **piányi-huò** cheap goods

In the face of so many exceptions to the rule of thumb, there is one strategy that you may use to avoid outright error. When in doubt about whether 的 **de** may be omitted after a stative verb, go ahead and include it. At worst, you may run the risk of sounding a bit wordy. In other words, expressions like the following are acceptable even though the use of 的 de is unnecessary:

新的衣服 **xīnde yīfu** *new clothes*　　　笨的孩子 **bènde háizi** *stupid kid*

大的苹果 **dàde píngguǒ** *big apple*　　　便宜的货 **piányide huò** *cheap goods*

On the other hand, omitting 的 de when it is necessary can result in unacceptable expressions like the following:

- ✗ 客气朋友 **kèqi péngyou** *polite friends*
- ✗ 聪明学生 **cōngming xuésheng** *smart students*
- ✗ 有意思题目 **yǒuyìsi tímù** *interesting topics*
- ✗ 贵书 **guì shū** *expensive books*
- ✗ 对答案 **duì dá'àn** *correct answers*

All of the above should have 的 de between the modifier and the noun.

4. Sometimes, the inclusion of 的 de creates a difference in meaning. For example:

no 的 de	with 的 de
中国朋友 **Zhōngguó péngyou** *Chinese friend*	中国的朋友 **Zhōngguóde péngyou** *China's ally*
老朋友 **lǎo péngyou** *old friend* (long-time friend)	老的朋友 **lǎode péngyou** *elderly friend*
美国人 **Měiguórén** *an American*	美国的人民 **Měiguóde rénmín** *American people*
大熊猫 **dàxióngmāo** *giant panda* (a species)	大的熊猫 **dàde xióngmāo** *a big panda*

If we compare the expressions in the first column with the ones listed in 1(a) (p. 325), the modifiers may not seem as integral to the nouns as those, but compared with the ones in the second column, they are definitely more integrated.

5. When multiple noun modifiers are used:

a. When a noun is modified by two or more *stative verb* phrases, the following rules apply: the longer ones generally precede the shorter ones. The last "detached" modifier (not including the one that is connected to the noun without an intervening 的 de) carries the "suffix" 的 de, and the preceding phrases have this option as well. As you read these examples, take note of the different ordering of modifiers in Chinese and English.

- 黄色的大房子 **huángsède dàfángzi** *a big yellow house*
- 那只黑白两色(的)、可爱的小狗 **nèizhī hēibái liǎngsè(de), kě'àide xiǎogǒu**
  or 那只可爱的、黑白两色的小狗 **nèizhī kě'àide, hēibái liǎngsède xiǎogǒu**
  that cute black and white puppy

- 有意思的、好看的美国电影 yǒuyìside, hǎokànde Měiguó diànyǐng
  American movies that are good and interesting

b. When a noun is modified by several different types of modifiers, the following word order is observed (refer to types of modifiers in the table on p. 324):

   i. a noun or pronoun indicating possession
   ii. a clause (may include phrase indicating time or location)
   iii. a verbal phrase
   iv. a phrase indicating time or location
   v. a stative verb

◆ 老王挂在客厅里的国画怎么不见了？
  Lǎo Wáng guàzài kètīnglide guóhuà zěnme bújiànle?
  How come that Chinese painting of Old Wang's that was hanging in the living room has disappeared?

◆ 我们晚上常看的那个电视节目被取消了。
  Wǒmen wǎnshang chángkànde nèige diànshì jiémù bèi qǔxiāole.
  That TV show that we often watch in the evening has been cancelled.

◆ 我每天都找机会用上老师当天教过的生词。
  Wǒ měitiān dōu zhǎo jīhuì yòngshang lǎoshī dāngtiān jiāoguode shēngcí.
  Every day I look for opportunities to use the new vocabulary that the teacher has taught us that day.

◆ 研究所第一年的课程最难。 **Yánjiūsuǒ dìyīniánde kèchéng zuì nán.**
  The courses in the first year of graduate school are the most difficult.

◆ 为了学习中文，我常常看有意思的、好看的中国电影。
  Wèile xuéxí Zhōngwén, wǒ chángchang kàn yǒuyìside, hǎokànde Zhōngguó diànyǐng.
  For the sake of practicing Chinese, I often watch good and interesting Chinese movies.

◆ 和我一起上大学的那些老朋友差不多都出国了。
  Hé wǒ yìqǐ shàng dàxuéde nèixiē lǎopéngyou chàbuduō dōu chūguó le.
  Almost all the old friends who went to college with me have gone abroad.

◆ 留在国内创业的那个同学后来成了最有成就的。
  Liúzài guónèi chuàngyède nèige tōngxué hòulái chéngle zuì yǒu-chéngjiù de.
  The classmate who stayed in China to establish a business became the most accomplished.

EXERCISES:

Translate the following sentences into Chinese:

1. The news we hear on TV is not necessarily true.
2. We used to live in that big white house next to the church.

3. <u>Our daughter, whom we adopted from China 20 years ago</u>, graduated from college this year!

> **ANSWERS:**
> 1. 我们在电视上看到的新闻不一定是真实的。
>   **Wǒmen zài diànshì-shang kàndàode xīnwén bù yídìng shì zhēnshíde.**
> 2. 我们从前住在教堂旁边的那个白色的大房子里。
>   **Wǒmen cóngqián zhùzài jiàotáng pángbiānde nèige báisède dà fángzili.**
> 3. 我们二十年前从中国领养的那个女儿今年大学毕业了！
>   **Wǒmen èrshí-nián qián cóng Zhōngguó lǐngyǎngde nèige nǚ'ér jīnnián dàxué bìyè le!**

15.3 Adding a specifier or number to a noun phrase with modifiers

Whenever a specifier (*this, that, these, those*) and/or a number precedes a noun, a measure word must be inserted as well (see 4.1). The resulting *specifier + number + measure* cluster may either precede the modifier or come right before the noun. Of these two possible options, the latter—with the *specifier + number + measure* cluster after the modifier—is more common in Chinese, which is the opposite of the usual word order in English.

♦ *The two landscape paintings hanging on the living room wall were painted by Old Wang himself.*
挂在客厅里的<u>那两幅</u>山水画是老王自己画的。(more common)
Guàzài kètīnglǐde <u>nèi liǎngfú</u> shānshuǐhuà shì Láo Wáng zìjǐ huà de.
<u>那两幅</u>挂在客厅里的山水画是老王自己画的。(acceptable)
<u>Nèi liǎngfú</u> guàzài kètīnglǐde shānshuǐhuà shì Láo Wáng zìjǐ huà de.

♦ *All four Chinese language teachers who taught me in college were excellent.*
在大学教过我的<u>那四位</u>中文老师都非常好。(more common)
Zài dàxué jiāoguo wǒde <u>nèi sìwèi</u> Zhōngwén lǎoshī dōu fēicháng hǎo.
<u>那四位</u>在大学教过我的中文老师都非常好。(acceptable)
<u>Nèi sìwèi</u> zài dàxué jiāoguo wǒde Zhōngwén lǎoshī dōu fēicháng hǎo.

Because nouns in Chinese have no singular/plural distinction, a noun modified by a long phrase may be interpreted in three ways: 1) as referring to all entities in the category; 2) referring to one or more specific entities; 3) ambiguous as to which of the two is intended. This is where specifiers and the adverb 都 **dōu** come into play. To avoid ambiguity, native speakers tend to include a specifier and/or the adverb 都 **dōu**.

♦ *In the past five years, Chinese students who come to study in the U.S. tend to be rich.*
这五年以来，来美国留学的中国学生通常都很富有。(all-inclusive)
Zhè wǔnián yǐlái, lái Měiguó liúxuéde Zhōngguó xuésheng tōngcháng <u>dōu</u> hěn fùyǒu.

♦ *Foreign scholars who study Chinese literature should be able to speak Chinese fluently.*

研究中国文学的外国学者都应该能说一口流利的中文。(all-inclusive)
Yánjiū Zhōngguó wénxuéde wàiguó xuézhě <u>dōu</u> yīnggāi néng shuō yìkǒu liúlìde Zhōngwén.

♦ *The Princeton professor who teaches Chinese literature speaks Chinese fluently.*

教中国文学的那位普大教授能说一口流利的中文。(a specific professor)
Jiāo Zhōngguó wénxuéde <u>nèiwèi</u> Pǔ-Dà jiàoshòu néng shuō yìkǒu liúlìde Zhōngwén.

or 那位教中国文学的普大教授⋯
   <u>Nèiwèi</u> jiāo Zhōngguó wénxuéde Pǔ-Dà jiàoshòu...

EXERCISES:

Translate the following sentences into Chinese:

1. <u>Foreigners who speak Chinese well</u> generally have many Chinese friends.

2. <u>The vegetables that you bought from that supermarket</u> are not very fresh.

3. <u>The four Chinese movies we saw in Chinese class this semester</u> are all very interesting.

ANSWERS:
1. 中文说得好的外国人通常有很多中国朋友。
   Zhōngwén shuōde hǎode wàiguó-rén tōngcháng yǒu hěn duō Zhōngguó péngyou.
2. 你在那个超市买的那些蔬菜不太新鲜。
   Nǐ zài nèige chāoshì mǎide nèixiē shūcài bú tài xīnxian.
3. 我们这个学期在中文课上看的那四部中国电影都非常有意思。
   Wǒmen zhèige xuéqī zài Zhōngwén kè-shang kànde nèi sìbù Zhōngguó diànyǐng dōu fēicháng yǒuyìsi.

15.4 Using 是⋯ shì... to assert a fact or to focus on a particular element

The preceding three sections were about the grammatical ordering of sentence elements. The two final two sections here are about another kind of ordering—how to confer primacy on a particular element within a sentence. The reason for doing this can be to convey concession or focus, to contrast two or more items, or to convey contradiction (against an assumption). There are two ways to accomplish this in Chinese, however, they are complementary and only one of them may be used in any given situation.

The first is to use the *topic + comment* sentence pattern (see 1.3, section 1). The second is the 是⋯ **shì...** pattern. If you already know about the 是⋯的 **shì...de** pattern, you may be momentarily confused at this point, wondering whether these two patterns are the same. Actually, 是⋯的 **shì...de** is a corollary of 是⋯ **shì...**, and we will get to that in the next section. For now, consider the following examples of the 是⋯ **shì...** pattern. As you read each sentence, identify the element being emphasized.

◆ *He IS very diligent, but his memory is too poor, [so] no matter how he studies he can't get it.*
他是很用功，可是记性太差了，怎么学也学不会。(concession)
Tā shì hěn yònggōng, kěshì jìxìng tài chà le, zěnme xué yě xué-bu-huì.

◆ *Elementary language textbooks ARE uninteresting, but nothing can be done about it.*
初级的语言课本是没有意思，可是没办法。(concession)
Chūjíde yǔyán kèběn shì méiyǒu yìsi, kěshì méi bànfǎ.

◆ *I want to help you, not to criticize you.* (emphasis is conveyed by intonation in English)
我是想帮助你，不是要批评你。(contrast, contradiction)
Wǒ shì xiǎng bāngzhù nǐ, búshì yào pīpíng nǐ.

◆ *It's not tomorrow that they are arriving, it's the day after tomorrow.*
他们不是明天到，是后天才到。(contrast, contradiction)
Tāmen búshì míngtiān dào, shì hòutiān cái dào.

◆ *I want to tell you about our company's newest product, not to necessarily sell it to you.*
我是想告诉你我们公司的最新产品，不是一定要向你推销。
(contrast, contradict)
Wǒ shì xiǎng gàosu nǐ wǒmen gōngsīde zuìxīn chǎnpǐn, búshì yídìng yào xiàng nǐ tuīxiāo.

When the main verb in a sentence is 是 **shì**, the way to superimpose the 是⋯ **shì...** pattern for emphasis is simply to put extra stress on the word 是 **shì**.

◆ *He IS a Chinese American, how can you say he is Chinese?*
他是美籍华人啊，你怎么说他是中国人呢？ (contradiction)
Tā shì Měijí Huárén a, nǐ zěnme shuō tā shì Zhōngguórén ne?
(The sentence-ending particle 啊 is an additional device for adding emphasis.)

◆ *Global warming IS an obvious reality, how come there are still people who deny this today?*
全球变暖是一个明显的事实，怎么今天还有人否认这一点呢？
Quánqiú biànnuǎn shì yíge míngxiǎnde shìshí, zěnme jīntiān hái yǒurén fǒurèn zhè yìdiǎn ne?

15.5 Using 是⋯的 shì... de when referring to completed actions or events

The 是⋯的 **shì...de** pattern is a corollary of the 是⋯ **shì...** pattern, in that it too is used to assert a fact, or to confer emphasis on a particular element in a sentence. The following example illustrates the difference this pattern makes in presenting a fact.

He arrived yesterday.   vs   It was yesterday that he arrived.
他昨天到了。 **Tā zuótiān dàole.**   他是昨天到的。 **Tā shì zuótiān dào de.**

The 是···的 **shì...de** pattern is applied to established facts or actions/events that have been completed. In this respect, it parallels the aspect marker 了 **le**, which indicates "completion of an action." It overlaps with the past tense in English, but is not equivalent to it (see 7.1). In other words, the concept of tense in English is replaced by the concept of aspect in Chinese. The three examples below illustrate the fact that 是···的 **shì...de** is not necessarily applied only to events in the past, and 是··· **shì...** is not necessarily applied only to events in the present and future.

♦ *Columbus wasn't headed for America, he thought he was headed for Asia!* (past) (focus on destination, contrasting Columbus' intention with the actual outcome.)
哥伦布<u>不是</u>要到美洲去，其实他以为他<u>是</u>到亚洲去。
Gēlúnbù <u>búshì</u> **yào dào Měizhōu qù, qíshí tā yǐwéi tā** <u>shì</u> **dào Yàzhōu qù.**
Note: Even though this is in the past, 要 **yào** and 以为 **yǐwéi** are not *actions* that can be *completed*. Hence the "是··· **shì...**" pattern is the correct one to use here.

♦ *The feeling that humans have for dogs is not the same as for other animals.* (present)
人对狗的感情跟对别的动物<u>是</u>不一样<u>的</u>。 (asserting an established fact)
Rén duì gǒude gǎnqíng gēn duì biéde dòngwù <u>shì bù yíyàng de</u>.

♦ *Eating dog meat in China can only be called inhumane; legally, it is not a crime.* (present)
在中国吃狗肉只能说是不人道，在法律上<u>是</u>没有罪<u>的</u>。
(asserting an established fact)
Zài Zhōngguó chī gǒuròu zhǐnéng shuō shì bù réndào, zài fǎlǜ-shang <u>shì méiyǒu zuì de</u>.

As you read each of the examples below, note the difference in meaning between the patterns 是··· **shì...** and 是···的 **shì...de**.

♦ *I would like to go with you, but I'm simply too busy.*
我<u>是</u>想跟你一起去，可是我实在太忙了。
Wǒ <u>shì</u> **xiǎng gēn nǐ yìqǐ qù, kěshì wǒ shízài tài máng le.**

♦ *She originally planned to get married next year, but later she decided to get married this year.*
她原来<u>是</u>打算明年才结婚<u>的</u>，可是后来决定今年就结婚了。
Tā yuánlái <u>shì</u> **dǎsuàn míngnián cái jiéhūn** <u>de</u>, **kěshì hòulái juédìng jīnnián jiù jiéhūn le.**

♦ *He was born in the U.S., so we can say he is a Chinese American.*
他<u>是</u>在美国出生<u>的</u>，所以我们可以说他是个美籍华人。
Tā <u>shì</u> **zài Měiguó chūshēng** <u>de</u>, **suǒyǐ wǒmen kěyǐ shuō tā shì ge Měijí Huárén.**

♦ *It was because she got pregnant that she dropped out of school.*
她<u>是</u>因为怀了孕而离开学校<u>的</u>。 **Tā** <u>shì</u> **yīnwèi huái-le-yùn ér líkāi xuéxiào** <u>de</u>.

♦ *At the time, I thought I would return to China when I graduated, but later I married an American and stayed.*
我当时是想毕业以后就回国，后来嫁给了一个美国人就留下来了。
Wǒ dāngshí <u>shì</u> xiǎng bìyè yǐhòu jiù huíguó, hòulái jiàgěile yíge Měiguórén jiù liú-xiàlai le.

The 是··· 的 **shì...de** pattern is normally a "frame" that begins and ends the verb phrase of the sentence. This is illustrated by the relevant examples above. However, there are two exceptions to this:

1. When the verb phrase of the sentence consists of a *verb + object*, the preferred position for 的 **de** is before the object of the verb.

♦ *It was two months ago that she arrived in Beijing.*
她是两个月以前<u>到</u>的北京。(preferred)
Tā shì liǎngge yuè yǐqián <u>dàode</u> Běijīng.
or 她<u>是</u>两个月以前到北京<u>的</u>。(acceptable)
Tā <u>shì</u> liǎngge yuè yǐqián dào Běijīng <u>de</u>.

♦ *They got married in a park, not in a church.* (emphasis on venue of the wedding)
他们是在一个公园里<u>结的婚</u>，不是在教堂结的。
Tāmen shì zài yíge gōngyuánlǐ <u>jié-de-hūn</u>, búshì zài jiàotáng jié de.
or 他们不是在教堂而是在一个公园里<u>结的婚</u>。
Tāmen búshì zài jiàotáng érshì zài yíge gōngyuánlǐ <u>jié-de-hūn</u>.

♦ *It was only last week that I bought this bike, how come it's broken down already?*
我是上个星期才<u>买的这辆自行车</u>，怎么已经坏了？(preferred)
Wǒ shì shàngge xīngqī cái <u>mǎide zhèliàng zìxíngchē</u>, zěnme yǐjīng huàile?
or 这辆自行车，我是上个星期才买的，··· (acceptable)
Zhèliàng zìxíngchē, wǒ shì shàngge xīngqī cái mǎi de,...

2. When the verb phrase is long, the 是 **shì** part of the "frame" may be understood and omitted. This seems ironic because 是 **shì** is the word that conveys the idea of assertion whereas 的 **de** simply "brings up the rear." In real life conversations, the aspect being emphasized is usually clear from context. Therefore, the omission of 是 **shì** does not lead to misunderstanding.

♦ Principal of a prep school to concerned parents:
Rest assured! Your child would absolutely not become addicted to drugs at our school.
你们放心吧！你们的孩子绝对不会在我们这所学校染上毒瘾<u>的</u>。
(firm assertion)
Nǐmen fàngxīn ba! Nǐmende háizi juéduì búhuì zài wǒmen zhèisuǒ xuéxiào rǎn-shàng dúyǐn de.

◆ *At the time, I thought she would return after two years, in the end she left and never came back.* (focus on "after two years")

当时我以为她两年以后就会回来的，结果她一去就再也没回来。

Dāngshí wǒ yǐwéi tā liǎngnián yíhòu jiù huì huílai de, jiéguǒ tā yí qù jiù zài yě méi huílai.

EXERCISES:

Translate the following sentences into Chinese:

1. I came by airplane, not by train.

2. Apple computers are an American brand, although most of them are made in China.

3. Although there are people who say Obama was not born in the U.S., he was in fact born in the U.S.

4. My Chinese was learned in Taiwan, not in mainland China. In that era, it was not possible for Americans to go to China.

ANSWERS:

1. 我是坐飞机来的，不是坐火车来的。or 我是坐飞机而不是坐火车来的。
   Wǒ shì zuò fēijī lái de, bú shì zuò huǒchē lái de. or Wǒ shì zuò fēijī ér bú shì zuò huǒchē lái de.

2. 苹果电脑是美国的品牌，不过多半是中国制造的。
   Píngguǒ diànnǎo shì Měiguóde pǐnpái, búguò duōbàn shì zài Zhōngguó zhìzào de.

3. 虽然有人说奥巴马不是在美国出生的，实际上他是在美国出生的。
   Suīrán yǒurén shuō Àobāmā bú shì zài Měiguó chūshēng de, shíjì-shang tā shì zài Měiguó chūshsēng de.

4. 我的中文是在台湾学的，不是在中国大陆学的。那个时代，美国人不可能到中国去。**Wǒde Zhōngwén shì zài Táiwān xué de, bú shì zài Zhōngguó dàlù xué de. Nèige shídài, Měiguórén bù kěnéng dào Zhōngguó qù.**

16 Speaking Like an Educated Person in Chinese

The final line from a Tang dynasty poem that has become a favorite Chinese phrase of all time is 更上一层楼 **gèng shàng yìcéng lóu**, meaning *to go up one more level*. This phrase applies to individuals who are already accomplished yet still aspire to achieve more. This chapter is intended for this breed of ambitious Chinese language learners.

The hallmark of a well-educated Chinese speaker is the ability to deliver paragraph-level discourse coherently and to nimbly incorporate set phrases like 更上一层楼 **gèng shàng yìcéng lóu** into their speech. This chapter delves into these two features of sophisticated Chinese speech. It is not a magic bullet, but it should give you the tools for continued self-improvement. The first two sections (16.1 and 16.2) below provide an introduction to the "nuts and bolts" of connected discourse; a topic which will receive a thorough treatment later in Part II. The last part of the chapter provides an overview of set phrases or sayings, called 成语 **chéngyǔ** in Chinese.

The "nuts and bolts" of connected discourse go by a number of names in Chinese. The label we will use here is 结构词 **jiégòucí** *structural words*—which to us comes closest to describing the function of these words that serve to frame the substance of discourse. It is this framing that lends clarity to the components and articulates their connections. The most common *structural words* like 因为··· 所以··· **yīnwèi...suǒyǐ...** are no doubt already in your repertoire. An additional 254 colloquial structures are covered in Part II of this book, and should provide you with all the essential patterns needed for extended discourse in Chinese.

Another Chinese term for these language tools is 虚词 **xūcí**, which literally means *empty words*. *Structural words* always include some "emptiness" in order to fulfill their structural function. However, they often, but not always, carry some substantive meaning as well. So they are actually a class of words whose meanings straddle the substantive and the structural. Language buffs refer to them as "semanto-syntactic" words. Whatever we call them, they reflect how the Chinese linguistic mind structures thoughts into sentences.

Structural words tend to be more difficult to translate into English than regular *substantive words*, and dictionaries often do not provide good definitions. To be sure, English has structural words as well, but they are more abundant and diverse in Chinese. Most of them do not have exact equivalents in English. For your convenience, we will provide rough English translations of these words. Wherever appropriate, we will also supplement these rough translations with brief explanations. Ultimately though, it is the examples that will provide the "immersive experience" needed to intuitively grasp the meanings of the terms.

Students at the advanced level generally understand *structural words* without much difficulty, but using them spontaneously in discourse requires deliberate practice. When we express ourselves in another language, we naturally think of the substantive elements first. Inserting *structural words* appropriately is a cultivated habit. There is always a gap between what we understand passively and what we can use actively. This phenomenon is especially true of structural vocabulary.

The majority of *structural words* in Chinese operate in pairs. An example is the partnering of 因为 **yīnwèi** *because* with 所以 **suǒyǐ** *therefore*. In real life conversations, as soon as the first of a duo is uttered, the listener is primed for the second shoe to drop. Even *structural words* that operate singly tend to be implicitly hitched to another clause. A sentence may also be framed by three *structural words*, such as 不要说···, 就是···, 也··· **búyào shuō..., jiùshi..., yě...** (*not to mention..., even... is...*). In this chapter, we will introduce the more common *structural words* that operate singly and in pairs. All of them will be illustrated with at least one example here, and will be reviewed in Part II with additional examples.

16.1 Using structural words: 16 basic "sentence frames"

Rather than presenting a random sampling of *structural words* here, we will focus on one theme: How Chinese speakers frame their discourse. We have chosen 16 *structures* (e.g. ways of "framing" thoughts into sentences) to illustrate two common characteristics of these expressions:

1) Their use indicates that the situation under discussion is complex and warrants discussion from different perspectives;
2) The reasoning does not follow a straight line toward the "target," but rather approaches it sideways or in a curve.

These two characteristics of "frames" formed by *structural words* enable the speaker to make a point without sounding argumentative, thereby speaking more effectively.

Each of the 16 structures in this section uses one of five approaches:

1) Conceding a point before making a counter argument;
2) Contrasting two situations;
3) Taking a given point one step further;
4) Using a rhetorical question to lead the listener to the speaker's point of view;
5) Using a negative or a double negative to drive home a point.

As you read the examples, try to identify the approach used by each of the following structures.

1. ···是···, 可是/不过··· **shì..., kěshì/búguò...** *granted..., but...*
    (可是 **kěshì** and 不过 **búguò** are interchangeable)

◆　金钱重要是重要，不过生活品质还是最重要的吧？
Jīnqián zhòngyào shì zhòngyào, búguò shēnghuó pǐnzhì háishi zuì zhòngyàode ba?
Granted money is important, but quality of life is still the most important, isn't it?

A variation of this pattern involves substituting 是 **shì** with 倒是 **dàoshi**, but there is a slight difference in nuance. 倒是 **dàoshi** implies that the speaker is conceding to a fact that runs counter to either his previous view or a commonly accepted view.

◆　你说的倒是有道理，可是在西方文化环境中，你的办法是行不通的。
Nǐ shuōde dàoshi yǒu dǎolǐ, kěshì zài Xīfāng wénhuà huánjìng-zhōng, nǐde bànfǎ shì xíng-bu-tōng de.
(Alright), what you say makes sense, but in the Western cultural environment, your way is not workable.

2. 固然…，但是/可是/然而… **gùrán…, dànshì/kěshì/rán'ér…** *admittedly…, and yet…; given the fact that…, still…* (This is a more formal version of the preceding structure.)

◆　事业成就固然重要，然而如果没有健康的心态，一切都是空谈。
Shìyè chéngjiù gùrán zhòngyào, rán'ér rúguǒ méiyǒu jiànkāngde xīntài, yíqiè dōu shì kōngtán.
Of course professional achievement is important, but without a healthy mentality, it's all meaningless.

3. 别以为…，其实… **bié yǐwéi…, qíshí…** *don't (mistakenly) think that…, actually…*

◆　别以为妈妈不上班，在家里照顾孩子就很轻松，其实那也是一份全职的工作！ **Bié yǐwéi Māma bú shàngbān, zài jiālǐ zhàogu háizi jiù hěn qīngsōng, qíshí nà yěshì yífèn quánzhíde gōngzuò!**
We mustn't think that it's easy-going for a non-working mother to stay at home taking care of the children, actually that too is a full-time job!

4. 不但…，反而(还)… **búdàn…, fǎn'ér(hái)…** *not only…on the contrary…*
This structure is a more eloquent variation of the familiar structure 不但…，而且… **búdàn…, érqiě…** *not only…, but also….* The phrase that begins with 不但 **búdàn** is in the negative, indicating that something that is expected is not happening. The follow-up phrase that begins with 反而 **fǎn'ér** states a further step in the direction initiated in the 不但 **búdàn** phrase. The pairing is what makes this structure more forceful. The substance of the sentence is not necessarily negative however (see second example below).

◆　我跟她道歉以后，她不但没有原谅我，反而决定要跟我分手了。
Wǒ gēn tā dàoqiàn yǐhòu, tā búdàn méiyǒu yuánliàng wǒ, fǎn'ér juédìng yào gēn wǒ fēnshǒu le.
After I apologized to her, not only did she not forgive me, on the contrary she decided to break up with me.

- 老师得知他缺课是因为家里出了事，不但没有责备他，反而给他补了课。**Lǎoshī dézhī tā quēkè shì yīnwèi jiālǐ chū-le-shì, búdàn méiyǒu zébèi tā, fǎn'ér gěi tā bǔ-le-kè.**
When the teacher learned that he missed class because something happened at home, she not only didn't reprimand him, she even gave him a make-up class.

5. 不是…而是… **búshì…érshì…** *it is not…, but rather…*

- 教授起的最重要的作用不是传授知识，而是唤起学生对学习的热情。**Jiàoshòu qǐde zuì zhòngyàode zuòyòng búshì chuánshòu zhīshi, érshì huànqǐ xuésheng duì xuéxíde rèqíng.**
The most important function of professors is not to transmit knowledge, but to inspire a love for learning in students.

6. 与其…，不如… **yǔqí…, bùrú…** *rather than…, it is better to…*
This structure is quite formal and eloquent. What follows 与其 **yǔqí** is *not as good as* what follows 不如 **bùrú**, hence whatever follows 不如 **bùrú** is *better than* whatever follows 与其 **yǔqí**. The example below and the ones in Part II of the book will help you get the hang of this rather convoluted structure. Your well-educated Chinese peers will surely be impressed if they hear you using it!

- 与其把闷气憋在心里，不如当面把问题说开。
Yǔqí bǎ mēnqì biēzài xīnli, bùrú dāngmiàn bǎ wèntí shuōkāi.
Rather than stifle resentment in silence, it would be better to talk through the issue face to face.

7. 别说…，就是…也… **biéshuō…, jiùshi…yě…** *not to mention…, even…is…*
不要说…，就是…也… **búyào shuō…, jiùshi…yě…** *not to mention…, even…is…*

- 有了孩子以后，别说旅行了，就是周末去看个电影也不行。**Yǒule háizi yǐhòu, biéshuō lǚxíng le, jiùshi zhōumò qù kàn ge diànyǐng yě bùxíng.**
After we had a child, we could not even go see a movie on the weekend, not to mention traveling. (Note the order of the latter two phrases in English is reversed from the Chinese.)

- 那么复杂的项目，不要说一个星期了，就是一个月也做不完。**Nàme fùzáde xiàngmù, búyào shuō yíge xīngqī le, jiùshi yíge yuè yě zuò-bu-wán.**
Such a complex project, we wouldn't be able to finish it in even a month, not to mention just a week.

8. 更不用说…了 **gèng búyòng shuō…le** *to say nothing of…; not to mention…*

- 那年经济不景气，连日用品的销路都受到影响，奢侈品就更不用说了。**Nèinián jīngjì bù jǐngqì, lián rìyòngpǐnde xiāolù dōu shòudào yǐngxiǎng, shēchǐpǐn jiù gèng búyòng shuō le.**
The economy was in recession that year, even the sale of daily necessities was affected, to say nothing of luxury goods.

9. ···，何况 ..., **hékuàng** *much less, let alone*

This structure is a more formal version of the preceding one. Its succinctness also makes it more eloquent.

🔹 世界上没有完美的人，何况年轻人，犯点错误是可以原谅的。
Shìjièshang méiyǒu wánměide rén, hékuàng niánqīng-rén, fàn diǎn cuòwù shì kěyǐ yuánliàng de.
There are no perfect humans in this world, let alone young people, making a few mistakes is forgivable.

10. 哪儿/哪里···(啊/呢)? **nǎr/nǎli...(a/ne)?** *rhetorical question conveying disagreement*

🔹 哪儿有这样的事啊？你在开玩笑吧？
Nǎr yǒu zhèyàngde shì a? Nǐ zài kāi wánxiào ba?
How can there be such a thing? You've got to be joking!

🔹 过奖了，我的汉语哪里能跟土生土长的中国人比呢？
Guòjiǎngle, wǒde Hànyǔ nǎli néng gēn tǔshēng-tǔzhǎngde Zhōngguórén bǐ ne?
Your praise is overdone, how can my Chinese be compared with a Chinese born and bred in China?
(This sentence is tongue in cheek, as it does in fact manifest native-level linguistic and cultural proficiency.)

11. 何必···(呢)? **hébì...(ne)?** *why must...?* (rhetorical)

🔹 当前全国各地都有发展的机会,你何必一定要留在一线城市呢？
Dāngqián quánguó gèdì dōu yǒu fāzhǎnde jīhuì, nǐ hébì yídìng yào liúzài yīxiàn chéngshì ne?
There are now opportunities for development throughout the country, why must you stay in a first-tier city?

12. 难道···(吗)? **nándào...(ma)?** *you don't mean...?* (incredulous)

This structure is a favorite among Chinese speakers. Even though it has already appeared in the previous section, it deserves a couple more examples here.

🔹 何必那么垂头丧气呢？难道有机化学不及格就不能学医了吗？
Hébì nàme chuítóu-sàngqì ne? Nándào yǒujī-huàxué bù jígé jiù bùnéng xué yī le ma?
Why be so crestfallen? You don't mean just failing organic chemistry will prevent you from studying medicine?

🔹 来自世界各国的留学生都能做到，难道美国本土的研究生就做不到吗？
Láizì shìjiè gèguóde liúxuésheng dōu néng zuòdào, nándào Měiguó běntǔde yánjiūshēng jiù zuò-bu-dào ma?
Foreign students from around the world can all do this, how could it be that native American graduate students are not capable of it?

13. 不得不 **bùdébù** *cannot but...*

This double negative structure is more eloquent than a positive sentence using 必得 **bìděi** *must*.

♦ 为了供她上大学,她的父母不得不节衣缩食。
Wèile gōng tā shàng dàxué, tāde fùmǔ bùdébù jiéyī-suōshí.
To support her college education, her parents had no choice but to tighten their belts (even with basic necessities like clothing and food).

14. 不是不···，是/可是... **búshì bù..., shì/kěshì...** *it's not that..., but rather...*

The first clause in this structure states a premise that will be refuted by the second clause.

♦ 真抱歉！我不是不肯帮忙，实在是力不从心。
Zhēn bàoqiàn! Wǒ búshì bù kěn bāngmáng, shízài shì lì-bù-cóng-xīn.
I'm really sorry! It's not that I'm unwilling to help, but in truth "my ability is not up to following my heart."

15. 非···不可/不行 **fēi...bùkě/bùxíng** *absolutely must...*; (lit. "not...will not do")

Like the 不得不 **bùdébù** structure, the double negative here is more powerful than a positive sentence using 必得 **bìděi** "must."

♦ 他是个慢性子，你要他做任何事，非提醒他三次不可。
Tā shì ge mànxìngzi, nǐ yào tā zuò rènhé shì, fēi tíxǐng tā sāncì bùkě.
He's a procrastinator, whatever you want him to do, you must remind him three times.

16. 非得/非要···才··· **fēiděi/fēiyào...cái...** *must...and only then..., have no choice but...*

The adverb 才 **cái** is the key word in this structure. If you have not totally mastered this word, this would be a good time to review it in 5.1, sec. 7. In this structure, the element stated before 才 is the indispensable requirement for the desired result.

♦ 看他呼吸困难的样子，非得叫个救护车才能及时送到医院急诊部了。
Kàn tā hūxī kùnnande yàngzi, fēiděi jiào ge jiùhùchē cái néng jíshí sòngdào yīyuàn jízhěnbù le.
Judging by the difficulty he has breathing, we must call an ambulance in order to get him to a hospital emergency room in time.

16.2 Structural words that operate alone

A characteristic of *structural words* demonstrated by the above example sentences is that they tend to come in pairs, just like nuts and bolts composed of two or more parts holding together physical structures. However, there are also many structural words that operate singly, and there are two common usages for them:

1) At the beginning of a two-part sentence, to set the stage or background for the key point of the sentence.

2) As an adverb, either before or after the subject, to indicate the "attitude" or mind-set of the speaker.

Below are examples of *structural words* used at the beginning of sentences. Take note of how these words articulate the relationship between the two parts of the sentence.

1. 对于 **duìyú** *toward, vis-a-vis*

♦ 对于那些愿意接受教育的少年犯，我们应该尽量多给予支持。
Duìyú nèixiē yuànyi jiēshòu jiàoyùde shàonián-fàn, wǒmen yīnggāi jìnliàng duō jǐyǔ zhīchí.
With regard to the juvenile delinquents who are willing to accept education, we should give them as much support as possible.

2. 关於 **guānyú** *concerning*

♦ 关于如何安置无家可归的市民，市政府刚推出了一个新方案。
Guānyú rúhé ānzhì wú-jiā-kě-guīde shìmín, shì-zhèngfǔ gāng tuīchūle yíge xīn fāng'àn.
On the issue of how to settle homeless people, the city government just came out with a new program.

Alternative: 市政府刚推出了一个关于如何安置无家可归市民的新方案。
Shì-zhèngfǔ gāng tuīchūle yíge guānyú rúhé ānzhì wú-jiā-kě-guī shìmínde xīn fāng'àn.

Note: The second sentence uses an alternative pattern, in which 关于···的 **guānyú... de** is a modifier of the noun. The first sentence, with the 关于··· **guānyú...** phrase set as the topic of the sentence, has a more clearly articulated structure.

3. 至于 **zhìyú** *as for*

♦ 美国人很喜欢看运动比赛。至于自己做锻炼，持之以恒的人就比较少了。 **Měiguórén hěn xǐhuan kàn yùndòng bǐsài. Zhìyú zìjǐ zuò duànliàn, chí-zhī-yǐ-héngde rén jiù bǐjiào shǎo le.**
Americans like to watch sports competitions. As for doing exercises themselves, there are fewer who stick with it.

4. 由于 **yóuyú** *due to*

♦ 由于进口商品的价格比较便宜，本国的工业很难发展起来。
Yóuyú jìnkǒu shāngpǐnde jiàgé bǐjiào piányi, běnguóde gōngyè hěn nán fāzhǎn-qǐlai.
Because imported goods are cheaper, domestic industries have a hard time developing.

5. 因此 **yīncǐ** *because of this, therefore*

♦ 本国的产品不如进口的便宜，因此，商店卖的日用品多半是进口
的。**Běnguóde chǎnpǐn bùrú jìnkǒude piányi, yīncǐ, shāngdiàn màide rìyòngpǐn
duōbàn shì jìnkǒude.**
*Domestic products are not as cheap as imports; therefore, most of the everyday
items sold in stores are imported.*

6. 除非 **chúfēi** *unless*

♦ 在中国，一个老人是不会单独生活的，除非他连一个家人都没有。
**Zài Zhōngguó, yíge lǎorén shì búhuì dāndú shēnghuó de, chúfēi tā lián yíge jiārén
dōu méiyǒu.**
In China, an old person would not live alone, unless he has no family whatsoever.

♦ 除非你把重男轻女的态度改掉，我是不会嫁给你的。
Chúfēi nǐ bǎ zhòngnán-qīngnǚde tàidù gǎidiào, wǒ shì búhuì jiàgěi nǐ de.
Unless you get rid of your sexist attitude, I will not marry you.

Note the two possible positions for the 除非⋯ **chúfēi...** clause in the above two
sentences. When 除非 **chúfēi** leads off the first clause in a two clause sentence, it
may also operate in tandem with 要不然 **yàoburán** *otherwise* in the second clause.

♦ 除非你非常热爱音乐，(要不然)当个音乐家不是那么轻松的。
Chúfēi nǐ fēicháng rè'ài yīnyuè, (yàoburán) dāng ge yīnyuè-jiā búshì nàme qīngsōng de.
*Unless you are passionate about music, otherwise, the life of a musician is not that
carefree.*

♦ 除非他在路上发生了问题，(要不然)今天晚上应该到了。
Chúfēi tā zài lùshang fāshēngle wèntí, (yàoburán) jīntiān wǎnshang yīnggāi dào le.
Unless he ran into some trouble en route, otherwise, he should be arriving tonight.

7. 如果 **rúguǒ...** or 要是 **yàoshi...** *if...*
The words 如果 **rúguǒ** and 要是 **yàoshi** are synonyms, but 要是 **yàoshi** is a bit
more colloquial.

♦ 如果你必须提早离校，可以请老师提前给你考试。
Rúguǒ nǐ bìxū tízǎo líxiào, kěyǐ qǐng lǎoshī tíqián gěi nǐ kǎoshì.
*If you need to leave school early, you can ask the teacher to give you the exam in
advance.*

A more colloquial way to express *if...* is putting ⋯的话 **...dehuà** at the end of the
clause, thus "framing" it from the back end. 如果⋯ **rúguǒ...** or 要是⋯ **yàoshi...** may
also be used in tandem with ⋯的话 **...dehuà**, thus framing the *if* clause on both ends.

♦ 你不能来的话，请早点儿告诉我。
Nǐ bùnéng lái dehuà, qǐng zǎodiǎnr gàosu wǒ.
If you cannot come, please let me know early.

- 如果我没走错路的话，就不会迟到了。
  Rúguǒ wǒ méi zǒu-cuò-lù dehuà, jiù búhuì chídào le.
  It I hadn't taken the wrong road, I wouldn't have been late.

In the following examples, the *structural words* are adverbs that indicate the "attitude" or mindset of the speaker toward the underlying background or context for the sentence. This class of adverbs may be positioned before or after the subject of the sentence.

8. 难道 **nándào** This literally means *difficult to say*, but is often translated as *do you really mean to say…?* It is a rhetorical way to express incredulity.

♠ 三年没见面了，难道你把我忘了！？ *or* …，你难道把我忘了！？
  Sānnián méi jiànmiàn le, nándào nǐ bǎ wǒ wàngle!? or …, nǐ nándào bǎ wǒ wàngle!?
  It's been three years since we've seen each other, can it be that you've forgotten me?!

9. 难免 **nánmiǎn** (lit., "difficult to be spared,") *unavoidable, inevitable*
A synonym of 难免 **nánmiǎn** is 免不了 **mǎin-bu-liǎo**. The two can be used interchangeably.

♠ 夫妻之间难免有时候会有矛盾。
  Fūqī zhījiān nánmiǎn yǒushíhou huì yǒu máodùn.
  Between husband and wife, it is inevitable that they will have disagreements at times.

10. 难怪 **nánguài** (lit., "difficult to take as odd,") *no wonder*
A synonym of 难怪 **nánguài** is 怪不得 **guài-bu-de**, and the two can be used interchangeably.

♠ 原来她父母都是音乐家，难怪她是个音乐天才。
  Yuánlái tā fùmǔ dōu shì yīnyuè-jiā, nánguài tā shì ge yīnyuè tiāncái.
  As it turns out, both of her parents are musicians; no wonder she is a musical prodigy.

11. 到底 **dàodǐ** (lit., "at the bottom,") *after all*

♠ 台湾的"国语"和大陆的"普通话"到底有什么不同？
  Táiwānde "guóyǔ" hé Dàlùde "pǔtōnghuà" dàodǐ yǒu shénme bùtóng?
  What, after all, is the difference between the "national language" of Taiwan and the "common language" of the Mainland?

♠ 到底是先有鸡还是先有鸡蛋，谁都不知道。
  Dàodǐ shì xiān yǒu jī háishi xiān yǒu jīdàn, shéi dōu bù zhīdao.
  Ultimately, no one knows if chickens came before eggs or vice versa.

16.3 Using ···而已 ...éryǐ at the end of a sentence to convey "that's all there is to it"

We single out the structure ··· 而已 **...éryǐ** in this section because it is unique in that it operates singly and comes at the end of a sentence. It is a term from literary Chinese that remains robust in contemporary discourse. Literally, it means *and that's the end*, implying that there is nothing more to be said. The literary flavor and the position at the end of the sentence make this term stand out as the most eloquent way to express the notion of *merely*.

♦ 在1949年，中国的人口大约是5.4亿而已。
 Zài 1949 nián, Zhōngguóde rénkǒu dàyuē shì 5.4 yì éryǐ.
 In 1949, China's population was only about 540 million.

♦ 我们不应该把"妇女能顶半边天"当作一个口号而已。
 Wǒmen bù yīnggāi bǎ "fùnǚ néng dǐng bànbiāntiān" dāngzuò yíge kǒuhào éryǐ.
 We should not take "women hold up half the sky" merely as a slogan.

The notion of *merely* may be further reinforced by an adverb (只是 **zhǐshì**, 不过 **búguò** or 就是 **jiùshi**), but it is still the 而已 **éryǐ** at the end of the sentence that delivers the punch.

♦ 那时候我不是真的想吸毒，<u>只是</u>想试试而已。
 Nà shíhou wǒ búshì zhēnde xiǎng xīdú, zhǐshì xiǎng shìshi éryǐ.
 At that time, I wasn't seriously thinking about taking drugs, I merely wanted to try it.

♦ 从前妇女在外工作<u>不过</u>是给家里添一点收入<u>而已</u>，并不是认真地发展自己的事业。**Cóngqián fùnǚ zài wài gōngzuò búguò shì gěi jiālǐ tiān yìdiǎn shōurù éryǐ, bìng búshì rènzhēnde fāzhǎn zìjǐde shìyè.**
 In former times, women worked outside of the home only to supplement their family's income, and not to seriously develop their own careers.

SUMMARY EXERCISES:

Consider these to be long-term exercises that you may do as you continue to progress in Chinese. If you have time now, it would be good to get started while this is all still fresh in your mind.

1. Go to Part II of the book and read additional examples of the structures introduced in this chapter.

2. Make up a sentence or two for each of the structures and try them out on native speakers.

3. As you listen to well-educated Chinese discoursing in paragraph style, take note of the structures that they use. In our era of the flourishing internet, talks on substantive topics can be found on the web, many with Chinese subtitles, including 凤凰视频 **Fènghuáng Shìpín**: http://v.ifeng.com/ (active as of February 2020)

16.4 The use of 成语 chéngyǔ: set phrases or sayings

Set phrases constitute a very rich part of the Chinese language. The speech of any well-educated Chinese tends to be spiced with a goodly dose of them. It's easy for students at the intermediate and advanced level to fall in love with them, for they are eloquent, humorous and unforgettable once you learn them. They tend to pop up ubiquitously at speech contests, and in fact some contestants display extreme wittiness in composing speeches consisting entirely of set phrases.

Such phrases exist also in English. Take for example: "A stitch in time saves nine," or "Penny wise, pound foolish." However, many of them are now seen as archaic or pretentious, whereas in Chinese they are still very popular.

The vast majority of Chinese set phrases come in four syllables, but due to their classical references and historical allusions, they pack in far more meaning than an ordinary phrase of comparable length. Spoken out loud, four-syllable phrases flow smoothly with the rhythm of the language. The earliest works of classical poetry, the 诗经 Shī Jīng, are essentially composed of four syllable lines. Even names of Chinese dishes, like 麻婆豆腐 mápó dòufu and 宫保鸡丁 gōngbǎo jīdīng, tend to have four syllables.

Some set phrases are obvious and need no explanation. Can you guess the meanings of the following four phrases from their literal meaning? Look them up in a dictionary to confirm your guesses.

set phrase	literal meaning	meaning
人山人海 rén-shān-rén-hǎi	"people-mountain-people-sea"	?
七嘴八舌 qī-zuǐ-bā-shé	"seven-mouths-eight-tongues"	?
手忙脚乱 shǒu-máng-jiǎo-luàn	"hands-busy-feet-chaotic"	?
胡说八道 hú-shuō-bā-dào	"reckless-speak-eight-talk"	?

Set phrases that are not obvious are even more fun, perhaps because they need to be acquired by learning the stories behind them—especially the ones that involve metaphors and historical allusions. Set phrases have three common characteristics that can help you acquire them and remember them once acquired.

1. Unlike in ordinary Chinese, where most words are bisyllabic, each word in a set phrase tends to consist of just one syllable. These single-syllable words also tend to be used in their original or classical sense. For example, 无 wú is used instead of 没 méi or 没有 méiyǒu to mean *do not have*, and 进 jìn is used in its literary sense of *to advance* rather than the more colloquial meaning of *to enter*. So knowledge of literary Chinese is very helpful in understanding set phrases. In fact, the relationship between set phrases and literary Chinese can be called 相辅相成 xiāngfǔ-xiāngchéng or *mutually enhancing*. The meanings of the following set phrases become clear once the original meanings of the individual syllables are understood. The only thing to

keep in mind is that some very familiar words are used in an unfamiliar literary sense. Some examples are 身 **shēn** *self*, 行 **xíng** *to walk, to go*, 了 **liǎo** *to end*, and 由 **yóu** *up to (so-and-so), to rest with (so-and-so), to go by way of.*

举一反三 **jǔ-yī-fǎn-sān**	*to draw multiple inferences from one example*
岂有此理 **qǐ-yǒu-cí-lǐ**	*what kind of reasoning is that?! nonsense!*
日新月异 **rì-xīn-yuè-yì**	*something new daily and monthly; rapid changes*
以身作则 **yǐ-shēn-zuò-zé**	*to set an example by one's own action*
身不由己 **shēn-bùyóu-jǐ**	*to have no control over what one can do himself or herself*
无家可归 **wú-jiā-kě-guī**	*to have no home to return to, homeless*
心不在焉 **xīn-búzài-yān**	*absent-minded, inattentive*
不了了之 **bù-liǎo-liǎo-zhī**	*to end something without resolving it*
不进则退 **bújìn-zé-tuì**	*no progress means retrogression*
后生可畏 **hòushēng-kěwèi**	*youths are to be regarded with awe*
信口开河 **xìnkǒu-kāihé**	*to let one's mouth run away; to say whatever comes to mind without due consideration*
逆水行舟 **nìshuǐ-xíngzhōu**	*to go against the current*
听天由命 **tīngtiān-yóumìng**	*to "listen to heaven, follow fate," to resign oneself to one's fate*

2. A large proportion of the four-character set phrases can be parsed into 2+2 pairs. The majority of the above examples fall into this category. Often the two parts are grammatically parallel, e.g. verb-object + verb-object; noun-verb + noun-verb; or noun-adjective + noun-adjective. The set phrases below illustrate this kind of parallelism in structure.

东张西望 **dōngzhāng-xīwàng**	*aimlessly looking in every direction*
忘恩负义 **wàng'ēn-fùyì**	*forgetting others' benevolence; ungrateful*
妻离子散 **qī-lí-zǐ-sàn**	*wife departed and children scattered, family broken up*
倾家荡产 **qīng-jiā-dàng-chǎn**	*to lose the family's fortune (through misdeeds or disaster)*
心灰意冷 **xīn-huī-yì-lěng**	*"heart ashen, will cool;" to be disheartened*
胡说八道 **hú-shuō-bā-dào**	*to talk utter nonsense, hogwash*
四通八达 **sìtōng-bādá**	*accessible to all directions*

3. A sizable proportion of set phrases are based on metaphors or historical stories. The metaphorical ones are easy to grasp. Here are just three examples:

set phrase	literal meaning	connotation
青出于蓝 qīng-chūyú-lán	"azure comes out of indigo"	*the student surpasses the teacher*
老马识途 lǎomǎ-shítú	"an old horse knows the way"	*an old hand is a good guide*
桃李满天下 táolǐ-mǎn-tiānxià	"peaches and plums all over the world"	*a teacher with former students (fruit of her labor) scattered far and wide*

The set phrases with historical or literary allusions are comparable to phrases like "Achilles' heel" or "Trojan horse" in English. They are based on historical tales or folktales, which makes them the most fun to learn. We will list just ten favorites here. Space limitation does not allow us to include the background stories. But they are readily available online. You may find them by searching the set phrase (in Chinese characters). Adding 中英对照 Zhōng-Yīng duìzhào after the set phrase will lead you to websites with the stories in English.[1]

set phrase	literal meaning	connotation
守株待兔 shǒu-zhū-dài-tù	"staying by a stump waiting for more hares (to come and dash themselves against it)"	*waiting foolishly for the most unlikely windfall*
南辕北辙 nán-yuán-běi-zhé	"intending to go south but headed north"	*acting in the opposite direction from one's purpose*
朝秦暮楚 zhāo-Qín-mù-Chǔ	"aligned with Qin in the morning but Chu in the evening"	*capricious, inconsistent, lacking sense of loyalty*
拔苗助长 bá-miáo-zhù-zhǎng	"pulling up a sprout to help it grow faster"	*killing something by excessive zeal*
掩耳盗铃 yǎn-ěr-dào-líng	"plugging one's ears while stealing a bell"	*deceiving oneself while doing something evil*
滥竽充数 làn-yú-chōng-shù	"superfluous mouth organ player filling the number"	*filling the ranks with incompetent people*
望梅止渴 wàng-méi-zhǐ-kě	"gazing into the distance at plums to quench one's thirst"	*to endure through dire straits by imagination, to satisfy unattainable hopes*
愚公移山 yúgōng-yíshān	"foolish old man moves the mountain"	*with sustained consorted effort, monumental projects can be accomplished*

---

[1] As an example, the background story for the first set phrase below can be found here:
http://www.gushi51.com/chengyugushi/zhongying/chengyu35088.html

set phrase	literal meaning	connotation
塞翁失马 **sàiwēng-shīmǎ**	"old man at the border pass loses his horse"	*a blessing in disguise*
四面楚歌 **sìmiàn-Chǔ-gē**	"surrounded by songs of Chu"	*besieged on all sides*

We can only include a very brief introduction to this very important aspect of the Chinese language. If it has inspired you to 更上一层楼 **gèng shàng yìcéng lóu**, there are many dictionaries and collections of stories associated with set phrases (成语词典 **chéngyǔ cídiǎn** and 成语故事 **chéngyǔ gùshi**) available to satisfy your curiosity and desire to speak more like a well-educated Chinese person.

Part II   254 Chinese Sentence Constructions You Should Know

Table of Contents for Part II

Preamble

When Chinese is taught as a foreign language, all the systematic features of grammar are generally introduced in the basic phase. Beyond this, the study of grammar becomes more and more an exercise in mastering a type of vocabulary called 结构词 **jiégòucí** *structural words*, which are the nuts and bolts that fasten the substance of discourse into coherent structures. An overview of these was presented in the final chapter of Part I. Here, in Part II, we present the 254 most frequently-used structures, in alphabetical order for easy search. You are no doubt already familiar with some of these structures, so the first step is to set aside those that you already know, and focus on learning the others.

Mastery of grammatical structures is not done by reading about them, but by hearing or reading examples of their usage as well as using them in one's own speech or writings. More so than ordinary vocabulary, *structural words* reflect how the Chinese linguistic mind works to fashion thoughts into sentences. Because of this, *structural words* are often difficult to translate into English, and you should take the translations provided here only as approximate renderings.

Each chapter ends with a set of translation exercises for you to put your knowledge into action. Depending on your Chinese proficiency level, these exercises will contain varying amounts of vocabulary beyond your repertoire. Don't let unfamiliar vocabulary become a stumbling block; by all means, look them up in any dictionary or reference device of your choice. Since the point of these exercises is to grasp the grammatical structures, the first step in translating a sentence is to identify the proper structure to use. If your Chinese proficiency is not up to doing these exercises, or if you simply don't have the time, the translation exercises together with the answer keys may also be used as an additional set of examples. Whatever stage you are at in your learning of Chinese, this part of the book will lead you to 更上一层楼 **gèng shàng yìcéng lóu** *to go up one more level*.

Chapter 17: Expressions 1–13

1. 按… àn... + *verb...* (to do something) according to...

♦ 他开始学做菜的时候总是按菜谱来做。
Tā kāishǐ xué zuòcàide shíhou zǒngshì àn càipǔ lái zuò.
When he began to learn to cook, he always followed the recipe.

♦ 这里的人不总是按规章办事。**Zhèlǐde rén bù zǒngshì àn guīzhāng bànshì.**
The people here don't always follow the rules.

♦ 跟他这样的人打交道很难，因为他常常不按规则出牌。
Gēn tā zhèiyàngde rén dǎ jiāodào hěn nán, yīnwèi tā chángcháng bú àn guīzé chūpái.
It is very difficult to deal with someone like him because he often doesn't follow the rules.

♦ 目前的社会还是按劳分配，将来有可能发展到按需分配。
Mùqiánde shèhuì háishi àn láo fēnpèi, jiānglái yǒu kěnéng fāzhǎndào àn xū fēnpèi.
In present-day society, things are allocated according to what each person contributes; in the future, perhaps society will develop to "to each according to his needs."

2. 按照 ànzhào *according to...*

♦ 按照中国人的习俗，过新年的时候要吃饺子，也要给小孩子红包。
Ànzhào Zhōngguórénde xísú, guò xīnniánde shíhou yào chī jiǎozi, yě yào gěi xiǎoháizi hóngbāo.
According to Chinese custom, at New Year's time we must eat jiaozi, *and children should be given red envelopes.*

♦ 要是他按照医生的建议吃药，那很快就可以恢复健康。
Yàoshi tā ànzhào yīshēngde jiànyì chīyào, nà hěn kuài jiù kěyǐ huīfù jiànkāng.
If he would take his medicine as the doctor suggested, he would quickly return to good health.

♦ 公司可以按照客户的要求设计个性化的产品。
Gōngsī kěyǐ ànzhào kèhùde yāoqiú shèjì gèxìng-huàde chǎnpǐn.
The company can design individualized products according to their clients' requests.

3. 本来 běnlái *originally, at first* (implying a change later)

♦ 他们本来住在这里，上个月搬到纽约去了。
Tāmén běnlái zhùzài zhèlǐ, shàngge yuè bāndào Niǔyuē qù le.
They used to live here but last month they moved to New York.

♦ 父母本来不同意她跟那个人结婚，后来改变了想法。
Fùmǔ běnlái bù tóngyì tā gēn nèige rén jiéhūn, hòulái gǎibiànle xiǎngfǎ.
At first her parents didn't agree to her marrying that man, but later they changed their minds.

♦ 深圳本来是个小渔村，现在变成了一个现代化的大城市了。
Shēnzhèn běnlái shì ge xiǎo yúcūn, xiànzài biànchéngle yíge xiàndài-huàde dà chéngshì le.
Shenzhen was originally a small fishing village, but now it has become a big modern city.

4. 毕竟 bìjìng *after all*

♦ 他毕竟是外国人，还不完全了解中国人的习俗。
Tā bìjìng shì wàiguórén, hái bù wánquán liǎojiě Zhōngguórénde xísú.
He is a foreigner after all, so he doesn't completely understand Chinese customs yet.

♦ 他毕竟在一家大公司工作，所以待遇很不错。
Tā bìjìng zài yìjiā dà gōngsī gōngzuò, suǒyǐ dàiyù hěn búcuò.
After all, he works in a big company, so his pay is not bad.

♦ 他们之间常常有误会，毕竟来自不同的文化背景。
Tāmen zhījiān chángcháng yǒu wùhuì, bìjìng láizì bùtóngde wénhuà bèijǐng.
They often have misunderstandings; after all, they come from different backgrounds.

5. 别说…, 就是…也 biéshuō…, jiùshi…yě… *not to mention…, even…*
In English translation, the two phrases linked by this structure are usually reversed from the Chinese.

♦ 这么重的活儿，别说是孩子，就是大人也做不了。
Zhème zhòngde huór, biéshuō shì háizi, jiùshi dàrén yě zuò-bu-liǎo.
With such a difficult task, even an adult couldn't do it, not to mention a child.

♦ 别说是10万块钱，就是一万我现在也拿不出来。
Biéshuō shì shíwàn-kuài qián, jiùshi yíwàn wǒ xiànzài yě ná-bù-chūlai.
I can't come up with even just $10,000 at this time, not to mention $100,000.

♦ 最近实在太忙了，别说平时不能休息，就是周末也得加班。
Zuìjìn shízài tài máng le, biéshuō píngshí bùnéng xiūxi, jiùshi zhōumò yě děi jiābān.
I've really been too busy recently. Even on weekends I have to work overtime, not to mention getting no rest on regular days.

6. 别以为…, 其实 bié yǐwéi…, qíshí… *don't think…, actually…*
This structure derives its strength from contrasting appearance with reality. See also #205 以为 yǐwéi and #143 其实 qíshí.

♦ 别以为贵的东西质量就一定很好，其实不一定。
Bié yǐwéi guìde dōngxi zhìliàng jiù yídìng hěn hǎo, qíshí bù yídìng.
Don't think that expensive things are all of good quality; actually, that's not necessarily so.

♦ 别以为三个月的假期很长，其实时间过得很快。
Bié yǐwéi sānge yuède jiàqī hěn cháng, qíshí shíjiān guòde hěn kuài.
Don't think that three months' vacation is a long time; actually, the time goes by very quickly.

◆ 别以为他看起来年轻就缺乏经验，其实他很有能力。
Bié yǐwéi tā kàn-qǐlai niánqīng jiù quēfá jīngyàn, qíshí tā hěn yǒu nénglì.
Don't think that just because he looks young he lacks experience; actually he is very capable.

7. 并不 bìngbù by no means…; not…at all (contrary to expectations)

◆ 许多父母并不真正了解孩子的心事。
Xǔduō fùmǔ bìngbù zhēnzhèng liǎojiě háizide xīnshì.
Many parents don't really understand their children's problems.

◆ 他们虽然住在美国，可是并不太会说英文。
Tāmen suīrán zhùzài Měiguó, kěshì bìng bú tài huì shuō Yīngwén.
Although they live in America, they really can't speak much English.

◆ 这个城市并不大，但是经济很发达。
Zhèige chéngshì bìngbú dà, dànshì jīngjì hěn fādá.
This city is by no means very big, but it is very developed economically.

8. 不但不/没···，反而(还)··· búdàn bù/méi…, fǎn'ér (hái)… not only not…, but even (on the contrary)…

This is the first of six structures that begin with 不但 **búdàn**. The 不/没 **bù/méi** is required in the first clause because it goes hand-in-hand with the 反而 **fǎn'ér** that begins the second clause.

◆ 妈妈不但不支持小孩子参加课外兴趣小组的活动，反而批评他浪费时间。
Māma búdàn bù zhīchí xiǎoháizi cānjiā kèwài xìngqù xiǎozǔde huódòng, fǎn'ér pīpíng tā làngfèi shíjiān.
Not only does the mother not support her child's participation in extracurricular activities; she even criticizes the kid for wasting time.

◆ 考试以前，小孩子不但不抓紧时间复习，反而整天上网玩游戏，父母怎么能不生气呢？
Kǎoshì yǐqián, xiǎoháizi búdàn bù zhuājǐn shíjiān fùxí, fǎn'ér zhěngtiān shàngwǎng wán yóuxì, fùmǔ zěnme néng bù shēngqì ne?
Not only does the child not use the time prior to an exam for review, she even plays online games all day long. How could her parents not be angry?

◆ 地区的紧张局势不但没有缓解，反而更加恶化了。
Dìqūde jǐnzhāng júshì búdàn méiyǒu huǎnjiě, fǎn'ér gèngjiā èhuà le.
Not only has the tension in the area not relaxed; on the contrary it has become even more serious.

9. 不但···，而且/并且(也)··· búdàn…, érqiě bìngqiě (yě)… not only…, but also…
不但 **búdàn** may be omitted, but having it in this two-part structure definitely strengthens the statement.

◆ 学中文不但很有意思，并且也很有用。
Xué Zhōngwén búdàn hěn yǒuyìsi, bìngqiě yě hěn yǒuyòng.
Not only is studying Chinese very interesting, it is also very useful.

◆ 留学不但可以提高外语水平，而且有机会结交世界各地的朋友。
Liúxué búdàn kěyǐ tígāo wàiyǔ shuǐpíng, érqiě yǒu jīhuì jiéjiāo shìjiè gèdìde péngyou.
Studying abroad not only improves one's foreign language competence, it also provides opportunities for making friends from around the world.

◆ 不但中国人过春节，而且亚洲一些别的国家也过春节。
Búdàn Zhōngguórén guò chūnjié, érqiě Yàzhōu yìxiē biéde guójiā yě guò chūnjié.
It is not only the Chinese who celebrate Spring Festival, there are also several other Asian countries that celebrate Spring Festival.

10. 不但…，连…也… **búdàn…, lián…yě…** *not only…, also…even…*

◆ 他不但把学过的中文忘得差不多了，连自己的中文名字也不记得怎么写了。 **Tā búdàn bǎ xuéguode Zhōngwén wàngde chàbuduō le, lián zìjǐde Zhōngwén míngzi yě bú jìde zěnme xiě le.**
Not only has he forgotten most of the Chinese that he learned, he can't even remember how to write his own Chinese name.

◆ 失业六个月以后，现在他不但没有工作，连积蓄也花光了。
Shīyè liùge yuè yǐhòu, xiànzài tā búdàn méiyǒu gōngzuò, lián jīxù yě huāguāng le.
After six months out of work, now he not only has no job, he has also spent most of his savings.

◆ 她在辩论中发挥出色，不但老师同学都为她喝彩，就连竞争对手也十分佩服。 **Tā zài biànlùn-zhōng fāhuì chūsè, búdàn lǎoshī tóngxué dōu wèi tā hècǎi, jiù lián jìngzhēng duìshǒu yě shífēn pèifu.**
She made an excellent showing in the debate. Not only did her teachers and fellow students all commend her, even her opponents showed great admiration for her.

11. 不但是…，也可以说(是)… **búdàn shì…, yě kěyǐ shuō (shì)…** *… is not only…, but can also be said to be…*

◆ 纽约不但是美国的金融中心，也可以说是世界的金融之都。
Niǔyuē búdàn shì Měiguóde jīnróng zhōngxīn, yě kěyǐ shuō shì shìjiède jīnróng zhī dū.
Not only is New York America's financial center, it can also be said to be the financial capital of the world.

◆ 对现代人来说，手机不但是联系家人和朋友的工具，也可以说是他们生活中不能缺少的伴侣。
Duì xiàndài rén láishuō, shǒujī búdàn shì liánxì jiārén hé péngyoude gōngjù, yě kěyǐ shuō shì tāmen shēnghuó-zhōng bùnéng quēshǎode bànlǚ.
For the modern generation of people, the cell phone is not only a tool for staying in touch with family and friends, it can also be said to be an indispensable companion in daily life.

♦ 出国留学不但是学习知识的好机会，也可以说是体验异国文化的
绝佳时机。**Chūguó liúxué búdàn shì xuéxí zhīshide hǎo jīhuì, yě kěyǐ shuō shì tǐyàn yìguó wénhuàde juéjiā shíjī.**
Not only is studying abroad an excellent opportunity for gaining knowledge, one can also say that it is an excellent time to experience foreign cultures.

12. 不但⋯，同时也⋯ búdàn..., tóngshí yě... *not only..., (but) at the same time...*

♦ 她不但在大学里念书，同时也在公司里实习。
Tā búdàn zài dàxuélǐ niànshū, tóngshí yě zài gōngsīlǐ shíxí.
Not only is she studying in college, she is at the same time doing an internship in a company.

♦ 跑马拉松不但锻炼身体，同时也磨练意志。
Pǎo mǎlāsōng búdàn duànliàn shēntǐ, tóngshí yě móliàn yìzhì.
Running a marathon not only strengthens your body, at the same time it also trains your will.

♦ 中美两国不但是合作伙伴，同时也是竞争对手。
Zhōng-Měi liǎngguó búdàn shì hézuò huǒbàn, tóngshí yě shì jìngzhēng duìshǒu.
The two countries China and America are not only cooperating partners, at the same time they are also competitors.

♦ 经过几十年的发展，中国不但已经成为了世界第二大经济体，同
时也在世界舞台上扮演越来越重要的角色。
Jīngguò jǐshí-niánde fāzhǎn, Zhōngguó búdàn yǐjīng chéngwéile shìjiè dì'èr dà jīngjìtǐ, tóngshí yě zài shìjiè wǔtái-shang bànyǎn yuèláiyuè zhòngyàode juésè.
Having gone through several decades of development, China has not only become the world's number two economic force, it has at the same time also become an increasingly important player on the world's stage.

13. 不但⋯，也/还⋯ búdàn..., yě/hái... *not only..., also...*

♦ 这家餐馆的菜不但味道很好，价格也不太贵。
Zhèijiā cānguǎnde cài búdàn wèidao hěn hǎo, jiàgé yě bú tài guì.
Not only is the food in this restaurant very tasty, the prices are also not expensive.

♦ 他不但是这部电影的导演，还在电影里扮演了一个小角色。
Tā búdàn shì zhèibù diànyǐngde dǎoyǎn, hái zài diànyǐngli bànyǎnle yíge xiǎo juésè.
Not only is he the director of this movie, he also played a small role in it.

♦ 去中国留学不但帮助他提高了中文水平，也加深了他对中国社会
的了解。**Qù Zhōngguó liúxué búdàn bāngzhù tā tígāole Zhōngwén shuǐpíng, yě jiāshēnle tā duì Zhōngguó shèhuìde liǎojiě.**
Going to China to study not only helped raise his Chinese language proficiency, it also deepened his understanding of Chinese culture.

EXERCISES: ▶

Translate the following sentences into Chinese, using the structures covered in this chapter:

1. What you say is reasonable. Let's just do it the way you suggest.

2. By American law, anyone born in America is an American.

3. At first he wasn't accustomed to life in America, but now he is quite used to it.

4. I still can't read a Chinese newspaper; after all, I've only studied Chinese for a year.

5. He could afford to buy even an airplane, not to mention a car.

6. Don't think Americans are all rich; actually there are also a lot of poor people in America.

7. The company's pay is not nearly as good as he had imagined it would be.

8. Not only is this student very smart, he also studies hard.

9. Not only does she not shrink back in the face of difficulties, on the contrary she becomes even more determined.

10. Not only is he usually very busy at work, he can't even take time off on weekends.

11. Not only are they the parents of the children, one can also say that they are their children's good friends.

12. Studying abroad not only increases one's knowledge, at the same time it broadens one's outlook.

13. Not only can he speak Chinese, he also speaks Japanese and Korean.

ANSWERS:

1. 你说的有道理，我们就按你说的做吧。
   Nǐ shuōde yǒu dàolǐ, wǒmen jiù àn nǐ shuōde zuò ba.

2. 按照美国的法律，在美国出生的人就是美国人。
   Ànzhào Měiguóde fǎlǜ, zài Měiguó chūshēngde rén jiùshì Měiguórén.

3. 他本来不太适应美国的生活，现在习惯了。
   Tā běnlái bú tài shìyìng Měiguóde shēnghuó, xiànzài xíguàn le.

4. 我还看不懂中文报纸，毕竟只学过一年的中文。
   Wǒ hái kàn-bù-dǒng Zhōngwén bàozhǐ, bìjìng zhǐ xuéguo yìniánde Zhōngwén.

5. 别说是汽车，就是飞机他也买得起。 Biéshuō shì qìchē, jiùshi fēijī tā yě mǎi-de-qǐ.

6. 别以为美国人都很有钱，其实美国穷人也不少。
   Bié yǐwéi Měiguórén dōu hěn yǒuqián, qíshí Měiguó qióngrén yě bù shǎo.

7. 公司的待遇并不像他想象的那么好。
   Gōngsīde dàiyù bìngbú xiàng tā xiǎngxiàngde nàme hǎo.

8. 这个学生不但很聪明，并且也很用功。
   Zhèige xuéshēng búdàn hěn cōngmíng, bìngqiě yě hěn yònggōng.

9. 在困难面前，她不但没有退缩，反而更坚强起来。
   Zài kùnnan miànqián, tā búdàn méiyǒu tuìsuō, fǎn'ér gèng jiānqiáng-qǐlai.

10. 他不但平时工作很忙，常常连周末也不能休息。
    Tā búdàn píngshí hěn máng, chángcháng lián zhōumò yě bùnéng xiūxi.

11. 他们不但是孩子们的父母，也可以说是孩子们的好朋友。
    Tāmen búdàn shì háizimende fùmǔ, yě kěyǐ shuō shì háizimende hǎo péngyou.

12. 出国留学不但增加知识，同时也开阔眼界。
    Chūguó liúxué búdàn xuéxí zhīshi, tóngshí yě kāikuò yǎnjiè.

13. 他不但会说中文，也会说日文和韩文。
    Tā búdàn huì shuō Zhōngwén, yě huì shuō Rìwén hé Hánwén.

Chapter 18: Expressions 14–26

14. 不到 + *quantity* **búdào** + *quantity less than...* (lit., "not reach...")

♦ 他们家的月收入不到一万元。 **Tāmen jiāde yuè-shōurù búdào yíwàn yuán.**
Their family's monthly income is less than ten thousand dollars.

♦ 三年前，这家公司的员工人数不到200人，现在已经超过了2000人。
Sānnián qián, zhèijiā gōngsīde yuángōng rénshù búdào liǎngbǎi rén, xiànzài yǐjīng chāoguòle liǎngqiān rén.
Three years ago this company had fewer than 200 employees; now they already have more than 2000 people.

♦ 他在这家公司工作的时间还不到三年，但是已经晋升为部门负责人了。 **Tā zài zhèijiā gōngsī gōngzuòde shíjiān hái búdào sānnián, dànshi yǐjīng jìnshēng wéi bùmén fùzérén le.**
He has worked in this company less than three years, but has already advanced to the position of a department manager.

15. 不得不 **bùdébù** *have to, must* (lit., "cannot not")

This structure is one of several that use a double negative to drive home a point. It is more forceful than using a positive word like 必得 **bìděi** "must." (see 16.1).

♦ 为了孩子上学方便，他们不得不在学校附近租房。
Wèile háizi shàngxué fāngbiàn, tāmen bùdébù zài xuéxiào fùjìn zūfáng.
For the sake of the children's convenience in attending school, they had to rent a home near the school.

♦ 出于安全考虑，主办方不得不改变了活动地点。
Chūyú ānquán kǎolǜ, zhǔbàn-fāng bùdébù gǎibiànle huódòngde dìdiǎn.
In consideration of safety, the people making the arrangements had to change the venue of the activities.

♦ 由于生产成本的上升，公司不得不提高产品的价格。
Yóuyú shēngchǎn chéngběnde shàngshēng, gōngsī bùdébù tígāo chǎnpǐnde jiàgé.
Due to the rising costs of production, the company had to raise the prices of their products.

16. 不得已 bùdéyǐ *to have no alternative* (implying great reluctance)

The meaning of this structure is similar to the preceding one (不得不 bùdébù), but it is slightly more formal.

♦ 她也是不得已才这样做的。 **Tā yě shì bùdéyǐ cái zhèiyàng zuò de.**
She did this because she had no alternative.

♦ 父亲失业之后，他们不得已才把房子卖了。
Fùqin shīyè yǐhòu, tāmen bùdéyǐ cái bǎ fángzi màile.
After the father lost his job, they had no choice but to sell their house.

♦ 他之所以放弃工作，也是不得已而为之。
Tā zhīsuǒyǐ fàngqì gōngzuò, yě shì bùdéyǐ ér wéi zhī.
He gave up his job because there was no way to avoid it.

♦ 在巨大的经济压力之下，他不得已选择了铤而走险。
Zài jùdàde jīngjì yālì zhīxià, tā bùdéyǐ xuǎnzéle tǐng ér zǒuxiǎn.
Under tremendous economic pressure, he felt that he had to take this risk.

17. 不管怎么···，都··· + verb, bùguǎn zěnme..., dōu... + verb *no matter how* (something is done), *still...; regardless of..., still...*

♦ 不管怎么走，我们都可以到达目的地。
Bùguǎn zěnme zǒu, wǒmen dōu kěyǐ dàodá mùdìdì.
No matter what route we take, we can reach our destination.

♦ 不管(政府)怎么控制，这几个大城市的流动人口都越来越多。
Bùguǎn (zhèngfǔ) zěnme kòngzhì, zhèi jǐge dà chéngshìde liúdòng rénkǒu dōu yuèláiyuè duō.
No matter what controls are put into effect (by the government), the transient population of these several big cities continues to increase.

♦ 一个地区不管怎么发展，都应该牢记"绿水青山就是金山银山"。
Yíge dìqū bùguǎn zěnme fāzhǎn, dōu yīnggāi láojì "lǜshuǐ qīngshān jiùshì jīnshān yínshān."
No matter how we develop a region, we must remember that "emerald water and green hills are equivalent to gold and silver mountains."

18. 不管···，只要···就··· bùguǎn..., zhǐyào...jiù... *regardless of/no matter..., if only.../as long as..., then...*

♦ 不管你对金融专业有没有兴趣，只要将来好找工作就可以认真考虑。
Bùguǎn nǐ duì jīnróng zhuānyè yǒu-méiyǒu xìngqu, zhǐyào jiānglái hǎo zhǎo gōngzuò jiù kěyǐ rènzhēn kǎolù.
Regardless of whether you are interested in majoring in finance, as long as it will help you get a job in the future, you should seriously consider it.

♦ 不管工作的待遇如何，只要有工作他就很满意了。
Bùguǎn gōngzuòde dàiyù rúhé, zhǐyào yǒu gōngzuò tā jiù hěn mǎnyì le.
No matter what the pay is, as long as he has a job, he is quite satisfied.

♦ 不管我们的计划成功与否，只要大家尽力就不会留下遗憾。
Bùguǎn wǒmende jìhuà chénggōng yǔfǒu, zhǐyào dàjiā jìnlì jiù búhuì liúxià yíhàn.
Whether our plan succeeds or not, as long as everybody tries their best, there will be no regrets.

19. 不过是　búguò shì　is only, merely

The meaning of this structure is quite different from the adverb 不过 **búguò**, meaning *however*.

♦ 她不过是个十岁的小孩子，父母不应该对她太严厉。
Tā búguò shì ge shísuìde xiǎoháizi, fùmǔ bù yīnggāi duì tā tài yánlì.
She is only a ten-year-old child; her parents shouldn't be too strict with her.

♦ 这不过是他个人的看法，并不代表大家都同意他的意见。
Zhè búguò shì tā gèrénde kànfǎ, bìng bú dàibiǎo dàjiā dōu tóngyì tāde yìjian.
This is only his personal view; it doesn't mean that everybody is in agreement with his opinion.

♦ 父母对孩子不切实际的期望往往不过是一厢情愿罢了。
Fùmǔ duì háizi búqiè-shíjìde qīwàng wǎngwǎng búguò shì yìxiāng-qíngyuàn bà le.
Parents' unrealistic hopes for their children are often no more than their own wishful thinking.

20. 不见得　bújiàndé　not necessarily (lit., "cannot be perceived")

♦ 美国人不见得都喜欢喝咖啡。
Měiguórén bújiàndé dōu xǐhuan hē kāfēi.
Americans don't necessarily all like to drink coffee.

♦ 有黑头发黑眼睛的人不见得都是中国人。
Yǒu hēi tóufa hēi yǎnjīngde rén bújiàndé dōu shì Zhōngguórén.
People with black hair and black eyes are not necessarily all Chinese.

♦ 经济发展太快对一个国家来说不见得是一件好事。
Jīngjì fāzhǎn tài kuài duì yíge guójiā láishuō bújiàndé shì yíjiàn hǎoshì.
Overly rapid economic development is not necessarily a good thing for a country.

♦ 人的一生中吃一点儿苦，受一点儿罪不见得是一件坏事。
Rénde yìshēng-zhōng chī yìdiǎnr kǔ, shòu yìdiǎnr zuì bújiàndé shì yíjiàn huàishì.
For a person to suffer some difficulties and endure a little hardship in their life is not necessarily a bad thing.

21. 不仅/不仅仅　bùjǐn/bùjǐnjǐn　not only

仅 **jǐn** is synonymous with 只 **zhǐ**, but it is stronger, and is usually used in the negative.

♦ 他们不仅是孩子的父母，也是他们的好朋友。
Tāmen bùjǐn shì háizide fùmǔ, yě shì tāmende hǎo péngyou.
They are not only the children's parents, they are also their good friends.

♦ 运动不仅锻炼身体，也磨练一个人的意志。
Yùndòng bùjǐn duànliàn shēntǐ, yě móliàn yíge rénde yìzhì.
Exercise not only toughens the body, it also tempers the will.

♦ 老师不仅仅传授知识，更要以身作则，言传身教。
Lǎoshī bùjǐnjǐn chuánshòu zhīshi, gèngyào yǐ-shēn-zuò-zé, yánchuán-shēnjiào.
Teachers not only impart knowledge; more importantly, they should be a role model, teaching by what they say and what they do.

♦ 上大学不仅仅是获得一纸文凭，也是开启个人心智的重要阶段。
Shàng dàxué bùjǐnjǐn shì huòdé yìzhǐ wénpíng, yě shì kāiqǐ gèrén xīnzhìde zhòngyào jiēduàn.
Going to college is not only for obtaining a diploma, it is also an important phase in developing one's personal wisdom.

22. 不仅如此, 还/也 **bùjǐn rúcǐ, hái/yě** *not only that, but also…*
不只 **bùzhǐ** may be used in lieu of 不仅 **bùjǐn** in this structure.

♦ 小芳学习认真，成绩优异。不仅如此，她还是一名运动健将。
Xiǎo Fāng xuéxí rènzhēn, chéngjì yōuyì. Bùjǐn rúcǐ, tā háishì yìmíng yùndòng jiànjiàng.
Xiao Fang is serious about her studies and has an outstanding record. And not only that, she is also quite an athlete.

♦ 近年来，国内的一些品牌质量不断提升。不仅如此，许多品牌更走出国门，畅销全球。**Jìnnián lái, guónèide yìxiē pǐnpái zhìliàng búduàn tíshēng. Bùjǐn rúcǐ, xǔduō pǐnpái gèng zǒuchū guómén, chàngxiāo quánqiú.**
In recent years some domestic Chinese brands have steadily improved in quality; and not only that, many brands have gone beyond the borders of China and now sell around the world.

♦ 中美两国在未来几年间将成为彼此最大的贸易伙伴。不仅如此，两国在政治，安全以及人文领域的交往也将日渐加深。
Zhōng-Měi liǎngguó zài wèilái jǐnián-jiān jiāng chéngwéi bǐcǐ zuìdàde màoyì huǒbàn. Bùjǐn rúcǐ, liǎngguó zài zhèngzhì, ānquán yǐjí rénwén lǐngyùde jiāowǎng yě jiāng rìjiān jiāshēn.
In the next few years the two countries China and America will become the greatest trade partners. Not only that, interaction in the realms of politics and security as well as in the cultural arena will gradually deepen.

23. 不论…都… **búlùn…dōu…** *no matter whether, regardless*
不论 **búlùn** is synonymous with 不管 **bùguǎn** in #17 and #18, and may be used interchangeably with 不管 **bùguǎn** in those structures, but it is more formal. See also #173 (无论…都… **wúlùn…dōu…**)

♦ 不论是中餐还是西餐，他们都吃得惯。
Búlùn shì Zhōngcān háishi Xīcān, tāmen dōu chī-de-guàn.
Whether it's Chinese or Western cuisine, they are used to eating it.

● 不论天气怎么样，我们都坚持锻炼。
Búlùn tiānqì zěnmeyàng, wǒmen dōu jiānchí duànliàn.
No matter what the weather is like, we will persist in our exercise.

● 不论谁当选美国总统，中美关系的大局都不会改变。
Búlùn shéi dāngxuǎn Měiguó zǒngtǒng, Zhōng-Měi guānxide dàjú dōu búhuì gǎibiàn.
Regardless of who is elected as the American president, the overall relationship between America and China will not change.

24. 不能不 **bùnéngbù...** *cannot not..., must...*

This structure is similar to #15 (不得不 **bùdébù**), but 不得不 **bùdébù** implies restrictions imposed by external circumstances, whereas 不能不 **bùnéngbù** may refer to one's own situation.

● 到了北京不能不去看一看长城，吃一吃北京烤鸭。
Dàole Běijīng bùnéngbú qù kànyikàn Chángchéng, chīyichī Běijīng kǎoyā.
Upon arriving in Beijing, one must go have a look at the Great Wall and eat some Peking roast duck.

● 现在一切发展项目都不能不重视环境保护。
Xiànzài yíqiè fāzhǎn xiàngmù dōu bùnéngbú zhòngshì huánjìng bǎohù.
Now all development projects must pay serious attention to environmental protection.

● 管理层做决定以前不能不先听取各方的意见。
Guǎnlǐ-céng zuò juédìng yǐqián bùnéngbù xiān tīngqǔ gèfāngde yìjiàn.
Before the management makes a decision, they must first hear the opinions of all sides.

25. 不然(的话) **bùrán (dehuà)** *otherwise*

的话 **dehuà**, meaning *if*, is dispensable because 不然 **bùrán** *otherwise* already implies a hypothetical situation. But the four-syllable 不然的话 **bùrán dehuà**, does not sound wordy, and in fact reinforces the notion of *if*. (see #55 的话 **dehuà**)

● 去中国以前你最好学一点儿中文，不然的话，没法跟本地人沟通。
Qù Zhōngguó yǐqián nǐ zuìhǎo xué yìdiǎnr Zhōngwén, bùrán dehuà, méifǎ gēn běndì-rén gōutōng.
Before you go to China, you should learn a little Chinese, otherwise you won't be able to communicate with the local people.

● 夫妻之间应该相互尊重，彼此信任，多些沟通，不然感情很难维系。
Fūqī zhījiān yīnggāi xiānghù zūnzhòng, bǐcǐ xìnrèn, duōxiē gōutōng, bùrán gǎnqíng hěnnán wéixì.
Husband and wife should have mutual respect, mutual trust, and frequent communication, otherwise it will be difficult to maintain a good emotional connection.

● 企业应该加快改革步伐，不然就会在市场竞争中被淘汰。
Qǐyè yīnggāi jiākuài gǎigé bùfá, bùrán jiù huì zài shìchǎng jìngzhēng-zhōng bèi táotài.
Enterprises should speed up their pace in reforms, otherwise they will be eliminated in market competition.

26. 不如 **bùrú** *not as good as* (See 14.2 for a discussion of this comparison structure in conjunction with other similar structures.)

♦ 按照中国人传统的观念，生女孩不如生男孩。
   Ànzhào Zhōngguórén chuántǒngde guānniàn, shēng nǚhái bùrú shēng nánhái.
   According to traditional Chinese custom, to give birth to a girl is not as good as giving birth to a boy.

♦ 一般来说，北方的冬天不如南方那么暖和。
   Yìbān láishuō, běifāngde dōngtiān bùrú nánfāng nàme nuǎnhuo.
   Generally speaking, winter in the north is not as warm as in the south.

♦ 虽然女性跟男性从事一样的工作，但是年薪往往不如男性的那么高。
   Suīrán nǚxìng gēn nánxìng cóngshì yíyàngde gōngzuò, dànshi niánxīn wǎngwǎng bùrú nánxìng nàme gāo.
   Although women do the same jobs as men, their annual salary is often not as high as for men.

♦ 你知道"百闻不如一见"是什么意思吗？
   Nǐ zhīdào "bǎiwén bùrú yíjiàn" shì shénme yìsi ma?
   Do you know what is meant by "hearing about it a hundred times is not as good as seeing it once"?

EXERCISES:

Translate the following sentences into Chinese, using the structures covered in this chapter:

1. His child is not yet five years old.

2. Because the dad changed jobs, they had to move.

3. During the time I was in college, I had no choice but to work in a restaurant for four years.

4. No matter what you say, parents should not beat their children.

5. Regardless of whether he has money or not, if you love him, you should marry him.

6. I was only kidding you; don't be angry.

7. Chinese people don't necessarily all can speak standard Chinese.

8. She is not only my colleague, but also my good friend.

9. This foreigner speaks Chinese very fluently; and not only that, he also has a deep understanding of Chinese history and culture.

10. Regardless of gender, in employment all should receive the same pay for the same work.

11. When college students choose a major, they surely must consider the question of employment after graduation.

12. You must be serious about your studies, otherwise it will be hard to get into a good college in the future.

13. As far as they are concerned, Western cuisine is not as good as Chinese.

ANSWERS:

1. 他的孩子还不到五岁。Tāde háizi hái búdào wǔsuì.

2. 因为爸爸换了工作，他们不得不搬家。
   Yīnwèi bàba huànle gōngzuò, tāmen bùdébù bānjiā.

3. 上大学期间，我不得已在餐馆打工打了四年。
   Shàng dàxué qījiān, wǒ bùdéyǐ zài cānguǎn dǎgōng dǎle sìnián.

4. 不管怎么说，父母都不应该打孩子。Bùguǎn zěnme shuō, fùmǔ dōu bù yīnggāi dǎ háizi.

5. 不管他有没有钱，只要你爱他就应该嫁给他。
   Bùguǎn tā yǒu-méiyǒu qián, zhǐyào nǐ ài tā jiù yīnggāi jiàgěi tā.

6. 我不过是跟你开个玩笑，别生气了。Wǒ búguò shì gēn nǐ kāi ge wánxiào, bié shēngqì le.

7. 中国人不见得都会说标准的汉语。
   Zhōngguórén bújiànde dōu huì zhuō biāozhǔnde Hànyǔ.

8. 她不仅是我的同事，也是我的好朋友。
   Tā bùjǐn shì wǒde tóngshì, yě shì wǒde hǎo péngyou.

9. 这个外国人中文说得很流利。不仅如此，他对中国历史文化也有很深的了解。Zhèige wàiguórén Zhōngwén shuōde hěn liúlì. Bùjǐn rúcǐ, tā duì Zhōngguó lìshǐ wénhuà yě yǒu hěn shēnde liǎojiě.

10. 不论男人还是女人，在工作上都应该同工同酬。
    Búlùn nánrén háishi nǚrén, zài gōngzuò-shang dōu yīnggāi tónggōng tóngchóu.

11. 大学生在选专业的时候不能不考虑毕业以后的就业问题。
    Dàxuéshēng zài xuǎn zhuānyède shíhou bùnéngbù kǎolǜ bìyè yǐhòude jiùyè wèntí.

12. 你要努力学习，不然的话，将来很难上好大学。
    Nǐ yào nǔlì xuéxí, bùrán dehuà, jiānglái hěn nán shàng hǎo dàxué.

13. 对他们来说，西餐不如中餐那么好吃。
    Duì tāmen láishuō, Xīcān bùrú Zhōngcān nàme hǎochī.

Chapter 19: Expressions 27–38

27. 不是···，而是··· búshì…, érshì… *it's not…, but rather it's…*

◆ 她感兴趣的专业不是经济，而是政治。
   Tā gǎn-xìngqude zhuānyè búshì jīngjì érshì zhèngzhì.
   The major that she's interested in is not economics but political science.

◆ 现在公司最需要的不是资金，而是有高学历的人才。
   Xiànzài gōngsī zuì xūyàode búshì zījīn, érshì yǒu gāo xuélìde réncái.
   What the company needs most now is not capital but personnel with advanced education.

◆ 她辞职不是因为待遇不好，而是因为没有升职的空间。
   Tā cízhí búshì yīnwèi dàiyù bù hǎo, érshì yīnwèi méiyǒu shēngzhíde kōngjiān.
   She didn't resign because of poor salary; it was because of the lack of room for advancement.

28. 不是A就是B **búshì A jiùshì B** *if it's not A, then it's B*

This structure implies that either A or B must be the case, i.e. there is no other alternative. The meaning is quite different from the preceding structure (不是···，而是··· **búshì..., érshì...**) even though the wording is very similar.

⦁ 这个小孩子不是看电视就是上网玩儿游戏，一点儿都不喜欢学习。
Zhèige xiǎoháizi búshì kàn diànshì jiùshì shàngwǎng wár yóuxì, yìdiǎnr dōu bù xǐhuan xuéxí.
If this kid is not watching TV, then he is playing games online. He doesn't like to study at all.

⦁ 我猜他们不是坐飞机就是坐火车来，应该不会自己开车。
Wǒ cāi tāmen búshì zuò fēijī jiùshì zuò huǒchē lái, yīnggāi búhuì zìjǐ kāichē.
My guess is that they are either flying or will come by train; they wouldn't be driving their own car.

⦁ 美国历来都是两党轮流执政，不是民主党就是共和党。
Měiguó lìlái dōu shì liǎngdǎng lúnliú zhízhèng, búshì Mínzhǔdǎng jiùshì Gònghédǎng.
In America the two parties have always alternated in controlling the government. If it's not the Democratic party, then it's the Republican party.

29. 不是···吗？ **búshì...ma?** *is it not...?* (rhetorical question)

⦁ 你不是四川人吗？怎么不喜欢吃辣的呢？
Nǐ búshì Sìchuānrén ma? Zěnme bù xǐhuan chī làde ne?
Aren't you Sichuanese? How is it that you don't like spicy food?

⦁ 今天不是周末吗？为什么不好好儿休息一下呢？
Jīntiān búshì zhōumò ma? Wèishénme bù hǎohāor xiūxi yíxià ne?
Isn't today a weekend day? Why not take a good rest?

⦁ 这个工作的待遇不是很好吗？为什么要辞职呢？
Zhèige gōngzuòde dàiyù búshì hěn hǎo ma? Wèishénme yào cízhí ne?
Isn't the salary for this job very good? Why do you want to resign?

30. 不是···能···的 **búshì...néng...de** *is not something that so-and-so can.../can be...*

⦁ 那么大的压力不是每一个人都能承受的。
Nàme dàde yālì búshì měi yíge rén dōu néng chéngshòu de.
Not everyone can stand such heavy pressure.

⦁ 这么高水平的技能不是轻轻松松地就能练成的。
Zhème gāo shuǐpíngde jìnéng búshì qīngqīngsōngsōngde jiù néng liànchéng de.
Such a high level of technical expertise is not something that can be easily acquired.

⦁ 这个历史遗留下来的问题，不是短时间内能解决的。
Zhèige lìshǐ yíliú-xiàlaide wèntí, búshì duǎn shíjiān-nèi néng jiějuéde.
This problem that has been left by history cannot be solved in a short time.

31. 不是···, 是··· **búshì…, shì…** *it's not…, it's…*

This structure is synonymous with #27 (不是···, 而是··· **búshì…, érshì…**), but it is milder and less formal.

♦ 加拿大的首都不是多伦多，是渥太华。
Jiānádàde shǒudū búshì Duōlúnduō, shì Wòtàihuá.
Canada's capital is not Toronto; it's Ottawa.

♦ 我们见面的时间不是星期六，是星期日。
Wǒmen jiànmiànde shíjiān búshì xīngqīliù, shì xīngqīrì.
It's not Saturday that we will be seeing each other; it's Sunday.

♦ 他们之间的矛盾不是钱的问题，是性格不合。
Tāmen zhījiānde máodùn búshì qiánde wèntí, shì xìnggé bùhé.
Their conflicts are not about money; it's that their personalities are incompatible.

32. 不是不···, 可是··· **búshì bù…, kěshì…** *it's not…not…, but…*

This structure uses a double negative to drive home a point. (see 16.1)

♦ 父母不是不支持她选文学作为专业，可是很担心她将来找不到工作。
Fùmǔ búshì bù zhīchí tā xuǎn wénxué zuòwéi zhuānyè, kěshì hěn dānxīn tā jiānglái zhǎo-bú-dào gōngzuò.
It's not that her parents don't support her choice to major in literature, but they are worried that she won't be able to find a job in the future.

♦ 我不是不愿意帮你，可是心有余而力不足。
Wǒ búshì bú yuànyì bāng nǐ, kěshì xīn yǒuyú ér lì bùzú.
It's not that I don't want to help you, it's just that "my heart is ample but my ability is inadequate."

♦ 这里的生活不是不好，可是离大城市太远，实在太单调冷清。
Zhèlǐde shēnghuó búshì bù hǎo, kěshì lí dà chéngshì tài yuǎn, shízài tài dāndiào lěngqīng.
Life is not bad here, but it is too far from a big city and really too monotonous and quiet.

33. 不要说···就是···也··· **búyào shuō…jiùshì…yě…** *not to mention/let alone…even…*

A synonym of 别 **bié** is 不要 **búyào** (in the sense *don't*). Thus, this structure is synonymous with #5 (别说···, 就是···也··· **biéshuō…, jiùshi…yě…**).

♦ 这么重的活儿，不要说小孩子，就是成人也做不了。
Zhème zhòngde huór, búyào shuō xiǎoháizi, jiùshi chéngrén yě zuò-bù-liǎo.
Not to mention a child, even an adult cannot undertake such a heavy task.

♦ 对富有的人来说，不要说汽车豪宅，就是私人飞机也买得起。
Duì fùyǒude rén láishuō, búyào shuō qìchē háozhái, jiùshi sīrén fēijī yě mǎi-de-qǐ.
For the very rich, they can afford to buy even a private plane, let alone a car or a fancy house.

♦ 对有的中国父母来说，为了孩子能到海外留学，不要说花光自己
的积蓄，就是卖房子也是值得的。
**Duì yǒude Zhōngguó fùmǔ láishuō, wèile háizi néng dào hǎiwài liúxué, búyào shuō
huā-guāng zìjǐde jīxù, jiùshì mài fángzi yě shì zhídéde.**
*To some Chinese parents, for the sake of sending their children abroad to study,
even selling their home is worth it, let alone using up all their savings.*

34. 才⋯就⋯ cái...jiù... only..., already...

才 and 就 were given the full treatment in Part I of this book because they are not
easily translated into English (see 5.1, sections 4 and 7). Either individually, or together as in this structure, their meaning is best grasped through example sentences
and actual usage.

♦ 他才16岁就上大学了。 **Tā cái shíliùsuì jiù shàng dàxué le.**
He was only sixteen when he started college.

♦ 他们才认识两个月就结婚了。 **Tāmen cái rènshi liǎngge yuè jiù jiéhūn le.**
They had only known each other for two months when they got married.

♦ 公司才成立三年就具备了相当的规模。
Gōngsī cái chénglì sānnián jiù jùbèile xiāngdāngde guīmó.
*The company was founded only three years ago and it has already achieved a
considerable scale.*

♦ 因为她能力超强，才进公司就受到了重用。
Yīnwèi tā nénglì chāoqiáng, cái jìn gōngsī jiù shòudàole zhòngyòng.
*Because of her outstanding abilities, she was given important responsibilities as
soon as she joined the company.*

35. 差不多 chàbuduō approximately; almost (not quite yet)

Note: This term has two meanings. *Approximately* is the intended meaning in the
1st and 3rd examples; *almost* is the meaning in the 2nd and last examples.

♦ 他学中文学了差不多两年了。 **Tā xué Zhōngwén xuéle chàbuduō liǎngnián le.**
He has been studying Chinese for about two years.

♦ 他才12岁，差不多跟爸爸一样高了。
Tā cái shíèrsuì, chàbuduō gēn bàba yíyàng gāo le.
He is only 12 years old and is almost as tall as his father.

♦ 四年大学的学费差不多要二十五万美元。
Sìnián dàxuéde xuéfèi chàbuduō yào èrshíwǔ-wàn Měiyuán.
Four years of college tuition is about $250,000.

♦ 为了去海外留学，孩子差不多花光了父母所有的积蓄。
Wèile qù hǎiwài liúxué, háizi chàbuduō huāguāngle fùmǔ suǒyǒude jīxù.
In order to go abroad to study, the child spent nearly all of his parents' savings.

36. 差一点儿、差一点儿没 **chàyìdiǎnr, chàyìdiǎnr méi** *almost..., nearly*

You may be puzzled at the same meaning for this pair, one in the positive and one in the negative. This oddity is illustrated in the last two examples. An explanation for this was given in 2.1 (part 7, point 2, p. 34). Be sure to read up on it.

♦ 因为工作表现不佳，他差一点儿被解雇了。
Yīnwèi gōngzuò biǎoxiàn bùjiā, tā chàyìdiǎnr bèi jiěgùle.
Because his work performance was not good, he was almost fired.

♦ 他酒后开车，差一点儿没出事儿。 **Tā jiǔhòu kāichē, chàyìdiǎnr méi chūshìr.**
Driving after drinking, he almost had an accident.

♦ 他们经常吵架，差一点儿没离婚。 **Tāmen jīngcháng chǎojià, chàyìdiǎnr méi líhūn.**
(Because of their) constant quarreling, they almost got divorced.

37. 趁 **chèn** *take advantage of...(to do something)*

♦ 大家都趁周末好好儿休息一下。 **Dàjiā dōu chèn zhōumò hǎohāor xiūxi yíxià.**
Everybody took advantage of the weekend to get a good rest.

♦ 他们趁在北京留学的机会到中国别的地方去看看。
Tāmen chèn zài Běijīng liúxuéde jīhuì dào Zhōngguó biéde dìfāng qù kànkan.
They took advantage of their time studying in Beijing to go see other places in China.

♦ 我们应该趁年轻多努力，要不然将来可能会后悔。
Wǒmen yīnggāi chèn niánqīng duō nǔlì, yàobùrán jiānglái kěnéng huì hòuhuǐ.
We should take advantage of our youth and be diligent, otherwise we might have regrets in the future.

38. 除非…(要不然)… **chúfēi...(yàobùrán)...** *unless... (otherwise) ...*

♦ 除非你会说这个国家的语言，要不然很难真正了解这里的文化。
Chúfēi nǐ huì shuō zhèige guójiāde yǔyán, yàobùrán hěn nán zhēnzhèng liǎojiě zhèlǐde wénhuà.
Unless you learn to speak this country's language, it will be very difficult for you to really understand the culture.

♦ 除非受过良好的教育，(要不然)一个人很难找到好的工作。
Chúfēi shòuguo liánghǎode jiàoyù, (yàobùrán) yíge rén hěn nán zhǎodào hǎode gōngzuò.
Unless a person has had a good education, it will be very difficult to find a good job.

♦ 除非老板给我加薪，(要不然)我会离开这家公司。
Chúfēi lǎobǎn gěi wǒ jiāxīn, (yàobùrán) wǒ huì líkāi zhèijiā gōngsī.
Unless the boss gives me a raise, I will leave this company.

EXERCISES:

Translate the following sentences into Chinese, using the structures covered in this chapter:

1. My birthplace is not Beijing, but Chongqing.

2. She is considering going abroad to study next year, either England or the U.S..

3. Isn't it already May? How come it's still snowing?

4. This complicated problem is not something that can be explained in just a sentence or two.

5. They are not New Yorkers, they're Californians.

6. It's not that the children don't want to obey their parents, but they often have their own ideas.

7. This problem is very complicated. It cannot be solved even in a year or two, let alone one or two months.

8. This kid is only three, her parents are already beginning to teach her to read.

9. I taught Chinese for almost 40 years, and have taught about 2,000 students.

10. Because the road was so clogged with traffic, I almost missed my plane.

11. Many American students take advantage of summer vacation to get a job and earn some money.

12. Unless you practice every day, you won't be able to learn a foreign language.

ANSWERS:

1. 我的出生地不是北京，而是重庆。**Wǒde chūshēngdì búshì Běijīng, érshì Chóngqìng.**

2. 她正在考虑明年出国留学，不是去英国就是去美国。
Tā zhèngzài kǎolǜ míngnián chūguó liúxué, búshì qù Yīngguó jiùshì qù Měiguó.

3. 不是已经五月了吗？怎么还下雪呢？**Búshì yǐjīng wǔyuè le ma? Zěnme hái xiàxuě ne?**

4. 这个复杂的问题不是一两句话能说清楚的。
Zhèige fùzáde wèntí búshì yīliǎngjù huà néng shuō-qīngchǔ de.

5. 他们不是纽约人，是加州人。**Tāmen búshì Niǔyuērén, shì Jiāzhōurén.**

6. 孩子不是不愿意听父母的话，可是他们常常也有自己的想法。
Háizi búshì bú yuànyì tīng fùmǔde huà, kěshì tāmen chángcháng yě yǒu zìjǐde xiǎngfǎ.

7. 这个问题比较复杂，不要说一两个月，就是一两年也不一定解决得了。
Zhèige wèntí bǐjiào fùzá, búyào shuō yīliǎngge yuè, jiùshì yīliǎngnián yě bù yídìng jiějué-de-liǎo.

8. 这个孩子才三岁，她父母就已经开始教她看书了。
Zhèige háizi cái sānsuì, tā fùmǔ jiù yǐjīng kāishǐ jiāo tā kànshū le.

9. 我教中文教了差不多四十年，教过差不多两千个学生。
Wǒ jiāo Zhōngwén jiāole chàbuduō sìshí-nián, jiāoguo chàbuduō liǎngqiān'ge xuésheng.

10. 因为路上很堵，我差一点儿误了飞机。**Yīnwèi lùshang hěn dǔ, wǒ chàyìdiǎnr wùle fēijī.**

11. 很多美国学生趁暑假打工挣钱。**Hěn duō Měiguó xuéshēng chèn shǔjià dǎgōng zhèngqián.**

12. 除非你每天练习，要不然学不好一门外语。
Chúfēi nǐ měitiān liànxí, yàobùrán xuébùhǎo yìmén wàiyǔ.

Chapter 20: Expressions 39–51

39. 除了…(以外)，…都… chúle...(yǐwài), ...dōu... *except for..., ...all...*

♦ 除了王明，别的同学都会参加今天的活动。
Chúle Wáng Míng, biéde tóngxué dōu huì cānjiā jīntiānde huódòng.
All of the classmates except Wang Ming will participate in today's activity.

♦ 除了海鲜以外，别的肉她都不吃。
Chúle hǎixiān yǐwài, biéde ròu tā dōu bù chī.
She doesn't eat any meat except seafood.

♦ 除了南极洲以外，其他几个大洲他都去过了。
Chúle Nánjízhōu yǐwài, qítā jǐge dàzhōu tā dōu qùguo le.
He has been to all of the continents except Antarctica.

40. 除了…(以外)，…还/也… chúle...(yǐwài), ...hái/yě... *aside from..., ...also...*

♦ 除了好好儿学习以外，你还应该多运动。
Chúle hǎohāor xuéxí yǐwài, nǐ hái yīnggāi duō yùndòng.
In addition to working hard on your studies, you should also exercise more.

♦ 很多学生除了上课以外，每个星期还有一两次实习。
Hěn duō xuéshēng chúle shàngkè yǐwài, měige xīngqī hái yǒu yìliǎngcì shíxí.
Many students participate in practicum once or twice a week in addition to their classes.

♦ 这里除了环境好以外，交通也很方便。
Zhèlǐ chúle huánjìng hǎo yǐwài, jiāotōng yě hěn fāngbiàn.
In addition to a good environment, transportation is also very convenient here.

41. 从…到…来/去… cóng...dào...lái/qù... *to come/go from...to...*

♦ 从中国到美国来留学的学生一年比一年多。
Cóng Zhōngguó dào Měiguó lái liúxuéde xuésheng yìnián bǐ yìnián duō.
There are more students every year coming from China to America for study.

♦ 改革开放以后，大批农村人从乡下到城里去打工谋生。
Gǎigé-kāifàng yǐhòu, dàpī nóngcūn-rén cóng xiāngxia dào chénglǐ qù dǎgōng móushēng.
Since (China's) Reform and Opening Up, legions of people have migrated from rural to urban areas to find work.

♦ 将来人们有可能从地球到外星球去定居吗？
Jiānglái rénmen yǒu kěnéng cóng dìqiú dào wàixīngqiú qù dìngjū ma?
Is it possible that in the future people will go from Earth to other planets to live?

42. 从···来说 **cóng...láishuō** *speaking from the perspective of..., as far as...is concerned*

♦ 从生活条件来说，农村跟城市还有明显的差距。
Cóng shēnghuó tiáojiàn láishuō, nóngcūn gēn chéngshì hái yǒu míngxiǎnde chājù.
As far as living conditions are concerned, there is still a clear gap between the countryside and the cities.

♦ 从经济发达的程度来说，中国的西部还比东部落后。
Cóng jīngjì fādáde chéngdù láishuō, Zhōngguóde xībù hái bǐ dōngbù luòhòu.
As far as economic development is concerned, China's western area is still more backward than the eastern area.

♦ 从经济发展的速度来说，世界上没有一个国家能跟中国比。
Cóng jīngjì fāzhǎnde sùdù láishuō, shìjiè-shang méiyǒu yíge guójiā néng gēn Zhōngguó bǐ.
In terms of the speed of development, there is no country in the world that can be compared to China.

43. 从···起 **cóng...qǐ** *from (a certain time) onward*

♦ 她从五岁起一直住在美国。**Tā cóng wǔsuì qǐ yìzhí zhùzài Měiguó.**
She has lived in America since age five.

♦ 我从下个学期起不在学校食堂吃饭了。
Wǒ cóng xiàge xuéqī qǐ bú zài xuéxiào shítáng chīfàn le.
From next semester on, I won't eat in the school cafeteria anymore.

♦ 从八十年代起，中国的经济一直在快速发展。
Cóng bāshí niándài qǐ, Zhōngguóde jīngjì yìzhí zài kuàisù fāzhǎn.
From the 1980s China's economy has continually developed rapidly.

44. 从···verb 起 **cóng...verb qǐ** *to start doing something from a certain point or time*

♦ 学中文都得从发音学起。**Xué Zhōngwén dōu děi cóng fāyīn xué qǐ.**
In studying Chinese one must begin with pronunciation.

♦ 这个电影我没有从头看起，所以到最后也没看懂。
Zhèige diànyǐng wǒ méiyǒu cóng tóu kàn qǐ, suǒyǐ dào zuìhòu yě méi kàn-dǒng.
I didn't see this movie from the beginning, so right to the end of it I didn't understand (what was going on).

♦ 中国改革开放的历史要从20世纪70年代末讲起。
Zhōngguó gǎigé-kāifàngde lìshǐ yào cóng èrshí shìjì qīshí niándài-mò jiǎng qǐ.
In talking about the history of China's Reform and Opening, we must begin from the late 70s of the 20th century.

♦ 我认为"保护环境，从我做起"这个说法非常好。
Wǒ rènwéi "bǎohù huánjìng, cóng wǒ zuò qǐ" zhèige shuōfǎ fēicháng hǎo.
I think the saying "Environmental preservation begins with me" is excellent.

45. 从来不⋯ **cónglái bù...** *never (do a certain thing or have a certain occurrence)*

♦ 这里的冬天从来不下雪。**Zhèlǐde dōngtiān cónglái bú xiàxuě.**
It never snows in the winter here.

♦ 他从来不抽烟，一直保持着良好的生活习惯。
Tā cónglái bù chōuyān, yìzhí bǎochízhe liánghǎode shēnghuó xíguàn.
He never smokes, always maintaining good life habits.

♦ 虽然生活不那么容易，可是她从来不抱怨。
Suīrán shēnghuó bú nàme róngyì, kěshì tā cónglái bú bàoyuàn.
Although life is not so easy, she never complains.

46. 从来没(有)⋯过 **cónglái méi(yǒu)...guo** *have never* (in the past)...

This structure corresponds to the preceding one (从来不⋯ **cónglái bù...**), but it refers to the past.

♦ 你从来没去过中国，中文怎么说得那么好呢？
Nǐ cónglái méi qùguo Zhōngguó, Zhōngwén zěnme shuōde nàme hǎo ne?
You have never been to China; how come you speak Chinese so well?

♦ 这个秘密她从来没有告诉过别人。
Zhèige mìmì tā cónglái méiyǒu gàosuguo biérén.
She has never told this secret to anyone else.

♦ 你从来没经历过那样的苦难，很难了解他们的想法。
Nǐ cónglái méi jīnglìguo nèiyàngde kǔnàn, hěn nán liǎojiě tāmende xiǎngfǎ.
(Since) you have never experienced such hardship, it is very difficult for you to understand their mentality.

47. 当⋯的时候/之时 **dāng...de shíhou/zhī shí** *when/at a time when...*

The time word 当时 **dāngshí** *at that time* can be associated with this structure.

♦ 当两个人有矛盾的时候，应该互相沟通。
Dāng liǎngge rén yǒu máodùnde shíhou, yīnggāi hùxiāng gōutōng.
When two people have a disagreement they should communicate with each other (and work it out).

♦ 当孩子成为父母的时候，才能真正体会为人父母的心情。
Dāng háizi chéngwéi fùmǔde shíhou, cái néng zhēnzhèng tǐhuì wéi rén fùmǔde xīnqíng.
It is only when children become parents that they can really understand the feelings of parents.

♦ 当两个国家出现贸易摩擦之时，贸易战的结果只会是两败俱伤。
Dāng liǎngge guójiā chūxiàn màoyì mócā zhī shí, màoyì-zhànde jiéguǒ zhǐ huì shì liǎngbài jùshāng.
When two countries have trade conflicts, the results of a trade war can only be that both sides lose.

48. 倒是···, 可是/不过··· **dàoshi..., kěshì/búguò...** *granted..., but...*

This structure is best studied in conjunction with its synonym #156 (···是···, 可是··· **...shì..., kěshì...**). Both structures use the strategy of conceding a point before making a counter argument, but there is a difference in nuance between them. 倒 **dào** means *contrary, inverted*, so 倒是 **dàoshi** implies that the fact to which the speaker is conceding runs counter to either his previous view or a commonly accepted view.

♦ 这家餐馆倒是不贵, 不过菜的味道也很一般。
   Zhèjiā cānguǎn dàoshi bú guì, búguò càide wèidao yě hěn yìbān.
   This restaurant is not expensive, but the food is very ordinary.

♦ 现在年轻人的机会倒是挺多的, 可是竞争也很激烈。
   Xiànzài niánqīng-rénde jīhuì dàoshi tǐng duōde, kěshì jìngzhēng yě hěn jīliè.
   There are now many opportunities for young people, but the competition is also fierce.

♦ 这些年来, 老百姓的物质生活条件倒是有了很大的改善, 可是心理上的压力似乎也比以前大多了。
   Zhèxiē nián lái, lǎobǎixìngde wùzhì shēnghuó tiáojiàn dàoshi yǒule hěn dàde gǎishàn, kěshì xīnlǐ-shangde yālì sìhū yě bǐ yǐqián dà duō le.
   In recent years the material living conditions for ordinary people have greatly improved, but the emotional pressures seem to be much greater than before.

49. *adj/adv* + 到···*adj/adv* + **dào...** *to the extent of...* (describing the extent of the preceding adjective or adverb)

♦ 大考期间, 他每天忙到没时间吃饭睡觉。
   Dàkǎo qījiān, tā měitiān mángdào méi shíjiān chīfàn shuìjiào.
   At final exam time, he was so busy every day that he didn't have time to eat and sleep.

♦ 这里的房子贵到大多数年轻人都买不起了。
   Zhèlǐde fángzi guìdào dàduōshù niánqīng-rén dōu mǎi-bu-qǐ le.
   Houses are so expensive here that most young people can't afford (to buy) them anymore.

♦ 中国还有一些边远地区落后到今天也用不上电。
   Zhōngguó hái yǒu yìxiē biānyuǎn dìqū luòhòudào jīntiān yě yòng-bu-shàng diàn.
   China still has some borderland areas that are so backward that (even) today they have no access to electricity.

50. 到···的程度 **dào...de chéngdù** *to the level/extent of...*

This is a synonym of the preceding structure. With 的程度 **de chéngdù** at the end, the phrase that describes the extent of an adjective or adverb is "framed" at both ends, making the sentence more complete.

♦ 这个好消息使他兴奋到一整夜都无法入睡的程度。
   Zhèige hǎo xiāoxi shǐ tā xīngfèndào yìzhěngyè dōu wúfǎ rùshuìde chéngdù.
   This good news made him so excited that he couldn't get to sleep for the whole night.

- 这位老师傅的技术熟练到闭着眼睛也不会出错的程度。
  Zhèiwèi lǎo shīfude jìshù shúliàndào bìzhe yǎnjīng yě bú-huì chūcuòde chéngdù.
  This old master is so expert that he wouldn't make a mistake even with his eyes closed.

- 这个城市的空气污染已经严重到影响老百姓健康的程度了。
  Zhèige chéngshìde kōngqì wūrǎn yǐjīng yánzhòngdào yǐngxiǎng lǎobǎixìng jiànkāngde chéngdù le.
  The air in this city is so polluted that it is affecting people's health.

- 上下班高峰时间，北京的地铁常常挤到人都快不能呼吸的程度。
  Shàng-xiàbān gāofēng shíjiān, Běijīngde dìtiě chángcháng jǐdào rén dōu kuài bùnéng hūxīde chéngdù.
  At peak rush hour when people are going to or from work, Beijing's subway is so crowded that one can hardly breathe.

51. 到…为止，… **dào...wéizhǐ, ...** *...up until.../as of...*(a certain time), ...

- 到去年为止，她已经去过世界上一百多个国家了。
  Dào qùnián wéizhǐ, tā yǐjīng qùguo shìjiè-shang yìbǎiduōge guójiā le.
  As of last year, she had already been to more than a hundred countries in the world.

- 到目前为止，两家公司还没有公布并购的细节。
  Dào mùqián wéizhǐ, liǎngjiā gōngsī hái méiyǒu gōngbù bìnggòude xìjié.
  Up to now, the two companies have not yet announced the details of their merger.

- 到今天早上为止，这次地震造成的伤亡人数增加到了2700人。
  Dào jīntiān zǎoshang wéizhǐ, zhècì dìzhèn zàochéngde shāngwáng rénshù zēng-jiādàole 2,700 rén.
  As of this morning, the number of people killed or injured by the earthquake has increased to 2,700.

EXERCISES:

Translate the following sentences into Chinese, using the structures covered in this chapter:

1. I have classes every day except Wednesday.

2. In addition to Chinese, he also speaks Arabic.

3. This weekend his parents will come from New York to Washington to see him.

4. As far as employment opportunities are concerned, big cities are of course much better.

5. I have decided that beginning tomorrow I will exercise for one hour every day.

6. In talking about American history, one should start from the era before European colonization.

7. She is in good health, (and) never gets sick.

8. They have been married for several decades and have never quarreled.

9. When you are busy and tired, don't forget to let yourself relax.

10. This test was not difficult, but it was a bit long.

11. During the interview, she was so nervous that she couldn't speak.

12. Her Chinese pronunciation is so good that it's like that of a native Chinese.

13. By the end of the first year, we have learned more than 600 Chinese characters.

ANSWERS:

1. 除了星期三，我每天都有课。**Chúle xīngqīsān, wǒ měitiān dōu yǒu kè.**

2. 除了中文以外，他也会说阿拉伯语。**Chúle Zhōngwén yǐwài, tā yě huì shuō Ālābóyǔ.**

3. 这个周末他父母要从纽约到华盛顿来看他。
    Zhèige zhōumò tā fùmǔ yào cóng Niǔyuē dào Huáshèngdùn lái kàn tā.

4. 从工作机会来说，大城市当然好得多。
    Cóng gōngzuò jīhuì láishuō, dà chéngshì dāngrán hǎo-de-duō.

5. 我决定从明天起每天运动一小时。
    Wǒ juédìng cóng míngtiān qǐ měitiān yùndòng yìxiǎoshí.

6. 美国历史应该从欧洲殖民时代之前说起。
    Měiguó lìshǐ yīnggāi cóng Ōuzhōu zhímín shídài zhīqián shuō qǐ.

7. 她身体很好，从来不生病。**Tā shēntǐ hěn hǎo, cónglái bù shēngbìng.**

8. 他们结婚几十年了，从来没吵过架。**Tāmen jiéhūn jǐshí-nián le, cónglái méi chǎoguo jià.**

9. 当你又忙又累的时候，别忘了放松自己。
    Dāng nǐ yòu máng yòu lèide shíhou, bié wàngle fàngsōng zìjǐ.

10. 这次考试倒是不难，不过有一点儿长。
    Zhèicì kǎoshì dàoshi bù nán, búguò yǒu yìdiǎnr cháng.

11. 面试的时候，她紧张到说不出话来。
    Miànshìde shíhou, tā jǐnzhāngdào shuō-bu-chū-huà lái.

12. 她的中文发音好到有如国人的程度。
    Tāde Zhōngwén fāyīn hǎodào yǒurú guórénde chéngdù.

13. 到一年级学期末为止，我们学了600多个汉字。
    Dào yìniánjí xuéqī-mò wéizhǐ, wǒmen xuéle 600-duōge Hànzì.

Chapter 21: Expressions 52–63

52. 到底 **dàodǐ** *after all* (lit., "reaching down to the bottom")

到底 **dàodǐ** is a high-frequency adverb, but it does not have a handy English translation. It implies getting to the bottom of a murky situation.

♦ 很奇怪，给她寄了生日礼物的人到底是谁呢？
Hěn qíguài, gěi tā jìle shēngrì lǐwùde rén dàodǐ shì shéi ne?
It's very strange, but who (after all) was it that mailed a birthday present to her?

♦ 这两个工作机会各有长短，我到底应该选择哪一个呢？
Zhè liǎngge gōngzuò jīhuì gè yǒu chángduǎn, wǒ dàodǐ yīnggāi xuǎnzé nǎ yíge ne?
There are advantages and disadvantages to these two job offers, and I don't know which one I should choose (after all).

● 听到他们突然离婚了，我们真不知道他们之间到底发生了什么事情。
Tīngdào tāmen tūrán líhūnle, wǒmen zhēn bù zhīdào tāmen zhījiān dàodǐ fāshēngle shénme shìqing.
We heard that they suddenly got divorced, but we really don't know, after all, what happened between them.

53. 到了···的地步 **dàole...de dìbù** *to the extent of...; have reached the point of...*
This structure is similar to #50 (到···的程度 **dào...de chéngdù**), but there's a slight difference in nuance. 地步 **dìbù** *step* implies a certain point in a progressively worsening situation, whereas 程度 **chéngdù** *degree* can be applied to a positive or negative situation.

● 他跟父母的关系很紧张，现在到了互相不来往的地步。
Tā gēn fùmǔde guānxi hěn jǐnzhāng, xiànzài dàole hùxiāng bù láiwǎngde dìbù.
His relationship with his parents is very tense; it has now reached the point where they don't interact with each other.

● 这里的空气污染太严重了，几乎到了令人无法呼吸的地步。
Zhèlǐde kōngqì wūrǎn tài yánzhòng le, jīhū dàole lìng rén wúfǎ hūxīde dìbù.
Air pollution is too severe here; it has almost reached the point where a person can't breathe.

● 这家公司一直经营得不太好，已经到了发不出工资的地步了。
Zhèjiā gōngsī yìzhí jīngyíngde bú tài hǎo, yǐjīng dàole fā-bu-chū gōngzīde dìbù le.
This company has been struggling all along; now it has reached the point where it cannot meet a payroll.

● 一些官员的腐败行为到了肆无忌惮，令人发指的地步。
Yìxiē guānyuánde fǔbài xíngwéi dàole sì-wú-jì-dàn, lìng rén fàzhǐde dìbù.
The corrupt behavior of some officials has become so brazen that it makes one bristle (with anger).

54. A的A，B的B，··· **A de A, B de B, ...** *this and that, various separate things*
This structure conveys the notion that the entities being discussed are varied and multitudinous. This structure can be extended to a third phrase, as in the last example.

● 家里老的老，小的小，都需要她一个人来照顾。
Jiālǐ lǎodelǎo, xiǎodexiǎo, dōu xūyào tā yíge rén lái zhàogu.
In the family, there are the old ones and the young ones, all needing to be cared for by her alone.

● 店里的鞋子大的大，小的小，没有合适我穿的。
Diànlǐde xiézi dàde-dà, xiǎode-xiǎo, méiyǒu héshì wǒ chuānde.
The shoes in the shop are all too big or too small; there aren't any that fit me.

♦ 一放假，学生们回家的回家，旅游的旅游，校园里很冷清。
Yí fàngjià, xuéshēngmen huíjiāde huíjiā, lǚyóude lǚyóu, xiàoyuánlǐ hěn lěngqīng.
As soon as vacation begins, students either go home or go traveling, leaving the campus deserted.

♦ 清早的公园里，唱歌的唱歌，跳舞的跳舞，打拳的打拳，做什么的都有。**Qīngzǎode gōngyuánlǐ, chànggēde chànggē, tiàowǔde tiàowǔ, dǎquánde dǎquán, zuò shénmede dōu yǒu.**
In the early morning in the park, there are people doing all kinds of things—singing, dancing, or doing tai chi.

55. ···的话 **...dehuà** *if...*

The two most common words for *if* are 如果 **rúguǒ** and 要是 **yàoshi**, but the "···的话 **...dehuà**" structure is just as common in colloquial Chinese. The content of the *if* phrase could be "framed" at either the front end with 如果 **rúguǒ** or 要是 **yàoshi**, or the back end with 的话 **dehuà**; a third alternative is to frame it at both ends (see #148 and #184). With any of these *if* structures, the adverb 就 **jiù** *then* often appears in the main clause, further linking it with the *if* clause.

♦ 天气好的话，很多老人都喜欢在公园里活动。
Tiānqì hǎo dehuà, hěn duō lǎorén dōu xǐhuan zài gōngyuánlǐ huódòng.
When the weather is good, many old folks like to do activities in the park.

♦ 幸运的话，我会得到这次实习的机会。
Xìngyùn dehuà, wǒ huì dédào zhèicì shíxíde jīhuì.
If I'm lucky, I will get the practicum opportunity this time.

♦ 顺利的话，我们再过一小时就可以到达目的地了。
Shùnlì dehuà, wǒmen zài guò yìxiǎoshí jiù kěyǐ dàodá mùdìdì le.
If things go well, we will reach our destination in just one (more) hour.

56. ···得不能再···了 **...de bùnéng zài...le** *cannot be...any further; as...as it can possibly get; ...to the extreme*

♦ 这个地方他住了快20年了，熟得不能再熟了。
Zhèige dìfang tā zhùle kuài 20 nián le, shúde bùnéng zài shú le.
He has lived here almost 20 years, and he knows everything that one can possibly know about this place.

♦ 这件衣服旧得不能再旧了，可他还不愿意扔掉。
Zhèijiàn yīfu jiùde bùnéng zài jiù le, kě tā hái bú yuànyi rēngdiào.
This piece of clothing is as old as it can possibly get, but he still doesn't want to discard it.

♦ 虽然他们不是孩子的亲身父母，可是对孩子真是好得不能再好了。
Suīrán tāmen búshì háizide qīnshēn fùmǔ, kěshì duì háizi zhēnshì hǎode bùnéng zài hǎo le.
Although they are not the child's birth parents, they are as good to him as any parent can possibly be.

57. adjective/adverb + 得连···也···(不/没)···   adjective/adverb de lián...yě...(bù/méi)...   so adjective/adverb that even...(not...)

♦ 孩子不听话，妈妈气得连饭都吃不下。
Háizi bù tīnghuà, māma qìde lián fàn dōu chī-bu-xià.
(Because) the kid was so obstreperous, his mom got so mad that she couldn't even eat.

♦ 这个学生的房间乱得连坐的地方都没有，但是他也不在乎。
Zhèige xuéshengde fángjiān luànde lián zuòde dìfang dōu méiyǒu, dànshì tā yě bú-zàihu.
This student's room is so messy that there isn't even a place to sit, but he doesn't care.

♦ 终于找到了理想的工作，他兴奋得连觉也睡不着。
Zhōngyú zhǎodàole lǐxiǎngde gōngzuò, tā xīngfènde lián jiào yě shuì-bu-zháo.
Having finally found an ideal job, he was so excited he couldn't even get to sleep.

58. 得以 déyǐ have a way to...; be enabled to...

♦ 得到一笔奖学金以后，他上大学的梦想终于得以实现了。
Dédào yìbǐ jiǎngxuéjīn yǐhòu, tā shàng dàxuéde mèngxiǎng zhōngyú déyǐ shíxiàn le.
After he received a scholarship, his dream of going to college finally could be realized.

♦ 经过几轮谈判，中美双方紧张的关系才得以缓和。
Jīngguò jǐlún tánpàn, Zhōng-Měi shuāngfāng jǐnzhāngde guānxi cái déyǐ huǎnhé.
It was only after several rounds of negotiations that China and the U.S. found a way to ease their tense relationship.

♦ 由于政府资金上的支持，这家濒临倒闭的企业终于得以度过难关。
Yóuyú zhèngfǔ zījīn-shangde zhīchí, zhèijiā bīnlín dǎobìde qǐyè zhōngyú déyǐ dùguò nánguān.
Thanks to financial support from the government, this nearly failed enterprise finally had a way to pull through its crisis.

59. 对···客气/公平/礼貌/etc. duì...kèqi/gōngpíng/lǐmào/... be polite/fair/courteous/etc. toward...

♦ 对长辈没(有)礼貌的孩子一点儿也不可爱。
Duì zhǎngbèi méi(yǒu) lǐmàode háizi yìdiǎnr yě bù kě'ài.
A child who is not polite/respectful toward his elders is not the least bit lovable.

♦ 不管客人来自什么社会背景，酒店的服务员都应该对他们客气周到。
Bùguǎn kèrén láizì shénme shèhuì bèijǐng, jiǔdiànde fúwùyuán dōu yīnggāi duì tāmen kèqi zhōudào.
Regardless of the guests' social background, the hotel staff should be polite and considerate toward them.

♦ 在公司里，男女同工不同酬对女性是不公平的。
Zài gōngsīlǐ, nánnǚ tónggōng bù tóngchóu duì nǚxìng shì bù gōngpíng de.
In a company, unequal pay for equal work between men and women is not fair to the women.

60. 对···来说 duì...láishuō *speaking from the perspective of...; as far as...is concerned*

♦ 对学生来说，考试虽然是一种负担，但也是复习的好机会。
Duì xuésheng láishuō, kǎoshì suīrán shì yìzhǒng fùdān, dàn yě shì fùxíde hǎo jīhuì
As far as students are concerned, although tests are a burden, they are also a fine opportunity for review.

♦ 对年轻人来说，大城市的生活更加丰富多彩。
Duì niánqīng-rén láishuō, dà chéngshìde shēnghuó gèngjiā fēngfù duōcǎi.
For young people, life in a big city is more enriching and colorful.

♦ 对美国来说，中国既是合作伙伴，也是竞争对手。
Duì Měiguó láishuō, Zhōngguó jìshì hézuò huǒbàn, yě shì jìngzhēng duìshǒu.
For America, China is a partner and a competitor.

61. 对于 duìyú *regarding; concerning; when it comes to*

♦ 对于孩子的教育，中国父母往往很愿意投资。
Duìyú háizide jiàoyù, Zhōngguó fùmǔ wǎngwǎng hěn yuànyì tóuzī.
When it comes to their children's education, Chinese parents usually are very willing to invest.

♦ 对于全球变暖的现象，有些人仍持怀疑的态度。
Duìyú quánqiú biàn nuǎnde xiànxiàng, yǒuxiē rén réng chí huáiyíde tàidù.
About the phenomenon of global warming, some people are still maintaining a skeptical attitude.

♦ 对于癌症研究，医学上还有很多尚未解决的疑问。
Duìyú áizhèng yánjiū, yīxué-shang hái yǒu hěn duō shàngwèi jiějuéde yíwèn.
In cancer research, the medical profession still has many unanswered questions.

62. 多么···！ duōme...! *how...!* (emphatic statement made by a rhetorical question)

♦ 在中国留学的那些日子多么难忘啊！
Zài Zhōngguó liúxuéde nèixiē rìzi duōme nánwàng a!
How unforgettable are the days that I was studying in China!

♦ 以前学的中文现在都忘了，多么可惜啊！
Yǐqián xuéde Zhōngwén xiànzài dōu wàngle, duōme kěxī a!
How sad it is that I have now forgotten all the Chinese that I once learned!

♦ 他小时候多么希望快快儿长大，可以独立生活！
Tā xiǎo shíhou duōme xīwàng kuàikuāir zhǎngdà, kěyǐ dúlì shēnghuó!
When he was little, how he used to wish that he could grow up quickly and live independently!

63. 多少 *verb* 一点儿 **duōshǎo** *verb* **yìdiǎnr** *(do/be something) to some extent/a bit*

In the context of this structure, 多少 **duōshǎo** means *more or less*.

♦ 因为我学过中文，所以看中文电视节目的时候，多少听得懂一点儿。
Yīnwèi wǒ xuéguo Zhōngwén, suǒyǐ kàn Zhōngwén diànshì jiémùde shíhou, duōshǎo tīng-de-dǒng yìdiǎnr.
Because I have studied Chinese, I can watch Chinese television programmes and understand a bit of it.

♦ 妈妈专门给你做的晚饭，虽然你不饿，还是多少吃一点儿吧。
Māma zhuānmén gěi nǐ zuòde wǎnfàn, suīrán nǐ bú è, háishi duōshǎo chī yìdiǎnr ba.
Since Mom has especially prepared supper for you, you should eat a bit even if you're not hungry.

♦ 虽然我们也有困难，但应该多少帮他们一点儿。
Suīrán wǒmen yě yǒu kùnnan, dàn yīnggāi duōshǎo bāng tāmen yìdiǎnr.
Although we have problems ourselves, we should help them a bit.

EXERCISES:

Translate the following sentences into Chinese, using the structures covered in this chapter:

1. He has talked for a long time, but (after all) we still don't know what he wants to say.

2. This old car has reached such a decrepit state that it's not worth repairing anymore.

3. As soon as class lets out, the children participate in various extracurricular activities: playing the piano, dancing, sports, all kinds of things.

4. When I have time, I call my parents every day.

5. This kid is lazy to the extreme. He doesn't want to do ANYthing.

6. These several weeks he has been so busy he couldn't even rest on the weekends.

7. Only after Reform and Opening did China's economy have a way to develop rapidly.

8. He is very polite to everybody.

9. For me, studying Chinese is interesting and also useful.

10. When it comes to choosing a field to major in, she is still feeling very conflicted.

11. How she longs for a happy family life!

12. I once lived in Shanghai for half a year, so I can speak a little Shanghainese.

ANSWERS:

1. 他说了半天，我们也不知道他到底想说什么。
   Tā shuōle bàntiān, wǒmen yě bù zhīdào tā dàodǐ xiǎng shuō shénme.

2. 这部旧车破烂到不值得修理的地步了。
   Zhèbù jiù chē pòlàndào bù zhídé xiūlǐde dìbù le.

3. 一下课，孩子们就参加各种各样的课外活动，弹琴的弹琴，跳舞的跳舞，运动的运动，做什么的都有。Yí xiàkè, háizimen jiù cānjiā gèzhǒng gèyàngde kèwài huódòng, tánqínde tánqín, tiàowǔde tiàowǔ, yùndòngde yùndòng, zuò shénmede dōu yǒu.

4. 有时间的话，我每天都给父母打电话。
   Yǒu shíjiān dehuà, wǒ měitiān dōu gěi fùmǔ dǎ diànhuà.

5. 这个孩子真是懒得不能再懒了，什么事情都不愿意做。
   Zhèige háizi zhēn shì lǎnde bùnéng zài lǎn le, shénme shìqing dōu bú yuànyi zuò.

6. 这几个星期他忙得连周末也不能休息。
   Zhèijǐge xīngqī tā mángde lián zhōumò yě bùnéng xiūxi.

7. 改革开放以后，中国的经济才得以快速地发展。
   Gǎigé-kāifàng yǐhòu, Zhōngguóde jīngjì cái déyǐ kuàisùde fāzhǎn.

8. 他对每一个人都很客气。Tā duì měi yíge rén dōu hěn kèqi.

9. 对我来说，学中文又有意思又有用。
   Duì wǒ láishuō, xué Zhōngwén yòu yǒuyìsi yòu yǒuyòng.

10. 对于选择什么学科作为专业，她心里还很矛盾。
    Duìyú xuǎnzé shénme xuékē zuòwéi zhuānyè, tā xīnlǐ hái hěn máodùn.

11. 她多么渴望有一个幸福的家庭！Tā duōme kěwàng yǒu yíge xìngfúde jiātíng!

12. 我以前在上海住过半年，多少会说一点儿上海话。
    Wǒ yǐqián zài Shànghǎi zhùguo bànnián, duōshǎo huì shuō yìdiǎnr Shànghǎihuà.

Chapter 22: Expressions 64–76

64. ⋯而⋯ ...ér... *and; but; moreover; however*

而 **ér** is a versatile word in classical as well as modern Chinese. It also appears as a component in words like 而且 **érqiě**, 反而 **fǎn'ér** (see #68), and 然而 **rán'ér** (see #83). Its function in this structure is to link two elements. The linkage could be adjoining (*and*), pivotal (*but*), or some other function illustrated below. Since it is a multi-function linkage word, its exact meaning can only be deduced from context.

◆ 学好中文不容易，而每天练习才能真正把中文学好。
   Xuéhǎo Zhōngwén bù róngyi, ér měitiān liànxi cái néng zhēnzhèng bǎ Zhōngwén xuéhǎo.
   It's not easy to learn Chinese, and it is necessary to practice every day in order to really learn it.

◆ 中国大陆使用的是简体字，而香港和台湾使用的是繁体字。
   Zhōngguó dàlù shǐyòngde shì jiǎntǐzì, ér Xiānggǎng hé Táiwān shǐyòngde shì fántǐzì.
   Simplified characters are used in mainland China, and traditional characters are used in Hong Kong and Taiwan.

♦ 身体健康才能保证有充沛的精力来工作，而良好的生活习惯是健康的基础。**Shēntǐ jiànkāng cái néng bǎozhèng yǒu chōngpèide jīnglì lái gōngzuò, ér liánghǎode shēnghuó xíguàn shì jiànkāngde jīchǔ.**
Only good health will guarantee that you will have sufficient energy to work, and good life habits are the basis of good health.

♦ 老百姓的生活水平有了较大提高，而生活环境却受到了严重的破坏。**Lǎobǎixìngde shēnghuó shuǐpíng yǒule jiàodà tígāo, ér shénghuó huánjìng què shòudàole yánzhòng de pòhuài.**
The standard of living for ordinary people has been improved, but our life environment has been seriously damaged.

65. ⋯而已 ...éryǐ ...and that's all

A thorough discussion of this structure appears in 16.3. You should find it enlightening and interesting!

♦ 妈妈认为我并不真正需要那么多东西，就是喜欢乱花钱而已。**Māma rènwéi wǒ bìng bù zhēnzhèng xūyào nàme duō dōngxi, jiùshì xǐhuan luàn huāqián éryǐ.**
Mom thinks I don't really need so many things, it's just that I like to spend money recklessly.

♦ 我在脸书上的朋友有好几百，但真正的知心朋友不过十几个人而已。**Wǒ zài liǎnshū-shangde péngyou yǒu hǎo jǐbǎi, dàn zhēnzhèngde zhīxīn péngyou búguò shíjǐge rén éryǐ.**
I have many hundreds of "friends" on Facebook, but as for really intimate friends, I have only a dozen or so.

♦ 大学毕业生的薪水只够每个月的生活费而已，哪里还有存款呢？**Dàxué bìyèshēngde xīnshuǐ zhǐ gòu měige yuède shēnghuó-fèi éryǐ, nǎlǐ hái yǒu cúnkuǎn ne?**
A college graduate's salary is only enough for living expenses. How could (I) have savings?

66. 凡是⋯都⋯ fánshì...dōu... all which..., all those who...

♦ 凡是学过的生词，她都记得。**Fánshì xuéguode shēngcí, tā dōu jìde.**
She remembers all of the vocabulary that she has studied.

♦ 凡是感兴趣的学科，不管实用不实用，你都应该试试。**Fánshì gǎn-xìngqù-de xuékē, bùguǎn shíyòng-bùshíyòng, nǐ dōu yīnggāi shìshi.**
Every subject that you're interested in, regardless of whether it's of practical use, you should give it a try.

♦ 凡是跟他一起工作过的人，都认为他是一个有能力的好人。**Fánshì gēn tā yìqǐ gōngzuòguode rén, dōu rènwéi tā shì yíge yǒu nénglìde hǎorén.**
Everyone who has worked with him feels that he is a competent, good person.

67. 凡是…就是… **fánshì…jiùshì…** *everything that…is precisely/must be…*

◆ 千万别以为凡是老师说的就是正确的。
Qiānwàn bié yǐwéi fánshì lǎoshī shuōde jiùshì zhèngquède.
Don't by any means think that everything the teacher says is correct.

◆ 有人认为，凡是贵的东西就是好东西，我不同意这样的看法。
Yǒu rén rènwéi, fánshì guìde dōngxi jiùshì hǎo dōngxi; wǒ bù tóngyì zhèiyàngde kànfǎ.
Some people think that anything that is expensive must be of good quality, but I don't agree with this view.

◆ 我不认为凡是被判过刑的人就是坏人。
Wǒ bú rènwéi fánshì bèi pànguo-xíngde rén jiùshì huàirén.
I don't believe that anyone who has been convicted of a crime is necessarily a bad person.

◆ 凡是不懂得尊重别人的人就是不值得别人尊重的人。
Fánshì bù dǒngde zūnzhòng biérénde rén jiùshì bù zhíde biérén zūnzhòngde rén.
People who don't understand respect for others are exactly the kind of people who don't deserve other people's respect.

68. 反而 **fǎn'ér** *on the contrary* (contrary to an assumption or common belief)
The notion conveyed by 反而 **fǎn'ér** is not easily expressed in English; therefore, the translations below can only be paraphrases.

◆ 很难写的字我都记住了，简单的反而忘了。
Hěn nán xiěde zì wǒ dōu jìzhùle, jiǎndānde fǎn'ér wàngle.
I have remembered all the characters that are difficult to write, while on the other hand, I have forgotten the simple ones.

◆ 在困难面前，他没有害怕，反而更勇敢了。
Zài kùnnan miànqián, tā méiyǒu hàipà, fǎn'ér gèng yǒnggǎn le.
In the face of difficulties he was not afraid but became even more courageous.

◆ 这个方法没有解决问题，反而使情况更复杂了。
Zhèige fāngfǎ méiyǒu jiějué wèntí, fǎn'ér shǐ qíngkuàng gèng fùzá le.
This method did not solve the problems, but even made the circumstances more complicated.

69. 反过来说 **fǎnguòlai shuō** *conversely, in other words*

◆ 中国人有个说法：良药苦口；反过来说，不苦的药是没有用的。
Zhōngguórén yǒu ge shuōfǎ: liángyào-kǔkǒu; fǎnguòlai shuō, bù kǔde yào shì méiyǒu yòng de.
The Chinese have a saying: "Good medicine is bitter in the mouth"; in other words, medicine that isn't bitter is useless.

♦ 中国有句老话，便宜没好货，反过来说，好货不便宜。
Zhōngguó yǒu jù lǎohuà, piányi méi hǎohuò, fǎnguòlai shuō, hǎohuò bù piányi.
China has an old saying: "There are no good things that are cheap"; or in other words, good things are not cheap.

♦ 中美保持良好关系对世界和平有利，反过来说，中美两国对抗对世界和平有害。**Zhōng-Měi bǎochí liánghǎo guānxi duì shìjiè hépíng yǒulì, fǎnguòlai shuō, Zhōng-Měi liǎngguó duìkàng duì shìjiè hépíng yǒuhài.**
Having China and America maintain good relations is beneficial to world peace; conversely, if China and America are antagonistic, that is detrimental to world peace.

♦ 一个国家货币升值的时候有利于扩大该国的进口，反过来说，货币贬值的时候有利于扩大该国的出口。
Yíge guójiā huòbì shēngzhíde shíhou yǒulì-yú kuòdà gāiguóde jìnkǒu, fǎnguòlai shuō, huòbì biǎnzhíde shíhou yǒulì-yú kuòdà gāiguóde chūkǒu.
If a country's currency appreciates, that improves that country's imports; conversely, if a country's currency depreciates, that aids exports.

70. 反正 **fǎnzhèng** *in any case* (lit., "either turned over or upright")

♦ 不知道他大学毕业以后有什么计划，反正不能再靠父母了。
Bù zhīdào tā dàxué bìyè yǐhòu yǒu shénme jìhuà, fǎnzhèng bùnéng zài kào fùmǔ le.
We don't know what plans he has after graduating from college. At any rate, he can no longer depend on his parents.

♦ 不管父母同意不同意，她反正要跟那个男的结婚。
Bùguǎn fùmǔ tóngyì-bùtóngyì, tā fǎnzhèng yào gēn nèige nánde jiéhūn.
Whether or not her parents agree, (in any case) she will marry that man.

♦ 戒不戒烟由你自己决定，反正抽烟对健康是有害的。
Jiè-bú-jièyān yóu nǐ zìjǐ juédìng, fǎnzhèng chōuyān duì jiànkāng shì yǒuhài de.
It's up to you whether to quit smoking or not; in any case, smoking is harmful to your health.

71. 非···不可/不行 **fēi...bùkě/bùxíng** *cannot...not..., absolutely must*
This is one of several frequently used structures that convey emphasis through a double negative (see 16.1). It is stronger than using 必得 **bìděi** *must* in a regular positive sentence.

♦ 这篇文章明天要交，今天晚上非写完不行。
Zhèipiān wénzhāng míngtiān yào jiāo, jīntiān wǎnshang fēi xiěwán bùxíng.
This article has to be turned in tomorrow; I really must finish writing it tonight.

♦ 要成为优秀的运动员，非坚持训练不行。
Yào chéngwéi yōuxiùde yùndòng-yuán, fēi jiānchí xùnliàn bùxíng.
If you want to become an excellent athlete, you must persevere in your training.

♦ 环境污染的问题非解决不可，不然老百姓的健康会受到很大的影响。
Huánjìng wūránde wèntí fēi jiějué bùkě, bùrán lǎobǎixìngde jiànkāng huì shòudào hěn dàde yǐngxiǎng.
The problem of environmental pollution must be solved; otherwise people's health will be seriously impacted.

72. 非得/非要···才··· fēiděi/fēiyào...cái... must...and only then...

This structure is a combination of the preceding structure with the adverb 才 **cái** (see 5.1, sec. 7). It states a condition that is absolutely necessary in order to bring about a certain outcome.

♦ 小孩子非要妈妈给买了冰淇淋才不哭了。
Xiǎoháizi fēiyào māma gěi mǎile bīngqílín cái bù kū le.
The child wouldn't stop crying until his Mama bought ice cream for him.

♦ 有些员工非要老板加薪才同意继续留在公司里工作。
Yǒuxiē yuángōng fēiyào lǎobǎn jiāxīn cái tóngyì jìxù liúzài gōngsīlǐ gōngzuò.
Some of the personnel would not agree to continue working in the company unless the boss gave them a raise.

♦ 在竞争激烈的现代社会，一个人非得受过良好的教育才有可能找到好的工作。 **Zài jìngzhēng jīliède xiàndài shèhuì, yíge rén fēiděi shòuguo liánghǎode jiàoyù cái yǒu kěnéng zhǎodào hǎode gōngzuò.**
In the intensely competitive contemporary society, a person must have a good education in order to find a good job.

73. 否则 fǒuzé otherwise, or else

否则 **fǒuzé** is a formal synonym of 要不然 **yàoburán** (#180). It is used frequently by well-educated Chinese. Both 否 **fǒu** *nay* and 则 **zé** *then* are words from literary Chinese. This term exemplifies how some fairly common words in modern Chinese could be derived from combining single-syllable words in literary Chinese.

♦ 父母不应该过分溺爱孩子，否则孩子将来很难独立。
Fùmǔ bù yīnggāi guòfèn nì'ài háizi, fǒuzé háizi jiānglái hěn nán dúlì.
Parents shouldn't spoil their children too much, or they would have a hard time being independent in the future.

♦ 在国外生活最好会说那个国家的语言，否则会困难重重。
Zài guówài shēnghuó zuì hǎo huì shuō nèige guójiāde yǔyán, fǒuzé huì kùnnan chóngchóng.
In living abroad, it is best to be able to speak the language of the country; otherwise (you) would face numerous problems.

♦ 中美之间应该避免贸易战，否则可能两败俱伤。
Zhōng-Měi zhījiān yīnggāi bìmiǎn màoyì-zhàn, fǒuzé kěnéng liǎngbài jùshāng.
China and America should avoid a trade war; otherwise both sides might suffer losses.

74. 干脆 **gāncuì** *simply, straightforwardly* (doing something without dithering)

♦ 他说话做事很干脆，不喜欢拖拖拉拉。
Tā shuōhuà zuòshì hěn gāncuì, bù-xǐhuan tuōtuōlālā.
He is very simple and direct in speech and actions; he doesn't like to drag things out.

♦ 饭馆的生意越来越难做，爸爸干脆关了饭馆，开起了优步。
Fànguǎnde shēngyì yuèláiyuè nánzuò, Bàba gāncuì guānle fànguǎn, kāiqǐle Yōubù.
As running a restaurant became more and more difficult, Papa simply closed the restaurant and started driving an Uber.

♦ 他上大学的时候就创办了自己的公司，后来干脆退学，一心一意经营公司去了。
Tā shàng dàxuéde shíhou jiù chuàngbànle zìjǐde gōngsī, hòulái gāncuì tuìxué, yìxīn-yíyì jīngyíng gōngsī qù le.
He established his own company while he was in college, then later he simply quit school and put all his efforts into managing his business.

75. 刚(刚) **gāng (gāng)** *just* (at such and such a time)

See 2.1, pt. 9 for a three-way comparison of 刚 **gāng**, 刚刚 **gānggāng**, and 刚才 **gāngcái**.

♦ 我们刚出门就下起雨来了。 **Wǒmen gāng chūmén jiù xià-qǐ-yǔ-lái le.**
We had just gone out the door when it started to rain.

♦ 她刚刚开始工作，还没有什么存款。
Tā gānggāng kāishǐ gōngzuò, hái méiyǒu shénme cúnkuǎn.
She has just started working and doesn't have much savings yet.

♦ 这家公司刚刚起步，很难说会不会成功。
Zhèijiā gōngsī gānggāng qǐbù, hěn nán shuō huì-búhuì chénggōng.
This company has just gotten started, so it's hard to say whether it will succeed or not.

76. 各 *verb* 各的 **gè** *verb* **gède** *each doing his own thing; each having its own characteristics*

♦ 在饭馆吃饭的时候，美国人通常各点各的，也各吃各的；而中国人喜欢一起吃。 **Zài fànguǎn chīfànde shíhou, Měiguórén tōngcháng gè diǎn gède, yě gè chī gède, ér Zhōngguórén xǐhuan yìqǐ chī.**
When eating in a restaurant, Americans mostly place their orders individually and eat their own selections, while Chinese prefer to share their food.

♦ 我跟朋友一起住的公寓有两个卫生间，所以我们各用各的。
Wǒ gēn péngyou yìqǐ zhùde gōngyù yǒu liǎngge wèishēngjiān, suǒyǐ wǒmen gè yòng gède.
The apartment that I share with a friend has two bathrooms, so we each use our own.

♦ 聚会的时候，大家都各玩各的手机，没什么交流，真是太没意思了!
Jùhuìde shíhou, dàjiā dōu gè wán gède shǒujī, méi shénme jiāoliú, zhēn shì tài méiyìsi le!
At the get-together, everybody played with their own cell phones and there was no interaction. It was really too pointless!

● 大都市和小镇各有各的好处和坏处。换句话说，各有利弊。
Dàdūshì hé xiǎozhèn gè yǒu gède hǎochù hé huàichù. Huàn jù huà shuō, gè yǒu lìbì.
Big cities and small towns each have their own pluses and minuses. In other words, there are pros and cons to each.

EXERCISES:

Translate the following sentences into Chinese, using the structures covered in this chapter:

1. Her parents hope that she will study medicine or law, but she is only interested in the arts.

2. You don't need to be that nervous, this is only a placement test.

3. Everyone who was born in America is an American citizen.

4. Don't by any means think that the news broadcasted by Voice of America must be true.

5. The younger brother has (unexpectedly) grown taller than his older brother.

6. Opportunities are left for those who are prepared, or (looking at it from the other side) those who are not prepared will not get the opportunities.

7. As far as I'm concerned, leaving earlier will be fine; in any case, I'm an early riser.

8. If you want to learn Chinese well, you absolutely must put in some hard work.

9. A good teacher must have patience.

10. People should take advantage of their youth to go out and see the world; otherwise they will have regrets in the future.

11. To repair this old car is very expensive. I think you should just buy a new car.

12. I had just gotten up when you phoned me.

13. Since your home is in a different direction from mine, let's just go our own way.

ANSWERS:
1. 她父母希望她学医或者法律，而她只对艺术感兴趣。
   Tā fùmǔ xīwàng tā xué yī huòzhě fǎlǜ, ér tā zhǐ duì yìshù gǎn-xìngqu.
2. 你们不必那么紧张，这不过是一个分班测试而已。
   Nǐmen búbì nàme jǐnzhāng, zhè búguò shì yíge fēnbān cèshì éryǐ.
3. 凡是出生在美国的人都是美国公民。
   Fánshì chūshēngzài Měiguóde rén dōu shì Měiguó gōngmín.
4. 千万别以为凡是美国之音广播的新闻就是真实的。
   Qiānwàn bié yǐwéi fánshì Měiguó Zhī Yīn guǎngbōde xīnwén jiùshì zhēnshíde.
5. 弟弟长得反而比哥哥高。**Dìdì zhǎngde fǎn'ér bǐ gēgē gāo.**
6. 机会是留给那些有准备的人的，反过来说，没有准备的人是没有机会的。
   Jīhuì shì liúgěi nèixiē yǒu zhǔnbèide rén de, fǎnguòlai shuō, méiyǒu zhǔnbèide rén shì méiyǒu jīhuì de.
7. 对我来说，早一点儿走没问题，反正我起得很早。
   Duì wǒ láishuō, zǎo yìdiǎnr zǒu méi wèntí, fǎnzhèng wǒ qǐde hěn zǎo.

8. 要学好中文非下苦功不可。Yào xuéhǎo Zhōngwén fēi xià kǔgōng bùkě.

9. 好老师非得有耐心才行。Hǎo lǎoshī fēiděi yǒu nàixīn cái xíng.

10. 人都应该趁年轻多出去看看世界，否则将来会后悔。
Rén dōu yīnggāi chèn niánqīng duō chūqu kànkàn shìjiè, fǒuzé jiānglái huì hòuhuǐ.

11. 这辆旧车子修起来不便宜，我看你干脆换一辆新的吧！
Zhèiliàng jiù chēzi xiū-qǐlai bù piányi, wǒ kàn nǐ gāncuì huàn yíliàng xīnde ba?

12. 你给我打电话的时候，我刚起床。Nǐ gěi wǒ dǎ diànhuàde shíhou, wǒ gāng qǐchuáng.

13. 你家跟我家是两个不同的方向，我们就各走各的吧。
Nǐjiā gēn wǒjiā shì liǎngge bùtóngde fāngxiàng, wǒmen jiù gè zǒu gède ba.

Chapter 23: Expressions 77–89

77. 跟A比(起来)，B⋯ **gēn A bǐ (qǐlai), B...** *compared to A, B...*

♦ 跟说中文比，写汉字难多了。**Gēn shuō Zhōngwén bǐ, xiě Hànzì nán duō le.**
Compared to speaking Chinese, writing Chinese characters is so much more difficult.

♦ 跟小地方比起来，大城市的生活更热闹，机会也多得多。
Gēn xiǎo dìfang bǐqǐlai, dà chéngshì de shēnghuó gèng rènào, jīhuì yě duō-de-duō.
Compared to a small place, big cities are more lively and there are more opportunities.

♦ 跟中国东部比起来，西部的发展没那么快。
Gēn Zhōngguó dōngbù bǐqǐlai, xībùde fāzhǎn méi nàme kuài.
Development in the western part of China has not been as rapid as in the eastern part.

78. A跟B差不了多少 **A gēn B chà-bu-liǎo duōshǎo** *A and B don't differ by much*

♦ 北京跟华盛顿的气候差不了多少，都是夏天热冬天冷。
Běijīng gēn Huáshèngdùnde qìhòu chà-bu-liǎo duōshǎo, dōu shì xiàtiān rè dōngtiān lěng.
The climates of Washington and Beijing are not very different; they are both hot in the summer and cold in the winter.

♦ 今晚参加比赛的两个球队的实力差不了多少，很难说谁赢谁输。
Jīnwǎn cānjiā bǐsàide liǎngge qiúduìde shílì chà-bu-liǎo duōshǎo, hěn nán shuō shéi yíng shéi shū.
There is not much difference in the strength of the two teams that are competing this evening. It's hard to say who will win and who will lose.

♦ 一些国产的小家电和进口的在质量方面差不了多少，可是进口的价格贵多了。**Yìxiē guóchǎnde xiǎo jiādiàn hé jìnkǒude zài zhìliàng fāngmiàn chà-bu-liǎo duōshǎo, kěshì jìnkǒude jiàgé guì duō le.**
The quality of some of the small electrical appliances made in China is not very different from imported items, but the imported things are much more expensive.

79. A 跟 B 一起(⋯) **A gēn B yìqǐ (...)** *A (does something) together with B*

◆ 他跟妻子是从小一起长大的，可以说是青梅竹马。
Tā gēn qīzi shì cóng xiǎo yìqǐ zhǎngdà de, kěyǐ shuō shì qīngméi-zhúmǎ.
He and his wife had grown up together since they were young; they can be said to be childhood sweethearts.

◆ 随着住房条件的改善，成年子女跟父母一起生活的家庭在逐渐减少。
Suízhe zhùfáng tiáojiànde gǎishàn, chéngnián zǐnǚ gēn fùmǔ yìqǐ shēnghuóde jiātíng zài zhújiàn jiǎnshǎo.
As living conditions have improved, the practice of adult children living with their parents has gradually declined.

◆ 在贸易问题上，美国跟中国应该一起努力，共同解决矛盾。
Zài màoyì wèntí-shang, Měiguó gēn Zhōngguó yīnggāi yìqǐ nǔlì, gòngtóng jiějué máodùn.
America and China should work together to resolve their conflicts on trade issues.

80. 根本 **gēnběn** *simply, utterly, fundamentally*

◆ 要是他对学中文根本没有兴趣，就不可能把中文学好。
Yàoshi tā duì xué Zhōngwén gēnběn méiyǒu xìngqù, jiù bù kěnéng bǎ Zhōngwén xuéhǎo.
If he simply has no interest in learning Chinese, then there's no chance that he will learn it well.

◆ 这些广告都很不真实，根本就是在欺骗消费者。
Zhèxiē guǎnggào dōu hěn bù zhēnshí, gēnběn jiùshì zài qīpiàn xiāofèi-zhě.
These ads are all very unreal; they are intended simply to cheat consumers.

◆ 中国政府出台了新的政策，希望从根本上解决环境污染的问题。
Zhōngguó zhèngfǔ chūtáile xīnde zhèngcè, xīwàng cóng gēnběn-shang jiějué huán-jìng wūrǎnde wèntí.
The Chinese government has launched a new policy, hoping to fundamentally solve the problem of environmental pollution.

81. ⋯，更不用说⋯了 **..., gèng búyòng shuō...le** *..., even less worth mentioning, not to mention...*

This is a two-step structure, in which a "platform" is first stated (in the first ellipsis), then the 更不用说 **gèng búyòng shuō** phrase takes the point one step further. It is a very effective way to make a statement. (see 16.1)

◆ 最近我连吃饭睡觉的时间都没有，更不用说去看电影了。
Zuìjìn wǒ lián chīfàn shuìjiàode shíjiān dōu méiyǒu, gèng búyòng shuō qù kàn diànyǐng le.
Recently I haven't had time to even eat and sleep, much less go to the movies.

◆ 他们两个人的关系很紧张，见面都不说话，更不用说一起合作了。
Tāmen liǎngge rénde guānxi hěn jǐnzhāng, jiànmiàn dōu bù shuōhuà, gèng búyòng shuō yìqǐ hézuò le.
Those two people's relationship is very tense. They don't even speak when they see each other, not to mention the possibility of working together.

◆ 这里的人连生活必须品都买不起，更不用说奢侈品了。
Zhèlǐde rén lián shēnghuó bìxūpǐn dōu mǎi-bu-qǐ, gèng búyòng shuō shēchǐpǐn le.
People here can't even afford the daily necessities of life, not to mention any luxuries.

82. 更加 **gèngjiā** *even more* (a stronger synonym of 更 **gèng**)

◆ 随着城市人口的增加，交通堵塞的情况也更加严重了。
Suízhe chéngshì rénkǒude zēngjiā, jiāotōng dǔsède qíngkuàng yě gèngjiā yánzhòng le.
As the city's population increases, traffic congestion becomes even more serious.

◆ 在经济进一步发展的同时，政府应该更加关注农村贫困人口的问题。
Zài jīngjì jìn yíbù fāzhǎnde tóngshí, zhèngfǔ yīnggāi gèngjiā guānzhù nóngcūn pínkùn rénkǒude wèntí.
As economic development moves forward, the government should become even more concerned with the problems of the rural poor.

◆ 由于全国多次发生校园枪击事件，学校现在更加重视校园的安全问题了。**Yóuyú quánguó duōcì fāshēng xiàoyuán qiāngjī shìjiàn, xuéxiào xiànzài gèngjiā zhòngshì xiàoyuánde ānquán wèntí le.**
Due to multiple cases of school shootings across the country, schools are now paying more attention to security in the schools.

83. 固然···，但是/可是/然而··· **gùrán..., dànshì/kěshì/rán'ér...** *of course/admittedly..., but...*

固然 **gùrán** is a formal word that means *no doubt*, so this structure is a more formal version of #48 (···倒是···，可是/不过··· **...dàoshi..., kěshì/búguò...**) and #156 (···是···，可是··· **...shì..., kěshì...**) All three use the strategy of conceding a point before making a counter argument (see 16.1).

◆ 发展经济固然很重要，但是也不能因此而牺牲环境。
Fāzhǎn jīngjì gùrán hěn zhòngyào, dànshì yě bùnéng yīncǐ ér xīshēng huánjìng.
Economic development is admittedly very important, but we can't sacrifice the environment because of that.

◆ 少数民族固然不再受歧视了，然而在政治上还缺少有力的代表。
Shǎoshù mínzú gùrán búzài shòu qíshì le, rán'ér zài zhèngzhì-shang hái quēshǎo yǒulìde dàibiǎo.
Granted minorities are no longer discriminated against, yet they still lack strong political representation.

◆ 人民的生活水平固然有了很大的提高，但是贫富不均的问题也越来越严重了。**Rénmínde shēnghuó shuǐpíng gùrán yǒule hěn dàde tígāo, dànshì pínfù bùjūnde wèntí yě yuèláiyuè yánzhòng le.**
Admittedly, people's standard of living has greatly improved, but inequality between the poor and the affluent is becoming more serious.

84. 怪不得 guài-bu-de *no wonder*

怪 **guài** in itself means *strange, odd*; thus, 怪不得 **guài-bu-de** literally means *cannot be considered odd*. This phrase is often coupled with another phrase that begins with 原来 **yuánlái**, meaning *as a matter of fact, as it turns out* (see #218). This is illustrated by the last two examples.

● 这家餐馆又好吃又便宜，怪不得生意那么好。
 Zhèijiā cānguǎn yòu hǎochī yòu piányi, guài-bu-de shēngyì nàme hǎo.
 This restaurant serves good food and is not expensive; no wonder it does good business.

● 怪不得他这些天都没去上班，原来是被解雇了。
 Guài-bu-de tā zhèixiē tiān dōu méi qù shàngbān, yuánlái shì bèi jiěgù le.
 No wonder he hasn't gone to work the past several days; as it turns out, he's been fired.

● 怪不得这家企业倒闭了，原来一直亏损。
 Guài-bu-de zhèijiā qǐyè dǎobìle, yuánlái yìzhí kuīsǔn.
 No wonder this enterprise has gone bankrupt; it was running a deficit all along.

85. 关于 guānyú *about, concerning*

A 关于 **guānyú** phrase may be used in two ways: 1) as a modifier of a noun (first example), 2) as the topic of a sentence (as in the latter two examples).

● 他看过很多关于第二次世界大战的电影。
 Tā kànguo hěn duō guānyú dìercì shìjiè dàzhànde diànyǐng.
 He has seen many movies about World War II.

● 关于男女平等的话题，同学们讨论得很热烈。
 Guānyú nán-nǚ píngděngde huàtí, tóngxuémen tǎolùnde hěn rèliè.
 The students had rousing discussions on the topic of male and female equality.

● 关于如何应对老龄化的问题，政府实施了新的人口政策。
 Guānyú rúhé yìngduì lǎolíng-huàde wèntí, zhèngfǔ shíshīle xīnde rénkǒu zhèngcè.
 Concerning the question of how to deal with the problem of aging, the government has instituted a new population policy.

86. 管⋯叫⋯ guǎn...jiào... *to call something/someone by the moniker of...*

● 为什么大家都管纽约叫"大苹果"呢？
 Wèishénme dàjiā dōu guǎn Niǔyuē jiào "Dà Píngguǒ" ne?
 Why does everyone call New York "the Big Apple"?

● 如果一个人做事情马马虎虎，我们可以管他叫"差不多先生"。
 Rúguǒ yíge rén zuò shìqing mǎmahūhū, wǒmen kěyǐ guǎn tā jiào "Chàbuduō Xiānsheng".
 If a person does things very haphazardly, we can say that he is "Mr. So-so."

◆ 许多人认为美国总喜欢干涉别的国家的事情，于是就管美国叫"国际警察"。**Xǔduō rén rènwéi Měiguó zǒng xǐhuan gānshè biéde guójiāde shìqing, yúshì jiù guǎn Měiguó jiào "Guójì Jǐngchá".**
Many people think America likes to meddle in other countries' affairs; therefore they call America the "International Policeman."

87. 果然 guǒrán *sure enough, as expected*

◆ 我这次比赛准备得不是很好，果然最后的成绩不太理想。**Wǒ zhècì bǐsài zhǔnbèide búshì hěn hǎo, guǒrán zuìhòude chéngjì bú tài lǐxiǎng.**
I wasn't very well prepared for this competition, so sure enough my final score was not ideal.

◆ 专家预测这次谈判将十分艰难，果然谈判的过程很不顺利。**Zhuānjiā yùcè zhècì tánpàn jiāng shífēn jiānnán, guǒrán tánpànde guòchéng hěn bú shùnlì.**
The experts predicted that these negotiations would be very difficult, and in fact the negotiations did not progress smoothly at all.

◆ 他说将来会回来娶她，果然没有食言。**Tā shuō jiānglái huì huílai qǔ tā, guǒrán méiyǒu shíyán.**
He said that (in the future) he would return and marry her, and sure enough he did not eat his words.

88. 过…的生活 guò…de shēnghuó *to live a life of…*

◆ 妈妈总是说，要想将来过上自己喜欢的生活，那现在就得努力。**Māma zǒngshì shuō, yào xiǎng jiānglái guòshang zìjǐ xǐhuande shēnghuó, nà xiànzài jiù děi nǔlì.**
Mom always said that if we want to live the life that we like in the future, we must work hard now.

◆ 他既不上学也不工作，整天过着无所事事的生活。**Tā jì bú shàngxué yě bù gōngzuò, zhěngtiān guòzhe wúsuǒ-shìshìde shēnghuó.**
He neither goes to school nor has a job, but lives a life of idleness all day long.

◆ 他从失业以后就一直过着朝不保夕的生活。**Tā cóng shīyè yǐhòu jiù yìzhí guòzhe zhāo-bù-bǎo-xī-de shēnghuó.**
Since he lost his job, he has lived a very (financially) insecure life.

89. 还是…吧 háishi…ba *(all things considered) it's best to…(after all)*

The combination of 还是 háishi *still* with 吧 ba (indicating a suggestion) conveys a conclusion reached after careful consideration of various options or pros and cons.

◆ 晚上一个人走路不太安全，你还是小心一点儿吧。**Wǎnshang yíge rén zǒulù bú tài ānquán, nǐ háishi xiǎoxīn yìdiǎnr ba.**
It's not very safe to be out walking on the street in the evening. You should be careful after all.

● 我们还是早一点儿出发吧，免得碰上交通高峰。
Wǒmen háishi zǎo yìdiǎnr chūfā ba, miǎnde pèngshang jiāotōng gāofēng.
We should get an early start, lest we get into rush hour traffic.

● 我担心她受不了，所以还是暂时别告诉她这个坏消息吧，
Wǒ dānxīn tā shòu-bu-liǎo, suǒyǐ háishi zànshí bié gàosu tā zhèige huài xiāoxi ba.
I'm afraid she won't be able to take it, so let's not tell her this bad news yet.

EXERCISES:

Translate the following sentences into Chinese, using the structures covered in this chapter:

1. Compared to learning Western languages, learning Chinese takes much longer.

2. In America, farmers' standard of living is not very different from city residents'.

3. After class every day, she often reviews her Chinese with classmates.

4. No matter what the parents say, the child simply doesn't listen.

5. He can't even manage himself, not to mention managing a company.

6. After they leave their parents and go off to college, children become even more independent than before.

7. Of course work is very important, but one should also pay attention to one's health.

8. He is always willing to help others; no wonder everybody likes him.

9. I like to read books about history very much.

10. Because Mom is very strict with the children, everyone calls her "tiger mom."

11. The weather forecast was very accurate. In the morning it said that it would snow in the afternoon, and sure enough it snowed in the afternoon.

12. Although he is very wealthy, he still likes to live a simple life.

13. The results of the competition have not yet been announced. You shouldn't be so optimistic yet.

ANSWERS:

1. 跟学西方语言比，学中文要花更长的时间。
Gēn xué Xīfāng yǔyán bǐ, xué Zhōngwén yào huā gèng chángde shíjiān.

2. 在美国，农民的生活水平跟城市人的差不了多少。
Zài Měiguó, nóngmínde shēnghuó shuǐpíng gēn chéngshì-rénde chà-bu-liǎo duōshǎo.

3. 每天下课以后，她常跟同学们一起复习中文。
Měitiān xiàkè yǐhòu, tā cháng gēn tóngxuémen yìqǐ fùxí Zhōngwén.

4. 不管父母说什么，小孩子根本不听。Bùguǎn fùmǔ shuō shénme, xiǎoháizi gēnběn bù tīng.

5. 他连自己都管不好，更不用说管理好一家公司了。
Tā lián zìjǐ dōu guǎn-bu-hǎo, gèng búyòng shuō guǎnlǐ-hǎo yìjiā gōngsī le.

6. 离开父母去上大学以后，孩子比以前更加独立了。
Líkāi fùmǔ qù shàng dàxué yǐhòu, háizi bǐ yǐqián gèngjiā dúlì le.

7. 工作固然很重要，可是也应该注意健康。
Gōngzuò gùrán hěn zhòngyào, kěshì yě yīnggāi zhùyì jiànkāng.

8. 他总是愿意帮助别人，怪不得大家都喜欢他。
   Tā zǒngshì yuànyì bāngzhù biérén, guài-bu-de dàjiā dōu xǐhuan tā.

9. 我很喜欢读关于历史的书。 **Wǒ hěn xǐhuan dú guānyú lìshǐde shū.**

10. 因为妈妈对孩子非常严格，所以大家都管她叫"虎妈"。
    Yīnwèi Māma duì háizi fēicháng yángé, suǒyǐ dàjiā dōu guǎn tā jiào "Hǔ Mā".

11. 天气预报很准，早上说下午要下雪，下午果然下雪了。
    Tiānqì yùbào hěn zhǔn, zǎoshang shuō xiàwǔ yào xiàxuě, xiàwǔ guǒrán xiàxuě le.

12. 他虽然很有钱，但还是喜欢过简单的生活。
    Tā suīrán hěn yǒuqián, dàn háishi xǐhuan guò jiǎndānde shēnghuó.

13. 比赛的结果还没有公布，你还是别那么乐观吧。
    Bǐsàide jiéguǒ hái méiyǒu gōngbù, nǐ háishi bié nàme lèguān ba.

Chapter 24: Expressions 90–102

90. 好像…，可是/其实… **hǎoxiàng…, kěshì/qíshí…** *it seems…, but/actually…*

◆ 她好像有心事，可是又不愿意跟我们说。
   Tā hǎoxiàng yǒu xīnshì, kěshì yòu bú yuànyi gēn wǒmen shuō.
   She seems to be troubled by a "matter of the heart," but she doesn't want to talk about it with us.

◆ 他们谈话的时候好像是老朋友，其实才第一次见面。
   Tāmen tánhuàde shíhou hǎoxiàng shì lǎopéngyou, qíshí cái dìyīcì jiànmiàn.
   When they talk, they seem like old friends, but actually this is the first time they have met.

◆ 他好像什么事情都不在乎，其实是一个周到细心的人。
   Tā hǎoxiàng shénme shìqing dōu bú-zàihu, qíshí shì yíge zhōudào xìxīnde rén.
   He may seem nonchalant about everything, but he is actually a very meticulous person.

91. 好像…似的 **hǎoxiàng…shìde** *it seems (as though)…*

◆ 她的眼睛又大又亮，好像会说话似的。
   Tāde yǎnjīng yòu dà yòu liàng, hǎoxiàng huì shuōhuà shìde.
   Her eyes are big and bright, as though they can speak.

◆ 大家都穿得很漂亮，好像今天过节似的。
   Dàjiā dōu chuānde hěn piàoliang, hǎoxiàng jīntiān guòjié shìde.
   Everybody got dressed up, as though today is a festival day.

◆ 他好像公司的老板似的，常常对别人发号施令。
   Tā hǎoxiàng gōngsīde lǎobǎn shìde, chángcháng duì biérén fāhào-shīlìng.
   He seems like the boss of the company, constantly ordering people around.

92. A和B一起(···) **A hé B yìqǐ (...)** *A (does something) together with B*

This structure is synonymous with #79 (A跟 **gēn** B一起 **yìqǐ**...).

♦ 申请大学的时候，孩子和父母一起商量，决定上哪一所大学。
  Shēnqǐng dàxuéde shíhou, háizi hé fùmǔ yìqǐ shāngliang, juédìng shàng nǎyìsuǒ dàxué.
  When applying for college, the child and his parents talked it over and decided which college he should attend.

♦ 在这家小公司里，员工和老板一起努力，为公司的发展出力。
  Zài zhèijiā xiǎo gōngsīlǐ, yuángōng hé lǎobǎn yìqǐ nǔlì, wèi gōngsīde fāzhǎn chūlì.
  In this little company, the workers and the boss are working hard together for the sake of developing the company.

♦ 他和邻居经常一起拼车上下班，这样又省钱又环保。
  Tā hé línjū jīngcháng yìqǐ pīnchē shàng-xiàbān, zhèyàng yòu shěngqián yòu huánbǎo.
  He usually shares a ride with a neighbor for going to and from work; this saves money and is good for the environment.

93. 何必···(呢)? **hébì...(ne)?** *why must...?* (emphatic statement made by a rhetorical question)

♦ 他不是小孩子了，你何必为他操心呢？
  Tā búshì xiǎoháizi le, nǐ hébì wèi tā cāoxīn ne?
  He's not a child anymore. Why should you worry over him so much?

♦ 小孩子不愿意弹钢琴就算了，大人何必逼他们呢？
  Xiǎoháizi bú yuànyi tán gāngqín jiù suàn le, dàrén hébì bī tāmen ne?
  If the children don't want to play the piano, just let it go. Why should the adults press them so?

♦ 天涯何处无芳草，你何必一定要留在纽约呢？
  Tiānyá héchù wú fāngcǎo, nǐ hébì yídìng yào liú zài Niǔyuē ne?
  There is fragrant grass everywhere; why must you stay in New York?

94. ···，何况··· **..., hékuàng...** *..., moreover, let alone, all the more*

Both 何 **hé** and 况 **kuàng** are rooted in literary Chinese. The meaning of the term has morphed quite far from the original meanings of the two components. This structure uses the strategy of first stating a point, then taking it one step further. (see 16.1)

♦ 这条路平时开车就不太容易，何况下雨天，你一定要十分小心。
  Zhèitiáo lù píngshí kāichē jiù bú tài róngyì, hékuàng xiàyǔ-tiān, nǐ yídìng yào shífēn xiǎoxīn.
  This road is problematic even in ordinary times; especially on a rainy day, you must be very careful.

♦ 谁都有可能出错，何况他刚开始在这里工作，还不太熟悉。
  Shéi dōu yǒu kěnéng chūcuò, hékuàng tā gāng kāishǐ zài zhèlǐ gōngzuò, hái bú tài shúxī.
  Anybody might make a mistake; moreover, he has just started working here and is not yet familiar with things.

♦ 对手的实力本来比他强，何况他今天有点儿不舒服，所以输球也在意料之中。**Duìshǒude shílì běnlái bǐ tā qiáng, hékuàng tā jīntiān yǒudiǎnr bùshūfu, suǒyǐ shūqiú yě zài yìliào zhīzhōng.**

His opponent is basically stronger than he is; moreover, he was not feeling very well today, so it's not surprising that he lost (the match).

95. 换一句话说 **huàn yíjù huà shuō** *in other words* (lit., "change a sentence and say it")

♦ 谁有困难他都想办法帮忙。换一句话说，他是个热心的好人。**Shéi yǒu kùnnan tā dōu xiǎng bànfǎ bāngmáng. Huàn yíjù huà shuō, tā shì ge rèxīnde hǎorén.**

Whenever someone has a problem, he will think of a way to help. In other words, he is a warm-hearted good person.

♦ 公司里男性的年薪往往比女性的高。换一句话说，今天的社会男女还不平等。**Gōngsīlǐ nánxìngde niánxīn wǎngwǎng bǐ nǚxìngde gāo. Huàn yíjù huà shuō, jīntiānde shèhuì nán-nǚ hái bù píngděng.**

In a company, men's annual salary is often higher than women's. In other words, in today's society men and women are still not equal.

♦ 不论在哪里，许多人都是手机不离手。换一句话说，手机已经是现代人生活中不可缺少的伴侣了。**Búlùn zài nǎli, xǔduō rén dōu shì shǒujī bù lí shǒu. Huàn yíjù huà shuō, shǒujī yǐjīng shì xiàndài rén shēnghuó-zhōng bùkě quēshǎode bànlǚ le.**

No matter where, for many people their cell phone never leaves their hand. In other words, the cell phone is already an indispensable companion in contemporary daily life.

96. …极了 **…jíle** *extremely…* (stronger than 非常 **fēicháng** "exceedingly")

♦ 最近我又是期末考，又是找工作，真的忙极了。**Zuìjìn wǒ yòushì qīmò kǎo, yòushì zhǎo gōngzuò, zhēnde máng-jíle.**

Now I'm taking final exams and job hunting too; I'm really exceedingly busy.

♦ 对我这个学生来说，那些名牌商品的价格贵极了。**Duì wǒ zhèige xuésheng láishuō, nèixiē míngpái shāngpǐnde jiàgé guì-jíle.**

To a student like me, those name-brand goods are extremely expensive.

♦ 过年的时候，家里的几十个亲戚都聚在一起吃吃喝喝，简直热闹极了。**Guòniánde shíhou, jiālǐde jǐshíge qīnqi dōu jùzài yìqǐ chīchī-hēhē, jiǎnzhí rènào-jíle.**

At New Year's time, dozens of relatives get together to eat and drink, and it is simply bustling in the extreme.

97. 即使…也… **jíshǐ…yě…** *even if…still…*

This structure is synonymous with #108 (就是…也… **jiùshi…ye…**), but it is slightly more formal. In both structures, the 也 **yě** is not dispensable, even though in a corresponding English sentence, the word *still* would be superfluous.

♦ 这么多功课，我即使不睡觉也做不完。
Zhème duō gōngkè, wǒ jíshǐ bú-shuìjiào ye zuò-bù-wán.
With so much homework, even if I don't sleep, I won't be able to finish it.

♦ 即使是名牌大学的毕业生也不一定都找得到好工作。
Jíshǐ shì míngpái dàxuéde bìyèshēng yě bù yídìng dōu zhǎo-de-dào hǎode gōngzuò.
Even graduates of famous universities won't necessarily be able to find good jobs.

♦ 即使遇到很大的困难，我们也决不放弃。
Jíshǐ yùdào hěn dàde kùnnan, wǒmen yě jué bú fàngqì.
Even if we run into serious obstacles, we will not give up.

98. 既···又··· **jì...yòu...** *both...and...*

This structure is synonymous with #215 (又···又··· **yòu...yòu...**), but is more formal, and more forceful due to its less frequent usage.

♦ 他既了解西方文化又熟悉中国的国情。
Tā jì liǎojiě Xīfāng wénhuà yòu shúxī Zhōngguóde guóqíng.
He understands Western culture and is also familiar with the national ethos of China.

♦ 利用太阳能发电，既节约能源又保护环境。
Lìyòng tàiyáng-néng fādiàn, jì jiéyuē néngyuán yòu bǎohù huánjìng.
Using solar energy to produce electricity conserves energy resources and protects the environment.

♦ 改革开放既改善了国内的经济体制，又打开国门吸引了外资。
Gǎigé-kāifàng jì gǎishànle guónèide jīngjì tǐzhì, yòu dǎkāi guómén xīyǐnle wàizī.
Reform and Opening improved the country's economic system and opened the nation's doors to foreign investment.

99. 既然···, 就··· **jìrán..., jiù...** *since/given that..., then...*

就 **jiù** in the second clause goes hand-in-hand with 既然 **jìrán**. It is not dispensable, even though in a corresponding English sentence, the word *then* would be considered superfluous.

♦ 既然你们是好朋友，就应该互相帮助。
Jìrán nǐmen shì hǎo péngyou, jiù yīnggāi hùxiāng bāngzhù.
Since you are good friends, you should help each other.

♦ 既然我们来了美国，就要努力适应这里的生活。
Jìrán wǒmen láile Měiguó, jiù yào nǔlì shìyìng zhèlǐde shēnghuó.
Since we have come to America, let's try hard to get used to life here.

♦ 既然公司重点培训她，她就要好好儿珍惜这个机会。
Jìrán gōngsī zhòngdiǎn péixùn tā, tā jiù yào hǎohāor zhēnxí zhèige jīhuì.
Since the company is providing her with special training, she should cherish this opportunity.

100. 既然···，怎么··· **jìrán..., zěnme...** *since/given that..., how come...?*

◆ 既然身体不舒服，怎么不在家里好好儿休息一下呢？
Jìrán shēntǐ bùshūfu, zěnme bú zài jiālǐ hǎohāor xiūxi yíxià ne?
Since you are not feeling well, why don't you stay home and get a good rest?

◆ 既然你对这个工作没兴趣，怎么还接受了呢？
Jìrán nǐ duì zhèige gōngzuò méi xìngqu, zěnme hái jiēshòule ne?
Given that you are not interested in this work, why did you accept (the job)?

◆ 既然你不再爱他了，你们怎么还在一起呢？
Jìrán nǐ búzài ài tā le, nǐmen zěnme hái zài yìqǐ ne?
Since you don't love him anymore, why are you (two) still together?

101. 假如···(就)··· **jiǎrú...(jiù)...** *if/supposing..., (then)...*

假如 **jiǎrú** is a synonym of 如果 **rúguǒ** and 要是 **yàoshi** (see #148 and #184), but there is a difference in nuance. 假 **jiǎ** means *to fake, to pretend, to simulate*, so 假如 **jiǎrú** actually means *supposing*, as though the hypothetical situation is not likely to happen. The example sentence here, when compared with those in #148 and #184, should reflect this difference in nuance. This structure is also used less frequently than 如果 **rúguǒ** and 要是 **yàoshi**.

◆ 假如天气不好，我们就不去爬山了。
Jiǎrú tiānqì bùhǎo, wǒmen jiù bú qù páshān le.
If the weather is not good, we won't go mountain climbing.

◆ 假如你明天没有时间，我们就另外找个时间见面吧。
Jiǎrú nǐ míngtiān méiyǒu shíjiān, wǒmen jiù lìngwài zhǎo ge shíjiān jiànmiàn ba.
If you don't have time tomorrow, we'll look for another time to meet.

◆ 假如我是一只小鸟，就可以飞到很远的地方去。
Jiǎrú wǒ shì yìzhī xiǎo niǎo, jiù kěyǐ fēidào hěn yuǎnde dìfang qù.
If I were a little bird, I could fly to a place far away.

◆ 假如你失败了，可能会失望；但假如你不尝试一下，就不知道你会不会成功。 **Jiǎrú nǐ shībàile, kěnéng huì shīwàng, dàn jiǎrú nǐ bù chángshì yíxià, jiù bù zhīdào nǐ huì-búhuì chénggōng.**
You might be disappointed if you fail, but if you don't try, you won't know whether you might succeed.

102. 简直 **jiǎnzhí** *simply, absolutely*

◆ 那个学生经常不上课，也不做功课，简直太不像话了！
Nèige xuéshēng jīngcháng bú shàngkè, yě bú zuò gōngkè, jiǎnzhí tài bú xiànghuà le!
That student often skips class, and he doesn't do his homework. It's simply ridiculous!

◆ 那个服务员的态度特别不好，简直气死人了！
Nèige fúwùyuánde tàidù tèbié bù hǎo, jiǎnzhí qìsǐ-rén le!
That attendant's attitude is especially poor; it is really infuriating!

◆ 那样的工作环境对他来说简直是如鱼得水。
Nèiyàngde gōngzuò huánjìng duì tā láishuō jiǎnzhí shì rú-yú-dé-shuǐ.
For him, that kind of work environment is simply like a fish in water.

▶ **EXERCISES:**

Translate the following sentences into Chinese, using the structures covered in this chapter:

1. He seems to be very busy, but we don't know what he has been busy with all day.

2. It suddenly got dark, as though there is about to be a big rain.

3. I worked together with Old Zhang for more than ten years; I understand him extremely well.

4. We are old friends; why be so polite?

5. He is always very tense about exams; today is all the more so because it's the semester's final exam.

6. After she went to college she became able to do everything herself. In other words, she became independent.

7. Compared to the food in the school cafeteria, meals at home are exceedingly delicious.

8. Even if her parents don't agree (to it), she still wants to marry Ol' Wang.

9. This student is both smart and industrious; He makes A's in all his courses.

10. Since he admits that he was wrong, let's just forgive him.

11. Since you don't like it here, why don't you move to some other city?

12. If I had a million dollars, I could retire now.

13. Your room is simply too messy. There is not even a place to sit down.

ANSWERS:

1. 他好像很忙，可是我们又不知道他整天忙些什么。
   Tā hǎoxiàng hěn máng, kěshì wǒmen yòu bù zhīdào tā zhěngtiān máng xiē shénme.

2. 天突然黑了，好像要下大雨似的。 **Tiān tūrán hēile, hǎoxiàng yào xià dàyǔ shìde.**

3. 我和老张一起工作了十多年了，非常了解他。
   Wǒ hé Lǎo Zhāng yìqǐ gōngzuòle shí-duō-nián le, fēicháng liǎojiě tā.

4. 我们是老朋友了，你何必这么客气呢？ **Wǒmen shì lǎopéngyou le, nǐ hébì zhème kèqì ne?**

5. 他考试的时候总是很紧张，何况今天是期末考试。
   Tā kǎoshìde shíhou zǒngshì hěn jǐnzhāng, hékuàng jīntiān shì qīmò kǎoshì.

6. 上了大学以后，她什么事情都可以自己做了。换一句话说，她变得独立了。
   Shàngle dàxué yǐhòu, tā shénme shìqing dōu kěyǐ zìjǐ zuò le. Huàn yíjù huà shuō, tā biànde dúlì le.

7. 跟学校食堂的饭菜相比，家里的饭好吃极了。
   Gēn xuéxiào shítángde fàncài xiāngbǐ, jiālǐde fàn hǎochī-jíle.

8. 即使父母不同意，她也要嫁给老王。 **Jíshǐ fùmǔ bù tóngyì, tā yě yào jiàgěi Lǎo Wáng.**

9. 这个学生既聪明又用功，门门功课都是A。
   Zhèige xuésheng jì cōngmíng yòu yònggōng, ménmén gōngkè dōu shì A.

10. 既然他承认自己错了，我们就原谅他吧。
    Jìrán tā chéngrèn zìjǐ cuò le, wǒmen jiù yuánliàng tā ba.

11. 既然你不喜欢这里，怎么不搬到别的城市去呢?
    Jìrán nǐ bù xǐhuan zhèlǐ, zěnme bù bāndào biéde chéngshì qù ne?

12. 假如我有一百万美元，现在就可以退休了。
    Jiǎrú wǒ yǒu yìbǎiwàn Měiyuán, xiànzài jiù kěyǐ tuìxiū le.

13. 你的房间简直太乱了，连坐的地方都没有!
    Nǐde fángjiān jiǎnzhí tài luàn le, lián zuòde dìfang dōu méiyǒu!

Chapter 25: Expressions 103–116

103. 结果 jiéguǒ *as a result, ended up*

◆ 他在面试的时候太紧张了，结果没得到那个工作机会。
  Tā zài miànshìde shíhou tài jǐnzhāng le, jiéguǒ méi dédào nèige gōngzuò jīhuì.
  He was too tense in the interview, with the result that he didn't get that job opportunity.

◆ 他坚持了很长时间也看不到成功的希望，结果就放弃了，实在可惜!
  Tā jiānchíle hěn chángde shíjiān yě kàn-bu-dào chénggōngde xīwàng, jiéguǒ jiù fàngqìle, shízài kěxī!
  He persisted for a long time but didn't see any hope of success, so he ended up giving up. That's too bad!

◆ 我朋友的工作压力很重，生活方式也不健康，结果年纪轻轻就得了重病。 **Wǒ péngyoude gōngzuò yālì hěn zhòng, shēnghuó fāngshì yě bú jiànkāng, jiéguǒ niánjì qīngqīng jiù déle zhòngbìng.**
  My friend was under a lot of pressure in his work, and his lifestyle was also unhealthy, so he ended up with serious illness when he was still young.

104. 借···机会 jiè...jīhuì *to take the opportunity of...to* (do something)

◆ 许多学生都借到中国留学的机会游览那里的名胜古迹。
  Xǔduō xuésheng dōu jiè dào Zhōngguó liúxuéde jīhuì yóulǎn nàlide míngshèng-gǔjì.
  Many students have taken the opportunity of studying in China to visit the important historical sites there.

◆ 他借参加学术会议的机会认识了几位有名的学者。
  Tā jiè cānjiā xuéshù huìyìde jīhuì rènshile jǐwèi yǒumíngde xuézhě.
  He took advantage of the academic conference to meet a few famous scholars.

◆ 许多人都借着房价上涨的机会赚了一大笔钱。
  Xǔduō rén dōu jièzhe fángjià shàngzhǎngde jīhuì zhuànle yí-dà-bǐ qián.
  Many people took advantage of the rising prices in real estate to reap a lot of money.

105. 尽管 **jǐnguǎn** *although, in spite of*

尽管 **jǐnguǎn** is a synonym of the more common word 虽然 **suīrán**, and the two may be used interchangeably in most situations. But when the subject in the follow-up clause is resolutely holding to a stance despite the reality stated in the first clause, 尽管 **jǐnguǎn** is the appropriate word to use (see the second example below).

◆ 尽管这次考试很难，但她还是考得非常好。
Jǐnguǎn zhèicì kǎoshì hěn nán, dàn tā háishi kǎode fēicháng hǎo.
Although this exam was very difficult, she still did very well on it.

◆ 他尽管上了岁数，但走起路来仍健步如飞。
Tā jǐnguǎn shàngle suìshù, dàn zǒu-qǐ-lù-lai réng jiànbù-rúfēi.
Although he is at an advanced age, he still walks spritely as if flying.

◆ 尽管他刚进公司，却因为工作能力很强而受到重用。
Jǐnguǎn tā gāng jìn gōngsī, què yīnwèi gōngzuò nénglì hěn qiáng ér shòudào zhòngyòng.
Although he just joined the company, (but) because he is very capable, he has been given important responsibilities.

◆ 尽管广告把这种产品说得千好万好，我还不敢完全相信。
Jǐnguǎn guǎnggào bǎ zhèizhǒng chǎnpǐn shuōde qiānhǎo wànhǎo, wǒ hái bù-gǎn wánquán xiāngxìn.
Although the ads say that this kind of product is wonderful, still I don't dare completely believe them.

106. 究竟···(呢)? **jiūjìng...(ne)?** *after all...?*

As an adverb, 究竟 **jiūjìng** is a synonym of 毕竟 **bìjìng** (#4) and 到底 **dàodǐ** (#52), but it is normally used only in questions. 究 **jiū** means *to investigate*, so 究竟 **jiūjìng** implies a conclusion reached after an investigation. 究竟 **jiūjìng** is also a noun, meaning *outcome*.

◆ 我们走错路了，现在究竟在哪里呢？
Wǒmen zǒucuò-lù le, xiànzài jiūjìng zài nǎli ne?
We have taken the wrong road. Where are we now, after all?

◆ 他们两个人为什么分手了呢？究竟是怎么回事儿呢？
Tāmen liǎngge rén wèishénme fēnshǒu le ne? Jiūjìng shì zěnme huí shìr ne?
Why did the two of them part ways? What was their problem after all?

◆ 这次比赛高手云集，究竟谁会最后夺冠呢？
Zhèicì bǐsài gāoshǒu yúnjí, jiūjìng shéi huì zuìhòu duóguàn ne?
There is such a crowd of outstanding players in this competition; who after all will be the final champion?

107. 究竟是···还是···? **jiūjìng shì...háishi...?** *after all, is it...or...? In the final analysis...*
This structure implies that the answer to the question is not clear. It has no parallel in the English language, and can only be paraphrased—not translated—into English. Hearing it and using it frequently will lead you to mastery of this structure.

- 我看不出来，你究竟是哥哥还是弟弟？
  Wǒ kàn-bu-chūlai, nǐ jiūjìng shì gēgē háishi dìdì?
  I can't tell after all whether you are the older brother or the younger brother.

- 去中国留学，我究竟应该去北京还是上海？
  Qù Zhōngguó liúxué, wǒ jiūjìng yīnggāi qù Běijīng háishi Shànghǎi?
  All things considered, where in China should I go to study, Beijing or Shanghai?

- 关于这个计划，领导究竟是同意还是不同意？
  Guānyú zhèige jìhuà, lǐngdǎo jiūjìng shì tóngyì háishi bù tóngyì?
  In regard to this plan, does the leadership agree with it or not?

108. 就是···也··· **jiùshi...ye...** *even if...still...*
Note of caution: The English terms *even* and *even if* sometimes cause students to confuse 连 **lián** with 就是 **jiùshi**, and by extension, this structure with #124 (连···也 **lián...yě...**). (see 2.1, sec. 15)

- 最近公司里很忙，就是周末我们也必须加班。
  Zuìjìn gōngsīlǐ hěn máng, jiùshi zhōumò wǒmen yě bìxū jiābān.
  Things are very busy at the company now. Even if it's a weekend we have to work overtime.

- 他非常固执，就是自己错了也很少承认。
  Tā fēicháng gùzhí, jiùshi zìjǐ cuòle yě hěn shǎo chéngrèn.
  He is very stubborn. Even if he is wrong, he is seldom willing to admit it.

- 为了孩子，许多母亲就是牺牲自己的事业也心甘情愿。
  Wèile háizi, xǔduō mǔqin jiùshi xīshēng zìjǐde shìyè yě xīngān-qíngyuàn.
  For their children, many mothers are perfectly willing to sacrifice their careers.

109. 就是···，又···呢? **jiùshi..., yòu...ne?** *even if...* (followed by a rhetorical question)
The word 又 **yòu** in this structure does not have a handy equivalent in English. It does not mean *again*, but simply reinforces the notion of *even if*. A rhetorical question is built into this structure for an emphatic effect.

- 在他看来，为了得到好成绩，就是不睡觉又有什么关系呢？
  Zài tā kànlai, wèile dédào hǎo chéngjì, jiùshi bú shuìjiào yòu yǒu shénme guānxi ne?
  As he sees it, for the sake of getting a good grade, what does it matter if he doesn't sleep?

- 为了更好的将来，就是现在吃一点儿苦，又算得了什么呢？
  Wèile gèng hǎode jiānglái, jiùshi xiànzài chī yìdiǎnr kǔ, yòu suàn-de-liǎo shénme ne?
  For a better future, what does it matter if we suffer a little now?

♦ 就是孩子错了，父母又何必那么生气呢?
Jiùshi háizi cuòle, fùmǔ yòu hébì nàme shēngqì ne?
Even if the child is wrong, (still) why do the parents have to be so angry?

110. 就算···也··· **jiù suàn...yě...** *even if...still...*

This structure is a less common synonym of 就是···也··· **jiùshi...ye...** (#108). The word 算 **suàn** "to count" adds the notion of "taking (something) into account," and implies that "even accepting a certain fact," the assertion still holds true.

♦ 在学生们看来，为了得到好成绩，就算两天不睡觉也很值得。
Zài xuéshengmen kànlai, wèile dédào hǎo chéngjì, jiù suàn liǎngtiān bú shuìjiào yě hěn zhíde.
As the students see it, in order to get good grades, even losing a couple nights' sleep is worth it.

♦ 就算他是公司的大老板，也不能这样不尊重下面的员工。
Jiù suàn tā shì gōngsīde dà lǎobǎn, yě bùnéng zhèiyàng bù zūnzhòng xiàmiànde yuángōng.
Granted that he is the top boss of the company, he still cannot be so disrespectful toward the employees under him.

♦ 就算我们遇到很多的困难，也不应该放弃，要相信我们一定能成功。
Jiù suàn wǒmen yùdào hěn duōde kùnnan, yě bù yīnggāi fàngqì, yào xiāngxìn wǒmen yídìng néng chénggōng.
Even though we encountered many obstacles, we still should not give up; we must believe that we definitely can succeed.

111. 就要···了 **jiù yào...le** *will soon..., is about to...*

♦ 就要毕业了，我还没找到工作呢!
Jiù yào bìyè le, wǒ hái méi zhǎodào gōngzuò ne!
We are about to graduate, and I still haven't found a job!

♦ 孩子就要离开家去上大学了，妈妈又高兴又难过。
Háizi jiù yào líkāi jiā qù shàng dàxué le, Māma yòu gāoxìng yòu nánguò.
The child is about to leave home and go to college; Mom is both happy and sad.

♦ 圣诞节就要到了，人人都忙着给亲朋好友挑选圣诞礼物。
Shèngdànjié jiù yào dào le, rénrén dōu mángzhe gěi qīnpéng- hǎoyǒu tiāoxuǎn shèngdàn lǐwù.
Christmas is almost here, and everyone is busy selecting (Christmas) presents for their friends and family.

112. 居然 **jūrán** *actually* (surprisingly)

居然 **jūrán** indicates that the outcome or reality is contrary to expectations. It is the antonym of 果然 **guǒrán** (#87). There is no precise equivalent for 居然 **jūrán** in English; the meaning *actually* is only an approximation.

♦ 看他并不很用功，居然考了满分，不是聪明就是作弊！
Kàn tā bìng bù hěn yònggōng, jūrán kǎole mǎnfēn, búshì cōngmíng jiùshì zuòbì!
Look, he isn't very studious, and yet he actually made a perfect score. Either he is very smart or he cheated.

♦ 好多年不见，她居然长得又高又漂亮，真是丑小鸭变成了美丽的天鹅！
Hǎo duō nián bú jiàn, tā jūrán zhǎngde yòu gāo yòu piàoliang, zhēn shì chǒu xiǎoyā biànchéngle měilìde tiān'é!
We hadn't seen her for many years, and she has indeed grown tall and pretty, really like an ugly duckling grown into a beautiful swan!

♦ 在那次车祸当中，汽车完全毁了，而他居然一点儿没受伤，真是万幸！
Zài nèicì chēhuò dāngzhōng, qìchē wánquán huǐle, ér tā jūrán yìdiǎnr méi shòushāng, zhēnshì wànxìng!
In that automobile accident, the car was totaled but he actually didn't suffer the slightest injury. It was amazing good luck!

113. 看来 **kànlai** *as far as we can see, apparently*

♦ 饭馆的生意一天不如一天，看来快要关门了。
Fànguǎnde shēngyì yìtiān bùrú yìtiān, kànlai kuàiyào guānmén le.
The restaurant's business is declining day by day; it looks as though it is about to close.

♦ 大赛前他一点儿也不紧张，看来是胸有成竹了。
Dàsài qián tā yìdiǎnr yě bù jǐnzhāng, kànlai shì xiōng-yǒu-chéngzhú le.
Before the big race/contest he is not the least bit nervous. He seems to have complete confidence.

♦ 最后的结果证明老张是对的，看来姜还是老的辣。
Zuìhòude jiéguǒ zhèngmíng Lǎo Zhāng shì duìde, kànlai jiāng háishi lǎode là.
The final results confirm that Old Zhang was right; it's clear that "old ginger is more spicy." (euphemism for elders with experience)

114. 可 *adjective* 多了   **kě** *adjective* **duō le**   *much more...(adjective)*

可 **kě** has a secondary meaning of *actually, for sure*. It is used mainly in colloquial speech. In this structure, it adds emphasis to a comparison between two entities.

♦ 跟从前比，这里的夏天可热多了。 **Gēn cóngqián bǐ, zhèlǐ de xiàtiān kě rè duō le.**
Summer here is much hotter than in the past.

♦ 大城市的生活比我们这个小地方的可有意思多了。
Dà chéngshìde shēnghuó bǐ wǒmen zhèige xiǎo dìfangde kě yǒuyìsi duō le.
Life in the big city is much more interesting than this little place of ours.

♦ 对刚开始学中文的人来说，发音声调比读书写字可重要多了。
Duì gāng kāishǐ xué Zhōngwénde rén láishuō, fāyīn shēngdiào bǐ dúshū xiězì kě zhòngyào duō le.
For someone who has just begun to study Chinese, pronunciation and tones are much more important than reading and writing.

115. 可不要/不能/别··· **kě búyào/bùnéng/bié...** *do not, cannot* (emphatic)

In this structure, 可 **kě** is used in the same sense as in the preceding structure. The same level of emphasis can be expressed in English either by intonation or by a phrase like *by no means, under no circumstances, etc.* The single word 可 **kě** in Chinese is much more succinct, but no less effective.

♦ 这一带不太安全，晚上可别一个人走路回家。
   Zhè yídài bú tài ānquán, wǎnshang kě bié yíge rén zǒulù huíjiā.
   This area is not very safe. Don't walk home alone in the evening.

♦ 吃什么药应该听医生的，可不能自己随便吃哟。
   Chī shénme yào yīnggāi tīng yīshēngde, kě bùnéng zìjǐ suíbiàn chī yo.
   You should listen to the doctor's advice about what medicine to take. Don't just haphazardly medicate yourself.

♦ 投资一定要小心，可不要为了高回报而冒太大的风险啊！
   Tóuzī yídìng yào xiǎoxīn, kě búyào wèile gāo huíbào ér mào tài dàde fēngxiǎn a.
   You must be careful in making investments. Don't take too much risk for the sake of getting high returns!

116. 可见 **kějiàn** *(as one) can see*

可见 **kějiàn** differs from 看来 **kànlai** (#113) in that it makes a direct connection between an observed fact and a conclusion, whereas 看来 **kànlai** presents a surmise based not necessarily on a great deal of evidence.

♦ 这个外国人说的中文，中国人都听不懂，可见学好发音声调很重要。
   Zhèige wàiguórén shuōde Zhōngwén, Zhōngguórén dōu tīng-bu-dǒng, kějiàn xuéhǎo fāyīn shēngdiào hěn zhòngyào.
   No Chinese can understand what this foreigner says in Chinese. From this, we can see that learning pronunciation and tones is indeed very important.

♦ 半年没来，这里的很多地方都认不出来了，可见变化实在是太快了！
   Bànnián méi lái, zhèlǐde hěn duō dìfang dōu rèn-bu-chūlai le, kějiàn biànhuà shízài shì tài kuài le!
   It's been only half a year since we were last here, and already there are many places that we don't recognize. From this, we can see that changes are happening very fast!

♦ 在许多行业里，男女并没有同工同酬，可见男女不平等的现象依然存在。**Zài xǔduō hángyèlǐ, nánnǚ bìng méiyǒu tónggōng-tóngchóu, kějiàn nánnǚ bù píngděngde xiànxiàng yīrán cúnzài.**
   In many professions, equal pay for equal work between men and women has not come into effect. Apparently, gender inequality still exists.

EXERCISES:

Translate the following sentences into Chinese, using the structures covered in this chapter:

1. It was already late when we started, and traffic was too heavy on the road; as a result we missed the plane.

2. I took the opportunity of summer vacation to go home and see family and friends.

3. Although they already have three lovely daughters, they still would like to have a son.

4. With so many different universities, which ones, after all, should I apply to?

5. After all, are China and America cooperating partners or competing opponents?

6. Even if I don't sleep tonight, I must finish this article.

7. Even if her parents object to her marrying that man, what can they do about it?

8. Even if he cannot get into a first rate college, he will still have many opportunities in the future.

9. It will soon be summer vacation. What plans do you have?

10. He actually forgot his girlfriend's birthday, and she is naturally very angry!

11. Apparently her parents don't like her boyfriend much.

12. The food that Mom prepares is much better than that of the school cafeteria.

13. If you go abroad for travel, don't forget to take your passport.

14. There are more and more Chinese going abroad for travel. Obviously, the Chinese people are wealthier than in the past.

ANSWERS:

1. 我们出发的时候已经晚了，路上又堵车，结果误了飞机。
   Wǒmen chūfāde shíhou yǐjīng wǎn le, lùshang yòu dǔchē, jiéguǒ wùle fēijī.

2. 我借着放暑假的机会回家看看亲朋好友。
   Wǒ jièzhe fàng shǔjiàde jīhuì huíjiā kànkan qīnpéng-hǎoyǒu.

3. 他们尽管已经有三个可爱的女儿了，可是还是想再生一个儿子。
   Tāmen jǐnguǎn yǐjīng yǒu sānge kě'àide nǚ'ér le, kěshì háishi xiǎng zài shēng yíge érzi.

4. 这么多不同的大学，究竟应该申请哪几所呢？
   Zhème duō bùtóng de dàxué, jiūjìng yīnggāi shēnqǐng nǎ jǐsuǒ ne?

5. 中美两国究竟是合作伙伴还是竞争对手？
   Zhōng-Měi liǎngguó jiūjìng shì hézuò huǒbàn háishi jìngzhēng duìshǒu?

6. 今晚就是不睡觉，我也得写完这篇文章。
   Jīnwǎn jiùshi bú shuìjiào, wǒ yě děi xiěwán zhèipiān wénzhāng.

7. 父母就是不同意她跟那个人结婚，又有什么办法呢？
   Fùmǔ jiùshi bù-tóngyì tā gēn nèige rén jiéhūn, yòu yǒu shénme bànfǎ ne?

8. 就算上不了一流的大学，他将来也会有很多机会。
   Jiù suàn shàng-bu-liǎo yīliúde dàxué, tā jiānglái yě huì yǒu hěn duō jīhuì.

9. 就要放暑假了，你有什么计划？ Jiù yào fàng shǔjià le, nǐ yǒu shénme jìhuà?

10. 他居然忘了女朋友的生日，她当然很生气！
    Tā jūrán wàngle nǔpéngyoude shēngrì, tā dāngrán hěn shēngqì!

11. 看来父母不太喜欢她的男朋友。**Kànlai fùmǔ bú tài xǐhuan tāde nánpéngyou.**

12. 妈妈做的饭菜比学校食堂的可好吃多了。
    Māma zuòde fàncài bǐ xuéxiào shítángde kě hǎochī duō le.

13. 你出国旅行的话，可别忘了带护照。**Nǐ chūguó lǚxíng dehuà, kě bié wàngle dài hùzhào.**

14. 出国旅行的中国人越来越多，可见中国人比以前富有了。
    Chūguó lǚxíngde Zhōngguórén yuèláiyuè duō, kějiàn Zhōngguórén bǐ yǐqián fùyǒu le.

Chapter 26: Expressions 117–129

117. 恐怕··· **kǒngpà...** *afraid that..., probably*

恐怕 **kǒngpà** literally means "afraid that." But like its English counterpart, it usually just means *probably*. The probable situation stated in the sentence is not something to be feared, though more often than not, it is a negative situation.

♦ 天那么黑，恐怕一会儿要下雨了。
  Tiān nàme hēi, kǒngpà yìhuǐr yào xiàyǔ le.
  The sky is so dark, it will probably rain in a little while.

♦ 现在已经八点了，恐怕我们赶不上九点半的飞机了。
  Xiànzài yǐjīng bādiǎn le, kǒngpà wǒmen gǎn-bu-shàng jiǔdiǎn-bànde fēijī le.
  It's already eight o'clock; I'm afraid we won't be able to catch the nine-thirty flight.

♦ 她的态度有点儿奇怪，恐怕我们之间有些误会。
  Tāde tàidù yǒudiǎnr qíguài, kǒngpà wǒmen zhījiān yǒuxiē wùhuì.
  Her attitude is rather strange. I'm afraid there has been a misunderstanding between us.

♦ 双方目前还存在很多分歧，恐怕很难达成共识。
  Shuāngfāng mùqián cúnzài hěn duō fēnqí, kǒngpà hěn nán dáchéng gòngshí.
  There are still a lot of disagreements between us; I'm afraid it will be very difficult to come to a mutual understanding.

118. 快/快要···了 **kuài/kuàiyào...le** *soon, just about to...*

♦ 学期快结束了，你的期末报告完成了吗？
  Xuéqī kuài jiéshù le, nǐde qīmò bàogào wánchéngle ma?
  The semester is ending soon; is your end-of-semester report completed yet?

♦ 妈妈快要过生日了，我给她买什么礼物呢？
  Māma kuàiyào guò shēngrì le, wǒ gěi tā mǎi shénme lǐwù ne?
  It is almost time for Mom's birthday. What shall I buy her for a birthday present?

♦ 他太太怀孕了，所以他快要当爸爸了！
  Tā tàitai huáiyùn le, suǒyǐ tā kuàiyào dāng bàba le!
  His wife is expecting, so he will soon be a dad!

119. 况且 **kuàngqiě** *and besides, moreover*

况且 **kuàngqiě** is a cross between 而且 **érqiě** and 何况 **hékuàng** (see #9 and #94). Its meaning is closer to 而且 **érqiě**, but it has the literary flavor of 何况 **hékuàng**. 而且 **érqiě** usually functions in tandem with 不但 **búdàn**, whereas 况且 **kuàngqiě** and 何况 **hékuàng** function independently.

♦ 今天我有点儿不舒服，况且天气也不好，就打算在家里休息休息。
　　Jīntiān wǒ yǒudiǎnr bùshūfu, kuàngqiě tiānqì yě bù hǎo, jiù dǎsuàn zài jiālǐ xiūxi-xiūxi.
　　I'm not feeling well today, and the weather is bad, so I plan to stay home and rest.

♦ 这家餐馆菜的味道不错，况且价钱也不贵，所以生意一直很红火。
　　Zhèijiā cānguǎn càide wèidao búcuò, kuàngqiě jiàqián yě bú guì, suǒyǐ shēngyì yìzhí hěn hónghuǒ.
　　The food in this restaurant is not bad, and it's not expensive either. So business has been great all along.

♦ 总经理年纪不小了，况且身体不太好，所以正考虑退休呢。
　　Zǒngjīnglǐ niánjì bùxiǎo le, kuàngqiě shēntǐ bú tài hǎo, suǒyǐ zhèng kǎolù tuìxiū ne.
　　The general manager is no longer young, and besides, his health is not good, so he is considering retiring.

120. ⋯来⋯ **...lái...** *(do something) in order to (do something else)*

♦ 今天，人们可以用手机来做各种各样的事情。
　　Jīntiān, rénmen kěyǐ yòng shǒujī lái zuò gèzhǒng gèyàngde shìqing.
　　Nowadays people can use a cell phone to do all sorts of things.

♦ 老师用"愚公移山"的故事来说明做事情要有恒心。
　　Lǎoshī yòng "Yúgōng-yíshān" de gùshi lái shuōmíng zuò shìqing yào yǒu héngxīn.
　　The teacher used the story of "The foolish old man who moved a mountain" to illustrate the importance of perseverance.

♦ 1976-2016年间，中国实行了"独生子女"的政策来控制人口的增长。
　　1976-2016 niánjiān, Zhōngguó shíxíngle "dúshēng zǐnǚ" de zhèngcè lái kòngzhì rénkǒude zēngzhǎng.
　　In the years 1976–2016, China maintained the "one child" policy to control population growth.

121. 老 + *verb phrase* **lǎo** + *verb phrase* *continually, to keep on* (being a certain way or doing something)

♦ 你怎么老记不住我的生日呢？ **Nǐ zěnme lǎo jì-bu-zhù wǒde shēngrì ne?**
　　How come you never can remember my birthday?

♦ 他不好好儿读书，老想赚大钱，后来就退学了。
　　Tā bù hǎohāor dúshū, lǎo xiǎng zhuàn dàqián, hòulái jiù tuìxué le.
　　He wasn't serious about his studies, and only kept wanting to make a lot of money. Later he dropped out of school.

♦ 父母不应该老批评孩子，而应该以鼓励为主。
  Fùmǔ bù yīnggāi lǎo pīpíng háizi, ér yīnggāi yǐ gǔlì wéi zhǔ.
  Parents shouldn't always criticize their children. They should focus on encouraging them.

122. 老是··· lǎoshi... *synonym of "老 lǎo + verb phrase" above*

♦ 他在工作上老是马马虎虎的，让人觉得他不太可靠。
  Tā zài gōngzuò-shang lǎoshi mǎmahūhūde, ràng rén juéde tā bú tài kěkào.
  He is always haphazard in his work, making people feel he's unreliable.

♦ 他跟别人说话的时候，老是一副自以为是的样子，令人讨厌。
  Tā gēn biérén shuōhuàde shíhou, lǎoshi yífù zì-yǐwéi-shìde yàngzi, lìng rén tǎoyàn.
  When he talks with other people, he always acts as though he thinks he is right about everything, making people feel disgusted with him.

♦ 这里明明写着不许停车，可老是有人不遵守规定。
  Zhèlǐ míngmíng xiězhe bùxǔ tíngchē, kě lǎoshi yǒu rén bù zūnshǒu guīdìng.
  (The sign) here clearly says "No parking," but there are always some people who don't respect the rules.

123. verb 了又 verb verb le yòu verb *to do (something) again and again*

♦ 我们找了又找，终于找到了要去访问的那位老大爷。
  Wǒmen zhǎole yòu zhǎo, zhōngyú zhǎodàole yào qù fǎngwènde nèiwèi lǎodàye.
  We looked and looked, and finally found the old man whom we wanted to interview.

♦ 那件衣服上的黑点，我洗了又洗，还是洗不掉。
  Nèijiàn yīfu-shangde hēidiǎn, wǒ xǐle yòu xǐ, háishi xǐ-bu-diào.
  I washed and washed, trying to get the black spots out of that piece of clothing, but they never came out.

♦ 他解释了又解释，女朋友还不肯原谅他。
  Tā jiěshìle yòu jiěshì, nǚpéngyou hái bùkěn yuánliàng tā.
  He explained again and again, but his girlfriend wasn't willing to forgive him.

♦ 女儿数学考砸了，妈妈安慰了又安慰，女儿还是很伤心。
  Nǚ'ér shùxué kǎozále, Māma ānwèile yòu ānwèi, nǚ'ér háishi hěn shāngxīn.
  (After) the daughter bombed on her math test, Mom tried and tried to soothe her, but the girl was still very disheartened.

124. 连···都/也··· lián...dōu/yě *even...still...*

To the mind of an English speaker, this structure may seem very similar to "就是···也··· jiùshi...yě..." (#108), but the two structures are quite distinct in Chinese. 连 lián is a coverb meaning *even* and 就是 jiùshi is a conjunction meaning *even if*. The object of the coverb 连 lián must be a noun phrase of some sort (including nominalized verbs). 就是 jiùshi introduces a subordinate clause in a two-clause sentence.

♦ 我最近忙得连吃饭睡觉的时间都没有。
Wǒ zuìjìn mángde lián chīfàn shuìjiàode shíjiān dōu méiyǒu.
I've been so busy that I haven't even had time to eat and sleep.

♦ 他连飞机都会开，开车当然没问题。
Tā lián fēijī dōu huì kāi, kāichē dāngrán méi wèntí.
He even knows how to fly an airplane; of course driving a car is no problem (for him).

♦ 这个年轻人提出的解决方案，连老练的专家们都很佩服。
Zhèige niánqīng-rén tíchūde jiějué fāng'àn, lián lǎoliànde zhuānjiāmen dōu hěn pèifu.
Even the seasoned experts admire the solution that this young person suggested.

125. 另外(又/还)verb··· **lìngwài (yòu/hái) verb...** *and in addition (do something more)*

♦ 妈妈送我到机场，另外又给了我几百块钱，告诉我要经常给她打电话。
Māma sòng wǒ dào jīchǎng, lìngwài yòu gěile wǒ jǐbǎikuài qián, gàosu wǒ yào jīng-cháng gěi tā dǎ diànhuà.
Mom saw me off at the airport, and then also gave me a few hundred dollars and told me to call her regularly.

♦ 我买的手机正在打折促销，价格便宜不少，商家另外又有赠品，很划算！
Wǒ mǎide shǒujī zhèngzài dǎzhé cùxiāo, jiàgé piányi bùshǎo, shāngjiā lìngwài yòu yǒu zèngpǐn, hěn huásuàn!
The cell phone that I'm buying is on sale, the price is greatly reduced, and the store is also giving away bonus items, so it's a real bargain!

♦ 在国外旅行的时候，她丢了钱包，另外还受了伤，真是祸不单行。
Zài guówài lǚxíngde shíhou, tā diūle qiánbāo, lìngwài hái shòule shāng, zhēnshì huò-bù-dānxíng.
While she was traveling abroad, she lost her purse, and was also injured. It was really a case of "tragedies not coming singly."

126. 没(有)(多大)关系 **méi(yǒu) (duōdà) guānxi** *doesn't matter (much)*

没关系 **méiguānxi** is a high-frequency phrase. The examples below show the variations that can be used to make your speech less monotonous.

♦ 只要你爱他，他现在不是很有钱没多大关系。
Zhǐyào nǐ ài tā, tā xiànzài búshi hěn yǒuqián méi duō dà guānxi.
As long as you love him, it doesn't matter much that he is not rich at this time.

♦ 电影开始前还有20分钟的广告，咱们晚一会儿到没关系。
Diànyǐng kāishǐ qián hái yǒu èrshí fēnzhōngde guǎnggào, wǒmen wǎn yìhuǐr dào méi guānxi.
Before the movie begins, there are 20 minutes of ads; it doesn't matter if we are a bit late.

♦ 第一次不成功也没有关系。有句话说得好，失败是成功之母。
Dìyīcì bù chénggōng yě méi guānxi. Yǒu jù huà shuōde hǎo, shībài shì chénggōng zhī mǔ.
It doesn't matter if you don't succeed the first time. There's a saying that is quite appropriate: "Failure is the mother of success."

127. 没想到 **méi xiǎngdào** *didn't realize..., unexpectedly, surprisingly*

没想到 **méi xiǎngdào** is typically used without a subject, i.e. the subject is understood. Comparing the English translations with the original Chinese in the examples below will show that understood elements of a sentence are more likely to be omitted in Chinese than in English. (see 1.3, sec. 2)

◆ 没想到这家看上去很普通的饭馆生意这么好！
  Méi xiǎngdào zhèijiā kàn-shàngqu hěn pǔtōngde fànguǎn shēngyì zhème hǎo!
  I never would've thought that this very ordinary-looking restaurant would have such good business!

◆ 他们曾经是好朋友，没想到现在谁也不理谁了。
  Tāmen céngjīng shì hǎo péngyou, méi xiǎngdào xiànzài shéi yě bù lǐ shéi le.
  They used to be good friends. One never would have thought that now they have become completely estranged.

◆ 这位老大爷平时生活很节俭，没想到他过世以后给学校捐了一大笔钱。 **Zhèiwèi lǎodàye píngshí shēnghuó hěn jiéjiǎn, méi xiǎngdào tā guòshì yǐhòu gěi xuéxiào juānle yídàbǐ qián.**
  This old gentleman usually lived very frugally. Who would have thought that on his death he would donate such a large sum of money to the school.

128. 免不了 **miǎn-bu-liǎo** *cannot avoid, can't help but...*

◆ 他最后没得到那个工作机会，免不了有点失望。
  Tā zuìhòu méi dédào nèige gōngzuò jīhuì, miǎn-bu-liǎo yǒudiǎn shīwàng.
  In the end he did not get that opportunity for a job, and he couldn't help being a bit disappointed.

◆ 两个人在一起生活，经常发生一些小矛盾是免不了的。
  Liǎngge rén zài yìqǐ shēnghuó, jīngcháng fāshēng yìxiē xiǎo máodùn shì miǎn-bu-liǎode.
  When two people live together, they can't avoid having some little disagreements now and then.

◆ 刚移民到一个新的国家，免不了要经历一个痛苦的适应过程。
  Gāng yímín-dào yíge xīnde guójiā, miǎn-bu-liǎo yào jīnglì yíge tòngkǔde shìyìng guòchéng.
  Upon moving/immigrating to a new country, one can't avoid going through a painful process of adjustment.

◆ 如果中美之间爆发贸易战，出现两败俱伤的结果是免不了的。
  Rúguǒ Zhōng-Měi zhījiān bàofā màoyì-zhàn, chūxiàn liǎngbài jùshāngde jiéguǒ shì miǎn-bu-liǎode.
  If a trade war erupts between China and America, both sides will inevitably suffer losses.

129. 免得··· **miǎnde...** *so as to avoid..., in order to be spared...*

◆ 我们早一点儿出发吧，免得天黑之前到不了。
Wǒmen zǎo yìdiǎnr chūfā ba, miǎnde tiānhēi zhīqián dào-bu-liǎo.
Let's leave a little earlier so as to avoid not arriving before dark.

◆ 在外国生活就应该多了解那里的文化习俗，免得闹笑话。
Zài wàiguó shēnghuó jiù yīnggāi duō liǎojiě nàlǐde wénhuà xísú, miǎnde nào xiàohuà.
When you live in a foreign country, you should understand their culture and customs, lest you make a fool of yourself.

◆ 你应该趁年轻多看看世界，丰富人生经历，免得将来后悔。
Nǐ yīnggāi chèn niánqīng duō kànkan shìjiè, fēngfù rénshēng jīnglì, miǎnde jiānglái hòuhuǐ.
You should see more of the world and add to your experiences while you're young, so as not to have regrets in the future.

EXERCISES:

Translate the following sentences into Chinese, using the structures covered in this chapter:

1. There is a surge in people traveling around Chinese New Year's time, I'm afraid train and air tickets will all be very expensive.

2. Winter will soon be here; I must buy a warm jacket.

3. Smoking is bad for one's health; also it wastes money; so you ought to quit smoking.

4. You could take part in more school activities to get to know new friends.

5. I'm not a child (anymore). Don't keep worrying about me!

6. Regardless of what he is doing, he always complains; so none of his colleagues wants to work with him (on projects).

7. He has tried and tried, and still couldn't quit his alcohol addiction.

8. This question is very difficult; even the teacher doesn't know how to respond.

9. We ordered four dishes, and then also added a soup.

10. This is only a quiz; it doesn't matter much if you don't do well on it.

11. She looks very young; I didn't realize that she was already the mother of two children.

12. After age seventy, one's memory can't help but decline a bit.

13. Do your homework first before watching TV, so as to avoid making Mom angry.

ANSWERS:
1. 春节期间旅行的人特别多，火车票、飞机票恐怕都会很贵。
   Chūnjié qījiān lǚxíngde rén tèbié duō, huǒchē-piào, fēijī-piào kǒngpà dōu huì hěn guì.
2. 冬天快来了，我得买一件暖和的外套！
   Dōngtiān kuài lái le, wǒ děi mǎi yíjiàn nuǎnhuode wàitào!

3. 抽烟对身体有害，况且很费钱，所以你应该戒烟。
   Chōuyān duì shēntǐ yǒuhài, kuàngqiě hěn fèiqián, suǒyǐ nǐ yīnggāi jièyān.

4. 你可以多参加一些学校的活动来认识新的朋友。
   Nǐ kěyǐ duō cānjiā yìxiē xuéxiàode huódòng lái rènshí xīnde péngyou.

5. 我不是小孩子了，别老为我担心！ **Wǒ búshì xiǎoháizi le, bié lǎo wèi wǒ dānxīn!**

6. 不管做什么，他老是抱怨，所以同事都不愿意跟他合作。
   Bùguǎn zuò shénme, tā lǎoshi bàoyuàn, suǒyǐ tóngshì dōu bú yuànyi gēn tā hézuò.

7. 他试了又试，还是没法子戒掉酒瘾。 **Tā shìle yòu shì, háishi méi fázi jièdiào jiǔyǐn.**

8. 这个问题很难，连老师也不知道怎么回答。
   Zhèige wèntí hěn nán, lián lǎoshī yě bù zhīdào zěnme huídá.

9. 我们点了四个菜，另外又加了一个汤。 **Wǒmen diǎnle sìge cài, lìngwài yòu jiāle yíge tāng.**

10. 这只是一次小考，成绩不理想也没有多大关系。
    Zhè zhǐshì yícì xiǎokǎo, chéngjì bù lǐxiǎng yě méiyǒu duō dà guānxi.

11. 她看起来很年轻，没想到已经是两个孩子的母亲了。
    Tā kàn-qǐlai hěn niánqīng, méi xiǎngdào yǐjīng shì liǎngge háizide mǔqin le.

12. 过了七十岁以后，记忆力免不了会有一点儿衰退。
    Guòle qīshísuì yǐhòu, jìyì-lì miǎn-bú-liǎo huì yǒu yìdiǎnr shuāituì.

13. 你先做功课再看电视，免得妈妈生气。
    Nǐ xiān zuò gōngkè zài kàn diànshì, miǎnde Māma shēngqì.

Chapter 27: Expressions 130–141

130. 明明 míngmíng *clearly, obviously*

明明 **míngmíng** is typically used in the first clause of a two-clause sentence, in which the second clause states a situation that contradicts the clear evidence presented in the first clause.

♦ 明明是他错了，可还要怪别人，真是不像话。
   Míngmíng shì tā cuòle, kě hái yào guài biérén, zhēnshì bú xiànghuà.
   It is obvious that he was wrong, yet he still wants to blame others; it's really ridiculous.

♦ 他卖的明明是假名牌，可价格却跟正品一样。
   Tā màide míngmíng shì jiǎ míngpái, kě jiàgé què gēn zhèngpǐn yíyàng.
   What he is selling is clearly fake, yet the price is the same as the genuine merchandise's.

♦ 这里明明写着不许抽烟，可还是有人视而不见。
   Zhèlǐ míngmíng xiězhe bùxǔ chōuyān, kě háishi yǒu rén shì-ér-bújiàn.
   It is clearly written here that smoking is prohibited, but there are still people who turn a blind eye to it.

131. 拿···来说 ná...láishuō *speaking of..., in terms of...*

♦ 拿老百姓的生活水平来说，现在比从前有了很大的改善。
   Ná lǎobǎixìngde shēnghuó shuǐpíng láishuō, xiànzài bǐ cóngqián yǒule hěn dàde gǎishàn.
   In terms of common people's standard of living, there has been great improvement from the past.

♦ 拿军事力量来说，中国还远远落后于美国。
Ná jūnshì lìliàng láishuō, Zhōngguó hái yuǎnyuǎn luòhòu-yú Měiguó.
In terms of military strength, China is way behind America.

♦ 拿自然环境来说，过去几十年的快速发展给这里造成了很大的破坏。
Ná zìrán huánjìng láishuō, guòqù jǐshí-niánde kuàisù fāzhǎn gěi zhèlǐ zàochéngle hěn dàde pòhuài.
In terms of the natural environment, the rapid development in recent decades has done a lot of damage to this area.

132. 哪儿/哪里···(啊/呢)? **nǎr/nǎli…(a/ne)?** rhetorical question conveying disagreement
哪儿 **nǎr** and 哪里 **nǎli** are interchangeable. Northerners tend to use 哪儿 **nǎr** and Southerners 哪里 **nǎli**.

♦ 我哪儿知道你在想什么啊？ **Wǒ nǎr zhīdào nǐ zài xiǎng shénme a?**
How would I know what you're thinking?

♦ 学文学哪儿有学经济那么容易找工作啊？
Xué wénxué nǎr yǒu xué jīngjì nàme róngyi zhǎo gōngzuò a?
How could a literature major find a job as easily as an economics major?

♦ 一个刚起步的小公司哪儿有能力跟大公司竞争呢？
Yíge gāng qǐbùde xiǎo gōngsī nǎr yǒu nénglì gēn dà gōngsī jìngzhēng ne?
How could a small startup company compete with a big company?

♦ 他去年才开始工作，自己哪里有能力在北京买房啊？
Tā qùnián cái kāishǐ gōngzuò, zìjǐ nǎli yǒu nénglì zài Běijīng mǎi fáng a?
He only started working last year, how could he have the resources to buy an apartment in Beijing?

133. 哪怕···也··· **nǎpà…yě…** *even if…, though…, granted that…*
There is logic to this seemingly odd use of the question word 哪 **nǎ**. By itself, the 哪怕 **nǎpà** clause within this two- or three-clause structure can be construed as a rhetorical question (see #132), meaning *not daunted by…*, i.e., *even under the unfavorable circumstances of….* But of course, native speakers simply treat it as an idiomatic way of speaking without analyzing it.

♦ 哪怕中文很难学，我也一定要把中文学好。
Nǎpà Zhōngwén hěn nán xué, wǒ yě yídìng yào bǎ Zhōngwén xuéhǎo.
Even if Chinese is very difficult to learn, I am determined to learn it well.

♦ 哪怕我们在政治上有不同的看法，也还是好朋友。
Nǎpà wǒmen zài zhèngzhì-shang yǒu bùtóngde kànfǎ, yě háishi hǎo péngyou.
Even though our political views are different, we are still good friends.

♦ 创业绝不是轻而易举的事情，哪怕不会成功，他也想试一试。
Chuàngyè jué búshì qīng-ér-yì-jǔde shìqing, nǎpà búhuì chénggōng, tā yě xiǎng shì-yishì.
To start a business is definitely not an easy thing, but even if he might not succeed, he still wants to make an attempt.

134. 难道···(吗)？ **nándào...(ma)?** *you don't mean to say...; how could it be...?*

This seemingly simple structure is one of the more difficult ones for students to master, but it is also one of the most worthwhile ones for students to make the effort to learn. It was mentioned in 16.2 as a structure that conveys the attitude of the speaker, so it speaks volumes. This rhetorical question structure is so well-used that the final particle 吗 **ma** can be understood and omitted.

♠ 这么好看的电影，难道你不喜欢？
Zhème hǎokànde diànyǐng, nándào nǐ bù xǐhuan?
Such a good movie, how could you not like it?

♠ 他抽烟抽得这么厉害，难道不担心他的身体健康吗？
Tā chōuyān chōude zhème lìhài, nándào bù dānxīn tāde shēntǐ jiànkāng ma?
He is such a heavy smoker, is he really not concerned about his health?

♠ 女人跟男人做一样的工作，难道不应该得到跟男人一样的年薪吗？
Nǚrén gēn nánrén zuò yíyàngde gōngzuò, nándào bù yīnggāi dédào gēn nánrén yíyàngde niánxīn ma?
When women do the same work as men, how could they not deserve the same salary as men?

135. 难怪 **nánguài** *no wonder* (lit., "hard to take as strange," i.e. not strange)

♠ 他花钱总是大手大脚，难怪工作了几年也没存什么钱。
Tā huāqián zǒngshì dàshǒu dàjiǎo, nánguài gōngzuòle jǐnián yě méi cún shénme qián.
He is always extravagant in his expenditures; it's no wonder that he has worked a few years but still has no savings.

♠ 公司管理混乱，缺乏激励机制，难怪留不住好的人才。
Gōngsī guǎnlǐ hùnluàn, quēfá jīlì jīzhì, nánguài liú-bu-zhù hǎode réncái.
The company's management is chaotic and it lacks an incentive system. No wonder it can't hold on to good talent.

♠ 这家餐馆菜品丰富，价格合理，服务一流，难怪生意一直红火。
Zhèijiā cānguǎn càipǐn fēngfù, jiàgé hélǐ, fúwù yīliú, nánguài shēngyì yìzhí hónghuǒ.
This restaurant has a broad selection of dishes, its prices are reasonable, and its service is excellent. No wonder its business keeps booming.

136. 难免 **nánmiǎn** *hard to avoid, can't help but, inevitably* (synonym of #128, 免不了 **miǎn-bu-liǎo**)

Despite the difference in the literal meanings of 免不了 **miǎn-bu-liǎo** (*unavoidable*) and 难免 **nánmiǎn** (*difficult to avoid*), there is really no difference between them. 难免 **nánmiǎn** is an example of how Chinese speakers tend to understate negative situations out of politeness. Another example is the non-difference between 有点困难 **yǒudiǎn kùnnan** *there's a bit of difficulty* and 没办法 **méi bànfa** *no way* or 行不通 **xíng-bu-tōng** *no go*.

● 谁都不是完美的，有时候工作中出错是难免的。
Shéi dōu búshì wánměi de, yǒu shíhou gōngzuò-zhōng chūcuò shì nánmiǎn de.
Nobody is perfect. An occasional error in our work is unavoidable.

● 虽然我准备得很好，但是面试的时候难免还会有点儿紧张。
Suīrán wǒ zhǔnbèide hěn hǎo, dànshì miànshìde shíhou nánmiǎn hái huì yǒudiǎnr jǐnzhāng.
Although I was well prepared, still when it came to the interview I couldn't help being a little nervous.

● 中美两国之间的贸易规模如此之大，出现贸易摩擦是难免的。
Zhōng-Měi liǎngguó zhījiānde màoyì guīmó rúcǐ zhī dà, chūxiàn màoyì mócā shì nánmiǎn de.
Given that the scale of Chinese-American trade is so large, it's unavoidable that trade friction would occur.

137. 难以 nányǐ difficult to...

● 爸妈都是为了孩子好，但是他们的教育方法让孩子难以接受。
Bà Mā dōu shì wèile háizi hǎo, dànshì tāmende jiàoyù fāngfǎ ràng háizi nányǐ jiēshòu.
Dad and Mom have their children's best interest in mind, but their educational methods are difficult for the children to accept.

● 这次事故造成的巨大伤亡和财产损失难以估量。
Zhèicì shìgù zàochéngde jùdà shāngwáng hé cáichǎn sǔnshī nányǐ gūliáng.
The huge number of casualties and massive property loss caused by this accident is inestimable.

● 中美贸易之间的纠纷与争端难以在短时间内解决。
Zhōng-Měi màoyì zhījiānde jiūfēn yǔ zhēngduān nányǐ zài duǎn shíjiān nèi jiějué.
The Sino-American trade disputes and conflicts cannot be solved easily in a short time.

138. 能···就··· néng... jiù... to...(do something) as long as it's possible
能不···就不··· **néng bù... jiù bù...** *to not...(do something) as long as it can be avoided*

● 你现在能买房子就快买吧，将来一定会更贵。
Nǐ xiànzài néng mǎi fángzi jiù kuài mǎi ba, jiānglái yídìng huì gèng guì.
If you can buy a house now, quickly buy one, as they will be even more expensive in the future.

● 你们能坚持就多坚持一下，救护员很快就到了！
Nǐmen néng jiānchí jiù duō jiānchí yíxià, jiùhùyuán hěn kuài jiù dào le!
Hold on a little longer if you can; rescuers will soon be here!

● 这个消息你能不告诉妈妈就先别告诉她，免得她着急。
Zhèige xiāoxi nǐ néng bú gàosu Māma jiù xiān bié gàosu tā, miǎnde tā zhāojí.
If you can avoid telling Mom this news, don't tell her yet, lest she be upset.

139. 宁可…也不…   **nìngkě...yě bù...**   *would rather...than to...*

In this structure, the situation stated after 也不 **yě bù** is always negative, while the situation stated after 宁可 **nìngkě** also tends to be negative, but not necessarily so (as in the second example). In other words, the structure is used most often to express a choice for the lesser of two "evils."

- 我宁可在家里睡觉也不想出去看那个无聊的电影。
  Wǒ nìngkě zài jiālǐ shuìjiào yě bùxiǎng chūqu kàn nèige wúliáode diànyǐng.
  I'd rather stay home and sleep than to go out to see that boring movie.

- 父母宁可让她有一个快乐的童年也不愿意逼她逼得太紧。
  Fùmǔ nìngkě ràng tā yǒu yíge kuàilède tóngnián yě bú yuànyi bī tā bīde tài jǐn.
  The parents prefer to let her have a happy childhood, rather than driving her too hard.

- 大多数老百姓宁可经济发展得慢一点也不愿意生活在被破坏了的环境里。 **Dàduōshù lǎobǎixìng nìngkě jīngjì fāzhǎnde màn yìdiǎn yě bú yuànyi shēnghuó zài bèi pòhuàilede huánjìngli.**
  A great majority of the people would rather have slower economic development than to live in a ruined environment.

140. 宁愿…也不…   **nìngyuàn...yě bù...**   *would rather...than to...* (synonym of #139)

- 他宁愿少赚一点儿钱也不想每天加班。
  Tā nìngyuàn shǎo zhuàn yìdiǎnr qián yě bùxiǎng měitiān jiābān.
  He would rather make a little less money than to work overtime every day.

- 她宁愿单身也不想嫁给一个不爱的人。
  Tā nìngyuàn dānshēn yě bùxiǎng jiàgěi yíge bú'àide rén.
  She would rather be single than marry someone she doesn't love.

- 我宁愿做一只在天空中自由飞行的小鸟，也不愿做一只牢笼里的苍鹰。 **Wǒ nìngyuàn zuò yìzhī zài tiānkōng-zhōng zìyóu fēixíngde xiǎoniǎo, yě bú yuàn zuò yìzhī láolónglǐ de cāngyīng.**
  I would rather be a little bird flying freely in the sky than an eagle in a cage.

141. 凭 **píng...+** *verb phrase* *relying on...to (do something); to...on the basis of...*

- 你凭什么说他不是一个好人？ **Nǐ píng shénme shuō tā bú shì yíge hǎo rén?**
  What evidence do you have that he is not a good person?

- 她希望凭自己的能力而不是父母的关系来找到自己感兴趣的工作。
  Tā xīwàng píng zìjǐde nénglì ér búshì fùmǔde guānxi lái zhǎodào zìjǐ gǎn-xìngqùde gōngzuò.
  She hopes to depend on her own abilities rather than her parents' connections to find work that she will be interested in.

- 这两个年轻人全凭自己的双手打造了幸福的家庭生活。
  Zhèiliǎngge niánqīng-rén quán píng zìjǐde shuāngshǒu dǎzàole xìngfúde jiātíng shēnghuó.
  These two young people have created a happy family life entirely by their own hands.

• 他们赢了这次比赛一半凭的是实力，另一半凭的是运气。
Tāmen yíngle zhèicì bǐsài yíbàn píngde shì shílì, lìngyíbàn píngde shì yùnqi.
Their winning this competition was half due to their real strength and half due to luck.

EXERCISES:

Translate the following sentences into Chinese, using the structures covered in this chapter:

1. You clearly know that she doesn't like you. Why do you keep giving her gifts?

2. In terms of weather, Chicago is not as pleasant as San Francisco.

3. We will soon have final exams, how could I have time to watch TV?

4. She really enjoys being a teacher. Granted that the salary is not high, she is still very enthusiastic about it.

5. Global warming is already quite obvious, how could you still be skeptical about it?

6. She is smart and loves to study, and she likes to help people. It's no wonder everybody likes her.

7. She didn't listen to what her parents said, so it was hard for them to not be angry.

8. This goal is too high; it will probably be difficult to realize.

9. It's snowing hard outside; don't go out if you can help it.

10. I would rather spend the time cooking than eat in the dining hall.

11. I'd rather get up a bit earlier than to be so rushed in the morning.

12. On what basis did this expert claim that this is not an authentic work of Van Gogh's?

ANSWERS:

1. 你明明知道她不喜欢你，为什么总给她买礼物呢？
   Nǐ míngmíng zhīdào tā bù xǐhuan nǐ, wèishénme zǒng gěi tā mǎi lǐwù ne?

2. 拿天气来说，芝加哥没有旧金山那么舒服。
   Ná tiānqì láishuō, Zhījiāgē méiyǒu Jiùjīnshān nàme shūfu.

3. 快要期末考试了，我哪里有时间看电视啊？
   Kuài yào qīmò kǎoshì le, wǒ nǎli yǒu shíjiān kàn diànshì a?

4. 她很喜欢当老师，哪怕年薪不高，她也很有热情。
   Tā hěn xǐhuan dāng lǎoshī, nǎpà niánxīn bù gāo, tā yě hěn yǒu rèqíng.

5. 全球变暖的现象已经很明显，难道你还怀疑吗？
   Quánqiú biànnuǎnde xiànxiàng yǐjīng hěn míngxiǎn, nándào nǐ hái huáiyí ma?

6. 她聪明好学，乐于助人，难怪大家都喜欢她。
   Tā cōngmíng hàoxué, lèyú zhù rén, nánguài dàjiā dōu xǐhuan ta.

7. 她没有听父母的话，他们难免有点儿生气。
   Tā méiyǒu tīng fùmǔde huà, tāmen nánmiǎn yǒudiǎnr shēngqì.

8. 这个目标太高了，恐怕难以实现。**Zhèige mùbiāo tài gāo le, kǒngpà nányǐ shíxiàn.**

9. 外面雪下得很大，今天能不出门就不要出门了。
   Wàimian xuě xiàde hěn dà, jīntiān néng bù chūmén jiù búyào chūmén le.

10. 我宁可花时间做饭也不要吃食堂的饭。
   Wǒ nìngkě huā shíjiān zuòfàn yě búyào chī shítángde fàn.

11. 我宁愿早一点儿起床也不要早上那么匆忙。
   Wǒ nìngyuàn zǎo yìdiǎnr qǐchuáng yě búyào zǎoshang nàme cōngmáng.

12. 这位专家凭什么说这幅画不是梵高的真品?
   Zhèiwèi zhuānjiā píng shénme shuō zhèfú huà bú shì Fán Gāode zhēnpǐn?

Chapter 28: Expressions 142–154

142. 其次···，再其次··· **qícì..., zài qícì...** *(top priority), then..., and then...*

This structure is used to state an ordering of priorities. The leading clause that precedes 其次 **qícì** states the top priority, usually with such wording as 首先 **shǒuxiān** *first and foremost* or 最重要的是 **zuì zhòngyàode shì** *the most important thing is.*

♦ 这家公司需要的人才首先要有责任心，其次有能力，再其次才是学历。 **Zhèjiā gōngsī xūyàode réncái shǒuxiān yào yǒu zérènxīn, qícì yǒu nénglì, zài qícì cái shì xuélì.**
   What this company needs in its personnel is first and foremost a sense of responsibility, and then ability, and finally academic qualifications.

♦ 创办一家成功的企业首先要有资金，其次需要人才，再其次需要良好的管理。
   Chuàngbàn yìjiā chénggōngde qǐyè shǒuxiān yào yǒu zījīn, qícì xūyào réncái, zài qícì xūyào liánghǎode guǎnlǐ.
   To create a successful enterprise, the first requirement is funding, and then personnel, and finally, good management.

♦ 健康的生活有三个基本条件，首先是合理的饮食，其次是适量的运动，再其次是要有良好的心态。
   Jiànkāngde shēnghuó yǒu sānge jīběn tiáojiàn, shǒuxiān shì hélǐde yǐnshí, qícì shì shìliàngde yùndòng, zài qícì shì yào yǒu liánghǎode xīntài.
   There are three basic requirements for a healthy life: first of all is a rational diet, second is an appropriate amount of exercise, and finally is a good mental attitude.

143. 其实 **qíshí** *actually, in fact*

In literary Chinese, 其 **qí** and 实 **shí** mean *its* and *reality*, respectively. 其实 **qíshí** introduces a reality that is contrary to appearances, and it is often used in tandem with a phrase that presents the false appearance. See #6 别以为···，其实··· **bié yǐwéi..., qíshí...**, and #90 好像···，其实··· **hǎoxiàng..., qíshí....**

♦ 他表面上很大方，其实是个小气鬼。
   Tā biǎomiàn-shang hěn dàfāng, qíshí shì ge xiǎoqìguǐ.
   On the surface he seems to be a generous person, but he is actually a penny pincher.

● 他自以为很聪明，其实他的一言一行同事们都看得很清楚，所以在公司里没有人愿意跟他合作。
Tā zì-yǐwéi hěn cōngming, qíshí tāde yìyán-yìxíng tóngshìmen dōu kànde hěn qīngchǔ, suǒyǐ zài gōngsīlǐ méiyǒu rén yuànyi gēn tā hézuò.
He thinks he is very smart, but his coworkers have clearly seen his every word and deed, and nobody in the company wants to work with him.

● 她的英文那么好，我还以为她是在美国出生长大的华裔，其实她是从中国来的留学生。 **Tāde Yīngwén nàme hǎo, wǒ hái yǐwéi tā shì zài Měiguó chūshēng zhǎngdàde Huáyì, qíshí tā shì cóng Zhōngguó láide liúxuéshēng.**
Her English is so good, I thought she had been born and raised in America, but she is actually a student from China.

144. 千万别/不要 qiānwàn bié/búyào *don't by any means*

● 这个坏消息千万不要告诉她，不然她会受不了的。
Zhèige huài xiāoxi qiānwàn búyào gàosu tā, bùrán tā huì shòu-bu-liǎo de.
Don't by any means tell her this bad news; otherwise she won't be able to bear it.

● 父母千万不要太宠爱孩子，对他们将来的发展不利。
Fùmǔ qiānwàn búyào tài chǒngài háizi, duì tāmen jiānglàide fāzhǎn búlì.
Parents should not by any means spoil their children too much, as it will be bad for their future development.

● 毒品是恶魔，千万别沾上它，否则会毁了自己和家人。
Dúpǐn shì èmó, qiānwàn bié zhānshàng tā, fǒuzé huì huǐle zìjǐ hé jiārén.
Drugs are a demon. Don't have anything to do with them, or they will destroy yourself and your family.

145. 前者…, 后者… qiánzhě…, hòuzhě… *the former…, and the latter…*

● 熊猫和猫熊说的都是panda。大陆用的是前者，而多半的台湾人习惯用后者。 **Xióngmāo hé māoxióng dōu shì "panda." Dàlù yòngde shì qiánzhě, ér duōbànde Táiwānrén xíguàn yòng hòuzhě.**
Both xióngmāo and māoxióng refer to panda. On the Mainland the former is used, while most Taiwanese are used to using the latter.

● 智商和情商是一个人成功的两个重要因素，很难说前者一定比后者更重要。 **Zhìshāng hé qíngshāng shì yíge rén chénggōngde liǎngge zhòngyào yīnsù, hěn nán shuō qiánzhě yídìng bǐ hòuzhě gèng zhòngyào.**
Both I.Q. and E.Q. are important factors in a person's success, and it is hard to say whether the former is definitely more important than the latter.

● 世界上有两种人，一种从他人索取，另一种给予他人。前者自私自利，后者乐于助人。 **Shìjiè-shang yǒu liǎngzhǒng rén, yìzhǒng cóng tārén suǒqǔ, lìngyìzhǒng jǐyǔ tārén. Qiánzhě zìsī zìlì, hòuzhě lèyú zhùrén.**
There are two kinds of people in the world, takers and givers. The former are selfish; the latter like to help others.

146. 任何···都··· **rènhé...dōu...** *any...(all)...*

Note that 都 **dōu** goes hand-in-hand with 任何 **rènhé**, i.e., it is indispensable, while its equivalent in English (*all*) is never used in the same context because it would be considered superfluous.

● 这个机器人好聪明，你有任何问题，它都可以解答。
Zhèige jīqìrén hǎo cōngming, nǐ yǒu rènhé wèntí, tā dōu kěyǐ jiědá.
This robot is very intelligent. It can answer any question that you might have.

● 任何一个国家的领土主权都不应该受到侵犯。
Rènhé yíge guójiāde lǐngtǔ zhǔquán dōu bù yīnggāi shòudào qīnfàn.
No country's territorial rights should be infringed upon.

● 法律面前人人平等，任何人都应该受到法律的约束。
Fǎlǜ miànqián rénrén píngděng, rènhé rén dōu yīnggāi shòudào fǎlǜde yuēshù.
All people are equal before the law, and everyone should be subject to legal restraint.

147. 仍然 **réngrán** *still*

The usage of 仍然 **réngrán** implies that a certain situation persists despite some contravening circumstance.

● 他现在有钱了，但仍然过着简朴的生活。
Tā xiànzài yǒuqián le, dàn réngrán guòzhe jiǎnpǔde shēnghuó.
He has become wealthy now, but he still leads a simple life.

● 虽然我们在会议上有过很多争论，但仍然是好朋友。
Suīrán wǒmen zài huìyì-shang yǒuguo hěnduō zhēnglùn, dàn réngrán shì hǎo péngyou.
Although we have had many arguments at meetings, we are still good friends.

● 改革开放四十多年了，这个边远的小山村仍然没有太大的改变。
Gǎigé-kāifàng sìshí-duō-nián le, zhèige biānyuǎnde xiǎo shāncūn réngrán méiyǒu tài dàde gǎibiàn.
After more than forty years of reform and opening, there has still not been much change in this small mountain village in the boondocks.

148. 如果···(的话) **rúguǒ...(dehuà)** *if...* (see #55···的话 ...dehuà)

● 如果明天下雨(的话)，我们就不去爬山了。
Rúguǒ míngtiān xiàyǔ (dehuà), wǒmen jiù bú qù páshān le.
If it rains tomorrow, we won't go mountain climbing.

● 如果政府不加大环保力度(的话)，环境污染会进一步恶化。
Rúguǒ zhèngfǔ bù jiādà huánbǎo lìdù (dehuà), huánjìng wūrǎn huì jìn-yíbù èhuà.
If the government doesn't put more effort into environmental protection, environmental pollution will worsen.

♦ 如果没有竞争(的话)，市场就没有优胜劣汰，企业也就不会进步。
Rúguǒ méiyǒu jìngzhēng (dehuà), shìchǎng jiù méiyǒu yōushèng-lièdài, qǐyè yě jiù búhuì jìnbù.
If there is no competition, the market will not be subject to the survival of the fittest, and enterprises will not make progress.

149. 甚至(于) shènzhì (yú) *even to the point of...*

甚 shèn and 至 zhì mean *extreme* and *to reach* in literary Chinese, so 甚至 shènzhì literally means *extreme to the point of...* It describes a situation that has become very intense or gone very far.

♦ 考试那两周我特别忙，有时候甚至(于)没有时间吃饭睡觉。 **Kǎoshì nèi liǎngzhōu wǒ tèbié máng, yǒu shíhou shènzhì(yú) méiyǒu shíjiān chīfàn shuìjiào.**
I was especially busy during those two weeks of exams, sometimes not even having time to eat and sleep.

♦ 在饭馆里碰见一位老同学，我甚至(于)忘了他的名字，特别不好意思。 **Zài fànguǎnlǐ pèngjiàn yíwèi lǎo tóngxué, wǒ shènzhì(yú) wàngle tāde míngzi, tèbié bùhǎo-yìsi.**
I ran into an old classmate in a restaurant, and I couldn't even remember his name; so embarrassing!

♦ 喜欢赌博的人大多赚不了钱，有的甚至(于)家破人亡。
Xǐhuan dǔbóde rén dàduō zhuàn-bu-liǎo qián, yǒude shènzhì(yú) jiāpò-rénwáng.
Most people who like gambling don't make money at it, some even end up with broken homes and family members scattered.

150. 省得 shěngde *lest, be spared from* (an unfortunate situation or having to do something)

♦ 你快把客厅收拾好，省得妈妈回来了生气。
Nǐ kuài bǎ kètīng shōushi-hǎo, shěngde Māma huílaile shēngqì.
Hurry up and tidy up the living room, lest Mom will be angry when she comes home.

♦ 我们最好早一点出门，省得在路上堵车。
Wǒmen zuì hǎo zǎo yìdiǎn chūmén, shěngde zài lùshang dǔchē.
We'd best leave early, lest we get into a traffic jam on the way.

♦ 我在网上买这些东西，快递都可以送到家里来，省得我们去超市了。
Wǒ zài wǎngshàng mǎi zhèxiē dōngxi, kuàidì dōu kěyǐ sòngdào jiālǐ lái, shěngde wǒmen qù chāoshì le.
I'll buy these things online and have them delivered by express, saving us the trouble of going to the supermarket.

151. 实际上 shíjì-shang *in reality, actually* (synonym of #143 其实 qíshí)
This is one example of the prolific construction "···上 shang." Other examples: 事实上 shìshí-shang *in reality* (#158), 表面上 biǎomiàn-shang *on the surface*, 原则上

yuánzé-shang *in principle,* 大体上 **dàtǐ-shang** *in general,* 法律上 **fǎlù-shang** *legally,* 基本上 **jīběn-shang** *basically,* 理论上 **lǐlùn-shang** *in theory,* 历史上 **lìshǐ-shang** *historically.*

♦ 这两家人表面上关系很好，实际上有很多矛盾。
  Zhèi liǎngjiā rén biǎomiàn-shang guānxi hěn hǎo, shíjì-shang yǒu hěn duō máodùn.
  On the surface these two families seem to have a good relationship, but in reality, there are many conflicts between them.

♦ 这块玉很贵，但实际上不值这个价钱。
  Zhèikuài yù hěn guì, dàn shíjì-shang bùzhí zhèige jiàqián.
  This piece of jade is very expensive, but actually it is not worth this price.

♦ 公司虽然还在运营，但实际上已经债台高筑了，很可能会倒闭。
  Gōngsī suīrán hái zài yùnyíng, dàn shíjì-shang yǐjīng zhàitái-gāozhù le, hěn kěnéng huì dǎobì.
  Although the company is still operating, but in reality it is under a great pile of debt and perhaps it is about to go bankrupt.

152. 使 shǐ to cause, to make, to lead to

♦ 在中国留学使我进一步了解了中国人与中国文化。
  Zài Zhōngguó liúxué shǐ wǒ jìnyíbù liǎojiěle Zhōngguórén yǔ Zhōngguó wénhuà.
  Studying in China led me to take another step in understanding Chinese people and their culture.

♦ 贸易上的摩擦使中美关系变得很紧张。
  Màoyì-shang de mócā shǐ Zhōng-Měi guānxi biànde hěn jǐnzhāng.
  Conflicts in trade have made the Sino-American relationship very tense.

♦ 这笔奖学金使这个农民工有了机会上大学，实现了自己的梦想。
  Zhèibǐ jiǎngxuéjīn shǐ zhèige nóngmín-gōng yǒule jīhuì shàng dàxué, shíxiànle zìjǐde mèngxiǎng.
  This scholarship gave this peasant (migrant) worker an opportunity to go to college, thus realizing his dream.

153. 使⋯成为⋯ shǐ...chéngwéi... to cause...to become...

♦ 那年参加夏令营使我们两个人成为了最好的朋友。
  Nèinián cānjiā xiàlìngyíng shǐ wǒmen liǎngge rén chéngwéile zuìhǎode péngyou.
  Going to summer camp that year made the two of us become the best of friends.

♦ 高等教育的目的就是要使年轻人成为对社会有贡献的人。
  Gāoděng jiàoyùde mùdì jiùshì yào shǐ niánqīng-rén chéngwéi duì shèhuì yǒu gòngxiànde rén.
  The objective of higher education is to make young people into contributing members of society.

● 网络的发展使"足不出户便知天下事"成为了现实。
Wǎngluòde fāzhǎn shǐ "zú bù chū hù biàn zhī tiānxià shì" chéngwéile xiànshí.
Development of the Internet has made "know everything in the world without going out the door" a reality.

154. 使得 **shǐde** *to bring about, to cause*

● 经济过快的发展使得这个地区的环境受到了很大的破坏。
Jīngjì guòkuàide fāzhǎn shǐde zhèige dìqūde huánjìng shòudàole hěn dàde pòhuài.
Overly rapid economic development has seriously ruined the environment of this area.

● 中国迅速发展的高铁网络使得老百姓的出行十分便捷。
Zhōngguó xùnsù fāzhǎnde gāotiě wǎngluò shǐde lǎobǎixìngde chūxíng shífēn biànjié.
Rapid development of a fast rail network in China has made travel very convenient for the people.

● 科技的发展，社会的变化使得语言里不断地增加新的词汇。
Kējìde fāzhǎn, shèhuìde biànhuà shǐde yǔyán-lǐ búduànde zēngjiā xīnde cíhuì.
Technical development and social change have brought about constant expansion of new vocabulary in our language.

● 吸毒使得他妻离子散，家破人亡。 **Xīdú shǐde tā qī-lí-zǐ-sàn, jiā-pò-rén-wáng.**
His use of drugs has caused his wife and children to leave him, and the family to be broken.

EXERCISES:

Translate the following sentences into Chinese, using the structures covered in this chapter:

1. The city that they hope to settle down in is Seattle, with San Francisco as their second choice, and Los Angeles after that.

2. She looks very young, but she is actually already the mother of two children.

3. It is not very safe here, so be sure not to let your child go out alone.

4. Stanford University and UC Berkeley are both in California. The former is private and the latter is public.

5. You can call me anytime.

6. This old man is more than seventy years old, but he still has a child's heart.

7. If I had not had the support of my family I would not have succeeded.

8. His work is secret. He can't even tell his wife about it.

9. We'll go to a restaurant to eat tonight, saving you the trouble of cooking (at home).

10. This doctor looks very young, but actually he is very experienced.

11. This good news made his parents exceedingly happy.

12. Reform and Opening made China become the second biggest economy in the world.

13. The one-child policy has caused the Chinese people to pay even more attention to early childhood education.

ANSWERS:

1. 他们希望定居的城市首先是西雅图，其次是旧金山，再其次是洛杉矶。
   Tāmen xīwàng dìngjūde chéngshì shǒuxiān shi Xīyǎtú, qícì shì Jiùjīnshān, zài qícì shì Luòshānjī.

2. 她看起来很年轻，其实已经是两个孩子的妈妈了。
   Tā kàn-qǐlai hěn niánqīng, qíshí yǐjīng shì liǎngge háizide māma le.

3. 这里不太安全，千万别让孩子自己一个人出门。
   Zhèlǐ bú tài ānquán, qiānwàn bié ràng háizi zìjǐ yígerén chūmén.

4. 斯坦福大学和伯克利大学都在加州，前者是私立的，而后者是公立的。
   Sītǎnfú Dàxué hé Bókèlì Dàxué dōu zài Jiāzhōu, qiánzhě shì sīlìde, ér hòuzhě shì gōnglìde.

5. 你任何时间都可以给我打电话。Nǐ rènhé shíjiān dōu kěyǐ gěi wǒ dǎ diànhuà.

6. 这位老先生年逾古稀，仍然保持着一颗童心。
   Zhèiwèi lǎo xiānsheng niányú gǔxī, réngrán bǎochízhe yìkē tóngxīn.

7. 如果没有家人支持(的话)，我是不会成功的。
   Rúguǒ méiyǒu jiārén zhīchí (dehuà), wǒ shì búhuì chénggōng de.

8. 他从事的工作是保密的，甚至(于)不能告诉他太太。
   Tā cóngshìde gōngzuò shì bǎomìde, shènzhì(yú) bùnéng gàosu tā tàitai.

9. 今晚我们上馆子去吃饭，省得你在家做饭了。
   Jīnwǎn wǒmen shàng guǎnzi qù chīfàn, shěngde nǐ zài jiā zuòfàn le.

10. 这位医生看起来还很年轻，实际上很有经验。
    Zhèiwèi yīshēng kàn-qǐlai hái hěn niánqīng, shíjì-shang hěn yǒu jīngyàn.

11. 这个好消息使他父母非常高兴。Zhèige hǎo xiāoxi shǐ tā fùmǔ fēicháng gāoxìng.

12. 改革开放使中国成为了世界第二大经济体。
    Gǎigé-kāifàng shǐ Zhōngguó chéngwéile shìjiè dìèr dà jīngjì-tǐ.

13. 独生子女政策使得中国人更注重幼儿教育了。
    Dúshēng zǐnǚ zhèngcè shǐde Zhōngguórén gèng zhùzhòng yòuér jiàoyù le.

Chapter 29: Expressions 155–166

155. 是···的 **shì...de** *asserting a fact or focusing on a certain aspect* (see 15.5)

◆ 你们是自己开车还是坐飞机来的？
Nǐmen shì zìjǐ kāichē háishi zuò fēijī lái de?
Did you drive your own car or come by airplane?

◆ 他和他太太是在交友网站上认识的。
Tā hé tā tàitai shì zài jiāoyǒu wǎngzhàn-shang rènshi de.
It was on a dating website that he and his wife met.

◆ 谷歌公司是由两个年轻人创办的。
Gǔgē gōngsī shì yóu liǎngge niánqīng-rén chuàngbàn de.
Google was in fact established by two young people.

156. ⋯是⋯, (可是)⋯   ...shì..., (kěshì)...   *granted...(but)...*

See note under #48 (⋯倒是⋯, 可是⋯   dàoshi..., kěshì...) for a comparison between these two similar structures.

● 智能手机方便是方便，(可是)用起来也浪费不少时间。
  Zhìnéng shǒujī fāngbiàn shì fāngbiàn, (kěshì) yòng-qǐlai yě làngfèi bùshǎo shíjiān.
  A smartphone is convenient alright, but using it wastes a lot of time.

● 我是应该减肥，可是又非常喜欢吃甜食。
  Wǒ shì yīnggāi jiǎnféi, kěshì yòu fēicháng xǐhuan chī tiánshí.
  It's true that I ought to lose weight, but I love eating sweets.

● 她的父母是逼得很紧，(可是)都是为了她将来能考上好的大学。
  Tāde fùmǔ shì bīde hěn jǐn, (kěshì) dōu shì wèile tā jiānglái néng kǎoshang hǎode dàxué.
  Her parents do drive her very hard, but it is all so that in the future she can get into a good college.

157. 是否   shìfǒu   *whether...or not*

● 她问自己是否真的愿意嫁给他。 **Tā wèn zìjǐ shìfǒu zhēnde yuànyi jiàgěi tā.**
  She asks herself whether she really wants to marry him.

● 你是否相信所谓的"缘分"？ **Nǐ shìfǒu xiāngxìn suǒwèide "yuánfèn"?**
  Do you believe there's such a thing as predestined affinity between people?

● 这个计划是否成功得看我们有没有足够的资金。
  Zhèige jìhuà shìfǒu chénggōng děi kàn wǒmen yǒu-méiyǒu zúgòude zījīn.
  Whether this plan will succeed depends on whether we have sufficient funds.

158. 事实上   shìshí-shang   *in reality, actually* (synonym of #151 实际上 shíjì-shang)

● 从年薪来看，男女事实上还没有完全平等。
  Cóng niánxīn lái kàn, nánnǚ shìshí-shang hái méiyǒu wánquán píngděng.
  Looking at it from the point of view of salary, men and women don't actually have complete equality yet.

● 虽然他们还住在同一个公寓里，但事实上已经离婚了。
  Suīrán tāmen hái zhùzài tóng-yíge gōngyùlǐ, dàn shìshí-shang yǐjīng líhūnle.
  Although they are still living in the same apartment, they have actually already gotten divorced.

● 虽然公司说上班的时间是从九点到五点，但事实上员工经常需要加班。 **Suīrán gōngsī shuō shàngbānde shíjiān shì cóng jiǔdiǎn dào wǔdiǎn, dàn shìshí-shang yuángōng jīngcháng xūyào jiābān.**
  Although the company says that we work from 9 a.m. to 5 p.m., actually employees often have to work overtime.

159. 顺便 shùnbiàn *conveniently* (on the way to doing something else), *to do something along the way*

◆ 他到北京出差，顺便回家看看父母。
Tā dào Běijīng chūchāi, shùnbiàn huíjiā kànkan fùmǔ.
On a business trip to Beijing, he will also go home to see his parents.

◆ 暑假里很多学生到中国去学中文，顺便去一些地方旅游。
Shǔjià-lǐ hěn duō xuésheng dào Zhōngguó qù xué Zhōngwén, shùnbiàn qù yìxiē dìfāng lǚyóu.
During summer vacation many students go to China to study Chinese, and also travel to some places along the way.

◆ 奶奶每天早上到公园去锻炼，回来的时候顺便去超市买菜。
Nǎinai měitiān zǎoshang dào gōngyuán qù duànliàn, huílaide shíhou shùnbiàn qù chāoshì mǎicài.
Every morning Grandma goes to the park for exercise, and on the way home she also goes to the market to buy groceries.

160. 说起…(来) shuōqǐ...(lái) *speaking of..., while mentioning...*

◆ 他平时话不多，可是说起他的研究课题来就停不下来。
Tā píngshí huà bù duō, kěshì shuōqǐ tāde yánjiū kètí lái jiù tíng-bu-xiàlai.
He usually doesn't have much to say, but when his research topic is mentioned, he can't stop (talking).

◆ 说起电脑游戏来，这个十几岁的小男孩真是个行家。
Shuōqǐ diànnǎo yóuxì lái, zhèige shíjǐsuìde xiǎo nánhái zhēnshì ge hángjiā.
When it comes to computer games, this young teenage boy really is an expert.

◆ 说起这些年在国外的经历，老张又悲又喜，一言难尽。
Shuōqǐ zhèixiē nián zài guówàide jīnglì, Lǎo Zhāng yòu bēi yòu xǐ, yìyán-nánjìn.
When talking about his experiences during these several years abroad, Old Zhang is both sad and happy; it's a long story that cannot be told in a few words.

◆ 这些老朋友说起文革时代的经历来，总是感叹不已。
Zhèixiē lǎopéngyou shuōqǐ Wén-Gé shídàide jīnglì lái, zǒngshì gǎntàn bùyǐ.
Whenever these old friends talk about their experiences during the Cultural Revolution, they can't stop sighing with emotions.

161. 虽然…，可是/但是… suīrán..., kěshì/dànshì... *although..., but/however/still...*
可是 kěshì or 但是 dànshì goes hand-in-hand with 虽然 suīrán, i.e. it is indispensable, even though its equivalent in English would be considered superfluous.

◆ 虽然很少有研究生能在一年内完成博士论文，但是他对自己还是很有信心。 **Suīrán hěn shǎo yǒu yánjiūshēng néng zài yìnián-nèi wánchéng bóshì lùnwén, dànshì tā duì zìjǐ hěn yǒu-xìnxīn.**
Although few graduate students can finish their doctoral dissertations within one year, he has a lot of self confidence (that he can do it).

♦ 她虽然跟男同事从事一样的工作，可是工资却比他们的低得多。
Tā suīrán gēn nán tóngshì cóngshì yíyàngde gōngzuò, kěshì gōngzī què bǐ tāmende dī-de-duō.
Although she does the same work as her male colleagues, her pay is much lower than theirs.

♦ 虽然全国大部分地区的生活水平有了明显的提高，可是还有很多偏远山区依然很贫穷。 **Suīrán quánguó dà-bùfen dìqūde shēnghuó shuǐpíng yǒule míngxiǎnde tígāo, kěshì hái yǒu hěn duō piānyuǎnde shānqū yīrán hěn pínqióng.**
Although the great majority of areas in the country have seen clear improvement in their standard of living, there are still a lot of distant mountain areas that are very poor.

162. 随着 suízhe *along with, as* (lit., "following")

♦ 随着收入的增加，老百姓的日常消费也明显地提高了。
Suízhe shōurùde zēngjiā, lǎobǎixìngde rìcháng xiāofèi yě míngxiǎnde tígāo le.
As income has increased, people's daily living expenses have also risen noticeably.

♦ 随着汽车数量的增多，城市交通堵塞的现象越来越严重。
Suízhe qìchē shùliàngde zēngduō, chéngshì jiāotōng dǔsède xiànxiàng yuèláiyuè yánzhòng.
As the number of automobiles has increased, traffic congestion in the city has gotten worse and worse.

♦ 随着社会老龄化日益严重，政府在养老问题上也面临越来越大的挑战。 **Suízhe shèhuì lǎolíng-huà rìyì yánzhòng, zhèngfǔ zài yǎnglǎo wèntí-shang yě miànlín yuèláiyuè dàde tiǎozhàn.**
As the aging of the population has become more serious by the day, the government is facing ever greater challenges in caring for the elderly.

163. 所 verb 的 suǒ verb de *that which..., those who...*

This structure is best learned from multiple Chinese examples, because it is impossible to translate into English. Although it sounds a bit literary, it is used quite frequently by Chinese speakers.

♦ 算命先生所说的(话)不一定可信。
Suànmìng xiānsheng suǒ-shuōde (huà) bùyídìng kěxìn.
What the fortune teller said is not necessarily believable.

♦ 她希望可以把在国外所经历的事情写成小说。
Tā xīwàng kěyǐ bǎ zài guówài suǒ-jīnglìde shìqing xiě-chéng xiǎoshuō.
She hopes to turn what she had experienced abroad into a novel.

♦ 在我们所参观过的名胜古迹当中，长城是最令人难忘的。
Zài wǒmen suǒ-cānguānguode míngshèng gǔjì dāngzhōng, Chángchéng shì zuì lìng rén nánwàngde.
Among the famous sites that we visited in China, the Great Wall is the most memorable.

164. 所谓···就是··· suǒwèi...jiùshì... *the so-called...is...*

Note: The 就是 **jiùshì** in this structure goes hand-in-hand with 所谓 **suǒwèi**, i.e. it would not do to replace it with just 是 **shì**. But 所谓 **suǒwèi** may be used in other contexts, e.g. 那个所谓"名校"只不过是个暴发户的私立学校。**Nèige suǒwèi "míngxiào" zhǐ búguò shì ge bàofāhùde sīlì xuéxiào.** *That so-called famous school is nothing but a private school for the nouveau riche.*

♦ 所谓"美国化"就是移民完全适应了美国文化。
   Suǒwèi "Měiguó-huà" jiùshì yímín wánquán shìyìngle Měiguó wénhuà.
   What "Americanization" refers to is immigrants completely adjusted to American culture.

♦ 中国文化里所谓的"孝顺"就是孩子完全服从父母的意志。
   Zhōngguó wénhuà-li suǒwèide "xiàoshùn" jiùshì háizi wánquán fúcóng fùmǔde yìzhì.
   What "filiality" in Chinese culture refers to is children totally obeying their parents' will.

♦ 所谓"小皇帝"就是那些在家里被大人过分宠爱的独生子女。
   Suǒwèi "xiǎo huángdì" jiùshì nèixiē zài jiālǐ bèi dàrén guòfèn chǒng'àide dúshēng zǐnǚ.
   A so-called "little emperor" is an only child who has been spoiled by adults' excessive permissiveness.

165. 实在太···了 shízài tài...le *truly too...*

♦ 我这个星期实在太忙了！ **Wǒ zhèige xīngqī shízài tài máng le!**
   I am really terribly busy this week!

♦ 你写的汉字实在太漂亮了！ **Nǐ xiěde Hànzì shízài tài piàoliang le!**
   Your Chinese characters are really excellent!

♦ 考试的时候我实在太紧张了！ **Kǎoshìde shíhou wǒ shízài tài jǐnzhāng le!**
   I was really too tense during the test!

166. 同时 tóngshí *at the same time, concurrently, ...while...*(doing two things concurrently)

Note: 同时 **tóngshí** functions as an adverb in the first two examples, and as a noun in the last two examples.

♦ 他们两个好朋友同时考上了北京大学。
   Tāmen liǎngge hǎo péngyou tóngshí kǎoshangle Běijīng Dàxué.
   Those two good friends were admitted into Peking University at the same time.

♦ 他是个好父亲，同时也是孩子的好朋友。
   Tā shì ge hǎo fùqin, tóngshí yě shì háizide hǎo péngyou.
   He is a good father, and also a good friend to his children.

♦ 在学校上课的同时，很多学生也在公司里或政府部门实习。
   Zài xuéxiào shàngkède tóngshí, hěn duō xuésheng yě zài gōngsīlǐ huò zhèngfǔ bùmén shíxí.
   Many students do practicum at a company or a government department while taking courses.

● 在经济快速发展的同时，很多地方的环境也遭到了破坏。
Zài jīngjì kuàisù fāzhǎnde tóngshí, hěn duō dìfangde huánjìng yě zāodàole pòhuài.
While the economy is developing so rapidly, the environment in many places is being ruined.

EXERCISES:

Translate the following sentences into Chinese, using the structures covered in this chapter:

1. It was last year that I graduated from college.
2. Learning Chinese is indeed difficult, but it is very interesting, and it's also useful.
3. I don't know whether he still remembers me.
4. He talks a lot, but in reality he doesn't do much.
5. When Dad goes to work every day, he also takes his son to school along the way.
6. When they speak of their own children, parents are generally all very proud.
7. Although Grandma is already over 80 years old, she is still in very good health.
8. With technological advancement, people's lifestyle has undergone great change.
9. The Chinese people that I am acquainted with are all very friendly.
10. The so-called "generation gap" is the divergence between people of different ages.
11. He speaks Chinese amazingly well!
12. She works every day, and at the same time has to look after two children.

ANSWERS:
1. 我是去年大学毕业的。Wǒ shì qùnián dàxué bìyè de.
2. 学中文难是难，可是很有意思，也很有用。
   Xué Zhōngwén nán shì nán, kěshì hěn yǒuyìsi, yě hěn yǒuyòng.
3. 我不知道他是否还记得我。Wǒ bù zhīdào tā shìfǒu hái jìde wǒ.
4. 他说得多，事实上做得很少。Tā shuōde duō, shìshí-shang zuòde hěn shǎo.
5. 爸爸每天上班的时候顺便把儿子送到学校去。
   Bàba měitiān shàngbānde shíhou shùnbiàn bǎ érzi sòngdào xuéxiào qù.
6. 说起自己家的孩子，父母一般都很自豪。
   Shuōqǐ zìjǐ jiāde háizi, fùmǔ yìbān dōu hěn zìháo.
7. 奶奶虽然已经八十多岁了，但是身体还很健康。
   Nǎinai suīrán yǐjīng bāshíduō suì le, dànshì shēntǐ hái hěn jiànkāng.
8. 随着科技的进步，人们的生活方式也发生了很大的变化。
   Suízhe kējìde jìnbù, rénmende shēnghuó fāngshì yě fāshēngle hěn dàde biànhuà.
9. 我所认识的中国人都很友好。Wǒ suǒ-rènshide Zhōngguórén dōu hěn yǒuhǎo.
10. 所谓的"代沟"就是不同年龄的人之间的距离。
    Suǒwèide "dàigōu" jiùshì bùtóng niánlíngde rén zhījiānde jùlí.
11. 他的中文说得实在太好了！Tāde Zhōngwén shuōde shízài tài hǎo le!
12. 她每天工作，同时还得照顾两个小孩子。
    Tā měitiān gōngzuò, tóngshí hái děi zhàogu liǎngge xiǎoháizi.

Chapter 30: Expressions 167–178

167. 万一　wànyī　*if by some slim chance* (lit., "one chance out of 10,000"), *in case*

♦ 我把电话号码给你，万一需要联系，就给我打电话。
Wǒ bǎ diànhuà hàomǎ gěi nǐ, wànyī xūyào liánxì, jiù gěi wǒ dǎ diànhuà.
I'll give you my phone number, in case you need to contact me, just give me a call.

♦ 开车坐车都得系好安全带，万一出了车祸，还有生还的可能。
Kāichē zuòchē dòu děi jìhǎo ānquán-dài, wànyī chūle chēhuò, hái yǒu shēnghuánde kěnéng.
Whether you are driving or riding as a passenger, you should fasten your seatbelt so that in case of a crash you might still come back alive.

♦ 他买人寿保险的目的很清楚，万一他出了意外，太太和孩子会有
一些保障。**Tā mǎi rénshòu bǎoxiǎnde mùdì hěn qīngchǔ, wànyī tā chūle yìwài, tàitai hé háizi huì yǒu yìxiē bǎozhàng.**
The reason he bought life insurance is very clear, in case something happens to him, his wife and children will have a little security.

168. 往往　wǎngwǎng　*frequently*

♦ 波士顿的冬天往往下很大的雪。
Bōshìdùnde dōngtiān wǎngwǎng xià hěn dàde xuě.
Boston winters often bring very heavy snow.

♦ 城里人往往看不起乡下人。**Chénglǐ-rén wǎngwǎng kàn-bu-qǐ xiāngxia-rén.**
Urbanites often look down on country folks.

♦ 不同文化背景的人之间往往容易产生误会。
Bùtóng wénhuà bèijǐngde rén zhījiān wǎngwǎng róngyì chǎnshēng wùhuì.
Misunderstandings often develop between people of differing cultural backgrounds.

169. 未必　wèibì　*not necessarily*

未必 **wèibì** is a slightly more formal way to say 不一定 **bùyídìng**, yet it is the term preferred by well-educated Chinese speakers. It may even be used in conjunction with 一定 **yídìng** for more emphasis, as in the first example.

♦ 有很多钱未必就一定幸福快乐。
Yǒu hěn duō qián wèibì jiù yídìng xìngfú kuàilè.
Having a lot of money does not necessarily mean good fortune and happiness.

♦ 年轻人经历一些挫折未必是一件坏事。
Niánqīng-rén jīnglì yìxiē cuòzhé wèibì shì yíjiàn huàishì.
For young people to experience some setbacks is not necessarily a bad thing.

♦ 广告做得漂亮，产品未必有广告说得那么好。
Guǎnggào zuòde piàoliang, chǎnpǐn wèibì yǒu guǎnggào shuōde nàme hǎo.
When the advertisement looks nice, the product may not be as good as the advertisement said.

170. 为的是… **wèideshì…** *in order to…, for the sake of…*

This structure and the next one (为了 **wèile**) are mirror images of each other. This structure states the purpose after the action, while the 为了 **wèile** structure states the purpose first. In terms of semantic content, the two structures are actually synonymous.

♦ 她换工作为的是能有时间多陪陪孩子。
Tā huàn gōngzuò wèideshì néng yǒu shíjiān duō péipéi háizi.
The reason she changed her job was to have more time to spend with her children.

♦ 他们移民到美国来为的是孩子将来有更好的机会。
Tāmen yímín dào Měiguó lái wèideshì háizi jiānglái yǒu gèng hǎode jīhuì.
They immigrated to America so that their children might have better opportunities in the future.

♦ 他一边学习一边打工，为的是减轻父母经济上的负担。
Tā yìbiān xuéxí yìbiān dǎgōng, wèideshì jiǎnqīng fùmǔ jīngjì-shangde fùdān.
He works while he studies, so as to lessen his parents' financial burden.

171. 为了… **wèile…** *in order to…, for the sake of…* (see note in #170)

♦ 为了学好中文，他打算去中国留学。
Wèile xuéhǎo Zhōngwén, tā dǎsuàn qù Zhōngguó liúxué.
In order to learn Chinese well, he plans to go to China to study.

♦ 为了有时间多陪陪孩子，她决定换一个工作。
Wèile yǒu shíjiān duō péipéi háizi, tā juédìng huàn yíge gōngzuò.
In order to have more time with her children she decided to change her job.

♦ 为了减轻父母经济上的负担，他一边学习一边打工。
Wèile jiǎnqīng fùmǔ jīngjì-shangde fùdān, tā yìbiān xuéxí yìbiān dǎgōng.
In order to lighten the financial burden on his parents, he works while he studies.

172. 为(了)…起见 **wèi(le)…qǐjiàn** *in order to…, for the sake of…*

This structure is a slightly more emphatic version of the preceding one. 起见 **qǐjiàn** adds the meaning *in view of…*, which makes the structure a bit more formal as well.

♦ 为了安全起见，请大家都系好安全带。
Wèile ānquán qǐjiàn, qǐng dàjiā dōu jìhǎo ānquán-dài.
For the sake of safety, please, everybody, fasten your seatbelts.

♦ 为了保密起见，连他太太也不知道他真正的身份。
Wèile bǎomì qǐjiàn, lián tā tàitai yě bù zhīdào tā zhēnzhèngde shēnfèn.
For the sake of secrecy, even his wife doesn't know his real status.

♦ 为了孩子上学方便起见，他们在学校附近租了一个公寓。
Wèile háizi shàngxué fāngbiàn qǐjiàn, tāmen zài xuéxiào fùjìn zūle yíge gōngyù.
To make it convenient for the children to go to school, they have rented an apartment near the school.

173. 无论···都··· **wúlùn...dōu...** *no matter.../regardless of..., still...*

This structure is synonymous with #23 (不论···都··· **búlùn...dōu...**), but 不论 **búlùn** is a bit less formal because 无 **wú** is a literary word. Structures #17 and #18 (with 不管 **bùguǎn**) are even more informal than 不论 **búlùn**.

● 无论他怎么解释，她都不相信。**Wúlùn tā zěnme jiěshì, tā dōu bù xiāngxìn.**
No matter how he explains it, she doesn't believe him.

● 无论是大人还是小孩都喜欢迪士尼的动画片。
Wúlùn shì dàrén háishi xiǎohái dōu xǐhuan Díshìníde dònghuà-piàn.
Whether it be adults or children, everyone likes Disney's animated cartoons.

● 无论是发达国家还是发展中国家都有保护环境的义务。
Wúlùn shì fādá guójiā háishi fāzhǎn-zhōng guójiā dōu yǒu bǎohù huánjìngde yìwù.
All nations, whether they are developed or developing, have the duty to protect the environment.

174. 先···，然后··· **xiān..., ránhòu...** *first..., then...*

In this structure referring to a sequence of two events, the subject in each may or may not be the same. This is in contrast to the next structure, 先···再··· **xiān...zài...**, in which there is only one subject for the two clauses.

● 我先认识了一个中国朋友，然后那个朋友又给我介绍了他的家人。
Wǒ xiān rènshile yíge Zhōngguó péngyou, ránhòu nèige péngyou yòu gěi wǒ jièshàole tāde jiārén.
I first made a Chinese friend, then that friend introduced me to his family.

● 他先一个人来了美国，然后他全家一个一个地也移民来了。
Tā xiān yíge rén láile Měiguó, ránhòu tā quánjiā yíge-yígede yě yímín lái le.
He first came to the U.S. by himself, then one by one, his whole family immigrated.

● 他先从银行借了钱，然后创办了自己的公司。
Tā xiān cóng yínháng jièle qián, ránhòu chuàngbànle zìjǐde gōngsī.
He first borrowed money from a bank, then founded his own company.

175. 先···，再··· **xiān..., zài...** *first..., then...*

This structure is slightly more colloquial than the preceding one (先···，然后··· **xiān..., ránhòu...**), and the 再 **zài** phrase does not have a separate subject. Note that 再 **zài** does not mean *again* here.

● 早上起床以后，我先洗澡，再吃早饭。
Zǎoshang qǐchuáng yǐhòu, wǒ xiān xǐzǎo, zài chī zǎofàn.
After I get up in the morning, I first bathe, then I eat breakfast.

● 学中文都得先学拼音，再学说话读书写字。
Xué Zhōngwén dōu děi xiān xué pīnyīn, zài xué shuōhuà dúshū xiězì.
In studying Chinese, one must first learn pinyin, then learn to speak, read and write.

◆ 她打算先工作几年再考虑结婚的事儿。
Tā dǎsuàn xiān gōngzuò jǐnián zài kǎolǜ jiéhūnde shìr.
She plans to first work a few years, then consider the question of getting married.

The two structures above may even be "stacked," to form 先···, 再···, 然后··· **xiān..., zài..., ránhòu....**

◆ 我早上起床以后，先去健身房锻炼，再洗澡，然后吃早饭。
Wǒ zǎoshang qǐchuáng yǐhòu, xiān qù jiànshēn-fáng duànliàn, zài xǐzǎo, ránhòu chī zǎofàn.
After getting up in the morning, I first go to the fitness room to work out, then take a shower, and then have breakfast.

◆ 中国的千禧一代(2000后)大多有很实际的想法：他们要先工作赚钱，再买房，然后才考虑结婚。
Zhōngguóde qiānxǐ yídài (2000 hòu) dàduō yǒu hěn shíjìde xiǎngfǎ: tāmen yào xiān gōngzuò zhuànqián, zài mǎi fáng, ránhòu cái kǎolǜ jiéhūn.
Most of China's millennials have this pragmatic view: they want to first work and make money, then buy an apartment, and only then consider getting married.

176. 限于 **xiànyú** *limited by/to; restricted by*

◆ 限于身高条件，她没能当上空中小姐。
Xiànyú shēngāo tiáojiàn, tā méi néng dāngshang kōngzhōng-xiǎojiě.
Due to height restrictions, she was not able to become an air stewardess.

◆ 限于资金不足，公司目前没法扩大规模。
Xiànyú zījīn bùzú, gōngsī mùqián méifǎ kuòdà guīmó.
Due to insufficient funds, the company cannot at the present time expand its scope.

◆ 这次的公司招聘不限于名牌大学的毕业生。
Zhèicìde gōngsī zhāopìn bú xiànyú míngpái dàxuéde bìyèshēng.
In the present recruitment drive, the company is not limiting eligibility to graduates of famous universities.

◆ 他从来没去过中国，因此对中国社会和文化的了解仅限于书本上的知识。**Tā cónglái méi qùguo Zhōngguó, yīncǐ duì Zhōngguó shèhuì hé wénhuàde liǎojiě jǐn xiànyú shūběn-shangde zhīshi.**
As he has never been to China, his knowledge of Chinese society and culture is limited to what he has read in books.

177. 向来 **xiànglái** *always* (in the past), *never before* (when used in the negative)

◆ 爷爷奶奶向来很宠溺孙子孙女。
Yéye nǎinai xiànglái hěn chǒngnì sūnzi sūnnǚ.
Grandpa and Grandma have always doted on their grandchildren.

◆ 她向来是个好学生，做什么事情都认认真真的。
Tā xiànglái shì ge hǎo xuésheng, zuò shénme shìqing dōu rènrènzhēnzhēnde.
She has always been a good student, taking seriously whatever she does.

♦ 投资银行年薪很高，向来很吸引大学毕业生。
Tóuzī yínháng niánxīn hěn gāo, xiànglái hěn xīyǐn dàxué bìyèshēng.
Investment banks' salaries are high and have always attracted college graduates.

♦ 这里的夏天向来不热，可是今年有点儿反常。
Zhèlǐ de xiàtiān xiànglái bú rè, kěshì jīnnián yǒudiǎnr fǎncháng.
Summers here have never been hot, but this year is a bit unusual.

178. 幸亏…，（要不然…） **xìngkuī…, (yàoburán...)** *fortunately..., (otherwise...)*

♦ 去机场的路上堵车堵得厉害，幸亏我们出发得早，要不然可能误了飞机。 **Qù jīchǎngde lùshang dǔchē dǔde lìhai, xìngkuī wǒmen chūfāde zǎo, yàoburán kěnéng wùle fēijī.**
On the way to the airport we encountered a serious traffic jam; fortunately we started out early, otherwise we might have missed the plane.

♦ 幸亏我会说中文，要不然在中国旅行不会那么顺利。
Xìngkuī wǒ huì shuō Zhōngwén, yàoburán zài Zhōngguó lǚxíng búhuì nàme shùnlì.
Fortunately I can speak Chinese; otherwise traveling in China would not be so convenient.

♦ 幸亏我很早就买了房子，现在的房价我根本买不起了。
Xìngkuī wǒ hěn zǎo jiù mǎile fángzi, xiànzàide fángjià wǒ gēnběn mǎibuqǐ le.
Fortunately I bought a house early on; otherwise with current house prices so high, I simply wouldn't be able to buy one.

♦ 幸亏我们的投资很多元化，要不然这次股市大跌会给我们带来不堪想象的损失。
Xìngkuī wǒmende tóuzī hěn duōyuán-huà, yàoburán zhèicì gǔshì dà diē huì gěi wǒmen dàilái bùkān xiǎngxiàngde sǔnshī.
Fortunately our investments are diversified; otherwise this stock market crash would incur unimaginable losses for us.

EXERCISES:

Translate the following sentences into Chinese, using the structures covered in this chapter:

1. When traveling, you should take along some of the most frequently used medicine so that in case you become ill, you will have it to use.

2. There is often a generation gap between parents and their children.

3. What the teacher says is not necessarily correct.

4. He went to study in China in order to learn Chinese well.

5. In order to give their children better opportunities many parents immigrate to America.

6. For the sake of fairness, my roommate and I take turns cleaning up.

7. You can ask me for help anytime.

8. I first visited a few schools before I decided which ones to apply to.

9. Our plan is to first go to New York, then go to Washington.

10. Due to limited of time and energy, we only saw a part of the zoo.

11. She has always been a good student, what happened to her this semester?

12. Many classmates in the dorm got the flu, fortunately I already got a flu shot.

ANSWERS:

1. 旅行的时候应该带一点儿常用的药，万一生病了，用得上。
   Lǚxíngde shíhou yīnggāi dài yìdiǎnr chángyòngde yào, wànyī shēngbìng le, yòng-de-shàng.

2. 父母和孩子之间往往有代沟。**Fùmǔ hé háizi zhījiān wǎngwǎng yǒu dàigōu.**

3. 老师所说的未必就是对的。**Lǎoshī suǒ-shuōde wèibì jiùshì duìde.**

4. 他到中国去留学为的是学好中文。**Tā dào Zhōngguó qù liúxué wèideshì xuéhǎo Zhōngwén.**

5. 为了给孩子更好的机会，很多父母移民来美国。
   Wèile gěi háizi gèng hǎode jīhuì, hěn duō fùmǔ yímín lái Měiguó.

6. 为了公平起见，我和室友轮流打扫卫生。
   Wèile gōngpíng qǐjiàn, wǒ hé shìyǒu lúnliú dǎsǎo wèishēng.

7. 无论什么时候你都可以找我帮忙。**Wúlùn shénme shíhou nǐ dōu kěyǐ zhǎo wǒ bāngmáng.**

8. 我先参观了一些学校，然后才决定申请哪几所大学。
   Wǒ xiān cānguánle yìxiē xuéxiào, ránhòu cái juédìng shēnqǐng nǎ jǐsuǒ dàxué.

9. 我们的计划是先去纽约，再去华盛顿。
   Wǒmende jìhuà shì xiān qù Niǔyuē, zài qù Huáshèngdùn.

10. 限于时间和精力，我们只看了动物园的一部分。
    Xiànyú shíjiān hé jīnglì, wǒmen zhǐ kànle dòngwùyuánde yíbùfen.

11. 她向来是个好学生，这个学期她怎么了？
    Tā xiànglái shì ge hǎo xuésheng, zhèige xuéqī tā zěnme le?

12. 宿舍里很多同学都得了流感，幸亏我已经打了预防针。
    Sùshèlǐ hěn duō tóngxué dōu déle liúgǎn, xìngkuī wǒ yǐjīng dǎle yùfángzhēn.

Chapter 31: Expressions 179–190

179. 要⋯了 **yào...le** *going to..., about to...*

This is a synonym of #118 (快/快要⋯了 **kuài/kuàiyào...le**), but a bit more colloquial. In both structures, the 了 **le** at the end of the sentence signifies an imminent change or onset of a new situation.

♦ 要放假了！ **Yào fàngjià le!** *Vacation is coming!*

♦ 我要当爸爸了！ **Wǒ yào dāng bàba le!** *I'm going to be a father!*

♦ 孩子要上大学了！ **Háizi yào shàng dàxué le!** *(My) child is going to college!*

180. 要不/要不然 **yàobù/yàoburán** *otherwise* [lit., "if not"]

This structure is synonymous with 不然 **bùrán** (#25), but it is a bit more colloquial. A even more formal synonym is 否则 **fǒuzé** (#73).

♦ 你最好把缺课的原因告诉老师，要不她会以为你无故旷课。
Nǐ zuìhǎo bǎ quēkède yuányīn gàosu lǎoshī, yàobù tā huì yǐwéi nǐ wúgù kuàngkè.
You had better tell the teacher why you missed class; otherwise she will think you cut class for no good reason.

♦ 孩子上大学不希望完全靠父母，要不然他们的经济负担就太重了。
Háizi shàng dàxué bù xīwàng wánquán kào fùmǔ, yàoburán tāmende jīngjì fùdān jiù tài zhòng le.
Children going to college hope they won't need to completely depend on their parents; otherwise their (the parents') financial burden will be too heavy.

♦ 美国人应该少吃快餐，要不然肥胖症的问题会越来越严重。
Měiguórén yīnggāi shǎo chī kuàicān, yàoburán féipàng-zhèngde wèntí huì yuèláiyuè yánzhòng.
Americans should eat less fast food; otherwise obesity will become more and more serious.

181. 要不是···，···就··· yàobushì..., ...jiù... *if it's not/were it not for..., then...*

A comparison with #178 (幸亏 xìngkuī...) is in order. These two patterns are similar in that they convey a turn in the outcome of an event due to an intervention. The difference between the two is that 幸亏 **xìngkuī** indicates a fortunate intervention, and is used only with a positive outcome (i.e. the intervention averted a negative outcome, and saved the situation from unfolding into a major or minor disaster), whereas this structure may be used with either a positive or a negative outcome.

♦ 要不是有了网络，我们的生活就不会那么方便。
Yàobushì yǒule wǎngluò, wǒmende shēnghuó jiù búhuì nàme fāngbiàn.
If it weren't for the Internet, our lives would not be so convenient.

♦ 她要不是大二时怀了孕，老早就大学毕业了。
Tā yàobushì dà-èr-shí huái-le-yùn, lǎozǎo jiù dàxué bìyèle.
If she hadn't gotten pregnant in the second year of college, she would have graduated long ago.

♦ 要不是这所大学给了我全额奖学金，我很可能就上了另外一所大学。
Yàobushì zhèisuǒ dàxué gěile wǒ quáné jiǎngxuéjīn, wǒ hěn kěnéng jiù shàngle lìngwài yìsuǒ dàxué.
If this university had not given me a full scholarship, I might very well have gone to a different university.

♦ 要不是因为独生子女的政策，中国的人口早就超过十四亿了。
Yàobushì yīnwèi dúshēng zǐnǚde zhèngcè, Zhōngguóde rénkǒu zǎojiù chāoguò shísìyì le.
Were it not for the one-child policy, China's population would long ago have exceeded 1.4 billion.

182. (要)不是…, 就是… **(yào)búshì…, jiùshì…** *if it's not…, then it must be…* (i.e. it's either…or…)

The structure may begin with either 不是 **búshì** or 要不是 **yàobúshì**, and there is no difference in their meaning, except that 不是 **búshì** is a bit more common. There is no relationship between this structure and the preceding one (要不是…, …就… **yàobushì…, …jiù…**).

♦ 你要不是看电视，就是玩电脑游戏，什么时候才做功课呢？
Nǐ yàobushì kàn diànshì, jiùshì wán diànnǎo yóuxì, shénme shíhou cái zuò gōngkè ne?
You're either watching television or playing computer games. When will you do your homework?

♦ 她总是抱怨，要不是钱太少，就是工作太累。
Tā zǒngshì bàoyuàn, yàobushì qián tài shǎo, jiùshì gōngzuò tài lèi.
She is always complaining; if it's not that she doesn't have enough money, it's that her work is too tiring.

♦ 我将来要不是在大学里当教授，就是在政府里工作。
Wǒ jiānglái yàobushì zài dàxuéli dāng jiàoshòu, jiùshì zài zhèngfǔli gōngzuò.
In the future I want to be either a college professor or a government employee.

183. 要么…, 要么… **yàome…, yàome…** *either…, or…* (choice between two options)

♦ 这种鱼有两种不同的做法，要么清蒸，要么红烧。
Zhèizhǒng yú yǒu liǎngzhǒng bùtóngde zuòfǎ, yàome qīngzhēng, yàome hóngshāo.
There are two different ways to cook this kind of fish; either steamed or braised in soy sauce.

♦ 上这门课的学生在期末有两个选择，要么写文章，要么考试。
Shàng zhèimén kède xuésheng zài qīmò yǒu liǎngge xuǎnzé, yàome xiě wénzhāng, yàome kǎoshì.
In this course students have a choice at the end of the term; either write a paper or take an exam.

♦ 女朋友跟他说："我们要么结婚，要么分手，没有第三种选择！"
Nǚpéngyou gēn tā shuō: "Wǒmen yàome jiéhūn, yàome fēnshǒu, méiyǒu dìsānzhǒng xuǎnzé!"
His girlfriend said to him: "We'll either get married or break up; there is no third choice!"

184. 要是…(的话) **yàoshi…(dehuà)** *if…*

See also #55 (…的话 **…dehuà**) and #148 (如果 **rúguǒ…**). 如果 **rúguǒ** is widely used in all regions of China, whereas 要是 **yàoshi** is used mainly in North China.

♦ 要是明天天气好(的话)，我们就去海边玩儿。
Yàoshi míngtiān tiānqì hǎo (dehuà), wǒmen jiù qù hǎibiān wánr.
If the weather is good tomorrow, we'll go to the beach for fun.

♦ 要是我是你(的话)，就去跟她好好儿谈一谈。
Yàoshi wǒ shì nǐ (dehuà), jiù qù gēn tā hǎohāor tán-yitán.
If I were you, I would just go and have a good talk with her.

♦ 要是双方都不妥协(的话)，问题就很难解决了。
Yàoshi shuāngfāng dōu bù tuǒxié (dehuà), wèntí jiù hěn nán jiějué le.
If the two sides won't compromise, it will be very difficult to solve the problem.

185. …也好，…也好，…(反正/都)… **…yěhǎo, …yěhǎo, …(fǎnzhèng/dōu)…** *whether it be…or…, in either case…* (see #70 反正 **fǎnzhèng**)

♦ 大人也好，小孩子也好，都喜欢看迪士尼的动画片。
Dàrén yěhǎo, xiǎoháizi yěhǎo, dōu xǐhuan kàn Díshìníde dònghuàpiàn.
Whether they are adults or children; everyone likes Disney cartoons.

♦ 自己开车也好，坐飞机也好，反正我们星期六以前得到纽约。
Zìjǐ kāichē yěhǎo, zuò fēijī yěhǎo, fǎnzhèng wǒmen xīngqīliù yǐqián děi dào Niǔyuē.
We can drive our own car or fly; either way we must be in New York by Saturday.

♦ 你弹钢琴也好，拉小提琴也好，反正你应该学一种乐器。
Nǐ tán gāngqín yěhǎo, lā xiǎotíqín yěhǎo, fǎnzhèng nǐ yīnggāi xué yìzhǒng yuèqì.
You can play the piano or a violin; in any case you should learn to play a musical instrument.

186. 一…比一… **yī…bǐ yī…** *more and more…; all very…*
In this structure, the element that follows 一 **yī** is a measure word (same measure word repeated). When that measure word denotes time (e.g. 天 **tiān**, 年 **nián**), the structure means *becoming more…by the (day/year)*, but there is also the implication that the situation is already quite entrenched. When the measure word denotes something else, it literally means *each one is more…than the next*, implying that the situation is quite intense for all of them.

♦ 学费一年比一年贵，所以孩子一出生，父母就得开始预备他将来上大学的费用。
Xuéfèi yìnián bǐ yìnián guì, suǒyǐ háizi yì chūshēng, fùmǔ jiù děi kāishǐ yùbei tā jiānglái shàng dàxuéde fèiyòng.
Tuition is getting more expensive every year; so as soon as a child is born, his parents must begin preparing for his future college expenses.

♦ 学生一个比一个聪明。 **Xuésheng yíge bǐ yíge cōngming.**
Students are all very smart, as though each one is smarter than the last.

♦ 这里的饭馆一家比一家贵。 **Zhèlǐde fànguǎn yìjiā bǐ yìjiā guì.**
All the restaurants here are very expensive, as though each one is more expensive than the last.

♦ 我选的课一门比一门有意思。 **Wǒ xuǎnde kè yìmén bǐ yìmén yǒuyìsi.**
All the courses I signed up for are so interesting that each one seems more interesting than the last.

187. 一···才··· **yī...cái...** *when something happens, it's only then that...*

The key to understanding this structure is in 才 **cái** (see 5.1, sec. 7). This structure has no equivalent in English, therefore the translations of the examples below can only be paraphrases.

♦ 朋友一打来电话，我才想起来我们今天要一起吃晚饭。
Péngyou yì dǎlái diànhuà, wǒ cái xiǎng-qǐlai wǒmen jīntiān yào yìqǐ chī wǎnfàn.
When my friend phoned me, it was only then that I remembered we were supposed to have dinner together this evening.

♦ 我一称体重才意识到最近长胖了。
Wǒ yì chēng tǐzhòng cái yìshidào zuìjìn zhǎngpàng le.
Only when I got on the scale did I realize that I had gained weight recently.

♦ 孩子一出生，他们才真正体会到做父母的责任。
Háizi yì chūshēng, tāmen cái zhēnzhèng tǐhuìdào zuò fùmǔde zérèn.
It was only when the child was born that they (truly) understood the responsibilities of being parents.

188. 一···就··· **yī...jiù...** *1) as soon as... (then)...; 2) whenever...*

Note the two different usages of this structure illustrated in the examples below.

♦ 我一回家，妈妈就做好吃的。 **Wǒ yì huíjiā, Māma jiù zuò hǎochīde.**
Whenever I return home (from being away), Mom prepares good food.

♦ 学校一放假，大部分学生就都离开了。
Xuéxiào yí fàngjià, dàbùfen xuésheng jiù dōu líkāi le.
As soon as school lets out for vacation, most of the students leave.

♦ 我一听到这个好消息就马上给父母打电话了。
Wǒ yì tīngdào zhèige hǎo xiāoxi jiù mǎshàng gěi fùmǔ dǎ diànhuà le.
As soon as I heard this good news, I called my parents right away.

189. 一···一···地 *verb* **yī...yī...de** *verb* *(to do something) one at a time; one by one*

As in #186, the element that follows 一 **yī** is a measure word (same measure word repeated).

♦ 学中文不可能一下子就学好，就像中国的一句老话说的，饭要一口一口地吃。
Xué Zhōngwén bù kěnéng yíxiàzi jiù xuéhǎo, jiù xiàng Zhōngguóde yíjù lǎohuà shuōde, fàn yào yìkǒu-yìkǒude chī.
It's not possible to learn Chinese in one fell swoop. As an old Chinese saying goes, you must eat your rice one mouthful at a time.

♦ 孩子一天一天地长大了，父母也感觉轻松一点儿了。
Háizi yìtiān-yìtiānde zhǎngdà le, fùmu yě gǎnjué qīngsōng yìdiǎnr le.
The child is growing up day by day, and his parents are feeling a little more relaxed.

● 读博士好像是一条很长的路，不过我相信只要一步一步来，总有
一天会成功的。

**Dú bóshì hǎoxiàng shì yìtiáo hěn chángde lù, búguò wǒ xiāngxìn zhǐyào yíbù-yíbùde
lái, zǒng yǒu yìtiān huì chénggōng de.**

*Studying for a Ph.D. may seem like a long road, but I believe as long as I take it
one step at a time, I will succeed one of these days.*

● 受经济危机的影响，这里的商店一家一家地关门了。

Shòu jīngjì wéijīde yǐngxiǎng, zhèlǐde shāngdiàn yìjiā-yìjiāde guānmén le.

The stores here have been affected by the economic crisis, and have closed one by one.

190. 一边···一边··· yìbiān...yìbiān... *concurrently doing...and...*

● 我喜欢一边跑步，一边听音乐。 **Wǒ xǐhuan yìbiān pǎobù, yìbiān tīng yīnyuè.**
I like to listen to music while I run.

● 很多大学生一边读书，一边实习。

Hěn duō dàxuésheng yìbiān dúshū, yìbiān shíxí.

Many college students do practicum while studying.

● 我们一边走一边聊天，不知不觉就到家了。

Wǒmen yìbiān zǒu, yìbiān liáotiān, bùzhī-bùjué jiù dàojiāle.

We chatted as we walked along, and before we knew it we had reached home.

EXERCISES: ▶

Translate the following sentences into Chinese, using the structures covered in this
chapter:

1. Winter is coming!

2. I can't drink tea in the evening, and not coffee either; otherwise I won't be able
   to sleep.

3. If it weren't for the parents' opposition, she would have married her boyfriend
   long ago.

4. If he's not in the library reading, then he's in the dormitory sleeping.

5. I have to get some exercise every day. I either swim or run.

6. If you don't feel well, you should stay home and rest.

7. Either Chinese or Western food is fine; I like both.

8. The restaurant's business is getting better and better; so I am getting busier by
   the day.

9. Only when I opened my backpack did I discover that my purse was missing.

10. Nowadays many people look at their cell phones as soon as they get up (in the
    morning).

11. One by one, the young people in this village went into cities to find jobs.

12. Every day Dad reads the paper while eating his breakfast.

ANSWERS:

1. 冬天要来了！ **Dōngtiān yào lái le!**

2. 我晚上不能喝茶，也不能喝咖啡，要不睡不着觉。
   Wǒ wǎnshang bùnéng hē chá, yě bùnéng hē kāfēi, yàobù shuì-bu-zháo-jiào.

3. 要不是父母反对，她早就跟男朋友结婚了。
   Yàobushì fùmǔ fǎnduì, tā zǎojiù gēn nánpéngyou jiéhūn le.

4. 他要不是在图书馆里看书，就是在宿舍里睡觉。
   Tā yàobushì zài túshūguǎnlǐ kànshū, jiùshì zài sùshèlǐ shuìjiào.

5. 我每天都得运动一下，要么游泳，要么跑步。
   Wǒ měitiān dōu děi yùndòng yíxià, yàome yóuyǒng, yàome pǎobù.

6. 要是身体不舒服（的话），就应该在家里休息。
   Yàoshi shēntǐ bùshūfu (dehuà), jiù yīnggāi zài jiālǐ xiūxi.

7. 中餐也好，西餐也好，我都喜欢。 **Zhōngcān yěhǎo, Xīcān yěhǎo, wǒ dōu xǐhuan.**

8. 餐馆的生意越来越好，所以我一天比一天忙了。
   Cānguǎnde shēngyì yuèláiyuè hǎo, suǒyǐ wǒ yìtiān bǐ yìtiān máng le.

9. 我一打开背包才发现我的钱包不见了。
   Wǒ yì dǎkāi bēibāo cái fāxiàn wǒde qiánbāo bújiàn le.

10. 现在很多人都是一起床就看手机。 **Xiànzài hěn duō rén dōu shì yì qǐchuáng jiù kàn shǒujī.**

11. 这个农村的年轻人一个一个地到城里打工去了。
    Zhèige nóngcūnde niánqīng-rén yíge-yígede dào chénglǐ dǎgōng qùle.

12. 爸爸每天都是一边吃早餐，一边看报。
    Bàba měitiān dōu shì yìbiān chī zǎocān, yìbiān kànbào.

Chapter 32: Expressions 191–204

191. 一点儿都/也不/没⋯ **yìdiǎnr dōu/yě bù/méi...** *not the least bit..., not even a bit...*
This structure could be preceded by 连 **lián** *even* with no difference in meaning (as in the second example), but the shorter form is much more common in colloquial speech.

- 她什么都吃，一点儿也不挑剔。 **Tā shénme dōu chī, yìdiǎnr yě bù tiāoti.**
  She eats everything. She's not at all picky.

- 这个星期特别忙，连一点儿空儿都没有。
  Zhèige xīngqī tèbié máng, lián yìdiǎnr kòngr dōu méiyǒu.
  I'm especially busy this week. I don't have any free time at all.

- 今天我有点儿不舒服，早上一点儿东西也没吃。
  Jīntiān wǒ yǒudiǎnr bùshūfu, zǎoshang yìdiǎnr dōngxi yě méi chī.
  I'm not feeling too well today. I didn't eat anything at all this morning.

192. 一方面⋯，另一方面⋯ **yìfāngmiàn..., lìng yìfāngmiàn...** *on the one hand..., on the other hand...*
This structure is similar to #190 (一边…一边⋯ **yìbiān...yìbiān...**) and #193 (一面⋯一面⋯ **yímiàn...yímiàn...**), but there are differences in nuance. 一边⋯一边⋯ **yìbiān...yìbiān...** implies that two actions or events are occurring at the same

time, whereas 一方面⋯，另一方面⋯ **yìfāngmiàn…, lìng yìfāngmiàn…** implies that two situations co-exist side-by-side, but the timing is not particularly relevant. 一面⋯一面⋯ **yímiàn…yímiàn…** is a hybrid between these two structures.

⦁ 他一方面很聪明，另一方面很勤奋，所以将来一定会成功。
   Tā yìfāngmiàn hěn cōngming, lìng yìfāngmiàn hěn qínfèn, suǒyǐ jiānglái yídìng huì chénggōng.
   On the one hand he is very smart, and at the same time he is very industrious, so he will surely be successful.

⦁ 我一边学习一边打工，一方面可以得到一些工作经验，另一方面也可以挣一点儿钱。**Wǒ yìbiān xuéxí yìbiān dǎgōng, yìfāngmiàn kěyǐ dédào yìxiē gōngzuò jīngyàn, lìng yìfāngmiàn yě kěyǐ zhèng yìdiǎnr qián.**
   I study and work at the same time, so that I can get some work experience and at the same time earn a little money.

⦁ 改革开放一方面发展了经济，提高了人民的生活水平，可是另一方面也带来了许多社会问题。
   Gǎigé-kāifàng yìfāngmiàn fāzhǎnle jīngjì, tígāole rénmínde shēnghuó shuǐpíng, kěshì lìng yìfāngmiàn yě dàiláile xǔduō shèhuì wèntí.
   Reform and Opening developed the economy and raised people's standard of living, but on the other hand it also brought about many social problems.

⦁ 智能手机一方面给人们的生活带来许多便利，可是另一方面也浪费了人们很多时间。**Zhìnéng shǒujī yìfāngmiàn gěi rénmende shēnghuó dàiláile xǔduō biànlì, kěshì lìng yìfāngmiàn yě làngfèile rénmen hěn duō shíjiān.**
   Smartphones bring many conveniences to our lives, but on the other hand they also waste a lot of our time.

193. 一面⋯一面⋯ **yímiàn…yímiàn…** *on the one hand..., and on the other hand...*

⦁ 一面开车一面打电话发短信都很危险，在某些地区还算是违法的行为。**Yímiàn kāichē yímiàn dǎ diànhuà fā duǎnxìn dōu hěn wēixiǎn, zài mǒuxiē dìqū hái suànshì wéifǎde xíngwéi.**
   Driving while making a phone call or texting is very dangerous, and also illegal in certain areas.

⦁ 她一面节食，一面运动，所以减肥的效果很好。
   Tā yímiàn jiéshí, yímiàn yùndòng, suǒyǐ jiǎnféide xiàoguǒ hěn hǎo.
   She diets and exercises at the same time, so her weight reducing program has very good results.

⦁ 他一面在餐馆打工维持生活，一面准备考GRE，申请研究所。
   Tā yímiàn zài cānguǎn dǎgōng wéichí shēnghuó, yímiàn zhǔnbèi kǎo GRE, shēnqǐng yánjiūsuǒ.
   He works in a restaurant to maintain his livelihood, but he is also preparing for the GRE for his application to graduate school.

194. 一时 **yìshí** *on the spot, at the moment, within a brief time, suddenly*

♦ 虽然我很喜欢这所房子，但一时拿不出那么多钱来。
Suīrán wǒ hěn xǐhuan zhèisuǒ fángzi, dàn yìshí ná-bu-chū nàme duō qián lái.
Although I like this house very much, I don't have that much money just now.

♦ 老板一时高兴，给每位员工发了一个大红包。
Lǎobǎn yìshí gāoxìng, gěi měiwèi yuángōng fāle yíge dà hóngbāo.
The boss was suddenly very happy, so he gave each employee a big red envelope (bonus).

♦ 她一时糊涂，尝试了毒品，结果染上了毒瘾。
Tā yìshí hútú, chángshìle dúpǐn, jiéguǒ rǎnshàngle dúyǐn.
In a moment of foolishness, she tried out some drugs, and subsequently became addicted.

195. 一向 **yíxiàng** *(have) always, heretofore; never before* (when used in the negative)
Synonym of #177 (向来 **xiànglái**).

♦ 我一向不喜欢吃辣的。 **Wǒ yíxiàng bù xǐhuan chī làde.**
I have never liked hot (spicy) food.

♦ 我爸爸一向对政治很感兴趣。 **Wǒ bàba yíxiàng duì zhèngzhì hěn gǎn-xìngqu.**
My dad has always been very interested in politics.

♦ 在美国，政府部门的工作一向不怎么吸引大学毕业生。
Zài Měiguó, zhèngfǔ bùménde gōngzuò yíxiàng bù zěnme xīyǐn dàxué bìyèshēng.
In the U.S., government jobs have never been all that appealing to college graduates.

♦ 老李一向助人为乐，有求必应。 **Lǎo Lǐ yíxiàng zhù-rén-wéi-lè, yǒu-qiú-bì-yìng.**
Old Li has always enjoyed helping people, and came through for others whenever he was asked.

196. 以…来说 **yǐ…láishuō** *considering…; when it comes to…; in terms of…*
This structure literally means *talking about something by way of…*, but Chinese speakers use it idiomatically without being conscious of its literal meaning.

♦ 以空气质量来说，目前中国大部分城市都受到不同程度的污染。
Yǐ kōngqì zhìliàng láishuō, mùqián Zhōngguó dàbùfen chéngshì dōu shòudào bùtóng chéngdùde wūrǎn.
When it comes to air quality, the majority of China's cities are all affected by varying degrees of air pollution.

♦ 以生活成本来说，中国的一线大城市已经达到了世界最高水平。
Yǐ shēnghuó chéngběn láishuō, Zhōngguóde yīxiàn dà chéngshì yǐjīng dádàole shìjiè zuì gāo shuǐpíng.
In terms of cost of living, China's first-tier cities have already reached the world's highest level.

♦ 以规模和实力来说，2018年中国已有120家企业进入了《财富》世
界500强。**Yǐ guīmó hé shílì láishuō, 2018 nián Zhōngguó yǐ yǒu 120 jiā qǐyè
jìnrùle Cáifù shìjiè 500 qiáng.**
*In terms of scale and strength (of enterprises), 120 companies in China have al-
ready entered the Fortune 500 in 2018.*

197. 以···为··· yǐ...wéi... to take...as..., to construe...as...

♦ 华盛顿的时间以美国东部时间为准。
Huáshèngdùnde shíjiān yǐ Měiguó dōngbù shíjiān wéi zhǔn.
Washington (DC) time takes America's Eastern Time as its standard.

♦ 普通话是以北京音为标准音，以北方方言为基础的语言。
Pǔtōnghuà shì yǐ Běijīng yīn wéi biāozhǔn yīn, yǐ běifāng fāngyán wéi jīchǔde yǔyán.
*Chinese takes Beijing pronunciation as the standard, and the dialect of North
China as its basis.*

♦ 从现在开始，政府工作以保卫蓝天为工作重心之一。
Cóng xiànzài kāishǐ, zhèngfǔ gōngzuò yǐ bǎowèi lántiān wéi gōngzuò zhòngxīn zhīyī.
*From now on, the government will take protection of the blue sky as one of the
focuses of its work.*

♦ 公司以提供高质量的服务为宗旨，把顾客的满意度放在第一位。
Gōngsī yǐ tígōng gāo zhìliàngde fúwù wéi zōngzhǐ, bǎ gùkède mǎnyì-dù fàngzài dìyīwèi.
*The company will take providing high quality service as it goal and give top pri-
ority to customer satisfaction.*

198. 以···为主 yǐ...wéizhǔ to take...as the main thing/as primary (a corollary of #197)

♦ 学校食堂以供应西餐为主。**Xuéxiào shítáng yǐ gōngyìng Xīcān wéi zhǔ.**
The school dining hall provides primarily Western meals.

♦ 这家公司的产品以家用电器为主。(这家公司以生产家用电器为主。)
**Zhèijiā gōngsīde chǎnpǐn yǐ jiāyòng diànqì wéi zhǔ. (Zhèijiā gōngsī yǐ shēngchǎn
jiāyòng diànqì wéi zhǔ.)**
This company produces primarily electrical home appliances.

♦ 在美国大城市里开出租车的司机以移民为主。
Zài Měiguó dà chéngshìlǐ kāi chūzū-chēde sījī yǐ yímín wéi zhǔ.
In the big cities of America taxicab drivers are primarily immigrants.

199. ···以来 ...yǐlái since (a certain time or event in the past)
See also #251 (自从···以来/以后 zìcóng...yǐlái/yǐhòu).

♦ 上大学以来，他学到了很多有用的知识，也认识了很多新朋友。
Shàng dàxué yǐlái, tā xuédàole hěn duō yǒuyòngde zhīshi, yě rènshile hěn duō xīn péngyou.
*Since he went to college he has acquired a lot of useful knowledge, and he has
made a lot of new friends.*

♦ 改革开放以来，中国人的生活水平有了很大的提高。
Gǎigé-kāifàng yǐlái, Zhōngguórénde shēnghuó shuǐpíng yǒule hěn dàde tígāo.
Since Reform and Opening, Chinese people's standard of living has greatly improved.

♦ 中美建交以来，两国关系时而处于蜜月期，时而落入低谷。
Zhōng-Měi jiànjiāo yǐlái, liǎngguó guānxi shí'ér chǔyú mìyuè-qī, shí'ér luòrù dīgǔ.
Since the establishment of formal diplomatic relations between China and America, the two countries have sometimes been in a honeymoon and sometimes fallen into an abyss.

200. 以免 yǐmiǎn... *in order to avoid..., lest...* (synonym of #129 免得 miǎnde...)

♦ 千万别经常熬夜，以免伤了身体。
Qiānwàn bié jīngcháng áoyè, yǐmiǎn shāngle shēntǐ.
By all means don't burn the midnight oil too often, lest you damage your health.

♦ 买卖股票要注意风险，以免损失太大。
Mǎimài gǔpiào yào zhùyì fēngxiǎn, yǐmiǎn sǔnshī tài dà.
In buying and selling stocks, one should pay attention to the risk in order to avoid big losses.

♦ 父母不能对孩子有求必应，以免把孩子惯坏了。
Fùmǔ bùnéng duì háizi yǒuqiú-bìyìng, yǐmiǎn bǎ háizi guànhuàile.
Parents can't grant their children's every wish, or they will be spoiled.

201. ···以前/以后 ...yǐqián/yǐhòu *before.../after...*

♦ 出国以前，我们得办护照签证。
Chūguó yǐqián, wǒmen děi bàn hùzhào qiānzhèng.
Before going abroad we have to get passports and visas.

♦ 下课以后，有的同学去图书馆学习，有的去食堂吃饭。
Xiàkè yǐhòu, yǒude tóngxué qù túshūguǎn xuéxí, yǒude qù shítáng chīfàn.
After class, some students go to the library to study, and others go to the dining hall and eat.

♦ 他们俩打算研究生毕业以后就结婚。
Tāmen liǎ dǎsuàn yánjiūshēng bìyè yǐhòu jiù jiéhūn.
The two of them plan to get married after they finish graduate school.

202. 以前···，后来··· yǐqián..., hòulái... *formerly, previously..., later...*

♦ 我以前对数学很感兴趣，后来决定以经济作为专业。
Wǒ yǐqián duì shùxué hěn gǎn-xìngqu, hòulái juédìng yǐ jīngjì zuòwéi zhuānyè.
I used to be very interested in mathematics, and later I decided to take economics as my major.

♦ 以前快餐很受欢迎，后来大家都知道吃快餐对健康有害。
Yǐqián kuàicān hěn shòu huānyíng, hòulái dàjiā dōu zhīdào chī kuàicān duì jiànkāng yǒuhài.
People used to like fast food very much, but later everybody came to know that fast food was harmful to their health.

♦ 深圳以前是个小渔村，后来变成了中国经济最发达的城市之一。
Shēnzhèn yǐqián shì ge xiǎo yúcūn, hòulái biànchéngle Zhōngguó jīngjì zuì fādáde chéngshì zhīyī.
Shenzhen was formerly a little fishing village, then later it became one of the most economically developed cities in China.

203. ⋯以上 **...yǐshàng** *more than..., above...* (usually inclusive)

♦ 这家公司50%以上的员工是女性。
Zhèijiā gōngsī bǎifēn-zhī-wǔshí yǐshàngde yuángōng shì nǚxìng.
In this company, over 50% of the employees are women.

♦ 年薪在十万以上就算是高收入了。
Niánxīn zài shíwàn yǐshàng jiù suàn shì gāo shōurù le.
An annual salary of one hundred thousand or more is considered high income.

♦ 65岁以上的老人可以享受票价优惠。
65 suì yǐshàngde lǎorén kěyǐ xiǎngshòu piàojià yōuhuì.
Persons 65 and older can enjoy the benefits of discounted tickets.

204. 以往⋯，（现在⋯） **yǐwǎng..., (xiànzài...)** *in the past..., (now...)*
以往 **yǐwǎng** is a literary synonym of 从前 **cóngqián**. Chinese speakers use it not so much to be formal, but to make the other party sit up and listen.

♦ 这一带的治安以往不那么好，现在好多了。
Zhè yídàide zhì'ān yǐwǎng bú nàme hǎo, xiànzài hǎo duō le.
In the past, public security in this area was not that good, (but) now it's much better.

♦ 以往大家只能通过写信互通信息，现在写信的人少之又少了。
Yǐwǎng dàjiā zhǐnéng tōngguò xiěxìn hùtōng xìnxī, xiànzài xiěxìnde rén shǎo-zhī-yòu-shǎo le.
In the past everybody could only communicate by writing letters; nowadays hardly anyone writes letters anymore.

♦ 以往这里是一大片田地，现在是高楼林立的商业中心了。
Yǐwǎng zhèlǐ shì yídàpiàn tiándì, xiànzài shì gāolóu línlìde shāngyè zhōngxīn le.
In the past this was a great expanse of agricultural fields; now it is a commercial center consisting of a forest of tall buildings.

EXERCISES:

Translate the following sentences into Chinese, using the structures covered in this chapter:

1. Summers are not the least bit hot here.

2. Attending a summer program in China can continue to raise one's Chinese proficiency, and at the same time prevent forgetting what one has learned before.

3. In order to reduce the burden on his family, he works while he is studying.

4. He asked me why I didn't want to marry him, but I didn't know how to answer him on the spot.

5. I have always liked sweets, so it's hard (for me) to lose weight.

6. Given your grades, you very likely won't be able to get into one of the best colleges.

7. Before 1980, the English curriculum in China took British English to be the standard.

8. This Chinese course takes listening and speaking as primary; reading and writing are only secondary.

9. Since school started this fall, his Chinese has improved greatly.

10. Let's leave a little earlier, so as to avoid missing the plane.

11. He likes to read a while before going to sleep.

12. We used to live in New York, then later we moved to San Francisco.

13. In America, only persons 21 or older may buy liquor.

14. In the past, most people rode their bicycles to work; now they all drive their cars or take public transportation.

ANSWERS:

1. 这里的夏天一点儿都不热。 **Zhèlǐde xiàtiān yìdiǎnr dōu bú rè.**

2. 去中国上暑期班一方面可以继续提高中文水平，另一方面可以避免忘记以前学过的中文。 **Qù Zhōngguó shàng shǔqībān yìfāngmiàn kěyǐ jìxù tígāo Zhōngwén shuǐpíng, lìng yìfāngmiàn kěyǐ bìmiǎn wàngjì yǐqián xuéguode Zhōngwén.**

3. 为了减轻家里的负担，他一面上学，一面打工。 **Wèile jiǎnqīng jiālǐde fùdān, tā yímiàn shàngxué, yímiàn dǎgōng.**

4. 他问我为什么不愿意嫁给他，我一时不知道怎么回答。 **Tā wèn wǒ wèishénme bú yuànyi jiàgěi tā, wǒ yìshí bù zhīdào zěnme huídá.**

5. 我一向喜欢吃甜食，所以很难减肥。 **Wǒ yíxiàng xǐhuan chī tiánshí, suǒyǐ hěn nán jiǎnféi.**

6. 以你的成绩来说，你很可能上不了最好的大学。 **Yǐ nǐde chéngjì láishuō, nǐ hěn kěnéng shàng-bu-liǎo zuì hǎode dàxué.**

7. 1980年以前，中国的英语课程以英国的英语为标准。 **1980 nián yǐqián, Zhōngguóde Yīngyǔ kèchéng yǐ Yīngguóde Yīngyǔ wéi biāozhǔn.**

8. 这门中文课以听说为主，读写只是次要的。 **Zhèmén Zhōngwén-kè yǐ tīngshuō wéi zhǔ, dúxiě zhǐshì cìyàode.**

9. 今年秋季开学以来，他的中文有了长足的进步。 **Jīnnián qiūjì kāixué yǐlái, tāde Zhōngwén yǒule chángzúde jìnbù.**

10. 我们早一点出发吧，以免误了飞机。 **Wǒmen zǎo yìdiǎn chūfā ba, yǐmiǎn wùle fēijī.**

11. 睡觉以前，他喜欢看一会儿书。**Shuìjiào yǐqián, tā xǐhuan kàn yìhuǐr shū.**

12. 我们家以前在纽约，后来搬到旧金山去了。
Wǒmen jiā yǐqián zài Niǔyuē, hòulái bāndào Jiùjīnshān qù le.

13. 在美国，21岁以上的人才可以买酒。**Zài Měiguó, 21 suì yǐshàngde rén cái kěyǐ mǎi jiǔ.**

14. 以往人们大多骑自行车上下班，现在都自己开车或坐公交了。
Yǐwǎng rénmen dàduō qí zìxíngchē shàng-xiàbān, xiànzài dōu zìjǐ kāichē huò zuò gōngjiāo le.

Chapter 33: Expressions 205–216

205. 以为 **yǐwéi** *to think/thought (incorrectly), misconstrue*

This word is derived from 以…为… **yǐ…wéi…** (#197), and it is another example of how fairly common words in modern Chinese can be derived from combining two single-syllable words in literary Chinese. See also #6 别以为…，其实… **bié yǐwéi…, qíshí….**

♠ 我以为今天的考试会很难，其实挺简单的。
Wǒ yǐwéi jīntiānde kǎoshì huì hěn nán, qíshí tǐng jiǎndānde.
I thought today's test would be very difficult, but it was actually quite simple.

♠ 他以为这个工作比较轻松，后来发现不是这么回事儿。
Tā yǐwéi zhèige gōngzuò bǐjiào qīngsōng, hòulái fāxiàn bú shì zhème huí shìr.
He thought this job would be relatively light, but later he discovered that it was not the case.

♠ 别看他整天开开心心的样子就以为他什么烦恼都没有。
Bié kàn tā zhěngtiān kāikāixīnxīnde yàngzi jiù yǐwéi tā shénme fánnǎo dōu méiyǒu.
Don't just go by his constant happy appearance and think that he has no worries. (Don't let his constantly happy appearance fool you into thinking that he has no worries.)

206. 以至于 **yǐzhìyú** *(even) to the extent that…*

♠ 这件事情发生得太突然了，以至于我无法做好心理准备。
Zhèijiàn shìqing fāshēngde tài tūrán le, yǐzhìyú wǒ wúfǎ zuòhǎo xīnlǐ zhǔnbèi.
This matter happened so suddenly that I had no way to be mentally prepared for it.

♠ 我的家乡这两年的变化太快了，以至于我都找不到三年前还很熟悉的路了。**Wǒde jiāxiāng zhèi liǎngniánde biànhuà tài kuài le, yǐzhìyú wǒ dōu zhǎo-bu-dào sānnián qián hái hěn shúxīde lù le.**
In the past two years my hometown has changed too rapidly, so that I can't even find roads that were very familiar to me three years ago.

♠ 网络上的新闻真真假假，以至于人们很难分清楚哪些是真的，哪些是假的。**Wǎngluò-shangde xīnwén zhēnzhēnjiǎjiǎ, yǐzhìyú rénmen hěn nán fēn-qīngchǔ nǎxiē shì zhēnde, nǎxiē shì jiǎde.**
News on the web is such a mixture of the real and the fake that people have a hard time distinguishing what is real and what is fake.

207. 因此 **yīncǐ** *because of this, therefore*

This structure is a good one to use if you want to perk up your Chinese speech with an alternative to the overused structure 因为···所以··· **yīnwèi...suǒyǐ...**.

● 王老师教课教得很好，人也很幽默，因此学生都喜欢他。
  Wáng Lǎoshī jiāokè jiāode hěn hǎo, rén yě hěn yōumò, yīncǐ xuésheng dōu xǐhuan tā.
  Professor Wang teaches very well, and he has a very good sense of humor; therefore students all like him.

● 每个人都有各自的特点，因此要互相学习，取长补短。
  Měige rén dōu yǒu gèzìde tèdiǎn, yīncǐ yào hùxiāng xuéxí, qǔcháng-bǔduǎn.
  Everyone has their own special characteristics; therefore they must learn from each other, and look for strengths in others to make up for one's own weaknesses.

● 他工作能力很强，态度又很认真，因此在公司里很受重用。
  Tā gōngzuò nénglì hěn qiáng, tàidù yòu hěn rènzhēn, yīncǐ zài gōngsīlǐ hěn shòu zhòngyòng.
  He is very capable and has a very serious attitude; therefore he is entrusted with important tasks in the company.

208. 因为···的关系 **yīnwèi...de guānxi** *because of..., due to...*

● 因为气候的关系，大批中国北方退休老人到海南过冬。
  Yīnwèi qìhòude guānxi, dàpī Zhōngguó běifāng tuìxiū lǎorén dào Hǎinán guòdōng.
  Because of the climate, a lot of retirees in North China go to Hainan for the winter.

● 因为工作的关系，他们常常在一起，时间长了就有了感情。
  Yīnwèi gōngzuòde guānxi, tāmen chángcháng zài yìqǐ, shíjiān chángle jiù yǒule gǎnqíng.
  Due to their work they are often together, and with the passage of time they developed affection for each other.

● 因为她很注意饮食，又常常运动的关系，她的身材依然保持得很好。
  Yīnwèi tā hěn zhùyì yǐnshí, yòu chángcháng yùndòngde guānxi, tāde shēncái yīrán bǎochíde hěnhǎo.
  Because she pays attention to her diet, and also exercises frequently, she has maintained a very good figure.

209. 因为···的缘故 **yīnwèi...de yuángù** *because (of)... (synonym of the preceding structure)*

There is a slight difference in nuance between #208 and #209: 关系 **guānxi** means *relevance* and 缘故 **yuángù** means *reason, cause*. These two words have very different meanings, but the two structures are interchangeable.

● 因为热爱美食的缘故，她希望将来当一名大厨。
  Yīnwèi rè'ài měishíde yuángù, tā xīwàng jiānglái dāng yìmíng dàchú.
  Because of her love of good food, she hopes to become a chef in the future.

● 因为爱情的缘故，她跟着先生搬到了南美洲定居。
  Yīnwèi àiqíngde yuángù, tā gēnzhe xiānsheng bāndàole Nán-Měizhōu dìngjū.
  It was love that made her move to South America to settle down there with her husband.

◆ 因为性格不合的缘故，他们结婚不到一年就离婚了。
Yīnwèi xìnggé bùhéde yuángù, tāmen jiéhūn búdào yìnián jiù líhūn le.
Because their personalities were incompatible, they got divorced less than a year after they were married.

◆ 因为健康亮了红灯的缘故，他决定辞去公司总经理的职务。
Yīnwèi jiànkāng liàngle hóngdēngde yuángù, tā juédìng cíqù gōngsī zǒngjīnglǐde zhíwù.
Because his health "flashed a red light," he decided to resign from being the company's CEO.

210. 用⋯做⋯ yòng...zuò... to use/take...as...

This structure is a more colloquial synonym of #198 (以⋯为⋯ yǐ...wéi...). But 用⋯做⋯ yòng...zuò... is preferred when referring to concrete physical objects, while 以⋯为⋯ yǐ...wéi... is preferred when referring to non-physical things. In this pattern, 作 zuò or 当作 dāngzuò may be used in lieu of 做 zuò.

◆ 为了环保，我们应该尽量用回收的废品做原材料。
Wèile huánbǎo, wǒmen yīnggāi jìnliàng yòng huíshōude fèipǐn zuò yuán-cáiliào.
For the sake of environmental preservation, we should insofar as possible use recycled waste as raw material.

◆ 你为什么总是用工作忙做借口，不回家陪陪家人呢？
Nǐ wèishénme zǒngshì yòng gōngzuò máng zuò jièkǒu, bù huíjiā péipéi jiārén ne?
Why do you always use the excuse of being busy at work to not come home and be with the family?

◆ 我打算用房子做抵押，从银行借贷两百万来创办自己的公司。
Wǒ dǎsuàn yòng fángzi zuò dǐyā, cóng yínháng jièdài liǎngbǎiwàn lái chuàngbàn zìjǐde gōngsī.
I plan to use the house as collateral and borrow two million from the bank to establish my own company.

◆ 他预备用自己的博士论文做第一本出版著作的基础。
Tā yùbèi yòng zìjǐde bóshì lùnwén zuò dìyīběn chūbǎn zhùzuòde jīchǔ.
He plans to use his own Ph.D. dissertation as the basis for his first published work.

211. 尤其是 yóuqíshì especially

◆ 这位教授对中国历史很有研究，尤其是清朝历史。
Zhèiwèi jiàoshòu duì Zhōngguó lìshǐ hěn yǒu-yánjiū, yóuqíshì Qīngcháo lìshǐ.
This professor is very knowledgeable about Chinese history, especially Qing dynasty history.

◆ 重男轻女的传统观念仍然存在，尤其是在农村地区。
Zhòngnán-qīngnǔde chuántǒng guānniàn réngrán cúnzài, yóuqíshì zài nóngcūn dìqū.
The traditional concept of valuing males over females still exists, especially in rural villages.

◆ 中国的房价这些年一直上涨，尤其是在北上广深这样的一线城市。
Zhōngguóde fángjià zhèxiē nián yìzhí shàngzhǎng, yóuqíshì zài Běi-Shàng-Guǎng-Shēn zhèyàngde yīxiàn chéngshì.
Housing prices in China have steadily risen in recent years, especially in the top-tier cities like Beijing, Shanghai, Guangzhou and Shenzhen.

212. 由于 yóuyú *due to..., because of...*

由于 **yóuyú** means the same thing as 因为 **yīnwèi**, but it is used singly rather than coupled with another structural word like 所以 **suǒyǐ**. The 由于 **yóuyú** structure is also a more eloquent alternative to the mundane structure 因为···所以··· **yīnwèi...suǒyǐ....**

◆ 由于他粗心大意，不负责任，才造成了这起严重的事故。
Yóuyú tā cūxīn dàyì, bú fù-zérèn, cái zàochéngle zhèiqǐ yánzhòngde shìgù.
This serious accident came about due to his carelessness and lack of responsibility.

◆ 由于经济的快速发展，中国在世界上也扮演着越来越重要的角色。
Yóuyú jīngjìde kuàisù fāzhǎn, Zhōngguó zài shìjiè-shang yě bànyǎnzhe yuèláiyuè zhòngyàode juésè.
Due to rapid economic development, China is playing an increasingly important role on the world stage.

◆ 由于他们成长的环境不同，接受的教育也不一样，难免常常有误会。
Yóuyú tāmen chéngzhǎngde huánjìng bùtóng, jiēshòude jiàoyù yě bù yíyàng, nánmiǎn chángcháng yǒu wùhuì.
Because they grew up in different environments and received different educations, frequent misunderstanding between them is unavoidable.

213. 有的···，有的··· yǒude..., yǒude... *some..., (and) some/others...*

This structure is always used within a context, i.e. 有的 **yǒude** always refers to an antecedent.

◆ 美式的potluck聚餐很有意思，每人带一个菜，有的带肉，有的带菜。
Měishìde potluck jùcān hěn yǒuyìsi, měirén dài yíge cài, yǒude dài ròu, yǒude dài cài.
American-style potluck dinners are interesting. Each person brings a dish; some bring meat and others bring vegetables.

◆ 大学毕业以后，同学们都各奔东西，从事不同的行业。有的为政府工作，有的做投资银行家，有的上研究所继续求学。
Dàxué bìyè yǐhòu, tóngxuémen dōu gè bēn dōng-xī, cóngshì bùtóngde hángyè. Yǒude wèi zhèngfǔ gōngzuò, yǒude zuò tóuzī yínháng-jiā, yǒude shàng yánjiūsuǒ jìxù qiúxué.
After graduating, classmates scatter east and west and pursue various occupations. Some work for the government, some become investment bankers, and some go to graduate school to continue their education.

● 大清早，很多老人都在公园里锻炼，有的跳舞，有的打太极拳，有的练剑。**Dà qīngzǎo, hěn duō lǎorén dōu zài gōngyuánlǐ duànliàn, yǒude tiàowǔ, yǒude dǎ tàijíquán, yǒude liànjiàn.**

Early in the morning many old people exercise in the park; some dance, some do tai chi, and some practice swordplay.

214. 有(一)点儿 yǒu(yì)diǎnr *a little* (followed by a stative verb) (see 2.1, sec. 8)

● 老师周末给学生那么多功课，实在有点过分。
Lǎoshī zhōumò gěi xuésheng nàme duō gōngkè, shízài yǒudiǎnr guòfèn.

The teacher gave the students so much homework over the weekend, it's really a bit excessive.

● 男朋友忘了给她买生日礼物，让她有一点不高兴。
Nánpéngyou wàngle gěi tā mǎi shēngrì lǐwù, ràng tā yǒu yìdiǎnr bù gāoxìng.

Her boyfriend forgot to buy her a birthday present, making her a bit unhappy.

● 他一个人住这么大的房子会不会感觉有点儿寂寞呢？
Tā yíge rén zhù zhème dàde fángzi huì-búhuì gǎnjué yǒudiǎnr jìmò ne?

Living alone in such a big house, won't he feel a little lonely?

215. 又···又··· yòu...yòu... *both...and...*

This structure may be extended to include a third 又 **yòu**, as in the last example below. See also #98 (既···又··· **jì...yòu...**).

● 他在参观大学的时候，看到宿舍楼里又脏又乱，让他大吃一惊，立刻就决定不申请那所大学了。
Tā zài cānguān dàxuéde shíhou, kàndào sùshè-lóu-lǐ yòu zāng yòu luàn, ràng tā dà chī yìjīng, lìkè jiù juédìng bù shēnqǐng nèisuǒ dàxué le.

When he was visiting a college, he was very taken aback to see that the dormitory was filthy and disorderly, so he immediately decided not to apply to that school.

● 兄弟俩小时候又打又闹，家里没有一天安宁的日子，长大后两个人却变成了铁哥们。
Xiōngdì liǎ xiǎo-shíhou yòu dǎ yòu nào, jiālǐ méiyǒu yìtiān ānníngde rìzi, zhǎngdà hòu liǎngge rén què biànchéngle tiěgēmen.

When the two brothers were small, they fought and quarreled; there was never a day of peace in the home. But after they grew up, they became very close buddies.

● 他的姨妈给他介绍了一个又聪明、又善良、又能干的对象，可他宁愿娶那个美貌的舞女。
Tāde yímā gěi tā jièshàole yíge yòu cōngmíng, yòu shànliáng, yòu nénggànde duì-xiàng, kě tā nìngyuàn qǔ nèige měimàode wǔnǚ.

His aunt introduced him to a prospective match who is smart, kind, and capable, but he would rather marry that good-looking dance girl.

216. 于是 **yúshì** *thereupon, as a result...*

于是 **yúshì** is a formal synonym of 所以 **suǒyǐ**. Like 由于 **yóuyú**, 于是 **yúshì** is a more eloquent alternative to the mundane structure 因为···所以··· **yīnwèi...suǒyǐ....** Both 于是 **yúshì** and 由于 **yóuyú** operate independently, i.e. not in tandem with another structural word.

- 父母发现她很有运动天赋，于是从小就培养她滑冰。
  Fùmǔ fāxiàn tā hěn yǒu yùndòng tiānfù, yúshì cóng xiǎo jiù péiyǎng tā huábīng.
  Her parents discovered that she had innate athletic talent, thereupon from a young age they gave her training in ice skating.

- 老王觉得自己的身体一天不如一天，于是决定该退休了。
  Lǎo Wáng juéde zìjǐde shēntǐ yìtiān bùrú yìtiān, yúshì juédìng gāi tuìxiū le.
  Old Wang felt that his physical health was declining day by day, so he decided that he should retire.

- 他们意识到两个人的性格很不一样，恐怕很难在一起生活，于是就分手了。
  Tāmen yìshidào liǎngge rénde xìnggé hěn bù yíyàng, kǒngpà hěn nán zài yìqǐ shēng-huó, yúshì jiù fēnshǒu le.
  They realized that the two of them had very different personalities, and probably would have a hard time living together, so they broke up.

EXERCISES:

Translate the following sentences into Chinese, using the structures covered in this chapter:

1. A lot of people think that Americans are all very wealthy, but America actually has a lot of poor people.

2. He was so very tired that he fell asleep just sitting there.

3. The two of them have very different lifestyles; because of this, they often have conflicts.

4. Because of the weather, the plane could not take off on time.

5. Because her parents were divorced, she grew up with her mother from the time she was small.

6. The city government is encouraging people to use bicycles as their primary mode of transportation.

7. I love Chinese food, especially Sichuan dishes.

8. Due to the rising incomes of ordinary people, their standard of living has also been greatly improved.

9. My classmates come from all over China; some are northerners and some are southerners.

10. I didn't eat breakfast this morning, and now I feel a little hungry.

11. This little restaurant is both good and inexpensive, no wonder it is very popular.

12. Both of his parents were very busy with their work, so they sent him to a boarding school.

ANSWERS:

1. 很多人以为美国人都很有钱，其实美国也有不少穷人。
   Hěn duō rén yǐwéi Měiguórén dōu hěn yǒuqián, qíshí Měiguó yě yǒu bùshǎo qióngrén.

2. 他实在太累了，以至于坐在那里就睡着了。
   Tā shízài tài lèi le, yǐzhìyú zuò zài nàli jiù shuìzháole.

3. 他们两个人的生活习惯很不一样，因此常常有矛盾。
   Tāmen liǎngge rénde shēnghuó xíguàn hěn bù yíyàng, yīncǐ chángcháng yǒu máodùn.

4. 因为天气的关系，飞机不能按时起飞。Yīnwèi tiānqìde guānxi, fēijī bùnéng ànshí qǐfēi.

5. 因为她父母离了婚的缘故，她从小是跟着妈妈长大的。
   Yīnwèi tā fùmǔ lí-le-hūnde yuángù, tā cóngxiǎo shì gēnzhe māma zhǎngdà de.

6. 市政府鼓励人们用自行车做主要的交通工具。
   Shì-zhèngfǔ gǔlì rénmen yòng zìxíngchē zuò zhǔyàode jiāotōng gōngjù.

7. 我很喜欢中国菜，尤其是川菜。Wǒ hěn xǐhuan Zhōngguó cài, yóuqíshì Chuāncài.

8. 由于老百姓收入的增加，生活水平也有了较大提升。
   Yóuyú lǎobǎixìng shōurùde zēngjiā, shēnghuó shuǐpíng yě yǒule jiàodàde tíshēng.

9. 我的同学来自全国各地，有的是北方人，有的是南方人。
   Wǒde tóngxué láizì quánguó gèdì, yǒude shì běifāng-rén, yǒude shì nánfāng-rén.

10. 我早上没吃早饭，现在感觉有一点儿饿。
    Wǒ zǎoshang méi chī zǎofàn, xiànzài gǎnjué yǒu yìdiǎnr è.

11. 这家小饭馆又好吃又便宜，难怪很受欢迎。
    Zhèijiā xiǎo fànguǎn yòu hǎochī yòu piányi, nánguài hěn shòu huānyíng.

12. 父母工作都非常忙，于是就送他上了寄宿学校。
    Fùmǔ gōngzuò dōu fēicháng máng, yúshì jiù sòng tā shàngle jìsù xuéxiào.

Chapter 34: Expressions 217–228

217. 与其···，不如··· yǔqí..., bùrú... *compared against..., it would be better to...; it's better to...than to...*

This structure has no English equivalent, hence the translations in the examples below are all paraphrases. For a discussion of this structure, see 16.1, sec. 6.

⬥ 与其自己开车，不如坐高铁，又快又安全。
Yǔqí zìjǐ kāichē, bùrú zuò gāotiě, yòu kuài yòu ānquán.
He considered driving his own car, but then he realized that it would be better to take a fast train, both faster and safer.

⬥ 与其整天空谈，不如行动起来。成功不成功，反正我们都应该尝试一下。**Yǔqí zhěngtiān kōngtán, bùrú xíngdòng-qǐlai. Chénggōng-bùchénggōng, wǒmen dōu yīnggāi chángshì yíxià.**
Rather than just talking about it all day, it would be better to take action. Whether we succeed or not, we should give it a try.

♦ 我们应该趁年轻努力学习，就像老话说的，与其老来悲伤，不如年少发奋。

Wǒmen yīnggāi chèn niánqīng nǔlì xuéxí, jiù xiàng lǎohuà shuōde, yǔqí lǎolái bēishāng, bùrú niánshào fāfèn.

We should study hard while we are young. As the old saying goes, it's better to exert your utmost when you're young than to be sad in old age.

218. 原来 **yuánlái** *after all, as it turns out* (lit., "originally")

The implication of 原来 **yuánlái** in this structure is a derived meaning of the term. Its primary meaning is *originally*, and that is the meaning shown in the next structure (原来···, 后来··· **yuánlái…, hòulái…**). In the context of the following examples, it implies a sudden realization of a fact that has been there all along (i.e. since the *beginning*), and that fact is what lies behind a certain manifestation.

♦ 难怪他特别能吃辣的，原来是四川人。

Nánguài tā tèbié néng chī làde, yuánlái shì Sìchuān rén.

It's not so surprising that he can eat such hot food; he's from Sichuan, after all.

♦ 原来他并不是我们要找的张大爷，我们搞错了。

Yuánlái tā bìng búshì wǒmen yào zhǎode Zhāng Dàyé, wǒmen gǎocuò le.

As it turns out, he's not the Old Mr. Zhang that we are looking for. We made a mistake.

♦ 原来这家公司几年前已经倒闭了，只不过没有人知道这个信息。

Yuánlái zhèijiā gōngsī jǐnián-qián yǐjīng dǎobì le, zhǐ búguò méiyǒu rén zhīdào zhèige xìnxī.

As it turned out, this company had already gone bankrupt several years ago. It's just that nobody knew about it.

219. 原来···后来··· **yuánlái…, hòulái…** *originally/used to be…, later on…*

♦ 原来我们关系特别好，后来慢慢地就没有联系了。

Yuánlái wǒmen guānxi tèbié hǎo, hòulái mànmānde jiù méiyǒu liánxì le.

Our relationship used to be especially good, but later we gradually lost contact.

♦ 原来他特别喜欢吃辣的，后来胃出了毛病，就不再敢吃辣的了。

Yuánlái tā tèbié xǐhuan chī làde, hòulái wèi chūle máobìng, jiù búzài gǎn chī làde le.

He used to especially like spicy food, but later he developed stomach problems, and then didn't dare eat spicy food anymore.

♦ 原来他对政治一点也不感兴趣，后来却一心一意要从政。

Yuánlái tā duì zhèngzhì yìdiǎn yě bù gǎn-xìngqù, hòulái què yìxīn-yíyì yào cóngzhèng.

Originally he had no interest at all in politics, but later he devoted himself to political work.

220. 越···越··· **yuè…yuè…** *the more…the more…*

♦ 中文我越学越有兴趣。**Zhōngwén wǒ yuè xué yuè yǒu-xìngqù.**

The more I study Chinese the more I am interested in it.

● 他是个工作狂，越忙越高兴。他要是一闲下来就心慌。
Tā shì ge gōngzuò-kuáng, yuè máng yuè gāoxìng. Tā yàoshi yì xián-xiàlai jiù xīnhuāng.
He is a workaholic; the busier he is the happier he is. If he suddenly finds himself at loose ends, he becomes flustered.

● 有的父母总喜欢逼孩子弹钢琴。有时候他们逼得越紧，孩子越不想弹。**Yǒude fùmǔ zǒng xǐhuan bī háizi tán gāngqín. Yǒu shíhou tāmen bīde yuè jǐn, háizi yuè bùxiǎng tán.**
Some parents always want to push their children to practice piano. Sometimes, the harder they push the less the children are willing to practice.

221. 越来越··· yuèláiyuè... *increasingly more..., getting to be more and more...*

● 因为网络越来越发达，世界变得越来越小。
Yīnwèi wǎngluò yuèláiyuè fādá, shìjiè biànde yuèláiyuè xiǎo.
As the web becomes more and more developed, the world becomes smaller and smaller.

● 改革开放四十年来，中国边远地区的交通越来越发达了。
Gǎigé-kāifàng sìshí-nián lái, Zhōngguó biānyuǎn dìqūde jiāotōng yuèláiyuè fādá le.
In the past forty years of reform and opening, transportation in the border areas of China has become more and more developed.

● 随着人们对健康饮食的了解不断深入，有机食品也越来越受欢迎。
Suízhe rénmen duì jiànkāng yǐnshíde liǎojiě búduàn shēnrù, yǒujī shípǐn yě yuèláiyuè shòu huānyíng.
As people's understanding of healthy diet continuously improved, organic foods have become more and more popular.

222. 再···还是··· zài...háishi... *no matter how...still...*

In this structure, 再 zài in the sense of *further* is extended to the implication of "no matter how much further...," i.e. *even at the most....* The English paraphrase *no matter how...* is very apt in this case.

● 孩子再不听话，父母还是有责任教育他们。就像老话说的，子不教，父之过。**Háizi zài bù tīnghuà, fùmǔ háishi yǒu zérèn jiàoyù tāmen. Jiù xiàng lǎohuà shuōde, zǐ bù jiāo, fù zhī guò.**
No matter how unwilling a child is to listen, parents still have the responsibility to teach him. As the old saying goes: Failing to teach a child is a father's fault.

● 我们出门在外，再安全的地方还是得小心才行。
Wǒmen chūmén zài wài, zài ānquánde dìfang háishi děi xiǎoxīn cái xíng.
When we are out (away from home), even in a very safe place, we still must be careful.

● 他的能力再强还是应该谦虚一点儿，总是那么骄傲让人讨厌。
Tāde nénglì zài qiáng háishi yīnggāi qiānxū yìdiǎnr, zǒngshì nàme jiāo'ào ràng rén tǎoyàn.
No matter how capable he is, he should still be a bit more modest. If he is always so arrogant, people will loathe him.

223. 再···也··· zài...yě... *no matter how... still...*

◆ 父母工作再忙也应该抽一点儿时间陪陪孩子。
  Fùmǔ gōngzuò zài máng yě yīnggāi chōu yìdiǎnr shíjiān péipéi háizi.
  No matter how busy they are, parents should find a little time to be with their children.

◆ 你再不喜欢他也不要伤他的心，人都是有自尊的。
  Nǐ zài bù xǐhuan tā yě búyào shāng tāde xīn, rén dōu shì yǒu zìzūn de.
  No matter how much you dislike him, you shouldn't hurt his feelings. Everybody has self respect.

◆ 创业初期，困难再大，我们也咬着牙坚持下来了。
  Chuàngyè chūqī, kùnnan zài dà, wǒmen yě yǎozhe-yá jiānchí-xiàlai le.
  During the initial period of the enterprise, no matter how great the difficulties, we gritted our teeth and persevered.

224. 再多···一下/一点儿/一会儿 zài duō...yíxià/yìdiǎnr/yìhuǐr *(do something) a little more/a little longer*

◆ 今天是周末，我再多睡一会儿，补补觉。
  Jīntiān shì zhōumò, wǒ zài duō shuì yìhuǐr, bǔbǔ jiào.
  Today is the weekend, I'll sleep a little longer to catch up on my sleep.

◆ 你再多坚持一下，救护车马上就来了。
  Nǐ zài duō jiānchí yíxià, jiùhùchē mǎshàng jiù lái le.
  Bear with it a little longer. The ambulance will be here soon.

◆ 别客气，再多吃一点儿，剩下来就浪费了。
  Bié kèqi, zài duō chī yìdiǎnr, shèng-xiàlai jiù làngfèi le.
  Don't be polite. Eat a little more. Anything left over will just be wasted.

225. 再加上 zài jiāshàng *and in addition (to the aforementioned)*

◆ 他们两个人非常勤奋，再加上一点儿运气，生意做得很红火。
  Tāmen liǎngge rén fēicháng qínfèn, zài jiāshàng yìdiǎnr yùnqi, shēngyì zuòde hěn hónghuǒ.
  The two of them are very industrious, and with the addition of a bit of luck, their business is going roaringly well.

◆ 医生建议他注意饮食，再加上适量的运动，很快就会恢复健康。
  Yīshēng jiànyì tā zhùyì yǐnshí, zài jiāshàng shìliàngde yùndòng, hěn kuài jiù huì huīfù jiànkāng.
  The doctor suggested that he should pay attention to his diet, and with an appropriate amount of exercise, he should quickly regain his health.

◆ 深圳有优越的地理位置，再加上政府的优税政策，因此很快就从一个小渔村发展成为了现代化的大都市。
  Shēnzhèn yǒu yōuyuède dìlǐ wèizhi, zài jiāshàng zhèngfǔde yōushuì zhèngcè, yīncǐ hěn kuài jiù cóng yíge xiǎo yúcūn fāzhǎn chéngwéile xiàndài-huàde dàdūshì.
  Shenzhen has an excellent geographic location, and with the government's preferential tax policy, it quickly developed from a little fishing village to a big modern city.

226. 再说 zài shuō *furthermore* (lit., "to speak further")

◆ 中文很有用，再说我对中国历史文化很有兴趣，所以就选了中文课。
Zhōngwén hěn yǒuyòng, zài shuō wǒ duì Zhōngguó lìshǐ wénhuà hěn yǒu-xìngqù, suǒyǐ jiù xuǎnle Zhōngwén kè.
Chinese is very useful, and in addition I am very much interested in Chinese history and culture, so I have signed up for a Chinese course.

◆ 你不应该跟他发火，他是为你好，再说又是长辈，你要理解他。
Nǐ bù yīnggāi gēn tā fāhuǒ, tā shì wèi nǐ hǎo, zàishuō yòushì zhǎngbèi, nǐ yào lǐjiě tā.
You shouldn't get angry at him. He is thinking of what's best for you, and besides, he is of the older generation. You should understand him.

◆ 纽约机会很多，再说也很国际化，因此对年轻人很有吸引力。
Niǔyuē jīhuì hěn duō, zài shuō yě hěn guójì-huà, yīncǐ duì niánqīng-rén hěn yǒu xīyǐnlì.
There are many opportunities in New York, and besides, it is very cosmopolitan. That's why it's so attractive to young people.

227. 再也不···了 zài yě bù...le *will never again...(from here on)*

◆ 他骗过我太多次了，我再也不相信他说的话了。
Tā piànguo wǒ tài duō cì le, wǒ zài yě bù xiāngxìn tā shuōde huà le.
He has deceived me too many times, I will never again believe what he says.

◆ 有了这次的经验教训，我以后再也不会上当了。
Yǒule zhèicìde jīngyàn jiàoxùn, wǒ yǐhòu zài yě bú huì shàngdàng le.
Having learned this lesson from experience, I will never let myself be taken advantage of again.

◆ 他们重新和好以后，两个人都表示以后再也不提离婚的事了。
Tāmen chóngxīn héhǎo yǐhòu, liǎngge rén dōu biǎoshì yǐhòu zài yě bù tí líhūnde shì le.
After they reconciled, both of them said they would not raise the question of divorce again.

228. 再也没(有)···过 zài yě méi(yǒu)...guo *to have never again (done something)*

◆ 上次大病以后，他再也没有喝过酒。
Shàngcì dàbìng yǐhòu, tā zài yě méiyǒu hēguo jiǔ.
After his last big illness, he never drank again.

◆ 他出国以后，我再也没有听到过他的消息。
Tā chūguó yǐhòu, wǒ zài yě méiyǒu tīngdàoguo tāde xiāoxi.
Since he went abroad, I have not heard any news of him.

◆ 这家明星企业三年前出现亏损以后，再也没有恢复过元气。
Zhèijiā míngxīng qǐyè sānnián-qián chūxiàn kuīsǔn yǐhòu, zài yě méiyǒu huīfùguo yuánqì.
After its losses three years ago, this star enterprise never recovered its vigor.

EXERCISES:

Translate the following sentences into Chinese, using the structures covered in this chapter:

1. If you plan to live here for several years, it would be better to buy a house than to rent.

2. No wonder they look so much alike, they are mother and daughter after all.

3. He was originally a peasant, but later, after going through a lot of hard work, he became a very successful entrepreneur.

4. My Chinese teacher is always saying, the more you practice the faster your progress will be.

5. I am recognizing more and more Chinese characters now.

6. His parents' expectations are too high. No matter how well he does, they are still not satisfied.

7. No matter how high the salary is, I'm not interested in a profession that requires 15 or 16 hours of work a day.

8. Let's wait a little longer. She should be arriving soon.

9. He is intelligent and diligent, and in addition he has a good teacher. Therefore he has learned Chinese very well.

10. Although this dress is a famous brand, it doesn't look good, and besides it is extremely expensive. I don't think I'll buy it.

11. He pledged to the doctor that he would not smoke any more.

12. We have had no more contact after the divorce.

ANSWERS:

1. 如果你打算在这里住几年，与其租房，不如买房。
   Rúguǒ nǐ dǎsuàn zài zhèlǐ zhù jǐnián, yǔqí zūfáng, bùrú mǎifáng.

2. 怪不得她们长得那么像，原来是母女俩。
   Guài-bu-de tāmen zhǎngde nàme xiàng, yuánlái shì mǔnǚ liǎ.

3. 他原来是农民，后来通过奋斗成为了很成功的企业家。
   Tā yuánlái shì nóngmín, hòulái tōngguò fèndòu chéngwéile hěn chénggōngde qǐyèjiā.

4. 我的中文老师总是说，你们练习得越多，进步得越快。
   Wǒde Zhōngwén lǎoshī zǒngshì shuō, nǐmen liànxíde yuè duō, jìnbùde yuè kuài.

5. 我认识的中文字越来越多了。 **Wǒ rènshide Zhōngwén zì yuèláiyuè duō le.**

6. 他父母的期望太高了，他做得再好，他们还是不满意。
   Tā fùmǔde qīwàng tài gāo le. Tā zuòde zài hǎo, tāmen háishi bù mǎnyì.

7. 这种每天工作十五、六个小时的职业，年薪再高，我也不感兴趣。
   Zhèizhǒng měitiān gōngzuò shíwǔ-liùge xiǎoshíde zhíyè, niánxīn zài gāo, wǒ yě bù gǎn-xìngqù.

8. 我们再多等一会儿，她应该马上就到了。
   Wǒmen zài duō děng yìhuǐr, tā yīnggāi mǎshàng jiù dào le.

9. 他又聪明又用功，再加上有位好老师，因此中文学得非常好。
   Tā yòu cōngming yòu yònggōng, zài jiāshàng yǒu wèi hǎo lǎoshī, yīncǐ Zhōngwén xuéde fēicháng hǎo.

10. 这件衣服虽然是名牌，但是样子不好看，再说又非常贵，我看别买了。
    Zhèijiàn yīfu suīrán shì míngpái, dànshì yàngzi bù hǎokàn, zàishuō yòu fēicháng guì, wǒ kàn bié mǎi le.
11. 他向医生保证，以后再也不抽烟了。
    Tā xiàng yīshēng bǎozhèng, yǐhòu zài yě bù chōuyān le.
12. 离婚以后，我们再也没有联系过。Líhūn yǐhòu, wǒmen zài yě méiyǒu liánxìguo.

Chapter 35: Expressions 229–241

229. 在⋯(的)过程中 zài...(de) guòchéng-zhōng *in the process of..., in the course of...*

♦ 在学习中文的过程中，她认识了不少中国朋友，其中一个后来成了她的丈夫。
Zài xuéxí Zhōngwénde guòchéng-zhōng, tā rènshile bùshǎo Zhōngguó péngyou, qízhōng yíge hòulái chéngle tāde zhàngfu.
In the process of learning Chinese, she made many Chinese friends, and one of them later became her husband.

♦ 在创业的过程中，他吃了不少苦，也获得了很多经验。
Zài chuàngyède guòchéng-zhōng, tā chīle bùshǎo kǔ, yě huòdéle hěn duō jīngyàn.
In the process of establishing his business, he endured a lot of hardship but also gained a lot of experience.

♦ 我们在相互了解的过程中，越来越相亲相爱。
Wǒmen zài xiānghù liǎojiěde guòchéng-zhōng, yuèláiyuè xiāngqīn-xiāng'ài.
In the process of coming to understand each other, we gradually developed a loving relationship.

230. 在⋯(的)情况下 zài...(de) qíngkuàng-xià *under the conditions/circumstances of...*

♦ 在缺乏资金的情况下，公司无法扩大规模。
Zài quēfá zījīnde qíngkuàng-xià, gōngsī wúfǎ kuòdà guīmó.
Lacking funding, the company could not expand its scope.

♦ 在目前市场不稳定的情况下，投资的风险是很大的。
Zài mùqián shìchǎng bù wěndìngde qíngkuàng-xià, tóuzīde fēngxiǎn shì hěn dàde.
With the current market volatility, investment risk is very high.

♦ 在证据不足的情况下，我们打不赢这场官司。
Zài zhèngjù bùzúde qíngkuàng-xià, wǒmen dǎ-bù-yíng zhèichǎng guānsī.
With such insufficient evidence, we cannot win this lawsuit.

♦ 在社会不断进步的情况下，我们也需要与时俱进。
Zài shèhuì búduàn jìnbùde qíngkuàng-xià, wǒmen yě xūyào yǔshí jùjìn.
With society continuously improving, we should also move ahead with the times.

231. 在···方面 zài...fāngmiàn *in the aspect of..., with respect to..., as far as...is concerned*

- 他在音乐方面很有天赋。
  Tā zài yīnyuè fāngmiàn hěn yǒu tiānfù.
  He has great natural talent for music.

- 中国政府在人工智能方面的研发投入不断加大。
  Zhōngguó zhèngfǔ zài réngōng zhìnéng fāngmiànde yánfā tóurù búduàn jiādà.
  The Chinese government is steadily increasing its investment in the research and development of artificial intelligence.

- 他没有什么真本事，但是在拉关系方面可以说是行家。
  Tā méiyǒu shénme zhēn běnshì, dànshi zài lā-guānxi fāngmiàn kěyǐ shuō shì hángjiā.
  He doesn't have any real ability, but when it comes to making personal connections, he is a real pro.

- 在环境保护方面，政府出台了许多新的举措，而且已初见成效。
  Zài huánjìng bǎohù fāngmiàn, zhèngfǔ chūtáile xǔduō xīnde jǔcuò, érqiě yǐ chū-jiàn-chéngxiào.
  The government has undertaken many new initiatives in the area of environmental protection, and furthermore some of them have already begun to show some results.

232. 在···看来 zài...kànlai *as (so-and-so) sees it*

- 在儿子看来，爸爸是世界上最令人敬佩的人。
  Zài érzi kànlai, Bàbà shì shìjiè-shang zuì lìng rén jìngpèide rén.
  As a son sees it, Dad is the most admirable person in the world.

- 在我看来，成家和立业这两方面很难兼顾。就像老话说的，鱼与熊掌不可兼得。
  Zài wǒ kànlai, chéngjiā hé lìyè zhè liǎng fāngmiàn hěn nán jiāngù. Jiù xiàng lǎohuà shuōde, yú-yǔ-xióngzhǎng bùkě jiāndé.
  As I see it, it's difficult to attend to establishing a family and developing a career at the same time. As the old adage says, you can't have both "fish and bear's paw" at the same time.

- 在许多人看来，为经济发展而牺牲环境很不值得。
  Zài xǔduō rén kànlai, wèi jīngjì fāzhǎn ér xīshēng huánjìng hěn bù zhíde.
  In the eyes of many people, to sacrifice the environment for economic progress is not worthwhile.

233. 在···上 zài...shang *in regard to..., on the issue of...*

- 他刚到外国留学，在生活上还有很多不习惯的地方。
  Tā gāng dào wàiguó liúxué, zài shēnghuó-shang hái yǒu hěn duō bù xíguànde dìfāng.
  He has just gone abroad to study, and there are many daily life things that he is unaccustomed to.

♦ 虽然我们在政治上的看法不一样，但还是好朋友。
Suīrán wǒmen zài zhèngzhì-shangde kànfǎ bù yíyàng, dàn háishi hǎo péngyou.
Although our political views are not the same, we are still good friends.

♦ 移民父母和在外国出生长大的孩子之间在语言文化上并不容易沟通。
Yímín fùmǔ hé zài wàiguó chūshēng zhǎngdàde háizi zhījiān zài yǔyán wén-huà-shang bìng bù róngyì gōutōng.
Immigrant parents and their children born and raised abroad have difficulties communicating both linguistically and culturally.

234. 在⋯(之)下 **zài...(zhī)xià** *under...*(circumstance, influence, guidance, care, etc.)
The 之 **zhī** in this structure is more likely to be used when the phrase that follows 在 **zài** is longer, thus lending a bit more "substance" to the back end of this structure. Being a word from literary Chinese, 之 **zhī** also makes the phrase more formal.

♦ 在她女儿的悉心照料之下，她逐渐恢复了健康。
Zài tā nǚ'érde xīxīn zhàoliào zhīxià, tā zhújiàn huīfùle jiànkāng.
Under her daughter's attentive care, she gradually recovered her health.

♦ 在老师的耐心讲解之下，他终于明白了这道题。
Zài lǎoshīde nàixīn jiǎngjiě zhīxià, tā zhōngyú míngbáile zhèidào tí.
With the teacher's patient explanations, he finally understood this question.

♦ 在任何情况下，我们都应该把人生安全放在第一位。
Zài rènhé qíngkuàng-xià, wǒmen dōu yīnggāi bǎ rénshēng ānquán fàngzài dìyīwèi.
Under all conditions, we should give top priority to personal safety.

235. 怎么⋯也/还是⋯ **zěnme...yě/háishi...** *no matter how..., still...*
This structure may be extended to "不管怎么⋯也/还是⋯ **bùguǎn zěnme...yě/háishi...**" without any change in its meaning.

♦ 不管我怎么安慰妈妈，她还是生爸爸的气。
Bùguǎn wǒ zěnme ānwèi Māma, tā háishi shēng Bàbade qì.
No matter how I try to console my Mom, she is still angry at Dad.

♦ 她一定要跟男朋友分手，我怎么劝也劝不住。
Tā yídìng yào gēn nánpéngyou fēnshǒu, wǒ zěnme quàn yě quàn-bu-zhù.
She is determined to break up with her boyfriend; no matter how I try to persuade her (not to do it), she cannot be persuaded.

♦ 房价一直上涨，政府怎么控制也控制不了。
Fángjià yìzhí shàngzhǎng, zhèngfǔ zěnme kòngzhì yě kòngzhì-bu-liǎo.
Housing prices continue to rise. No matter how the government tries to control it, it doesn't work.

236. 怎么样 **zěnmeyàng** *how; How about it? How's that?*
The first two examples use this phrase in its primary meaning of *how*. The latter two examples illustrate an idiomatic usage of this phrase. 怎么 **zěnme** (without 样 **yàng**)

may be used in lieu of 怎么样 zěnmeyàng when it is followed by something else (as in the second example), i.e. not before a pause.

◆ 他们以后的日子怎么样，我现在很难预测。
Tāmen yǐhòude rìzi zěnmeyàng, wǒ xiànzài hěn nán yùcè.
As to how their life will be hereafter, it's hard for me to predict at this point.

◆ 我们怎么(样)才能顺利渡过这个困难时期呢？
Wǒmen zěnme(yàng) cái néng shùnlì dùguò zhèige kùnnan shíqī ne?
How can we smoothly get through this difficult period?

◆ 我们七点在餐馆见面，怎么样？
Wǒmen qīdiǎn zài cānguǎn jiànmiàn, zěnmeyàng?
Let's meet at the restaurant at seven o'clock, how about it?

◆ 怎么样？你现在知道"不听老人言，吃亏在眼前"了吧？
Zěnmeyàng? Nǐ xiànzài zhīdào "bù tīng lǎorén yán, chīkuī zài yǎnqián" le ba?
Well? Now do you see how you would come to grief if you don't listen to the advice of the elderly?

237. 怎么这么/那么··· zěnme zhème/nàme... *how come it is so...?!*
This rhetorical question usually conveys a complaint, but not always.

◆ 今年夏天怎么全世界都这么热，是不是老天爷开烧烤大会了？
Jīnnián xiàtiān zěnme quán shìjiè dōu zhème rè, shì-bushì Lǎo Tiānyé kāi shāokǎo dàhuì le?
Why is the whole world so hot this summer? Is the Old Man in Heaven having a barbecue party?

◆ 你怎么这么不听话，看你把妈妈气得都吃不下饭了！
Nǐ zěnme zhème bù tīnghuà, kàn nǐ bǎ Māma qìde dōu chī-bu-xià-fàn le!
How come you are so disobedient? Look how you have made Mom so mad that she can't even eat!

◆ 大象，大象，你的鼻子怎么那么长？妈妈说，鼻子长才漂亮！
Dà Xiàng, Dà Xiàng, nǐde bízi zěnme nàme cháng? Māma shuō, bízi cháng cái piàoliang!
Elephant, elephant, why is your nose so long? Mommy said, a long nose is what makes you pretty!

238. 这样一来 zhèyàng yìlái *given this, thus, with this one move*

◆ 爷爷奶奶答应来帮忙带小孩，这样一来，小两口就可以放心去上班了。
Yéye Nǎinai dāying lái bāngmáng dài xiǎohái, zhèyàng yìlái, xiǎo liǎngkǒu jiù kěyǐ fàngxīn qù shàngbān le.
Grandpa and Grandma agreed to come and help with the children, thus the young couple could go off to work without worry.

◆ 朋友聚会的时候，大家都加了微信。这样一来，相互联系就方便多了。
Péngyou jùhuìde shíhou, dàjiā dōu jiāle Wēixìn. Zhèyàng yìlái, xiānghù liánxì jiù fāngbiàn duō le.
When our friends got together, we all joined WeChat, and thus it became much more convenient for us to stay connected.

◆ 公司改革了激励机制，赏罚分明。这样一来，员工的积极性比以前高多了。
Gōngsī gǎigéle jīlì jīzhì, shǎngfá fēnmíng. Zhèyàng yìlái, yuángōngde jījíxìng bǐ yǐqián gāo duō le.
The company restructured its incentive system to make rewards and penalties clear, thus the employees' initiative rose quite a bit from before.

239. 这一下子 zhè yíxiàzi *suddenly at that moment, all of a sudden*

◆ 孩子上大学去了以后，家里突然安静下来了。这一下子，妈妈还真怀念那以往热闹的家庭气氛了。
Háizi shàng dàxué qùle yǐhòu, jiālǐ tūrán ānjìng-xiàlai le. Zhè yíxiàzi, Māma hái zhēn huáiniàn nà yǐwǎng rènàode jiātíng qìfēn le.
After the kid went off to college, the house suddenly became quiet. At that moment, Mom began to miss the rowdy family atmosphere of the past.

◆ 努力了好几年，太太终于怀孕了！这一下子，双方父母乐坏了。
Nǔlìle hǎojǐnián, tàitai zhōngyú huáiyùn le! Zhè yíxiàzi, shuāngfāng fùmǔ lè-huàile.
After several years of effort, the wife finally became pregnant! At that point, the parents on both sides became ecstatic.

◆ 爸爸的公司倒闭了，他也因此下岗了。这一下子，家里的经济来源就断了。**Bàbade gōngsī dǎobì le, tā yě yīncǐ xiàgǎng le. Zhè yíxiàzi, jiālǐde jīngjì láiyuán jiù duàn le.**
Dad's company went bankrupt, so he lost his job. All of a sudden, the family's economic source was cut off.

◆ 春节前夕，北京城里的打工族都回家过年了。这一下子，北京人才感觉到少了农民工，生活还真不方便！
Chūnjié qiánxī, Běijīng chénglǐde dǎgōng-zú dōu huíjiā guònián le. Zhè yíxiàzi, Běijīng-rén cái gǎnjuédào shǎole nóngmín-gōng, shēnghuó hái zhēn bù fāngbiàn!
Before New Year's, all the migrant workers went home for the New Year, and suddenly Beijing residents realized that life without the peasant workers was very inconvenient!

240. 正好 zhènghǎo *by happy coincidence, right at that moment*

◆ 下周放春假，我正好可以休息休息，最近实在太累了！
Xiàzhōu fàng chūnjià, wǒ zhènghǎo kěyǐ xiūxixiūxi, zuìjìn shízài tài lèi le!
Next week is spring break, just the right time for me to get some rest. I have really been too tired recently!

● 我跟同事正好都住在同一个小区，所以上下班我们经常互相搭车。
Wǒ gēn tóngshì zhènghǎo dōu zhùzài tóngyíge xiǎoqū, suǒyǐ shàng-xiàbān wǒmen jīngcháng hùxiāng dāchē.
I live right in the same neighborhood as my colleague, so we often share rides to and from work.

● 我觉得自己很幸运，因为我从事的工作正好也是我感兴趣的领域。
Wǒ juéde zìjǐ hěn xìngyùn, yīnwèi wǒ cóngshìde gōngzuò zhènghǎo yě shì wǒ gǎn-xìngqùde lǐngyù.
I feel very fortunate because my work is right in the field that I am interested in.

● 朋友来华盛顿看我，正好碰上樱花盛开的时候，我们就一起去赏花了。 **Péngyou lái Huáshèngdùn kàn wǒ, zhènghǎo pèngshang yīnghuā shèngkāide shíhou, wǒmen jiù yìqǐ qù shǎng-huā le.**
My friend came to Washington to see me, and as luck would have it, it was right at cherry blossom time, so we went together to enjoy the blossoms.

241. 正在 zhèngzài *right in the midst of, just at that moment, just then*

● 我们的女儿正在中国留学呢，你到北京的时候可以找她帮忙。
Wǒmende nǚ'ér zhèngzài Zhōngguó liúxué ne, nǐ dào Běijīngde shíhou kěyǐ zhǎo tā bāngmáng.
Our daughter is studying in China right now. When you land in Beijing, you can ask her to help you.

● 父母得知女儿申请到奖学金的时候，正在为她的学费发愁呢。
Fùmǔ dézhī nǚ'ér shēnqǐng-dào jiǎngxuéjīnde shíhou, zhèngzài wèi tāde xuéfèi fāchóu ne.
When the parents found out that their daughter got a scholarship, they were at that very moment worrying about her school tuition.

● 中美双方正在就贸易纠纷进行谈判。
Zhōng-Měi shuāngfāng zhèngzài jiù màoyì jiūfēn jìnxíng tánpàn.
China and America are just now in the midst of negotiating trade disputes.

EXERCISES:

Translate the following sentences into Chinese, using the structures covered in this chapter:

1. In the process of adjusting to college life, my daughter has become more independent and more mature.
2. Under the situation of worsening air pollution in the city, many people are considering moving to the suburbs.
3. In the aspect of math education, the U.S. cannot compare with most advanced nations in the world.
4. As many middle aged and older people see it, physical health is more important than anything.

5. If you have problems with your studies, you can ask the teacher for help.

6. Under his parents' influence he also became a scientist.

7. No matter how I say it, that foreigner does not understand.

8. What would you like to do this winter break? Let's go together to Hainan Island for fun, how about it?

9. Why is this test so difficult? I'm afraid I won't be able to pass.

10. After the term got under way, I dropped a course. Having done this, I had time to go and look for a practicum.

11. That novel she wrote won a prize; all of a sudden, she became a famous author.

12. The day my daughter was born was right on my 30th birthday. From now on, we can celebrate our birthdays on the same day!

13. I was sleeping just when you phoned me.

ANSWERS:

1. 在适应大学生活的过程中，我的女儿变得更独立、更成熟了。
   Zài shìyìng dàxué shēnghuóde guòchéng-zhōng, wǒde nǚ'ér biànde gèng dúlì, gèng chéngshú le.

2. 在都市空气污染越来越严重的情况下，很多人考虑把家搬到郊区去。
   Zài dūshì kōngqì wūrǎn yuèláiyuè yánzhòngde qíngkuàng-xià, hěn duō rén kǎolù bǎ jiā bāndào jiāoqū qù.

3. 在数学教育这方面，美国比不过世界上多半的先进国家。
   Zài shùxué jiàoyù zhè fāngmiàn, Měiguó bǐ-bu-guò shìjiè-shang duōbànde xiānjìn guójiā.

4. 在许多中老年人看来，身体健康比什么都重要。
   Zài xǔduō zhōng-lǎonián-rén kànlai, shēntǐ jiànkāng bǐ shénme dōu zhòngyào.

5. 你要是在学习上有问题，可以多请教老师。
   Nǐ yàoshi zài xuéxí-shang yǒu wèntí, kěyǐ duō qǐngjiào lǎoshī.

6. 在父母的影响下，他也成为了一名科学家。
   Zài fùmǔde yǐngxiǎng-xià, tā yě chéngwéile yìmíng kēxué-jiā.

7. 我怎么说，那个外国人还是不懂。 Wǒ zěnme shuō, nèige wàiguórén háishi bùdǒng.

8. 你今年寒假想做什么？我们一起去海南岛玩儿，怎么样？
   Nǐ jīnnián hánjià xiǎng zuò shénme? Wǒmen yìqǐ qù Háinándǎo wánr, zěnmeyàng?

9. 这次考试怎么那么难，我恐怕过不了了。
   Zhèicì kǎoshì zěnme nàme nán, wǒ kǒngpà guò-bu-liǎo le.

10. 开学以后，我退了一门课。这样一来，我就有空去找一个实习的工作了。
    Kāixué yǐhòu, wǒ tuìle yìmén kè. Zhèyàng yìlái, wǒ jiù yǒukòng qù zhǎo yíge shíxíde gōngzuò le.

11. 她写的那本小说获奖了，这一下子，她就成了一位知名的作家。
    Tā xiěde nèiběn xiǎoshuō huòjiǎngle, zhè yíxiàzi, tā jiù chéngle yíwèi zhīmíngde zuòjiā.

12. 我女儿出生的那天正好是我三十岁生日，以后我们可以同一天过生日了。
    Wǒ nǚ'ér chūshēngde nèitiān zhènghǎo shì wǒ sānshísuì shēngrì, yǐhòu wǒmen kěyǐ tóng-yìtiān guò shēngrì le.

13. 你给我打电话的时候，我正在睡觉。
    Nǐ gěi wǒ dǎ diànhuàde shíhou, wǒ zhèngzài shuìjiào.

Chapter 36: Expressions 242–254

242. 之所以···是因为···(的缘故) **zhīsuǒyǐ...shì yīnwèi...(de yuángù)** *the reason why...is because.../is due to the reason that...*

This is a fairly formal structure which lends gravity to both the cause and result of a situation. It is a good option to use when you want a more eloquent alternative to the mundane structure 因为···所以··· **yīnwèi...suǒyǐ....**

♦ 她之所以那么难过是因为没能考上她最希望上的大学。
Tā zhīsuǒyǐ nàme nánguò shì yīnwèi méi néng kǎoshang tā zuì xīwàng shàngde dàxué.
The reason she feels so bad is because she was not able to test into the college that she had most hoped for.

♦ 投资之所以有风险是因为市场总是在变化波动当中。
Tóuzī zhīsuǒyǐ yǒu fēngxiǎn shì yīnwèi shìchǎng zǒngshì zài biànhuà bōdòng dāngzhōng.
The reason investment is risky is because the market is always changing and unstable.

♦ 中美关系之所以那么重要是因为中美两国是世界上最大的两个经济体。**Zhōng-Měi guānxi zhīsuǒyǐ nàme zhòngyào shì yīnwèi Zhōng-Měi liǎngguó shì shìjiè-shang zuì dàde liǎngge jīngjì-tǐ.**
The reason why Sino-American relations are so important is because the two countries China and America are the world's two biggest economic entities.

243. ···之一 **...zhīyī** *one of the...*

♦ 万里长城是世界建筑史上的奇迹之一。
Wànlǐ Chángchéng shì shìjiè jiànzhù-shǐ-shangde qíjì zhīyī.
The Great Wall is one of the world's architectural wonders.

♦ 科学研究已经证实，造成全球变暖的原因之一就是人类的活动。
Kēxué yánjiū yǐjīng zhèngshí, zàochéng quánqiú biànnuǎnde yuányīn zhīyī jiùshì rénlèide huódòng.
Scientific research has confirmed that human activity is one of the reasons behind global warming.

♦ 中国政府在治理污染时所面临的挑战之一就是如何在发展与环保之间找到平衡点。
Zhōngguó zhèngfǔ zài zhìlǐ wūrǎn shí suǒ miànlínde tiǎozhàn zhīyī jiùshì rúhé zài fāzhǎn yǔ huánbǎo zhījiān zhǎodào pínghéng-diǎn.
One of the challenges that the Chinese government faces in managing pollution is finding the point of balance between development and environmental protection.

This structure does not go beyond one, i.e. there is no ···之二 **...zhī'èr**, etc. An ordinary sentence pattern may be used to express a number higher than one, but the meaning becomes a bit ambiguous. Here are two examples:

⬧ 苹果和葡萄是我最喜欢的两种水果。
Píngguǒ hé pútao shì wǒ zuì xǐhuande liǎngzhǒng shuǐguǒ.
Apples and grapes are two of my favorite fruits.
or: *Apples and grapes are my two favorite fruits.*

⬧ 长城和运河是世界历史上最伟大的两个工程。
Chángchéng hé Yùnhé shì shìjiè lìshǐ-shang zuì wěidàde liǎngge gōngchéng.
The Great Wall and the Grand Canal are two of the greatest engineering feats in world history.
The Great Wall and the Grand Canal are the two greatest engineering feats in world history.
(Common sense should lead to the first interpretation.)

244. 值得 zhíde worthy, worthwhile

⬧ 在我看来，不管花多少时间和精力学中文都是值得的。
Zài wǒ kànlai, bùguǎn huā duōshǎo shíjiān hé jīnglì xué Zhōngwén dōu shì zhíde de.
As I see it, learning Chinese is worth any amount of time and effort.

⬧ 在你看来，一个职业妇女为了养育孩子而牺牲自己的事业值得吗？
Zài nǐ kànlai, yíge zhíyè fùnǚ wèile yǎngyù háizi ér xīshēng zìjǐde shìyè zhíde ma?
As you see it, is it worth it for a professional woman to sacrifice her career in order to raise her children?

⬧ 先辈勤劳节俭的美德值得当代人学习。
Xiānbèi qínláo jiéjiǎnde měidé zhíde dāngdài-rén xuéxí.
Our forebears' virtues of hard work and frugality is worthy of emulation by the present generation.

245. 只···就··· zhǐ...jiù... only..., and then/already...

⬧ 一般来说，老年人睡眠都减少了，每天晚上只睡5-6个小时就够了。
Yìbān láishuō, lǎonián-rén shuìmián dōu jiǎnshǎo le, měitiān wǎnshang zhǐ shuì 5-6 ge xiǎoshí jiù gòule.
Generally speaking, old people tend to sleep less; five or six hours a night is sufficient.

⬧ 他高中修了很多学分，所以只用了三年就大学毕业了。
Tā gāozhōng xiūle hěn duō xuéfēn, suǒyǐ zhǐ yòngle sānnián jiù dàxué bìyè le.
He had taken a lot of college-credit courses in high school, so he was able to graduate from college in only three years.

⬧ 以前从上海坐火车到昆明要55个小时，现在坐高铁只要8个小时就到了。 **Yǐqián cóng Shànghǎi zuò huǒchē dào Kūnmíng yào 55 ge xiǎoshí, xiànzài zuò gāotiě zhǐ yào 8 ge xiǎoshí jiù dào le.**
It used to take 55 hours to go from Shanghai to Kunming by train, but now taking the high speed train one would arrive in just eight hours.

246. 只好… **zhǐhǎo…** *can only…; have no choice but…* (lit., "the only good thing to do is…")

- 冰箱里空空的，什么吃的都没有了，我只好叫外卖了。
  Bīngxiāngli kōngkōngde, shénme chīde dōu méiyǒu le, wǒ zhǐhǎo jiào wàimài le.
  The refrigerator is empty. There is nothing at all to eat, so I'll just have to order some carry-out.

- 我喜欢的蓝色已经卖完了，只好买了绿色的。
  Wǒ xǐhuande lánsè yǐjīng màiwánle, zhǐhǎo mǎile lǜsède.
  The blue one that I liked were sold out, so I could only buy a green one.

- 末班车已经走了，她只好搭出租车回家了。
  Mòbān-chē yǐjīng zǒule, tā zhǐhǎo dā chūzū-chē huíjiā le.
  The last bus had already left, so she had to take a taxi home.

247. 只要…就… **zhǐyào…jiù…** *whenever / as long as…, then…*

A note of caution: The meaning of this structure is quite different from the literal meaning of 只要 **zhǐyào** *only want* or *only if.*

- 只要有假期，他就会安排出门旅行。
  Zhǐyào yǒu jiàqī, tā jiù huì ānpái chūmén lǚxíng.
  Whenever there is a vacation, he will arrange to go traveling.

- 只要我们不放弃，就有成功的希望。
  Zhǐyào wǒmen bú fàngqì, jiù yǒu chénggōngde xīwàng.
  As long as we don't give up, there is hope for success.

- 只要一谈起国家大事，父子俩就争得面红耳赤。
  Zhǐyào yì tánqǐ guójiā dàshì, fùzǐ liǎ jiù zhēngde miànhóng-ěrchì.
  Whenever that father and son talk about national affairs, they argue until their faces turn red and ears become crimson.

248. 只有…才… **zhǐyǒu…cái…** *it is only…that…*

The negative corollary of this structure is 只有…才不… **zhǐyǒu…cái bù…** (see the last example).

- 平时我得上班，只有周末才有时间做些室外活动。
  Píngshí wǒ děi shàngbān, zhǐyǒu zhōumò cái yǒu shíjiān zuò xiē shìwài huódòng.
  On ordinary days I have to go to work; it is only on the weekends that I have time for a little outdoor activity.

- 只有工作过两年的人才能申请这个MBA项目。
  Zhǐyǒu gōngzuòguo liǎngniánde rén cái néng shēnqǐng zhèige MBA xiàngmù.
  Only people who have worked for two years may apply to this MBA program.

- 科技发展得太快了，一般的工人只有不断学习新技能才不会被淘汰。**Kējì fāzhǎnde tài kuài le, yìbānde gōngrén zhǐyǒu búduàn xuéxí xīn jìnéng cái búhuì bèi táotài.**
  Technology is developing too rapidly. Ordinary workers must continuously learn new skills or they will become obsolete.

249. 只有…没有… zhǐyǒu…méiyǒu… *have only…and no…, there is only…and no…*

- 要是我们的生活里只有快乐没有悲伤该多好啊！**Yàoshi wǒmende shēnghuó-lǐ zhǐyǒu kuàilè méiyǒu bēishāng gāi duō hǎo a!**
  How wonderful it would be if there were only happiness in our lives and no sadness!

- 在中国传统的大家庭里，孩子只有服从父母的命令，没有反抗的权利。**Zài Zhōngguó chuántǒngde dà-jiātíng-lǐ, háizi zhǐyǒu fúcóng fùmǔde mìnglìng, méiyǒu fǎnkàngde quánlì.**
  In the traditional Chinese big family, children could only obey parents' orders; they had no right to protest.

- 所谓极昼，就是只有白天没有黑夜，这是在南北极可以看到的自然现象。**Suǒwèi jízhòu, jiùshì zhǐyǒu báitiān méiyǒu hēiyè, zhè shì zài nán-běijí kěyǐ kàndàode zìrán xiànxiàng.**
  The so-called "midnight sun" is the natural phenomenon that occurs at the North and South Poles, where there is only daylight, and no dark of night.

- 在中国，上高中三年级的学生都在为考大学做最后的冲刺。他们的生活里只有学习，没有娱乐。**Zài Zhōngguó, shàng gāozhōng sānniánjíde xuésheng dōu zài wèi kǎo dàxué zuò zuìhòude chōngcì. Tāmende shēnghuó-lǐ zhǐyǒu xuéxí, méiyǒu yúlè.**
  In China, students in the third year of senior high school are in the final sprint of preparation for college entrance exam. Their life consists of studying only, no recreation.

250. 至于 zhìyú *as to*

- 我已经尽了最大的努力了，至于能不能得到那个工作机会还很难说。**Wǒ yǐjīng jìnle zuì dàde nǔlì le, zhìyú néng-bùnéng dédào nèige gōngzuò jīhuì hái hěn nánshuō.**
  I have already put forth my best efforts. As to whether I can get that job, it is as yet hard to say.

- 凡事只要尽力就好，至于结果好坏，就听天由命吧。**Fánshì zhǐyào jìnlì jiù hǎo, zhìyú jiéguǒ hǎohuài, jiù tīngtiān-yóumìng ba.**
  One can only try one's best in everything. As to whether the result will be good or bad, we can only wait for heaven to determine our fate.

- 参加比赛的几支球队势均力敌，至于哪队将夺得冠军仍无法预测。**Cānjiā bǐsàide jǐzhī qiúduì shìjūn-lìdí, zhìyú něiduì jiāng duódé guànjūn réng wúfǎ yùcè.**
  The several teams competing in this contest are well matched. As to which team will eventually capture the championship, there is still no way to predict that.

251. 自从…以来/以后 **zìcóng…yǐlái/yǐhòu** *(ever) since…* (some specific time or event)
See also #199 (…以来 …**yǐlái**). This structure means the same thing with either 以来 **yǐlái** or 以后 **yǐhòu**, but 以来 **yǐlái** has more of the sense that the situation has persisted up to the present.

♦ 这一带自从修了地铁以来，僻静的郊区很快地热闹起来了。
   Zhè yídài zìcóng xiūle dìtiě yǐlái, pìjìngde jiāoqū hěn kuàide rè'nao-qǐlai le.
   Since the construction of the subway to this area, this isolated suburb has quickly become quite bustling.

♦ 自从改革开放以来，中国已经发生了翻天覆地的变化。
   Zìcóng gǎigé-kāifàng yǐlái, Zhōngguó yǐjīng fāshēngle fāntiān-fùdìde biànhuà.
   Since reform and opening, China has already undergone momentous earth-shaking changes.

♦ 自从有了孩子以后，她的整个心思都放在养育孩子上了。
   Zìcóng yǒule háizi yǐhòu, tāde zhěngge xīnsī dōu fàngzài yǎngyù-háizi-shang le.
   Ever since she had a child, her entire psyche has been focused on nurturing the child.

♦ 自从出了车祸以后，她心里就有了阴影，很长一段时间不敢开车了。
   Zìcóng chūle chēhuò yǐhòu, tā xīnli jiù yǒule yīnyǐng, hěn cháng yíduàn shíjiān bù gǎn kāichē le.
   Ever since the automobile accident, there has been a dark shadow in her consciousness, and for a very long time she did not dare drive a car.

252. 总是… **zǒngshì…** *always, constantly*

♦ 他做事总是拖拖拉拉的，不到最后一分钟不着急。
   Tā zuòshì zǒngshì tuōtuōlālāde, bú dào zuìhòu yìfēnzhōng bù zhāojí.
   He procrastinates in everything he does, never getting anxious until the last minute.

♦ 她是家里的掌上明珠，父母对她也总是有求必应。
   Tā shì jiālǐde zhǎngshàng-míngzhū, fùmǔ duì tā yě zǒngshì yǒuqiú-bìyìng.
   She is the "bright pearl on the palm" in her family. Her parent always consent to whatever she wants.

♦ 这些富二代花钱总是大手大脚的，互相攀比。
   Zhèixiē fù-èr-dài huāqián zǒngshì dàshǒu-dàjiǎode, hùxiāng pānbǐ.
   These "second generation rich" (born rich) always spend extravagantly and compete with each other (in their acquisitions).

253. 总算 **zǒngsuàn** *after all is said and done, in the final accounting*
This is an idiomatic term with no equivalent in English. It conveys the sense that a positive outcome has been achieved, but only barely.

♦ 这次考试考得很不错，总算没白花那么多时间复习。
   Zhèicì kǎoshì kǎode hěn búcuò, zǒngsuàn méi báihuā nàme duō shíjiān fùxí.
   I did quite well on this test. All that time I spent reviewing was after all not wasted.

◆ 为了孩子上学，父母东借西借，总算把学费凑够了。
Wèile háizi shàngxué, fùmǔ dōng-jiè-xī-jiè, zǒngsuàn bǎ xuéfèi còugòu le.
For the child's schooling, the parents borrowed here and there and finally gathered enough money for tuition.

◆ 他读了八年博士，今天终于毕业了，他的苦日子总算熬出头了。
Tā dúle bānián bóshì, jīntiān zhōngyú bìyè le, tāde kǔ rìzi zǒngsuàn áo-chūtóu le.
He studied eight years for his Ph. D., and today he finally graduated. Having struggled through hard times, he is finally seeing brighter days.

◆ 虽然车祸让他失去了一条腿，但总算把命保住了。
Suīrán chēhuò ràng tā shīqùle yìtiáo tuǐ, dàn zǒngsuàn bǎ mìng bǎozhù le.
Although he lost a leg in the auto accident, but at least his life was saved.

254. 总之 **zǒngzhī** *in a word, in brief, in short* (lit., "summing it up")

◆ 不管他做什么总是比别人做得好。总之，可以说他是一个天才。
Bùguǎn tā zuò shénme, zǒngshì bǐ biérén zuòde hǎo. Zǒngzhī, kěyǐ shuō tā shì yíge tiāncái.
In whatever he does, his performance is always better than others. In short, we can say he is simply very talented.

◆ 吸烟不但对自己不好，也对别人的健康有害。总之，吸烟有百害而无一利。**Xīyān búdàn duì zìjǐ bùhǎo, yě duì biérénde jiànkāng yǒuhài. Zǒngzhī, xīyān yǒu bǎihài ér wú yílì.**
Not only is smoking bad for oneself, it is also harmful to other people. In a word, it carries a hundred harms without a single benefit.

◆ 新的一年，祝您工作顺利，身体健康，家庭幸福！总之，一切顺心如意！ **Xīnde yìnián, zhù nín gōngzuò shùnlì, shēntǐ jiànkāng, jiātíng xìngfú! Zǒngzhī, yíqiè shùnxīn rúyì!**
For the New Year, we wish you success in your work, good health, and family happiness! In short, may all your wishes be fulfilled!

◆ 今年经济形势不乐观，就业竞争激烈，总之，毕业生找工作难度很大。**Jīnnián jīngjì xíngshì bú lèguān, jiùyè jìngzhēng jīliè, zǒngzhī, bìyèshēng zhǎo gōngzuò nándù hěn dà.**
The state of the economy this year is not optimistic, and competition for jobs is fierce; it all adds up to great difficulties for graduates in finding jobs.

EXERCISES:

Translate the following sentences into Chinese, using the structures covered in this chapter:

1. The reason why everybody loves giant pandas is because their movements are a lot like pudgy little kids.
2. Scrambled eggs with tomatoes is one of my favorite Chinese dishes.

3. What's so good about wearing branded clothing? Is it worth spending so much money?

4. This movie was too boring. I fell asleep after watching it for only half an hour.

5. I have to turn this article in tomorrow, so I have no choice but to work on it through the night.

6. As long as the children are healthy and happy, the parents will rest at ease.

7. Only if I succeed in getting a fellowship will I be able to go to China to study.

8. In my whole life, I have never met a person who has only strong points and no faults.

9. I only know that he is Sichuanese; as to where in Sichuan he is from, I have no idea.

10. Ever since I had a dog, my state of mind has been much better than before.

11. Whenever students have a problem, Teacher Gao always patiently helps them.

12. Although she did not get into Peking University or Tsinghua University, she did at least pass the entrance exam to some university.

13. Teacher Wang gives students appropriate challenges but does not make them feel too pressured. In sum, she really understands her student's mentality.

ANSWERS:

1. 大家之所以喜爱大熊猫是因为它们的动作很像胖胖的小孩子。
   Dàjiā zhīsuǒyǐ xǐ'ài dà-xióngmāo shì yīnwèi tāmende dòngzuò hěn xiàng pàngpàngde xiǎoháizi.

2. 西红柿炒鸡蛋是我最喜欢的中国菜之一。
   Xīhóngshì chǎo jīdàn shì wǒ zuì xǐhuande Zhōngguó cài zhīyī.

3. 穿名牌到底有什么好处？值得花那么多钱吗？
   Chuān míngpái dàodǐ yǒu shénme hǎochù? Zhíde huā nàme duō qián ma?

4. 这个电影太无聊了，我只看了半个小时就睡着了。
   Zhèige diànyǐng tài wúliáo le, wǒ zhǐ kànle bànge xiǎoshí jiù shuìzháo le.

5. 这篇文章明天要交，只好今天晚上熬夜了。
   Zhèipiān wénzhāng míngtiān yào jiāo, zhǐhǎo jīntiān wǎnshang áoyè le.

6. 只要孩子健康快乐，父母就放心了。 Zhǐyào háizi jiànkāng kuàilè, fùmǔ jiù fàngxīn le.

7. 只有申请到奖学金，我才能去中国留学。
   Zhǐyǒu shēnqǐngdào jiǎngxuéjīn, wǒ cái néng qù Zhōngguó liúxué.

8. 我一辈子都没遇到过一个只有优点没有缺点的人。
   Wǒ yíbèizi dōu méi yùdàoguo yíge zhǐyǒu yōudiǎn méiyǒu quēdiǎnde rén.

9. 我只知道他是四川人，至于四川什么地方，我就不清楚了。
   Wǒ zhǐ zhīdào tā shì Sìchuān-rén, zhìyú Sìchuān shénme dìfang, wǒ jiù bù qīngchǔ le.

10. 自从我养了一只狗以来，我的心情就比从前好多了。
    Zìcóng wǒ yǎngle yìzhī gǒu yǐlái, wǒde xīnqíng jiù bǐ cóngqián hǎo duō le.

11. 学生有问题的时候，高老师总是很耐心地帮助他们。
    Xuésheng yǒu wèntíde shíhou, Gāo lǎoshī zǒngshì hěn nàixīnde bāngzhù tāmen.

12. 虽然她没考上北大或清华，但总算考上一所大学了。
    Suīrán tā méi kǎoshang Běi-Dà huò Qīnghuá, dàn zǒngsuàn kǎoshang yìsuǒ dàxué le.

13. 王老师给学生适当的挑战，但又不让学生感觉压力太大，总之，她很了解
    学生的心理。 Wáng Lǎoshī gěi xuésheng shìdàngde tiǎozhàn, dàn yòu búràng xuésheng gǎnjué
    yālì tài dà, zǒngzhī, tā hěn liǎojiě xuéshengde xīnlǐ.

Index